This book belongs to: _____

A HISTORY OF THE LONG BEACH NAVAL SHIPYARD, ROOSEVELT BASE and REEVES FIELD N.A.S.   Revision "B"

Purpose of Revision "B"

Since publication of the first edition (Revision "A") more historical data was found and needed to be added in. Also this larger size allows for more photos that have "hopefully" been enhanced or rescanned for better clarity. Original scanning from old newspaper clippings leaves a lot to be desired even with Photo Shop helping the best it (or "I") can.

Appendix C eliminates several pages of photos of various shipyard plaques as most of them are now aboard the Battleship USS *IOWA* (BB-61) in San Pedro for a future LBNSY museum. Also Appendix D has had the grid list of buildings removed. Most people wouldn't need it but if you want it, use the first edition. This helps leave room for an index that was sorely needed and noted by some reviewers. Now, I may have skipped over a couple of names. If so, my apologies. After all, I'm only human and 80 years old.

In Chapter 11, I cut out all of the conversation as it was, well, TMI (Too Much Information). Also, in Chapter 19 I have deleted all of my poor Income Tax "jokes" and just stuck to the facts. And I have added Chapter 34 of some random thoughts not specifically relating to LBNSY.

Any major changes in the text (and some photos) will be identified by **"B"** at the start of a paragraph where the changes, additions or corrections have been done. Otherwise about 80 to 90% of the text is the same as in the first edition.

The author (a Founding Member of the Pacific Battleship Center) aboard the USS *IOWA* (BB-61), now in San Pedro, California as a museum ship and educational center, "guarding" Generals Patton, Eisenhower, MacArthur and FDR.

TABLE OF CONTENTS

CHPTR #	TITLE/SUBJECT	PAGE
	DEDICATION	4
	ACKNOWLEGMENTS	5
	INTRODUCTION	6
1	Dry Dock 1	9
2	Herman the German	15
3	Titan vs. Hercules	24
4	Atomic Bombs	28
5	The Apprenticeship	33
6	Pop Up	39
7	Swing Shift	49
8	Trieste and White Sands	55
9	CURV	58
10	Quapaw	60
11	Hazmat	62
12	Sealab II	67
13	DSRV	75
14	S.A.C.S and Cecil & Ollie	83
15	AAV7 Track Mods & Benny Suggs	90
16	News & Entertainment Media	95
17	Shipyard Security & Thefts	97
18	Shipchecks	99
19	NSC - Naval Supply Center	105
20	Ghosts and Sea Monsters	113
21	--Get Out of this C*S* Outfit?	118
22	Winds, Fires and Floods	124
23	Earthquakes	129
24	When Your Number is Up	137
25	The New Jersey in 1968	141
26	Calling All Battleships	151
27	Battleship Class Problems	167
28	Missouri's Barbette Crack	188
29	Turret II Incident on Iowa	191
30	Armor, Stealth, Ship Stability	193
31	Reeves Field	204
32	Roosevelt Base	216
33	The Final Count	226
33A	The Beginnings of the Shipyard	229
33B	LBNSY in her Prime	232
33C	The Final Blows	246
34	Around The Scuttlebutt	251
	Epilogue - Retirement	274

Page	
277	APPENDIX A: Chronological list of all dockings at LBNSY from 1942 to 1996.
356	APPENDIX B: Special or noteworthy dockings at LBNSY.
368	APPENDIX C: Crests and Logos
372	APPENDIX D: Shipyard maps
384	APPENDIX E: List of all apprentice graduates from 1947 to 1991.
451	APPENDIX F: List of commanding officers.
464	APPENDIX G: Roster of Officers & CPO's at Reeves Field NAS in 1942
474	APPENDIX H: Deck log of one day on board USS Missouri (BB-63)
479 - 481	Index: Alphabetically by ship / Alphabetically by person

DEDICATION
I hereby dedicate this edition of my book to my late wife, Julia.

She was a great supporter of the work I and the rest of Long Beach Naval Shipyard did to finally bring an end to the Cold War. She was a victim of the "COLD" war when her fellow Hungarians revolted against the Socialistic rule of the Soviet Union in 1956. Only 10 years old at the time in her home town of Kaposvar, she joined in at least with moral support. Her mother was a writer of children's short stories and would read them on Sunday mornings over the public radio. So it was "a given" for her to help take over the radio station knowing its layout and how to operate some of the equipment. But when the Soviet troops moved back in with reinforcements and newer T-54 tanks, Julia, her 11 year old brother Miklos and her mother had to escape to Austria. Their efforts were often slowed down by machine gun and rifle fire aimed at them. America had dropped its quota of Hungarians but her mother chose to go to Caracas, Venezuela instead to join relatives there. That forced them to stay for over eight years to get back on the quota list. They finally arrived in California but had to wait five years to become American citizens. I'll never forget when she was finally sworn in and received her official document; she yelled "Now I can Wote". No, that is not a typo because in the Hungarian language the "V" is pronounced as a "W". Her English still took a while to improve but she was finally quite fluid in three languages. She liked the kinds of work we did at LBNSY and even joined me on a family day cruise of the USS *Tarawa* (LHA-1) and the USS *New Jersey* (BB-62). She also supported the Pacific Battleship Center in gaining ownership of the Battleship *Iowa* now a 20 minute drive from our home.

She was very patient with me in writing the first edition. But as time went on working on this edition in 2016 she started having fits of anger that was not like her at all. It is unfortunate that the media does not make symptoms of upcoming heart failure that are more prevalent in women than in men more public. In the evening of December 15th, her heart gave out and sent her to Heaven. But my wife, partner, crew mate, mother of our daughter and grandmother of four, will always be in my heart

Forgive the quality of the photo. I scanned it from her USS *Iowa* Crew Member badge.

AKNOWLEDGMENTS

There are scores of people I would like to personally thank for contributing to this book with their personal support, providing photos and personal accounts. Some pleaded and goaded me into writing this book. I thank them for the years of effort I put into it and their stories and reviews. The hardest part came every time I think I have typed the last period and suddenly recall another incident that is worthy of recording for posterity. I have also spent a small fortune on shop plaques I have purchased, though many were donated for a standing museum display I thank those people also. All of them are now aboard the Battleship USS *IOWA* (BB-61) for a future LBNSY museum on board.

I must first thank Joseph G. Saltalamacchia III ("Salty") who found a couple of shoeboxes of negatives in a dumpster just before the shipyard's final closure and he gave me access to all of them. "Salty's" father also worked at the shipyard and they were a typical example of blood relation family working together in the shipyard "family". Most of all "Salty" acquired the database on all of the dry dockings performed at LBNSY and spent many hours reviewing it and correcting typos before uploading it to me to become Appendix A.

And if it wasn't for Rosie Pominville (a member of our reunion committee) for perfecting EXCEL charts we would not have Appendices A and E.

Thanks goes to Vaughn Garvey who gave me a photo copy of a 1985 listing of special dockings and notes that make up the Appendix B. After retiring from the shipyard, Vaughn joined Earthtech to oversee the sale of shipyard equipment. When I needed to take some photos of the buildings before demolition, Vaughn opened the gate for me and personally drove me wherever I wanted to go.

In the "Memories" book handed out during the closing ceremonies, I scanned many of the photos from the book, but Joe Sotis happened to have the entire set of negatives that were used for the photos. They had sat in his garage for over three years so he let me have all of them.

Special thanks to Bob Cooper for providing me the machinist's point of view and the flooding problems they had in the machine shop. I must also thank Bob Zimmerman for providing me with the grid index of shipyard buildings so I could identify them on the maps I reconstructed.

Many photos are from my personal collection of photos taken during open house holidays. That's not counting photos donated by other fellow employees.

I thank Gordon Douglas who hates to see history thrown away. After I retired he came to my house with a footlocker full of records, memos and drawings he found in my old file cabinets. Many of those items I used either as reference or for drawings to scan and trace for clear, uncluttered illustrations.

I thank Steve Gwinn for dropping off three boxes of newspaper clippings and several years of the LBNSY weekly newspaper, The *Digest*. I now could complete the list of graduate apprentices for appendix E which was started when Garvey loaned me a ledger of the first thirty years of graduates that was found in an abandoned desk by Gate 5.

Of course I must thank my wife, Julia, for her patience over the years it took me to write this book. She did not object to the time and effort I was putting in, but she knew an engineering type like me is constantly making changes and improvements. "Stop", she said. "Send in what you have now because if you don't, you will never be satisfied." And she's right. Here I am now with "Revision B".

INTRODUCTION

The Introduction in the first edition starts off with a word-for-word copy of an "official" description of the Naval facilities and is too long winded and takes up 7 pages. So this Revision "B" will just summarize it and I'll add in italics needed clarification..

On a web site hosted by the National Technology Transfer Center (NTTC), a boring History of the Long Beach Naval Shipyard is given. The figures on work force and ongoing projects date this about 1992 and were issued by our Code 140. In transcribing the document I deleted the last paragraphs that "rambled" on about the Self Help program. Ron Malin, of the Self Help design section, wrote that up but between his desk and final issue some telex gizmo dropped a couple of sentences and the entire conclusion. Ron was not a happy camper. Comments in *italics* are mine to update or clarify the line item. If you start to nod off before getting to Demographic Data, skip to the end of the transcription and pick it back up at my personal description. Basically I'll just list the main items and if you want to look them up on the Internet (or buy my 1st edition), be my guest

****

HISTORY (*From the Internet*): Before World War II it was apparent that a major anchorage and operation area was needed in the Long Beach-Los Angeles/San Pedro area. Public Law 667 authorized establishment of a fleet operating base, as well as land acquisition, harbor breakwater, buildings and other accessories. The Second Deficiency Bill of 1940 provided 19.8 million dollars for this work, and the naval dry docks, Terminal Island was established. The location was ideal since it is within the doubly protected west basin of the Port of Long Beach and yet only minutes away from the open sea. On 18 December 1940, a one-dollar check was given to the city of Long Beach for the acquisition cost of surface rights. Construction of the Moreel dry dock permitted ship work to begin on 7 April 1942. In 1945 an inner breakwater was constructed to protect ships against the surge of open seawaters.

In truth we knew something was going on well before the 1940's. Chapter 31 goes into greater detail of the Naval Air Station we had on the Los Angeles side of the city borders. It was opened as a small "civilian" air field in 1927. Before the year was out the Naval Reserve started pilot training at the field though their headquarters were at the Submarine Base in San Pedro. Then in 1935 the Navy took complete control of Allen Field and renamed it Reeves Field.

During World War II, the naval dry docks provided routine and battle damage repairs to a parade of ships.. *From 1941 to the end of 1945 Dry Dock repairs were done on 405 ships and crafts of all types. That's not counting on hundreds of ships that only needed pier side work done.*

Peak employment of 16,091 civilian employees was reached in August 1945.

It was intended to lease dry docking facilities to Bethlehem Steel *(that had a shipyard facility on the west end of Terminal Island)*; but, on 9 February 1943, SECNAV established the facilities as the US Naval Dry Docks, Roosevelt Base, California. The name of this facility was changed to Terminal Island Naval Shipyard on 30 November 1945. The name became Long Beach Naval Shipyard (NSY) in March 1948.

The Long Beach NSY was placed in an inactive status on 1 June 1950. The Korean War began less than one month later. Reactivation of the shipyard was directed on 4 January 1951. Since then, the shipyard has provided fleet support in the Southern California area. The Long Beach NSY workload today *(circa 1992)* consists dominantly of overhaul and maintenance of non-nuclear surface ships of the US Navy.

(Critical interpretation of the above paragraph: We did work on nuclear ships but NOT on their nuclear plants. To be nuclear certified, all we had to do was transfer trained and licensed nuclear plant mechanics, and their special tools and equipment, down from Bremerton and we would have been nuclear certified until their job was done and went back up to Puget Sound)

MISSION: *To serve the Fleet.*

LOCATION: The Long Beach NSY is located at Terminal Island between the cities of Long Beach and San Pedro and is about 23 miles south of the Los Angeles International Airport.

SIZE: The LBNSY industrial area covers 109 acres; of the total 214 owned. There are 120 permanent, 52 semi-permanent and 11 temporary buildings for a total of 183 buildings. *(All of the temporary buildings and some of the semi-permanent buildings were demolished to reduce depreciation value that was added to the man-day rate set by NAVSEA).* There are 17 shop work areas and 2.4 million square feet of covered building space. The shipyard has three graving docks and three industrial **piers** *(**Piers 1, 2 and 3 but excluding Pier Echo. The wooden Pier 4 was removed totally and Pier 6 was designated as part of the Naval Station in 1982 to allow missile loading of the Battleships. Pier 5 was merely a stub pier with a derrick to load garbage barges**).*

"B" Check the last maps of the shipyard in Appendix D. Then take an ant-acid when you realize the Political involvement that caused the demise of the shipyard. Also the next 3 paragraphs deleted as extraneous descriptions.

LBNSY has a well-planned modernization and military Program to meet critical needs to improve waterfront capabilities and facilities to provide flexibility to workload changes and technological advances for fleet support. The Facilities and Maintenance Dept. has four shops to support the Naval Hospital, Naval Station, Naval Supply Center, San Diego; and local DOD activities; with Navy housing at Seal Beach, Los Alamitos, San Pedro and Long Beach.

WORK FORCE/PAYROLL: Long Beach employed *(circa 1992)* about 4,300 civilians and is considered a major industry in the area. Payroll estimated at about $182.4 million annually.

2.3.2.2 DEMOGRAPHIC DATA

POPULATION: The shipyard's work force is mainly from the Long Beach-Los Angeles-San Pedro area but also other counties; Los Angeles (73.8%); Orange (21.5%); Riverside (2.5%); Sand Bernardino (1.9%) and San Diego (0.3%).

SKILL BASE: 7 percent of the work force requires initial training. About 28 percent are moderately skilled. About 66 percent can be categorized as highly skilled *(thanks to our Apprentice Program that graduated 2,870 people as skilled "mechanics").*

TRANSPORTATION ACCESS: The main thoroughfare to the shipyard on was the Long Beach Freeway (I-710) *(via the Gerald Desmond that replaced the Pontoon Bridge)* the Harbor Freeway (I-110) *(via the San Pedro ferry boat, then Vincent Thomas bridge).* These freeways can be reached from many other Southern California freeways. *(Ford Avenue Bridge also provided vehicular access and rail access. In WW II the bridge also had light rail tracks for Pacific Electric "Red Cars" operated by the U.S. Maritime Commission.)*

LOCAL INDUSTRIES:
COMPETATIVE - Southwest Marine - Al Larson Boat - San Pedro Boat - Willard Marine, Inc. *(Bethlehem Steel closed after an employee strike. Southwest Marine took over the property, Todd Shipyard's last Navy contract was building the last FFG-7 class ship. Fellows and Stuart went bankrupt after LBNSY pulled two ships out due to poor workmanship on one and not even starting a conversion job with the other ship.)*

Other private industries in the area make it difficult to retain a quality work force due to less than competitive wages paid by the Long Beach NSY. The problem exists primarily with the skilled craftsmen and engineers. Some of these industries are: McDonnell-Douglas Corp *(taken over totally by Boeing, which is also closing shop since the first edition of this book) - Hughes Aircraft, North American Rockwell – Northrop Aviation (which was turned into a movie studio and has now been bulldozed flat for something else)* – TRW - Varied other industries.

COMPLIMENTARY – Private industries that complement the shipyard: Southwest Marine, Al Larson Boat, San Pedro Boat. *(Also a number of private design agencies, such as Forster and Rados that did farm-out/farm-in drafting services for the shipyard's design division)*

****
Yawn!

Borrr – ing. If all you want to know about the shipyard is the cut-and-dry figures stated above, then you don't need to read this book. But then, you won't know what the shipyard really was like..

I spent over 39 years of my adult life as an employee at the Long Beach Naval Shipyard. I started there in 1954 as a shipfitter apprentice and retired in 1994 as a Naval Architecture Technician with credit for one Navy Patent, two Beneficial Suggestion Awards, one Outstanding Achievement Award and four Superior Achievement Awards. I already had the minimum time and age requirements in and wanted to extend my service another six months for an even forty years. However, I was offered a golden parachute and the shipyard was preparing for its third and final round with the Base Realignment and Closure (BRAC) committee. I had seen enough of the handwriting on the walls to tell me it wasn't going to make it through the last round. Therefore, by taking the "early" out, I would give one of my younger coworkers a few more months of paychecks.

I am somewhat of an expert on *Iowa* class Battleships, since retirement I have been in contact with many Battleship enthusiasts. After responding to a query, my answer was so long and I thought to throw in humor saying I should write a book. Well, Revision "A" is available and this Revision "B" is an add-on, clarification, addition and/or confirmation of certain items. It is not a book just about me. It is a book about the people who served the Shipyard. Some friends have said that some of those people would not be who they are without me. I thank you for that compliment, but I'm sure they would have made it somehow with or without me. But if my guidance, influence or advice has made one of them a better person or a better asset to the Navy, then I owe it to those that did the same for me.

CHAPTER 1
DRY DOCK 1

One of the most dramatic structures at LBNSY was the huge Dry Dock 1. Its official name was the *Morreel* dock. It was over a thousand feet long, one hundred and forty feet wide and originally fifty-five feet deep. It could berth the largest Aircraft Carriers and Battleships in the Navy. The shipyard had two other smaller dry docks that could berth up to a light Cruiser each. There were also several floating dry docks usually berthed out at pier 4 and each could hold Destroyers, Frigates and Submarines including a *Los Angeles* class Nuclear Submarine. **"B" But that is unrecorded as it was classified.**

But Dry Dock 1 was our pride and joy, along with the German Crane. However, the shipyard suffered a problem called subsidence. As oil was being removed from beneath the shipyard by slant drills, the soil under the dry dock settled until the north end of the dry dock was unacceptably lower than the south end. As a matter of fact, the entire shipyard at its northeast corner was sunk below sea level. By the time lawsuits forced the oil companies to repressurize their wells to prevent further sinking, the street at the north end of Dry Dock 1 was sixteen feet below sea level. Walls had to be built up above street level around all three dry docks. As the years went by, double walls with a second story street between them encircled Dry Dock 1. Extra concrete also had to be poured into the bottom of the dock for two reasons. One was obviously to level the bottom of the dock and make the bottom thicker so the overall depth would not be too great. The second was that stresses from subsidence on the dock floor finally gave way to the weight of the *Iowa* when she was docked there in December of 1945 and the concrete floor cracked.

It's really strange that the oil companies had to be forced, by legal action, to pump salt water back down into their wells to repressurize the area. It was actually beneficial to them because the water brought more oil up into the sandy sponge that formed the oil field and they could extract much more oil than expected.

A design study, this author was involved in, showed that we could dock the world's largest Aircraft Carriers of that time. Only the *Eisenhower* would require double high blocks to ensure a safe clearance on each side for her bilge keels.

The *Queen Mary* was docked there. That caused some problems with private contractors. There were even pickets outside the gates protesting that the Navy was doing private work. Well, normally the Navy would not do private work. But one fact conveniently overlooked by the protestors was that to prepare the ship the way the owners wanted, she had to be dry-docked. The nearest dry dock besides Long Beach that could take her was in San Francisco and that was a Navy dock also. Then there was Bremerton, Washington, another Navy dock. National Steel in San Diego had not built their large graving dock yet for ship construction (and even after it was built they refuse to use it for repair and overhaul work). So, the *Morreel* dock was the only dry dock available on the West Coast to take the ship.

All crane work had to be done with the Navy yard cranes including the removal of the ship's four propellers. One went back onto its strut for display. Three of the propellers were totally removed. One went to the Los Angeles County Museum, one to Disneyland and the third, finally in 1995, went to the Los Angeles Maritime Museum across the bay in San Pedro. Most other modifications were designed, built and installed by private contractors after the ship left the dry dock.

There were a couple of jobs, on the "*Queen*", that was assigned to our design division because they were directly dry dock related. For one thing, all of the intake and discharge openings below the ship's waterline had to be blanked off with bolted or welded steel plates. The only drawings available that showed where all the underwater openings are were old-fashioned blueprints (white lines on a blue background).

The types of reproduction equipment we had then would not be able to make legible copies off of the blue prints. Therefore John Bauer was tasked to trace the blueprints onto reproducible vellum. John is an excellent draftsman and, though it was a strain on his eyes even with a small light table to shine through the blueprint, he did a very nice tracing showing both sides of the hull of the ship and the locations for every shell opening.

Just as he was almost finished with the drawing, John walked out to the dock to look at the ship. He looked up at the funnels (smoke stacks) and said, "Oh sh*t!" He came back to the office and dug out a book from the technical library that had pictures of the "*Queen*". Sure enough, *The Queen Mary* has three funnels but the drawing given to John to trace had four funnels. It was the *Queen Elizabeth*. Now, the hulls are almost identical, except for the locations of many of the underwater openings. So, after procuring the correct blueprint of the correct ship from the Cunnard Lines in England, John traced it all over again.

While the *Queen Mary* was still in dry dock, one propeller was to be left in place and was supposed to be turned slowly by an electric motor. Unfortunately the motor turning concept, designed by an outside private agency, didn't work. Additionally, LBNSY had some design work to do in relation to the in-place propeller. We were to design a cut for an archway through the shell of the ship and also design a watertight box to be welded to the outside of the ship so visitors could walk in and look down at the propeller in the water. A transparent deck was installed in the box and a steel walkway was installed around it for the visitors. To prevent corrosion of the bronze propeller, the enclosure below the deck would be filled with fresh water.

The structural design section was tasked to design the box-like enclosure and was assigned to Gary Cook. John Priftakis was the lead engineer to check all calculations. John was originally from Greece, and after retirement, moved back to Greece for a while. His engineering degree was actually in Naval Architecture when he graduated from MIT in 1944. Gary was a young engineer with a degree in Civil Engineering. But he was real sharp with a good sense of humor and was also a good skeet shooter. Gary and his wife though had a higher love and that was raising Labrador Retrievers. He eventually quit the Civil Service to raise his dogs.

Gary was pushed into a time crunch on the design of the box and when his first submittal of the drawing went to John for checking, he was rather anxious. The chief engineer, Phil Finkelstein, insisted it had to be on his desk at such and such time on so and so date because big shots from England were going to be there to review it.

John put aside all other work, checked and red lined corrections to be made and rechecked Gary's calculations on water pressure, weight loadings, etc. By this time Gary was getting rather anxious and made the changes as fast as possible. He only had a few hours to do them and still had to have John do a final check and then get three copies made before going to Finkelstein's office. They are down to minutes now and Finkelstein is calling on the phone for those plans. Gary ran the drawing down to reproduction himself and got a special order to have check prints made ahead of everybody else. He ran back upstairs and was folding the check prints while Finkelstein was calling again. He ran them down to Phil Finklestein's office (our Chief Entineer) and announced, "Here's the Queens Box."

Then he looks around and sees all knighted British VIPs from England glaring at him for such a demeaning remark of their Sovereign. Finkelstein laughed about it, but I think that was then Gary seriously considered raising Labradors.

"B"   However, as of this month of March 2017, the various owners of the Queen lacked almost total maintenance of the hull and various machinery in the ship. It has been estimated to cost about 300 MILLION dollars to repair her. The biggest problem is that we no longer have a Dry Dock for her. So, no matter what repairs can be done inside, without a Dry Dock to seal the outside, the ship is a loss.

The first Battleship to have repairs done in Dry Dock 1 was the USS *Nevada* in WW II. In 1946, *Nevada* was again at the shipyard to be prepared as an atomic bomb target ship for Test Able at Bikini Atoll. Many large ships were docked in Dry Dock 1 and served the Battleships *Arkansas* (BB 33), *Texas* (BB 35), *Nevada* (BB 36), *West Virginia* (BB 44), *Iowa* (BB 61), *New Jersey* (BB 62) and *Missouri* (BB 63).

We never had any nuclear carriers in that dry dock, but the largest conventionally powered carriers had their major repair work done in it that included the *Yorktown* (CV 10), *Hornet* (CVS 12), *Bennington* (CVS 20), *Kearsarge* (CV/CVA/CVS 33), *Bataan* (CVL 29), *Philippine Sea* (CV 47), *Ranger* (CV 61), *Ticonderoga* (CVA 14), *Lexington* (CVA 16), *Bon Homme Richard* (CVA 31), *Oriskany* (CVA 34), *Shangri La* (CVA 38), *Coral Sea* (CVA 43) and *Constellation* (CVA 64). Some escort Carriers were also docked in the *Morreel* dock but most were small enough to also fit in dry docks 2 and 3. Most LPH's were put in Dry Dock 1 though twice we were able to fit one into dry dock 2 even if it was a tight squeeze. The LHA's are as big as a WW II carrier so Dry Dock 1 berthed the *Tarawa* (LHA 1), *Belleau Wood* (LHA 3) and *Peleliu* (LHA 5) for their overhauls.

When the *Constellation* was in dry dock, we had an open cage personnel elevator at the north end of the dock. The stern of the carrier towered over us even when we were at the top and it was like being lowered to a subterranean world as we descended to the bottom of the dock. It is like a small city down there with supervisor shacks, stowage areas, parking for Bobcat skip loaders, rolling staging, welding rod issue booth, paint shack and just about anything else you needed for the bottom work. Everything, that is, except restrooms. You had to climb that fifty-five feet back up (or take the elevator if it was working) to go to the head.

The last major size carrier we had in Dry Dock 1 was the *Ranger* when she was demilitarized after decommissioning. She was actually decommissioned in her home port of San Diego, and then towed up to Long Beach to have her sea water injection and discharge openings sealed, catapult tracks covered, weather deck machinery removed and stowed on the hangar deck and finally sealed up for her final tow to Bremerton.

One of the very last times the dry dock was used was to dock the German Crane so another floating crane outside the dock could dismantle and lower the center jib boom. The very last time Dry Dock 1 was ever used was to dock a large floating dry dock named the *Steadfast*. Over the life span of the shipyard, Dry Dock 3 docked 757 ships, Dry Dock 2 docked 779 ships and Dry Dock 1 docked 1,120 ships and crafts of various types.

Dry Dock 1 was to be the only World War II built portion left of the Long Beach Naval Shipyard. But the Port of Long Beach could not find a reputable tenant to operate it and the eighteen acres around it. So it has also been filled in and now no one can tell that there ever was a Naval so there is no way to tell there every was a super dry dock on Terminal Island.

So, how do you build one of the world's largest Dry Dock?
You start off with a lot of steel framing then figure out a way to pump the water out.

Then you follow up with jillions of tons of concrete & re-bar. Well, you get the idea.

Above photos donated by an anonymous "yardbird".

The first Battleship USS *Nevada* (BB-36) to be in Dry Dock 1 in February of 1943.   Courtesy: "Salty"

Press release photo of USS *Iowa* (BB-61) entering Dry Dock 1 in December of 1945.
Author's collection purchased on Ebay

The *Queen Mary* in Dry Dock 1 with the German Crane nearby

Another view of the *Queen Mary* with the "box" installation on the port side for propeller viewing.
Courtesy: John L. "Jack" Whitmeyer

A well packed Dry Dock 1 from July 1 to July 30, 1945. (10) LCI's: L17, L19, L190, L192, L195, L2, L41, L42, L43 & L46. (1) Destroyer: USS *Mustin* (DD-413). (1) Escort Carrier: USS *Petroff Bay* (CVE-80).
Author's collection

CHAPTER 2
HERMAN THE GERMAN

Another pride and joy was the German Crane (YD-171). It was a self-propelled floating crane built in Bremerhaven, Germany in 1941. The crane was originally designed in 1912 for use in the First World War but construction was stopped. In the late 1930's, however, Hitler specifically ordered four of the cranes to be built. One was destroyed in an Allied Air Raid, another was captured by the British but capsized in the English Channel, another was taken by the Soviet Union and never heard of since (some distant photos have claimed to have identified it but the Jib Booms are totally wrong) so the only one left alive was ours at LBNSY.

It used a luffing screw mechanism, sort of like a gigantic rack and worm gear, to extend or pull in the main jibs for heavy lifts. It could lift four hundred metric tons. The ten-ton jib boom extending above the main jibs was two hundred and eighty feet in the air at its lowest position. It would rise up to three hundred and seventy four feet when the main jibs were cranked in for very heavy lifts.

The crane was confiscated from Germany as a war prize. It was totally dismantled and was towed to Long Beach. Other shipyards had big hammerhead cranes for shipbuilding, but Long Beach had no heavy lift capabilities. After all, the shipyard was built as a wartime need in only about three years. The crane barge was set down in Dry Dock 1 at the south end by the watertight caisson. Then the crane structure was reassembled. Another floating crane, the converted Battleship *Kearsarge* ex (BB-05), was used to lift the highest pieces up into place. All new concrete counterweights were cast. Four hundred tons of concrete at the bottom of the machinery house and two hundred tons in a cantilevered extension called the pendulum. During an air raid over Germany the pendulum received a direct hit and was blown off. You could walk around several spots of the deck and see where war damage had been repaired with clad welding.

Reassembly of the Crane was completed in January of 1948. An engineer from Germany, Louis Dietz, was brought over to assist in translating the crane plans into English. Many shipyard workers of that time related how impressed they were with Dietz as he spoke perfect American style English with no trace of an accent. The crane was finally put into service on December 31, 1948 after extensive testing was done.

A contest to give the crane a name was won by a lady in one of the offices naming it "The *Titan*". But most people called it "*Herman the German*". A couple of years later, however, it was discovered that another heavy lift crane was already named "*Titan*". So we changed "*Herman's*" name to "*Titan II*".

All of the original German signs and label plates were kept in place. The barge section carried a crew of twenty-two men and had its own Galley and berthing areas. Its propulsion was by three Voith-Schneider cycloidal propellers powered by constant-speed AC motors (540-kw, 850-volt, 3-phase, 50-Hz). The motors were powered by diesel-generators. In 1969 the original German-made Mannerheim diesels (375-rpm, 900-hp driving 800-kva, 850-volt, 50-Hz Seimens generators) were replaced by American built General Motors diesels (750-rpm, 1,200-hp driving Ideal electric generators at 1,062-kva, 850-volt, 50-Hz). This conversion cost $317,650.

But the propeller system remained the same. It was a very unusual propeller system as well.. Looking at one of them from the bottom of the dry dock, you would see three circular plates in the bottom of the hull. Arranged around each plate were six propeller blades, each about six feet long that looked more like long skinny rudders. Actually, those blades were variable pitched blades and as the whole unit rotated the blades would constantly change their pitch so the barge would go any direction you wanted it to go. It could do five knots in any direction, including sideways. It had self-compensating ballast tanks so as the crane made a heavy lift the tanks would counter flood automatically to keep the crane level.

Above the propellers and inside the barge were circular glass plates etched with degrees around the perimeter. At one time the Germans decided to divide up the circle into 400 degrees giving each quadrant 100 degrees. That way azimuth angles could be transmitted in decimals and be less confusing when coupled with time units of minutes and seconds. These glass plates were etched with the German circle of 400 degrees. When doing some structural repairs on the barge, this author verbally noted this to the workers and cautioned them to protect those plates. Alas, a couple of nights later somebody had dropped a staging plank on one of them and cracked the glass all the way across. Whether it was ever properly replaced is not known. Another piece of history destroyed because of irresponsibility.

In the early 1950s a tugboat sank in Los Angeles Harbor just off of Todd Shipyards. The crane, being totally self-propelled, went over from Long Beach to Los Angeles and lifted the two hundred and sixty-ton boat out of the water to carry it over to a floating dry dock. This was not a first of its kind of lift for the crane either. One of our Planners acquired a photograph of the crane taken in World War II, when the Germans still owned it, lifting a small Norwegian submarine out of the water. All in a day's work for Herman.

Perhaps her most famous lift was when Howard Hughes enormous two hundred and twenty-ton flying boat *Hercules* (commonly called the *Spruce Goose*) was floated out of its hangar. The crane picked it up to put it on land for repairs and preparation as a museum attraction over by the *Queen Mary*. Then the crane picked up the plane again several months later and placed it on a barge so it could be floated over to a new dome shaped hangar. When the Battleship *New Jersey* had to have the one hundred and eighteen ton center gun barrel of Turret II replaced, the German Crane was the one to take the old one out and put the new one in.

The crane was also used for very high lifts as well as very heavy lifts. When the USS *Bon Homme Richard* (CVA-31) was undergoing repairs, the highest antenna on the mast, a discus shaped satellite-receiving antenna, had to be replaced. It is not very heavy, but would be very dangerous to remove just by hanging onto the ladder even with safety belts. I was up on that mast, inspecting another installation, when suddenly I felt the staging, surrounding the mast structure, shaking from being bumped. I looked over and there was a personnel box hanging from the center ten-ton jib about ten feet from me. In it was three very serious looking mechanics and a very worried looking rigger because the two-hundred ton hooks of the crane below us were banging into the mast staging. The crane operator must really have had the fits as well, though his cab was high enough to see what was going on, he was actually on the OTHER side of the pier. The operator had to pull back on the jibs, move the crane down the pier a few feet, then reach out with the jibs again so he could get the personnel box up to the antenna.

I got off that mast as fast as I could. By the time I got down to the flight deck, the crane was in a better position and the mechanics were reaching out toward the antenna to unbolt it. By the time I got out on the brow, those mechanics had probably set a record in disconnecting that antenna as the crane was already bringing them back down to the pier.

1976 & 1981 brochures, handed out during a shipyard open houses, lists the crane's major lifts and is copied below. However a few clarifications and additions have been added to it.

Test lifting gear of LCU – 425 tons. (Bi-annual test of crane)
Transferring nine 16"/50 gun barrels for possible re-gunning of New Jersey in 1968 -- 118 tons EACH.
Pop Up launcher for Polaris underwater missile firing tests - 240 tons
YC-473 barge into Dry Dock for conversion to Wigwam atomic bomb carrier – 110 tons
3 Squaw midget submarines for Wigwam atomic bomb tests – 300 tons each.
Steam locomotives for Korea – 110 tons (each).
Transformers from Japan, Sweden and West Germany for LAWP – 160 to 280 tons each.
SEALAB II underwater exploration habitat – 240 tons.
Salvaged sunken tug in Los Angeles Harbor – 260 tons.
Steel casting for Niles planer – 112 tons (two lifts).
First Atomic reactor on West Coast for San Onofre power plant – 325 tons.
Erection bulk loader San Pedro – 170 ton and 215 ton lifts.
Prefabricated deckhouse on commercial oiler Ticonderoga at Todd Shipyard – 200 tons.
Move portal cranes from Los Angeles and Long Beach harbor to LBNS – 180 tons each.
Water barge at Pier G in Long Beach – 200 tons.
Container crane at Pier J in Long Beach – 150 ton and 45 ton lifts.
20 October 1980 - moved the Howard Hughes Flying Boat H-4 – 440,000 pounds.
"B" Lifting nine (9) 16"/50 gun barrels (one at a time) that were retrieved from Subic Bay Naval Base that were originally sent there to re-gun the New Jersey during the Viet Nam War. Each barrel weighs 118 standard tons each. Two barrels were sent to the China Lake Naval Test Center in the Mojave Desert for some project that was never carried out. Each truck that carried one barrel used a flatbed trailer that had 24 wheels to support the weight. A smaller floating crane, however, made a "wrong turn" at the end of the Mole and decided to off load the barrel on the side lawn of the Los Angeles Maritime Museum just 5 miles away.

Many people wondered what it would be like to climb up to the top of the German Crane. This author had that experience and will now depart from second or third party descriptions to give the reader a personal account of that adventure.

Being young, adventurous, foolish and not afraid of heights, I always wanted to climb up to the aircraft warning light at the top of the crane. The year I graduated from the apprenticeship, 1958, I was given the opportunity to realize my dream. New stop limit switches had to be installed up in the structure of the booms. The new American made Cutler-Hammer switches of course required new foundations of shaped steel plates to be welded onto the side beams of the main jibs. Any shipfitter or welder who wanted the job had to first pass a physical at the dispensary. I passed as well as Chuck Hastings and Dave Dickson who also graduated in my class. They were "lucky" enough to climb up there the day before I reported aboard.

Our first task together was to haul up the welding leads to the two hundred and fifty-foot level. The riggers had reeved a line through a single block (pulley) at the joint of the jibs and then through a block on the deck of the barge. We would tie the line to the end of the welding lead and start pulling it up. We formed a chain gang of line pullers and as we got near the end of the barge would run forward to get another bight on the line. We had to do that twice, once for the welding lead and once for the ground lead. Then we hauled up our tool bags and the limit switch foundations the same way.

Our supervisor, Charlie Callahan, gave us all safety belts. But the crane is huge and all access above is by inclined, rather than vertical, ladders with solid handrails. The jib booms have catwalks with handrails on them and I felt very comfortable up there. So I left my safety belt in the operator's cab because it was too bulky. It was a beautiful sight from up there. The air was clear and no bosses to bother you. I wished I had a camera with me to take abstract photos of the crane structure from those angles. I even climbed all the way up to the aircraft warning light and satisfied my fantasy, without a safety belt. The riggers who worked that crane all the time never bothered with safety belt either.

Climbing up the crane I found several more areas of repaired battle damage. It was a tough crane. Of the four built, one was completely destroyed in an air raid, a second was lost by the British when they tried to tow it across the English Channel and a third incomplete crane was taken by Russia and never heard of again for several years until it was supposedly photographed in Vladivostok. I have my doubts about that photo as it was taken at quite a distance and the main jib booms angled outwards instead of being parallel. Therefore, as far as we know, Herman was the only one of its kind left.

Our welder, Dave Kaiawalu from Hawaii, was busy with a job on deck. Plus his mind was on a luau he was organizing for the weekend. I told him that when he was ready, he could tie his tool bag and welding hood on the line and we would pull it up from up above. After about an hour waiting for Dave, I started back down to see what his delay was. Just then, he was arriving at our level, two hundred and fifty feet above the deck, huffing and puffing. He had his tool bag with his welding stinger and two cans of rod and was wearing his heavy welding hood on his hard hat. Obviously he hadn't paid attention to me when I told him he could tie those things on the end of the line down below.

Dave was pretty fatigued and didn't notice the height at first. He only remarked how heavy his welding hood had become. We attached his stinger to the welding lead and walked out onto the jib. Suddenly Dave looks over the side down to pier 6 below us. There were some automobiles there as a transport ship further out on the pier was getting ready to deploy. Dave gulped and said, "Christ. I bought a couple of cars like that for my kids for Christmas. How high up are we anyway?"

"About two hundred and fifty feet", I answered. At that moment, the crane barge gently bumped the wood fenders alongside the pier and the structure shook for a few seconds. "Hey! This thing is shaking!" Dave exclaimed.

"Yeah." I replied. "If it didn't bend some, it would shatter like glass." Just a little exaggeration there on my part. Well, being part Irish, my sense of humor often gets to me.

Dave then dropped down to one knee, quickly attached the line from his safety belt to the lower handrail and hung onto the upper hand rail with one hand. He would NOT let go of that upper rail. When he had to weld, I had to push his hood down over his eyes and he would weld with one hand. And I wasn't even leaning against anything. After a while, Dave did get accustomed to the height and was starting to enjoy the sights.

As mentioned earlier, there was a transport ship below us getting ready to deploy the next day. The stern of the ship was under the ends of the main jibs of the crane. We had to weld a limit switch foundation out there and our experience with previous foundations told us that big globs of welding slag was going to hit the deck of that ship. There was a Marine walking his post on the fantail and we yelled down to him to get out of the way. The jibs dip down from their main knuckle and were only about two hundred feet above the Marine.

But he couldn't hear us or couldn't tell where the voices were coming from. So we decided to do a couple of quick tack welds first. I would lean over the jibs to try to guess when the sentry's route would take him out of the way of the falling sparks. Then I would give the okay to weld a one-inch long tack to hold the foundation in place. The glowing globs of molten metal and slag would spiral down like slow tracers toward that Marine. Well, at least he was wearing a helmet liner. The globs would hit the deck just behind him. He stopped, looked around and wondered what that noise was. We yelled some more, but to no avail. So we welded another tack. SPLAT! SPLAT! SPLAT! The Marine stopped and stared at the deck intensely. We were now starting to get hoarse from our yelling and he still couldn't hear us. Well, we couldn't wait and that foundation had to be production welded in place so mounting holes could be drilled for the switches. Finally, some of the splats landed in front of the sentry and he looked up to see several more heading toward him like tracer bullets. He ran forward about fifty feet and glared up at us. At least he kept his M-1 Carbine shouldered.

Even before the BRAC decided to close the shipyard, one of the handwritings on the wall was to deactivate the German crane and find another user for it. In 1995 the crane was partially dismantled to be towed to Panama. The center ten-ton jib was detached and rigged down between the twin two-hundred ton jibs and secured for the tow. I saw the crane the day before the tow and it looked like it was hanging its head in shame. Like a child who had done its best but was now rejected and being thrown out in the street. Friends asked me if I was going to return the next day to see it towed out. There was no way I could bring myself to witness that. Instead, I stayed home, broke out a bottle and lifted a toast in honor of the best piece of crane design and engineering anyone had ever seen.

The Crane effortlessly lifting 110 ton steam locomotives in 1955 for shipment to South Korea. "Digest"

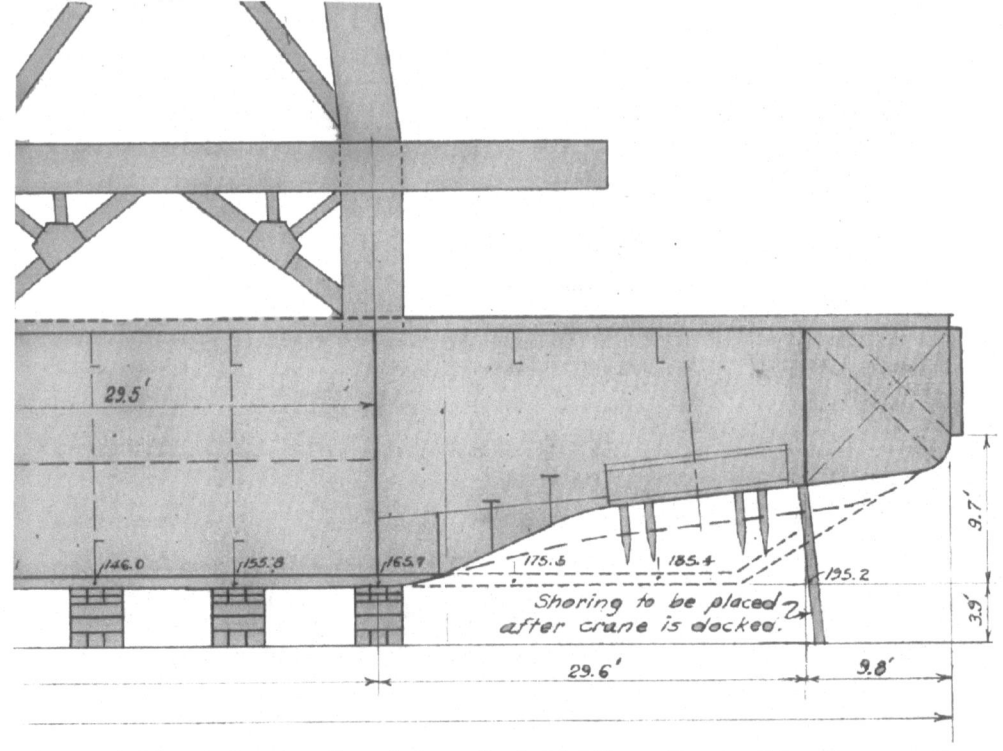

This air view shot from 1956 shows the enormous height of the German Crane and its ability to reach across the pier to ship masts on the other side.
Courtesy: "Salty"

The Variable Pitch propellers (a.k.a. Cycloidal Propellers) of the German Crane

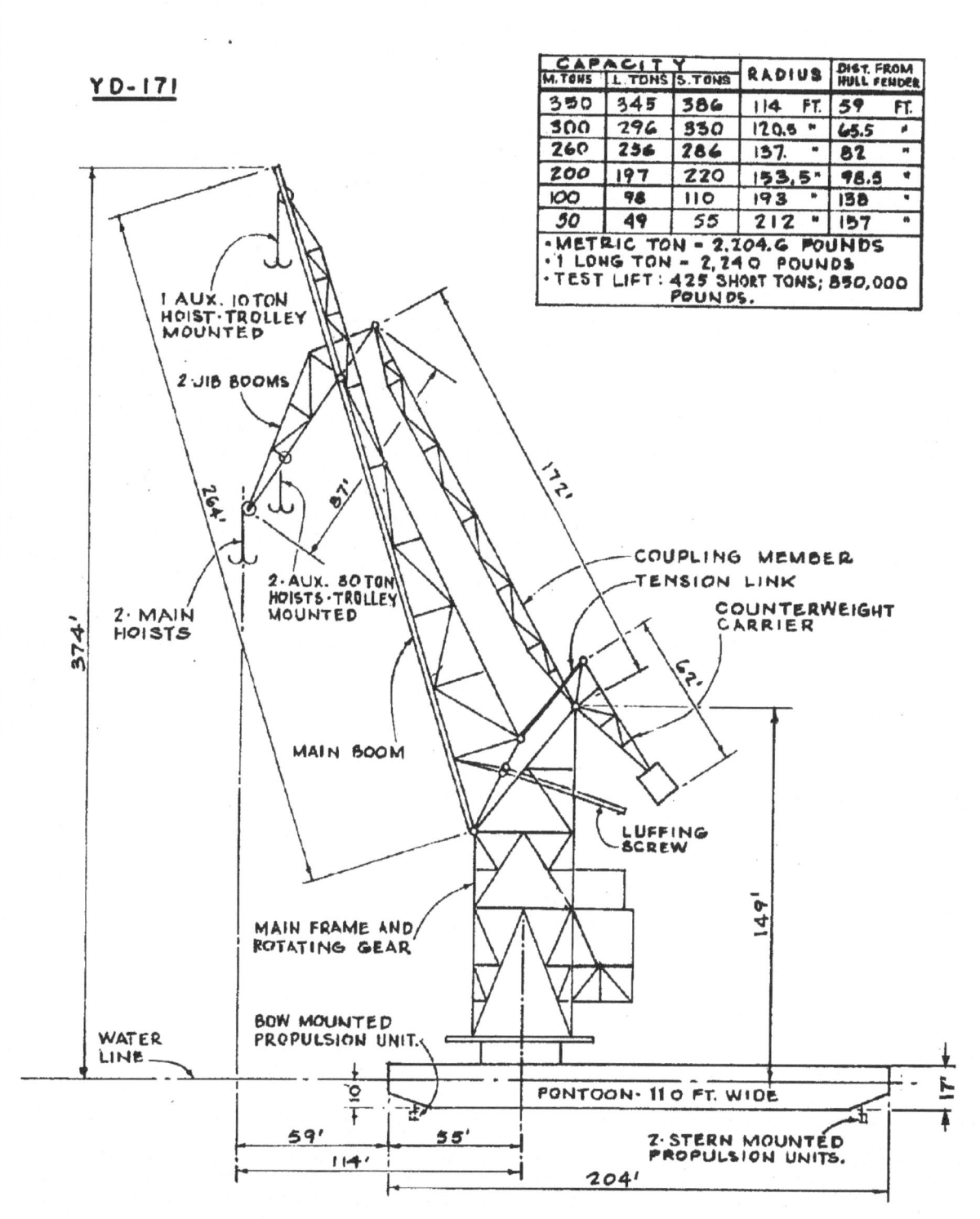

Fig. 4-3: This diagram of the German Crane and its lifting capacities was always included in handouts to visitors interested in the crane.

From the author's personal collection.

Two giants working together. TITAN II and USS *New Jersey* preparing to end the Cold War.

Being towed away to Panama. Auf Wiedersehen mine freund. Courtesy: Argonautics Marine Engineering

Titan II in Panama now without the 10 ton centerline jib boom.

The photo above was taken by Diane Duacsek. She is the daughter of Captain Anthony W. Duacsek, C.O. of LBNSY from August 14, 1973 to August 19, 1975. As of 2016/17 she is the recording secretary of the LBNSY picnic reunion committee. While on vacation, you will notice that she wore a special T-Shirt just for the occasion of photographing *Titan*. Once a yardbird, Always a yardbird.

CHAPTER 3
TITAN vs. *HERCULES*

Sounds like the title to a "sword and sandal" movie, doesn't it? As mentioned earlier, the official name of the German Crane was YD-171 *Titan*. What many people don't know, however, is that the official name of Howard Hughes' giant flying boat was the H-4 *Hercules*. It was more commonly known as the *Spruce Goose*, a name coined by the press because it was mostly constructed of wood. Ironically, no Spruce was used in the plane at all. Hughes stored the plane in a huge hangar on the east side of Pier Echo.

In 1980, the land the hangar was on was to be taken over for more active port use rather than stowage of the airplane. The plane would be moved near the *Queen Mary* inside a huge display dome. Getting the plane out of the hangar was difficult because the land had sunk a bit due to subsidence. Picking up the plane to put it the other side of the channel could only be done by the German Crane.

Actually, the need to move the plane out of the hangar went back to the 1970's when the Navy was to "confiscate" it for unfinished work by the Hughes Company. Back then, there were doubts that the plane even existed. However, Jim Bibeau, the supervisor of the fittings design section, was assigned to be the lead structural engineering supervisor for figuring out a way of lifting the plane out of the water. He came back from the hangar with some real sharp black and white photos of the plane in perfect condition. Because of the subsidence lowering the small dry dock the plane was in, John Bauer was tasked to draw a barge-like cradle and lift plane.

The project got shelved, however, when the legal problems between Hughes and the Navy were settled. But by 1980, Howard Hughes was dead, the port wanted the land for a fueling dock and the Hughes Company wanted to get rid of their white elephant.

The move was done in October of 1980 and many of us watched it from the east windows of building 300. Jim Bibeau was the lead engineer again overseeing the lift with Bob Riha assisting. Bob's son, Bob Riha Jr. (a former child actor) was climbing all over the crane and hangar with dozens of cameras doing a photo spread for publication. When the plane finally emerged from the hangar, a boat pulled it out into the bay a short distance for show and positioning for the lift. The propellers had been removed, probably so Hughes' former co-pilot wouldn't turn over the engines and take off one more time for a short hop. But as the hours went by and the crane had not done the pick up yet, we knew something was amiss. But, by the next morning, the plane was finally up on land.

The following month, Jim Bibeau and I went to Pascagoula, Mississippi to check on the *Kidd* class Destroyers that Ingalls was adding aluminum & Kevlar appliqué armor to. Now, there isn't much to do in Pascagoula after the sun goes down except to eat dinner, go to your hotel room and watch TV. On our second night, Jim called me over to his room and he had this stack of notes and a very rough draft of a report on the move of the airplane. The editor of the shipyard weekly newspaper, *The Digest*, had asked him to write an article on it. But Jim said, "Dick. You're a better writer than me. Can you put these notes in some sort of sensible order and come up with something? Not tonight, though. Next week would be fine."

"Sure". I answered. "Not much on TV tonight anyway." So, I went back to my room and wrote out one of my usual long-winded reports. I told Jim the reason I do that is because it's much easier to edit out superfluous sentences than try to add them into the margins for final typing.

However, the November 21st edition of *The Digest* printed my entire write up word for word (except the first three paragraphs which are a consolidation of notes between the editor, Jim Bibeau and myself) along with two pages of photos. The following is an exact transcription of that article.

****

To move the world's largest airplane, the world's largest self-propelled floating crane, the U.S. Navy's YD-171, was called into service. The YD-171 Titan crane and the Hughes Flying Boat, Hercules, have been neighbors ever since the YD-171 arrived at the Long Beach Naval Shipyard after being captured from the Germans during World War II. While the crane dominated the skyline in Long Beach Harbor, the airplane was secluded from view in a metal hangar on Pier E.

The YD-171 has been called upon many times to make special lifts for private concerns, but this lift would be the largest (in size, not weight) as the enormous plane measures 219 feet long, with a wingspan of 320 feet. It was also the first time hundreds of newsmen from around the world, television cameras and dignitaries would assemble to observe a job assignment while light planes, helicopters and the Goodyear blimp watched overhead.

Meetings and conferences between the Shipyard and the plane's owners and contract movers took place over the past few months. Captain J.A. Gildea, Shipyard Commander, assigned Art Green, code 224, as Liaison Coordinator and Tom Logan as Production Controller. Rigger General Foreman Curtis L. Halk was tasked with the lift, Structural and Fittings Branch Head James L. Bibeau was assigned engineering duties and General Foreman Harold Johnson was in charge of crane operations.

On the morning of October 29, 1980, the giant Hughes Flying Boat, H-4 Hercules (popularly called the Spruce Goose), left its hangar on Pier E after a seclusion spanning nearly a third of a century. On the evening of October 30, 1980, the giant U.S. Navy floating crane, YD-171 Titan (popularly called the German Crane), lifted the H-4 out of the water and set it down in a temporary storage area on Pier E.

During that time, speculation, rumors and jokes ("They found another will under the windshield wiper and are reading it.") abounded as to why an expected 10 hour transfer took two days. The total operation was beset with one technical complication after another. To clarify the situation, here are a few facts. Much of the first day was spent getting the plane out of its hangar, problems of flooding the dry dock and opening the rusty gates had to be surmounted. It was not brought alongside the YD-171 until 4:50 PM due to difficulties lifting the cradle out of the dock. The special lifting cradle required extensive modifications. The modifications took all night - adding spreader beams, rigging air bags and support drums.

The H-4 weighs 230,000 pounds; the cradle, another 150,000 pounds. The total lift of 190 tons was half the YD-171's 385 ton working load. However, because of the airplane's enormous size, the main hooks of the Titan would not have enough hoisting distance to lift the Hercules high enough out of the water to land on the pier. This was overcome by providing an assist with the 30 ton hoists through an ingenious double bridle rig. This necessitated some modifications to the cradle by adding padeyes and blocks for the 30-ton hooks that would lift the cradle to the main hoist pendants.

By 10:00 AM on the 30th, the cradle was on the channel bottom ready for positioning the H-4 over it. By the time the plane was cautiously moved up the channel by tugs and turned, it was 12:05 PM when the first mooring line was attached.

There was difficulty in holding the plane in position, even with a four-point moor, as she is highly responsive to wind and current. She had become partially airborne the week before inside her old hangar which acted like a wind tunnel after the sides were cut out.

Mating the cradle to the hull of the H-4 was an extremely tricky move that caused many aborts of the lift. The problem was finally solved by timing the cradle lift with the hauling of the airplane toward the crane. At 6:54 PM the cradle was perfectly mated and by 7:30 PM the YD-171 was underway, traversing the channel to Berth 118 with the Hercules safely carried like a stork with a baby. At 8:10 PM the "Spruce Goose" was on dry land. At 9:05 PM the spreader bar was set down on the pier. The Navy rigging was then returned to the deck and the YD-171 retired to the Shipyard to resume normal duties involving ships of the U.S. Navy.

All the shipyard employees involved - from the riggers and crane operators to the photographer and audio visual specialist - worked as a team with the safety of the airplane and everyone and everything involved uppermost in their minds. They took painstaking care to insure that the load was delicately balanced and snugly secured. It touched land without a scratch.

As the plane eased out of the water the crane operator sounded his air whistle. Tug boats in the Harbor followed suit and sounded their horns with the typical greeting to an ocean liner coming into port. The move was dubbed as "the second flight" of the Spruce Goose. And, indeed it was, as many dignitaries climbed out of the cabin after landing on dry land. The first flight occurred on November 2, 1947 when Howard Hughes flew the airplane for 60 seconds over Long Beach Harbor.

The Spruce Goose is now being shrouded with a special covering for protection against the elements. The plane's engines will be put back in shape for a final taxi next September to a new hangar next to the Queen Mary where she will become a tourist attraction. At that time, the YD-171 will again be summoned into service.

****

After that article was written, the plane was moved into its huge dome shaped hangar near the Queen *Mary*. It served as an attraction for many years and was even in one scene of the movie *The Rocketeer*.

For the tourists, a metal catwalk was placed athwart ships through the fuselage and visitors could only walk through and view the immense size by looking forward or aft. A wax mannequin of Howard Hughes was placed in the pilot's seat and as visitors climbed the stairways they could see "him".

But there is something very haunting about that plane and "haunting" is the correct word to use. At the time of the move, there was litigation going on over authenticity of various wills supposedly left by Howard Hughes. One man claimed to have picked Hughes up one night in the Nevada desert, not knowing who he was, and produced a will given to him years later as thanks. A movie was even made of it called *Howard and Me*. Interestingly, he was the former son-in-law of Meredith West, one of our secretaries (also a WW II Marine veteran who marched in FDR's funeral). Therefore, the abundance of wills created a joke by Bill Dickson about finding another one under the instrument panel of the plane.

Jim Bibeau was a very religious person. But he swore with his hand raised that as they were trying to position the plane for the lift, and when the sun hit the windshield just right - you could see Howard Hughes himself sitting in the pilot's seat. Jim of course suspected there was some sort of a flaw in the glass pane of the windshield. Perhaps slow liquid creep being stored for so many years distorted it just a bit. But still, he said it was the eeriest thing he had ever seen and several other people also saw it.

The plane served as a moderately successful tourist attraction for many years. Then one of the latter operators of the *Queen Mary/Spruce Goose* tourist center decided it was too expensive to maintain. So, the plane's wings were removed and the whole thing was hauled on a barge up to Oregon to be reassembled. The empty dome has been used mostly as a sound stage for movies, most notably as the bat cave for one or two of the Batman movies. The *Queen Mary* is still having problems drawing enough visitors even with a *Titanic* display on board. The city brought in an old Russian Submarine to boost interest even though that sub lost money when it was on display in Australia for two years. The German Crane was hauled down to Panama to continue service there. The Naval Station and Naval Shipyard have been bulldozed for a "Parking Lot" for a container shipping terminal.

"B" Jim Bibeau retired around 1990 but later died in 2006 from Alzheimer's Disease. Tom Logan died at the age of 62 from auto accident injuries. Bob Riha died in October of 1997 but his son (Bobby Jr.) now works as a photo-journalist for a major newspaper. Bobby even joined me in 2011, to ride the *Iowa* from Benicia to Richmond, California to begin her refurbishment before going to her final home in San Pedro in 2012. Perhaps the words eerie, haunting, ghostly and fatalistic used to describe the vision of Howard Hughes could be supplemented by one other word; **CURSE**. That is if you believe in that kind of stuff.

This is the most commonly issued photo of Titan picking up Hercules at night. In color its very eye catching but even in grayscale it is still very impressive.
                                  US Navy photo

CHAPTER 4
ATOMIC BOMBS

OPERATION CROSSROADS:
LBNSY was involved in two atomic bomb tests. The first was in 1946 and was the famous tests at Bikini Atoll in the Pacific named Operation *Crossroads*. The shipyard's involvement was mostly to prepare two target ships for the tests and outfit non-target support ships that monitored the tests.

"B" The first Battleship to have repairs done in Dry Dock 1 was the USS *Nevada* in WW II. In 1946, *Nevada* was again at the shipyard to be prepared as the main target ship for the Atomic Bomb Test Able at Bikini Atoll. This author has a personal connection with Test Able as a cousin of mine; Major Woodrow (Woody) Swancutt was the pilot of the B-29 that dropped the bomb in that test. Well, Vern R. Swancutt was my grandfather, therefore my mother's maiden name was Margaret Swancutt. All from Iowa and/or Nebraska. So, in a way I was also involved in that project, 2,000 miles away however.

"Woody" preparing to take off for Bikini

"Woody" at the controls as we listened on radio.

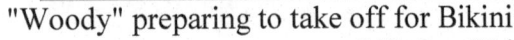
Stills from "Trinity and Beyond - The Atomic Bomb Story"

"B" We lived in Milwaukee then and listened to the bomb drop on the radio. We sat as close as we could to the floor model Philco in the corner so we could hear cousin Woody. He announced approaching the target ships and when the bombardier said "Bomb away" all we could hear was static as Woody kicked in full power, full rudder and full ailerons to bank the plane away from the falling bomb. Then there was a lot more static when the bomb went off blanking out all radio transmissions from its EM pulse. After the static subsided, Woody could be heard again and we breathed a sigh of relief. He later took command of the Air Force Base, near Roswell, New Mexico, that trained Bomber crews how to drop Atomic Bombs. That was well **after** the famous (or infamous) "Flying Saucer" incident. He later retired as a two-star General.

There was some flap about missing *Nevada* by a wide margin. The "Fat Man" (Plutonium) type bomb used with a **parachute** was uncooperative with wind drift. But, that miss was a blessing in disguise. Years later we were ordered to study films of how well the *Nevada's* hull survived the blast and how certain types of machinery got torn loose from their foundations. This prompted the Navy to devise better shock mountings that is now known as Grade A shock resistance to withstand a near miss of a nuclear warhead.

The *Nevada* was painted with Red Lead so the bombardier could pick it out from the rest of the armada. Some publications have said it was a special red paint designed for the atomic radiation because it contained lead. Don't believe everything you read. It was only common lead based "Red Lead" primer paint normally used on all steel ships and was the right color to paint a "Bulls Eye".

The shipyard also modified an LCU to be the support vessel allowing a bomb to hang underneath it for the underwater blast of test Baker. The second ship that was prepared by the shipyard was the German Cruiser *Prinz Eugen*. New York Naval Shipyard had already stripped some guns off for evaluation but many of her German crew were still on board. This leads to an interesting story about Don Foster, a shipfitter supervisor, whom I worked for a number of times and was even in my car pool.

One evening during lunch on swing shift I saw Don doing some drawings for modifications to his house. However, the plastic triangles of his drafting set were marked with Nazi emblems of the Eagle over a Hakenkreuz (commonly called a Swastika). Naturally I asked where he got that equipment.

He told us he got it off the German Super Cruiser *Prinz Eugen* when it was in Long Beach in 1946 before being taken out for the atomic bomb tests. He said he decided to take a little time away from his regular duties to board the ship and do some "skylarking". Most of the German crew were still aboard and still in full uniform.

Don was walking down the deck and a German Warrant Officer starts to stare at him and walks up to him. He reads the name on Don's work badge, sticks out his hand and exclaims, "Don Foster. I thought it was you. I haven't seen you in years."

It turned out that both this German Warrant Officer and Don were shipmates together aboard the Battleship *Nevada* **before** WW II. They both opened their shirts to display their chest tattoos of a baby with boxing gloves all *Nevada* sailors had to have at that time. Don was a seaman apprentice then while the German was a baker apprentice aboard *Nevada*. After they got out of the US Navy, the German went back to Germany to visit his family. Next thing he knew he was drafted. But when it was found out he served in the United States of America Navy, he was transferred to the KriegsMarine and made a Warrant Officer, in charge of the Bakery aboard the *Prinz Eugen*. Well, being old friends, Don got the grand tour of the ship. He met the ship's Kommandant (Kapitan zur See Brinkmann) and was given some very interesting and rare souvenirs including that drafting set.

What irony. *Nevada* was in Long Beach at the same time as well. Here were two former crewmen of that ship that later wound up on opposite sides of the war, then their ships are almost side by side and designated to be atomic bomb targets.

After tests Able and Baker were completed, some of the target ships were towed back to the United States for study. Most returned ships went to Bremerton or San Francisco, later to be sunk at sea, and a few went to Norfolk for study. But no target ship was ever sent to Long Beach. So for radiological purposes, Long Beach was kept pretty clean.

Some support ships that were outside the test area did return to Long Beach to resume their regular duties. This author worked on some of them, as a shipfitter, but never thought anything about their proximity to the atomic blasts. It really wasn't until after I retired and had joined the RAB that reminded me of those ships. Any military installation slated for closure is required to have a radiological investigation done. Bob O'Brien of Digital Systems Research headed the investigation of the Naval Complex and was well qualified as a retired DOD employee with many years of nuclear experience at Mare Island Naval Shipyard. They did a very thorough study and briefed the RAB in detail of their findings and what they were looking for. One of the criteria that they were concerned with was work done on any ships that were in attendance of Test Baker at Operation *Crossroads*.

Test Baker was a very, very dirty bomb and spread a radioactive mist over many ships that were downwind. All other ships that were used in other Pacific tests were not contaminated (or contaminated enough) to be harmful to crews and shipyard workers when undergoing later repairs or overhauls.

Reviewing the lists of ships used during Operations, *Crossroads*, *Wigwam*, *Redwing*, *Sandstone* and *Hardtack*, I was amazed at how many I personally worked on and never realized there may have been some danger from ignored radioactive contamination. Ship names that are very familiar to LBNSY were USS *Curtis* (AV-4), USS *Mt. McKinley* (AGC-7), USS *James E. Kyes* (DD-787), USS *Navasota* (AO-105), USS *Monticello* (LSD-35), USS *Floyd B. Parks* (DD-884), USS *Perkins* (DDR-877), USS *Collett* (DD-730), USS *DeHaven* (DD-727), USS *Moctobi* (ATF-105), USS *Cree* (ATF-84), USS *Cacapon* (AO-52) and USS *Lansing* (DER-317) just to name a few.

But it was the ships present during Test Baker that was the biggest concern such as USS *Haven* (AH-12), USS *George Clymer* (APA-27), USS *Henrico* (APA-45), USS *Blue Ridge* (AGC-2), USS *Turner* (DD-834), USS *Laffey* (DD-724), USS *Lowry* (DD-770), USS (DD-725), USS *Walke* (DD-723), USS *Allen M. Sumner* (DD-692) and USS *Ingraham* (DD-694), again just to name the few. As a result of the intense radiation hazard from that underwater burst, President Truman ordered Test Charlie to be cancelled.

USS Nevada being visited for the last time before Operation Crossroads.   "Digest" 1946

OPERATION *WIGWAM*:

Operation *WIGWAM* was the second special project that was assigned to LBNSY with Operation *CROSSROADS* being the first. When I hired in as an apprentice, this was the first special project I worked on. 39 years I worked on every special project assigned to the shipyard. So, the reason I wrote in Woodrow Swancutt in the preceding chapter is because he was a relative of mine. I now can claim I was involved in every special LBNSY project starting as a 10 year old listening to a relative dropping an atomic bomb.

Test *Charlie* was to be a deep-water detonation (at or near Bikini) in 1,200 to 2,000 feet of water, but President Truman ordered it cancelled because of the deadly "rain" test *Baker* created. However, when President Eisenhower was in office the test was reinstated in 1954 under the name of Operation *Wigwam*. A smaller group of ships were used in that test and only two of them were downwind from the blast site. They were USS *George Eastman* (YAG-39) and USS *Granville S. Hall* (YAG-40). We are told that they were heavily shielded and actual exposure to radiation was extremely small. Yet neither one of those ships were ever to report back to LBNSY for any repairs or overhauls, thus keeping the shipyard very clean of possibly contaminated ships. Most of the other ships, however, did have later availabilities with most of them requiring dry dock work. Out of the twenty-six ships used in Operation *Wigwam*, fourteen of them had dry dock work done after the test. One of them was dry docked just two months after whereas all the others had dry dock availabilities spread out over several years afterwards. Again, no one ever thought anything of it at the time. As a matter of fact, the full list was never made public for many years.

When I first reported for work in 1954 I was assigned to the layout section that scribed and center punched steel plates that had to be cut, rolled, bent, etc. The first items I worked on in layout were for diver's ladders on *Wigwam* that I was the surface support barge (ex YC-473) for *Squaw* which were three newly built unmanned midget submarines at LBNSY for the test. They had no propulsion but a lot of cameras. They looked like British X-craft midget submarines that mined the *Tirpitz*.

One of the three unmanned midget submarines built by LBNSY for Operation Wigwam to test effects of an underwater Atomic Bomb to take out a submarine "Wolf Pack". U.S. Navy photo

I thought I was really getting into some secret stuff because I was told that the atomic bomb test was just to be on the other side of Catalina Island. I found this hard to believe that they would be telling an 18-year-old first year apprentice this. But it was true. In 1996 a documentary movie, on DVD, was made of those early atomic tests, *Trinity and Beyond–The Atomic Bomb Story*, shows many atmospheric and underwater tests with a lot of scenes recently declassified. It even has an interior scene of a *Squaw* being crushed from the *Wigwam* detonation. It also identified the *Wigwam* bomb was a 35-kiloton bomb detonated at 2,000 feet in 16,000 feet of water just 450 miles Southwest of San Diego on 14 May 1955.

Above water contamination from the blast was almost a non-event in that radiation dissipated rapidly. The fireball never broke surface but sent up a small mountain of radioactive water. Some spray from the surge drifted over the *Eastman* and *Hall* but the intensity was very small, much less than at 35,000 feet in a modern jet liner. But layers of contaminated water remained for several days below the ten-foot depth. This is of concern because the intake scoops on the bottoms of steam-powered ships would have ingested the radioactive water.

Detonation of the Wigwam bomb. The fireball never reached the surface. Squaw 3 (foreground) had no damage and was later used as a SONAR calibration echo off of San Diego. U.S. Navy photo

The barge that was converted by LBNSY to hang the Wigwam bomb underneath. US Navy photo

CHAPTER 5
THE APPRENTICESHIP

This is probably an appropriate time to describe the apprenticeship program that many people trained under. It began in 1943 with the first graduates receiving their journeyman's certificates in 1947. The apprenticeship first started off as a two-year training program but when the war ended was extended to four years. All apprentices were given the choice to stay with the two-year program or transfer to the four-year program. Nearly all of them chose the four-year program because it offered more training and two more years of guaranteed employment.

My choice of hiring on as an apprentice is perhaps a typical example of most non-vets that applied. Most Navy veterans knew of its existence and benefits when their ship was assigned to LBNSY but in my case I heard about it through my stepfather who was a mechanical engineer there. In February of 1953 he took the whole family down to the shipyard for its open house. It was very interesting, especially touring a certain ship at pier one, the Battleship USS *Wisconsin* (BB-64). The complex towering superstructure, the thickness of the Turret armor, the pride the crew had made a very deep impression on me. It sure was a lot different than that cramped submarine that was on display a few years before when we were still living in Milwaukee. It was berthed in the Milwaukee River alongside Gimbel's department store. About a year after the war, the Navy brought in an LST that had been modified as a memorial to WW II. You entered through the bow doors and the first thing you would see was a captured Baka suicide rocket plane.

But this Battleship was something else. Then there were the other warships and the shops that built, repaired and modified them. I thought it might be an interesting place to work. The following year I picked up an application card at the Post Office and sent it in. The mail delivers a form 57 from the Government for my apprenticeship application. I filled it out in pencil and sent it in. In August I am ordered to go to the shipyard to take my Civil Service exam in old cafeteria number 2, near Dry dock 3. By September the family is still trying to figure out how to buy my books for El Camino Junior College when I get orders to report to work on 13 September 1954. A Friday the 13th, by the way.

On that first day at work, we were escorted back into cafeteria 2 to be given a pep talk and short description of what trades were open yet and what kind of work they entailed. Thurman G. Wade, the apprentice coordinator for the shipyard, gave the talk. He explained that during the school year, we would work at the shipyard five weeks and go to Long Beach City College for one week.

That was a whole forty-hour week too. But we discovered that the classes given would only apply for a journeyman's certificate. To earn an AA degree, there were two or three more classes we needed to take at night but they could be spread out over the next four years. Most of us took those classes and also earned AA degrees. Wade described each trade rather well. The group I was in was the non-vets that passed the Civil Service exam. All veterans were brought in the day before and had first choice at the openings. Wade would not say how many openings were left in each shop, but he would cross them off the board as they were filled.

Wade listed our names by score, with the highest first. After giving the briefing, he would then call each person by his score and ask them which shop they wanted. Ed Butler was number one and he picked the boiler shop. Les Hartzell was number two and he picked the wood shop. Then Wade crossed the wood shop off the black board. Ouch! That was the shop I wanted. But I was number 3 and still needing a job so I picked the shipfitter shop. If I couldn't build wood boats, I wanted to build the steel ships themselves. And a buck forty-five an hour was nothing to sneeze at in those days either. So, Shop 11, here I come.

Of all the new apprentices, twelve selected the shipfitter shop. Over the next four years, some quit for various reasons. Naturally we struck up friendships with fellow apprentices in the other shops, especially during our classroom sessions at the City College when many of us had the same teacher. We got to know almost every one and followed our individual progress through our years at LBNSY. Most of us finished up in the design or planning divisions as did several other grads from previous and following years.

Most of us who graduated from the apprenticeship stayed at the shipyard. Of those who stayed, all but a few finished up their careers as top supervisors, designers or planners. There were some who merely used it as a stepping-stone toward another career and needed the AA degree first. For example, when our group graduation picture was taken, there was a tall black man standing next to me. I really didn't know who he was because he started as a sheetmetal apprentice a year after everyone else. He crammed all of his classes into three years to get the degree ASAP. He later left the shipyard to join the Long Beach Police Department as a patrol officer. Years later, a friend of mine was talking about that man who rose in the ranks of the Police Department. I showed him the graduation picture and he said, "Yup. That's Charlie Usury. Long Beach Chief of Police." He served as Chief for a full eight years.

Our first day at reporting to work in our selected shops required us to check in with the shop apprentice supervisor. Our supervisor was George T. Davis Jr. who was also the trade theory instructor at LBCC for shipfitters, sheetmetal workers, boilermakers and blacksmiths. His shipyard office was upstairs in the shipfitter shop, building 128. The welding apprentice supervisor, Ted Walker, also had his desk in the same office. We would report in every morning either to be assigned a supervisor to work for or shoot the bull. Those of us who had to work out on the piers couldn't do that of course, but we were generally rotated through shop assignments enough times we got to know all the senior apprentices as well. If we worked in the shop, we also went up to George's office for lunch and more bull sessions.

Being the mid 1950's, most Korean War veterans at the shipyard were also hired. We had the great opportunity to work with WW II vets and even a few World War I vets. Shipfitter Dan E. Scally was in the Navy in WW II and served aboard a Destroyer off the coast of southern California. A Navy blimp spotted a Japanese submarine west of Catalina Island and radioed the position to Scally's Destroyer. The DD came in and laid a pattern of depth charges that got the sub. Somewhere, just a few miles west of Catalina, which is only twenty-six miles and within sight of San Pedro, is a Japanese submarine lying on the ocean floor.

In the second year of apprenticeship, the curriculum called learning some of the other trades. What a relief it was to get away from the Bayflex hand grinders for a while. It seemed that some of the mechanics we were assigned to only considered us as common helpers and we had to do all the grinding for them.

The first five weeks of the second year we spent in welding school. At the end of the training we were then qualified as Tack Welders, meaning we could weld steel structures in place with one or two-inch long tack welds but not do production welding. As time went on though, our welding skills improved and we often did small production welding jobs.

In 1956 some apprentices were loaned to the design division. The design section assigned me was Code 250F, where we designed masts, antenna platforms, rigging systems, mooring systems, towing rigs, anchor handling, etc. My Supervisor, Bill Harris, was of short stature and was an NCO fighter pilot in the First World War. He never talked of any combat he was in, but did like to talk about airplanes. He flew a Neuport and did tell us of the time he crashed one on takeoff.

Another thing that I impressed Bill with was my fearlessness of heights. I enjoyed climbing to the tops of masts to take measurements for another antenna support to be added or even a better ladder than the one I had just climbed up on. Bill was also fearless of heights. Some years later, after I transferred up from the shop to design, Bill and Tom O'Connell were inspecting a bomb elevator on an Aircraft Carrier. The problem reported was that it would hang up on the rail about half way up. The elevator shaft was a steel trunk with both vertical and horizontal framing around all four sides. The horizontal stiffeners were only about two feet apart and could be climbed like a ladder. Bill started climbing on up and when he looked down at Tom, he asked, "Are you coming up?" Tom just replied, "No thank you. You're doing just fine." That was shortly before Bill's 70th birthday when he had to leave under the rules of mandatory retirement we had then.

After returning to the shops, we were now respected a bit more and often given our own jobs without a journeyman to watch over and grade us. Upon finishing the apprenticeship in September of 1958, we were given our journeyman certificates. However, since most of us took the extra college courses required for an AA degree, we already received those degrees the previous June at Long Beach City College. The ceremonies were complete with robes and mortarboards, which made our families quite proud.

After we earned our certificates, we were given some lapel pins that said "Graduate Apprentice" on them. An Apprentice Alumni Association was formed and most of us joined it. The dues were only about five dollars a year. The Association had very little influence over shipyard management or improvement of apprentice training. Its meetings had more of an air of school reunions than lobbyist sessions. After all, by 1958 only 434 people had graduated from the apprenticeship. We organized dinners and picnics and even had some input as how apprentice training could be improved. But we never tried to act like a union.

Then the spoiler came on the scene. He claimed he was a graduate apprentice from the electrical shop but was very union minded. According to the listings of each and every person who graduated between 1947 to 1991 his name cannot be found anywhere. If he graduated from another shipyard, he never made that clear. He tried to get more power for the electricians union but as part of the Metal Trades Council that vowed a "No Strike" promise in their contract he couldn't get very far. Then he became president of the Apprentice Alumni Association and tried to run it like a union instead of a social organization. He would spend at least one day a week in the shipyard commander's office delivering his "demands" for the unions and the associations he was involved in. That killed the Apprentice Alumni Association and eventually he quit the shipyard and became president of a union local outside the shipyard.

However, over the years 2,870 people are listed as graduate apprentices from the Long Beach Naval Shipyard. That's 2,870 skilled tradesmen of who most advanced on up to supervisory type positions. The apprenticeship was a Godsend to most of us. It guaranteed four years of employment as no apprentices were ever laid off during Reductions in Force. It did not give you a deferment from the military but while on active duty your position was held open for you. We received a Junior College education while being paid for it at the same time. We learned not one but several skilled trades throughout the four years. A shipfitter for example, learned various methods of steel fabrication using various tools and machinery. He learned welding, gas cutting, drafting, planning, rigging and was also trained to operate the bridge cranes in the shop in case of an emergency.

Most of all, we all learned teamwork.

The 1958 Apprentice Class with their AA degrees from Long Beach City College. Most went on into supervision, design or planning. The author is 2nd from the right in the top row.   Author's collection

In order to save tuition funds at LBCC, classroom training was set up in Building 100 that also served the audio-visual group (photographers) and the Transportation Shop. You can see that the west building for the transportation shop has already been leveled for demolition.   Photo by author 23 June 2000

But we also had fun. This photo is of the Shop 11/26 slow pitch soft ball team that won the shipyard championship in 1958 (the last year of my apprenticeship). Though I was the worst player, we only lost one game (to Shop 72 of course who played slow pitch, regular soft and regular hard ball).

This author is fourth from the left in the back row at a "strapping" 145 lbs. Unsigned and kneeling 2nd from left is Robert "Bob" Reynolds who was just in his 2nd year (he graduated as a shipfitter in 1961). First bat boy from the left sitting is 9 year old Randy Dillenbeck. He was the son of Ralph Dillenbeck (far right kneeling) who was our coach. Ralph was a pneumatic tool operator and I once worked with him on a riveting gang. Randy is a Viet Nam Vet and a member of Lakewood VFW Post 8615.

Just how many of us are still around? Just two of us that I know of for the past 58 years, I'm still around and so is our bat boy, Randy Dillenbeck, a Vice Commander of VFW Post 8615 and I'm past Commander of American Legion Post 560.

Author's personal photo.

Nor has age stopped us from attending LBNSY annual reunion picnics. Photos below are of the 2015 picnic. Usually over 230 meal tickets are sold for ex-"yard birds" and their families.

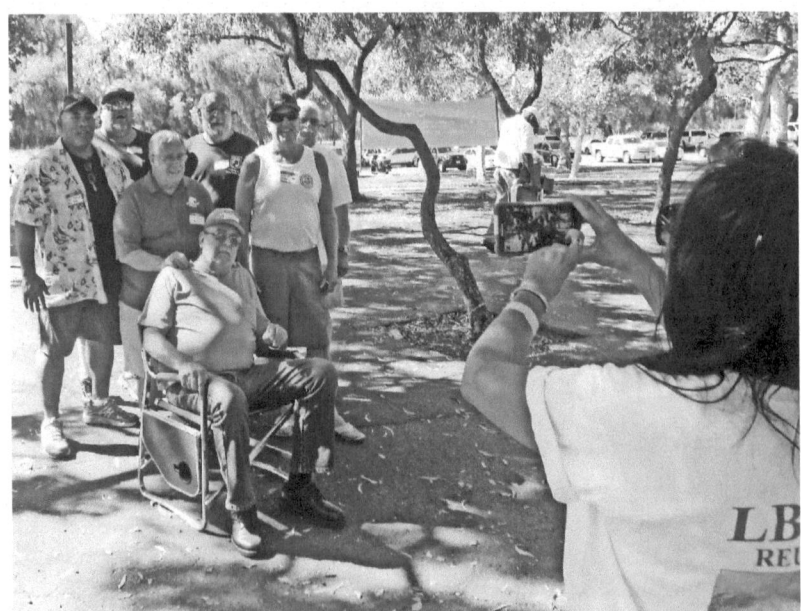

You just can't keep a "YARDBIRD" down.

CHAPTER 6 : POP UP

The shipyard's longest lasting big special research project was to design and build the surface support vessels for project Pop Up. Pop Up was the project name given for the testing programs of the *Polaris* missile and later modified for the *Poseidon* and *Trident* missiles Fleet Ballistic Missiles (FBMs). Besides the test missiles, the main components of the test equipment consisted of a Launch Vessel, Surface Support Vessel, Retrieval Vessel, Launch Tower and Translator Tower.

The first *Launch Vessel* was built at Mare Island Naval Shipyard, north of San Francisco and shipped to Long Beach. Basically, it was two vertical cylinders fit inside each other. The outer hull was shaped very much like a wooden spool you buy in the yardage store for sewing thread. The inner cylinder was the cylindrical launching tube for the missile.

LBNSY designed and built the next two *Launch Vessels* as the first one could only handle the 60-inch diameter A-1 *Polaris* missile. The next Launch Vessels had to finish up the A-2 *Polaris* portion of the program and be big enough to change out launch tubes to take the larger 74 inch diameter C-3 *Poseidon* missile. Therefore they were built as three tubes with the smaller tube capable of being removed to use the next tube for the larger missiles.

The Surface Support Vessel, formerly known as the *Staging Vessel*, was basically two 500-ton lighters (barges) attached together at the stern with a bridge-like deckhouse to form a catamaran. The aft port corner of the vessel would support a Baldwin-Lima crane mounted on a pedestal rather than on tracks. The supporting structure for the pedestal was an array of stanchions made from steel pipes that pretty well took up most of the compartments below. Those who had to work on the vessel dubbed that array "Sherwood Forest".

The port barge had an open topped deckhouse that the missile could be stowed in for pre-launch preparations. The starboard barge housed the berthing compartments, galley, mess hall and conference room. A small recompression chamber was installed on the starboard upper deck for the divers.

Between the barges hung a huge shovel-like framework that looked quite a bit like the kelp-cutting tool of vessels that clear harbors of kelp. Though its official name was the Launch Vessel Support Device, it was more commonly known as The Kelp Cutter. When in transit to the launch site, off San Clemente Island, the Kelp Cutter would be pulled up by the crane between the barges. When in use, it would hang between the barges with its shovel end level. The crane would then lower the Launch Vessel onto the Kelp Cutter. Then the missile would be loaded into the Launch Vessel and the Kelp Cutter lowered so the loaded Launch Vessel could be floated out to the launch area.

The Launch Vessel would be positioned over a launch "pad" which was actually a towering octagonal framework made of large diameter pipes that were underwater and secured to the ocean bottom to stake piles 185 feet down. A Skaggit winch on the shore of San Clemente Island would pull the Launch Vessel down to the top of the "pad" so the top of the Launch Vessel would be about the same depth below the water surface as periscope depth of a submarine. The hatch covers of the Launch Vessel would open, a web-like pattern of primer cord would cut open the dome-shaped Styrofoam seal, a small hydrazine rocket at the bottom would ignite creating a high pressure bubble of steam and gases which would then "Pop Up" the missile like a huge pop gun. Now you know why the operation was called Pop Up.

In the first tests, the missile would jump out of the water and fall back down, often sideways flattening out the sides. So a method of retrieving the missiles by catching them in mid-air was devised and LBNSY was tasked to design and build it.

The Retrieval Vessel was another catamaran and formerly named *Fish Hook*. Again, it was two 500-ton lighters side-by-side but fastened with seven large steel bridge trusses. On top of the trusses and at one end of the vessel, we installed a 185-foot tall fixed crane boom. Behind the boom, and on top of the trusses, we installed hydraulic arresting gear normally used for catching airplanes landing on carriers. The wire from the arresting gear went up to the head of the boom and down to hold up a huge teepee shaped net over the launch center of the missile.

The missile would be launched from underwater, without rocket fuel of course, and be caught in the net. The center of the net actually had a large steel ring and one time a missile hit so dead center that the nose jammed into the steel ring and a circular crease was formed into the steel nose cone. That nose cone was brought into the shop and I was given the job to weld up the crease and grind it smooth. I liked the idea of actually working on one of the missiles even if it was only a boilerplate test model.

Fish Hook looked very unstable with that tall tower leaning out over one end. However, the stability of *Fish Hook* was very meticulously calculated by Paul Cartegena of our scientific section. He was an extraordinary engineer and mathematician. He did the weight and moment calculations for *Fish Hook* vessel and Mother Nature helped him prove it was not as top-heavy as it looked. That 185 foot tall fixed boom towering above the barges made it look like the slightest swell would capsize it. I was fairly certain it wouldn't because, while I was on swing shift, I was with a team of shipfitters and welders installing steel bars for the concrete caps to go over decomposed granite in the ballast tanks. But it still looked unstable.

A proof of the vessel's stability was when a hurricane pushed some very high winds far enough north, to San Clemente Island and ripped *Fish Hook* from her moorings. After the winds subsided, we could not find *Fish Hook* anywhere and thought it had swept out to sea and capsized. Then we got a call from Mexico. Our *Fish Hook* was south of Ensenada and hung up on some rocks. Paul led a team to Mexico and retrieved the vessel. It only had one hole punched in one of the ballast tanks from the rocks and was still "seaworthy" for the tow back to Long Beach.

Later a different method of catching the missiles in mid-air was devised. The arresting gear wire of *Fish Hook* was attached to the missile's nose and would wind up as the missile shot out of the water. Then it would "catch" it as it fell back down. We could use the same birds over and over again for a long time.

After all the static shots proved we could pop missiles up out of submarine tubes and the booster would ignite just after the bird cleared water, it was time to test the system from a moving Launch Vessel to simulate a submarine at about five knots.

The *Translator* was another great design and construction project by LBNSY. In place of the static octagonal tower the *Translator*, that looked like an upside down truncated triangle, was bolted to the launch pad foundation. On top of the *Translator* was a set of tracks with a sled on them. The sled would be at one end of the tracks with a *Launch Vessel* on it and when pulled over to the other end; the missile would be launched. Movement of the sled was simple actually. A buoyancy tank underneath the sled and inside the *Translator* structure pulled it. A wire rope was reeved from the tank to the sled and when an explosive bolt holding the tank was sheared, the tank would rapidly rise and pull the sled down the track while the bird is launched.

The Naval Ordnance Test Station (NOTS) oversaw the entire Pop Up program, as well as some other special projects. The NOTS acronym was sometimes confused with the Naval Overseas Transport Service of the First World War, so the name was changed to the Naval Underwater Weapons Center (NUWC). The Navy is obsessed by acronyms so NOTS became Naval Underwater Weapons and Research Center (NUWRC) and Naval Underwater Center (NUC). I will refer to them only as NOTS.

One of the problems that perplexed NOTS was why the *Launch Vessel* would jump up off of the support when a missile was fired. It wasn't until I was in design that John DeFries of NOTS got funding for us to do a study on it. We watched several films of underwater launches and determined a chronology of events. The *Launch Vessel* would jump up seven feet when held down with new and unused wire ropes. Each jump after that would be less until about a two foot jump was standard. When the wire ropes were replaced it would start all over again with a seven-foot jump. We first suspected that it was not just the loss of the weight of the missile that gave the Launch Vessel extra buoyancy, it was also the loss of water momentarily until the missile cleared the tube plus new wire ropes were not pre-stretched yet.

I calculated the amount of extra buoyancy the *Launch Vessel* would gain the instant the missile cleared the tube and before water could rush in behind. John Priftakis, in the structural section, then calculated how much the new wire rope stretches by the loss of tonnage of both missile and water were to instantly pull on it. Sure enough a seven-foot jump would occur. After the *Launch Vessel* was settled back to the support stand again, the wire rope had now had its initial pre-stretching and the next jump would only be four feet and the rest them only about two feet after all the pre-stretching was done. Comparing our calculations with the films and NOTS records, the mystery of the jumping *Launch Vessels* was solved.

I did all kinds of work on the Pop Up equipment from just plain grunt work as an apprentice shipfitter to developing redesigns of the *Staging Vessel*. I was even a substitute cameraman on the first *Trident* C-4 launch. It had been a number of years since the launch equipment had been used since the last *Poseidon* test so I was sent out to San Clemente Island to observe the rigging, note any improvements needed and observe the launch of the first C-4 *Trident* missile. It was a *Translator* launch and everything seemed to be ready, except the cameraman. He had more cameras than people, so he gave me a quick instruction of how to operate the 16 millimeter high speed camera for slow motion.

One thing of interest was there were no Russian Trawlers out there this time. It was not a secret launch and was primarily just to test the existing equipment. During the *Polaris* days, however, a Russian Trawler was just a few miles out observed every **classified** launch. Non-classified launches did not interest them. Finally, the Navy decided to have a tanker or cruiser stationed between the launch site and Trawlers to block their view.

San Clemente Island is an oddity in itself. It is totally owned and controlled by the Navy and used as a test center for various underwater experiments such as the Pop Up program. It is also used as a target. The North side of the island is almost a straight line, forming the edge of an earthquake fault. Various ships have used that side of the island for target practice, including the USS *New Jersey* in 1968. The island is basically all rock but those 16-inch shells would leave a crater 75 feet across and 25 feet deep. It also had its own "National Forest" of just seven trees of scrub oak. Animal life was mostly goats that were transported over there decades before by ranchers. One old Billy always gave us problems by standing in the middle of the narrow one lane road, usually just around a blind bend, and blocking what traffic we had there. But, nobody was allowed to shoot them. The only people who carried guns on the island were Marine security forces. They are allowed to shoot people but not goats.

Another "Rube Goldberg" type design I had to come up with for Pop Up was to design some 190-foot tall camera towers to photograph the *Polaris* and *Poseidon* missiles at various depths during launch. The towers would be anchored on stake piles in around the launch site with a service platform just above water. The towers were large sections of pipe running straight up like single stack chimneys with guy wires attached well below the surface so as not to interfere with boat and crane traffic. Each tower was made up of three sections of pipe, each about 70 feet long. Divers would have to bolt the sections together while a floating crane above tried to hold them steady. Using a couple of cardboard toilet paper tubes cut in two at forty-five degree angles as a guide, I was able to design inner alignment pipes to aid the divers in fitting the tower sections together without having to strain to twist them in place for bolt hole alignment.

When it came time to start considering tests of the D-5 *Trident* missile, we were faced with a number of problems being that the *Staging Vessel* and the Kelp Cutter were too small. I was tasked to do a feasibility study of what kinds of modifications would need to be done to the *Staging Vessel* to accept the larger D-5 *Trident Launch Vessel* as well as stow one D-5 in the ready space on the port barge. To begin with, I had to design an entirely new and larger "Kelp Cutter". To support the extra weight and reinforce the connecting structure of the two barges, John Priftakis designed a buoyancy tank that would be welded to the bottom of the connecting structure. John also provided all the structural and stability calculations needed. However, he noted that the extra weight back aft would increase the vessel's stern trim.

Both barge hulls already had cast concrete ballast up forward (as mentioned earlier). But it wouldn't be enough with the weight of a loaded *Launch Vessel* resting on the larger Kelp Cutter even with the additional buoyancy tank aft. Originally, I had only intended to cut out the forward section of the port deckhouse to accommodate the longer D-5 missile. Instead, I designed Jumboized hulls by cutting the bows off of both barges, move them forward eight feet fill in the space with a new section. This rebalanced the *Staging Vessel*, added much-desired workspace in the ready area of the missile and added more berthing and offices to the starboard barge.

Fred Hock and Isaac Cavalier did all the engineering calculations for the rigging and fittings and the feasibility study was completed and issued to NOTS. It was quite a thick book, about 2 inches thick, of sketches and calculations. It would have worked too, until the *Staging Vessel* was put into dry dock for its regular inspection that showed some of the hull plating had corroded to only half of its original thickness. The Kelp Cutter also had some holes corroded through into its buoyancy tanks. The Baldwin-Lima crane was starting to show its age even after we repaired and reinforced it for the C-4 *Trident* tests. The small recompression chamber was never used too much, but it was now too old and long past certification.

The final blow to the "jumbo-ization" was that the *Translator* for the *Polaris* and *Poseidon* size missiles would be too tall for the much larger D-5 *Trident* missiles. A new *Translator* would also have to be designed and built and that final cost was the budget killer. As a result, only static tests of the D-5 were done off of Florida instead of San Clemente. Translated shots actually had to wait until the first *Ohio* class sub was available and the tests were done from it.

The Pop Up program then wound down to a complete halt in the late 1970's with the *Fish Hook*, *Staging Vessel*, the *Launch Vessels* and *Translator* being cut up for scrap. It was hoped to save the *Fish Hook* for use as a fixed-boom floating derrick of some sort, but such a limited use would not warrant the cost of upkeep. The NOTS/NUWC/NUWRC/NUC building between piers 1 and 2 was torn down in the 1990's as a depreciation cost savings and the other offices and stowage facilities out on the Mole were abandoned.

Now, all of the *Polaris/Poseidon* Fleet Ballistic Missile submarines have been inactivated and several already cut up for scrap. Even some of the *Trident* boomers are being slated for mothballs. They did their bit. They served their country. Not a single FBM had to be launched in anger. Pop Up was a resounding success in contributing to ending the Cold War. It can be compared to a catch phrase used by those who object to outlawing ownership of personal firearms. "It is better to have a gun and not need it, than it is to need a gun and not have it." Which is also true with a First Aid Kit.

The catamaran Staging Vessel built from two barges for the Pop Up program. In the well between the two hulls you can see one of the forks of the "Kelp Cutter" raised up in stowage position. Photo taken in 1960 without the control van or the recompression chamber deckhouse installed yet.   "Digest"

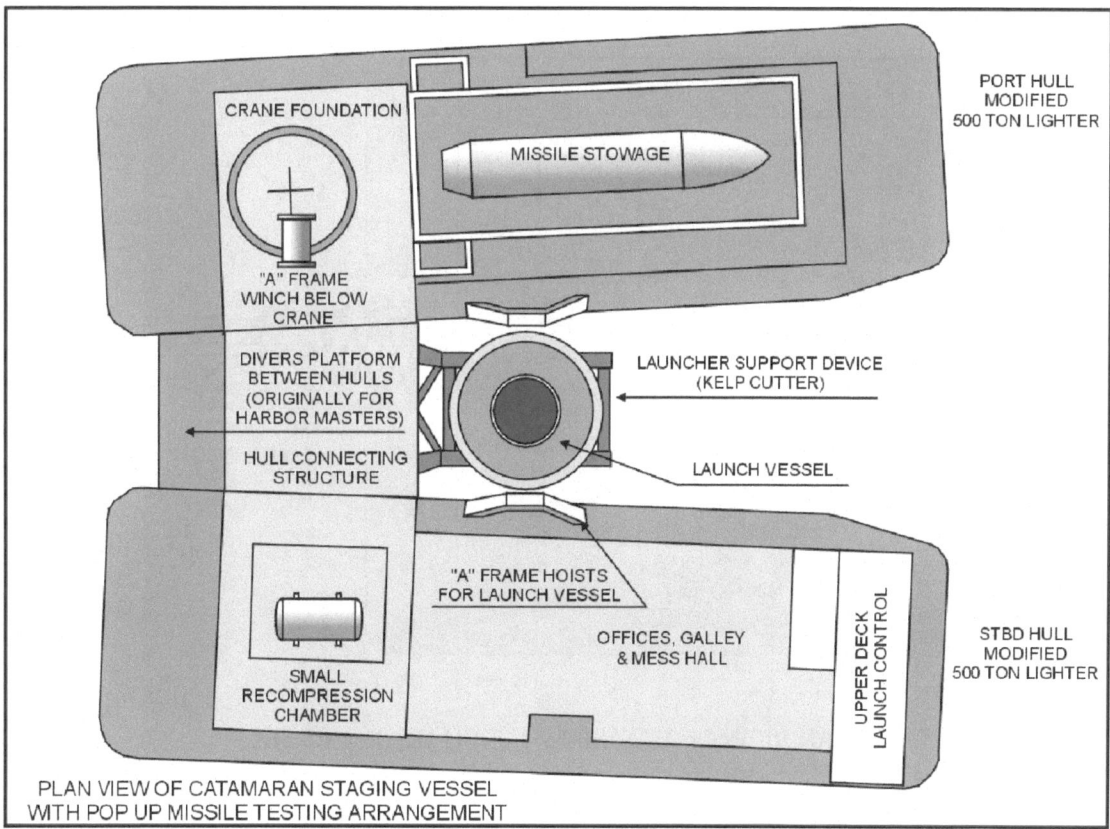

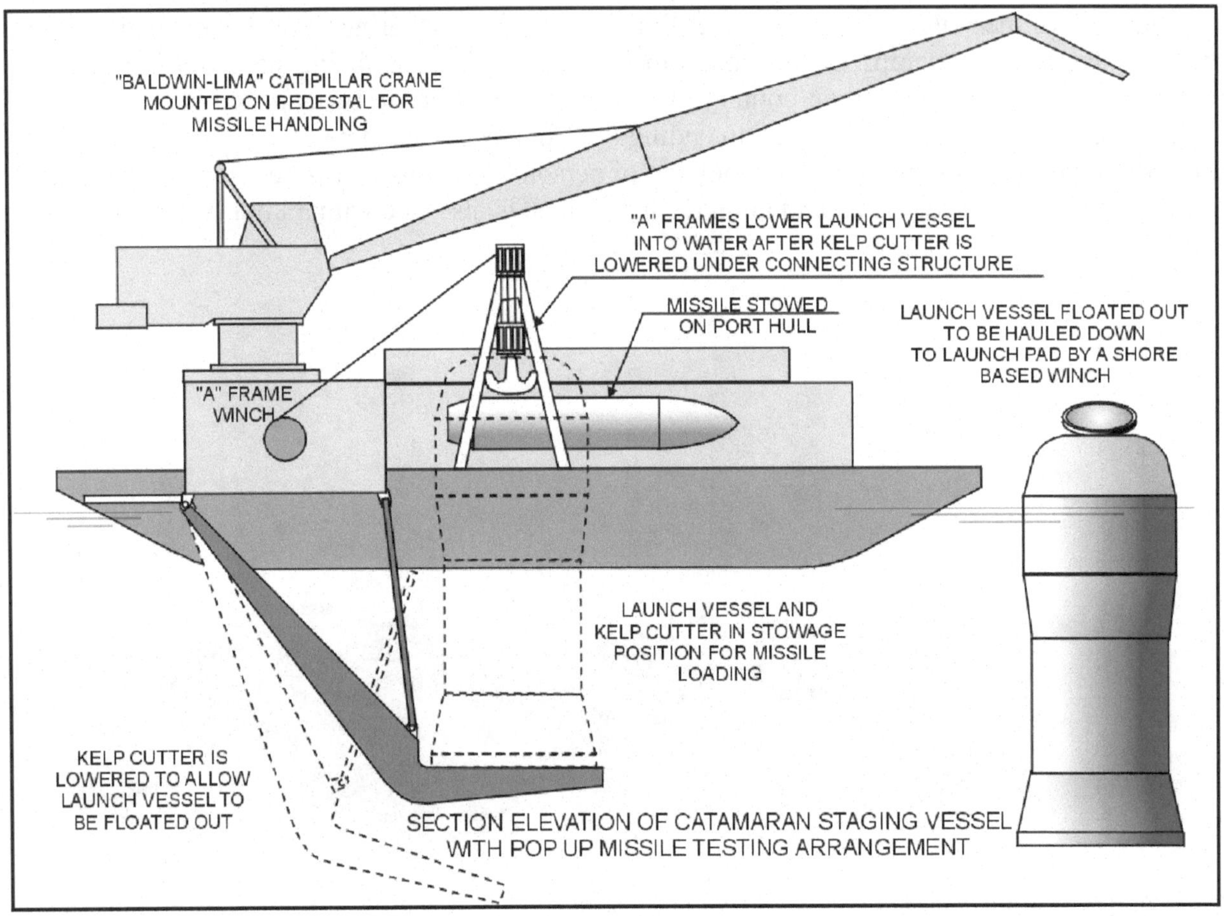

Section Elevation of Catamaran Staging Vessel with Pop Up Missile Testing Arrangement

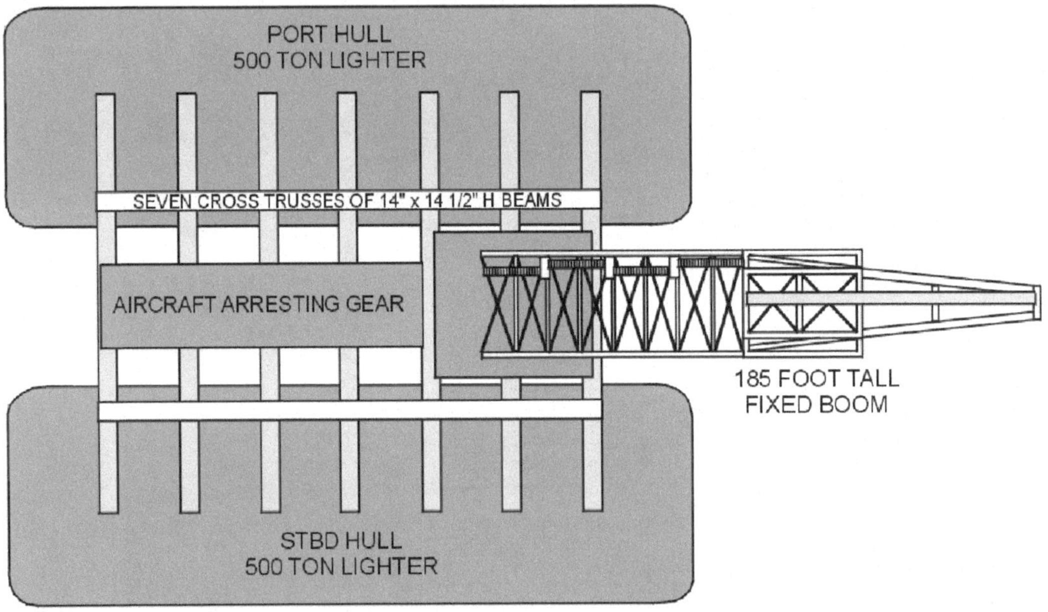

- "BALDWIN-LIMA" CATIPILLAR CRANE MOUNTED ON PEDESTAL FOR MISSILE HANDLING
- "A" FRAMES LOWER LAUNCH VESSEL INTO WATER AFTER KELP CUTTER IS LOWERED UNDER CONNECTING STRUCTURE
- MISSILE STOWED ON PORT HULL
- LAUNCH VESSEL FLOATED OUT TO BE HAULED DOWN TO LAUNCH PAD BY A SHORE BASED WINCH
- "A" FRAME WINCH
- LAUNCH VESSEL AND KELP CUTTER IN STOWAGE POSITION FOR MISSILE LOADING
- KELP CUTTER IS LOWERED TO ALLOW LAUNCH VESSEL TO BE FLOATED OUT

Plan View of Catamaran Fish Hook Vessel

- PORT HULL 500 TON LIGHTER
- SEVEN CROSS TRUSSES OF 14" x 14 1/2" H BEAMS
- AIRCRAFT ARRESTING GEAR
- 185 FOOT TALL FIXED BOOM
- STBD HULL 500 TON LIGHTER

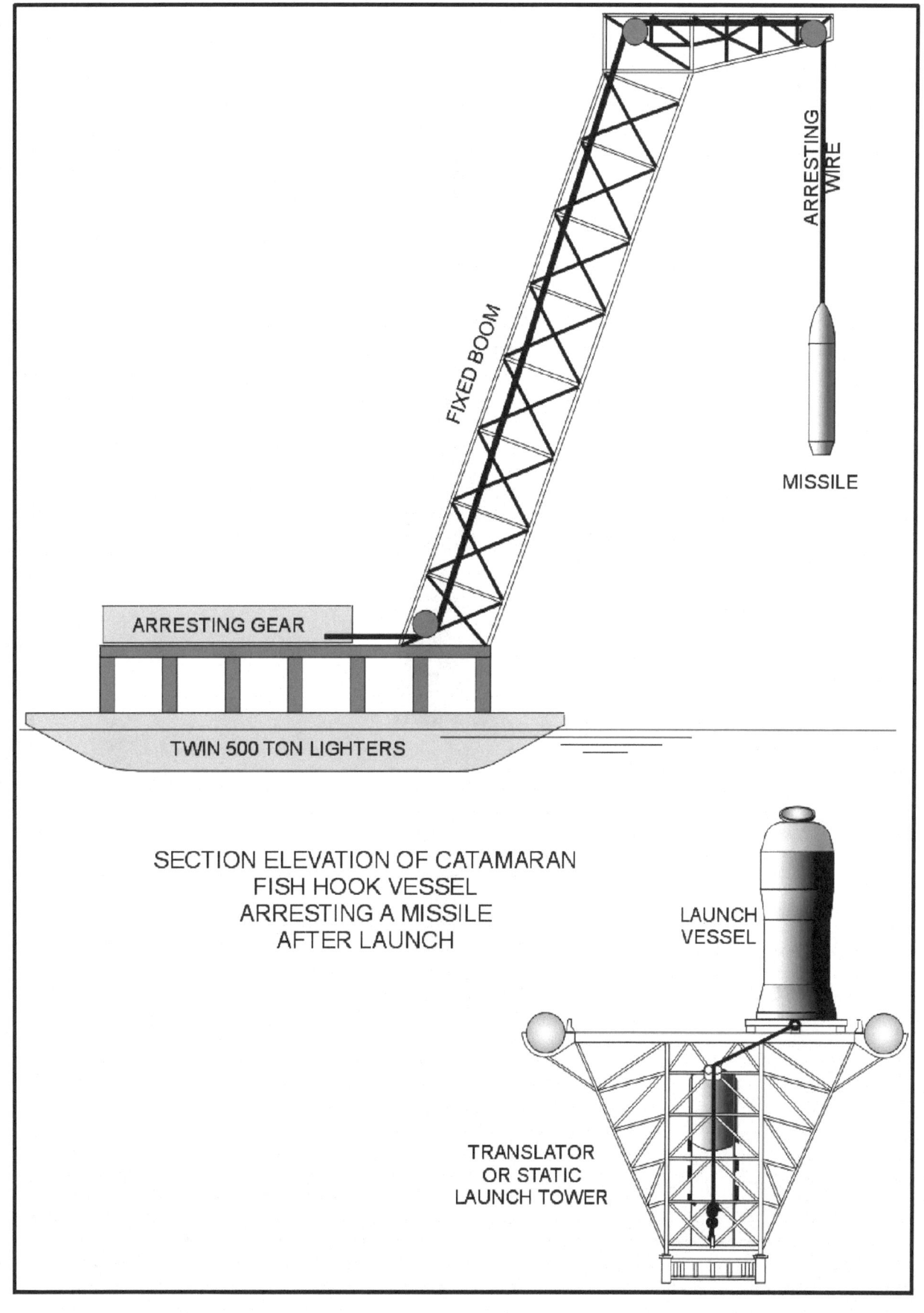

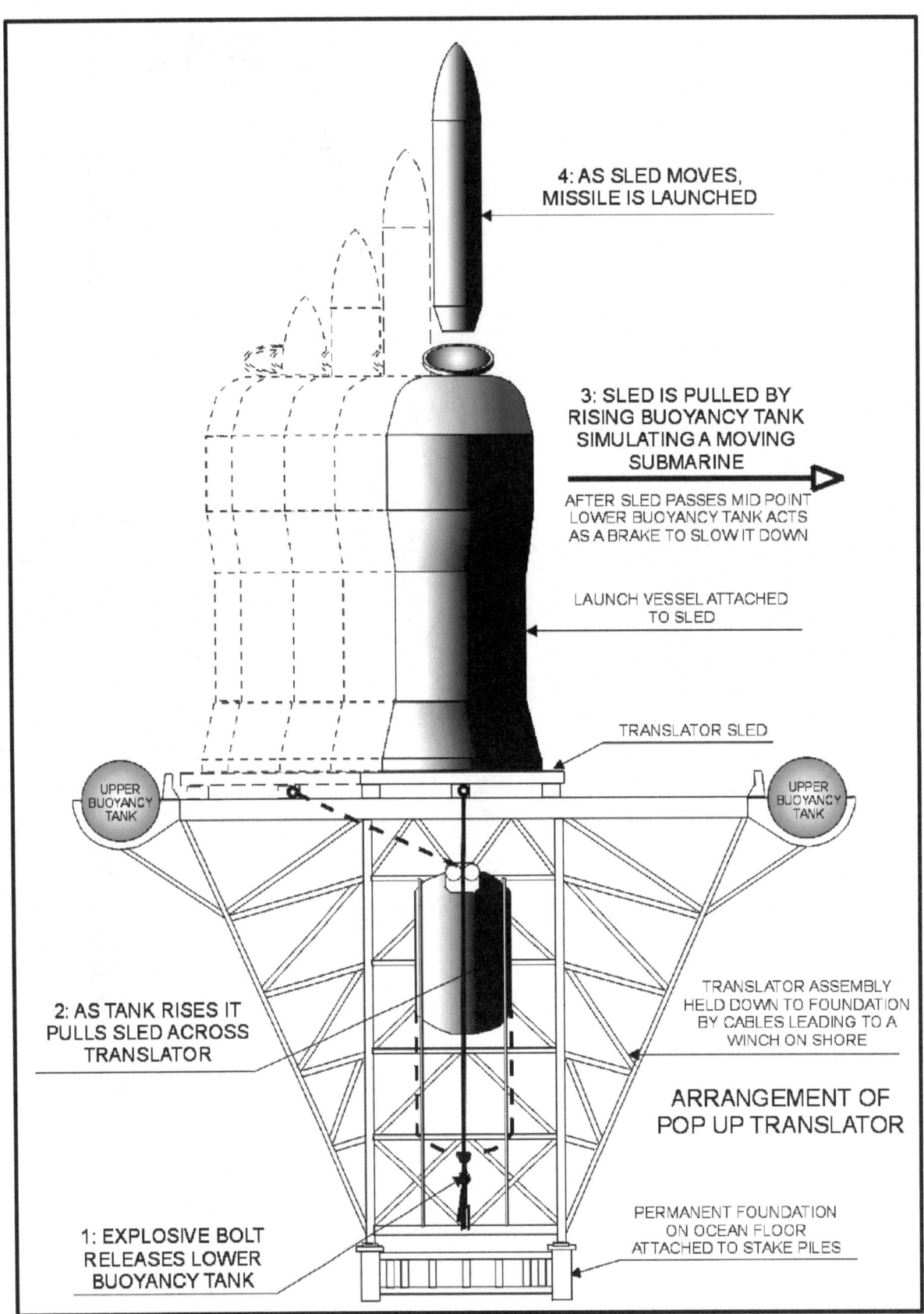

This illustration is showing a Polaris A-2 being launched. To launch a Poseidon A-3 the inner tube had to be removed from the launcher. Yes, it was **DESIGNED** that way. Later this same rig was also used to launch a Trident C-4. To launch a larger Trident D-5 would have required building an entirely new launch vessel and major modifications to the Staging Vessel. Preliminary drawings and calculations had already been done but it was decided to be cheaper to launch from a REAL Trident Submarine.

"B" *Fish Hook* catching a missile. Photo was taken from the Staging Vessel and the source says it was a Poseidon missile in 1967. I doubt that as I think it was a translator test of the first C-4 Trident (based upon the off-white color with no stripes like Polaris & Poseidon birds. I make that claim because I was at the test and the photographer needed somebody familiar with movie film to run the slow motion camera. So, that is me, second from the right with the camera tripod.   Photo from the Internet

A 1967 photo of the Launch Vessels and Translator built by LBNSYL to R: Launch Vessel 2, Open frame Static Tower, Launch Vessel 3, Translator Tower, Enclosed "Shed" for assembly & programming Missiles. Launch Vessel 1 (shaped like an hour glass) built by Mare Island not in picture. They were also used to launch Trident C-4 missiles. Photo by Author during an "open house" of LBNSY

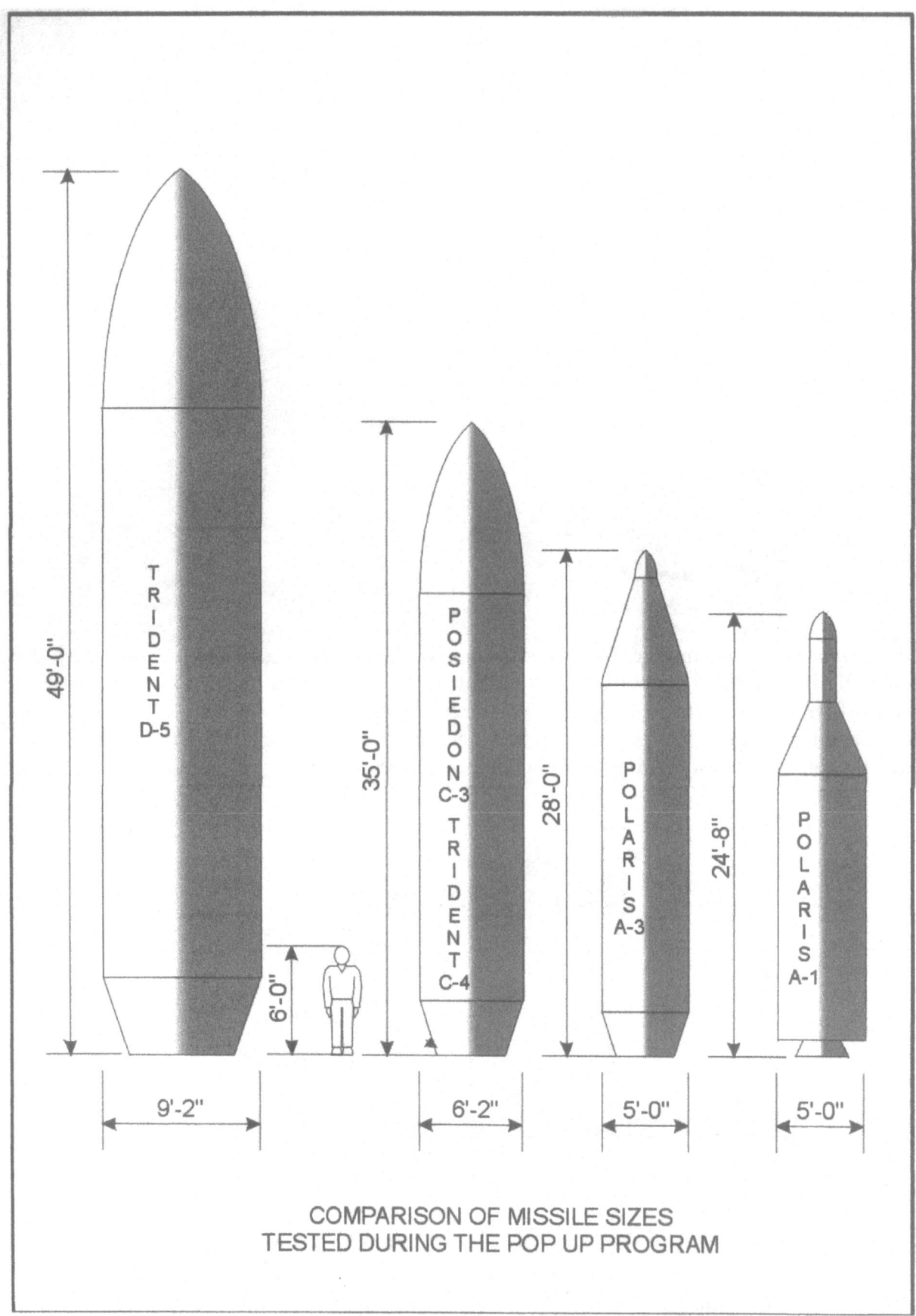

COMPARISON OF MISSILE SIZES
TESTED DURING THE POP UP PROGRAM

Just for you readers that want a quick reference in sizes of our Fleet Ballistic Missile Program, we started off with the Polaris A-1 ("A for "Attack"?) and progress through to the Poseidon C-3 and the Trident C-4 ("Catastrophe"?), finishing up with the Trident D-5 ("Doomsday"?).   Author's drawings

CHAPTER 7: SWING SHIFT

This is probably a good spot to describe what swing shift was like at LBNSY. This is my impression of some of the greatest and most dedicated people I ever worked with. After graduating from the apprenticeship in 1958, there was a call out for shipfitters to work the swing shift for a short while. Well, I was single and it paid an extra ten cents an hour so I volunteered.

Don Foster was the shipfitter leadingman for swing and I had worked with him before. He was even in my car pool for a while and was a congenial passenger if you didn't mind his once in a while sermons. Don was a recovered alcoholic and religion helped him stay away from the bottle. Don's personal sport, however, was Judo. Not the combat type martial art that you see in the action movies, but the sportsman's Judo that relied almost entirely on balance, timing and leverage.

I got to like swing shift very well. It was made up of a skeleton crew of shipfitters, welders, one team of riggers with crane operator and almost no electricians, machinists or ventilation installers. We would get our turnover work orders from day shift, report to the ship and find all the material there waiting to be installed.

You see, WAITING was the main problem we had with day shift. A pallet load of foundations and parts would sit on the pier for hours, or days, while you waited for a team of hand riggers to get it aboard the ship. After you got the materials in the part of the ship they needed to go, then you usually had to wait until a combination welder was available to do the acetylene cutting and arc welding.

I recall working day shift, on a destroyer in upper SONAR, near the end of my third year of apprenticeship. It took me four days to install one steel table-like foundation in the corner of a compartment. It was only about 2 by 2 feet square, and I had it scribed to fit the corner where it went. But before I could cut it to fit, a pipefitter tapped my shoulder and said I couldn't put it in because he had piping to go in the exact same corner. We contacted our supervisors who then contacted their supervisors who then contacted design. Then design would come out and determine how the piping could be re-routed around the equipment my foundation was to support. The next day I finally got a burner to cut the edges to fit any discontinuity of the bulkhead plating.

As we started to weld it in place, an electrician tells me that he has a large wireway going in that same corner. We contacted our supervisors who then contacted their supervisors who then contacted design. Then design would come out and determines I can cut out a six inch by six-inch quarter circle corner of the foundation to allow the wireway to pass behind.

The next day I cut out the corner and got the foundation tack welded in place. Then a sheet metal worker tells me that he has a ventilation duct to go in that corner. We contacted our supervisors who then contacted their supervisors who then contacted design. Then design would come out and determines that the duct work can be re-routed around the foundation but not in the same place as the already re-routed piping.

I was seriously thinking that after I graduated from the Apprenticeship to look for work elsewhere where I wouldn't waste taxpayer's money waiting for some boo-boos to be cleared up.

On swing I did not have to wait for a welder as one was assigned to me specifically just for that job. I could install an entire compartment of foundations in one evening and go home, dog tired, but feeling I really accomplished something for my eight hours and the taxpayers got what they paid for.

I also found swing more convenient to pursue daytime needs. Working the night shift allowed me time to get shopping done during the day without the traffic snarls and crowded stores. But it didn't do much good for my social life having only Saturday and Sunday nights off. Also I had to get excused from Monday night National Guard drills. As time went on, the Guard instituted more all-day Sunday drills or weekend drills so I didn't miss that many Monday nights. Usually I would make up the drill by doing work at the armory during the day such as catching up paperwork as my duty as Truck Master. Or just going up to the Torrance Police target range to practice my pistol and rifle shooting.

On swing, we had a great team to work with. We got to know each other better than those we worked days with because we were a smaller crew. We mustered for our shift at the front of the shop where we got our turnovers. Most of us were close enough to piers and ships to come in for our half-hour lunch and play cards in the upstairs locker room. That was a great time for everyone to swap war stories. They never talked much about their combat experiences at home but they felt they were in like company at the shipyard. Most were veterans of World War II and since I was a tank crewman in the National Guard they considered me as one of their own though I had never been in combat - yet.

We were a mixed bunch of personalities too. Les Davis was one of the best shipfitters you could find. He always had a cigar in his mouth and always ready with a joke. Les was in the Navy before the war and claimed he may have been the first American to beat up a Japanese soldier. He was on liberty, in China, and got drunk one night. He was still teed off about the bombing the *Pinay* and while walking back to his ship he spotted a Japanese anti-aircraft machine gun nest along the beach. There was only one Japanese soldier in it so Les hopped over the sandbags and nearly beat the poor guy to death.

Jack Scoggins always looked tired out. Well, he also had a chicken ranch he ran during the day. No one will forget the day he came in, started to change into his work clothes and found he still had his pajamas on. Scoggins was not afraid of dirt either. (I guess a chicken rancher wouldn't really notice it anyway). He could install an entire set of zinc cathodic plates on the hull of a destroyer in one evening. In those days the 23 pound zinc plates had steel tabs sticking out so you could weld them to the hull (later bolt on zincs were developed). They had to have a thick coat of zinc oxide paste troweled on them as a bond between the zinc plate and the steel hull. Most of the zincs were overhead on the bottom of the hull by the propellers and it was a very messy job holding them in place for the welder while the zinc oxide dripped down your arms, back of your collar and in your lap. But Scoggins didn't mind it a bit.

Lyle Waggoner was a relatively old man. He was tall, thin and very quiet. But what a memory he had. You could walk aboard a ship and pass the compartment where he was to install some foundations and you would see him sitting on a low sawhorse bent over studying the blueprint. If you walked back a half-hour later, he would be in the same position. "Oh oh", you would think, the poor old guy fell asleep. Suddenly he would rise up, fold the blueprint and put it in his back pocket then would proceed to do the installation perfectly, without ever having to take the plan out of his pocket again. He totally **memorized** it.

Charlie Steiner was our wise cracking insult comedian. He was a WW II Marine, short, had a big nose, big (false) teeth, big smile and a huge sense of humor. He never called anybody by his right name. He called me Land Grabber for so long some of the other swing shift workers who came on a few years later thought that really was my name.

One of Charlie's favorite foils was George Alpazzar, one of our swing shift welders of Cuban birth. Charlie always called Alpazzar, "Apple Sauce" or just plain "Al". Poor Alpazzar, he always took it in stride, sometimes seeming "bothered" about it. But Steiner said he wouldn't do it if he didn't think Alpazzar couldn't take it. Then Charlie told me about what that tiny little Cuban did during the war.

One night at lunchtime Alpazzar verified the story and told me what he did when he was in the US Army fighting in Europe. A unit was isolated well up front and running low on ammunition. Volunteers were called for to take a quarter ton trailer load of ammo to the unit. Alpazzar and two other men volunteered. He said they were all too drunk at the time to know any better because the first place they would "liberate" in a town would be the winery. They loaded the jeep with any and all weapons they could, including a Bazooka, because they were going to have to skirt around the German lines to get to the stranded unit.

Driving up the road, an explosion suddenly flipped the jeep and trailer over into a ditch. The other two men were killed and Alpazzar was wounded. As he cleared his head and sat up, he saw a German tank moving toward them from over a low hill to the left of the road. The German gunner in that tank was pretty good, hitting a moving target as small as that jeep. Alpazzar retrieved the Bazooka from the trailer, loaded it himself and torched the tank. Then he walked, limped or crawled back to his own lines. With the tank now gone, a relief party was able to get another load of ammunition up to the isolated unit. He was awarded a Silver Star for his deed.

Floyd Bevis was a shipfitter helper and eventually made journeyman mechanic. Floyd and I worked together before a number of times on days and he finally got assigned to swing. Since Floyd was originally from Bremerton, Washington, Steiner usually called him "Webfoot". Other times he would just call him "Bevo". Floyd and I were also hunting partners and went on a number of deer hunts up in the High Sierras.

Floyd served in the Navy aboard the USS *Ammen* (DD-527), a *Fletcher* class ship that had five single mounts of 5"/38 guns. Floyd was first pointer in mount 53 that just aft of amidships and faced forward over the torpedo tubes toward the aft stack. A Japanese *Francis* twin-engine bomber gave the *Ammen* the dubious honor of being the first Destroyer to be attacked by a Kamikaze. The plane came in on the port side with its right engine out which probably saved the bridge and bridge officers it was aiming for. Floyd tracked that plane all the way in until it plowed into the ship's smokestack.

Seven crewmen of the *Ammen* died from that attack. The *Francis* broke in two and the tail section was still sitting on the ship with the tail gunner raking the quarterdeck with his machine gun. Floyd received only a minor injury from banging his forehead against the gun sight as the ship jolted from the shock of the hit.

Years later, the *Ammen* was rammed by the USS *Collet* (DD-730) and 11 crewmen were killed. The collision took place just south of Long Beach and we heard about it on the radio on the way to work. The ships were pulling in just after we clocked in and we went out to the quay wall to watch them. The *Collet* was coming in backwards as most of her bow was totally crushed. *Ammen* came in bow first with a severe list to port where it was gashed open almost at amidships. Floyd stood there on the quay wall with tears in his eyes. All he said was, "That's MY ship. She sinks HARD."

That night many of us had to board both ships to take the bodies off that were trapped behind torn and folded shell plating and bulkheads. *Collet* hit at about thirty degrees off of perpendicular with the upper third of her bow bent over to port and tearing away superstructure bulkheads on *Ammen* above main deck. The middle third of *Collet's* bow bent to starboard and scraped down the side of *Ammen* caving in several feet of shell plating. The lower third bent to port and broke off inside *Ammen's* boiler room. It really sounded unbelievable that a section of the *Collet's* bow had broken off inside the *Ammen* like a brittle arrowhead. Naturally I had to inspect that broken bow section myself the next night when *Ammen* was in Dry Dock 2.

Floyd asked for permission to work on that ship. By that time Don Foster had retired and Bill "Pal" Ashford was the supervisor. Both he and Neal Blake, the welding supervisor, knew of Floyd's WW II connection to the ship and gave him "expediting duties" to collect repair requests and double check the material lists as it was delivered. In other words, they gave him all the time he wanted to just wander around the ship and talk to the crewmen about all of their past experiences.

Ammen was being prepared for decommissioning anyway, so only a simple cofferdam (a steel blister) was welded over the hull gash and she was sold for scrap. *Collet* had just had her Fleet Repair And Modernization (FRAM) done so we put a new bow on her. Actually, it was the bow off of the unfinished DD-791 a Destroyer of the same class.

I mentioned Bill Ashford's nickname as "Pal". He was a chubby gentleman always with a smile and a very vivid imagination. He subscribed to Scientific American and was always trying to invent something. But he rarely ever called anyone by name. He always would come up to you and say, for example, "Hey, Pal. Could you take the truck out and pick up the guys at pier 4 tonight?" Or, "Say, Pal, we need and extra shipfitter on the outside slab tonight and I'd like to have you work with, uhh, Davis." Yup, that's the key. Bill could not readily remember people's first names. So, everybody was "Pal" and it became his nickname as well.

Among our welders and burners on swing, Keith "Bubbles" Clarson was heavy set and if he grew a full beard he would have been a perfect Santa Claus. Frank Nikolai was a bit chubby but dark haired and proud of his son, Don, who was a motorcycle officer on the Torrance Police Department. Frank was always cheerful until one day when his son was run over by a drunk driver. Though Don survived, he had to retire on a disability because the injuries were so severe.

The first Beneficial Suggestion Award I ever received was a shared award of about fifty dollars with Frank. He and I "invented" a jig-like device to hold the cylinder halves of sea chest waster sleeves together for welding more easily than trying to pin them down on a square-holed assembly slab.

Our overall prankster was Johnny Grant, a tall, lean welder who loved Tuna fishing and would take off a month every year to sign on a Tuna boat out of Alaska. He built a beautiful home in Long Beach but eventually sold everything and moved to Alaska permanently. As a practical joker he often would tape an opened sardine can underneath an office desk. One night he picked a fish out of a dry dock, right after it was emptied, and kept sticking it in some welder's glove or shipfitter's toolbox. When it wound up in Davis' toolbox however, Les got the last laugh by putting it on top of the electric heater under the passenger seat of Grant's Buick.

Dick Ellis was an expert oxy-acetylene cutter, auto mechanic and pretty good with a hunting rifle as well. He was from Arkansas and spoke with the appropriate accent. As an auto mechanic, Dick did a great job overhauling my '56 Plymouth. In WW II he was an Army truck driver on the Burma-Lido road --- many times. He always equiped the trucks with twin .50 caliber machineguns mounted on top of the cab. He said there were areas of the road where the Japanese were still covering it and he had to use the machine guns more than once but he never elaborated on any details.

Pat Casey was another artist with an acetylene torch and a golf nut, owned a home by the ninth tee of a golf course and after retirement turned semi-pro.

Bill Dummond, though in his 60's, was so good with a torch he got an outstanding award for being able to literally wash off a steel sleeve that was frozen to a bronze propeller shaft without leaving a single scorch mark in the shaft.

Those were only a handful of the great craftsmen I had the pleasure of knowing and working with. Many became good friends and several had many common interests such as joining the gun club and participating in rifle, pistol and shotgun shooting. I wish I could name them all but it would take up far too much room even if I could correctly remember their names. I guess just calling anyone "Pal" was sufficient enough.

There were a number of jobs I worked on out on the ships. One of the most memorable was where we had to line an entire compartment with lead on the Submarine Tender USS *Neureus* (AS-17). The compartment was a void space that was to be converted into a shielded "vault" to store waste radioactive materials from nuclear submarines. Some of the lead shielding was four inches thick and packed in tight with lead wool around the edges. However, with all the lead dust and fumes within that compartment, some of us wound up with lead poisoning if we didn't wear the proper clothes and respirators.

When Don Foster suddenly retired on a disability, actually due to a back injury he received while riding the tail end of a toboggan in the mountains, I was made temporary supervisor for two weeks. Floyd did my work in the layout section while I sat in the office filling out the time cards and job sheets. Well, I had to come in a bit earlier as well to read the turnovers and assign them to workers. Then at the end of the shift I had to review, comment and sign the turnovers.

After a regular supervisor was assigned, I spent most of my remaining swing shift time in the layout section. Besides using templates developed in the Mold Loft, many items had to be done from scratch based only upon plans or a rusty chunk of ship that was to be "duplicated". Pump foundations were the most common items cut out of a ship and sent to the shop to be copied and built new.

Perhaps the most dangerous job I had on swing was to build a replacement end for the yardarm of an Aircraft Carrier. A helicopter had come in a bit too close and clipped the end of the yardarm off. I had to climb out on the end of that yardarm about ninety feet above the flight deck with no safety belt to check the diameter of the broken end so I could make up a new piece in the shop. I sometimes wonder why I'm still alive today.

We also did a lot of cumshaw work on swing. Cumshaw (Kum-Shaw) is Mandarin Chinese for "Something extra" or a "tip". When time permitted, and we had excess material to do it with, we would build items for ships in trade for coffee. Sometimes it was just rat guards or a non-standard item for the Captain's cabin, such as a stainless steel frame for an aquarium.

But not all cumshaw was for personal pleasure. One night, MacEneany brought in a small curved aluminum plate, sort of boomerang in shape, had a number of screw holes in it and was broken in two. Mac explained it belonged to a friend of his who had to wear an artificial leg. This plate was the attachment piece at the top of his wooden leg but would break quite often. They were not expensive to replace, but the time it took to get it replaced restricted the man too much. So, Mac asked if I could duplicate it out of a stronger metal. I did it gladly and made it out of stainless steel. As I learned later, it never broke again.

Nor was all cumshaw illegal. Some was "official" such as one night I had to make steel lifting straps for a full size fiberglass replica of a Polaris missile that was to be displayed in front of the Administration building. Another official cumshaw job was to build a shipping guard out of steel plate to protect a SONAR dome when it was transported on a truck.

It was on swing when I was first assigned to do a secret job. I was a bit surprised when I reported in to work one afternoon and Bill Ashford called me to one side to say the FBI had cleared me and he had a special job for me to do. I had no idea what the job was about and merely packed my tool bag and headed off for an Aircraft Carrier on Pier 1 to report to the supervisor of the ending day shift for my turnover.

He led me down several decks into the ship, identified me to an armed Marine standing guard and showed me the space where I had to lay out the installation of some deck doublers. The doublers were merely flat "H" shaped steel plates, about half an inch thick, to be welded directly to the deck to increase the deck strength for some foundations of some sort to be welded on top.

It took the whole night to do the layout, center punch the outlines of the doublers and grind the deck welds flush so the doublers would fit metal-to-metal. I couldn't see anything on the plan that indicated what the secrecy of the installation was. It wasn't even marked Confidential. Next to that space was a workshop where there were always two or three crewmen going over a procedures review and I inadvertently overheard something about a "Blue Goose" and a "Silver Streak".

A few months later, I was visiting a friend of mine and his brother was home on leave from the Navy. The brother was stationed aboard another Carrier out of San Diego and as the beer flowed we started talking shop. I mentioned the remarks of Geese and Streaks and he just looked at me and asked, "Are you sure they said 'Blue Goose' or 'Silver Streak'?"

"Yeah, I think that was it. I wasn't really there to listen in on their conversations though."

He explained, "The 'Blue Goose' is the inert practice model of a streamlined atomic bomb to be carried under the belly of a fighter bomber. The 'Silver Streak' is the real McCoy." Cripes! I then realized that I had installed the bases for the Atomic bomb stowages aboard that ship.

My days as a sledgehammer mechanic ended in July of 1964 when I reported to Building 147 as a temporary GS-7 draftsman for a six-month detail. After the detail ended, a GS-5 position was opened up and I grabbed it for a permanent transfer into design.

But those six years as a shipfitter on swing were my most memorable and rewarding of all my blue-collar days. I still call myself an ex-sledgehammer mechanic and even when doing home projects either of wood or metal, I have learned to never force anything into place. I just get a bigger hammer.

CHAPTER 8: TRIESTE & WHITE SANDS

Another special project the shipyard was involved in was converting an Auxiliary Repair Dock (ARD) to be the surface support, or "mother", ship for the bathyscaph *Trieste*. August Piccard had designed the bathyscaph many years before and I recalled reading about it in my grade school newsletters. I later bought his book, *In Balloon and Bathyscaph*, to bone up on the history of its development. The Krupp factory built Piccard's first pressure sphere for the *Trieste I*. Terni in France built his later and improved version for *Trieste II* that the US Navy used.

The bathyscaph worked like a blimp, but underwater. Where the gasbag of a blimp carries helium, a lighter than air gas, for buoyancy or "floating" in air, the tank above the bathyscaph sphere was filled with gasoline. Gasoline, being a liquid, would not compress from the water pressure at any depth and it still remained lighter than water. Steel ball bearings inside cylindrical tanks within the gasoline "bag" would provide ballast to get the bathyscaph down to depth. An magnetic valve would drop sufficient ball bearings for buoyancy for bottom exploration or for return to the surface.

The job assigned to Long Beach Naval Shipyard was to convert the ARD-20 into the surface support, or "mother", ship for the *Trieste*. An ARD looks something like a Great Lakes ore carrier with a stubby bow with the entire superstructure up forward. It has a stern gate that can be lowered and ballast tanks to allow it to partially submerge, leaving just four feet of freeboard, so it can dock small ships for repair. Actually, ARD's are no more than floating dry docks but with an enclosed high bow section to make towing easier.

But this ARD was not going to be towed. Instead it would be self-propelled and three Murray-Thuygursen Harbor Masters that we installed. Also a huge gasoline tank was built into the forward end of the well deck to resupply the bathyscaph. A 70-ton pedestal mounted crane was installed on the aft end of the port wing wall with an extended boom, which Fred Hock and I designed, with a reduced maximum load of 35 tons.

The ARD was named the USS *White Sands* by its commanding officer, Cdr. Watts. The ship would flood its well deck, open its stern gate and rig the bathyscaph in or out. It also mounted a large double drum traction winch with a stowage reel behind it to hold 25,000 feet of 9-inch circumference double braided nylon rope. The Sampson Rope Company made the single length of nylon rope. The *Trieste II* was stowed aft and the gasoline tank with the built in steel shot tanks well forward. Between them some of the well deck area stowed towing lines and barrels of steel shot for the bathyscaph's ballast. Between was stowed - well - something else. We were never told what those circles were on the arrangement drawing what was there. All we knew was the traction winch was to lower them down to the bottom of the ocean. What the bathyscaph had to do with it, we weren't told either.

The stowage reel was designed to hold 25,000 feet of rope and was mounted just forward of the double drum traction winch. Actually, the original specifications called for only 20,000 feet of rope, but I didn't think that would be far enough to reach the bottom of the Marianna Trench. So I said it should be 25,000 feet and the company that built the reel took my word for it. I was only a GS-7 draftsman and nobody told me what it was really going to be used for.

We tested the winch and reel systems at Ballast Point submarine base in San Diego. I was placed in charge of the tests and everything worked quite well, even when we pulled up the fifty thousand pound weight too far and snapped the rope. Dropped that big block of lead all the way to the bottom fifty-six feet down and literally buried it in the muck. Well, the ship's divers needed to put in some bottom time anyway.

Another test we did was to validate the polyurethane floats I designed for the battery recharging cable and steel shot hose that would be floated out behind the *White Sands* to the *Trieste II* for replenishment-at-sea rather than having to dock the bathyscaph every time. The way *Trieste II* was to be replenished was *White Sands* would lower the stern gate and float out the battery recharging cables and shot hose to refill the steel shot tanks. The gasoline hose for the floatation ballast floated by itself quite well however.

We went out about twenty miles from Long Beach and used the Diver's boat to simulate the bathyscaph. All equipment tested out great and *White Sands* carried *Trieste II* for several years on deep ocean exploration missions. Or so we were told. A few years later, a technical journal finally described what those circular things were that were stowed on the well deck and had to be lowered by the double drum winch.

They were nuclear powered SONAR units to monitor any and all submarine traffic. The ARD planted them all over the ocean floors of EVERY ocean using the bathyscaph to spot them, or maybe even flip the "On" switch. They were planted in a specific grid and would last for years transmitting back info of passing submarines, friend or foe. At no time then, could a Soviet submarine get close to American shores without it being tracked already from hundreds of miles out.

The *White Sands* was to be replaced later by the USS *Point Loma* (AGDS-2). But Fellows and Stewart ship repair yard, that had the contract to do the conversion, never touched the ship after it had been there for over two months. Also, they did a very poor job on repairs and modifications to the USS *Higbee* (DD-806). Don Fraser was walking out on the pier one day to inspect some item on the *Higbee* and he noticed that the new topmast that had just been installed was at least five degrees out of vertical athwart ships. Fore and aft, it was okay, but transversely it was unacceptably crooked. Don reported it upon his return and the Navy, already frustrated with no work being done on *Point Loma*, said that was it and pulled both ships out of Fellows and Stewart the following week. The next morning I picked up the newspaper and saw the headlines that Fellows and Stewart had filed for bankruptcy. I think *White Sands* has been scrapped but the *Trieste II* is now a museum display in Keyport, Washington.

ARD-20 in Dry Dock being modified to be the Trieste II surface support ship.   "Digest" Feb 18, 1966

Bathyscaphe Trieste II at Mare Island NSY for the USS White Sands (ARD-20).   Author's collection

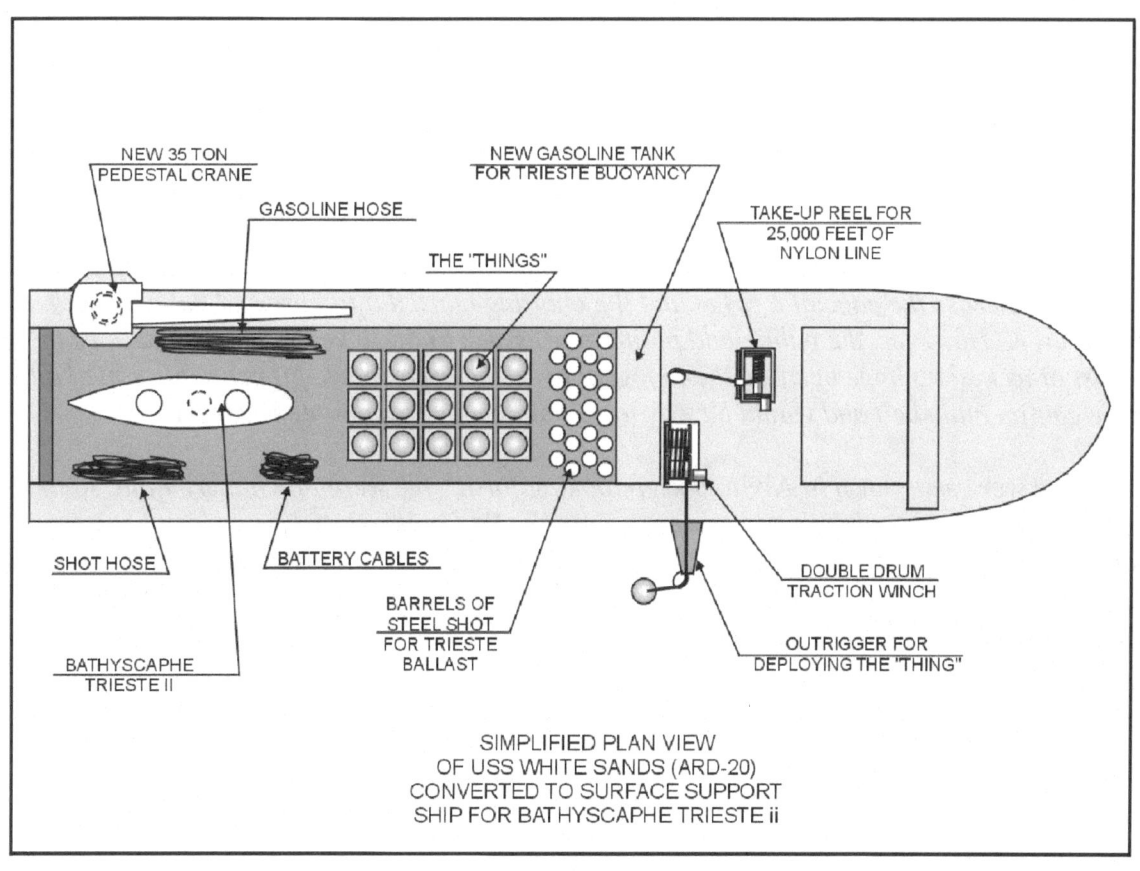

CHAPTER 9: CURV

Another deep-sea project LBNSY was involved in was *CURV* (Controlled Underwater Recovery Vehicle), which was a remote operated submersible that didn't look anything like a submarine or exotic research vehicle. It was a box-like framework of tubing with some long cylinders on top for buoyancy (that were later redesigned as pressurized square tubes) and a bunch of fancy instruments and tools below. The main tools were a camera and an articulated arm with a very versatile "claw". The claw could be replaced with a curved clamp that was sized for the diameter of a torpedo body.

The torpedoes *CURV* recovered were all inert practice torpedoes. If a live torpedo with a warhead were launched at a target but missed or the detonator failed, it would just be left on the bottom of the ocean unless it was in an area that could endanger ships or divers. Otherwise they are left alone to decompose. But the inert practice torpedoes could be used over and over again and it was economical to recover them. Finding them was a little tricky and they generally had an acoustic "beacon" for the *CURV* to home in on. It was also found that Dolphins could find the spent torpedoes faster and would lead *CURV* right up to them. Animal rights activists, however, took it wrong and thought Dolphins were being put at lethal risk to recover "**live**" torpedoes. As said before, we left the live ones alone to decompose underwater. Also, the Dolphins never actually recovered a torpedo because it was too heavy for them to lift back to the surface. Some tests were done where the Dolphin would attach the recovery clamp to the torpedo, but they didn't always put it at the right balance point. Today acoustic homing devices are much better and we do not use the Dolphins that much anymore.

On one of Jacques Cousteau's dives with his manned Diving Saucer, *CURV* was there for assistance and they made quite a show of the manned sub and the unmanned vehicle meeting hundreds of feet down and shaking hands -- er -- I mean --"claws".

CURV was connected to a surface support ship by an umbilical that provided power and, most importantly, data-link with the cameras and thrusters. The most fame *CURV* got was recovering the Hydrogen Bomb that was lost off of Palomares, Spain. Later I had the luck to meet the pilot of the submersible *Alvin* who actually found the bomb after they thought they lost it forever in a deep water canyon. We met in the bar of the Yacht Club Inn motel in San Diego near Point Loma. We were there attending a Marine Technology Society convention and we struck up a conversation. After I told him of what work I did on *CURV*, he felt I would be interested in his story of how the bomb was really found.

"When the bomb was first found, only a nylon line was used to try to raise it to the surface. But the line dragged across the edge of a ledge and the chaffing caused it to part and the bomb was thought to be lost forever. However, the public and political pressure to try to keep finding it kept us there even though most of us had no hope because the topography of the area showed it probably rolled off the edge of the continental shelf and would be way too deep for any reasonable recovery.

"So, we were sent down in Alvin *to keep looking for it. We were down there quite some time and the co-pilot needed to take a break and grab some lunch. So I took over while he was having a sandwich. I found a track, really just a shallow groove in the silt that looked like something may have rolled down the slope. The track could have been caused by anything, such as part of the bomber. But I followed it anyway because there was nothing else to guide me.*

"My co-pilot was just sitting back, with his sandwich and ignoring what I was doing. Suddenly I saw the bomb; all wrapped up in its parachute like a shroud. I just stopped Alvin and sat back to relax. My co-pilot didn't pay much attention at first and finally he asked, 'What are we stopped for?'

"I said that it wasn't any sense to go any further. He asked, 'Why not?'

"I replied that it's because the bomb is sitting right here by our window.

"His sandwich went flying and he scrunched his body over mine to look out the port. Then he got on the radio to report finding the bomb.

*"However, we were supposed to go by code words because Russian ships were also monitoring our communications. If we found the bomb, we were to use the code words that we found the instrument panel of the bomber. But he forgot the code and reported that we had found a **rusty nail**.*

"The mother ship responded by 'A what?'

"A rusty nail, we repeated.

'You mean the bomb?' was their reply. So much for code words. 'Yes. The bomb.'

"Well, when all had settled down, then came the problem of retrieving it. It was decided to use CURV. They had to build a special, but jury-rigged, clamp to fit the bomb that was a much larger diameter than the torpedoes CURV normally picks up.

"I'll tell ya, if that bomb was a couple of hundred feet further down that slope, they would never have got it. The umbilical was stretched to its limit and on the last wrap of the winch drum. But we got that sucker."

CURV I (Cable-controlled Underwater Recovery Vehicle). LBNS did some support work for testing this undersea Robot. It's primary use was to recover practice torpedoes up to a depth of only 2,000 feet. But it gained fame by recovering a lost H-bomb at a depth of 2,800 feet. A later variation, CURV III, with a 20,000 foot working depth rescued the two-man crew of the Pisces III in 1973.   SSC San Diego Robotics

CHAPTER 10: QUAPAW

Though not exactly out of the ordinary or even very special, the overhaul of the Fleet Tug USS *Quapaw* (ATF-110) deserves special mention. Since I previously told about the Navy pulling ships out of a private yard for shoddy work, *Quapaw* falls into this category.

The ship was being overhauled at a small shipyard on Terminal Island. They contracted to do a major overhaul on *Quapaw* including a total overhaul of her diesel-electric engine. The ship was driven by a huge electric motor turned by diesel-generators. To pull the rotor of the electric motor out required removing a fair size chunk of aft superstructure and cutting a large temporary access hole in the main deck just forward of the main towing winch.

I was instructed to go over to the yard and sit in on a review of X-rays they had taken of the welds of the temporary access. That was sort of an out of the ordinary request as normally the Navy yard's metallurgist and welding inspector would do that. I assumed, incorrectly, that they would be at that review also. But the higher ups knew something I didn't and they were keeping it to themselves for the moment. All I was to do was nod my head, say "Ohh" or "Ahh" at the appropriate times and take notes.

At the review meeting, they displayed scores of X-ray films of every inch of weld around that temporary access. There was no question there were problems. There were illegal patches from previous work, illegal weld butt junctures, slag inclusions and internal cracks throughout. The bottom line was that the private yard wanted an extension on the contract, and more money, to remove that entire deck area and replace it with new steel. At least that's what they said.

It turned out that was just a cover-up for a very sloppy job they did on the rotor. Instead of sending the rotor to a Westinghouse plant for proper dipping and baking, they merely slapped lacquer onto the windings. After it was installed with the temporary access all welded up and the superstructure back in place, their first test went to direct ground. What they really wanted was an excuse, as well as time and money, to pull that rotor back out and get the job done right the second time around.

We didn't fall for it and we pulled *Quapaw* out of their yard and put it at LBNSY. I then did a thorough study of the deck patch, pulled all the plans available and came up with two recommendations of repair. Either way, the rotor was going to be pulled out but I could just cut a minimum size access or go whole hog and replace a major chunk of main deck plating.

When I gave my briefing and recommendations to the ship's Captain, I was under the assumption that *Quapaw* was going to be reduced in service to just reserve status. So the minimum access cut would be sufficient. However, the Captain said that the ship's next assignment was beach gear work that would require full deck strength to support the towing winch. I immediately agreed with him and we proceeded to make major repairs to the deck while the rotor was being properly overhauled.

And I am very happy we did so. You see, when the Battleships *New Jersey* and *Missouri* were towed from Bremerton to Long Beach for their reactivations, *Quapaw* was assigned as a back-up tug. On each one of those tows, the main tugs pooped out and that little ATF with the creaky riveted hull took over and brought those ships home.

"B" She was later sold to a towing company along with the *Moctobi* in my home state of Wisconsin. But lack of use and proper maintenance finally forced her to sink at her pier. It's really a shame because as much as I love Battleships, there is a special place in my heart for the USS *Quapaw*.

The USS *Quapaw* (ATF-110). She towed *New Jersey* from Bremerton in 1982 and Missouri in 1984.

Honors and Awards

Quapaw received four battle stars for World War II service, five for the Korean War, and seven for the Vietnam War. You can look up all of her citations on the Internet.

USS *Quapaw* towing *New Jersey* from Bremerton to Long Beach in 1982. Photos from a Quapaw website.

CHAPTER 11: HAZMAT

Every industrial complex uses some sort of hazardous materials (HAZMAT). Shipyards are no exception. Whether we were working in the shops or in the design division we were aware of various HAZMAT in use. Asbestos was the most prominent on most people's minds which will be explained later.

It wasn't until after I retired and joined the Restoration Advisory Board (RAB) to oversee identification and remedial actions to be taken with HAZMAT at the Naval Complex did I realize how many materials are considered hazardous to human health. Even spilled dry cleaning fluids from a former laundry at the Naval Station created concern. I was somewhat amazed to find out how many dump sites there were around the complex that had to be investigated and cleaned up. There were four areas out on the Mole that required investigation and one of them actually had to be dug up and hauled off to an authorized disposal area.

Another question came up in a RAB meeting about the possibility of Radium paint contamination. One of the shipyard officers stated that the yard was never contracted to make new dial faces and there was probably no Radium painting done. However, I countered that and wrote a report based upon casual conversations I had with a former car pool member. Al Pearce worked in building 129 that was the electrical shop at the time. He mentioned that at times damaged dial faces were brought in and some Radium painting was done for repair and touch up.

Fortunately, the shipyard was being surveyed for radioactive contamination just as a matter of course. It was not part of the BRAC or CERCLA requirements but since some Bikini Atomic Bomb picket ships had work done on them at the shipyard after the tests, and we had a couple of nuclear powered cruisers stop by for a few days, it was a Navy requirement to check out the complex for radioactive contamination.

My report of Radium painting touch up was taken seriously and building 129 was thoroughly checked. Up on the third floor they found a sink and about one hundred feet of drainpipe contaminated with Radium. All items were safely removed and properly disposed of in deep holes bored through the layer of prehistoric concrete that lays far below the surface. Probably at a former Air Base, such as one Southwest of Salt Lake City, Utah. I'm pretty sure of another one -- but -- well, that is still classified.

The investigation of HAZMAT contamination was a long-term project starting back in the 70's with the drilling of exploratory wells throughout the shipyard. The most concern was contamination of ground water and its impact on human use. Fifteen Areas Of Concern (AOC's) were identified and exhaustively studied except for Site 7.

Site 7 was actually the entire harbor bottom and technically titled the West Basin. However, the Navy contractor had sub-contracted the basin studies to another laboratory. But that laboratory was replaced through a hostile take-over from yet another laboratory based in Carmenita.

By the time we got the first draft report on site 7, the Carmenita premises had been vacated and most of the records could not be found. Therefore the first draft report raised very extreme concerns at the RAB meetings. One of the members was a former supervisor of a chemical analytical laboratory and found the report to be incomplete and very unprofessional. Another member was the head of Earth Corps, an environmental right wing group, and he even filed intent to file suit over the report and brought his lawyer to one of the meetings.

The report showed maps of the harbor bottom outlining various areas of specific types of contamination. It showed high concentrations of silver around pier Echo, pier 6, pier 7 and pier 15 but it had no idea where the silver came from. I stood up and said, "If you would have just interviewed a few of the old timers, like me, you would know exactly where that silver came from." I later detailed my response in writing and am now part of the public record. Pier Echo often had support ships berthed there such as AOE's. Piers 6 and 7 had two hospital ships berthed there, the *Haven* and the *Repose*, at various times. Pier 15 often berthed a Destroyer tender. All of those ships had full photographic shops on board and the hospital ships had full X-ray developing labs. The silver was from the Silver-Nitrate developing chemicals that were merely pumped overboard into the harbor.

Silver is an element that normally poses no threat to human health. However, the report claimed it studied air view photos of the shipyard over many years of its existence. If that was true, then how could they not identify hospital ships berthed for over twenty years at piers 6 and 7 and not relate the Silver-Nitrate chemical used to develop X-ray film to the silver concentrations on the harbor bottom? So I studied the report more thoroughly. Over several days, page-by-page and field note by field note.

My next red flag was the locations of sample corings of the harbor bottom. Each "deep" coring was fifteen feet deep into the silt. But there were only eight corings and only one of them at the end of a pier. That coring sample showed heavy petroleum contamination all the way down to the fifteen-foot depth. That should have raised questions and prompted corings at the ends of all the other piers. Instead the contractor claimed that would not have been within the "random" pattern selected. One would think a geometric grid would provide the most accurate plotting of any and all layers of silt and contamination rather than a "random" pattern.

I wrote a report to the RAB on the area of the West Basin that seemed to be almost deliberately overlooked. That was the area where pier 4 used to be. It was an old wood pier that would often be submerged at high tide (thanks to subsidence). With the pier now gone, that area would have been a perfect site for several corings and dredge samples. Anything and everything that ever fell into the water during the shipyard's existence would be represented there. Materials that soaked deep would be found because the pulling of the pier pilings would have brought them closer to the surface. **"B" But, pier 4 was not part of the "random" pattern and several people, that should have known, did not even know the pier actually existed, even with aerial photos where it stood out like a sore thumb.**

All other bottom samples were only four inches deep. Though hundreds were taken, a four-inch depth only picks up the surface of the harbor bottom that is constantly changing due to tidal or ship propeller actions. That would not give a true indication as to what kinds of materials may have been deposited over the last half century and seeped below into the muck well below the four inch samples. But even those samplings raised another red flag to me being that of tributyltin contamination.

All of the lab tests on Flounder and White Croaker retrieved from the West Basin showed they contained tributyltin. When <u>sterile</u> clams were exposed to the harbor silt, they contracted tributyltin contamination. Yet, the executive summary of the report said that there were no tributyltins in the harbor and no action was required because it was claimed that tributyltin only lasts about thirteen days.

I wrote a report that for several years the Navy, as well as private ship operators, has been using anti-fouling bottom paints containing tributyltin **<u>fluoride</u>**. The Navy, or anyone else trying to keep their ship hulls free of barnacles and other marine fouling, would not waste their time and money on something that was going to last less than two weeks. The tributyltin compounds and impregnation methods used were designed to last **up to five years** between dry dockings.

I'm happy to say we did our job. The prime contractor back tracked on the site 7 report and relisted it for further study later coming out with a more accurate report. The Port of Long Beach picked up where the Navy contractor left off and did a much more thorough and detailed investigation before any major dredging was done.

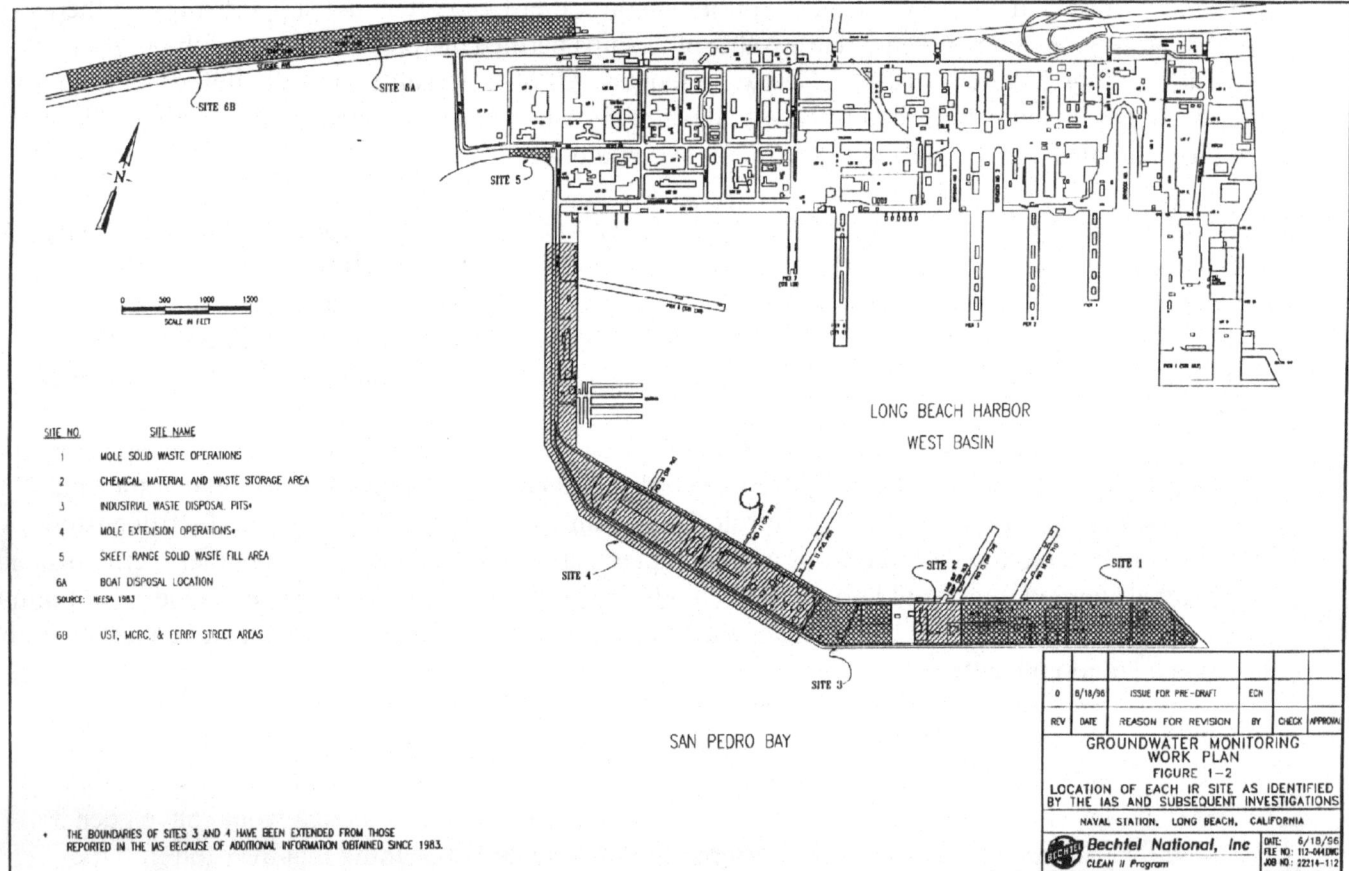

The toxic waste area map presented to the Restoration Advisory Board. Author's collection

Now, all of the above studies only had to do with any contamination that was below ground level. Therefore, asbestos was only noted when found in dumpsites. The asbestos problem is really something else and will take a while to explain.

To begin with, asbestos is a natural material mined from a special type of rock. It has a fibrous structure that is woven into cloth. It has excellent heat resistance and is an excellent fire retardant material. It has been used for ages as insulation in buildings, fire fighter suits and on hot piping, particularly steam piping.

Some types of piping are a mixture of asbestos fibers and fine cement. At one time some sewer pipes were made of asbestos instead of tile. Some time ago the city was doing some excavating in the street along the West side of my home. I noticed some broken sections of asbestos pipe had been dug up and were just lying on top of the dirt pile. Neighborhood children walking by were picking up some of those pieces and throwing them around. I commandeered a metal asbestos warning sign from the shipyard, mounted it on a stake in the dirt pile and wrapped up all the asbestos pipe shards I could find in a plastic bag.

The next day, the sign and bag disappeared. I assumed that the city-contracted crew just junked it. However, the following day the sign reappeared and remaining shards of piping were removed. Apparently the work crew took a sample in to their headquarters and confirmed that the remnants indeed contained asbestos and caution should be taken.

Insulation on ships is much different than buildings and sewers. Thermal insulation on the overheads and bulkheads is fiberglass. In the old days it was cork but fiberglass boards are much better. Insulation around hot water, cold water, chill water may have had asbestos blankets wrapped around the piping, covered with a non-asbestos topping and wired in place. However, all steam piping was assuredly wrapped with asbestos, then a non-asbestos wrap coat and then painted.

We never thought too much of asbestos being a hazardous material. We found the asbestos blankets, which came on long rolls about 3 or 4 feet wide, to be very handy for all kinds of purposes. The main purpose was to spread out blankets on the wood staging planks so hot slag from welding and acetylene cutting would not burn the wood. The asbestos blankets also protected furniture and flooring in the ships.

"B" But around 1977 or 1978 the head doctor at the dispensary of the Naval Station, **Dr. Shelton**, had done an extensive study on the caustic properties of minute asbestos fibers getting into the lungs of workers. These fibers are usually created whenever asbestos is cut and, being so small, become airborne for short periods of time and can be inhaled. The problem is, once they get into your lungs, they don't get back out. Some people have better natural filtration systems than others do. Exactly what sets immune people aside from susceptible people to asbestosis is still being studied. **Dr. Shelton** decided to start that study and had every employee, military and civilian, field worker and office worker, examined for asbestosis.

Everyone, including secretaries who never worked close to the ships, were X-rayed as many of the office workers often came in contact with shop workers who may have come to the office with asbestos particles on their clothing where a ceiling fan could blow the asbestos dust all over the room.

When reports of our X-rays and blood works came back, the doctor would inform you whether or not you had asbestosis. But if he saw something else out of the ordinary, he would inform you of that also and recommend you to see your family physician. For example, Meredith West's report showed she had a diaphragmatic hernia, which explained why she always had such "stomach aches".

However, people that were diagnosed with asbestosis were then given the option to apply for a disability retirement. However, it was not given to them immediately. They had to present proof that they worked in an asbestos environment sufficient years to contract the disease. Dave Dickson asked me if I could remember the names of some of the ships we worked on when we were apprentices. So, the next day I brought in my four-year collection of apprentice logbooks that listed each ship and the precise dates I had worked on them.

I worked those same ships Dave did at about the same time. Plus swing shift where we cut our own lengths of asbestos blankets while the welder was setting up. But, for some reason, I was not susceptible to the disease. Many who were not around asbestos very much were infected but then there were those around it almost all the time who were immune. It is still a perplexing problem.

Though it was a Navy doctor who brought the asbestos problem to the surface and started correctional programs to eliminate asbestos from the work place, the "News Media" blamed the Navy for the problem. Asbestos is not just a Navy problem. It is a problem with all commercial ships, buildings, etc. **It was the United States Navy that decided to tackle the problem**. But rather than being lauded to take the first steps it was accused instead of "causing" the problem.

LBNSY was also the first to develop safe procedures for removal and disposal of asbestos insulation. The compartments, where removal is to be done, are sealed off with plastic sheets to prevent airborne particles of asbestos from entering other spaces. The removal workers are dressed from head to toe in nearly airtight suits resembling the inspection team in the movie *E.T.-The Extraterrestrial*.

"B" In the first edition of this book, I wrote a word for word discussion a friend of mine had with another person on the problems with working with hazardous material. But I'm deleting it from this edition because I need more space for more photos and validated events.

During the Battleship reactivation days on *New Jersey* and *Missouri*. Asbestos was removed from those ships by the ton, but only as much as needed to be for any piping removals or modifications. It was just not cost effective and too time consuming to remove and replace 100% of the asbestos insulation aboard the ships ("If it ain't broke, don't fix it" philosophy). So, some asbestos still remains on them, but as long as it remains encased in its plastered non-asbestos outer layers it is perfectly safe.

I resigned from the RAB in 1998, finishing up my last year as community co-chair. I feel I did my duty by identifying a Radium contamination site in Building 129 and joining with other "activists" to force a more thorough re-study of the Harbor bottom.

Typical HAZMAT suits (Left: Santa Clara Fire Dept ----------. Right: LBNSY type Asbestos insulator).

CHAPTER 12: SEALAB II

One special project that caught the public's eye, and did not require the security of need-to-know restrictions, was the "Man-In-The-Sea Program" of the US Navy. Actually, the more publicity the Navy got, the better. Jacques Cousteau started it off in the early fifties with his underwater habitat where divers lived for days or weeks at a time. He filmed a documentary of that experiment called *World Without Sun*. At one theater where it was shown the theater manager had an interesting sense of timing. The first feature was Disney's excellent production of *20,000 Leagues Under the Sea* and the second feature was *World Without Sun*. It was stimulating to the imagination to watch a movie that was a science fiction story written in the mid-19th Century followed by a true documentary showing how we were catching up to science fiction in almost exactly 100 years.

Watching the divers at work at the shipyard was always a treat. Once in a while, somebody would drop an expensive piece of structure over the side that would be too expensive to make over again so the divers had to go down for it. Those were the old days where they still wore the old Mk V hardhat suits with the heavy brass helmet, lead weight belt and lead weighted shoes. So, they were pretty interesting to watch.

When the Navy launched its "Man-In-The-Sea" program, they started off small with *SEALAB I*. That experiment was done in the Caribbean with a small habitat only about 90 feet down. It was a cigar shaped structure and rather blah looking compared to Cousteau's star shaped, multi-room house he built a few years before.

Then *SEALAB II* came along with a much more complex agenda of tests and experiments, as well as a lot more publicity. The Naval Ordnance Test Station (NOTS) out of China Lake and San Clemente Island was the Navy unit to head the program with their contract agent of Westinghouse out of Sunnyvale providing field engineering.

Mare Island Naval Shipyard built the habitat, as they were experienced submarine builders to begin with. It was a steel cylinder of HY-80 steel twelve feet in diameter and twenty-four feet long. The ends were designed as ASME pressure tank caps of one-inch thick HY-80 steel formed by using high explosives to transfer a shock wave through the water that would press them into shape within a concrete mold.

This method of explosion forming was touted quite highly in various technical journals as the largest pressure vessel ends to be formed this way. Actually the basic process was over a hundred years old, on a much smaller scale shaping water pitchers, cuspidors and chamber pots.

A conning tower was added, as the habitat was to be towed out to its test site off of La Jolla, and extensive framework and support legs were added to the bottom. The framework also supported several heli-ox breathing bottles. At the depth the aquanauts were to work at, 240 feet down, normal air would not do. Therefore they used a mixed gas of helium and oxygen instead of atmospheric type air, which is high in nitrogen. Helium, being much lighter than nitrogen, can work its bubbles out of a diver's blood stream much faster, thus reducing decompression time and preventing the bends.

A surface support vessel was needed to lower and raise the habitat as well as provide supply and communication services to the aquanauts. Since the Pop Up program had wound down after the *Poseidon* missile had become a regular part of our weapons inventory, it was decided to use the Pop Up *Staging Vessel*, owned by NOTS, as the support vessel for *SEALAB*. This is where LBNSY came into the picture as we were the designers of the *Staging Vessel* and it was berthed in our West Basin.

It already had the basic facilities of berthing, messing, a crane and a small recompression chamber on board. We removed the Kelp Cutter, converted the Launch Vessel winch and A-frames to rig the habitat lowering/raising wire down and under the *Staging Vessel* to a fixed boom off the aft end.

It was my job to design that boom. Bill Harris was my supervisor of the fittings design section and he did the engineering calculations. His calcs showed that the beam provided by NOTS wasn't going to be quite strong enough, basing it upon a three-to-one factor of safety. I'm a 3-dimensionall thinker so just off-handedly I suggested welding in chock plates every ten or twelve inches inside the beam to make it more like a box beam with a centerline keel. Bill turned to look at me almost wild eyed, wondering where I had come up with that idea. I was only a shipfitter just out of the shop with only an AA degree and no formal engineering classes. He then said, "Not a bad idea. It just may work." A couple of hours later he had redone his calcs and we would have over a three to one factor of safety.

Another odd thing that NOTS and Westinghouse came up with was a way of dampening the waves and swells bobbing the *Staging Vessel* up and down while lowering the *SEALAB* habitat. Once the habitat was flooded to negative buoyancy and submerged, it would put excess strain on the lowering wire and associated rigging as the *Staging Vessel* bobbed. Also, sitting it in the correct spot on the ocean floor would be quite tricky. So, George Perrington of Westinghouse came up with the idea of running the lowering wire underneath the bridge section connecting the two barges with a counterweight hanging from it, then up to the lowering boom. Water resistance and negative buoyancy of the habitat would prevent it from bobbing up while the wire tightened and the counterweight acted as a shock absorber. A tensiometer would also be installed on the wire rope to monitor the tension and adjust the speed of the winch in lowering and hoisting cycles so the counterweight could do its job.

Our assistant chief engineer, Graydon Abbot, was not convinced it would work. After sitting in on a meeting where he voiced his doubts, I stopped by the hobby shop on the way home that evening and picked up some balsa wood sheets. I also brought home some basic plans of the *Staging Vessel*. That night, I built a 1:96 scale model of the staging vessel. It included the main decks of both barges, keels, transverse bulkheads (no shell plating), the connecting structure, the deckhouses (without tops), the A-frames that would guide the winch wire and finally the handling boom. For the *SEALAB* habitat, I merely used a cardboard toilet paper roll. For the counterweight, I stripped the lead bullet out of an 11-millimeter Remington cartridge. I screwed a picture frame eye into it and ran some fishing line as the lowering wire from the A-frame through the counterweight, up to the end of the boom and down to the cardboard roll. I finished the model about 0300 in the morning. After only three hours sleep, I went to work at my regular time of 0800 and took the model into Graydon's office and showed him how the counterweight dampening system would work.

He was not only convinced but even more amazed at how fast I had built that model to have on his desk less than sixteen hours after the meeting. We kept that model around the office for a couple of years, until somebody put some books on top of it and crushed it.

The Navy Captain in charge of the whole *SEALAB* experiment was George Bond. His second in command was Captain Walter Mazzone (pronounced Mah-ZONE-ee) of the Navy medical department. Bond and Mazzone developed and tested the free ascent method to escape from a downed aircraft that had sunk to a deep depth. I saw a TV special on it where Captain Bond strapped himself into the cockpit of an airplane that was secured to the deck of a submarine. After the sub dove to over 200 feet he opened the canopy, inflated his Mae West and shot to the surface. However, to prevent air embolism (the bends) he continued to exhale as hard as he could all the way up.

Captain Bond was generally pretty busy with the basic scope of the *SEALAB* experiment and PR. But Captain Mazzone hung around the NOTS office out between piers one and two quite a bit along with Commander Scott Carpenter, former astronaut, who was also going to be a team leader of the aquanauts. I got to know and work with Mazzone and Carpenter of course, but I was more closely teamed up with George Perrington and Joe Berkich of Westinghouse. Joe Berkich was a very energetic type of engineer whereas George was more of an imaginator like me. But it was Berkich and Mazzone who had the authority to order anything the rest of the team felt they needed.

They were so wrapped up in the *Staging Vessel* that George and John DeFriest, from NOTS, joked that the *Staging Vessel* should be renamed the *Berkone* (pronounced Bur-CONE-ee) after Berkich and Mazzone. Some news reporter was nearby one day when they were calling the *Staging Vessel* that and the next thing we knew was that the Surface Support Vessel for the *SEALAB II* was now the USS *Berkone* (but pronounced Bur-CONE without the "ee" sound at the end). Don't believe everything you read in the papers or hear on TV.

A larger recompression chamber, built by the Dixie Manufacturing Company, had been installed in the bay of the port barge where *Poseidon* and *Polaris* missiles were once stowed and prepped for launch. It was a double chamber allowing a medical officer to go in and out, using the outer chamber for faster decompression since he would only be in the main chamber for a few minutes with the more slowly decompressing aquanauts. That extra chamber came in handy after the first two-week stint of men living 240 under water. One of the aquanauts, Robert C. "Bob" Sheats, was getting a little old for deep diving and the air was not working out of his system fast enough. So, he was kept in the main chamber for a couple of more days while the rest of the crew finished their decompression, of only a few hours, in the outer chamber. Well, he DID celebrate his 50th birthday while down in SEALAB II. **"B"**

Bob was a Navy diver during World War II and was stationed in the Philippines when the war started. He was captured by the Japanese and forced to dive in Manila Bay to recover the gold that the Filipinos had dumped there. He had lots of interesting stories about that. Such as how they would weaken the crates just enough so they would break open upon surfacing and dump all the gold coins back down into the Bay again.

One of the *SEALAB* experiments was to use a Dolphin to supply tools and equipment to the divers. The Dolphin's original name, when he was trained up at Point Magu, was Tough Guy because it took him longer to learn his "tricks" than the other Dolphins. But once he learned them, he would do them flawlessly every time. His name was shortened to "Tuffy" for his *SEALAB* assignment and got along well with the aquanauts. One diver simulated being lost and upon sending out a special signal, Tuffy swam right over to him and led him back to the habitat.

But Tuffy wasn't the only non-human critter involved with *SEALAB*. Sam (later found out to be a Samantha rather than a Samuel) the Sea Lion joined the crew as well. Sam was a wild Sea Lion that inhabited the shores of La Jolla along with several other Sea Lions and are known to be the clowns and mimics of the marine world. Sam would hang around the *Berkone* and watch all the activity. As the small Galiazzi type diving bell was used for short-time personnel transit was lowered or raised, Sam would follow it. Sam was also curious as to what Tuffy was doing and would follow him around as well. The aquanauts got quite accustomed to Sam looking over their shoulder while doing one of the underwater experiments.

Since the internal mixed gas pressure of the habitat was the same inside as the water pressure outside, the bottom hatch was left open for fast entry and egress. One day, Sam poked her head up into the habitat and looked around. She found that as an opportunity to take in some "fresh" air. But the helium mix gives the vocal chords a very high-pitched tone. Humans sound like Donald Duck when they talk and are almost unintelligible. Sam gave out a bark that did not sound right at all to her and she dove out of sight.

We were all worried about her because she didn't show up for two or three days. Our first assumption was that when she took in her replenishment of air, she was not aware that it was at nearly 107 pounds per square inch as opposed to the less than 15 pounds at sea level. Therefore we feared that she surfaced too fast and burst her lungs.

She was found loafing around a marker buoy a few days later, captured with a tranquilizer gun and given a full medical examination. That's when they found Sam was a she instead of a he. She appeared to be in good shape and probably, by instinct, used Captain Bond's free ascent method of exhaling the higher-pressure air on the way up. But she didn't like being chased, tranquilized and tagged so her activities around the *Berkone* were more at a distance and she didn't go down into the habitat again either.

One of the experiments was to have a three-way radio communication with astronauts in a Gemini capsule orbiting over 100 miles up and Jacques Cousteau in his underwater habitat, *CONSHELF III*, in the Atlantic. The hook-up worked pretty well. To make the "Donald Duck" voices sound more intelligible; the speakers would breathe some pure oxygen first to thicken up the air in their vocal chords.

Interestingly, there are some words that are more understandable in a helium atmosphere than others. It appears that profanity comes across loud and clear. Now, it has been said that most deep-sea divers only have a 250-word vocabulary that can be said in mixed company. So, Captain Bond claimed that at least one-third of the communications from his divers was perfectly clear to understand.

However, since then the voice problem was solved by developing a triple gas mixture of Oxygen, Helium and Nitrogen. Just enough Nitrogen is introduced to bring voice tones down to more normal as well as the diver's microphone equipment was also modified.

SEALAB II also made some firsts such as testing the first underwater voice communication equipment and the first tests of Foam-In-Place salvage of an F-86 Sabre jet fuselage.

One of the best pieces of existing equipment that found constant use, both during *SEALAB* and the Pop Up program, was an underwater camera and casing developed by the movie actor, Jon Hall. He was noted for his South Pacific rolls as a Polynesian and his TV series as a doctor in East India, *Ramar of the Jungle*. Little did the public know that SCUBA diving was not only his past time but also an avocation that led to his development of an underwater camera. We used his cameras quite extensively on the Pop Up programs as well as *SEALAB II*.

Unfortunately *SEALAB III* was not so successful. It was a disaster. When NOTS tagged LBNSY to re-modify the *Staging Vessel* and *Fish Hook* back for the Trident C-4, a **new** Commanding Officer of the shipyard rejected the job because he thought we were too small and inexperienced to handle it. It took some time to convince him that WE were the shipyard that designed and built all of that to begin with.

He also rejected the job to convert a Landing Ship Medium (LSM) to be the *SEALAB III* surface support vessel with blisters added to the sides for greater stability and additional deck space. But the C.O. had his way on that one so NOTS and Westinghouse had to scramble for another design agent and the project was at least a year late getting underway.

By that time the "Man-In-The-Sea" program was not getting the full publicity as in the earlier years. The public was more interested in the moon flights than underwater laboratories. The *SEALAB II* habitat was converted into *SEALAB III* and the first tests were to be done at the same 240-foot depth as before. Then it would be moved deeper to 400 feet for more experiments. But the delay caused an acceleration of the program and the 400-foot depth was selected for all tests, by-passing the initial 240-foot dive.

Shortly after the habitat was set down, a diving bell followed with three divers to release the crane rigging. The water was icy cold and for some reason the hot water supply from the bell for the hot water suits was cold as well. Two of the divers also wore wool long johns under their hot water suits with a heavy-duty wet suit over that. One of the divers however, Berry L. Cannon, did not wear long johns. Soon after exiting the bell, he disappeared. The other divers found him within a few minutes, but by that time hypothermia had set in and he was beyond help.

"B" *This is heart breaking as Berry was an Aquanaut on both SEALAB I and SEALAB II.*

By standard procedure, the Navy suspended all dives beyond 85 feet until a full investigation of Cannon's death could be done. This also restricted all dives for the *Trident* program that were up to 185 feet. In the meantime, the habitat, with only partially blown ballast, was sitting on the bottom with the crane still hooked up to it.

Bill Goodman, of NOTS, told me later they decided to yank the habitat up by the brute force of the crane. They had a tensiometer on the lifting wire to tell them if they were getting too close to the breaking strength. Bill said he was within seconds of canceling the lift as the tensiometer was approaching "red line" and the corner of the hull of the floating crane was actually under water. Suddenly the crane rose back up to an even keel and the tensiometer went back down showing a normal loading for lifting the habitat.

That ended the Navy's "Man-In-The-Sea" program, at least for underwater living quarters. The Navy still operated the Bathyscaph *Trieste* for research and planting special equipment on the ocean floor. *NRS-1*, *Alvin*, Cousteau's *Diving Saucer* and *CURV* are really vehicles for short-term dives with no intent of forming underwater cities as envisioned by science fiction writers.

Some thought *SEALAB II* would be the apex of their careers at Long Beach Naval Shipyard. We thought it could never top anything else we could do as we designed its rigging systems and worked with some of the Nation's most experienced and famous deep-sea divers. However, other very interesting projects came along: the DSRV and the Battleships. Long Beach Naval Shipyard rose to the challenge with each and every one of them, thinking nothing could ever top the last project we successfully completed.

Shop 64 patternmakers built a detailed model of Sealab II with transparent Lucite. Left to right: Don Mutru, Jack Young, Dave Kawagoye & Bill Galayda. Head patternmaker Clarence Bailey was not pictured. "Digest"

SEALAB II on a barge at LBNSY shortly before being placed in the water to be towed to La Jolla, CA. "Herman is at the right of the photo ready to do the lift, as usual. "ONR Report ACR-124"

"Tuffy". Our trained Porpoise wearing a harness and awaiting orders for a job to do.

"Sam" (Samantha) a "wild" Sea Lion that volunteered to keep tabs on our Human divers.
Above photos from ONR Report ACR-124

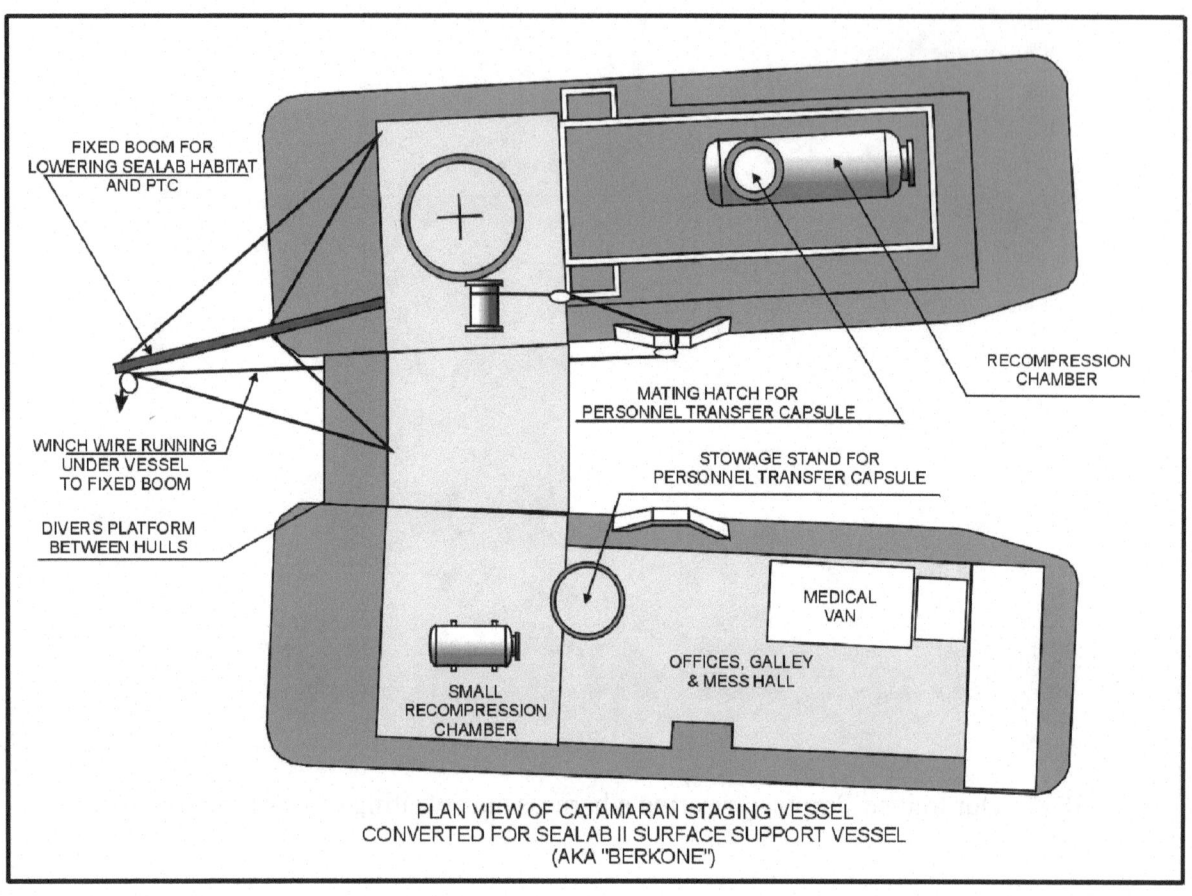
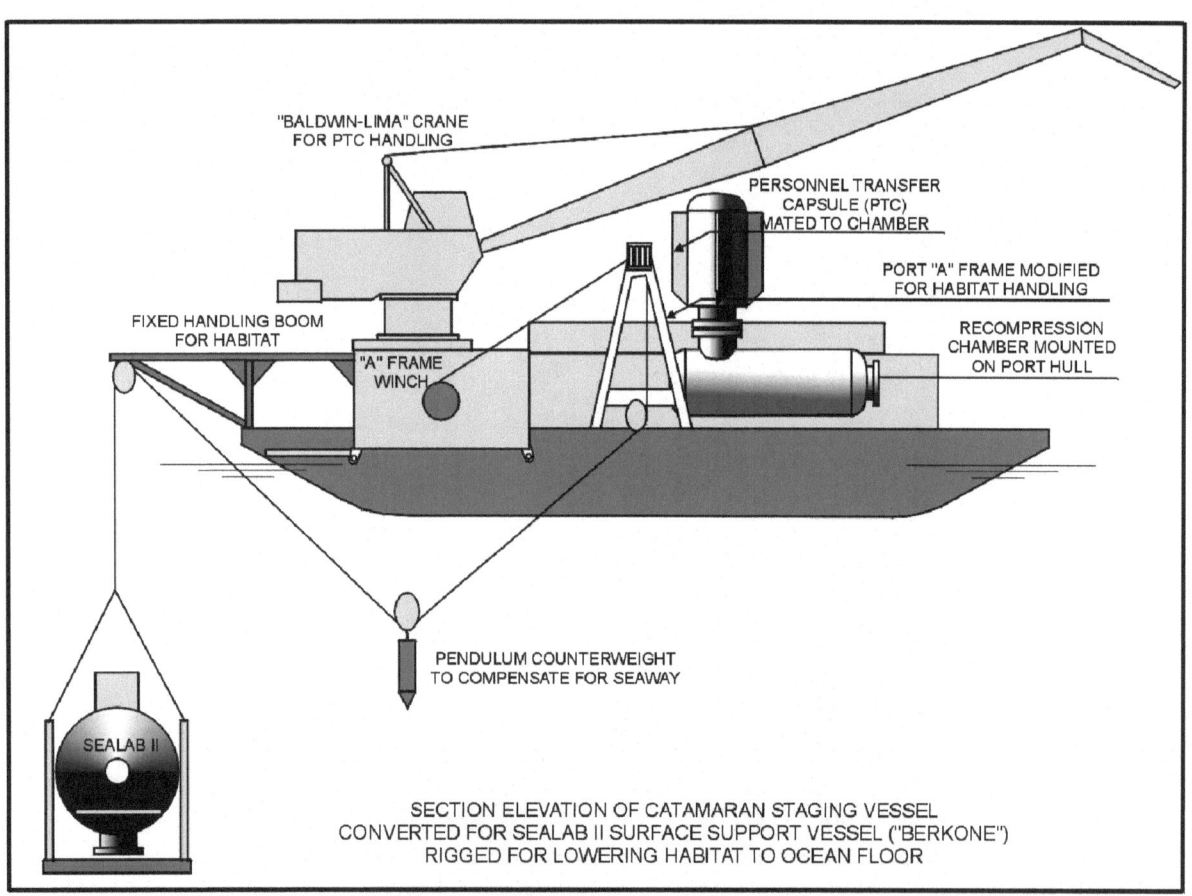

Plan view & Profile view of SEALAB rigging systems. Author's CAD drawings

CHAPTER 13: DSRV

One last chapter on deep-sea projects the shipyard was involved in but over thirty years later has created some controversy as to what it really was all about. I am referring to the Deep Submergence Rescue Vehicle (DSRV) that was specifically designed to rescue submariners from a sunken submarine that had **not** gone below its crush depth.

The project actually got started in the early 60's after the submarine USS *Thresher* (SSN-593) dove to her destruction on 10 April 1963. She hit bottom, well below crush depth, at about a hundred miles per hour so there was absolutely no chance of having any survivors. But it gave a wakeup call to the Navy about the need to have a rescue system for our modern deep diving submarines. Yes, it also tightened up on fabrication and welding procedures for submarines but as for rescue, the only thing the Navy had was the McCann Rescue Chamber. The McCann could only hold seven survivors and two operators at a time and could not operate anywhere near the deepest operational depth of a modern submarine. The only time the McCann was ever used, in a real rescue operation, was when the USS *Squalus* (SS-192) went down in May of 1938 and it took four trips of the McCann to rescue the survivors. Modern submarines dive much deeper and have much larger crews, thus making the McCann rescue chamber totally inadequate. LBNSY was tasked to do some initial studies, though we were not a submarine yard. During our studies I ran across a set of plans for a larger spherical rescue chamber that could hold twelve survivors. But it was never built and would still be totally inadequate.

Later, the Navy came out with the idea of having a small submarine, rather than a diving bell, capable of operating at depths up to 5,000 feet as the ideal rescue vehicle. Basically, the DSRV is three spheres connected in line. The forward sphere is the command and control cabin. The center sphere is the primary rescue chamber with a bell shaped collar on the bottom to mate to a submarine escape hatch. It also had an upper hatch leading to a conning tower above. The third sphere is another survivors' compartment bringing the vehicle's total rescue capacity up to twenty-four survivors. The propulsion system was aft of the third sphere and the entire assembly was enclosed within a streamlined (cigar-shaped) free flooding fiberglass hull. It would have floodlights, SONAR, anomaly sensors, cameras, double manipulators, communications and just about anything you would want in an all-purpose rescue vehicle that could **also do research work to pay for itself in between rescue operations**.

Two DSRVs were built as well as two very special (and extremely complex) catamaran mother ships. The DSRV-1 (*Mystic*) and USS *Pigeon* (ASR-21) were based on the West Coast while the DSRV-2 (*Avalon*) and USS *Ortolan* (ASR-22) were on the East Coast. Oh yes, the DSRV–1 and its mother ship have also been used in two movies; *Gray Lady Down* and *Hunt for the Red October*.

The Naval Underwater Research and Development Center (NURDC, formerly called NOTS) was the lead agency coordinating the development and testing of the DSRV. Long Beach's involvement was in the initial DSRV testing and its ability to mate to a mockup of a sunken submarine. Lockheed Missile and Space systems had designed and built a Simulated Distressed Submarine (SDS) with an open framework the size and shape of the top half of a real submarine. A sheet-metal mock-up of a submarine sail (a.k.a. Conning Tower) was mounted on it as well as an escape hatch with mating ring. The sail and mating ring could be rotated to a 45-degree list simulating a submarine not sitting level on the ocean floor. Our job was to design a way of getting the SDS down to the bottom of the ocean off of San Clemente Island. It was to be anchored to stake pile 5 at the 185-foot depth where the Pop Up launch towers had been. A hauldown beam had to be attached to the top of the stake pile and wire ropes (steel cables to you non-rigger oriented readers) would be reeved through a system of sheaves (large pulleys to you non-rigger oriented readers) from the SDS, fed through the hauldown beam and up to a Skaggit winch on the shore of the island.

The design of the hauldown beam was quite a challenge. First we designed a two-piece box structure that would bolt onto the top of the stake pile. Instructions strongly specified that everything had to be pre-assembled then disassembled in the shop first as the divers were only to have a twenty-minute bottom time for each stage of assembly. In truth, the divers often extended their bottom times to thirty or forty minutes and changed to the appropriate decompression tables. However, we did our best to create sub-assemblies that could be put together by teams of divers within twenty minutes.

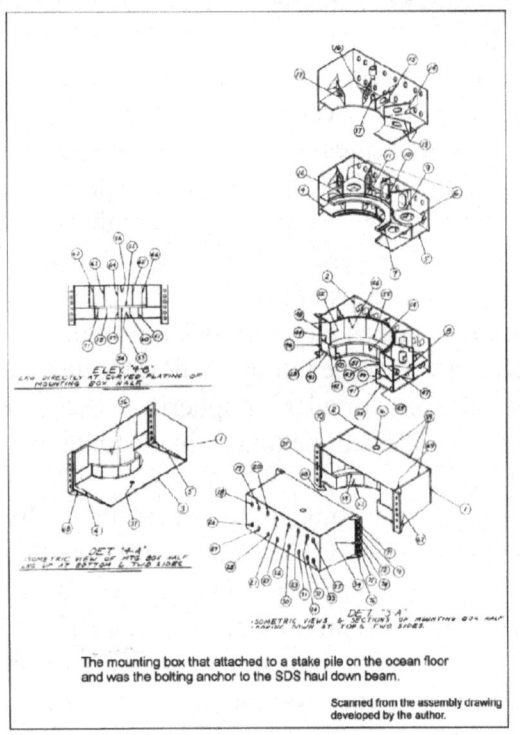

The mounting box that attached to a stake pile on the ocean floor and was the bolting anchor to the SDS haul down beam.
Scanned from the assembly drawing developed by the author.

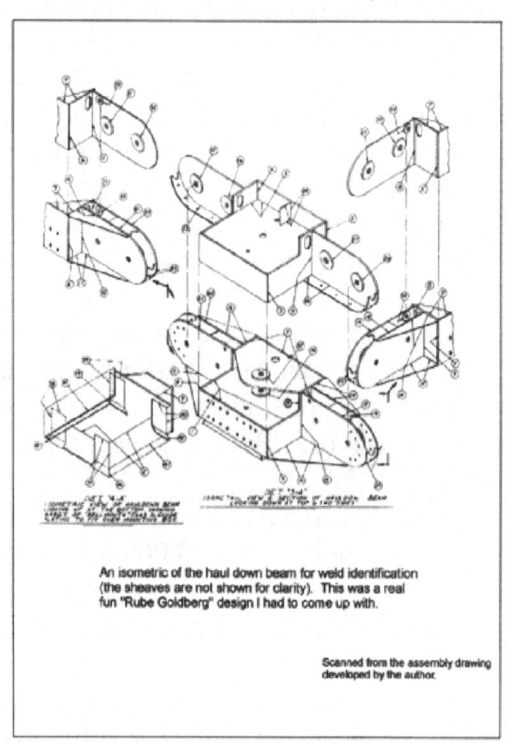

An isometric of the haul down beam for weld identification (the sheaves are not shown for clarity). This was a real fun "Rube Goldberg" design I had to come up with.
Scanned from the assembly drawing developed by the author.

The hauldown beam itself would then be lowered, by a floating crane, and bolted to the box anchor on the stake pile. Two wire ropes would be reeved through the sheaves of the hauldown beam and led toward shore to a Skaggit winch that would do the actual hauling down of the SDS. The assemblies would be very complex with a very specific fabricating procedure. Therefore, I included isometric views of the items both when assembled and in exploded views. Sort of like the directions in an airplane model kit. Besides being imaginative, I was fortunately an expert draftsman.

In the titles and General Notes of the drawings, we originally abbreviated Simulated Distressed Submarine as SDS, which normally would have been perfectly acceptable. However, it was not **politically** correct at that time because of an anti-American organization called Students for a Democratic Society (SDS). So, we had to erase almost all of the General Notes and rewrite them spelling out Simulated Distressed Submarine.

We were also required to document all engineering calculations for the rigging systems. The complete set of calculations is one-inch thick in a 3-ring notebook folder and consisted of the efforts of Fred Hock, Isaac Cavalier, David Limbert, Donald Lichti, Charles Dietl and myself. In the process, I also invented a new engineering formula.

The main beams at the top of the DSRV were made of titanium. Welded to those beams were titanium lifting padeyes only one-inch thick. A DSRV weighs about 78,000 pounds, but when lifted out of the water, several tons of water are still within the free flooding hull. I had to design a lifting bridle for picking the DSRV up out of the water. NURDC ordered the lifting bridle to be designed for 60 long tons (134,400 pounds) working load, which would require a test load of 268,800 pounds.

Standard steels would not be strong enough if their sizes had to be reduced to fit the small titanium pad eyes. Load tests nearly sheared the shackle bolts on our first designs. The biggest problem was designing steel rings, called Garland Rings to spread out the lifting wires to the padeyes. They had to be small enough to attach the rigging and still be strong enough to hold the test loads. Of our first set of rings, one of them stretched a quarter of an inch proving that the existing formula available to design them was inadequate.

Thanks to my Supervisor, Jim Bibeau, who found some 1947 experiments done with garland rings and Don Lichti who suggested to use plastic section modulus instead of the standard elastic, I was able to reverse engineer the original formula shown in the text books. The old formulas were envisioning the steel rings in tension whereas in actuality, due to their circular shape, were in compression. With that formula, presented to NURDC, steel garland rings could be accurately designed for strength and steel type. NURDC accepted it, particularly since it was reviewed and signed by Andrew Pyka, the engineering teacher at Cerritos Junior College. Mr. Pyka was a registered civil engineer in the three western states and a former Navy diver. With Navy diving being high on his list of interests, he didn't even charge a fee.

In a nutshell, this is how you should revise the old formula: Use the modulus of **PLASTICITY** instead of **ELASTICITY**. Then SWAP the two constants around. Your result will be within 5% of an actual test to break the ring. As simple as that sounds, it took me almost 2 weeks to figure that out. As for what steel to use, I first selected Crucible D-6 from Colt Industries (yes, the makers of the 1911 pistol). But we found in Mil-Specs that 300M would be the correct steel to use.

My design of the SDS hauldown beam earned me the nickname as being the shipyard's resident "Rube Goldberg". However, the *Pigeon* and *Ortolan* arrangements of cranes, hoists, winches, rigging, diving bells and recompression chambers make Rube Goldberg pale by comparison. My hat is off to those designers, whoever they were and whatever padded cells they must be in by now.

Spy Sub? Now we come to the cloak and dagger stories. It has been claimed that the DSRV was not designed to be a rescue vessel but a spy submarine instead. This accusation was publicly aired on a NOVA episode on television, first broadcast on January 19, 1999. The show overall was done very well including interviews with former American submarine crewmen who were actually on spy missions such as those carried out by the USS *Halibut* (SSN-587). The *Halibut* was officially identified as a "research" submarine after she completed all *Regulus* missile tests. In reality it was converted to a spy submarine capable of carrying Remote Operated Vehicles (ROV's) launched through a special bottom hatch while still submerged. ROV's are small remote controlled submarines equipped with cameras and manipulators to attach monitoring devices to underwater communication cables.

I didn't see the original broadcast but caught a repeat later that same year and was surprised to hear that the DSRV was really a spy submarine. The accuser was Sherry Sontag, an investigative journalist (after her death, an obituary in the newspaper titled her as an **extremist**). Ms Sontag, with Christopher Drew, co-wrote the book *Blind Man's Bluff*. It claims to reveal the untold secrets of spy missions our submarines have been used for. Though the book does not **specifically** claim the DSRV was a spy sub, the TV shows state it as "fact". Obviously the show's writers knew absolutely nothing about the extensive work we did in developing the DSRV and its surface support ships as very sophisticated rescue **and** research vessel combinations. The idea of using it as a spy vehicle never entered our minds though we did add capabilities to make it a research vessel as well to pay for itself in between rescue missions (that we hoped would never come). On TV, Ms Sontag was quite vocal about the DSRV being a fake rescue vehicle on the show **but** her book isn't quite as direct though she claimed the reason for its construction was a "fantasy" to get funding for sophisticated submarine spy missions.

In Ms Sontag's book, she was almost gleeful in "exposing" the "fact" that the DSRV shown, in a photo in the book, secured to the rear hull of *Halibut* was not a real submarine at all but a fake submarine. All of us from the lowest rank on up knew it was just a boiler plate model only for testing sea worthiness of a real DSRV if it was deployed by a "standard" submarine rather than its surface support ship. Perhaps because of the pictures of the "DSRV" on *Halibut* do not show any propeller **"gave it away"** to anyone who knows nothing about ships. I did find the book an interesting, or rather, entertaining, to read. Some of the stuff in it we already knew about of course. Such as the *Halibut* was not just a spy submarine either but a test bed for other systems such as the *Regulus* missile program. Similarly the USS *Norton Sound* (AVM-1) was a test bed for the Basic Point Defense Missile System (BPDMS) and the first installation of a Vertical Launch System (VLS) for missiles.

So, tell us something we DON'T know.

The infamous "fake" submarine described in "Blind Man's Bluff". It was actually the Hull Test Vehicle (HTV) to test rigging and handling gear and was common knowledge.   Author's collection

Curiously, a re-broadcast of the show in April of 2002 was heavily edited and makes one wonder if two different scripts were used as there were additions, deletions and inconsistencies between the 2002 show and the 1999 show. On an even later NOVA show, supposedly just on submarines. John Craven who was the "director of a spy project" was interviewed as well. The way the shows were edited leads the viewer to believe that the DSRV was a full-blown spy submarine. In one scene of the sinking of the Russian submarine *Kursk*, the narrator claimed the Russians did not call for the DSRV because they were afraid of its spying capabilities.

If you put the expose' type editing off to one side and ignore the dramatic narrator, you will note that neither Sherry Sontag, Christopher Drew or John Craven actually said the DSRV was itself a spy submarine as the *Halibut* was with its ROV's. They do claim, however, that the purpose of the DSRV was a "fantasy" and its sole purpose was to provide a clandestine funding program for the development of submarine spy equipment. What's surprising about that? There was an open checkbook to develop, build and deploy two vehicles with their very sophisticated surface support ships to rescue crews of ANY Nation's submarines that have **not** gone below crush depth. Such hardware had to jump years ahead of the normal funding time it would take to develop the highest state of the art. Naturally the intelligence community would want a few "samples" shipped their way for installation on true spy subs.

As for the DSRV itself to do spy work in Soviet waters is total fantasy. Its limited range of the would require the launch ship to be within Mk-1 eyeball distance of the shoreline. To launch from a full size submarine was possible but the slow speed of only 4.1 knots of the DSRV would certainly make it highly vulnerable and not able to outrun a Soviet torpedo as the *Halibut* had to do once.

However, I must concede that since I was never privy to the inner workings of the CIA, NIA, FBI, NIS (now NCIS), ONI, OSS, KGB, NKVD, SMERSH, THRUSH, Roswell, Hangar 18 or Area 51 I cannot say that the DSRV was never used covertly. Most of us in the design end of DOD spend most of our working hours inventing ways to kill the enemy, sink his ships, shoot down his airplanes, blow up his tanks and vaporize his cities. But to be given an open checkbook to design and build a life saving system really turned on our thinking caps and we took the challenge with zeal.

Sadly the *Pigeon* and *Ortolan* have been inactivated and stricken from the rolls and headed for the scrap yard. The DSRV's have also been inactivated and we no longer have a deep sea rescue system for manned submarines that are not below their crush depth. **"B" They were to have been replaced with the new Submarine Rescue, Diving and Recompression System (SRDRS). But I've only seen artist's drawings of what it might look like and as far as I know, not a single one has even begun to be built.**

I certainly hope none of our submarines experience a sinking where a DSRV would be joyously welcomed. We know the system works as the last test was in 1999 where the DSRV *Avalon* participated in a rescue exercise with a Japanese submarine simulating the distressed boat. All countries, including the Soviet Union, were provided the drawings and specifications to build and install universal mating hatches on their submarines. But it's been a very long time since any submarine has actually sunk above its crush depth where a rescue could be made.

Well, that is only counting American submarines. The Soviet Union/Russia has had more than its share of incidents. There was the K-429 in 1983, the K-219 in 1986 and the K-278 (*Komsomolets*) in 1989. Last but not least was the K-141 (*Kursk*) in 2000.

But that can never, ever, happen again. Can it?

Answer: Yes it can and already has.

On 8 January 2005 the USS *San Francisco* (SSN 711), a *Los Angeles* class nuclear powered attack submarine, grounded itself in route from Guam to Australia. She was in a normal submerged transit traveling at flank speed and the grounding slowed her almost instantly to only 4 knots. Of the 137 crewmen aboard, 60 were injured with 2 of them with extremely serious injuries. One of them died just before being taken off the ship by rescue personnel. Additionally, another 22 crewmen were injured badly enough that they could not return to duty. That is over half the crew knocked out of action. The ship was able to surface and return to Guam but only at 8 knots. After berthing in Guam on 10 January, she was one degree down bubble (down by the bow) with a 0.8 degree list to starboard. Her aft draft was 27'-10" where it normally would measure 32'-0".

If she had hit more severely, say ripping the bottom open on a submerged rock as *Missouri* did in Hampton Roads, she may not have been able to surface. A DSRV would be required to perform the rescue. Unfortunately, both ASRs (*Pigeon* and *Ortolan*) and both DSRVs (*Mystic* and *Avalon*) have been decommissioned

The USS Pigeon (ASR-21) in the "Ships Graveyard" in Suisun Bay, California. Photo by author; Oct, 2006

A real DSRV on its transport trailer. Letting the air out of the tires allows it to be loaded into a C-5A and it could be taken to any coastline in the world for a rescue mission   Author's collection

Design and Operational Requirements

Summarized, the vehicle design requirements are

Transportation weight	60,000 lbs. (maximum)
Length	50 ft. (maximum) transportable on a C-141A
Beam	8 ft.
Personnel	Operation crew: pilot, co-pilot and medical corpsman
Rescue capability	Up to 24 crewmen
Pressure range	Control sphere 0.8-3.7 atmospheres absolute. Rescue and mid-spheres 0.8-5.0 atmospheres absolute
Life support	Environmental control 24-hour minimum
	Emergency individual life support 3-hour minimum
Pressure hull	Inner hull consists of three interconnecting 7.5 ft. diameter spheres of HY-140 steel

Operational requirements are:

Operating depth	3,500 ft. (minimum)
Collapse depth	5,250 ft. (minimum)
Ascent/Descent rate	100 ft./minute
Speed submerged	5 knots (maximum)
Speed submerged "piggyback"	15 knots
Submerged endurance	3 knots for 12 hours
Maneuverability	Hover in one knot current
Mating attitude	All systems operable at 45° solid angle

Fig. 4—Checking out the equator of the transfer tank during machining to remove excess stock after welding.

Fig. 5—Inspecting the aft hemisphere of the forward sphere prior to welding.

Hourglass Welding Procedure

The automatic downhand gas tungsten arc welding operation that we used to join the two hourglass assemblies of the pressure hull was selected because of its inherent characteristics of producing weldments of high quality and reliability.

The procedure was qualified to U.S. Navy Specification 0900-006-9010 which included the preparation and testing of four explosion bulge and two explosion tear test plates. These plates met all specification requirements. Sun Ship, the first fabricator to apply the GTA process to HY-140 welding, amassed a wealth of data on the mechanical properties, both in tension, compression and toughness of both the weld and weld heat affected zone. All the data demonstrated that GTA welds in HY-140 were of a higher quality, higher toughness than welds made with any other welding process.

The welding parameters to be used (11 volts, 340 amps, welding speed 8 in. per minute and wire feed 48 in. per minute) will allow completion of the weld in approximately 12 passes. The weld will be X-rayed to both half and full level and will be ultrasonically inspected at full level. All inspection techniques have been fully demonstrated to the applicable LMSC and U.S. Navy specifications.

Subsequent to the final acceptance of the weld seam, the welded assembly will be contour machined to achieve a true spherical contour in the area of the weld. This final machining operation is necessary on seven weld seams of the pressure hull. These areas are inaccessible to inside welding/machining operations which would normally be used to reduce the distortion in the final configuration. The same technique of final contour machining after welding was used on the *Deep Quest* pressure hull.

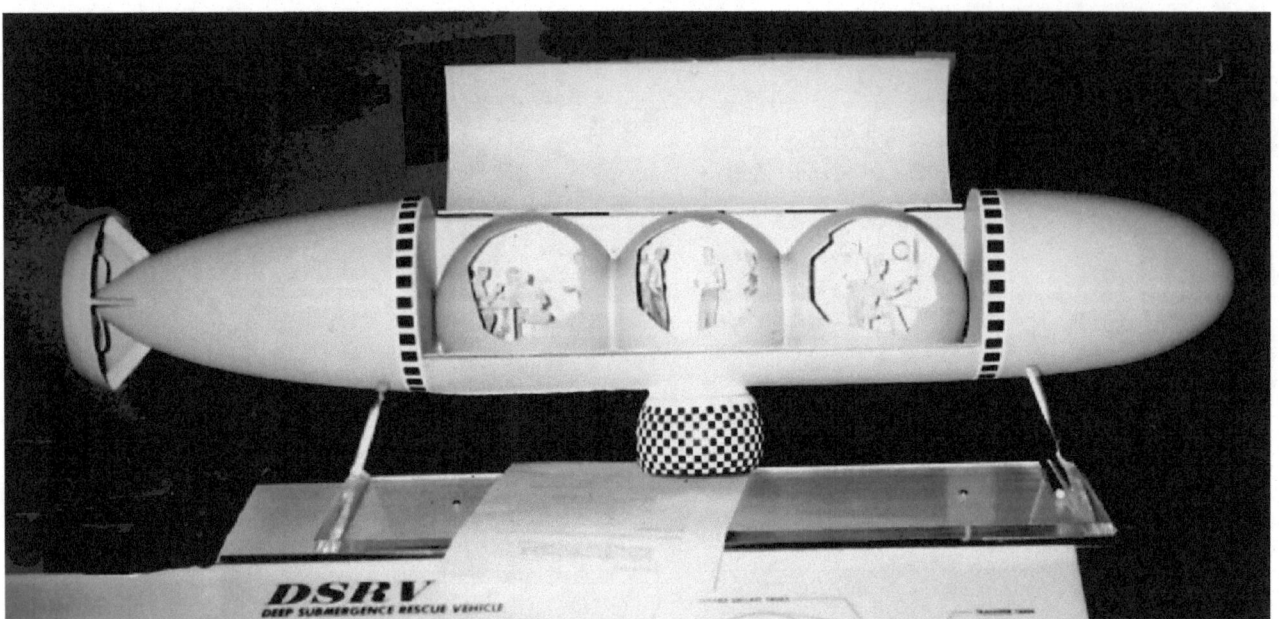

A scale model of the DSRV at a Marine Technology Society convention. Photo by author

Mystic (DSRV-1) being lowered into the water for a test run WITH the properly designed Garland Rings based upon this authors "invention" of a more accurate strength formula. Author's collection

CHAPTER 14: S.A.C.S., CECIL & OLLIE

S.A.C.S.: When looking at an air view photo of the shipyard, an oddly shaped pier is seen at the Pier 11 location on the inside of the Mole. It is a very narrow pier running northeast by north and perpendicular to the shoreline of the Mole and then doglegs slightly to the North to a circular pier with a wide opening at its northeast quadrant.

The actual name of this pier is the **Shipyard Accuracy Check Site** though it was often erroneously (but technically correct) called the SONAR Accuracy Check Site. It was designed and operated by the Naval Electronics Laboratory (NELC) to calibrate bow mounted SONAR transducers. A ship would be positioned with its bow SONAR in the exact center of the circle and held in place with mooring lines. Rather than the ship pinging its own SONAR on a target, a SONAR transducer was mounted on a vertical carriage that rolled around the inside of the circular pier. To my knowledge, that was the only calibration site of that type ever built. It was an ingenious idea and every ship on the West Coast with a bow mounted SONAR was calibrated there. The S.A.C.S. pier wasn't very glamorous or heroic as compared to some of the other shipyard functions and projects, but it was still a very unique feature and provided an important service to the fleet.

The transducer could be lowered on a set of rails to a depth of nearly forty feet. But in 1973 NELC decided to extend the depth another fourteen feet and I was given the job of redesigning the carriage. They also wanted a couple of extra features such as a winch mechanism to tilt the transducer up at a twenty-degree angle. That was really a "fun" job to work on and further enhanced my nickname of "Rube Goldberg". But it also gave me an opportunity to demonstrate my skill at isometric drawings to clarify assemblies of the tilting mechanism and guide rollers.

I was also tasked to redesign parts of the wood catwalk of the pier (mounted on octagonal concrete pilings) and I enjoyed doing that but learned there is a vast difference in nomenclature of carpentry from ship architecture. For example, what ship designers call a waterway bar along the edge of a ship's deck is called a toe board or kick plate along the edge of the pier's walkway by carpenters.

The pier during its time when bow mounted SONAR domes could be calibrated   Courtesy: "Salty"

The pier in a state of decay, July, 2001. Note the collapsed section at the far right. Photos by author

An enlarged section of the caved in part of the SACS pier.
Please forgive the blurriness as zooming in often fouls up the focus of the lens. Photo by author

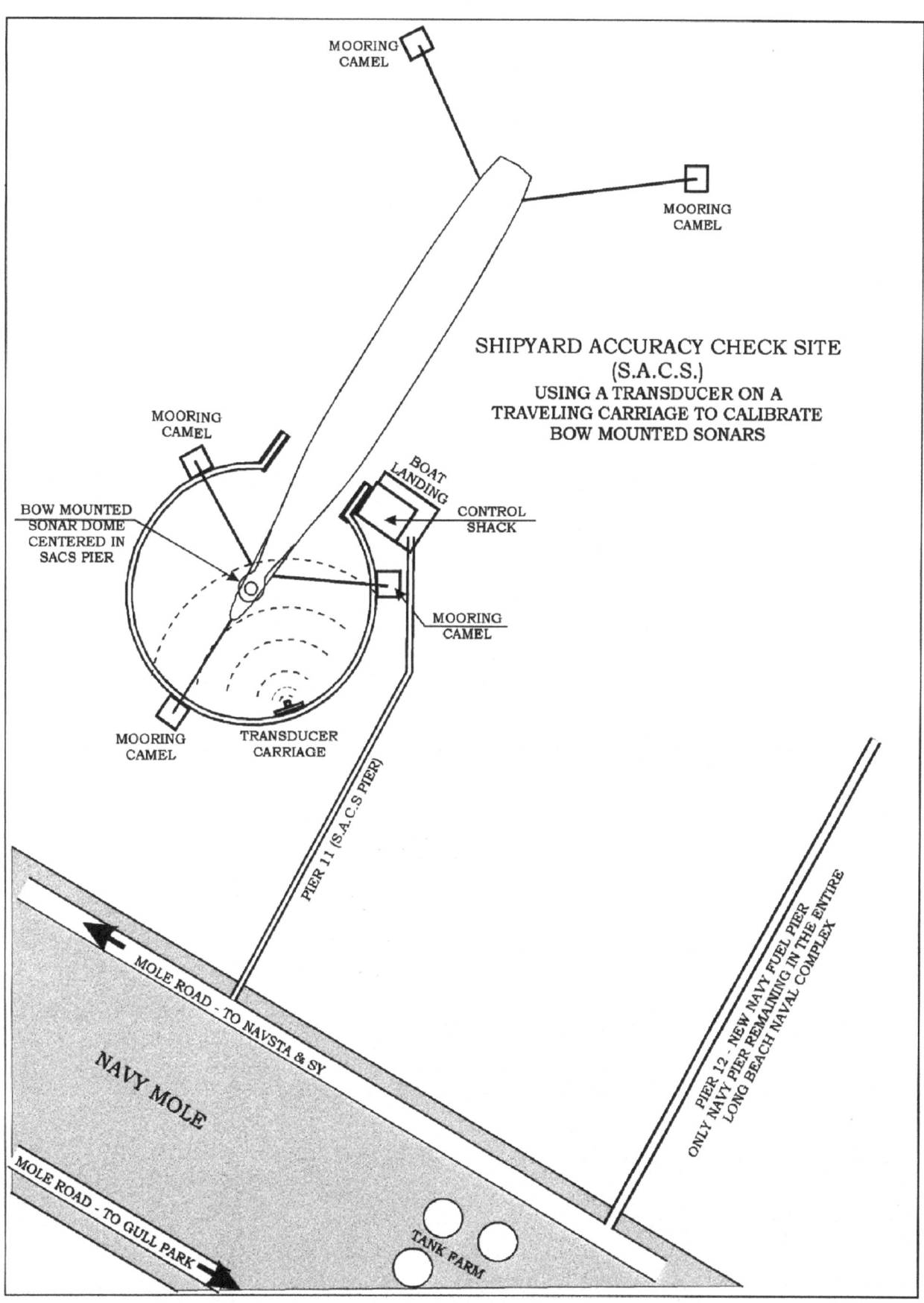

This is the way the SACS Pier worked. But it's totally gone now and travelers cannot get past the NAVY fuel pier because it is guarded by the US ARMY.

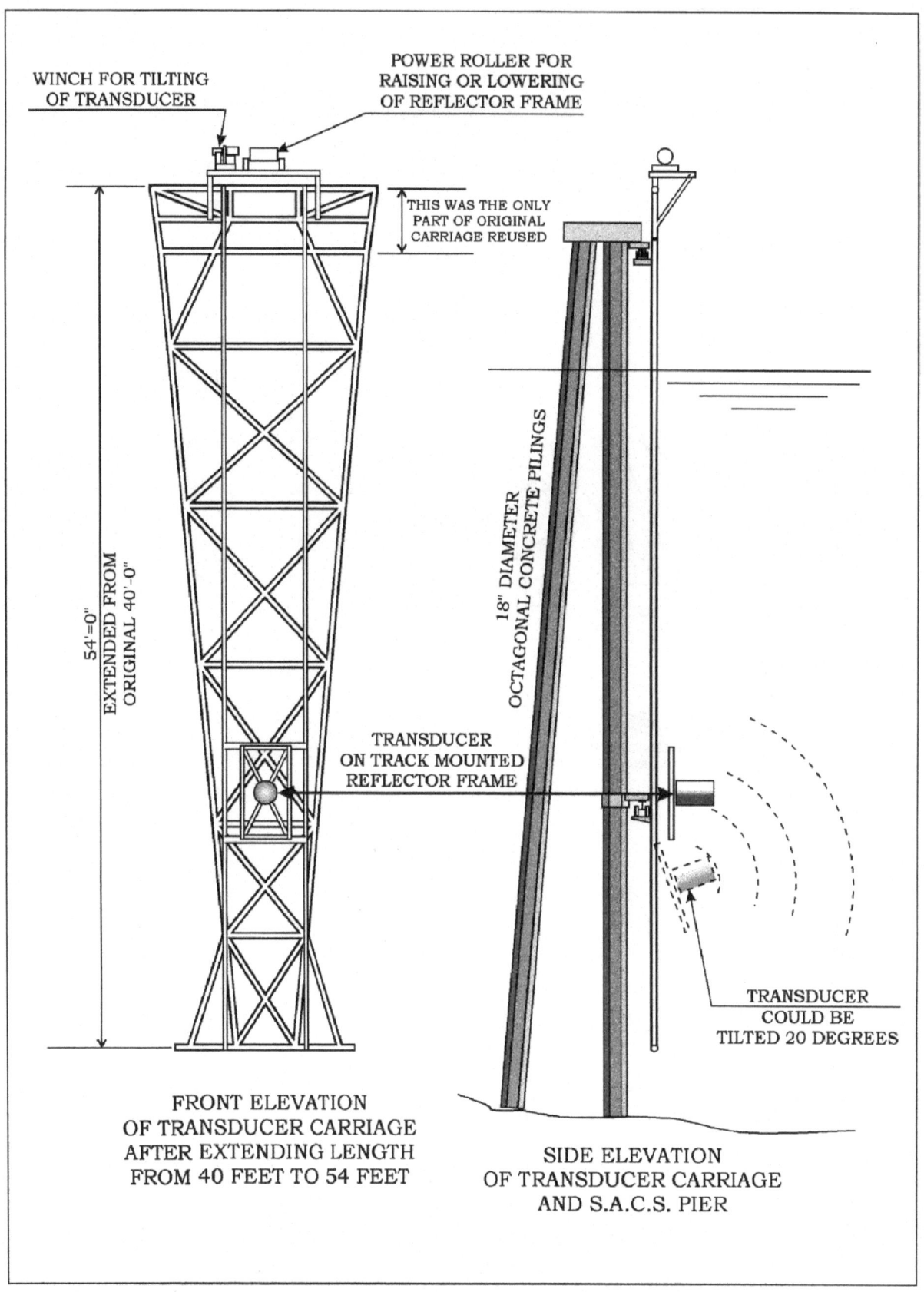

The Transducer Carriage that circled the pier and pinged ship's bow mounted SONAR for accurate calibration.

CECIL & OLLIE: *Cecil* and *Ollie* are the tongue in cheek names I gave to a couple of oil containment booms Bob Riha and I had to design (from old TV puppet shows featuring "Cecil the Seasick Sea Serpent" from "Beanie" and "Ollie the Dragon" from "Kukla, Fran and Ollie"). When an oil island blew off of Santa Barbara, the slick started moving down the coast toward Los Angeles and Long Beach. Somebody had an idea that if we could put a floating boom across the channel entrances of the outer breakwater, we would prevent the oil slick from coming ashore into the Wilmington, San Pedro and Long Beach harbors.

What had to be designed had to be assembled quickly from readily available materials. The Oil Company said it could provide us with all the 55-gallon drums we wanted if they were to be used as floats. Drill casing pipe would also be provided for ballast.

Bob toyed around with all kinds of boom ideas including using telephone poles for the upper segments of the booms. But they would not be high enough to prevent any splash over and the logs themselves may contaminate the waters with the creosote preservative they were soaked in.

Bob finally came up with a quickie design that basically consisted of an oil boom made up in segments. Each segment was a four-foot by eight-foot sheet of marine plywood with four oil drums, two on each side, clamped to it. That would be our upper part of the segment. The lower part was a sheet of Herculon with a loop at the bottom to hold a piece of casing pipe for ballast. Each segment would be attached with a curtain of Herculon. The towing stresses, however, would be taken up by one-half inch diameter wire ropes clamped to the drum straps on the plywood.

We were provided the harbor drawings of the breakwater and measured the distance of the openings at Angel's gate (Los Angeles entrance) and Queens gate (Long Beach entrance named after the *Queen Mary*). For the heck of it, I named the Angels gate boom *Cecil the Seasick Sea Serpent* (after the puppet on the *Beanie* children's TV show) and the Queens gate boom I named *Ollie the Dragon* (after another puppet from the *Kukla, Fran and Ollie* show).

A test section of the boom was made up and tested. It did look something like a sea serpent being towed through the water. However, they were never installed for two reasons. One being that the breakwaters were so porous that the oil slick would probably seep through anyway. Second being that the oil slick never got to Long Beach.

However, two other oil spills, one in the Gulf of Mexico and one in the Caribbean, did use our drawings to manufacture oil containment booms quickly and efficiently. I recall Phil Perkins, our personnel supervisor at the time, calling me and asking that I get four copies of those drawings IMMEDIATELY and deliver them to Phil Finkelstein's office. I did so and they were shipped out to the East Coast that day. A few months later, *Ocean Industry* magazine wrote up their use and even included our drawing numbers along with a photo and a sketch. So even though Bob's design was not needed to protect the Los Angeles and Long Beach harbors, we were all very proud and happy to see those booms used successfully elsewhere.

"B" Today, rubberized plastic booms are used as they can be flattened out and rolled up on deck until the clean-up boat gets to the oil spill and then inflated to trail behind the boat. So why did we go to so much effort back then? Simply because the inflatable designs were not "invented" or produced yet. This Navy design was an emergency job (with available oil drums for buoyancy and casing pipe for ballast) and could be assembled right away with all materials needed already in existence.

TSF oil boom built for San Juan Harbor.

Boom being rigged up to Chevron's spill.

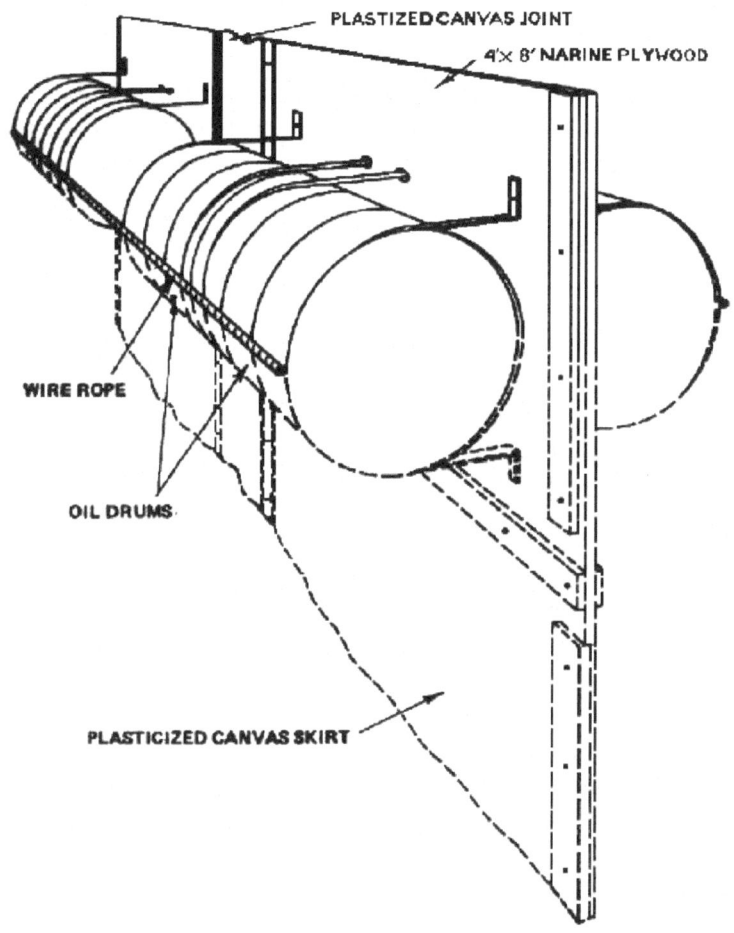

Diagram and photos from an article by Captain W. F. Searle, Jr. USN in Ocean Industry magazine, July 1970

Oil containment boom being tested by NAVSEA. Courtesy: Mike Said NAVSEA.

CHAPTER 15: AAV7A1 TRACK MODIFICATIONS AND BENNY SUGGS

One job we tried to land with the Marine Corps was to modify the track supports on their Amphibious Armored Vehicles (AAV) commonly called "Alligators" (which was the LVT-1 back in WW II). The FV's are tank-like, full tracked vehicles that can float in water and even have thrusters for water propulsion. They were designed and built by Food Machinery Corporation (FMC) and totally replaced all tracked amphibious vehicles in this country and some foreign countries as well. Their bodies are aluminum armor and powered by a diesel engine.

Land travel for the AAV's was expected to be no more than a few miles in from the beach until other motorized transport could be landed. However, in Desert Saber they were used as cross-country personnel carriers and ordered to travel hundreds of miles inland. That type of travel highlighted some serious flaws in the suspension system. Each road wheel is mounted on a bracket that is mounted on a torsion bar. The torsion bar is encased inside a torsion tube that extends almost all the way the width of the vehicle underneath sheet metal floor plates. That "almost" across was the big problem. Although the torsion tube is fixed to the hull at the side the road wheel is on, it is not fixed to anything at the other end. Hours of grinding across the Arabian and Iraqi deserts caused many track failures as well as the bouncing ends of the torsion tubes beating against the bottom of the floor plates. Tracks, torsion bars, road wheels, rear idler wheels and even the forward drive wheels often had to be replaced and it put quite a strain on the repair and maintenance system.

FMC also builds the M-2 and M-3 Bradley Armored Infantry and Armored Cavalry vehicles (actually light tanks of aluminum armor) with a much better track suspension system. The Bradley tracks are two inches wider and the torsion bars go all the way across and fixed to the hull on the other side.

Somebody finally had the bright idea that the Bradley tracks and suspension should be put on the AAV's. But it sounds easier than it is. With the tracks being two inches wider, the center of the road wheels, idler wheel and drive wheel would have to be moved one inch further away from the hull. Also, the mounting pads for the torsion bar brackets had a completely different bolting pattern and slightly different location. Also the Bradley type tracks used small track suspension wheels to allow proper track tension whereas the original tracks just sagged down between the drive wheel and idler wheel.

Someone, tasked to come up with a design, did a marvelous job designing semi-insert/doubler plates to be welded to the hulls to support the track fittings. By semi-insert, I mean that a section of plating was milled out in the shape of the insert but only half way through the aluminum armor plate. The insert/doublers were then welded into those milled areas and bored for the torsion bars. Then bolt holes were drilled and tapped in the proper places. The rear idler, however, took a full depth insert to give that end of the hull more reinforcement as well.

One AAV7A1 was modified that way and it was given a 10,000-mile test out in the Nevada and California deserts. The idlers only had to be replaced once. On the old suspension system, they would have had to be replaced up to four times with the drive wheels and road wheels and torsion bars also needing at least one change out.

I inspected that vehicle at Camp Pendleton and was quite impressed with it. Yes, I was obviously selected to be project leader on that job because I used to be a tank driver and was certified as a Tank Weapons mechanic on M-41s, M-47s and M-48's at Fort Irwin.

First, a group of planners and design types were sent out to Barstow to inspect the Marine maintenance facilities there. The project manager giving us the tour was Jake Blasco, an old friend of mine from the shipyard. He was also a graduate apprentice welder from LBNSY.

The plan was that the Barstow depot would pull the engines and tracks off the vehicles and ship them, by train, to a facility that would do the hull modifications to accept the new tracks. FMC was too busy building Bradleys plus some prototype armored vehicles that would be somewhere in between a Bradley and an Abrams. It was also the desire of the Marines that we keep the program in-house with the Navy.

The only hard part was, they wanted the full speed runs to put out two hundred vehicles a year. The Marines had almost 1,400 vehicles and foreign countries have about 700 more. Just doing the Marine vehicles would be a seven-year contract. Eight actually including a one-year start up construction of tools, dies and jigs.

We ran into problems with our machinist people who said they could do all the milling on their huge Niles machine, but that they would only be able to do 50 vehicles a year because of other uses for that machine. Perhaps, if other shipwork was low, they could do as many as 100 vehicles a year.

That was totally unsatisfactory. My German/Irish stubbornness refused to say, "No we can't do it" and I designed a semi-assembly line that also won me a superior accomplishment award. On 11 X 17 sketch paper I designed a line of four workstations (support jigs to hold the vehicle and tools) that could be set up on the assembly slabs of the shipfitter shop. A special step of each of the modification would be done at each station and the shop bridge cranes would move the vehicles from station to station. A fifth station was also included to do hull repair work on vehicles that hit rocks and damaged the aluminum armor. I also designed the tool holders and templates required to guide routers for the millwork. I then wrote up a set of procedures listing how many men it would take for each phase starting from offloading the vehicles from the flat cars to rolling them back on. J.B. Larkin, the superintendent of the shipfitter shop, was very impressed with the layout and wanted that job badly. It would keep men employed and be something a little different as well.

Unfortunately, we did not get the job. As I was told, it was a budgetary problem that stopped the program. Otherwise, it was going to keep the shipyard open another seven to eight years. It has been mentioned by some, in retrospect, that would have kept it open too long for somebody that wanted it closed in much less time than that. But that's only speculation and rumor with no proof at all behind it.

Presently, the vehicles are slowly being modified with the new tracks and are re-identified as AAV7A1 RAM/RS. According to the January 2000 issue of the Journal of Military Ordnance, the US has 1,322 AAV7A1s. The current contract calls for converting 680 of them with an option for another 377. The remaining 265 are not slated for conversion. As of October of 1999, only 63 vehicles had been modified. If LBNSY had gotten the contract in 1992 and tooled up before starting full production of 200 vehicles a year starting in 1993, such an important and long term contract may very well have taken LBNSY off the BRAC list. Starting in January of 1993 and finishing in December of 1999 is seven years on the nose. Therefore, before the year 2000, Long Beach Naval Shipyard would have finished all 1,322 vehicles instead of only 63.

"B" Sorry folks, but being a tank crewman (M41A1 Walkers) and qualified as a tank weapons "expert", I couldn't help myself but to describe this job we wanted to do that would have kept the shipyard open for at least ANOTHER **SEVEN** YEARS. LBNSY would have to be taken OFF of the BRAC list of military bases to be closed.

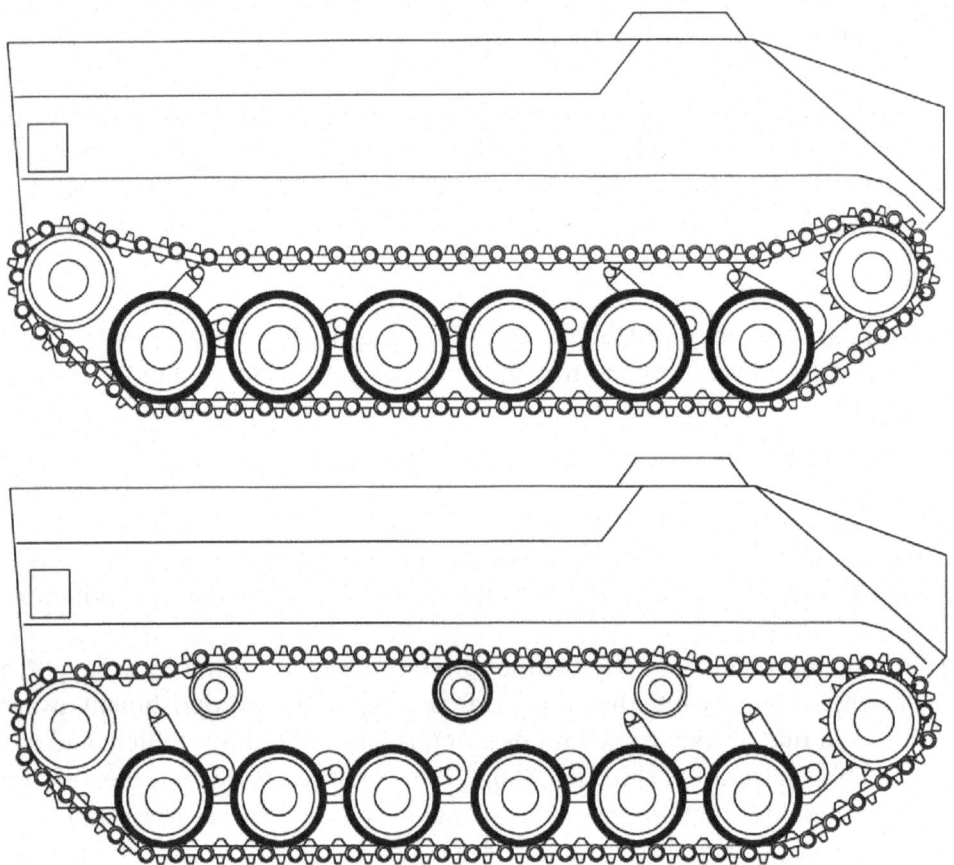

AAV-7 track differences: The top view shows the "as built" version with No track support rollers and non-secured torsion tubes for the suspension. The bottom view shows the modifications using the M-2 and M-3 Bradley Track suspension system with anchored torsion bars and support rollers.

A typical assembly cradle as proposed by LBNSY to do the track modifications for the Marine's AAV-7 vehicles that would have kept the shipyard in business at least another seven years.

Scanned from the author's original proposal sketches.

BENNY SUGGS: We also had a Beneficial Suggestion (Benny Sugg) program. If you could devise a better way of doing it and presented the idea (or preferably the finished product) on a Benny Sugg you would receive a cash award if the idea was adopted. The award would be based upon a percentage of a year's savings and in some cases more if other shipyards also adopted your idea. I have received two Benny Sugg awards including one while in design. But the award of the century just has to go to Larry Quatrone of the ventilation design section. Larry was a graduate apprentice from the sheet metal shop but just the look in his eyes would tell you that he was a deep thinker and very attentive to detail.

One of the ventilation maintenance problems aboard a ship is the ingestion and retention of dust in the ductwork. This is especially true of ships deployed to the Middle East where dust storms often cover the Arabian Gulf and the Red Sea. Even with large filters over the air intakes, very fine dust particles work their way into the duct runs to eventually settle down in various seams and joints. If any moisture gets into the ducts, even finer dust just from the ship's compartments also get trapped and restrict airflow as well as possibly being a bacterial culture bed. Cleaning out the duct runs periodically was time consuming and that segment of the vent system might have to be shut down for several hours while crewmen ran long-handled brushes through (like cleaning a gun barrel) and trying to vacuum up the loosened dust particles. By the time they got the vacuum hoses inside the duct, the dust would settle back down into the same nooks and crannies the earlier brushing dislodged them from.

Larry spent many months designing and testing a brush and vacuum system where the dust particles could be picked up by the vacuum while still airborne after being dislodged by a spinning brush head of nylon bristles (like a weed-eater). The system consists of two units each weighing less than 25 pounds. The flexible brush shaft and the vacuum hose can reach as far as 25 feet back into most duct runs requiring only a diffuser or maintenance access plate to be removed every 50 feet. Therefore 25 feet of duct cleaning can be done in a matter of minutes either by ship's force or by shipyard personnel during where it might take an hour or more working around the bends and trying to blow out remaining loose particles that a vacuum could not get before.

Awards are based upon a first year's savings and it was found that Larry's machine saved the Navy $3,366,242 in its first year. For that tremendous amount of time and material saved, Larry was awarded $20,000 and was eligible for additional awards if his system was adopted by other agencies.

That just goes to show the inventiveness of some of the people we had at LBNSY. There was no question that we were the "Can Do Shipyard".

Technically, receiving such an award could also earn at least a Meritorious Achievement medal and ribbon. But that is strictly up to the base commander to award either and or a check only. Obviously a check helped the personal budget better. However (as with the Cold War Medal), you could buy it yourself.

Larry Quatrone (on the right) receiving a check for $5,000 for his invention of a very efficient device for cleaning ventilation ductwork. His Supervisor, Glen Cox (on the left) presenting Larry the first check of $20,000 for saving the Navy $3,366,242 in the first year of its use alone.

Larry's duct cleaning devise that feeds the cleaning bristles and the vacuum hose at the same time rapidly cleaning up dust and dirt that can pollute the compartments the vent system provides for.

Photos scanned from the August 25, 1989 edition of the LBNSY DIGEST.

CHAPTER 16: THE NEWS & ENTERTAINMENT MEDIA

Movies & TV: It was not unusual to see some movie company doing a few days of filming either on the Naval Station or at the Shipyard. Scenes for war movies were done quite often at the shipyard. Scenes for "D-Day, 6th of June" were filmed on Pier 6 with the Hospital Ship *Haven* as the backdrop. The premiere episode of "Man from Atlantis" starring Patrick Duffy included scenes on the Naval Station.

Sometimes we were tasked to install WW II vintage 20mm machineguns on decks of ships for authenticity. "Navy Log" regularly filmed there as well as "Silent Service" using the old Submarine *Sawfish* at the Naval Station. "Midway" used some stock footage of the shipyard and a couple of scenes were filmed out on the Mole (you could see the 185-foot tower of the *Fish Hook* in the background).

Stock footage was used in three scenes of "The Navy versus the Night Monsters", a low budget sci-fi with Mamie Van Doren and Bobby Van. Under the original title of "The Night Crawlers", at each scene of the shipyard the narrator would specifically identify it as the Long Beach Naval Shipyard. But when the film was transferred onto VHS, the voice identity was muted out. I guess the Navy thought the film wasn't all that complimentary.

"Gone in Sixty Seconds" showed a car crashing through Gate 1 at the Naval Station. After the shipyard was closed, a remake of that movie also had a car chase, this time racing down the narrow alley between the machine shop and the pipe shop. "Lethal Weapon IV" has a car crashing into a building, racing around, and crashing out the other side. It was the vacated Administration Building 300.

The scene from "Lethal Weapon IV" where Linda Marshall's Plan Files office used to be.
You can see the air bags to catch the car on the right.   Photo from LBNSY Website

News Broadcasts: The Shipyard also appeared on the evening news a few times. Of course, the news media covered the dry-docking of the *Queen Mary* and the pickets from private industry protesting that they didn't have a dry dock big enough. Our greatest news coverage was where the unions were staging solidarity rallies against the BRAC when the shipyard was up for vote on closure.

We were spot lighted during the *SEALAB II* program, where they pronounced the name of the Surface Support Vessel incorrectly. Perhaps our greatest positive exposure was the recommissioning of the USS *New Jersey* with President Reagan presiding over the ceremony.

We were also incorrectly fingered for asbestos hazards where we were doing more than anyone else in any other industry to protect our workers and get rid of all asbestos.

Kept out of the Headlines: There were a couple of boo-boo type incidents also. Fortunately, none of them made the papers. When we were reactivating *New Jersey*, a worker was in one of the 16-inch projectile magazines where an inert projectile was in stowage. While waiting for a co-worker to show up, he started chipping lightly at the light blue paint, signifying an inert round, on the shell. But as the paint chipped off, he found olive drab underneath with a wide yellow band near the nose. That color combination identified it as a high capacity (explosive) round. The order went out immediately to evacuate the ship. A bomb disposal team was called in to inspect the shell. It turned out that at one time it was a live round but had the explosive and fuses removed to make it inert. Then it was painted over in the appropriate blue for a **Blind Loaded Plug (BLP)** practice round.

A few years before that, however, a "live" round was fired from the 5-inch gun of a Destroyer. Larry Marsh, a former rigger and now a test inspector, was walking up Pier 2 one evening after finishing a test when a Destroyer, on Pier 3, fired the round over his head. No, they weren't shooting at him. But he could hear the projectile whish-whoosh through the air toward Newport Beach. What had happened was the gun crew was doing a practice loading drill with what they thought were inert drill rounds of solid brass. Because of the heavy electronics now taking up topside spaces, all ships had their practice loading machines removed as weight savings. Therefore, loading drills were done with the actual guns. It was a dummy projectile fired out of the gun when the crew thought they were using a dummy (but "live") powder case. Fortunately it landed harmlessly at sea.

Thank goodness those incidents were never put in print. The moral of this chapter is not to believe everything you read in the papers or see on TV.

Incidentally, the dent in the left side of Turret II on the USS *Iowa*, I believe was caused by an inert round of about 5-inch caliber. I'm not saying it was an accidental practice round from one of own ships, but an inert round fired by enemy artillery. When trying to achieve a high rate fire, sometimes you just use what is closest to you to load. A similar incident happened when the HMS *Exeter* fired an 8-inch practice round at the DM *Graf Spee* that was found later (and shockably) by a German officer when he heard something rolling under his bunk.

"B" The "dent" is typical of a high velocity projectile literally melting upon impact with an immovable "wall" of face hardened Class A armor plate. The actual explosive hit (same side of turret) was much lower and tore up the weather seal assembly that was repaired leaving only a few shallow spots of where the tempered armor was merely chipped off.

CHAPTER 17: SHIPYARD SECURITY AND THEFTS

Security: Sometimes the news media got hold of stuff that amazed us. When the first Polaris missile was launched during project Pop Up out on San Clemente Island, films were shown at the shipyard behind closed doors in the auditorium. Mike Malia, my step dad, was present during the screening and before they left, they were ordered that what they had seen was not to leave that room. Secrecy was of the utmost concern. "Pop" came home and that night, after dinner, turned on the evening news. You guessed it. **The EXACT same film was on the six-o'clock news.**

Physical security of the shipyard was always in question. Generally security was left up to the Shipyard Security Police but supplemented with Marines guarding the gates. Officers John Daly and Joe Loparco of the Security Police were shooting champions and were also members of the shipyard gun club. The other Security officers often gave cause for worry with some never even cleaning their guns. We always felt more secure around the Marines though their pistols were not loaded, except for two loaded magazines in their ammo pouch.

One evening at quitting time, a woman was driving out the main gate (Gate 5) and a man ran up to her car and pulled her out at the stoplight. It was her ex-husband who started beating up on her. The Security Cop stood there wondering what to do. Not the Marine though as he ran 50 yards up the hill, loading his .45 at the same time. He knocked the man to the ground and stuck the pistol muzzle in his mouth and held him there until the City Police arrived. You DON'T argue with a Marine -- **EVER**.

Around 1956 two prisoners escaped from the brig on the Naval Station. The Marines literally cordoned off the entire Naval Station and Shipyard and doubled all gate guards. All were in full battle dress with **LOADED** M-1 Garands **WITH** fixed bayonets. Each and every car had to stop at the gate, the driver had to get out and open the trunk so they could inspect for stowaways. Every nook and cranny of every building was searched. By the second day, one was captured and the other shot to death while trying to climb over the eight-foot high chain link fence.

When the Naval Station was reduced in status to a Naval Support Facility (previously it held the highest status as a Naval Base) the Marines were moved out. Reeves Field was turned back over to the city of Los Angeles when the lease ran out so a lot of officers housing were left vacant. Without Marines at the gates we only had the civilian security police that was later phased out in favor of hiring a private guard agency. We objected to having "Rent-a-Cops" for such an important Defense installation. After two years of complaints, a security police department was established again.

For many years, we could drive our cars through the shipyard, and with the proper pass, park them on the pier near the ship we were to inspect. Many of the shops even had small parking lots around them. Then, in the interests of "security", a Controlled Industrial Area was established with eight-foot high chain link fences around it. Love the "CIA" acronym. It had nothing to do with spies but did offer some boundary in case terrorists attacked the Shipyard. A special wire rope barricade was built at the main gate (Gate 5) that could be raised to stop a vehicle. It had to be hand-cranked by a gate guard but because it was so slow a company of motorized infantry could cross over before it was high enough to stop anything.

During Desert Storm, flat bed trailers were parked across the entrances of the other gates, but **only on weekends**. Five foot cubes of Concrete docking blocks were also used as barricades, **but only on weekends**. It was "comforting" to know that we could work Monday through Friday in absolute safety without barricades as terrorists apparently only worked on Saturdays and Sundays. Go figure.

Thefts: The Naval Investigative Service (not to be confused with Naval Intelligence) was more concerned with thefts of government material than they were with spies. They didn't care about the guy who took home a few bolts and nuts to fix his car or use on a home project. More hardware was spilled overboard from ships than ever stolen. Their interest was people who were stealing items for sale.

The worst case was when a shipment of a rare metal alloy was stored in the foundry for some special castings. The ingots weighed about 30 to 40 pounds apiece and the quantity was carefully inventoried. When the expeditor noticed some ingots were missing and there was no job record showing any of the special castings being made, NIS was called in and they set up surveillance with cameras on top of one of one of the four two-story office building that is actually inside the main shop building. At the end of swing shift at 0100 hours in the morning they photographed a man, from another shop, walking in and rolling up an ingot inside his coveralls that he carried out the gate under his arm. They didn't stop him immediately because they wanted to find out what he was doing with them. A couple of nights later, the man became bolder and rolled up two ingots in his coveralls. They finally had to stop him on the night he parked his car inside the shipyard and he picked up the entire pallet load of ingots with a forklift and loaded them into his trunk. That was when he was stopped at the Main Gate.

It turned out he was selling them to a metal salvage dealer. He lost his job and probably spent some time in Federal Prison. What happened to the dealer though is not known but he is probably much more cautious about whom he buys "scrap" from. As the old saying goes, it only takes one bad apple to spoil the entire basket.

"B" Now, for clarity, NIS stood for **N**aval **I**nvestigative **S**ervice that investigated criminal activity within the Navy. When the USS *Iowa* had her turret "incident", naturally NIS was called in. But the general public thought it was the Naval INTELLIGENCE Service. Wrong acronym. **ONI** is Office of Naval Intelligence. So the NIS had to add the "C" (for Criminal) in their acronym to separate the differences. This was even explained, somewhat, on one of the episodes of "NCIS" on TV, but even then they had to be cautious as not to relate to what event prompted them to change the name and acronym. They did not mention it was because of confusion as to what Agency was called in to investigate possible criminal activity that caused the propellant to ignite in the turret of the *Iowa*.

CHAPTER 18: SHIPCHECKS

Quite often design personnel, planners and often shop mechanics have to travel to another shipyard to do a pre-arrival shipcheck to make sure what was drawn up on the plans will fit the ship. Most shipchecks out of LBNSY were to San Diego and within driving distance. Many others required air travel with most being within the Continental United States.

The first time I ever flew on a plane was in 1965 and it was for checking the Bathyscaphe *Trieste* up in Mare Island, California for the ARD conversion job we were assigned to do. There were only two of us to go to Mare Island for that inspection. As we were waiting in the terminal to board the plane, we saw newspaper headlines about a Boeing 727 that had crashed. And we were flying to Frisco on a 727. However, I found the flight very enjoyable and was looking forward to the return flight. Afterwards I saw a coupon in the paper for Cessna that for only five dollars you could get a one-hour flying lesson. So I learned how to fly Cessna airplanes. My instructor was originally from Germany and came over to this country initially as an auto mechanic in Ohio. Years later, he finally retired as a Captain for Capitol Airways and was a self-made millionaire through some apartment complexes he owned in Pennsylvania. Only in America.

But I'm not going to bore you with my personal flying experiences, though a couple were a bit harrowing. My foreign travel accounted for two trips to the Philippines, one to Taiwan (all with overnight stop-overs in Tokyo or Taipai) and one to Greece.

On the way to P.I., we had a one-night layover in Tokyo. I had a friend in the Air Force stationed at Tachikawa and I went to visit him and his family. When I returned to my hotel, I paused in the lobby to watch the TV to see the astronauts of Apollo 8 (that gave the Genesis reading on Christmas Eve) board the Carrier after their splashdown. It was late at night but all on-duty hotel staff, including cab drivers from outside, were watching it. When it was over, I couldn't get out of my seat as the desk clerk ran over and asked me, "Are you an American?"

I answered, "Yes I am." He then grabbed my hand shaking it hard, "Congratulations. You beat the Russians." Then he called everybody else over, "This man is an American."

All I could do was humbly say, "Thank you." I was never so proud to be an American in all my life and that feeling has not left me. Here were people who, as a child in World War II, I hated with bitterness, but here I am, in the heart of their Capitol City having my hand shaken off, patted on the back and sincerely congratulated "just for being an American."

"B" I do have to add one more personal item to this. One of Apollo 8's crewmembers was James Lovell. He was also Commander of Apollo 13 that coined the phrase, "Houston. We have a problem here". I was always intrigued by Captain Lovell because we went to the same High School (Solomon Juneau High) in Milwaukee, Wisconsin. Unfortunately, not in the same years (he being 8 years older than me) but he would stop by once in a while just to look around one more time.

On another shipcheck to P.I., Bob McClosky was the party chief. He had never been out of the country before in his life so I wound up as his tour guide. Bob was an electrician's helper in Pearl Harbor when the Japanese attacked. He said that being 6 foot 4 made him a good target as a Japanese plane actually chased him down the pier. He was running like hell and turned his head to watch the machine gun bullets chip little craters in the concrete right alongside of him. But he wasn't the target.

There was a Destroyer at the end of the pier and he could see the ship's guns firing at the plane directed by a Marine gunnery officer.

Bob ran into the electrical shop and stood by the outer wall that was actually hundreds of small glass windowpanes. He could look through the windows at the ship and saw the gun crew opening up on the planes' second pass. This time the plane "dropped its bomb" (or so Bob thought) and an entire panel of 8" X 12" windows fell on top of him as he just flattened out on the floor with the glass shattering on top of him. He didn't get even a scratch.

Note: Researching Bob's story, the ship at the pier was the USS *Bagley* (DD-386). It had claimed to have shot down three airplanes and opened fire on a torpedo bomber trying to use the pier shop buildings as cover. It's torpedo dropped on the dock and then the plane crashed just after Bob ran into the electrical shop. So the explosion he heard was probably the jettisoned torpedo.

A trip to Taiwan lasted us about three weeks. We had to inspect a Destroyer in Kaohsiung and another one if it came in from the Tonkin Gulf. We had Thanksgiving dinner aboard ship but before that day, the second Destroyer came into harbor with a harbor pilot in command. However, the harbor pilot did not allow for a 20-knot wind and they sideswiped our ship. Their high-mounted portside anchor ripped open the bulkheads of the ASROC missile magazine right below my feet. The signalman I was talking to earlier took off for the other side but I stayed and, like the dumb engineering type I am, I watched the whole thing with interest.

The corner ripped out of the ASROC magazine.
(Ship's names purposefully omitted)   Photo by author.

However, the trip back home really had us saying our prayers. We were on a Boeing 747 with Northwest Orient when those planes were still pretty new. The 747 has a greater lift to weight ratio than any of the other jumbo jets. Rather than a cylindrical fuselage with just the wings sticking out, the 747 has a lot more flat bottom than the other planes that allows greater lift, but also more susceptible to air turbulence.

Most of the flight was overnight and on most other types of planes you could pull up two or three armrests to make a bed in the back rows. But this particular model allowed removal of only one armrest. Also, the tail of the plane is bouncier than the front and we were flying through some rough weather. Make that very rough weather. Trying to sleep back aft was to no avail. Every time we hit some rough updrafts, I was awake. Looking forward, most of the rest of the passengers were watching the movie and the flickering lights coming past the galley and the shaking plastic luggage compartments above did not reinforce my confidence in Boeing's claim of bomber-like construction.

As dawn broke, we all moved as far forward as we could. The cabin attendants started serving breakfast and only the first five rows got served. It was almost impossible to drink any coffee before it jumped out of the cup. Jim Mauler was overly impressed with the way the wings flapped and would point it out every time. We yelled at him that he could watch the flapping wings all he wanted, just shut up about it. Those of us who had a higher tolerance for alcohol than most other people do didn't even order a single beer on that flight.

I finished my breakfast and just got out of my seat to go to the rest room. It's a good thing I was still gripping the armrest of the aisle seat I was in. Suddenly that 747 went straight up in the air and I pulled myself back into the seat, but still facing aft. As the plane got to the top of that thermal, she dropped off and I saw two cabin attendants go weightless and pull themselves into seats. The remaining breakfasts were still in the galley and they, too, went weightless and crashed to the deck as the plane leveled out. We all got FLUB STUBS for breakfast in Honolulu. Mitch asked if they would be good at the bar. The cabin attendants said they had liquor on board and they would even give it to us free. We still declined. Yet I must give Boeing credit that their 747 is one tough airplane.

"B"   As a sub-note, the last time I saw a Boeing 747 it was carrying the Space Shuttle *Endeavor* to Los Angeles. The advertised flight plan was to fly over the *Queen Mary* but the pilots saw a much more interesting ship first.

Of course, the BATTLESHIP USS *IOWA* (BB-61)

My only European trip was to Athens, Greece. We were supposed to go to the Isle of Rhodes, but the ship, an LPH, changed its schedule. The trip only lasted a week and I didn't do as much shopping in town that I would have liked. At the time, I didn't believe in credit cards but over there B of A and MasterCard were the norm. I did get a Sunday off to tour some of the ancient ruins.

We all had permission to take one week of vacation leave to tour any other part of Europe we wished at the end of the shipcheck. Harry Levy was our Party Chief and being Jewish he brought his wife with him as they were going to go to Tel Aviv to celebrate Yom Kippur. Mike Bartow was going to go to Cairo to photograph the Pyramids.

When I boarded the plane to come back to the U.S., we noticed guards at the airport carrying sub-machineguns. After finding my seat, I picked up a newspaper and discovered that while I was at the office of the Greek Shooting Federation the day before discussing big-game hunting in California, Egypt had attacked Israel.

Well, Mike didn't get to take pictures of the Pyramids. Harry Levy was in the middle of the Mediterranean, headed for Jerusalem instead of to Rhodes where his wife went ahead. Harry, and the remaining members of the shipcheck party, were dumped on Crete and had to find their own way back to either Athens or Rhodes. Harry didn't have any way of contacting his wife in Rhodes so by the time he got there (from Crete via Athens) she was a bundle of nerves.

One thing I did learn about my limited foreign travel however is that almost everybody you meet speaks English. I met one shopkeeper in Athens who spoke American style English perfectly because his wife was an American. U.S. shipchecks are too numerous to count. I have lost track as to how many times I have been to San Diego and Norfolk. The first time to Norfolk was during a hot, muggy July and the ship didn't even want us on board the first day because they were having a nuclear security inspection. The ship often had intruder alerts and shut down the ventilation to the compartments we were in. Not good when the temperature is 105 degrees with 85% humidity.

"B"   The only shipcheck I had in Philadelphia was on the Battleship *Wisconsin*. I was the party chief on that inspection trip and spent part of my birthday on top of her mast.

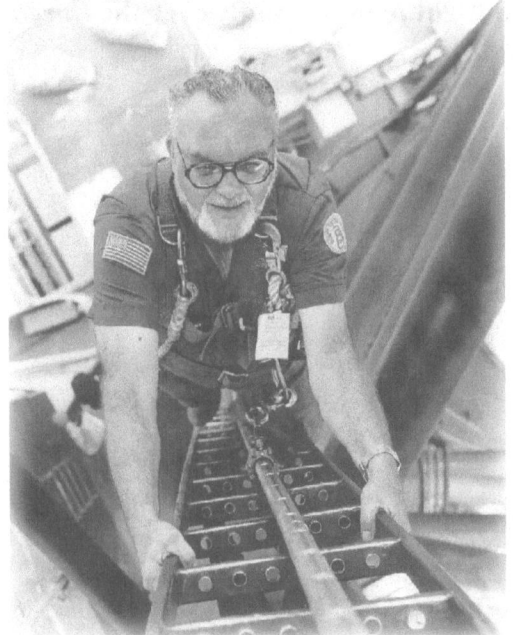

I was much younger (late 50's) and in better shape then.   Photo by Ship's Photographer

"B"   Since both *New Jersey* and *Missouri* were home ported at LBNSY, I have spent one or more birthdays aboard those ships. But, as many times as I inspected *Iowa* either in Norfolk or in the "Ghost Fleet" by Benicia, I never spent a birthday on her.

The crew celebrates Dick Landgraff's 80th birthday!
Until 2016 in San Pedro   Photo by Sue Scmidt - Volunteer Director

The first group checking the USS *Missouri* (BB-63) in Bremerton. January of 1982.
This author is on the far right.

Our largest group checking *Missouri* in February of 1983.

Names that I can remember:
1: **William Lee Upshaw** (Eng Tech - Master Model Builder)
2: **Gene Rose** (Coordinator)
3: **Paul Apodaca** (NAVSEA overseer - Lt. USN Viet Nam)
4: **Richard Landgraff** (Strl Config Mgr - BB 61 Class - USAR tank commander)
5: **Don Wolcott** (Mech Confit Mgr - BB 61 Class - USMC WW II - also served on USS *Maryland* & USS *North Carolina* - he was aboard the *North Carolina* when hit by a Long Lance torpedo)
6: **Homer Dixon** (Civilian Supe Confit Mgr BB 61 Class - USN Korea USS *Orleck* DD-996)
7: **George Stashak** (Co Config Mgr BB 61 Class - USN Viet Nam - Aircraft Carriers)
8: **Al Perry** (Elex Config Mgr BB 61 Class - USAF Bombadier crewman)
9: **LtCdr Tom Raines** (Navy Config Mgr Supe - USN Viet Nam - Rtrd as Full Cdr).
10: **Jose Aquilar** (Mech Eng Tech - Lt. Peruvian Navy)
11: **John E. Bauer** (Strl & Arrgt's Eng Tech - USMC Korea)
12: **John Kurai** (Elex Tech)
13: **Ray Covarrubias** (Elex Tech - Inspected BB 63, 62 & 61 for museums - Docent USS *Midway* in San Diego, CA.)
14: **Al Weschelberger** (Elex Tech - In Europe his Boy Scout Troup was drafted into Hitler Youth)
15: **Louis Horompoly** (Elex Tech - 1956 Hungarian Freedom Fighter)
16: **Mike Said** (Strl Engr - later transferred to NAVSEA Survivability Design {Armor Plating}.
17: **Brian Persons** (Strl Engr - later transferred to NAVSEA and was top Supe of all Naval Surface Ships).

We were the most DEDICATED Engineers and Technicians who brought the Battleships BACK.

CHAPTER 19: NSC - NAVAL SUPPLY CENTER

"B" removed poorly conceived "jokes" about Income Taxes.

There were two large concrete buildings (that were gleefully blown up in early 1999) set in about the middle of the Naval Complex more or less on the border between the Naval Shipyard and the Naval Station. They were very bleak-looking gray buildings with very few windows in them. They looked more like a better use would have been to imprison violent criminals in solitary confinement rather than being the center of material receiving and distribution to the Pacific Fleet.

They were NSC, the Naval Supply Center but often referred to as the Navy Sabotage Center. Every few months the shipyard's weekly newspaper, *The Digest*, would have a picture and article about some supply center employee or supervisor getting some award for saving the taxpayers money. Most shipyard people had absolutely no idea of where they saved any money at any time. At my end of the food chain was where I saw how they wasted thousands upon thousands of taxpayer dollars in the form of countless wasted man-hours and extra material.

Let's take a typical job, say the HALON fire suppression system in the main machinery spaces of the Battleship *New Jersey* (actually any ship would suffice for this example, but this one really got our dander up). The Ship Alteration (SHIPALT) specified the cylinders (steel bottles), valves, hoses and fittings to be made by the Ansul manufacturing company. Kidde also manufactures an equally efficient and reliable HALON system. But, the cylinders, fittings, hoses, etc. are all different sizes therefore requiring two different designs of foundations, supports and piping. Since one manufacturer's cylinders are fatter and shorter than the other is, it obviously won't fit in a foundation or support designed and built for the taller, slender ones and vice versa.

You are starting to get the picture now I think. In accordance with the SHIPALT, which was <u>our</u> "non-deviation" guidebook for design, we designed the foundations, supports and piping for Ansul. It takes several engineers and technicians several days to locate appropriate places within the four fire rooms and four engine rooms for all the cylinders required and three to four weeks for several draftsmen and engineers to develop the installation drawings of locations and foundations. From the drawings the shop lays out the hundreds of individual pieces of steel that is then cut to size, shaped and welded into each foundation assembly. Several pallets are filled with all the foundations and sent out to the ship where the field workers need a few more weeks install all of them in their proper places. The planners wrote up a material procurement list that orders Ansul equipment in accordance with the SHIPALT.

But Supply never sees the drawings and is **not** required to buy Ansul as ordered on the procurement list. Why? Because Kidde makes a "similar or equal" product. Oh yes. We designers are required <u>**by law**</u> to put **"similar or equal"** on the material ordering list of our drawings so somebody doesn't buy a box of carpet tacks from his brother-in-law. That way, everything has to go out for bid. Supply is required to request bids from at least three manufacturers and buy from the lowest bidder. In this case, there are only two manufacturers so selecting the winning bidder is easy, at least for NSC. It also makes no difference that we have a schedule to meet. Nor does it make a difference that NAVSEA **ordered** Ansul. Supply is **not** required to follow SHIPALT and is not answerable to NAVSEA. Also it makes no difference that Ansul may have already built the equipment and it's on their loading dock waiting for the purchase order. Kidde probably bid a couple of bucks lower and will deliver within ninety days, which is an acceptable delivery time as far as Supply is concerned. So, just about the time the last weld has cooled off the installed foundations, Kidde HALON cylinders and fittings are delivered.

Remember what I said earlier? They won't fit.

Do we go back to Ansul and buy what's waiting for us on the loading dock? Want to be locked up in Leavenworth? That's illegal and we are not allowed to claim sole source or propriety.

We then have to redesign the foundations, which will require the technicians and engineers to go back out to the ship and find different locations that the Kidde equipment will fit in. Then the existing foundations must be cut out and new foundations built and installed. **"B" A quick estimate would require about 170 man-days the of $425.00 per man per day would cost about $72,250.00 to do the foundation system all over again. You can assume that the original installation also cost almost the same but would have to be cut out (at extra cost) and scrapped adding more taxpayer dollars to the job.**

So, the entire "finished" installation cost a total of roughly $108,000.00 taxpayer dollars. All because NSC is not required to follow SHIPALT, read drawings or ask how critical it is.

When we shipchecked the *Missouri* later for reactivation, our foundations design section, under the leadership of Brian Persons, did a meticulous check of the ship. I had to give a presentation at the end of the shipcheck to NAVSEA and Pentagon personnel and showed them Brian's shipcheck package of sketches. It was about five inches thick of one page after another of detailed sketches of the areas of the engine rooms and fire rooms that HALON cylinders could be placed. That is, if they were of the manufacture NAVSEA said we would get. Needless to say I stressed the point of getting the right items for the design. Fortunately, there are ways around supply and NAVSEA got us the right equipment by some other means.

Now, I can't say all people in Supply were on another World. Most of them were, but one who wasn't was Mary Miller, one of the supervisors in Supply, and a member of one of the car pools I was in. Mary's husband was a Chief in the Navy when they were first married. So, she learned practicality real quick. She was also a humorous person and we enjoyed her company in the car pool. When she was promoted to supervisor, we gave her a small whip to hang up by her desk. Which she did and had a lot of fun with it.

In those days, we could drive our cars through the shipyard to pick up car pool passengers. One day, as she got in the car, she asked us to drive a different route to another gate. Jerry Fopiano was the driver that day and my step-dad, Mike Malia, and I sat in back. Jerry stopped where Mary asked him to and she pointed over to a large pile of anchor chain lying on a heister pallet. She asked us if we knew of any ship that needed brand new 2 ¼-inch anchor chain. Jerry was the supervisor of the Allowances section that may have some insight of a ship's needs, but he didn't know of such a need for any ship in the yard at the time. Mike was in the Mechanical Test section that tested anchor windlasses but didn't know of a ship that needed it. I was working in the Fittings section that designed anchoring systems and at that time only needed slightly larger anchor chain, because the smaller chain would not fit.

We asked her why. Well, about a year before, a Destroyer came in for a limited repair availability and requested replacement of its anchor chains. They put in all the proper paper work and Supply ordered new anchor chain through the normal channels. A year later, the chain is finally delivered. Mary contacted the ship, which was based at the adjoining Naval Station, but they didn't need it anymore. They got tired of waiting and found some used anchor chain out on the Mole.

So, what is Mary supposed to do with twelve shots of anchor chain? At 15 fathoms (90 feet) per shot that is 1,080 feet of anchor chain or about one-fifth of a mile long. If she can't find another ship that can use it within 30 days, she must schedule it for "salvage". In other words, send it to the scrap yard. Sadly to say that no other ship at that time needed the chain and it was finally shipped out as scrap never having been aboard a ship or dipped in seawater.

"B"   Or so I can only assume. Being brand new, it may have been "stored" for a while first. The next page quotes Bob Cooper's search for a motor they needed in the Machine Shop.

When the submarine tender *Proteus* (AS-19) came in, one of the jobs I was assigned was to design a new pressure head, with adapter plates, for their antenna test tank. The antenna test tank is a high pressure cylinder extending down a couple of decks into the ship. A submarine antenna would be attached to the bolt-on head of the tank and hung upside down in the tank that was filled with water. Then air pressure would be applied to simulate pressure greater than the maximum diving depth of the submarine to make sure the antenna joint did not implode or even leak.

New antennas had been developed for some of the newer submarines and the older adapter plate on the pressure head was not designed for all of them. I designed a new dome shaped pressure head, forged from class 1023 steel and two new adapter plates to be forged from higher strength class 8630 steel since they were flat and could not be too thick in order to mount the antenna plugs. I calculated it would take a 1,000-pound chunk of 1023 steel to forge out the pressure head and two 500-pound chunks of 8630 steel for the adapter plates. There was no problem finding some 1023 steel for the dome forging. It was the procurement of the 8630 steel that gave me heartburn.

I got a call from the forge shop to come on down and see what Supply bought for them. Well I went down there, walked into the forge shop and the supervisor took me over to the back of the shop where I stopped and just stood there in utter shock.

What I am looking at is a full bloom of 8630 steel, two feet by two feet by twelve feet long weighing 23,500-lbs. And we only needed a couple of 3-inch thick chunks of about 500 pounds each cut off the end.

I asked him what the hell happened. He said he checked with supply's inspector and found out that the first item shipped in was rejected because it looked like it may have been welded in the middle. We couldn't care less about a weld in the middle because we only had to cut off a piece of one end. I later looked up that inspector and voiced my concern over the fact he didn't call me. He just shrugged his shoulders.

After we cut what we needed off the end of that bloom, it was supposed to go back to supply for re-use, return or "salvage" (scrap). By law we were not allowed to stockpile material. We either used it or we scrapped it. Fortunately, the machine shop was in the process of building a new foundation for cold working pressure rollers on their shaft turning machine. So the remainder of the bloom was turned into a very stable foundation and not scrapped.

BUT LET'S BE FAIR:
In all fairness, there were some people in the supply center that hated to see perfectly good material, some of it brand new, sent to the scrap yard. So items for salvage were stored in one part of one of the buildings for a while hoping they could be used.

Bob Cooper, a machinist supervisor, told me of one incident where that came in handy. *"The DD-963 class Destroyers and CG-47 class Cruisers (same hull and propulsion plants for both) were driven by variable pitch propellers. Each propeller had three hydraulic pumps servicing them for varying the pitch on the blades. Two of those pumps were motor driven and when we started doing repair on the Destroyers that required overhauling the pumps, we were also tasked to test those pumps before reinstalling them in the ship.*

"But we didn't have a shop-mounted motor big enough to turn the pumps. A supervisor in charge of the job knew the supervisor in charge of the salvage pile over in supply and that person called me and asked what we needed. I replied that we need a 300 horsepower electric motor, run off of 440 volts AC and turn about 1800 revolutions per minute. The person told me to come on down to supply as they may have a salvaged motor lying around there. I went to supply and was shown dozens of motors, pumps and various other machinery awaiting their trip to the scrap yard. Sure enough, we found one that fit our specifications and the next morning it was delivered to the machine shop.

"A foundation was quickly designed and built for it and within 72 hours after being given orders to test the hydraulic pumps we had a test rig set up using that salvaged motor. That rig remained in service from 1985 to 1995 when the shipyard was closed."

Besides our own heartburn with our local supply center, there are ways of buying material and parts without going through them. Mechanicsburg, Pennsylvania is a virtual warehouse of military parts. Items that are going to be of repetitive orders or direct replacements of broken or worn parts are stockpiled at Mechanicsburg. But that is not always a blessing either.

All Navy ships have shore power receptacles installed so they can still run all electrical systems while tied up at the pier which allows the ship to shut down their on-board generators. Especially handy if the generators are being overhauled at the time. On one class of Destroyers, the new shore power receptacle panel, taking six cables, was to be located in the aft end of the superstructure deckhouse. These cables are not your standard extension cords as they have to carry large amounts of electricity and are therefore as big as a man's wrist. Obviously, they don't bend too easily either.

I was given the general layout of the receptacle panel and the location of its installation that was the corner of a ventilation plenum chamber. The design was quite difficult because the receptacles the SHIPALT called for were the "straight through" types which caused the cables inside to make a large bend before going down through the deck to the ship's switchboard.

I went over to the electrical design section and told Rick Jensen that the structural installation would be much easier and take up a lot less room if they used ninety-degree receptacles. Rick agreed full heartedly. However, they weren't allowed to use them. "Why not?" I asked.

Rick answered, "Because Mechanicsburg has a large supply of the straight through models and they have to be used up before they are allowed to issue any of the others."

For my final horror story, when we were officially tasked to do the detail design work for reactivation and modernization of the Battleship *New Jersey* in 1981, Captain Champlain of NAVSEA, in charge of the program, gave a very encouraging speech. He said that the ship will go out on time and that if anybody says we can't until their special requirements are met or their special black box is installed, that they should see him first. He will decide if it would impact our schedule and budget.

Then our balloons burst, in the very same meeting with Champlain sitting there not saying a thing, when the Captain in charge of the Supply end got up and gave his speech. He will not accept sole source and all material purchases must be made through the standard channels of going out for bids.

"We're dead," I thought to myself. And we almost were too.

When Supships Boston delivered the guidance drawings and basic scantlings, I took all the structural drawings home and laid them out on my living room floor, dining room table and breakfast bar by the kitchen. With an architect's scale, my trusty TI 35 calculator and a big stack of note paper I listed how many square feet of each thickness and type of steel plate would be needed and how many lineal feet of each size and type of steel structural beams would be needed. By 9:00 PM that night I had a rough material list of around 400 tons of HY-80 armor plate of various thicknesses, 400 tons of Ordinary Strength steel plate of various thickness and 400 tons of structural members of tee beams, angle bars and flat bar.

I went in to work the next morning and transferred all of my notes onto the standard Advanced Material List (AML) forms. My biggest concern was procurement of the HY-80 plate. We bought quite a bit for the magazine armor plating of the *Tarawa* a few months before and had to wait for it quite a while because it was bought through the normal supply system.

While thumbing through a technical magazine, I found that ARMCO steel in Texas was advertising a commercial equivalent of the HY-80 and HY-100 series of steels. Maybe we could use that if its chemical content and physical qualities met MIL-SPEC of the HY steels.

At about that moment Ron Stewart and Bill Fedak, upstairs in the Planning and Estimating section code 231, called and asked if I could come up with an Advance Material List by next week. They were a bit shocked when I told them I already have the list and will have it on their desks within five minutes. I think that is when they got their first real impression of how I was going to dedicate myself to this project of bringing the Battleships back.

Bill Fedak was also a graduate shipfitter apprentice and we were in the same graduating class of 1958. He stayed in the shops longer than most of the other graduates did and bounced back and forth between foreman and shop planner a couple of times before finally transferring up to topside planning. He was also a chief in the Naval Reserve and was very enthusiastic about getting the Battleships out. When I dropped off the AML, I also dropped off a copy of ARMCO's ad for their commercial equivalent steels. Not being the shy type (ever know a Navy Chief that was shy?), Bill called ARMCO the next morning. When ARMCO realized that this steel was going to be used to bring back the first of four Battleships, they said they would not sell the commercial equivalent. Instead, they would make the whole batch in strict accordance to MIL-SPEC and delivered within 45 days after receipt of order. Wow! Now, that's service.

But as far as NSC was concerned, getting a Battleship out ahead of schedule was not logical.

Weeks went by, we worked 10 to 12 hours a day, 8 to 10 hours on Saturdays to get the plans out. The plans for the construction and installation of major deckhouses called for most of them to be built of HY-80 steel. HY-80, ranging from 1/4 inch to 1 1/2 inches, would mostly be used as "clad" armor over existing armor or existing ordinary strength steel bulkheads and decks. By the time the removals of the old 40mm gun mounts and other structures were done however, no steel plate of any sort, HY or ordinary, had been delivered. Fortunately, we had several 3/4-inch thick HY-80 plates left over from the *Tarawa* job and the shops used them to build two of the four Tomahawk equipment room deckhouses.

Then, one morning, I got a call from Tom Logan of our Production Controller department. I was needed in a meeting with our supply personnel in regards to the HY-80 armor plate for the *New Jersey*. The meeting divulged the fact that the first half of the order would be shipped between 30 to 45 days. The second half of the order would be shipped 45 days after that. Therefore, I was asked what thickness or thicknesses would be the most crucial to have first.

I answered the 3/4 inch thick HY of course as we had at least two more deckhouses to build as well as other structures and clad armor requiring that size of steel. I then commented, "We are already using up material from the *Tarawa* to meet our schedule. Bill Fedak and I, several weeks ago, found that ARMCO would have shipped the entire order within 45 days after receipt of order. Why is it taking so long?"

A very sourpuss faced woman stated; "We are purchasing the material through the standard bid process from Lutjens."

"What about ARMCO with its almost immediate 45 day delivery?"

"We didn't send a bid request to ARMCO."

"Why not?"

"We didn't have to."

Oh, the thoughts that went through my mind such as the urge to kill. Tom noticed my look of "justifiable homicide" in my eyes and signaled me to just sit back.

NOW HERE IS WHERE THE PROBLEM LIES:
Now, in all honesty, I cannot put the full blame on Supply. They do have a tough job in trying to follow all the rules, regulations and laws that govern their actions. Auditors are constantly monitoring them to make sure all rules are strictly followed, regardless of how stupid they are. For the most part, Congress made those rules and laws supposedly for the protection of the taxpayer and for fairness in purchasing parts and material for the government. The laws were made to prevent any "conflict of interest" between a government employed purchasing agent and a relative that may be a potential vendor. The laws were made to distribute fair shares of purchases from all companies rather than just one monopoly. The laws were made to give the taxpayer the best deal by buying from the lowest bidder.

On the surface, this seems okay, but in reality it leads to delays in completing the project and often at greater expense to rebuild parts of the ship so what was purchased will actually fit. It would have only taken a stroke of the pen in 1981 to allow us to bypass the normal bid procedure and buy directly from ARMCO for absolutely critical material (armor plate) to meet an absolutely critical completion date (45 days delivery vs. 120 by the time we got the first shipment from Lutjens). But some Congressmen would have raised hell about that if they thought vendors within their districts would get cut out of the action. As it is, many Congressmen from the middle states of the country were against the Battleship reactivations because few or no industries within those states had anything to contribute.

In the late 1980's another purchasing law was passed to favor the local small businessman over nationwide big boys. In every engineering office, there is a copy of the McMaster-Carr catalog. It is 6 inches wide by 9 inches tall and (the copy I have at home) is 2 3/4 inches thick containing 2,559 pages of thousands of items. Those items range from gasket material in bulk to individual nuts and bolts to springs, castor wheels, ladders, valves, pipe fittings, switches, nails, etc., etc. It is an extremely handy catalog offering a one volume listing of any special piece of hardware that is not listed in MIL-SPEC (or too hard to find in MIL-SPEC because of the weird way the military describes an item).

McMaster-Carr has warehouses in Georgia, Illinois, New Jersey and Santa Fe Springs, California (Just a 45 drive from the shipyard). The warehouses stock all of the items listed in the catalog. One phone call and the items can be on your receiving dock within a couple of days -or less.

For designs where such hardware items would cost less than a certain amount of money (I think it was $5,000), going out for bids was no longer required. However, McMaster-Carr was considered a major company and we were not allowed to order directly from them. According to the new laws, we have to order from a small local supplier who in turn will merely buy from McMaster-Carr but add thirty to forty percent for "handling". So where are we saving taxpayer's money there?

One last note on NSC is needed however. When it came time to demolish the buildings in 1999, explosives were set to implode them. However, the demolition crew did not take into account that they were built to withstand aerial attack sufficiently to suffer only localized damage at each bomb hit. When the explosives went off, the upper two-thirds of each building collapsed only on the north sides. They came to rest thirty degrees out of vertical. They were as stubborn as the people who worked in them.

The two main Naval Supply Center buildings as photographed by author in 1968

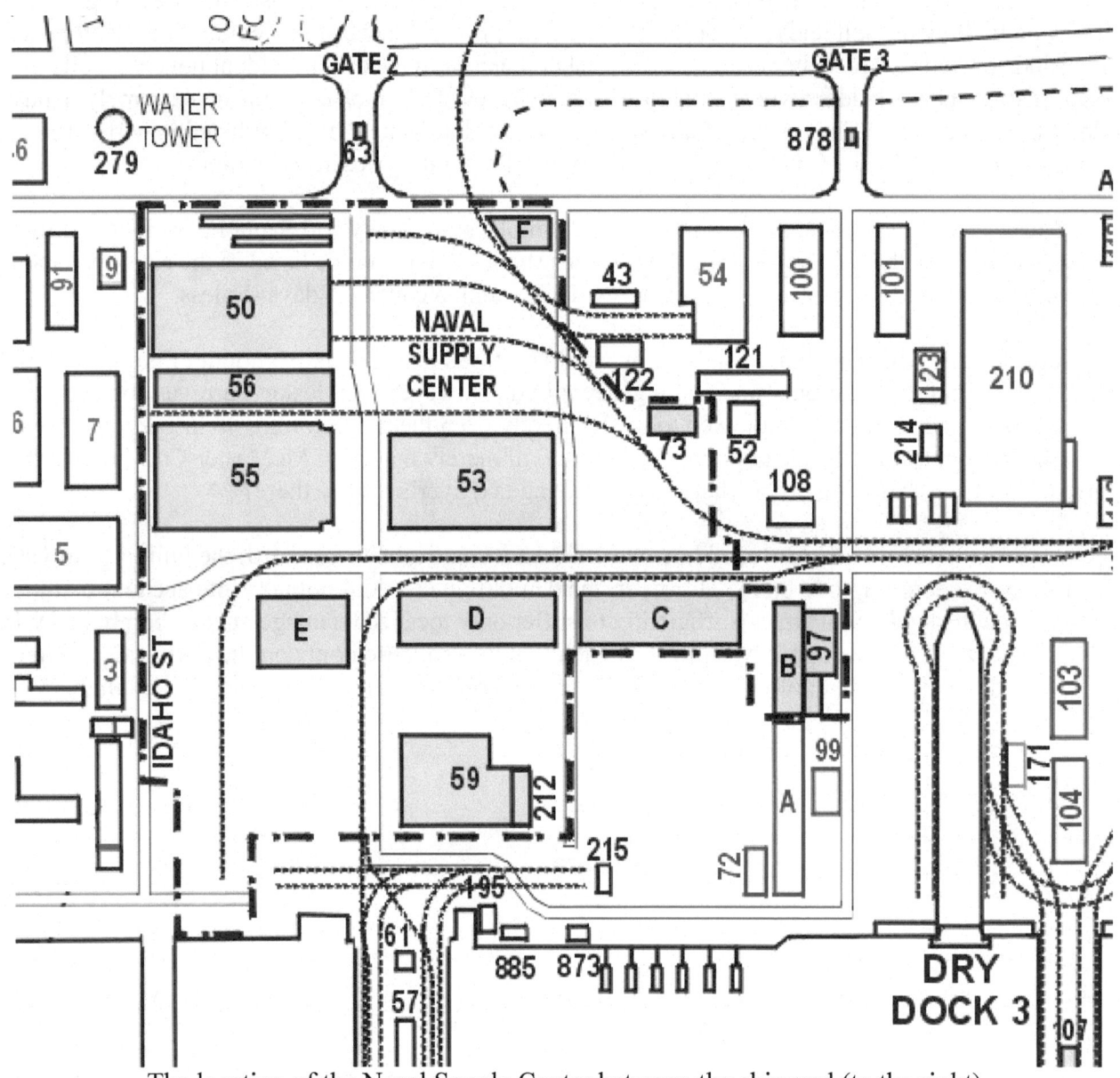

The location of the Naval Supply Center between the shipyard (to the right) and the Naval Station (to the left). CAD Map by author

CHAPTER 20: GHOSTS AND SEA MONSTERS

GHOSTS: I mentioned the spookiness of Howard Hughes giant flying boat in an earlier chapter. That most likely sparked memories of stories of ghosts aboard ships like those that supposedly haunt the *Queen Mary*. So, I thought I would devote this chapter to experiences others, as well as I, have had with so-called ghosts. And as we are dealing with the fantastic, I may as well add in one true sea monster story when a mysterious creature tried to "eat a Destroyer".

On an active ship, alive with the crew, shipyard workers and the hustle of all the work being done, there are no thoughts of ghosts or the ship being haunted. But on an inactivated ship, especially at night on the swing or graveyard shift, it can be real eerie.

The first time I worked on inactivated ships at night was typical. We had two stricken Destroyers, *Heywood L. Edwards* (DD-663) and *Richard P. Leary* (DD-664), that were to be given to Japan and they were in dry dock 3 to have more plates bolted over the underwater shell openings to assure water tightness for the tow. It was early March of 1959, the weather at night was very damp and I was suffering from a bad cough. Don Foster, my supervisor, did not want me in the night air and said I should be home instead. But, there I was so he assigned me fire watch duty aboard the ships while the shipfitter, Scoggins, and the welder, Nikolai, welded the studs on the hull for bolting the extra closure plates.

I reported aboard ship with a fire extinguisher and noted that only one of the shipyard security guards was on the fantail in a security shack. Scoggins and Nicolai, in the dry dock below the ship, would tap on the shell plating with a hammer to signal where they would be welding and I would track down the area from the inside by the sound. I would return their taps with a hammer and I would stand by to make sure the heat of the welding coming through did not start the paint or any grease on fire.

Scoggins and Nikolai were not the kinds of guys to dilly-dally around. They weren't speed demons, but once they set a pace, it was unrelenting until the job was done. Before I could really settle down, they would tap on the shell that they were done and ready to move to the next opening for sealing. I would tap back that I understood, picked up my hammer and fire extinguisher and moved forward listening for their next series of taps. While I was there, I also looked around the compartments trying to find memories of the last crew that were often left on ships when they were inactivated.

A Hedy Lamar pin-up was still inside the door of one locker, but that was about all. I should have "salvaged" that pin-up, it would be worth a fortune today. The ship was pretty clean otherwise. Near lunchtime, at 2030 hours, Scoggins gave the old "Shave and a Haircut - Two bits" tap signaling they were heading back to the shop for lunch. Well, I brown-bagged my lunch and headed up for the quarterdeck by the guard shack. The guard said his shift was over and he took off. I saw Scoggins and Nikolai trudging up the dry dock stairs to get to the shop in time for the half-hour lunch break. I was the only living person on board that ship, appropriately, "in the dead of night".

Great. I wolfed down my sandwiches and started touring the ship. Most of the main lights were on so I didn't have to use my flashlight very much. It was really interesting to walk around and look at the berthing areas where sailors once slept and their mess hall where they took meals maybe only during a lull in battle. All I had to do was sit down, relax, and I could hear an old phonograph playing the Andrews Sisters. Over on the table in the corner, you can hear a couple of sailors playing Acey-Deucy. That is, if you wanted to hear them. To me, that ship was a museum and a memorial to the crews that served on her.

What was that noise? Something went "clank" up forward. I'm the only one here though. I think. Oh well, probably my imagination. Suddenly something just made a creaking sound. Not really in a specific spot either. But I'm the only one here. Or am I?

Okay, I'm a science fiction fan, made straight A's in all my science classes and I want to be an engineer. What made those noises? Besides ghosts of the crew.

Well, let's see. It's getting close to 2100 hours. The night air is getting cooler. Oh yeah. Now I remember that first summer as an apprentice in 1955 when I worked on that new aluminum deck of the USS *Lowe* (DE-325). In the cool morning, that deck was nice and flat. But by lunch time, not only was the unpainted aluminum so hot that it would burn through the soles of our work boots and it was also buckled and humped so badly from heat expansion that it was almost useless as a deck.

That was when we used 6061-type heat-treated aluminum. The welding would take the heat treat out and it would be soft and weak within three inches of all welds. And it would expand like the dickens too. (We later switched to 5086 annealed type of aluminum and solved most of those problems).

So, even though this was a steel ship I was on that night, its structure was shrinking just ever so slightly as the night air cooled it off. Plus having a few thousand rivets holding it together didn't help keep her being very "solid" either.

I observed an even more interesting case of metal expansion and contraction in 1993 when we had to realign the tracks of the cargo weapons elevators of the helicopter assault ship USS *Essex* (LHD-2). The six Cargo/Weapons used a four guide rail arrangement rather than the standard two rail and the installation was so poorly done, looking down at them from an upper deck was like looking at "H" shaped snakes. Then one day a Shop 38 team realigned the tracks of elevator 3 perfectly early that morning using (previously installed) piano wires as index guides. When I checked it about mid-morning, with special gauges we had made up in the tool and die section, it was slightly out of alignment. Not drastically out of alignment but enough to fail an inspection. But when we went back about noon to fix the tracks, they were back in perfect alignment again. Now remember, the *Essex* is a steel ship, all welded (no rivets) but very box like in hull shape. The elevators I was inspecting were on the Starboard side that was receiving the heat of the morning sun. As the sun rose, it warped the tracks just a thirty-second of an inch out of alignment. After the sun passed overhead, that side of the ship cooled and the tracks "shrunk" back into shape.

Aircraft Carriers are perhaps the spookiest. They are big, boxy and prone to making all kinds of noises as the hull flexes either at sea or as the temperatures of the days and nights change. One time, Kenneth "Tiny" Miller and Art Goldberg were checking out an inactivated Carrier. Tiny was from the ventilation design surveying the vent ducts and Art was a planning coordinator making the inventory list. When they realized that they were the only two living humans on board the ship and noises were still coming up from its innards, Art said to hell with the list and got off as fast as he could.

My last time I was alone aboard an inactivated carrier was the USS *Kearsarge* (CV/CVS 33). I spent many nights aboard that ship on swing shift working her while in service. She was another one of our pride and joy. During a regular overhaul, we rebuilt the catapult tracks and installed all new track boundary plates. On an emergency availability, after running down a Soviet Submarine from San Francisco Bay, we had to replace some of the beams under the Main Deck that got warped from chasing that sub half way across the Pacific Ocean, with her four escort Destroyers, to prove to the Russians that they could not outrun our ASW team.

When *Kearsarge* was inactivated, I was tasked to design the towing bridle for it. After I sadly did my ship check, I wandered around a bit. Though it was daylight, it was lunchtime and everybody else left the ship. Except me. I took that opportunity to look the old gal over one last time. In a compartment ready to be sealed, I found a black board and some chalk. I wrote the date my kid brother's prom was held aboard that ship ("thanks" to the originally "reserved" hotel that screwed up the dates) and closed the door.

Creak! Groan! Snap! Yup. The ghosts are still there, even in the daytime.

A couple of years later, *Kearsarge* was towed back down from Bremerton and berthed at the south quay of Pier Echo. There she was cut up for scrap, right within sight of the south windows of Building 300 where I worked. The mast and island were cut down within a matter of days. Then the weeks crept by as the hull was eaten away by the cutting torches a few hundred pounds at a time. A lift platform, sort of like a floating dry dock but without the sidewalls, was set under the hull and she was raised out of the water for the final chopping up. It wasn't long before the USS *Kearsarge* was nothing but a pile of scrap metal at the railroad stop across the street. Hopefully the ghosts left rather than being cast into park benches.

So, there you have it folks. The ghosts you hear aboard old and vacant ships are really just the sounds of the hull, decks and bulkheads contracting as the day turns into night and expanding as the night turns into day. I believe that the ghostly sounds on the *Queen Mary* are only that especially it being an almost totally riveted hull that is more "flexible" than an all welded hull.

The apparitions though are another matter. No ghost is ever seen directly by the viewer. They are always "just caught sight of" within the viewer's side vision. I have seen one myself that way in my own home but I still doubt their existence. I asked my optometrist about the eye picking up light frequencies from the side that cannot be seen directly. He said that due to the shape of the lens and the image landing along the edges of the cones and rods inside the eye, that is possible and some study has been done on it. But nothing was conclusive yet.

SEA MONSTERS: Now let me tell you about a real sea monster that tried to "eat a Destroyer". However, the size of appetite, in reality, is a result of humorous descriptions thrown around during informal discussions. In 1972 the USS *Stein* (DE-1065) came into the shipyard to have her rubber bow mounted rubber SONAR dome replaced. It was badly damaged with cuts, gashes and abrasions all over it. I wasn't involved in the investigation of the damage but some years later somebody asked me about it and I found a copy of the divers' report in a file folder of the *Stein*. The report was very cut and dry describing the damage in abrupt terms with no personal opinion as to the cause. Off the record, the divers said the damage looked like bite marks from a very large animal.

Submarines also reported that rubber coatings on some of their hulls were also heavily damaged with a pattern of gashes that looked like bites from a large creature of some sort. But there was no way that any official Navy report was going to say something like that.

Then in 1976 a Navy recovery boat, retrieving a parachute from an aerial weather instrument, snagged the first specimen of what was determined to be our rubber-eating sea monster. What they had scooped up in the parachute off of Hawaii was a Megamouth Shark (*Megachasma pelagios*). Since then, many more specimens have been captured and necropsies have been able to determine their diet and life style. Photographs have been taken of Megamouths underwater and I have even seen a set of photos where three Whales were bouncing one around like a volley ball during daylight hours.

Megamouth is a bottom dwelling shark during the daylight hours and drifts along between six hundred and one thousand feet down. Its head is disproportionately larger than the classic streamlined shark and a photograph of just the front half would indicate a much longer animal than it really is. The largest specimen captured, so far, is slightly less than sixteen feet. Well, maybe that is pretty big after all being just two feet shorter than my pickup truck.

The huge mouth is lined with hundreds of small teeth in several rows looking more like a large wood rasp than a carnivore's eating machine. As a matter of fact, Megamouth is not a meat eater. It rises to the surface at night to feed on plankton-like organisms. Some of those organisms grow as marine fouling on rubber SONAR domes. Comparison of bite patterns to ship damage and finding bits of rubber in the stomach of one Megamouth solved our "Destroyer-eating sea monster" mystery.

Megamouth was not attacking our ships but was feeding off the marine growth on the rubber surfaces much as a human would gnaw on a spare rib. What attracts the Megamouth to the rubber instead of the steel hull of the ship is still a mystery. I suspect it is the tributyltin fluoride impregnation of the rubber, intended to kill barnacles, that attracts Megamouth either by taste or by smell. Though tributyltin fluoride is a potent toxin, it may just be salad dressing to Megamouth as the Mongoose is immune to Cobra venom.

So there you have it folks. Sea monsters do exist. No, they are not like Godzilla or the giant Kraken. They are monsters in mystery only until the mystery is solved.

"B" The very first photo of a Megamouth shark taken underwater.   Photo by: Bruce Rasner

Good thing Megamouth is not a meat eater.

The type of rubber SONAR dome that a Megamouth gnawed on.

The "cut and dry" diver's report of the Sonar dome damage:

RTF:mmm (972)
22 September 1972

MEMORANDUM

From: Code 970
To: Code 213

Subj: USS STEIN (DE-1065) Sonar Dome; underwater inspection of

Ref: (a) J. O. 13031-10016 - K.O. 002

1. In accordance with reference (a), the underwater inspection of STEIN was conducted by Shop 72 Divers on 14 September 1972; findings were as follows:

   a. Starboard Side

   (1) Approximately 12' aft of bow centerline on the topside of the dome, the rubber covering has many cuts in an area 15 inches wide by 29 inches long.

   (2) Centerline anchor extends 1¼" downward on the starboard side.

   (3) Heavy sea growth on starboard side.

   b. Port Side

   (1) Approximately 15' aft of the bow center at the top edge of the dome, the rubber covering is missing from an area 12" long by 20' wide.

   (2) Approximately 25' from bow and 14" down from the top edge, the rubber covering is missing from an area 30" long by 10" wide.

   (3) Approximately 7' aft of bow centerline and 10" from top edge of the dome, a damaged area 2' wide by 24' long appears like very small cuts and in places is shredded.

   (4) Approximately 12' 6" aft of bow centerline and approximately 8' from top edge of the dome, an area 12" long by 3" at widest is loose and has a "flap" of rubber existing.

   (5) Approximately 33' from after end of the dome an area 4" long by 1" wide has several "cuts".

   (6) About 8" below item No. 5, one "cut" 3/4" wide by 2" long.

   (7) Moderate sea growth appears on the port side.

   (8) Numerous point blisters were found on the lower portion of the hull aft of the dome.

CHAPTER 21: HOW DO I GET OUT OF THIS C*S* OUTFIT?

Many of our designs have been complimented as examples of extraordinary imagination. We appreciate that and, all modesty aside, are very proud of some of the "Rube Goldberg's" we came up with. Some of them however, stretched the limits of fantasy design to say nothing of logical design.

Top honors for illogical design goes to the topmast modifications we had to do to mount the Mk-105 TAC antennas on some FFs and DEs in November of 1973. Picture a flat, fan-shaped piece of aluminum plate with four "coffee cups" sitting on their sides along the curved edge of the fan with their open tops facing out. Imagine two of these assemblies in line with each other facing opposite directions about three feet apart. Connecting those two assemblies is an aluminum pipe about four inches in diameter. Welded to the center of the pipe is a circular mounting plate, eighteen inches in diameter, with bolt holes in it.

That arrangement works extremely well, mounted on top of a pole, in the barren desert where the antennas were tested. It is that arrangement that was contracted but as a **non-deviation design**.

Now we had to mount those antennas on the polemast (a.k.a. topmast). Don Fraser had it fairly easy for the FF-1040 class of ships he was assigned. The antenna assembly would mount on the very top of the polemast in place of the URD-4 antenna. Then he designed the modification to actually wrap around the support pipe so a mounting plate could be installed above for reinstallation of the URD-4.

I had the greater challenge on the *Brooke* class DEGs starting with USS *Ramsey* (DEG-2/FFG-2). I had to mount the antenna at about the center of the polemast. I looked at it and said, "Easy. We just cut that aluminum pipe and mount the forward and aft halves on each side of the polemast."

Wrong. We cannot modify the antenna at all. "Why?" I naturally asked. The answer was, "The manufacture would void the warranty on the antennas then." I looked at my perpetual calendar to note that I still had seventeen years and eight months to go before minimum retirement eligibility.

I was finally able to design an enormous spacer assembly that would allow the Mk-105 TAC antenna to actually stick through the polemast, yet maintain enough strength in the spacer so the mast would not break in two. To make the modification, the polemast had to be removed entirely from the ship and taken to the shop for major modifications just to mount the Mk-105 TAC antenna. And then reinstall it on the ship.

The part that really brings tears to your eyes is that all six ships of the *Brooke* class had to have that modification done when all it would have taken was a hack-saw and a couple of pieces of aluminum plate welded on each side of the polemast.

My illustrations on the next page were not copied from my original drawing. But this nightmare has burned it into my memory so well that I cannot forget it -- even though I want to.

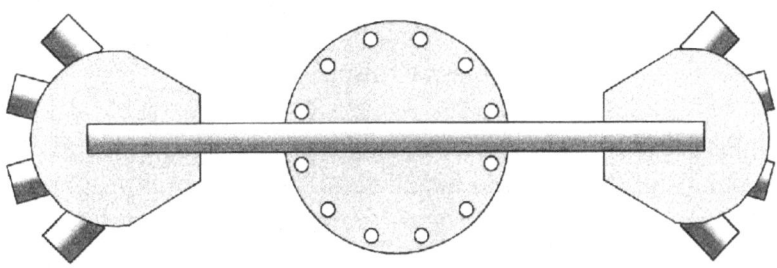

PLAN VIEW OF A MK-105 TAC ANTENNA
WE WERE NOT ALLOWED TO MODIFY THE MANUFACTURER'S
BOLTING PLATE OR SUPPORT PIPE IN ANY WAY AS THAT
WOULD VOID THE WARRANTY

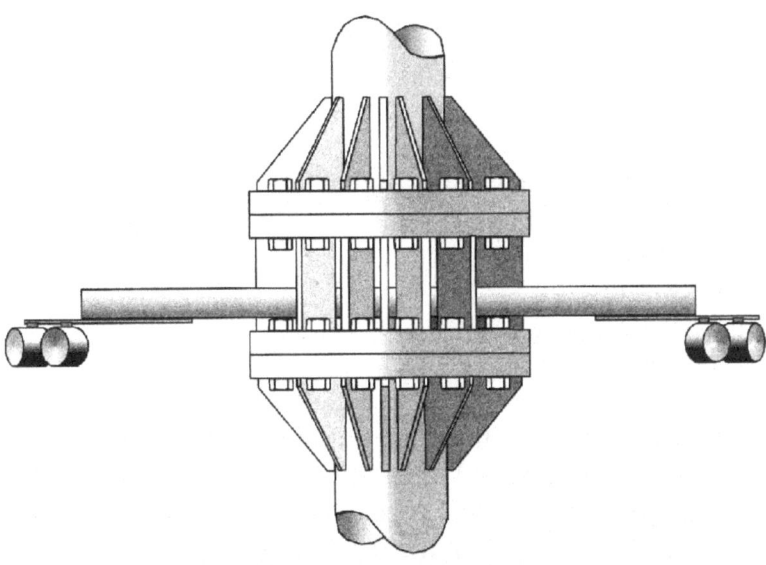

ELEVATION VIEW OF MOUNTED MK-105 TAC ANTENNA
WE HAD TO CUT THE TOPMAST IN TWO AND INSERT A HEAVY
ADAPTER PIECE TO ALLOW THE ANTENNA TO PASS THROUGH

Besides illogical designs, there were times when we were just in the wrong place at the wrong time and prompted other people to wish their retirement date would come up faster. Val Pena, the supervisor of our machinery design section, had that wish once. We were tasked to install a prototype Controllable Pitch Propeller (CPP) on the USS *Barbey* (FF-1088) for testing of CPP drive systems of the upcoming gas turbine powered ships.

Gas turbines normally run at a single, constant speed turning the shaft at a constant rate of revolutions per minute and in only one direction. The speed of the ship is increased or decreased by changing the pitch on the propeller blades instead of driving the propeller shaft at higher or lower revolutions. By running at a constant speed they are most fuel-efficient and can still turn out 22,500 horsepower. But none of these ships had been built yet so a prototype propeller with variable pitch blades was designed by a commercial company but to be installed and tested by LBNSY.

Val had a large display case set up in his design section that had tubes of different colored lights to show what hydraulic lines would be activated during certain phases of the propeller's operation. The *Barbey* was selected to be the test ship for the installation of the prototype CPP.

Though steam powered, she was a single screw ship (one shaft with one propeller) that could simulate the single screw *Oliver Hazard Perry* class of Frigates being planned and later the twin screw *Spruance* class Destroyers and *Ticonderoga* class Cruisers.

It took Val with his engineers and the mechanics from the shops several months to iron out all the installation and test details of the CPP and installed on the ship. A portlight (circular window) was installed in a watertight trunk in the hull of *Barbey* so cameras could record the propeller in operation. When the ship went out on her first trials, the jubilation from Val and his engineers could be felt all over the building.

Everything was working perfectly, at least until it came time to test from full ahead to full reverse. A normal steam-powered ship goes in reverse by bringing the shaft to a stop then shifting the reduction gear into reverse to turn the shaft in the opposite direction. But *Barbey* had to simulate a gas turbine powered ship where the shaft turns only one direction at the same speed all the time and reverse accomplished only by changing the pitch of the propeller blades.

Well, to cut to the chase, it turned out that of the dozens of bolts holding the five propeller blades in place, there was one - just one - bolt that had a forging flaw in it.

"For want of a nail a shoe was lost
"For want of a shoe a horse was lost
"For want of a horse a message was lost
"For want -----." Well, you get the idea.

The turbulence created by the propeller blades turning from full ahead pitch to full reverse pitch was too much for that one bolt. It sheared and threw the blade out of balance which then caused it to shear the rest of the bolts and when it broke away from the propeller hub it collided with at least one other blade, breaking that one off. With two of the five blades gone, the shaft was so far out of balance the other three also snapped all their bolts. One of the blades smashed the 1-½ inch thick glass of the portlight and flooded the trunk destroying the camera inside (but the film was saved).

Val's expression of perpetual smiles turned to the longest mope imaginable. We didn't think he would ever be happy again. However, as time went on, the lessons learned from those tests developed super strong Controllable Pitch Propellers that are used on several classes of ships today.

That still didn't make Val really happy until the Battleships were brought back. Working on those enormous boilers, steam turbines and reduction gears put him in his element again to give them his very personal TLC.

For the last nightmare of this chapter, sometimes no matter how hard you try, no matter how perfect your finished product is, you just cannot beat the hierarchical system. This is the case of the four-legged quadrupod masts on the FF-1052 class Frigates. When the first of the ships deployed, almost immediately complaints came in of how "limber" the quad-masts were. They would shake and twist violently and adversely affected the efficiency of the antennas mounted on them.

The *Knox* class Frigates used a structure amidships called a Mack that was a combination of the ships mast and stack. The base was a slightly tapered truncated cone supporting a RADAR room on top that looked like the tank of an old wooden water tower. Stack exhausts were vented out through funnels at the top of the structure that also supported the SPS-40 RADAR antenna and the quad-mast.

The quad-mast had almost no tapering from the base of the four legs to the top and was really more a vertically mounted box girder than anything else. Additionally, the four main legs of the quad-mast were all aluminum angles instead of pipe or tube. Pipe was always the best structural shape to build masts with because stresses from the centroid (center of the pipe) were equal in all directions. It was a bit more difficult to template and fit the joints of pipes, but it was a much stronger shape than angle bars.

The "skinny" mast was more like an oil well derrick. That kind of structure would be fine if sitting on solid ground. But mast structures on warships have to remain stiff when a ship pitches ten degrees and rolls thirty degrees in a one-hundred knot wind all at the same time. Additionally that mast has to absorb hull vibrations and resist the heat from the exhaust gases of the main propulsion machinery.

The worst aspect of this mast was its location on the ship placed it dead center over the ship's hull frequency. Every structure has a potential natural frequency within it and though it may appear to be solid and unmoving, if you placed a tuning fork at the exact center of the frequency waves, it will vibrate from induction. I found this out one day when I had to climb up to the top of a mast of a 1052 to take some measurements. While up there I definitely felt the mast was swaying and twisting. This was particularly noticeable since the ship was sitting solidly on concrete blocks in an unmoving dry dock.

Of course NAVSEA came up with a "suggested" fix, which was to attach guy wires (stays) to the mast to stiffen it. First of all outriggers would have to be designed to allow a wide enough spread of the stays to provide the stiffness required. Secondly, the stays could not be metallic wire at all in the vicinity of all those antennas. It was decided to use rods of resin-reinforced fiberglass that would not interfere with the antennas.

Bob Riha had a better idea and made up some sketches of a new quad-mast built out of pipe and with a wider spread to the legs. The higher ups sort of liked the idea and turned the sketches over to an engineer, Moises (Mo) Rael, to do the calculations. Bob then collected scraps of cardboard and wood dowels with which he built a 1:48 scale model of the entire Mack and his new mast design. He put the finish coat of paint on the model about a week before Mo came up with his final summary. Mo's off-the-record analysis was that Bob's design was so strong and so stable that the calculations were a waste of time.

The design was accepted by NAVSEA to fix some of the ships until they could finalize their tests of the fiberglass backstays. This is where the hierarchy steps in. Out of the forty-five ships of the class, fifteen of the ships (eleven West Coast and four East Coast) received LBNSY (Bob Riha) design quad-masts. Other ships may also have received the stronger mast but I can only confirm those I have found photos of that show it. Then NAVSEA decided that the design of the fiberglass stays on only the polemast were cheaper and did well enough to reduce secondary whipping of the polemast that added to the stresses of the four-legged girder mast below. No attempt was made to back stay the four-legged girder because there were no existing places spread out sufficiently to attach the bottom ends of the stays.

Many of us still think there was a bit of jealousy mixed in with the decision. It was just unheard of that a non-degreed technician could design a mast superior to anything their engineers could without having to do a single algebraic equation.

You win some and you lose some. Actually in the long run, because of the pride people had at Long Beach Naval Shipyard, I think we came out even if not ahead.

Robert L. (Bob) Riha (a.k.a. "Chiefie") at his desk when this author took his photo in 1967. He was a genius at some of the toughest designs assigned to LBNSY Such as the Oil Containment Booms and the superior mast for the 1052 class Frigates.

A young Bob Riha on active duty a few wars ago. Photo courtesy Bob ("Bobby") Riha Jr

The original NAVSEA design mast on the USS Lockwood (FF-1064).
It is quite obvious that it would be very vulnerable to twisting. Author's collection

The ("Bob Riha") mast on the USS *Sims* (FF-1059) is obviously much stronger than the original design.

CHAPTER 22: WINDS, FLOODS AND FIRES

WINDS: No matter where you live in this world, you will be subject to some form or forms of natural disasters that are peculiar to that area of the planet. In Florida you have hurricanes, in Kansas you have tornadoes and in California we have earthquakes plus a few others of more rarity such as small tornadoes, Santa Ana winds, brush fires, drought and floods.

In the southern California area, once or twice a year we get what are called the Santa Ana winds. The air currents change and bring winds in from the high desert. As the winds push over the San Bernardino Mountains, they rush back down into the lowlands toward the coastline. They can occur anytime during the year often taking out many trees. The worst aspect of those winds is the dust they kick up. I recall one time when we were working on a tanker in Dry Dock 1; the dust was so thick it was difficult to make out the other end of the dry dock if you were standing at one end. One shipfitter remarked that it was like they were sandblasting the ship without any tarps to cover the dust.

The shipyard itself never suffered any serious wind damage except for one year when the shipyard commander, a football fan, had a large canvas sign hung over the fifth floor windows of Building 300. It faced north toward the Gerald Desmond Bridge and it said GO NAVY in support of the upcoming Army-Navy game. Weights were added to the bottom hem to keep it flat in the breeze. Unfortunately the gentle breeze turned into a high wind and several glass windows on the fifth floor had to be replaced.

Now, you wouldn't think that a ship tied to a pier would have much to worry about. Wrong again. The USS *Brooke* (FFG-1) was moored to the concrete quay of Seal Beach when severe Santa Ana winds raced through for a couple of days. Bernie Jankowski, from our planning coordination section, drove by Seal Beach on the way home from work and he could easily see the ship slamming repeatedly against the concrete. Over one hundred feet of shell plating from the main deck to the second deck needed replacing as well as all of the stainless steel galley cabinets in the CPO quarters.

Tornadoes are an extreme rarity in California. Most times you see dust devils out in the farm fields or desert. However, around 1950, a small tornado was reported to tear up the *Porgy and Bess* set on a Hollywood movie lot. Most meteorologists said it was merely a strong wind or dust devil. The people who were there on the set however disagreed with the experts who were not there. Later though, another extremely rare wind condition was found to strike our area once in a great while and that is a Microburst. Simply speaking, a Microburst is an upside down tornado that lasts from a few seconds up to a few minutes. One tore up a thirty-foot tall "Christmas" tree (a **real** tree) in the city of Paramount.

In December of 1982 a real tornado actually touched down in LBNSY. I had taken a week off to rest up from the long hours reactivating *New Jersey* and I was sitting at my dining room table with an Apple II Plus computer I borrowed from Bill Reid trying to write some memoirs of the ship reactivation.

The tornado first touched down at the northwest end of Dry Dock 1, ripped up a corrugated metal tool shed and kept hopping northwards. It touched down again on Downey Avenue in north Long Beach at about South Street and went right up the centerline of Downey to Artesia Boulevard where it broke apart coming into contact with the 91 Freeway overpass. I live on the northeast corner of La Jara Street and Downey about three hundred yards north of where it did its last touchdown and one hundred fifty feet east of the centerline of Downey Avenue. The twister knocked power out throughout the neighborhood, the house and windows shook as if in an earthquake and the computer went down. A short while later, the power came back on and I was able to retype the pages I lost by not hitting Control S as often as I should. I had to turn on the news to discover what really happened.

The following week, the tail end of a hurricane out of Mexico buffeted us. The *New Jersey* had gone out on her first sea trial, but the winds and waves were too high to do her high-speed run. She was now tied up to Pier 1 and waiting for a fuel spill test to be done on the helicopter deck. Bruce Mason, from NAVSEA and formerly from our firefighting piping section, and I were walking out to the pier to perform the test. But the "waning" winds left over from the hurricane were just too much for us. We were dodging pieces of corrugated fiberglass roofing and strips of light aluminum sheet metal from the scrap bins as we were leaning heavily into the wind. I looked up at the ship and noticed a seagull above trying to fly south. Poor thing was exerting full throttle to his wings and just not moving an inch. He finally peeled off and let the wind take him North toward the machine shop. When we boarded the ship, even this behemoth of a Battleship was swaying in the wind so we cancelled the test until that afternoon.

FLOODS: Flooding is something else though, especially when one end of the shipyard is sixteen feet below sea level. Dikes around the East End of Terminal Island pretty well keep the water out but as subsidence increased, flooding of the dry docks during docking or undocking of a ship often flooded out parts of the shipyard. Heavy rains also flooded out parts of the shipyard, that were below sea level, so pumps were installed more for rain flooding than ocean flooding. Pumps at the north end of Dry Dock 1 usually kept parking lot H, the lowest part of the shipyard, clear. But one year they failed and cars at the northeast corner were totally submerged. And that is the worst case of shipyard flooding I ever saw.

That is outside in the parking lots. Building 132 was different however. That building, our main machine shop, was the very first major shop building erected. It originally housed the shipfitter shop and blacksmith shop until their separate structure, building 128, was built. Bob Cooper was a supervisor machinist and he wrote a newsletter for machinists called *The Sandcrab*. In one of his editions he describes the flooding problems of the machine shop quite well.

"The main problem was that the roof drains were all plugged down under the street by sandblasting sand that had drifted down into them over the years. The roof drains themselves contributed to the problem. The drains were large cast iron pipes that were strapped to the frame structure of the building. The frame was actually massive H beams that supported the bridge cranes. The roof kind of sat on top of this framework.

"These pipes simply ran up the columns and just before they reached the roof they "doglegged" away from the column into the box-like collection sump in the roof structure itself. Many of these sumps were buried inside the sidewalls of the building but some were exposed on the inside, particularly over the valve section on the main aisle. This was a pretty good design except that during earthquakes the roof shook at a different frequency than the steel frame underneath thereby breaking most of the pipes at the dogleg.

"Because the pipes were plugged up at their bottoms, when it started to rain they would fill up and after some time would start to leak furiously through the dogleg breaks at the top floor. Remember, in a building a little over 650 feet long by a little over 300 feet wide we would have lots of water to dispose of.

"The pipes in the middle of the building would leak massively and the inner walls on the sides would lift up an inch or two allowing literally rivers of water to gush out from underneath the partition. Because we didn't have any floor drains the water would simply move through the various machine sections downhill (the Northeast corner of the building was eleven feet lower than the Southwest corner because of subsidence) finally going underneath the wood block flooring in the Turret lathe section where it would leak through the floor onto the Niles planer on the main floor below. Because the wood flooring soaked up so much water, the leaking would go on for a couple of weeks.

""All this was usually over and done within two or three hours and would generally occur between 5 and 8 o'clock in the morning. By the time the top brass reported for work, all there was to be seen were wet floors. I would go down to the "head shed" (upper management offices) and complain but all I got was the "ho hums" until they moved the Automatic Combustion Control shop onto the floor and the problem became more personal then".

FIRES: California is also very dry in the summer with almost no rain at all. Maybe there is a light shower once in a while but generally we are dry as a bone. Wild fires are the greatest danger we face then and hundreds of homes have been lost as a result. However, the shipyard had almost no vegetation, almost all of the shops have metal roofs and there was never a lack of having enough fire hydrants and water supply. We could use the seawater and firefighting pumps on the ships if necessary to put out any fires.

Fires are something the Navy takes very seriously, especially aboard ship. I was working on a tanker once, while an apprentice, trying to install a small insert into the steel plating of the ship's transom (aft end). Then I heard, "Fire, fire, fire. This is not a drill." The next thing I knew was the compartment filling up with the ship's crew donning EBAs (Emergency Breathing Apparatus) and running fire hoses down the ladder way. This was just seconds after a shipyard welder shot up the ladder. I kid you not; it took less than a minute for the ship's damage control party to assemble. But of course, a fuel tanker can be a very vulnerable ship to a fire.

What had happened was the welder was down in the trim tank on the port side, opposite of the compartment side I was on, when some of his welding sparks ignited a pool of not yet dried fresh paint at the bottom of the tapered tank. He dropped his gear and ran up to the quarterdeck to report the fire and the crew responded so fast there wasn't even enough time for smoke to come out of the hatch and warn me that something was wrong.

Building fires can be something else though. We had a small fire department with three or four fire trucks located at the Naval Station and the fire fighters there did their best with what they had. But some fires can be too aggressive even for the most well trained professionals. Therefore, when a fire alarm was turned in to the Naval Station, it was also turned in to the Long Beach City Fire Department. The Naval Station fire fighters had just five minutes to call the city to tell them they had everything under control or it was a false alarm. If five minutes passed without such a call, the city would then dispatch units to assist.

In the 1940s the wood-frame shiplap sided BOQ on the Naval Station was just a pile of ashes only fourteen minutes after the fire started. The original shipyard's wood Administration building and original wood Cafeteria One, just thirty feet south of the Administration building, were also rated as only fourteen minute buildings. It was even surmised that the Administration building would go in less than ten minutes because of the tons of paper inside of drawings, records, manuals and notes throughout both floors from one end to the other. We had thousands of ship drawings on several different types of paper and almost every one was rolled. Rolled paper is an ideal fuel for fire as the hole inside the paper roll draws a draft of fresh air through and the paper literally flares instead of just burning. Try it sometime in your fireplace, barbeque or campfire with the cardboard rolls from paper towels. They make excellent kindling.

It was about 1968 when that theory was almost proven. In the early hours of the morning, an electrical malfunction set the Cafeteria on fire. The Naval Station Fire Department responded immediately and seeing a major structure on fire called in for city assistance without waiting for the five-minute delay. But it was to no avail as the Cafeteria was just a stack of charred framework and a pile of ashes within fourteen minutes. Normally the Administration Building would have gone as well, but as luck would have it the prevailing winds had reversed that morning and were blowing in a southerly direction away from the Administration Building.

Later, temporary cafeteria facilities were set up in a Quonset hut across the street by Dry Dock 1 while a brand new cafeteria was built, out of glass and concrete. A new Administration Building was constructed up on Pier Echo and the old one was torn down. But as equipment and training improved we came to respect our Fire Fighters quite well. I have personally seen their professionalism in responding to one of my supervisors suffering from a heart attack and another time when one of my coworkers had an epileptic seizure.

The subsidence problem (centered at the Edison Plant in the background) started causing severe flooding problems as shown in this 1954 photo at the top of the hill outside of Gate 5.   Courtesy: "Salty"

When the pumps failed during a heavy rain in 1983, Parking Lot H at the lowest point of the shipyard became known as "Lake H". Author's collection scanned from a Polaroid photo

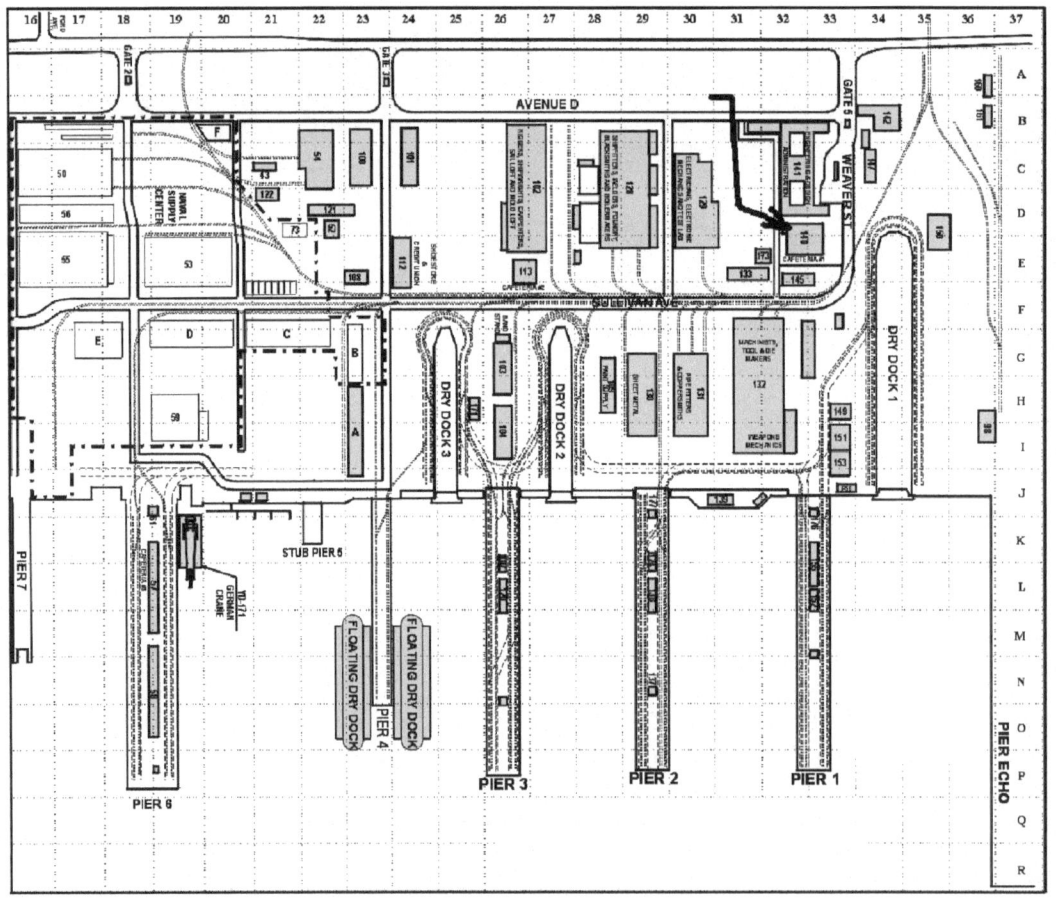

The original Cafeteria 1 that burned down to the ground in 14 minutes just a few feet south of the Main Administration & Design building.

CHAPTER 23: EARTHQUAKES

Most people from the East Coast and the Mid-West have never experienced an earthquake. However, California is seismically very active with earthquake activity as it is on the Eastern edge of what geologists call The Rim of Fire that encircles the Pacific Ocean. Oddly, the strongest earthquake ever recorded was in Missouri and it changed the course of the Mississippi River. However, that was in the 19th century and there are not any people around anymore to tell about it. The first quake I ever felt was around 1946 when Milwaukee, Wisconsin had its second "official" quake. I was in 5th grade at the time and it was just a fast rumble. First we thought Allis Chalmers (about a mile south) had blown up.

After our family moved to California in 1951 we felt our first California earthquake, which was the 7.5 magnitude Kern County earthquake, commonly known as the Tehachapi earthquake, on 21 July 1952. In more recent years earthquakes have been getting closer to home. The 6.6 magnitude San Fernando earthquake, also known as the Sylmar earthquake, on 9 February 1971 was only about 40 miles north of Long Beach.

In those quakes, no bouncing was experienced at first, just the rolling of the land below our feet. More recent quakes were all close enough or powerful enough that we felt the bouncing off the ground first, then the rolling. During the 5.9 magnitude Whittier Narrows quake, which is very close to Long Beach, at 0742 on 1 October 1987, I was at my desk talking on the phone to a mechanic out on the *New Jersey* on Pier one. I was by the large plate glass windows and the floor started jumping under my feet. Then the building started to rock. I told the mechanic, "We're having an earthquake. I'll call back later." I grabbed my hard hat as drop ceiling panels and their framing started falling down and I got away from the windows toward the aisle. It was an interesting rolling too. First the building rocked north and south, seemed to settle a little, then it rocked east and west. The second rocking, however, was the building recentering itself on the rollers it was built on just for that type of phenomena.

The building was evacuated while inspectors looked it over. We all had to stay out in the parking lot for several hours, so a number of us drove home to check on our houses and family. Most of us returned just before they cleared us to re-enter the building. Most damage was radial cracks in the plaster from the square corners of doorways and where the steel stairs are bolted to the concrete walls in the stairwells. The worst damage was around the concrete & steel vault on the third floor that held our confidential materials. There were a number of ugly cracks around it, but all superficial.

Even people aboard the *New Jersey* felt the quake, but that was because she was tied to the pier and the rolling waves transferred their action through the mooring lines to the ship. The worst thing that really happened during that quake was that the USS *Leahy* (CG-16) in dry dock 3 had some of her docking blocks jiggle out from underneath her. Doug Hamilton had to gather a team of brave people real fast to get tractors down into the dry dock to push the blocks back in place and drive wedges in to secure the ship. Doug never moved so fast in his life, but he got that ship secured before any serious aftershocks hit.

Most people were at home when the 7.3 Landers quake hit in the morning of 28 June 1992. A few hours later, at 0805 hours, the 6.4 Big Bear quake hit. But damage to the shipyard was insignificant though some of the cracks in Building 300 lengthened a bit more. It was just not cost efficient to plaster over superficial damage as future earthquakes would just open them up again.

It was on 17 January 1994 when the 6.7 Northridge earthquake hit at 0430 in the morning. It did little or no damage around Long Beach, but many homes, apartments and commercial buildings were heavily damaged or destroyed up in the San Fernando Valley area. On January 21st, a Friday night, and a week and a half before my retirement was to become effective, I was watching the evening news where they were reporting FEMA's problem of not having enough personnel to fill out the disaster relief forms of the earthquake victims. I snorted, "My God! We must have a thousand people at the shipyard who know how to fill out forms. Why the hell don't they use us?" Somebody must have read my mind or I was reading someone else's mind. The next morning I got a phone call from Don Lichti around 10:00 AM. He called and asked if I would like to volunteer to help the disaster victims in filling out their forms. I agreed and was told to report to a certain school auditorium in Pasadena for instructions.

I got up to the auditorium early and had a heck of a time finding a place to park. The lots were jammed with a lot of cars with LBNSY passes on them. I walked into the overflowing auditorium and recognized many the people there. Long Beach Naval Shipyard was answering the call of people in need. Also answering the call were volunteers from other Federal and State agencies. Name any agency, their people were there overfilling the 1,730 seating capacity of the auditorium.

There were so many that another class was scheduled for the next day to handle the literally thousands of people making that extra effort for our fellow man. Most of us noted three cracks in the ceiling of the auditorium, each about eight feet long directly over the sign up tables. Those tables were lined up of people willing and anxious to sign up for assignment to a Disaster Assistance Center (DAC).

Louis Rodriguez, the president of the International Federation of Professional and Technical Engineers (IFPTE) local 174 was there with Darryl Neft, the vice president, and several other union members signing up for the Santa Monica DAC. Isaac Cavalier, the supervisor of our Scientific Section, signed up for the Ventura DAC.

I signed up for DAC 4 in Van Nuys just two miles from my brother's house. I had talked to Jack earlier in the week to see how they fared in the quake. He said he wanted somebody with an engineering and construction background, like mine, to make a quick check of his house and the parking garage of the hospital he worked in. Well, I had the chance now to do that and maybe sign him up for a SBA disaster loan. It had some ladder-step cracks in a couple of the interior brick walls and some bricks fell off his chimney, but it was all repairable and there was no danger of the house collapsing from aftershocks. I stayed in their small guesthouse in back and regardless of how late I got in from the center, they always had dinner ready for me.

I reported to DAC 4 on Sunday morning. So did fourteen other shipyard workers. We were crowded into the gymnasium of the Van Nuys Recreation Center. Our tables were, more or less, centered on the floor. Surrounding us, and pressed against the walls, were assistance tables for HUD, SBA home loans, SBA business loans, Individual and Family Grants (IFG), Crisis Counselors, Building Inspectors, Disaster Disability Insurance, Department of Water and Power, Veterans Assistance, Disaster Unemployment, Social Services, Insurance assistance, Legal Counselors, Internal Revenue Service, California Franchise Tax Board, County Tax Assessor and finally the Exit Interview Table.

There were a few other assistance tables as well, but the tables mentioned above were the most needed to send various "clients" to. We were advised **NOT** to call them "victims." The people lined up there for help were "clients" or "applicants". That was a wise decision as we were often their first shoulders to cry on.

As well as all the other volunteers, I found my fellow shipyard workers have very broad shoulders. I wrote down their names from one of the daily sign-in sheets as, being the senior employee there, I was more or less their liaison and leader. I don't know what shops Donald Hong and Henry Don were from, but they were there. So was Paul DeVries (head metallurgist), Dave Mason (welding inspector), Cecil Heath (Leader Electronics Mechanic), Terry Plunket (Foreman Electronics Mechanic), Abel Ayon (Foreman Woodworker), and Victor Maldonado (Leader Woodworker). Also from the woodworking shop were Lawrence White, Gerald Spears, Joe Wesolowski, Daniel Fletcher, John Sanchez and Eddie Salamante.

That first day on the job had its "Murphy's Laws" of course. The short forms we were trained with the night before were not available yet. So we had to retrain ourselves to fill out the long forms. When the short forms were supplied the next day, we were able to revert back to the fewer questions, at least until they ran out later in the week. However, by that time we had filled out so many of them that we just knew instinctively which areas to skip over on the long forms. Several of us admitted to waking up in the middle of the night dreaming about those forms.

"Crowded" is too gentle of a description of the gymnasium. With all of the volunteers, assistance officials and applicants you couldn't pack sardines in a can tighter than that gym. However, a few yards north of us in the outfield of a baseball diamond, a 10,000 square foot circus-type tent was being erected to serve as our interview center and also to house the Salvation Army. A similar, but slightly smaller, tent was erected north of that one as a shelter for applicants whose apartments had been destroyed and they had to sleep outside until assigned other living quarters.

We put in eleven hours that first day; not counting the time it took to drive up there from Long Beach. That was our **shortest** day. Tuesday ran fourteen hours and Wednesday ran thirteen hours. After the Salvation Army moved its operations to Victory Boulevard, to relieve the congestion inside the tent, we were able to shorten our days to "only" twelve hours.

But I cannot complain. The full time FEMA personnel still put in another four to six hours after we left. HUD didn't close its table until an hour or two before midnight. Joe Chavez, the FEMA center manager, had two red phones on his table and a cellular phone strapped to his belt. But he was always available. One of his sidekicks, Donna, was a beautiful brunette whose hair hung below her shoulder blades. You could tell she was the athletic type and she certainly needed every ounce of her stamina and athletic abilities. Because Joe was so busy with other things, Donna was the one we would go to for help because she could think on her feet and knew exactly what she was doing. Needless to say, she was highly respected by all.

At DAC 4 we moved into the tent on Monday morning. We had a lot more room, but the work itself did not get easier. However, there were countless other volunteers there just trying to make things easier for everyone all around. The California Conservation Corps provided scores of able-bodied young people to serve as escorts and gofers. Several of them wound up at tables as interviewers just like us.

The Los Angeles Police Department and the California National Guard provided security. That Monday started to warm up and we now had a supply of short forms. Later in the evening though, the temperature dropped and it started to rain. Not good for the applicants forced to live in the open.

It was also that day that we realized we were going to have some serious language problems. Victor Maldonado is fluent in normal conversational Spanish, but translating some of the legalese of the Privacy Act (that we had to read to each applicant) and the technical terms to describe property damage were stretching Victor's talents. Instead of staying at a hotel or friend's house, he drove back home to Long Beach each night and stayed up a couple of more hours cracking the language books.

One of my applicants was a well-dressed and attractive Chinese woman with her two children. However, she spoke only Mandarin and very little English. We had no Chinese translators yet but her eight year old daughter was very fluent in both languages and I was able to interview her and fill out the forms with very little trouble.

Then I had an elderly couple who were Ukrainian refugees. The man spoke broken English well enough so I was able to process their application. I was thankful because we had only one FEMA person there who could speak Russian and he was very busy with the Russians and Armenians. I wasn't any help in languages as I only know a few words of German, but not all of them can be said in mixed company.

Though the Armenians speak Russian, they don't want to because they hate the Russians. Therefore our lone translator (who also spoke several other languages except Armenian) explained to them that they either spoke Russian with him or go back home until we can find an Armenian interpreter. They spoke Russian.

I wondered if we would get any Hungarian applicants. Louis Horompoly, from our electrical design section, was from Hungary but assigned to the Northridge DAC. Isaac Cavalier, our Scientific Section supervisor, was also at Northridge and he can speak Hebrew, Egyptian and French. My wife, Julia, is fluent in Hungarian and Spanish but she was unavailable to help because of her job commitments.

By Tuesday I thought that every Armenian west of the Mississippi was lined up at DAC 4. But there was this little boy from the neighborhood named Robert, running from table to table translating Armenian for us. He was short for fifteen years old and looked no more than twelve. But his command of both English and Armenian was exemplary. He originally came down there that day to help his parents get their forms filled out. Then he noticed that we needed somebody as an interpreter and, without even asking, would run over to a table where Armenians were applying and translate for us. He didn't go home until around 8:00 that night.

On Wednesday at 9:30 the next morning, Robert was there and ready to serve. Later that evening, an Armenian girl showed up and was also helping us. Her name was Anna and was Robert's cousin. We didn't see Robert again after Wednesday because Anna and three more teen-age Armenian girls came in to take his place. Two of the girls worked the interview tables in the tent and the other two worked the assistance tables in the gym. By the time us interviewers were ready to leave around 8:00 or 9:00 PM when the interview line closed, those girls would still be there until the last Armenian client had left. The actions and dedication of those Armenian teenagers lifted my spirits and I wish each one could be given some sort of medal.

It was also on Wednesday that the Army provided interpreters from its special language unit. We now had translators for Russian, Chinese, Korean, Viet Namese, Spanish and German from the Army. By Thursday the Marine Corps provided more interpreters including a Chaplain who spoke Korean. Also, more bilingual or multi-lingual volunteers from State and Federal agencies were arriving to help out. One of them was fluent in Hebrew, French and Greek.

Oh yes. We had one other language problem and that was with Farsi, the official language of Iran (but preferred by its natives to be called Persia). One of our interviewers was struggling with a Persian woman and it just so happened that the client I was interviewing was also Persian but she also spoke excellent English. Though she had waited over an hour in line before getting seated at my table, she willingly went over to the other table to help in translation.

By the middle of the week, Tuesday or Wednesday, the weather had turned against us. The chill started setting in by late afternoon requiring propane heaters to be placed around the tent. On Thursday the winds picked up and starting tearing the lashings loose on the tent sides forcing many of us to leave our tables to tie the canvas panels back down. A generator that worked most of the time provided lighting after dark. Afterwards regular line power was hooked up and our lighting was much more dependable.

Aftershocks? Oh yes. I think it was Wednesday around 9:30 in the morning when a 4.0 galloped through our tent. I was filling out a client's application when that happened. Most of the people around did their "Ooohs" and "Aaahs" and "Whoas" while I just sat there and continued with the questions. My client looked at me rather strangely and I merely said, "I've lived in California for forty-two years. This is nothing." My calmness put them at ease and I wasn't just putting on an act either. After four decades or so of being bounced out of bed or rocked in an upper floor of a building, you sort of steel yourself against such things. Sort of like what the British did during the Blitz.

After the Salvation Army moved out of the tent, the waiting lines outside of DAC 4 got considerably shorter. It was not intended to set up our DAC as a food and clothing distribution center but as an application-clearing house for those that needed loans or grants to rebuild or find a place to live. Yet we still got some people who only wanted food and clothing. So I learned how to start my interview with a couple of quick questions without wasting an application form. If they just wanted a handout I would give them the directions to the Salvation Army center on Victory Boulevard.

We also had to be careful not to pre-judge an applicant just by their looks. Though they may look like beggars, they may just be distraught and no running water for a shave. A young man came in one afternoon with a very discouraged look on his face and in his tone of voice. He was there a few days before, but it was before FEMA really got its act together, he was sent directly to the SBA loan tables rather than going through the interview first. Since he was a wage earner rather than on SSI or Welfare, it was thought he didn't need to apply for a grant. His building was red tagged and he was out of work until he could find a place to live. His job, believe it or not, was as a Drug and Alcohol Rehabilitation Counselor. Due to the error in procedure, all he got was a run-around, no loan, no grant, nothing.

As we learned over the past few days, this kind of a person we give a little more attention to and take some more time to accurately fill out his application. His first mistake was listing all of his last year's wages including overtime and bonuses. "Only your base pay" I reminded him. I juggled a few figures around but his earnings still required he see the SBA table first. But they were so close to the bottom of the formula that would allow you to apply for a government grant, I theorized that he would be passed over for a loan and sent to the grant table instead. Also, being technically SBA qualified I was able to escort him past the other long line and directly to the table. He recognized the person in charge and said he met him before. I said, loud enough for the SBA official to here, "Yes, but I suspect your corrected application will be too close to call and he will send you to the government grants table."

I wished him luck and went back out to the tent to interview more applicants. Less than two hours later, he came back into the tent with an armload of papers, a smile on his face and a dance to his step. He said they did exactly as I thought they would. He got the grant he needed, the unemployment and tax information he needed and, most important of all, a place to live at the same price he was paying before. He came in just to personally thank me and shake my hand for making that extra effort to help him out.

I never felt so good in all my life.

Some of the applicants brought in photos of their property damage. One lady had pictures of the red tagged apartment building she used to live in. However, she didn't know if she could claim her car because basically only the rear window was broken. I looked at the picture and there was her car, in the apartment carport, with the second floor walkway from between two of the buildings sticking through the rear window like a giant spear. The rest of the building was leaning precariously over her car but stopped just one foot short of crushing it. She thought that if the walkway could be removed, she could back her car up and drive off. Building removal doesn't quite work that way. I wrote her car off as a total loss.

Another client showed me pictures of his chimney that came down through the roof and was now sticking through the floor of his living room. He thought his house was safe because it used a piling type foundation instead of a cast concrete footing. I sent him to the building inspectors anyway but have kept in mind that a piling support would be much better. You would never have to worry about a foundation footing or a slab floor cracking that would write your house off as a total loss.

The low incidence of injuries was surprising to me. On Tuesday a medical center was set up in the center of the tent with four or five registered nurses with a supply of bandages, disinfectants and over-the-counter cold and flu medicines. Most of their business was treating people with colds or sore throats, particularly those that had to live in tent cities. But I had one client who tried to pass off his injury "only" as a gash in his leg when he had to jump over a wrought iron fence to get away from his apartment building during the quake. I took a look at his leg and saw the red lines of infection starting to spread out in his veins and, after finishing his application, I took him immediately over to the medics. The nurses thanked me for recognizing a problem that would only have gotten much worse.

The Crises Counselors were kept pretty busy also giving solace or even a shoulder to actually cry on. If the main quake and the seemingly unceasing aftershocks didn't stress a person out, the waiting in lines and the embarrassment of status reduction to charity handouts would. I had one lady who was obviously stressed out by all those factors. She started to cry a couple of times as I was filling out her application. Upon finishing, I said, "Instead of waiting in any of those other lines, I think you should see our stress counselors. Instead of these legal forms, you need to talk to somebody where you can just let it all out." So I took her inside the gym and to the private room set aside for the counseling. A little while later I walked by and the counselors were still with her as she was crying her heart out.

On Saturday, the 29th, all interviewers were called in to a special 8:00 AM meeting. We were to break off in splinter groups to meet with special stress counselors to handle our problems as well. Naturally the volunteers from LBNSY formed their own group and we met around a table in the tent. Now, we certainly appreciated the fact that these counselors came out to help us. Just having them just being there lifted our morale. But, they didn't know what kind of "Battleship Tough" people make up the work force of Long Beach Naval Shipyard. They didn't know that in the previous days whenever FEMA wanted us "Feds" to gather in a group or identify ourselves, one of us (often me) would call out, "Long Beach Naval Shipyard. The 'Can Do' shipyard."

After our counselor introduced himself and explained his purpose, he asked if anybody had something to say. I felt I knew these co-workers of mine well enough to start it off.

"My name is Dick Landgraff. I'm perhaps the senior employee here and the only one from the engineering department at this center. Hundreds of others from the engineering department and all the shops in the shipyard are now scattered throughout Southern California right now at the other disaster centers.

"As most of you already know, this coming Tuesday will be my last day as an employee of the Department of Defense and I will be retiring after over thirty-nine years of service at the Long Beach Naval Shipyard. Though I never thought that my last week of Federal Employment would be spent working in a Disaster Assistance Center.

"When it comes to stress, we know what stress is with the fears of the shipyard being put on the Base Closure Commission list. I have seen these people at our rallies and I have seen them at meetings where they try to give a speech supporting the shipyard. They are not professional speechmakers. Neither am I but I'm a bit of a ham so I get up there and also give a speech.

"But most importantly, we are a very proud group of people. I have personally worked on a number of projects, in the past third of a century or so, that I have been very proud to have been a part of. Those include the Polaris and Poseidon missile test programs, SEALAB II, the Bathyscaph Trieste surface support ship and, most recently, the elevator repair job on the USS Essex. That was a seemingly impossible job but we got that ship out on time and she was able to load her weapons and cargo on schedule.

"Most of us received the call to volunteer our services to assist FEMA on Friday night or Saturday morning. I was very pleased to see perhaps hundreds of my co-workers in Pasadena on Saturday night for the training class.

"For the most part, this has been the most rewarding experience of our lives. Yesterday I had one client who was given the run-around a few days before and was very upset by having to do it all over again. Less than two hours later he was smiling and personally made the effort to come over to this tent and shake my hand in thanks.

"And several of us here have had that same experience and it really makes you feel good that you have truly helped someone. However, in my thirty-nine years of service, I have NEVER been so proud of my fellow co-workers as I have been this past week.

"Gentlemen, I salute you."

Long Beach Naval Shipyard was the "Can Do" shipyard. We could do anything at any time. We could rebuild a Battleship. We could design and build a missile test support system. We could re-tube any boiler. We could fix any elevator. Or, as in the case of the Northridge earthquake, we could just reach out, lend a helping hand and offer a shoulder to cry on.

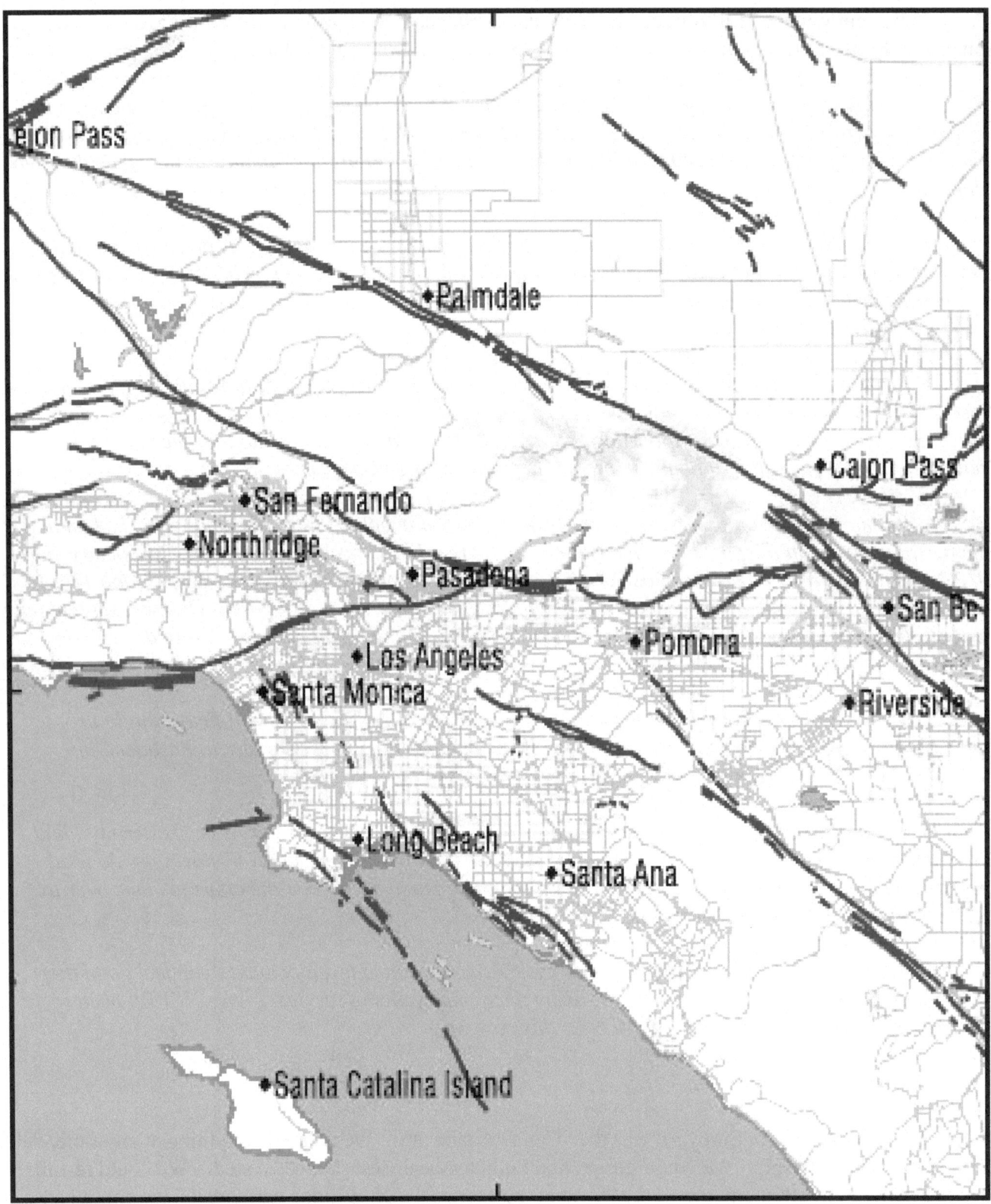

The fault map of the Los Angeles/Long Beach area. The long, almost straight one through Palmdale is the infamous San Andreas Fault. The one running through the "g" and above the "n" in Long Beach is the Newport-Inglewood fault that caused so much damage in the 1933 Long Beach Earthquake and caved in part of Torrance High School in 1934. Today, it runs directly under the interchange of the 710 and 405 freeways. Just WHO were the "geniuses" that designed that interchange?   USGS map

CHAPTER 24: WHEN YOUR NUMBER IS UP

Being a heavy industrial complex, the shipyard was not without injuries and deaths. As an apprentice I heard a couple of the old timers talking about a fatal accident that occurred across the channel at Todd shipbuilding. They lamented about the accident but said that there is about one death a month over at one of the private shipyards whereas, because of the strict safety regulations and the better construction of the Navy yard, we "only" had about one death a year.

Unfortunately, there have been several shipyarders whose luck ran out. Sometimes by errors of their own, sometimes by errors on the part of others or sometimes it was for their number to come up.

One of the times we had multiple fatalities in a single incident involved the test of a steam accumulator aboard a Destroyer. My stepfather, Mike Malia, from the machinery test section was assigned to perform the test. He inspected the accumulator within its small compartment of the boiler room but the machinists still had some more work to do. So, Mike went up to the Chief's mess for some coffee while the three machinists finished their work. Just then the accumulator blew up and killed all three machinists. I don't think it was ever determined just what caused the accumulator to blow. Basically, it was a case where the number was up for those three men, but not time for Mike Malia yet.

A double fatality that I personally witnessed was when I was a second year apprentice working aboard a Destroyer at Pier 2. Another Destroyer was tied outboard of the one I was on and three crewmen of that ship were assigned to paint the bow plating. Now, we have specially designed floating staging on steel rafts to float alongside ships just for that kind of work. However, somebody jury-rigged a floating stage by nailing dry dock staging to a wood raft camel. The camel was only supposed to be used as a floating spacer between a ship and pier or between ships moored alongside each other. The staging was standard Tube-Lox assembled from pipe and clamps and was mounted on two 2 X 12 planks merely for footing while sitting on the bottom of a dry dock. Those two items were never meant to be put together as a floating stage and who did it is unknown to me.

The camel was tied to the ship but NOT the staging. The sailors were wearing life jackets and safety belts. But two of the sailors tied themselves to the staging instead of the ship's liferails just a couple of feet above their heads. The third sailor was apprehensive about the stability of the contraption and had not tied his safety line to anything yet when a small harbor tug did a turnaround between Piers 2 and 3.

The wake of the tug's turn started rocking the staging violently and it capsized, carrying all three sailors with it. However, the one who had not tied his safety line yet was able to swim free and come up to the surface. A shop 99 electrician on the pier immediately kicked off his shoes and dived in to try to rescue the other two sailors. A sailor aboard the ship I was on dove off the bow also in a rescue attempt. But the murky water from the silt stirred up by the tug made it impossible to find the victims. A crane was called over and the hook was attached to the camel to upright the rig. However, as it did so, the staging ripped off the camel as it was only nailed to the wood rather than bolted.

About half an hour later, the dive boat arrived and it took the diver several minutes before he could find the staging as it had drifted in its fall toward the pier and was directly in front of the bow of the inboard Destroyer I was on. As the crane lifted the staging to the surface, the bodies of the two sailors were still tied to it. This was definitely a case of an accident waiting to happen. Somebody did an illegal assembly of two items that should never have been near each other. Somebody did not rig the mooring lines of the camel properly. The crewmen on the staging did not receive proper instruction as to where they should tie their safety lines. It was stupidity on the parts of several people.

Or maybe, that was just a bad luck ship. About a week later, another crewman was using a high speed, hand-held Bayflex grinder with a carbide disk to clean off a deck space for new terrazzo covering. To reach around legs of stowage racks, he removed the guard cover. The disk, at about 4,500-rpm, shattered and, because there was no guard cover to stop it, a jagged chunk of it cut into the sailor's groin. It sliced off part of his scrotum, but I later learned he would still be able to father children though with only one testicle. But it was still stupidity on the part of the injured for removing the guard on the grinder. A week after that, I saw another sailor being carried off between two husky men in a fireman's chair carry. His pants leg was ripped open exposing his lower thigh and upper calf that were scalded by boiling water. I saw him a couple of days later, hobbling around with his leg heavily bandaged up.

Then there is the type of person you don't want to stand too close to. We had a man in shop 64 that seemed to have a black cloud follow him around wherever he went. His first accident was while working in a dry dock and an oil barrel rolled off the side of the ship and struck him. Fortunately, the barrel was spinning end over end and caught him on the outer spin and merely broke his shoulder that also gave him a sore neck for quite a while.

His second accident, which was partly his fault, was when he was riding on the side of a stage-moving tractor. This is an illegal procedure but two others were doing the same thing and the driver did not stop them. They were driving down Pier 1, while it was under reconstruction to be raised because of subsidence. A two-foot section of concrete pier had not been butted together yet and the tractor went down into the hole throwing all three riders off. The bad luck guy broke an arm in that one.

His third and final accident, before quitting the shipyard, was while working in the shop where his supervisors figured he would be safer there. Wrong. While ripping a board on a table saw, the blade hit a knot splitting the board and sending a lance-like piece through his side.

One of the most gruesome fatal accidents we had occurred aboard an Aircraft Carrier. An electrician's helper was on a narrow crawl space by one of the aircraft elevators when somebody activated the hydraulic stanchions to raised position. He was lying right on top of one of the stanchions and it impaled him against a low overhang. Yes, the stanchion controls should have been tagged out or inactivated at another control point. Blame had to be shared by victim, the mechanic he was working with, their supervisor and the person who activated the stanchions.

A very poignant, as well as gruesome, death was that of an elderly shipyard worker who only had a few months to go before retirement. When I first started at the shipyard in 1954, the tops of the dry docks were level with the street. Only handrails and chains kept people from falling in. The open rails and chains, however, allowed a person climbing back out of the dock a clear view of any truck or crane traffic going by. The tracks for the portal cranes were only about four feet away from the edge of the dry dock and overhangs of the crane structure and wheel trucks closed that gap to only about one foot.

But, due to subsidence, whenever a ship was docked or undocked, the northeast part of the shipyard would flood. Dry Dock I finally had twenty-foot high double walls built around it. Dry Dock 2 had a six-foot high wall built around the edge and Dry Dock 3 a four-foot high wall. Because of these walls, it was difficult to see if a crane was coming by as you got to the top of the steps at the steel gate in the wall. The steps are actually recessed into the sides of the dry dock walls, so vision to traffic above is totally blocked. Oh yes, there are signs at the top of the steps to look out for cranes. But this person was in his sixties and by the time he climbed those forty-five steps to the top, he was exhausted and didn't see the crane coming around the corner from behind him as he stepped through the gate.

Believe it or not, this was the fault of bean counters. Prior to that incident it was a requirement to have a trackwalker accompany any of those track mounted gantry cranes and be within a couple of steps of one of the four emergency stop buttons at the corners of the crane. The trackwalkers job was to walk along with the crane as it was moving to make sure nobody got in the way when exiting a dry dock. But some cost-conscious office decided that was "feather-bedding" and warning signs at the gates would be sufficient and much cheaper. However, after this man was crushed against the dry dock wall, the trackwalker billets were opened up again.

"B"

STEADFAST (AFDM 14) in drydock.

On the left side of this photo you can see how close the Crane tracks are to the dry dock wall.

Our divers have perhaps the most hazardous jobs of all, yet their accident rate is extremely low because they never work alone, always work in teams and follow every safety precaution in the book and some not in the book yet. They are employed as riggers, but are also qualified as welders, mechanics and metal workers as well as certified divers. They are trained in the old MK-5 "Hard Hat" suits before even looking at SCUBA or MK-1 rebreather gear.

Up until the 1960's, almost all underwater work done by our divers was in the "Hard Hat" suits. It was a very good suit and even with 120 pounds of helmet and weights, it could be inflated with compressed air to control buoyancy for working underneath a ship. But the lines of air hose and comm wire made that suit hazardous as a loop to the bottom could get snagged on some junk lying in the silt.

Eventually, SCUBA started to replace the old suits and *SEALAB II* led the way in developing underwater, wireless communication. By the time the shipyard closed, Mk-1 rebreather gear and SCUBA were the standard.

But during the reactivation and modernization of the Battleship *New Jersey*, in 1982, something went wrong. One of our divers, Mike McCarthy, was under the ship, at Pier 1 and didn't come back up. When the emergency divers went down to look for him, they found his body at an intake scoop for the boilers. There are splitter bars across the opening so large objects could not be drawn into the three-foot diameter pipe. If it had been activated, the draw of the water would have been strong enough to pin a man there. However, investigation found that the injection pumps had not been activated. So it is still a mystery as to what actually happened to Mike to trap him in that sea scoop.

Every shop had a sign, with number cards, showing how many days they had gone without a lost time accident. Now, that includes non-fatal injuries as well as fatalities. A lost time accident is where the victim has been injured seriously enough to need time off from work to recuperate. Most injuries were minor enough to allow the victim to return to work the same shift though perhaps with stitches as what happened to me once on swing shift. But, being a heavy industry those things happen. More often than not, it is human error that causes this. Generally, it is the victim that gets most of the blame though often others who contributed to creating the hazardous situation can also be identified.

Then we have lost coworkers who were completely innocent but were victims of someone else's complete irresponsibility. Manuel Quintana was one of those lost by irresponsible actions of a stranger. We were just starting to allow flextime for people in Building 300 who rode in carpools consisting of shop personnel who got off fifteen minutes earlier. Manuel took advantage of the shift in hours to not only satisfy his carpool partner but it gave him an opportunity to get home a little earlier for his children. His death occurred on the Gerald Desmond Bridge when a car, coming from the opposite direction and driven by a drunken driver jumped the center divider, literally sailed over one car and tee-boned into the car Manuel was in. Both Manuel and the driver were decapitated. What happened to the DUI who caused their deaths? He climbed out of the wreckage on his own but cussing about losing his car.

Then there are the deaths that nobody can do absolutely anything about. During the modernization of *New Jersey*, the Rigger Leader for the installation of all of the heaviest items, especially the armor plate over Combat Engagement Center, was Alfred LeBlanc. Those plates are just under a ton each and he manhandled them himself to make sure everything went exactly where it should go. He was as tough as they came. **Battleship Tough**.

Al spent twenty-two years active duty in the Navy before coming to the shipyard as a civilian rigger. With fifteen years shipyard time in as well as his Navy time, he was very close to retirement. When the *New Jersey* went out on her first sea trial, Al was assigned a bunk to ride the ship and serve as the lead rigger for any testing (such as release of the life rafts). Though he had very little to do at sea, We always had a lead mechanic aboard from every shop when doing full assessments on major sea trials. Also he was proud to have been selected as one of the ship riders. As he was boarding the ship, he recalled his thirty-seven years of service and said, *"Well, when I go to sea on this one, I will have been on them all."*

On September 27, 1982, Al claimed to be feeling very tired and went to his bunk for a nap. There, he died peacefully in his sleep. No fault could be laid on anyone. There was no accident. No one made any mistakes. It's just that Alfred LeBlanc's number was up.

CHAPTER 25
THE *NEW JERSEY* IN 1968

Okay, some of you readers who prompted and pushed me into writing this book only want to read about the Battleships. Well, this chapter will deal with LBNSY involvement with the USS *New Jersey* (BB-62) when she was reactivated in 1968. Some details of the Battleships I have already covered in other chapters. Therefore I will (hopefully) not repeat myself.

Though the shipyard worked on other Battleships during and shortly after World War II, and even did an overhaul on the *Iowa* in the 1950's, I can only address the work we did on those gorgeous examples of engineering and construction from 1968 to 1991. Those are the times I worked on them and can give you some firsthand accounts.

When *New Jersey* was reactivated in 1968 for her Viet Nam duty, Philadelphia Naval Shipyard was the planning and reactivation yard. Shortly after she arrived at LBNSY, planning yard status was **transferred** to LBNSY as we were expected to be her homeport over the next few years.

I was a GS-9 engineering draftsman in the Fittings design section and Jim Bibeau was my section supervisor. When I heard about the Big J coming in, and some final antenna and fittings work that needed to be done, I walked up to Jim at his desk and said, "Jim. I want the *New Jersey*."

He shrugged his shoulders, winced a bit and replied, "Technically, a GS-11 can be a project leader. Not a GS-9."

I argued, "But if I have the Battleship, I can prove my project leader capabilities."

Jim thought about it for a moment then said, "Well, officially Bob Riha will be the project leader. But otherwise, she's your ship."

The *New Jersey* first arrived in California by way of San Diego. Rod Theobald, from the Structural section, and I went down there for a shipcheck of items still needed to be done before her deployment to Southeast Asia. As I was driving down the highway toward the Coronado Bridge, I could look across the channel and see the Battleship berthed at Pier Juliet on North Island. She almost seemed dwarfed by a Carrier in front and an AOE in back. But as I walked up toward the brow (Gangway or Gangplank to you land lubbers), her size became very apparent. The ships are large, but their freeboard (height from the waterline to the main deck) is quite low and the compact (though very tall) superstructure gives them the appearance of seeming smaller or further away. I had heard that the far away effect was an inadvertent design feature that, hopefully, may confuse enemy range finders on shore. The optical range finders may be correct in calculating a range of, say, 20,000 yards but the observer may think the ship is at least 24,000 yards away. Thus, his first rounds of shore fire would be too far over. The ship would then have time to set her guns on the shore batteries that would be too late in adjusting for the optical illusion of being further away than she really was.

When the *New Jersey* arrived at Long Beach, Bob Riha and I went out to the end of Pier Echo to watch her come in. She was an impressive, and massive, sight as she entered the channel between the end of the Mole and Pier J. As she tied up to the pier, Bob, a former crewman of the Cruiser *Columbus*, said, "Well, the Navy is secure again." As an interesting side note, Jim Bibeau also served aboard the *Columbus* as well as John Bauer's father.

The most important job we had was to finish the installation of the AN/ULQ-6B Electronics Countermeasures (ECM) antennas to be mounted on the outriggers at 09 level. Crawling out there was no fun but I still had little fear of heights. Since I was more than 50 feet (more like 70 feet) above the first "splatter" deck should I fall off, I was paid 10% high pay for each day I had to crawl out there.

The next most important job was relocating the padeyes on top of Turret II for the ammunition Replenishment-At-Sea tripod. Mike Kolb, a young engineer recently hired, designed the padeye relocations.

Two 35-foot whip antennas were to be mounted above the bridge windows at 05 level. According to NAVELEX guidance drawings, they were to be at a permanent forward tilt of about 15 degrees. Normally, we would have designed a support platform of solid plating but I was concerned about muzzle blast from Turret II if it should be trained inboard at its most extreme limits and highest elevation. We did not have all of the structural drawings shipped in from Philadelphia yet, so I went out to the ship and asked the Turret captain what the limit of traverse was. He shrugged his shoulders and said "That's a good question. I don't even know for sure so let's climb into the turret and read the dials." So we both climbed into the Turret to check the limit marks on the azimuth indicator.

I did not know then that the elevation of the barrels were restricted to 42 degrees (to prevent excessive loading on the roller path) and drew a plan view of the Turret rotated 140 degrees back with the muzzles up at 45 degrees. I then superimposed the 05 level and was able to measure a distance from the muzzles to where the antennas would be.

In the technical library we only had one manual on muzzle blast of Navy guns. No other studies were done until 1982 when the *New Jersey* was reactivated again. I turned the job of calculating muzzle blast over to a real sharp engineer from Milwaukee, Wisconsin, Fernando G. Gonzales. Yes, a Hispanic from my own hometown. He even habitated Sharkey's Tavern where my family used to hang out.

I sketched up a drawing of a platform with ¾-inch diameter holes punched in a quilt-like pattern and had Dante P. Mangione draw the plan. The holes would allow overpressure from the muzzle blast to pass through the support plating without ripping it off of the bridge front.

One of the lesser jobs we had was to install mounting brackets for overside floodlights. The lights were for security while the ship may be in a RVN harbor but infested with NVN or VC frogmen.

One day, while up on 04 level checking some minor items, Captain Snyder was giving a briefing to some planners about some improvements he would like to have. One thing he pointed out was that the peepholes in the 04 level of the Conning Tower did not have their crank-up windows as the 05 level did. He said, "They (*the North Vietnamese*) have nothing over there that can sink this ship. But they can hurt it. The fireball from a major caliber warhead can go right through those peepholes and injure or kill people behind them. I would like to see something done about that."

I did some sketches later to offer as peephole protection. As I said, the original plans and microfilms had not come in from Philly yet. In 1981, I finally found the plans that designed the peephole covers. But as of 1990, when the ship was decommissioned forever, nothing was ever done about it.

The very last thing the shipyard did to the ship, on the day before it deployed to WESTPAC, was to cut off the 40mm gun tubs on the Main Deck forward of Turret I. So, when you view pictures of the *New Jersey* from her Nam period, if the gun tubs are there that is before she came to Long Beach. If the gun tubs are gone, that is after deployment.

Overall, the 1968 modifications to the ship were almost insignificant. Though the 20mm guns were removed in the Korean War, the 40mm guns remained until Viet Nam. Philly removed them but kept the gun tubs. The tub on 01 level, starboard of Turret II was temporarily used as a "swimming pool" for a photo op. Then the ship's doctor put it off limits because it had no recirc system and wasn't chlorinated.

The deckhouse "ears" were installed to enclose the electronic gear and provide a support base for the AN/ULQ-6B ECM antenna outrigger frameworks between 09 and 010 levels. A couple of CHAFFROC launchers were installed on 03-½ level. A helicopter flight deck was added 8 inches above the main deck aft of Turret III.

Air conditioning improvements consisted only of package A/C units placed in some compartments near any doorway to provide air. Some electronics upgrading was done to support the latest in RADAR and radio communications including adding that ugly DISCONE/DISCAGE antenna up on the bow. Admiral Halsey's cabin on 02 level was kept intact and furnished as a memorial but his Flag Plot on 03 level was void of equipment and designated only as an Unassigned Space.

I got to know one of the electronics officers aboard the ship, a Lieutenant Wilkinson. He was a very congenial gentleman and gave me a *New Jersey* tie clasp as a gift. Before the ship deployed, he asked if there was anything else he could do for me. I asked that one of their 16-inch shells be written up with my sister-in-law's name on it, Kinga Biro who had to be left behind in Hungary at the age of two when her mother, brother and older sister (my wife) escaped in 1956. I was told later, though I don't know how true it is, that it was that shell that took 20-feet off the top of a mountain in Viet Nam taking out a critical observation post.

One story I heard about the ship seemed too good to be true and I passed it off as a scuttlebutt joke. But years later, Steve Torres who was a crewman aboard the USS *Bronstein* (FF-1037) confirmed that it actually did happen.

One night, in the Gulf of Tonkin, the *Bronstein* was on patrol and spotted a ship approaching on RADAR. By signal lights, *Bronstein* challenged the ship. "This is a United States warship. Identify yourself or you will be fired upon."

Bronstein received no reply and sent out the challenge again, **twice**. After the third challenge the New Jersey replied: "This is the United States Battleship *New Jersey*. You may fire when ready."

Now, the above has been debunked as an "Urban Legend" and the incident never happened. However, Steve swore up and down that it really did happen and the bridge crew was nearly falling on the deck laughing that they had just challenged a Battleship. But proper signaling techniques and code words were used instead of the above version as told today. A Battleship normally would never have identified herself by her actual name and would have used her code name instead (I have heard it was *On Rush)*. Also her escort, the USS *England* (DLG-22), should have also been within *Bronstein's* RADAR scan. Though IFF (Identification, Friend or Foe) electronic signals would have been transmitted from *New Jersey*, as a matter of procedure, until identification could be confirmed, *Bronstein* still had to challenge the ship.

It could have been a cargo ship carrying war materials to Haiphong. It could also have been a merchant ship converted into an unarmored cruiser/raider like the German Q ships *Atlantis* and *Penguin* of World War II. So, the *Bronstein* was merely carrying out standard procedures.

Then one evening, some years ago, I received an email from a Battleship enthusiast back east. He contacted Admiral Snyder, the *New Jersey's* commanding officer at the time of the purported incident, to ask if the story was true or not. Here is his answer:

"I do not remember the name of the ship but do remember the skipper was a Lieutenant.

"My policy was not to release messages without my personal O.K. My OOD ignored the first two messages from the small Naval vessel since they had her on radar and the visual call sign identified the sending ship. But when the flashing light message saying 'unknown vessel identify yourself or we will open fire' my OOD called me right away. The reason I had our signalmen use the 24-inch searchlight is that I was slightly ticked that the other Naval vessel (sending ship) should have been able to tell the difference between a Battleship on radar and a North Vietnam gun runner or fishing boat.

"I was in the habit of not signing messages with our name since the message always had a heading telling who sent it and to whom it was addressed. I admit my reply was rather tense and not in the best Naval tradition but we on the **New Jersey** *felt nothing could hurt us and the crew enjoyed my reply which was 'AA (standing for 'unknown vessel') NEW JERSEY. BB 62. OPEN FIRE WHEN READY, FEAR GOD, DREADNOUGHT.'*

"I do not think your quote is that far off."
J. EDWARD SNYDER JR.

Well folks, there you have it, straight from the Commanding Officer of the *New Jersey*.

Quite a number of old time Battleship people worked on the Big J that year. The structural planner was John McFaul who was a shipfitter back in the New York Naval Shipyard (Brooklyn) in WW II. His most memorable job on a Battleship was installing the foundations for the 20mm guns on the USS *South Dakota* (BB-57). There have been numerous debates as to just how many anti-aircraft guns were on that ship because in one battle she single handedly took out no less than twenty-six Japanese airplanes. So, since John was the man that installed all the machine gun foundations, I asked him how many guns he installed. His answer was, "I put so many on that ship, I really lost count. I had a wood mock-up of the foundation and a pier full of guns. My helper and I just went around setting the mock-up down, checked the periphery of the gun swing simulating a gunner in his back-strap harness and set a permanent steel foundation in that place. Other shops that were to have a vent duct or pipe or a goose-necked handling davit installed had to place their helpers over those spots for fear I would put a machine-gun there." John added, "I put so many guns on that ship that some folks at the shipyard wanted to rename her the USS *Porcupine*." So there you have it, historians. Even the man who mounted all those guns put so many down even **he** lost count.

Bob Hartley in our plan coordination section made sure he was on the *New Jersey* team, both in 1968 and in 1981. Bob was a gunners mate in the main batteries of the USS *Texas* (BB-35). He was pretty proud of that ship as it served in both World Wars, **"B"** the Vera Cruz embargo (Halls of

Montezuma) and crippled the Barbary Pirates (The Shores of Tripoli). You "Devil Dogs" know what **that** means.

You would think that by 1981 most of the old Battleship sailors would prefer to sit back in their rocking chairs and just read about the recall of the ships. Bob Ballinger of NAVSEA was not going to sit in a rocker as he served on the *Wisconsin* in WW II. Also there was an electrician on loan to us from Philadelphia who served on the *Indiana*. I'll be telling you about Don Wolcott who served on both the *Maryland* and *North Carolina* in a later chapter.

And those are only the people I personally met and worked with. How many other Battleship sailors from the past wars answered the call may never be known. It's just something about those ships that keeps bringing them back.

It was very disappointing to hear that the *New Jersey* was going to be decommissioned again so soon in 1969. During her deployment, she was able to cover the entire width of Viet Nam where North and South meet. The country is only about 20 miles wide at that point and the ship's guns were able to lob shells into Cambodia to take out the Ho Chi Min trail. She was so impressive that the peace talks came to a halt because the communist North Vietnamese considered her too imposing and refused to continue negotiations unless she was pulled out.

Perhaps "imposing" is not the right word. I believe "effective" is a more accurate description of the Battleship's value over there.

If you check the dates, about the time *New Jersey* was bombarding the Ho Chi Min trail across the entire width of Viet Nam, the Cambodian government had a quick turn-around of leadership. While their pro-communist leader was visiting Peking, they formed an anticommunist government and asked President Nixon to send in armored units to take out the trail on its western end. For all effective purposes, the Viet Nam war came to a halt because the Ho Chi Min trail was blocked on the west by tanks and decimated on the east by the *New Jersey*.

The political ploy by the communists to remove the Battleship hit the right chords in a non-supportive Congress swayed by crying "Flower Children" that were actually dupes of communist propaganda.

To think that the reactivation of only one Battleship was so effective it was made a high priority issue at the peace talks. One can only wonder what the discussions would have been if we reactivated all four Battleships, sailed them into Haiphong Harbor, under appropriate fighter air cover, and rearranged their waterfronts and industrial centers. The shelling could be done without touching the "friendly" ships in harbor except popping the eardrums of the crews. Then all Henry Kissinger would have to ask for at the peace talks would be what date the North Vietnamese would like to sign the peace treaty written under our terms.

As an aside, here is *New Jersey's* "HIT LIST":

New Jersey's record for Viet Nam cruise.
GUN DAMAGE ASSESSMENT, (1968 - 1969 Combined)
MAIN BATTERY
Structures destroyed - 439
Structures damaged - 259
Bunkers destroyed - 596
Bunkers damaged - 250
Artillery sites neutralized - 19
Automatic weapons, AA and mortar sites silenced - 35
Secondary explosions - 130
Roads interdicted - 26
Meters of trench lines rendered unusable - 1,925
Cave and tunnel complexes destroyed - 75
Enemy killed in action (confirmed) - 136
Enemy killed in action (probable) - 17
Troop movements stopped - 12

SECONDARY BATTERY
Structures destroyed - 56
Structures damaged - 92
Bunkers destroyed - 59
Bunkers damaged - 73
Artillery sites neutralized - 2
Mortar sites silenced - 6
Waterborne Logistic Craft (WBLC) destroyed (Sea Dragon) - 9
Secondary explosions - 46
Roads interdicted - 26
Enemy killed in action (confirmed) - 1o
Enemy killed in action (probable) - 7

When *New Jersey* was ordered for deactivation, I lamented a comment I made to Rod Theobald the previous year when we were inspecting her in San Diego. Both Rod and I felt very privileged to be working on her and I noted, sort of off-handedly, that "This may be the last Battleship ever to serve again." When she was decommissioned in Bremerton, I was angry with myself for being so accurate in my prediction.

But twelve years later, I was never so glad as to have been so wrong.

Perhaps the most popular photo of *New Jersey* during her Viet Nam deployment is this one of her firing the center barrel of Turret II. That barrel got used more than the other eight as it always fired the first "Sighting In" round which often did the job just by itself.   Naval Historical Center photo #NH90639

The same photo above has been used in all kinds of souvenirs including a decorative plate this author bought in the Scandinavian tourist town of Solvang, California. Author's collection

The *New Jersey* at LBNSY in 1968. She was at the South end of Pier Echo with her escort USS *England* (CG-22) ahead. Photo by Denny Beauregard

The *New Jersey* in Panama Canal enroute to LBNSY. The AN/ULQ-6B antennas are not yet installed nor the twin 35 foot whip antennas at the 05 level and the forward 40mm gun tubs are still in place.

Photo by Robert M. Cierl in NavSource Online

The *New Jersey* after final outfitting at LBNSY with the AN/ULQ-6B and the 35 foot whip antennas installed. Photo by Robert M. Cierl in NavSource Online

CHAPTER 26: CALLING ALL BATTLESHIPS
For the reader: There are some minor revisions too small to rate a "B" notation.

In 1981, rumors started going around that the *New Jersey* was going to be reactivated again. In 1970 we shipped all of the Battleship plans back to a storage facility in St. Louis. Suddenly they all showed up "on our doorstep" which gave some credence to the rumors. John Shuey (the supervisor of plan files) and Robert "Bob" Blount (our personnel supervisor) didn't know what to do with them. Bob retired but when he was told about this book, he wrote a letter describing that first encounter with the drawings.

"Reading about the New Jersey *plans brings back a lot of memories – some good. I can close my eyes and see John Shuey on the flatbed trailer that brought them to LBNSY. I got a phone call from some guy in Supply that nine pallets of boxes had arrived and they wanted to know what to do with them. When John, Jan Kirk and I got there, they were still on the trailer.*

"I was already in trouble for getting the plans, and I didn't have any place to put that many, especially if we had to sort them when we took them out of the boxes. Somebody in Code 140 finally came up with a little building at the end of Pier Echo and we just put them on the floor out there.

"Because the shipyard commander didn't want to get them in the first place, I couldn't get any overtime to get them in the system, or really, do anything with them – and all those civilians who were hot to trot to have them just looked the other way when I asked for help (they didn't want to be connected with only a "rumor"). I didn't get out of the doghouse until the ship was officially assigned, and really, I didn't get out then because I had "embarrassed" Code 100 and 200. It came back to haunt me several times over the next few years."

In hindsight, we can now sort out the confusion and communications losses relating to the shipment of the drawings. After the *New Jersey* was inactivated in 1969, we boxed up all the Battleship drawings and stored them in Audavee Bransford's office/art studio. Audie was our shipyard artist that painted portraits of people and ships as well as general graphics arts in the form of posters or retirement cartoons. Audie wasn't too happy about that huge pile of boxes stacked up where his storage nook should have been and was quite happy to see them shipped to St. Louis for "permanent" storage.

When the drawings were shipped back to us in 1981, the reason for confusion lay in the fact that very few remembered that we were **now** the official planning yard for the Battleships. I had a copy of the planning yard assignment letter that I had kept on file since 1968 for a memento and distributed copies to Bob and a few others.

The shipyard commander at the time, Captain Gildea, was viewing the talk of reactivating the *New Jersey* as just a rumor. Washington never informed him, until later; that it was not just a rumor and the project was going to be much more complex than he could imagine. Later, Captain Gildea became one of the greatest supporters of the Battleship Program, but I suspect he was still ticked off that lower echelon people under his command knew more about the truth of the Battleships than he was told.

Finally the drawings were transferred up to the third floor plan files in Building 300 and pigeonhole storage was found for them. Then John Shuey got an order from NAVSEA to make copies of all the drawings, including microfilm reels, and send them to Supships Boston. This upset many of us because we were supposed to be the planning yard. We wondered how Boston got into the act. As it turned out, Supships Boston was to develop the general guidance drawings and Long Beach would develop the detail drawings based upon the guidance drawings.

In the structural section, where I had transferred to in 1976 when promoted to GS-11, we were finishing up the designs of the aluminum appliqué armor for the *Spruance* class Destroyers. At about the same time, the shops were finishing up installation of the ammo magazine armor for the USS *Tarawa* (LHA-1). Lastly, Nate Fernandez was finishing up the structural modification designs on the USS *Norton Sound* (AVM-1) for the first Vertical Launch System (VLS) module installation.

In May of 1981 I walked into Jim Bibeau's office who was now the branch supervisor in charge of three design sections, Fittings, Structural and Foundations. I said, "Jim, I hear the Battleship *New Jersey* is coming back out. I want her. You let me have her, though unofficially, in 1968 and I want her again."

Jim said, "Well, those are just rumors so far. But let me think about it." As I turned and started out the door, Jim said, "You got her."

In the last week of June, we were all planning how to spend our Independence Day weekend when Jim called me into his office. He said that he was supposed to go up to Bremerton with Tom Bowles, our chief design engineer, and Homer Dixon, the supervisor of our fire control and weapons section. They were to leave on July 5th but he had another conference to go to in San Diego so he wanted me to go in his place.

The trip to Bremerton, according to what he was told, was just a management walk-through on the *New Jersey* to see if reactivation was plausible. Since I was going to be the structural project leader and was an experienced designer in fittings, masts, antenna platforms or anything that had a wire rope or synthetic line attached, I would be a proper replacement for him. Also, while I was there, would I do him a favor and deliver a package of drawings to Supships Seattle. They were for a different class of ship, but I could get them there faster than through regular shipping channels.

Just a walk-through? I reminded Jim of that Battleship reactivation feasibility study, done by Rosenblatt Design Agency, that he gave me to read a couple of weeks before. He just shrugged and said that was only a general concept and nobody had any idea yet on what to do. So Jim actually was hoping that the rumors were true and assigned this ex-tank driver to a ship where it takes **four** M41-A1 tanks and **one M75 armored personnel carrier** to weigh as much as only **one** of the 16"/50 gun barrels. **"B"** I corrected the number of tracked vehicles above and I still have my old driver's I.D. for them.

As the plans became available in plan files, I had collected a copy of the Booklet of General Drawings and a few others that I thought would be handy on the shipcheck. I also packed a new set of blue coveralls that I had sewn a LBNSY patch on. Oh and we were also told to bring our hard hats. For just a walk-through?

I flew up to Seattle with Tom and Homer, rented my own car because of the errand I had to run up to Supships at the North end of Seattle. When I delivered the plans, my contact man said they envied us for getting the Battleship and we were probably picked instead of them because of the problems they had with the *Enterprise*. He also wished us Luck in keeping within the 365-million dollar budget.

I just said I'm sure the *Enterprise* had nothing to do with the decision as we had already been assigned Planning Yard status in 1968. I was a bit dumbfounded however, as he just told me more about what was going on than our own shipyard commander, chief engineer and all others at Long Beach knew. As I rode the ferry across Puget Sound to Bremerton, I wondered just what really was coming off. The only thing I was fairly certain of now was that the Battleship *New Jersey* was going to be reactivated and Long Beach Naval Shipyard was going to do the job.

The next morning, Tom, Homer and I boarded the *New Jersey* at the inactive ship pier in Bremerton. Across the pier was the *Missouri* that still provided public visitor access to the forward part of the main deck and 01 level, where the surrender plaque was. Tom was in his casual suit and Homer was also just wearing casual attire. They looked at me rather strangely as I was in my coveralls with brief case full of plans, measuring tape and Polaroid camera.

We were ordered to assemble in the wardroom on the main deck. That wardroom was absolutely packed with people, none of whom I knew. As informal introductions went around, I found they were from NAVSEA, NAVELEX, NAVWEPS, Supships Boston, Rosenblatt, Gibbs & Cox, John J. McMullen and a few others I have forgotten.

Standing in the center of the room, in blue coveralls similar to mine, was a stocky, middle-aged man with a small mustache. He introduced himself as Ray Schull who was the head Program Manager for the reactivation **and** modernization of the Battleships. He announced that modernization would consist of installing eight Armored Box Launchers (ABL's) for thirty-two TOMAHAWK cruise missiles, four sets of four cell Harpoon launchers for sixteen HARPOON anti-ship cruise missiles, central air conditioning, four CIWS anti-missile "Gatling" guns, new RADAR and communications facilities with a new mast and new electronics spaces.

Then he said, ***"By January of 1983, the Battleship* New Jersey *will be reactivated, modernized and in commission.***

"By January of 1984, the Battleship* Iowa *will be reactivated, modernized and in commission.

"By January of 1985, the Battleship* Missouri *will be reactivated, modernized and in commission.

"And by January of 1986 the Battleship* Wisconsin *will be reactivated, modernized and in commission."

You could have heard a pin drop in that wardroom. Everyone was totally stunned. Then you could hear the whispers of response, more to themselves than to anyone else around them. But the most predominant expression was, "We are going to have a **REAL** Navy again."

The rest of the week was a madhouse with people crawling and climbing all over that ship. I even went across the pier to the *Missouri* and had the female officer on board let me back through the chain link gates aft so I could get some overall side shots of *New Jersey*. Some of the visitors looked at me sort of weird though. By that time the word was out that *New Jersey* was going to be pulled out of Bremerton. Seeing some of us engineering types from *New Jersey* now aboard *Missouri* got them spooked into thinking we were going to grab the *Missouri* from them as well. Actually, we were, but not for another two years and we were specifically **ordered** not to say anything like that.

The biggest arrangement problem we had was where to put all eight Tomahawk ABL's. You see, when the Navy decided to bring the Battleships back out, Captain Biers, who was then in charge of the initial concepts before being taken over by Captain Champlain, the original modernization called for only four ABL's and two sets of Harpoon launchers. Also, Congress was promised that the reactivation and modernization of the first ship would only be 365 million dollars. Congress agreed to the price, but only if we **doubled up** on the Tomahawks and Harpoons. When we finished *New Jersey* with the extra weapons, (added on by Congress) we completed the ship with a Champlain taste on a Biers budget. Thanks to Bobby Wilson (HAVC design) for coming up with that analogy.

Removing the four aft 5"/38 gun mounts allowed room to build port and starboard deckhouses to support four of the ABL's. The quad 40mm gun tubs port and starboard of the after stack, that were originally designed to be supports for boat cranes, were large enough to take two Harpoon racks each, thus giving Congress its 16 Harpoons. But it was finding acreage for the other four ABL's that was the worst problem. I even considered mounting them on top of Turrets II and III in place of the 40mm gun tubs that were to be removed anyway. But fixed cable and air supply runs of the Tomahawk programming and launching system squashed that idea very quickly.

About the only place we could find room was amidships on the 03-½ level. Two ABL's each would be placed port and starboard and facing outwards (as they are shown in the movie "Under Siege" which is **very** wrong).

Now, the way an ABL works is that just 35 seconds before firing it raises up to a 35-degree angle. The exhaust of the booster is 6,000 degrees Kelvin and contains about 20% Hydrochloric acid. Jim Snyder, the Structural Program Manager from NAVSEA, asked me if it would be possible to build an armored "wall" in between the port and starboard launchers that would also support ablative material to resist the heat and acids of the boosters.

That shield would be right on centerline and over a main vent intake to the main machinery spaces. Protective louvers that would close when an ABL was raised would be installed over those intakes at frame 115. As it is, they were anyway though in hindsight I don't think they were really that necessary.

And here is why. While looking down at the deck from the 05 level, I suddenly had a wild idea. So I suggested, "Why don't we mount the launchers facing each other? You are not going to fire both port and starboard launchers at the same time, so when you raise one, it fires over the top of the others. Just like the Harpoons do now on the *Spruances*. All I need to do then is design a low deflector shield on the outboard sides of the deckhouse to protect the small boats stowed below."

I like the looks some people get on their faces when such a simple solution to a previously impossible problem is offered. Even to this day Nat Choate, who was the Machinery Program Manager from NAVSEA, says that was talked about for weeks afterwards and everyone was almost in shock at the simplicity of it.

The fun really began after we got back to Long Beach and it changed many people's lives forever. I reported to Jim Bibeau's office to tell him what really was going to happen with the Battleships. He said he was already briefed by Tom Bowles and asked if I thought I could still handle the job.

"Watch me."

At that time, we had no permanent section supervisor in the Structural section. Throughout the next year and a half, three engineers sat in as temporary supervisors; Dean Archambeau, Isaac Cavalier and Jim Kaping. But the orders from Jim Bibeau were "The only job we are working is the *New Jersey*. Dick is in charge. Your temporary Supervisor will sign your time cards and handle personnel problems." Thank goodness they would handle the personnel problems because we did have one hard case of a new hire. I won't say any more about that because I would rather forget it.

While waiting for Boston to develop the guidance drawings that gave us time to finish up other ship projects and clear the decks for the Battleships. A hiring program was instituted to bring in trainee draftsmen and I was asked to give a class on compartment numbering. Only one person in that class, Lee Upshaw, cared to pay attention to what I was trying to teach and he also seemed to be very knowledgeable about Battleships. He looked vaguely familiar, but I couldn't place him at the time.

Lee was assigned to the Structural section under me and I found his historical knowledge of Battleships extremely useful. On the side he has a ship model building shop where he builds fiberglass hulls and casts resin fittings and gun mounts for other model builders. When it comes to ship histories, he is blessed with total recall. Also his personal familiarity to me was solved when I found out he was an apprentice gunsmith in one of the gun shops Chuck Dietl and I were part owners of five years before. Today we are still good friends and he is doing quite well with his ship model shop.

When it came to designing the CIWS mounts, Nate Fernandez was the logical choice as he had designed them for several other ships. Nate had a "smart-alec" personality but a hell of an engineer.

Anything I designed in armor modifications I immediately turned over to Mike Said for review and comments. Though Mike was not experienced with ricocheting bullets, shell case splinters or grenade fragments as I was, he was a very quick study. A few years later he transferred back to Washington, D.C. into the Survivability branch of NAVSEA.

Over in the Fittings section, right next to our structural section, Jeff Arthurs took on the design of the new tripod mast. But he did it strictly by computer using only centroids of the members. Not the way us old timers would have done it, but it worked.

Before the reactivation and modernization era of the *Iowa* class Battleships started, all drawings that designed the ships from the keel up and including their modifications throughout WW II, Korea and Viet Nam totaled 2,693 drawings comprised of 2,992 sheets. Almost all of them were categorized under the old "S" group system. Some drawings required two or more sheets, but under the "S" group system, a single drawing could be over twenty feet long. The BACD (Basic Alteration Class Drawing) system incorporated by the late 60's, required drawings to be made up in separate sheets with no sheet longer than 48-inches. This allowed a framing size for photographing onto microfilm.

By the time the last Battleship was decommissioned in the 1990's, the new SIDS (Ship Individual Drawing System) added another 13,443 drawings comprised of 40,992 sheets. It also added 2,749 "flat files" (test memos, change notices, etc. of letter or legal size) comprised of 49,647 sheets. Those numbers are quite accurate thanks to Captain John Pickering (the last commander of the shipyard) and Linda Marshall (supervisor of plan files) for supplying me the lists.

We worked ten to twelve hours a day from Monday through Friday and at least eight hours on Saturdays. Some of us were also called in on a few Sundays to solve some special problem that came up.

Computers were still in their juvenile age of development. We had a cute little Olivetti on a rolling stand to do basic engineering calculations using magnetic strips to program the formulas on. CAD computers were just being installed and I found their methods of drawing extremely slow and, frankly, boring. It wasn't until the late 80's when Rick Meza, Vince Concepcion and Don Lichti programmed them with more efficient ways of plugging in lines and dimensions.

For text writing and record keeping, many of our clerical staff was still using word processing only type computers with Wang being the most predominant though one secretary in the piping branch used a Tandy computer from Radio Shack with the noisiest daisy wheel printer imaginable.

Most of us project leaders still used pencil and paper to keep track of plan schedules, dates and man-hours used for each job order. Bill Reid in the mechanical piping section got the edge on everybody by using his personal Apple II Plus computer for plan scheduling. He would bring it in every day packed in a special set of carrying cases and slung as saddlebags over the rear of his motorcycle.

I first met Bill a couple of years before when I was assigned to teach a one week class on shipboard freehand sketching to eighteen new hired engineers. Bill was one of my "students" along with Jeff Arthurs, who later became supervisor of the fittings section, and Glen Cox, who later became assistant chief engineer. Bill and I became very good friends and when the shipyard closed he was able to transfer up to an Air Force base in Great Falls, Montana which was also his hometown.

The shop personnel worked six days a week, minimum. A large percentage also worked Sundays regularly to get that first Battleship out on time and under budget.

Talking about the budget, this was almost another screw up on the part of Washington. Prior to assigning the *New Jersey* to Long Beach, Captain Gildea was never officially ordered to take the ship. But he was extremely happy to get her and kept the towing receipt as a personal memento when he retired. He was also told that the budget was set at 365 million dollars.

But the funding letter had still not arrived by the time the ship docked. By that time, the design section was geared up and already started the removal drawings. So, Captain Gildea took the bull by the horns and said he would pay for the reactivation and modernization out of his overhead funds. He just wanted to be paid back when the ship was commissioned. Normally, funding is paid at a manday rate of (at that time) about 425 dollars per man per day. What Gildea did was pay at the manday rate with overhead funds. Then when he sent the bill to NAVSEA, he charged actual cost and made a 2.1 million dollar profit for the shipyard.

That was the first time in history that a Naval shipyard ever made a profit, and **legally** allowed to keep it too. Al Brauer, the Financial Program Manager for NAVSEA, just couldn't believe that would happen. Of all his years of counting beans, he was sure that our cost would be way over budget. We not only did it under budget, we kept the change.

Not that we didn't have any concerns about it though. The *New Jersey's* budget was actually a little too low because it was assumed (by people that know absolutely nothing about ship's air conditioning systems) that very few A/C changes would be done since she already had some air conditioning installed in 1968. They thought all we had to do was pull out the 146 package units (sit next to open doorways) and use the same ductwork.

There is a big difference between package air units (like you put in a window) and a centralized system consisting of eight 125-ton duplex York air conditioning plants installed on the 3rd deck. From those plants, the chilled water goes through a piping system to distribute cooled air from 48 overhead mounted cooling coils and 68 deck mounted fan coil units. Almost every vent duct had to be replaced, especially in areas that were heavily modified.

The ventilation of the remaining six 5"/38 mounts was changed from exhaust only to a recirculating system. Therefore the new supply ducts going into the ready service rooms had to be built of armor. But they couldn't just be an armored tube since the design was more of fragment protection than direct hit protection. If a piece of shrapnel came in one end of a straight duct, it could go on through to the space it is supposed to protect. So I sat down and came up with basic shapes for various armored ducts that would have at least two 90-degree turns in them to trap shrapnel. A separate drawing was developed for the 5"/38 ducts because of their larger size and unique locations. To improve airflow at the turns, I called for 16-gauge stainless steel sheet to be curved and tack welded in the corners. Air would flow more efficiently and a fragment would be "allowed" to penetrate the sheet metal to be trapped in the square corner behind it.

Now here is the real story of how we were able to fund the reactivation of *New Jersey*. Lieutenant Commander John Pickering (later to be the last commanding officer of the shipyard and retiring as a full Captain) was assigned to LBNSY as the COMSURFPAC representative. He was lounging by the pool at the Allen Center officers club when the shipyard Type Commander phoned him. The Type Commander had just gone over the extra costs involved to install all the latest required air conditioning systems and was not exactly on the "cool, calm and collected" side by the figures. He ordered Pickering to get his "butt" up to building 300 immediately and figure out some way to dig up another fifty million dollars.

Well, John was no dummy but even he initially thought it was impossible. However, he found postponed jobs, cancelled jobs, deleted shipalts, early finished ship availabilities, etc. that already had funding advanced but not yet been returned. John miraculously found forty eight million dollars.

That was probably another thorn in the sides of the Capitol Hill people. They were probably snickering at us behind our backs fully expecting LBNSY to fold under and not get the job done on time or charged with some sort of crime when it had to ask for cost overruns. Well, Long Beach Naval Shipyard doesn't go down that easy, not when you have people who really wanted to support the Battleship program.

It was in 1982 when we started preliminary shipchecks of the *Missouri* while she was still mothballed in Bremerton. Our first trip consisted only of twelve people from Long Beach to assist Supships Boston for two weeks. It was cold and miserable and we expected to get a lot of antagonism from the local residents for taking "their" Battleship away from them. But before the week was out, the Boston group was called back because of problems with the *Iowa* drawing schedules and contract problems with Ingalls Shipbuilding.

The Long Beach group had set up office in Admiral Halsey's cabin on the 02 level. There were still conference tables up there that we could lay our drawings out on and we got Bremerton to put a heater into the space. When the shipcheck was aborted, we stacked most of our drawings up into categorized piles and expected to find them there upon resuming the shipcheck a few months later. It was a little over a year before we returned, but in full force of 125 people. By that time I had received a temporary promotion to GS-12 as the Configuration Manager for the Hull, Structures, Armor and Space Control conversions.

Don Wolcott was also promoted to Machinery/Mechanical Configuration Manager. He served aboard the USS *Maryland* (BB-46) and the USS *North Carolina* (BB-55) in World War II. Aboard *North Carolina* he was at his 40-millimeter gun station when a Japanese Long Lance torpedo blew a hole into the forward 16-inch magazines of the ship.

Al Perry was our electrical/electronics Configuration Manager. He served in the Air Force as a machine gunner in B-29 bombers. Prior to coming to work at the shipyard, he did electrical engineering work at TRW.

George Stashak got the job as a general Configuration Manager. George served aboard the USS *Hancock* (CV-19) during the Viet Nam war. He had also worked as an engineer for a petroleum company and lived in Iran for a while. He had some interesting stories about his time in the Middle East. One thing he did observe was that the topography of Iran forced about 90% of its industry and trade to be located within twenty miles of the coastline. Naturally he had to emphasize that observation with the fact that the main guns of a Battleship can reach nearly twenty-six miles.

Homer Dixon was our civilian supervisor. Homer was a good-ol-boy from Texas and served in the Navy in the Korean War. At one time he was an artillery spotter for the Battleships.

LCDR Tom Raines was our uniformed supervisor. Tom served in the Viet Nam war and was our ship superintendent for the reactivation of *New Jersey*. Tom made full commander during our stint and later retired from the Navy and moved back to Ames, Iowa to earn a doctorate.

Paul Apodaca from JJMA was assigned as our NAVSEA liaison. Paul was a retired naval officer and a full-blooded Muscalero Apache. Paul had a good sense of humor and you always had to watch out for being pulled in by one of his jokes. He also had an absolutely gorgeous daughter that was an international fashion model. She visited us a couple of times and as she would walk down the hallway you could hear all male heart beats increase.

Dick Blanchard was appointed to be our logistics manager. Dick stood about five foot eleven, dark hair with a slight wave, square jawed and with a great sense of humor. This sense of humor kept him mentally balanced as he was at Pearl Harbor during the attack, at the age of only seven years old.

Dick's father was in the Navy and they were living in married officers housing on base at the Ewa MCAS. Dick and two friends were walking to Sunday school when the attack came. Just ahead of them was a Marine standing guard duty at a gate in a chain link fence. A Japanese plane strafed the street and its machine gun bullets literally cut the Marine in two just in front of the three boys. Dick said he ran home so fast that his feet never touched the ground.

Note: In researching the Pearl Harbor casualty list, the Marine Dick saw killed was PFC Edward Stephen Lawrence, one of three Marines killed at EWA. PFC Lawrence was on standard sentry duty and cut down by the opening shots of the attack and never had a chance to use his rifle and display any action worth a write-up in the logs. I think the Naval Historical Center should correct this omission.

When we returned to shipcheck *Missouri* in Bremerton, Boston was now out of the picture except for guidance drawings. When we opened Halsey's office however, we found all of the drawings had been jammed into a closet. I then recalled that it was that compartment that was used in a scene for "Winds of War" with Robert Mitchum. The ship was also used for other scenes in the same show. The igloo-shaped dehumidification enclosures over the 40mm gun tubs were removed and the gun barrels reinstalled for exterior shots.

We spent five cold and damp weeks in Bremerton on that shipcheck. Morning dew on the decks would be frozen as we boarded and we had to watch our step every inch of the way. Many people slipped and fell on the icy decks or slipped down steel ladders wetted by our boots.

Near the end of every day, the Configuration Managers had to report to a meeting with NAVSEA personnel, led by Ray Schull. We would advise them of the percentages of drawings checked, how many *New Jersey* drawings would be applicable, how many *Iowa* drawings would be applicable and any problems that we may have found.

One problem I brought up was CEC. On *New Jersey* and *Iowa*, CEC took over the starboard two-thirds of the Admiral's quarters on 02 level. The remaining third, on the port side, was to be an unassigned space with the supposed intent of opening it up later for an expanded CEC. However, right after *New Jersey* was commissioned, a "Tiger Team" came in and took over the compartment. They installed several electronic consoles in the space, tapped into CEC power systems and even CEC air conditioning ductwork we had running through that space.

Our guidance for *Missouri*, however, was to take over about three-fourths of the Admiral's quarters, starting from the port side, but still leave a small "unassigned" space on the starboard side. After laying out the above history, I said, *"Look Ray. I don't care and don't even want to know what that equipment is that is going to be put in there. But, structurally speaking, I would like to know how much it weighs so it can be added in correctly to our stability calculations. Al Perry would like to know what electrical power requirements are of the equipment so we can give you dedicated power supply rather than tapping off of CEC. Don Wolcott would like to know the heat dissipation of the equipment so we can size air conditioning to serve it. The New Jersey crew complained bitterly about that space on their ship robbing CEC of some of its air conditioning. If it is necessary to put an extra fan-coil unit in, then we can do that and all support services will be properly balanced."*

Ray just sort of stared at me in shock and he turned to the other NAVSEA reps. Jim Snyder had sort of a puzzled look on his face (apparently he didn't know anything about that equipment either). Nat Choate had a big grin because he knew I hit not just a nerve but an important function of the ship that had fallen through the cracks.

Ray asked all of us Long Beach personnel to step out into the passageway for a few minutes while he discussed the problem I brought up. When we were called back in, he explained that the space was to be used as a "Spook Room" where the Intelligence section worked to intercept and decode "enemy" radio traffic. He agreed that it was an oversight, brought on by an overzealous sense of security that cut us out of the loop on the other two ships. He also admitted that there were reports from *New Jersey* of the loss of sufficient air conditioning due to the installation of the intelligence equipment.

Therefore we would be provided with all the information we needed upon our return to Long Beach. As it turned out, it was much for the better. We were able to design the space with the double acoustic insulation required to prevent unauthorized personnel from hearing what was going on inside. We found a space, the next deck down, for another fan-coil unit that would be able to serve both CEC and TACC (the "official" acronym for the Spook Room). The Intelligence officer was so pleased to be part of the shipyard design and installation he was almost jumping for joy. Finally, he was able to work in a space that was properly laid out, with proper ventilation, proper lighting, sufficient power and proper security.

After *Missouri* was towed to Long Beach, we ran into another communication problem, but with the shops this time. They assumed that *Missouri* was going to be an exact duplicate of *New Jersey* and began manufacturing armored doors ahead of time. This was fine, but they wound up building one more 1.5" thick armored door for CEC than needed. On *New Jersey*, four armored doors led into the space, two from the weather and two interior doors from the transverse passageway on the aft side of CEC. The port weather and interior doors were used only for the Spook Room.

On *Missouri*, however, we deleted the port interior door. Intelligence personnel going into TACC entered either through CEC or the weather door on the starboard side. The port weather door was still necessary but we no longer needed a port armored door on the aft transverse bulkhead.

The extra door was kept in the shop and erected on a display stand for visitors to view during shipyard open houses. So, it didn't go to waste. But as the shipyard was scheduled for closure, it was sent out to the scrap yard.

During one of our meetings with NAVSEA and Pentagon officials, one of the Navy Captains expressed official concern of being able to man the *Missouri* even with a small pre-commissioning crew. Ron Ashe, our weapons shop General Foreman who personally reactivated the guns, said, "No problem. We will man her ourselves if need be." We all nodded in agreement.

Our configuration manager group was also ordered to inspect *Iowa* (several times) in Norfolk and *Wisconsin* in Philadelphia for configuration control. I found *Wisconsin* to have followed configuration control the best, and the ship was in the best shape of all four. Also, *Wisconsin* had four vestibule type deckhouses added on the port and starboard sides on the 03 and 04 levels to provide out of the weather access to the bridge. Shop sketches designed the deckhouses so no official drawings were available. Therefore I sketched them up and developed a "class" drawing from them later at Long Beach as NAVSEA was writing a SHIPALT to have them installed on the other three ships.

Wisconsin was in dry dock at the time of our shipcheck so I was able to inspect her bottom sides and compare them to *New Jersey* and *Missouri*. The only thing I found wrong with the Avondale Shipyard dry dock work (when reactivated by Ingalls) was the cutting of two-inch diameter holes in the twin keels for water cooling of the shaft bearings. In our West Coast ships, we followed Philly's 1968 method of drilling hundreds of .75 inch diameter holes instead so fish would not go into the twin keels, spawn when grown and create a school of fish that could bugger up the propeller shafts going through.

There were a number of other proposed SHIPALTS being written before inactivation threats started looming up on the horizon. One was to enlarge the doors and hatches to the escape trunks from the main machinery spaces. Each trunk had an eighteen-inch diameter hatch at the top that was to be changed out to twenty-one-inch diameter hatches. The original guidance for the doors down below, however, was to enlarge the trunks to take Elliason balanced doors.

After checking both *Missouri* and *Wisconsin*, I found that trunk enlargement would cause heavy-duty remote operating gear for the main scoops to be modified as well. Several other interferences would drive the cost up or actually make the change impossible. My solution that was adopted by NAVSEA was to leave the trunks themselves alone but just put larger standard doors in. The existing doors were simple 18 X 36 four-dog doors, a wee bit small for by today's standards. My solution was to replace them with 21 X 66 quick acting doors cut down from standard 26 X 66 doors.

While inspecting the trunks on *Missouri*, I had a young engineer with me assisting in the measurements. I decided to do an impromptu test of the ease or difficulty of opening the existing four-dog door. I dogged the door down tightly with a dogging wrench and first timed the engineer, standing only two feet away, as he opened it. It only took him ten seconds. Then I redogged the door and timed a (more practiced) sailor from six feet away open it. It took him only eight seconds.

To me, Elliason doors are more of a hindrance than an advantage. In some trunks only one person at a time can go in and must close it before he can reach the escape ladder. The other crewmen must wait until he is out of the way. After measuring up the existing trunks and interferences I decided a modified fast acting type door was faster in that it could remain open to allow all crewmen to enter the trunk and start climbing the ladder. Only the last man in would have to close the door behind him.

Now, I just have to tell you about the neat solution Danny Rios had for compressed air supply to the Harpoon handling booms. We graduated from the apprenticeship at the same time but he as a pipefitter. He was an ex-Marine who served in the Korean War and hired on as a pipefitter apprentice after his hitch. After a few years in the shop as a mechanic, he transferred up to the design division as a draftsman, as many of us did.

Earl Naval Weapons Center had come up with some guidance to install equipment that would reload the Harpoons and Tomahawks either at sea or at ports that did not have the proper cranes. For the Harpoons, two jib booms would be mounted, one on each side of the after stack with air powered (90 psi) monorail winches to lift the armored Harpoon canisters out of their shipping containers and set them in the launchers. The physical arrangement was rather straightforward and did not present any serious problems for Neil Cole and Peggy Wong in fittings design.

For the Tomahawk loading, that was a more complex arrangement created by Earl NWHC. It used a large rolling "A" frame on tracks to pick up the canistered missiles (All Up Rounds or AURs) and load them on the extended launching trays of the Armored Box Launchers. The "A" frame also required a 90 psi air powered winch.

The problem was getting low-pressure (LP) air of 90 to 120 pounds per square inch (psi) up to the air winches on the booms and "A" frame. All of the ship's air compressors are way down inside the hull for protection. By the time the air got all the way up above the 03 level, the pressure would drop to useless. If the LP air compressors are also being used for other purposes, such as air powered tools, the pressure drop would be even greater. NAVSEA tasked us to find a spot above main deck where we could install an LP air compressor closer to the Harpoon handling booms. We found a fairly clear deck area on 02 level starboard just under the forward overhang of the aft Tomahawk deck. The overhang would give the compressor some weather protection, but we would still have to design and install bulkheads around it for total weather protection and noise reduction. Air compressors are inherently very noisy machines.

In the Configuration Manager section, I was sitting in for Don Wolcott who was on travel when Danny came up to me with an idea. BAM! Talk about a simple solution to a complex problem. At the next scheduled meeting with NAVSEA when they came out for their briefing, I had Danny present his solution and again it was a pleasure seeing the astonished looks on the faces of the "experts", as well as pleasure in finding a very economical answer.

Danny's solution was to use the ships Medium Pressure (MP) air compressor to serve the Harpoon and Tomahawk handling winches. The MP air compressor puts out between 150 and 200 psi and simple regulators up by the loading areas would reduce it to the proper working pressure of 90 psi. The only other function of the MP air compressor was to provide gas ejection air to the 16-inch guns when they fire. The ejection air blows out smoke and embers from the barrel so they would not drift back inside the Turret when the breech is opened. Obviously, we would not be firing the guns during a missile load-out, so the MP air compressors would not be in service for anything else.

It is now time to address the value of all that hard work, millions of dollars spent on the Battleships and what their actual contribution was to winning the Cold War.

I ran across a report of an interview of the Admiral of the Soviet Fleet Sergei I. Gorshkov. The interview was supposedly taken after Admiral Gorshkov witnessed the firing exercises of the USS *Iowa* in the Baltic Sea during BALTOPS 85. I was not able to confirm the accuracy of the statement, at that time, but it was distributed widely and never refuted.

"B" *"You Americans do not realize what formidable warships you have in those four ships. We have concluded after careful analysis that these magnificent vessels are in fact the most to be feared in your entire Naval arsenal. When engaged in combat, we could throw everything we have at those ships and all of our firepower would just bounce off or be of little effect. Then when we are exhausted, we will detect you coming over the horizon and then you will sink us."*

USS IOWA (BB-61)
Firing a Broadside during NATO BALTOPS '85
1 October 1985

At that time I personally doubted that Admiral Gorshkov said anything like that in precisely those exact words. He had spent his entire military career devoted to building up the Soviet Navy to be the most powerful Navy in the world. Even if the statement was true, he would not admit the vulnerability of his Navy to the "invincibility" of the Battleships even if all four ganged up on his fleet. However, it would be possible he may have said something like that referring to a less powerful Navy such as a third world country and an overzealous copywriter exercised some artistic license.

Even if the entire quote was the figment of someone's imagination, it got passed around as truth. The quote has appeared in publications touting the superiority of the Battleships and was a great morale booster in this country. Undoubtedly a version was passed around in Russia as a morale buster. Coincidentally, at that time the Russian people seriously questioned the extreme cost of their modern military when all the Americans had to do was resurrect four World War II "relics" to put the entire Soviet Navy to shame. I searched the Internet trying to confirm the quote but I could not even find a denial to it. Because Admiral Gorshkov, nor anyone else of Soviet authority has ever denied it, just the lack of denial has lent feasibility that he may very well have said something similar to that. In fact, shortly after BALTOPS 85 the Soviet Fleet quickly reduced its profile in the Baltic **and** North Atlantic, withdrawing their feared *Kirov* class nuclear powered Battle Cruisers (that are basically non-armored).

"B" Then, around the year 2013, **BINGO**. I finally found a **CONFIRMATION** of that quote from the RAF museum describing the Admiral's personal history and his most significant quotes. Sure enough, that was one of them word for word.

That was exactly what the citizens of Russia **wanted** to hear and began to seriously question the validity of expanding or even keeping communist philosophies through military presence beyond Russia's borders. Then the East Germans, who didn't slip into Austria through Hungary, began taking sledge hammers to the Berlin wall. Then they took bulldozers to that wall and even former President Reagan went over there and chiseled out a couple of chunks for himself. Then the citizens of Moscow **staged** their final revolution and the Soviet Army made only a couple of token defenses. It was all a show. On a TV newscast it showed where Moscow citizens blockaded a street with old cars, furniture, and anything they didn't need. A Soviet Army armored vehicle tried to run over the blockade but couldn't get to the top. The give-away that it was staged because both the civilians AND the soldiers were standing around almost casually taken pictures (and probably bets) of the event. Then President Gorbachev went to turn in his communist party card, he found ------ no one was in the office.

WE **WON** the Cold War just as President Reagan said we would. There is no question in my mind that it was the Battleships that won the Cold War. Whether the Admiral's quote was accepted as accurate or not, the presence of the Battleships drove the Soviet Fleet back to its home ports. Nor is there any question that the efforts and dedication of the people of LBNSY who led their reactivation won the Cold War. Unfortunately, LBNSY may be the greatest casualty. It was declared as excess property and slated for demolition. It's now a parking lot to make room for a container terminal that the city of Long Beach originally wanted to lease to the China Ocean Shipping Company (COSCO) that is run by the (communist) People's Republic of China. The irony of that needs no further explanation.

It was the author's idea to have the amidships Tomahawk ABL's face each other instead of outboard. This saved the weight and the cost to build a "Fire Wall" on centerline if the launchers faced outboard. Since you will fire only one missile one at a time from only one of the eight ABLs, we just shoot over the tops of the ones in front.

Photo by author while at sea.

BB-62 before and after modernization. The emergency anchor in the bull nose was for her tow to Long Beach. Next docking the forefoot skeg and Paravane eye were removed.   US Navy Photos by Sophie Chase

"B"   Installing a renewed propeller on one of **our** Battleships

"B" Don Herr (lower-right) balancing one of *Missouri's* giant propellers. Photo courtesy of Don Herr

All four original props were removed and replaced by repaired and re-annealed propellers.
  #1 STBD Outboard-4 blades, 18'-3" dia., 39,792 lbs. Serial #5232
  #2 STBD Inboard-5 blades, 17'-0" dia., 40,032 lbs. Serial #5237
  #3 PORT Inboard-5 blades, 17'-0" dia., 43,290 lbs. Serial # 18570 (also marked *ESSEX)* .
  #4 PORT Outboard-4 blades, 18'-3" dia., 40,725 lbs. Serial # 5235
  . Weights and sizes noted by author when the propellers arrived at LBNSY.

"B" Don Herr & this author today. Hmmm, where did all that grey hair come from?

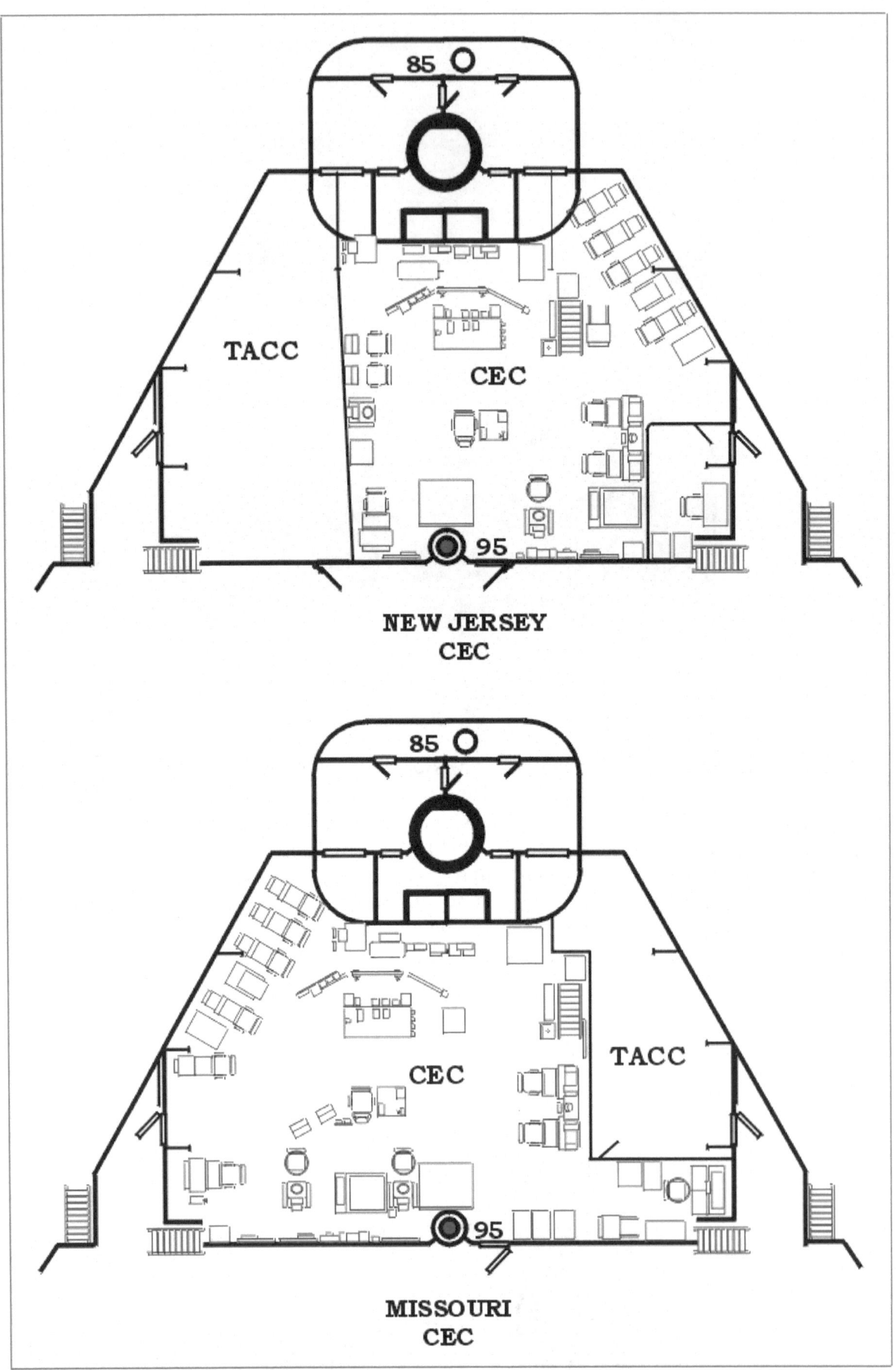

The differences in CEC arrangements. Author's personal CAD drawings

CHAPTER 27: BATTLESHIP CLASS PROBLEMS

On any class of ship, there will be some design or construction problems that will be repeatable on several ships of the class. We try to identify such problems as soon as possible and provide not only fixes to the ships having them but also preventive fixes for future ships of the class. The configuration manager section was assigned to investigate any class problems on the Battleships. We expected some problems may crop up with the modernization items, but were surprised to find a couple dating back to the original ship design.

Hull Corrosion: One, somewhat expected, class problem was hull corrosion. At the time of reactivating the first of the Battleships, the only method approved was sacrificial hull zincs bolted to selected places on the hull of the ship. When we reactivated *New Jersey*, the only guidance we had was the 1968 Philadelphia zinc pattern that was presumed to give the hull a two to three year protection against cathodic corrosion. So a drawing was developed merely duplicating the 1968 pattern. Shortly afterwards, I was tasked to write a Shipalt to install a much more extensive pattern of zincs as well as adding zincs to the sea chest openings and on the lower decks of all machinery spaces and shaft alleys. I wrote that Shipalt and directed the development of the drawings.

When *New Jersey* was dry docked after **FIVE** years at sea, versus three, her hull corrosion was quite severe with many of the zinc anodes being completely depleted. The Shipalt of the new zinc pattern was installed and the ship went back out to sea after extensive hull repairs and rivet replacements had been made. Then NAVSEA came out with guidance for a different pattern of zincs that we installed on *Missouri*. After that was done, NAVSEA decided to replace the sacrificial zinc anodes with the active Impressed Current Cathodic Protection (ICCP) system using energized platinum anodes to neutralize the electrical current that would cause cathodic corrosion.

The cathodic corrosion laboratory in Key West, Florida bought nine-foot long fiberglass hulls for their model tests. They would sheath the hull in thin metal and then spot where the anodes should go with scaled down working models. When they came out to Long Beach to describe how they did their studies, they mentioned that they were using a fiberglass model hull that they bought through a mail order catalog. I couldn't help laughing and pointed over to Lee Upshaw and said, "He's the guy who built them for you." Since then, they have bought quite a number of hulls from Lee including a hull of the *Nimitz* class Aircraft Carriers.

Now, there was no conflict of interest here. Lee had been in the model building business for a number of years before coming to work at the shipyard. Also, he started the master hull of the *Iowa* class at least a year before hiring in. But his fiberglass hulls are large enough and accurate enough that the Key West people said he was the only game in town when it came to getting accurate hulls that met their requirements. Also, Lee sold them at catalog price rather than jacking the cost up to soak the taxpayers.

I was personally tasked to develop the drawings for installation of the ICCP system. We used *New Jersey* as the base ship since she was at the pier at the time and we could check where to put the control unit. However, her schedule in port didn't allow installation at that time so *Iowa* was the first to receive the ICCP Shipalt, followed by *Missouri* and *Wisconsin* in that order. *New Jersey* was to get ICCP installed at her next dry docking, but that event was unfortunately changed for inactivation instead.

When we reactivated *New Jersey*, we found the bellmouth around the paravane eye to be heavily corroded. The paravane eye, also known as the forefoot skeg, was a steel casting shaped like a padeye lying flat and protruding forward from the "chin" of the bow. A seven-inch pipe ran up from the bellmouth opening through the forepeak tank to the main deck for guiding a chain that held paravane wires for mine sweeping. The paravanes looked something like torpedoes but were towed on each side of the ship. The fins on the paravanes kept them away from the ship and, hopefully, the tow wires would snag onto the anchor wires of mines. As the mine's anchor wire was pulled along the paravane wire, it would be hooked into a cutting device to cut the mine loose and allow it to float to the surface to be detonated by rifle fire.

But mines had come a long way since then. Though anchored mines of the stereotyped "horned" steel balls were of First World War design and extensively used in the Second World War and Korean War, they were now considered "old hat" compared to modern influence mines that lay in wait on the bottom for a passing ship above.

During the 1981 dry docking of *New Jersey*, I made up sketches of how to remove the paravane eye and chain pipe. The bulbous bow would then be inserted with one-inch thick steel plate. However, time and cost restraints allowed only a small steel plug to be welded up inside the chain pipe. The deep pitting around the bellmouth in the cast steel eye would be clad-welded and ground reasonably smooth.

When *New Jersey* was dry docked again in 1987, the paravane eye and pipe, including the welded plug, were so heavily corroded that a six-inch long crack-like hole was eaten through and the forepeak tank was flooded. Being a configuration manager, by that time, gave me the authority to convince NAVSEA that this was a serious problem and they finally authorized total removal of the paravane eye and chain pipe. We left the small paravane handling winch in place on deck however, as the crew had reactivated that themselves and found it a real handy tool for rigging items up forward.

When we dry docked *Missouri*, her paravane eye/forefoot skeg was not as badly corroded. However, I attributed that to the fact she had much less mileage on her than the *New Jersey*. I was rather proud of myself after seeing the finished product of paravane eye removal on *New Jersey*. Her bow was now the nice, smooth bulbous bow originally envisioned by David Taylor for greater efficiency in going through the water. The shops did an excellent job and I was looking forward to her next dry docking that would prove the effectiveness of a cleaner hull and with less corrosion problems.

Then Iran started laying the old-fashioned type mines around the Persian Gulf (a.k.a. Arabian Gulf by non-Iranians such as Egyptians and Arabians). These mines were made in North Korea, patterned after Russian mines that were copies of American mines of World War II vintage. I then received a phone call from the Mine Warfare Group in Panama City, Florida. They asked if the Battleships were still capable of deploying paravanes to sweep for mines. This was less than a week after New Jersey was undocked without a paravane eye. Some days it doesn't pay to get out of bed.

Corrosion on the Battleships was thoroughly monitored after that. Before *Missouri* was scheduled to receive the ICCP installation, I accompanied our shipyard divers on a three-day underwater inspection of the ship. I monitored the inspection of the anodes via underwater television, operated the VCR to record the inspection. Vino Namura and Tom Sorenson were the lead divers though three others worked with them as relief/ safety divers and support crew. We inspected each and every one of the zincs and replaced those that were not dissolving properly.

We also inspected the propellers and rudders for damage or corrosion and we kept meticulous notes of the inspection for our official Dive Report.

The Paravane Eye on the Forefoot of the *New Jersey*. The 7" IPS chain pipe running up through the forepeak tank was constantly corroding out. US Navy photo by Sophie Chase

In the left photo the Paravane Eye casting has been cut off but you can still see heavy corrosion around the mouth of the chain pipe. In the right photo the Forefoot is filled with an insert and is now smooth. Sections of the 7" IPS pipe are on the dock floor. But that size was deleted in about 1942 so the *Missouri* and *Wisconsin* had 8" IPS chain pipe installed. . US Navy photos by Earl Lester

Bilge keel damage was not a problem with the Battleships, but a problem with the Panama Canal Authority that refused to consider them as an interference with the curved corners of the Gatun Locks.
US Navy photo by Sophie Chase

Author inspecting the fully repaired bilge keels and the new zinc cathodic pattern used before the Impressed Current Cathodic Protection Shipalt was written and installed on the other three Battleships.
US Navy photo by Sophie Chase

A section of the centerline flat keel after having pits welded up and before grinding. The circular weld above is one of hundreds of 18-inch diameter holes cut into the ship's hull for tank cleaning. The holes were laid out one by one by Eric Pfefferkorn (aka "Pop Corn") before his retirement while he was still in his seventies, or eighties. He was an "old" man when the author (at the tender age of 18) first worked for him in the dry docks and here he was nearly 30 years later still at it.   US Navy photo by Sophie Chase

Bulkhead 36 cracks: A very interesting class problem hit one Sunday morning as I was lying in bed reading the comic's when the phone rang. It was Bill Fedak who was called in that morning to inspect a bulkhead crack in a fuel tank on *New Jersey* that occurred during her deployment to Lebanon. As I kept spare sets of coveralls, hard hat and steel-toed boots at home, I merely answered "I'll be there in 25 minutes". Thankfully there isn't much freeway traffic on a Sunday morning.

New Jersey's fuel tanks had been thoroughly cleaned of the old bunker oil to accept Navy Distillate (a.k.a. DFM) and her overflow and contaminated fuel tanks were perfectly clean before the ship's orders to "visit" Lebanon. Commander Callibriessi (ship's MPA) decided to top her off to 105% capacity for her run across the Atlantic and Mediterranean to Lebanon. He did this by using the clean overflow tanks and clean contaminated tanks as extra fuel tanks. In doing so, however, heretofore unknown cracks in the forward end of the overflow tanks at bulkhead 36 leaked fuel into the forward storeroom. Inspection of the leaks found hairline cracks just under the 3rd platform plating at the center of each tank. We also found a hairline crack above 2nd platform on the starboard side and an old repair weld. I sketched up a temporary patch repair but said I would need to do a thorough study of the original drawings on Monday when plan files was open.

I pulled the bulkhead 36 plan out of files Monday morning and studied it carefully. I found that the bulkhead plating thickness and the stiffener sizes gradually reduced the higher up they were in the tank. As there would be less pressure near the top, **if** ever filled, the thinner the plating and the smaller the stiffeners needed to be. That kept the overall weight of the ship down to meet the London Treaty restrictions.

I then made up a sketch for a more permanent fix with an insert and additional stiffening. I took that sketch, along with the sketches of the *New Jersey* cracks, out to the *Missouri* and inspected her bulkhead 36. Lo and behold, she also had cracks very similar to those on the Big J. It was like looking at carbon copies except the port and starboard cracks under 3rd platform were a little further inboard. I also found port and starboard repair welds of cracks under the 2nd platform in almost the identical places as on *New Jersey*.

Don Wolcott was preparing to go back to Norfolk to inspect the machinery spaces on *Iowa*, so he took copies of the sketches with him to check out the bulkhead. He called back a couple of days later and said he found almost identical cracks on that Battleship as well. There was a crack under the 3rd platform on the port side only almost identical to *New Jersey*. But he also found corner cracks under the 2nd platform further outboard port and starboard.

I wrote a Technical Issue Overview very quickly and personally contacted NAVSEA that we have a class problem. Not serious yet, but a problem just the same. In the official report we surmised that the bulkhead was acting like a diaphragm plate between torpedo bulkheads 2 and 3. I also noted in the report my experience aboard *New Jersey* during her first sea trials where I felt the bow twisting very slightly when she was on her full speed run. I was down in the forward areas while the ship was doing 31 plus knots in a perfectly, glassy calm sea. Having a good sense of balance, I was surprised to feel the bow, forward of frame 36, twisting ever so slightly. I stood there for some time analyzing the effect and listening closely for creaking of any joints or rivets. Hearing nothing, I assumed it was a natural feature of the ship. The almost imperceptible torque would not have been noticed if the ship was in a higher sea. I brought other people down and they confirmed we had a slight twist in the bow. But when the bulkhead 36 cracks were later found on two other BBs it was apparent, that their cause was the slight torque in the bow.

I then studied the bulkhead 36 construction drawing again. It was perplexing that everything else on those ships was designed so well and so tough. It was bothersome to think that the original designers overlooked this potential weakness should the overflow tanks be topped off. Though I knew everyone involved in the development of that drawing was either dead or too old to remember any details, I glanced at the signature block anyway just to see the names.

Then I glanced at the date the drawing was signed off: **December 5, 1941.**

I literally plopped back down into my chair with my mouth agape. I looked at revisions done after that date, but they were of minor nature that would not delay construction. It was then easy to imagine the thoughts and actions of the designers of that day and the following three days.

Friday, 12-5-1941, quitting time: *"Well, that plan is finally out. Sure would have liked to have made that plating a little thicker in case those tanks are ever topped off."*

"Yeah but the engineers have the weight down to the tenth of a pound to meet the Treaty limitations. Besides, I don't think they will ever put that much fuel in them."

Saturday, 12-6-1941: *"I think I'll go out and buy our Christmas tree today. I'm a little tired of reading about that war in Europe and Sunday's paper is going to be full of it as usual."*

Sunday, 12-7-1941 (on the radio): *"We interrupt this program to bring you a special announcement. Pearl Harbor is under attack by Japanese warplanes."*

Monday, 12-8-1941, before starting hour: *"No more major changes and no more weight limitations. Let's get those Battleships built and headed for Tokyo."*

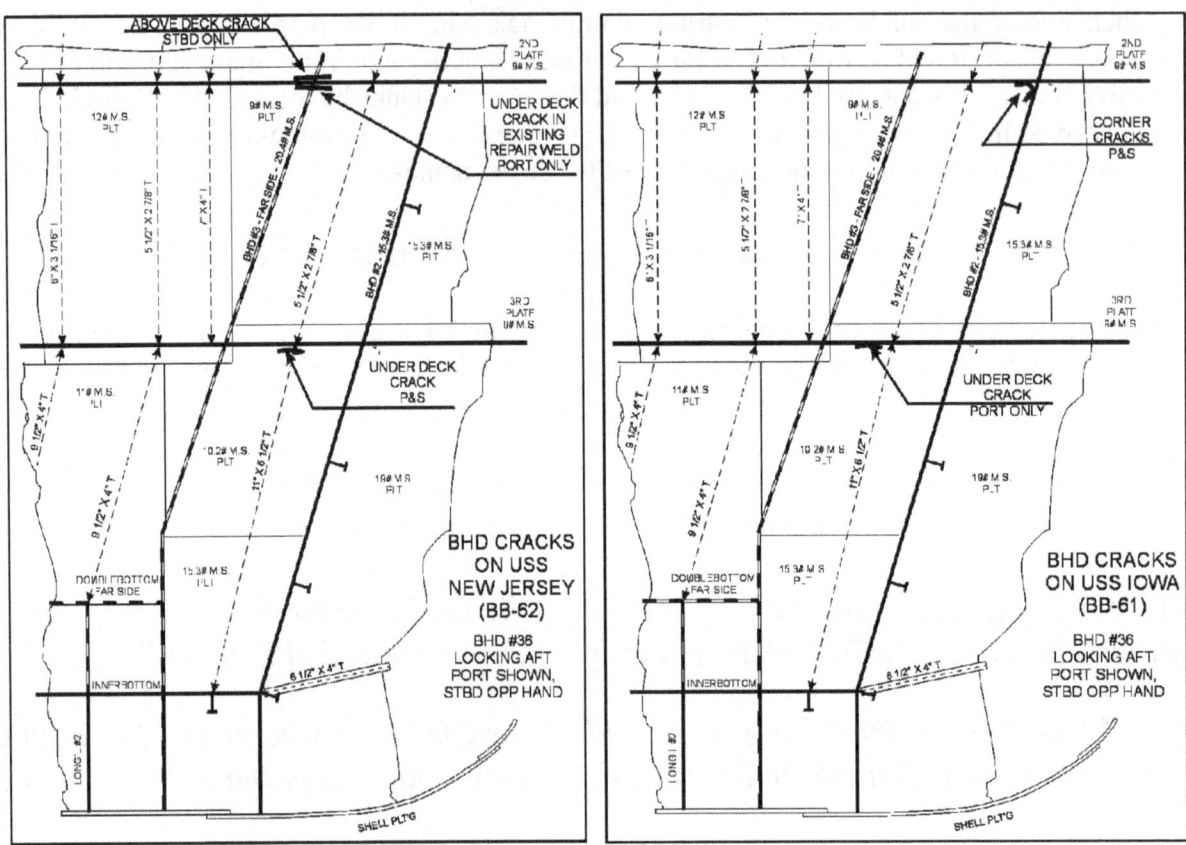

Left sketch: Bulkhead 36 cracks on *New Jersey* Right sketch: Bulkhead 36 cracks on *Iowa*.
CAD drawings by author from his field sketches

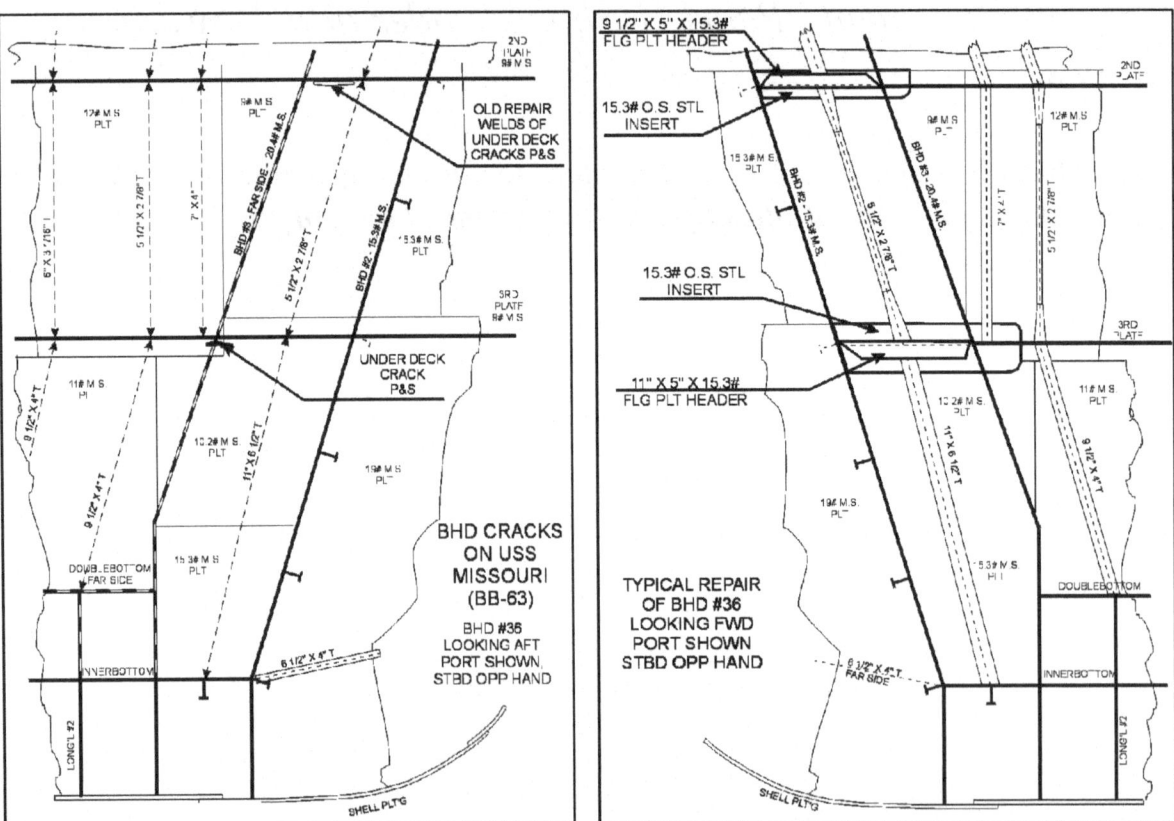

Left sketch: Bulkhead 36 cracks on *Missouri* Right sketch: Repair and reinforcement of Bulkhead 36 on all *Iowa* class ships including *Wisconsin*. CAD drawings by author from his field sketches

Boat Winches: Though procurement of the winches for the port boat-handling boom would not normally be classified as a class problem, the way we purloined two of them for *Missouri* and *Wisconsin* borderlines the subject. *New Jersey* already had a suitable winch on the port side of main deck at about frame 140 that was installed in 1968. We replaced the boom and added new topping and vang winches. The main hoisting winch was okay though. Where NAVSEA found a winch for *Iowa* I do not know, but when it came time to find one for *Missouri*, the fun really started.

I received a phone call from NAVSEA with a request to send an engineer and a planner-estimator to Houston, Texas and inspect a used Western Gear winch that had been offered for sale. Since boat-handling design was done in Eddie Felipe's section, I sent him accompanied by a man from the mechanical P&E section. However, Eddie's travel orders had a typo in them. They said he was to go to Houston to inspect a wench (spelled with an "e" instead of an "i"). Bill Dickson just **had** to make a cartoon out of that one.

Eddie came back with his report. The winch (not wench) was for sale for $30,000. But, it did not have a controller or master switch that would need to be purchased new at around $5,000. Plus, the planner estimated it would cost $12,000 to overhaul and repair the winch (not wench) completely as it had been sitting in a vacant lot, overgrown with weeds, for several years. So, we are talking about $47,000 for that one winch for the *Missouri* only and nobody knew where to find one for *Wisconsin* yet. A brand new winch would cost about $54,000 so the choice was really the toss of a coin with only a $7,000 difference between an old wench – er – winch and new unused virgin wench – er – winch.

Sorry. Even us "historians" gotta have some fun sometime.

Gordon Douglas went down to the technical library and pulled out the Technical Manual on that model of winch. He literally ran back up the stairs and plopped it down on my desk and said, "Look at the ships these winches were issued to."

Right there on the front cover it listed the USS *Albany* (CG-10), USS *Chicago* (CG-11) and USS *Columbus* (CG-12) that had been converted over from all gun heavy cruisers to Guided Missile Cruisers. Two Western Gear winches, of the identical model needed, had been installed on each of those ships. As luck would have it, the decommissioned *Chicago* was right across the pier from *Missouri* in Bremerton during our shipcheck. The next half-hour was spent collecting the books of 8 X 10 color photos several of us took during that shipcheck. BINGO, we found a photo that showed *Chicago* in the back ground with both winches in plain view.

I contacted Pat Ennis in Bremerton to set up a procedure to "cannibalize" those winches for both the *Missouri* and *Wisconsin*. At that time, the city of Chicago was considering taking the cruiser as a museum ship and we would have to replace those winches with something that looked the same. Fortunately, *Missouri* had four similar C. H. Wheeler winches on board. But C. H. Wheeler was bought out by Baldwin-Lima-Hamilton around 1960. In turn, Jered Brown Bros. bought out Baldwin-Lima-Hamilton. The motors were Vickers type and no longer parts supportable. This is based upon the detailed and invaluable research Gordon Douglas did. The foundations for the Wheeler winches were the same as the Western Gear winches so they could easily replace the ones on *Chicago*. I then contacted our Type Desk and they started the request for cannibalization of equipment from an inactive ship.

I contacted NAVSEA and told them to forget about that winch in Houston. I found two almost brand new winches, with their controllers and master switches and was having them shipped to Long Beach. The entire cost of removing both the Western Gear winches from *Chicago*, shipping them down to Long Beach and trucking two Wheeler winches back up to Bremerton only cost $7,000. Basically the difference between buying only one new winch against buying and overhauling one old winch of doubtful dependability.

When the truck left Bremerton on a Friday morning, Type Desk called me and gave me the time of departure. Jokingly, I asked for them for the driver's CB handle so I could track him down the I-5. The following Monday morning, while driving down the 710 freeway on the way to work, I noticed a truck ahead of me carrying two winches. I speeded up a tad and sure enough, there were the winches and the name of Prefab Transport on the door of the truck cab. As I pulled off the freeway onto the snake-like transition roads of Pico and Water streets that would lead to the on ramp of the Gerald Desmond bridge, I noted in my rear view mirror that the truck was pulling off onto the shoulder. I made a U-turn, went back, U-turned again and pulled in front of the truck. No cops around thank goodness.

I asked the driver what was wrong and he answered, "Nothing's wrong, except I don't know how to get to the shipyard from here." I laughed and said, "No problem. Those are MY winches. Follow me and I will lead you up to the supply gate." Yes, I "personally" brought those winches into the shipyard. Many people congratulated me at my cost savings efforts for procuring two winches, with their controllers and master switches for a fraction of the cost of a used broken-down winch.

But, that is not the end of the story. We selected one winch, cleaned it up and installed it on *Missouri*. The other winch was sent to Cheatham for use on *Wisconsin*. However, during a phone conversation I had a couple of years later with a counterpart at Supships, Pascagoula, apparently NAVSEA got stuck buying that broken down winch in Houston anyway. He said they had to go to Houston and literally dig it out of the weeds. Then they never could get it to work right. So NAVSEA sent down a newer winch from Cheatham that worked great. After recovering from my urge to kill, I told him the story of the winches. The replacement winch NAVSEA sent down was actually the winch I originally took off the *Chicago* for the *Wisconsin*. I guess there are some times that it doesn't make any difference how hard you try, something or somebody is going to screw it up anyway.

The proper boat boom winch cannibalized from the USS *Chicago* (CG-11) is installed on the *Wisconsin* as was its sister winch was installed on the *Missouri*.

Bill Dickson's cartoon of Eddie Felipe

NIXIE transom openings: The NIXIE torpedo decoy system is an updated version of the old T-Mk6 decoys where a noise-making "fish" is trailed behind the ship and emits noises to draw an enemy torpedo toward it. Previous installations on other ships of the T-Mk6 mounted the winch on the weather deck of the ship's fantail. This was not ideal, but on most ships you just didn't have the room down below especially when some of them were equipped with SONAR units that also trailed behind the ship. There are just so many pounds of potatoes you can put in the sack before they spill over.

While shipchecking *New Jersey* in Bremerton in 1981, the Boston design guidance people were scratching their heads trying to decide if the old 40mm gun tub sponsons on the fantail would be sufficient. The biggest problem with the tubs was that they were very close to the water and the rooster tail of the ship at full speed would probably send too much spray up into the NIXIE winch and electrical control boxes.

I had just inspected the boat and airplane crane machinery room, on centerline and the next deck down, for total removal. While I was standing next to the Boston group as they were discussing the pros and cons of the gun tubs I suggested in an "off-the-cuff" manner, "As long as we are totally removing the B&A crane, why don't we mount the NIXIE winch down below and trail the fish out through an opening in the transom?"

I had absolutely no idea what the size of the NIXIE winch was or how much other support equipment went with it, but I scored another bulls eye on that shipcheck. Shoe horning the winch into the former B&A crane machinery compartment wasn't too much of a problem. Designing the transom openings, however, caused more headaches than you can imagine.

First we had to provide two transom openings so a second noisemaker fish could be deployed as the first one is hauled in. Jeff Arthurs in the Fittings section took on the task of computer designing the chafing bolsters made out of steel pipe to provide large radius edges for the NIXIE cable to ride on. The next design problem had to do with the water tightness of the opening doors and cable hole (called a scuttle as, in effect, it acted like one). The doors had to be large enough to pass the decoy through, then closed and sealed except for the scuttle which was a two-piece collar to fit around the NIXIE cable. The scuttle collar did not have to be absolutely watertight during decoy deployment, but had to have a watertight cover when NIXIE was not in use.

Now, all four Battleships were supposed to be as much alike as possible. Jeff's transom bolster design was pretty much adopted for the other three ships, so on the outside all four ships look the same. But the doors and cable passing holes on the inside is a whole different story - a story that got started with the first sea trial of *New Jersey* and got blown all out of proportion.

I was not on the first sea trial but when the ship returned one discrepancy that got a number of people shook up, especially Jeff Arthurs, was that the transom openings leaked heavily and the deck of the winch room was flooded. The transom opening installation was done by farm in shipfitters and machinists from Todd Shipyard in San Pedro. Some of us first thought the bad installation was typical of private shipyards that might not meet the quality of public shipyards. However, that thought is more prejudice than fact. The mechanics from Todd actually did a first class installation (of course, they were working on a BATTLESHIP and no shoddy work will be seen) and were very concerned about the report of leaks.

One day while checking the *New Jersey* on some structural additions, I went back into the NIXIE room while the Todd people were chalk testing the transom doors. The chalk test showed a seal all the way around. It was assumed that the dull knife-edge that is supposed to press into the gasket was not high enough and the beating of the water from the rooster tail forced its way past the gasket. So Jeff directed a modification to the knife-edge to ensure a better seal.

While on the ship's second sea trial, I was awed by the rooster tail churning up under the rounded transom by the time we hit 26 knots. I went down to the NIXIE room to check on the transom openings. We were up to 28 knots by then and the stern end of the ship was vibrating tremendously. Imagine driving down over a hundred miles on railroad tracks at 35 miles per hour but on the TIES instead of the RAILS. That's how the vibration felt. Naturally I was assuming that vibration might have had something to do with the transom opening leaks.

Upon entering the NIXIE room I immediately found the deck wet with seawater. A sailor was sitting near the transom openings and had sheets of wrapping paper spread out to absorb the water. I asked him "Where are the transom doors leaking at?"

"They don't leak as far as I can tell." He replied.

"Then where is all that water coming from?"

"It squirts into the compartment every time I open one of the cable passing scuttles every fifteen minutes."

"Why are you opening the scuttles?"

"Because I was told to open them to make sure nothing else was leaking."

I didn't ask who told him to do that. But I did have the fleeting urge to kill something.

Well, as long as the deck was wet anyway I thought I should check one of the cable passing scuttles as well. I undogged the cover on the port opening and looked down through that one-inch diameter tube at the gorgeous power of that Battleship churning up foam like Niagara Falls. Then a glob of water hit the opening and, like a broken lawn sprinkler, squirted me directly in the face.

The sailor was doing his best to hold his laughter, but I laughed first, closed the scuttle and wiped my face and glasses with a shop towel on the bench. I then wrote my report, or tried to write it, on the nearby vibrating workbench about what the actual cause of the wetness in the NIXIE room.

But, for some reason my report was either never seen by anyone outside of LBNSY or (most likely) was totally ignored. Ingalls Shipbuilding, reactivating the *Iowa*, took the first report of leakage as an excuse to design their own type of passing scuttles for the NIXIE.

When we reactivated *Missouri*, her passing scuttles were a modification of *New Jersey's* as reports back from *Iowa* indicated that the Ingalls design had some other problems. When *Wisconsin* was reactivated, she had a totally different design than any of the others.

What made the problem even more difficult was that neither the *Iowa's* or *Wisconsin's* doors and scuttles were designed on NAVSEA standard drawing formats but by shop sketches. We had to take poor photocopies of those sketches and try to redraw them on standard plan formats for official documentation and record. That was not easy to do. When I transferred the *Wisconsin* design, I merely cut out the details and pasted them onto sheets of drawing paper. Then I had reproduction make a mylar copy of it. It wasn't very neat looking, not always to scale and I wasn't too proud of it. But the time I was allowed to transfer that data was too short to allow a detailed hand drawn copy. Well, at least they all work, I think.

The transom openings look simple from the outside – but not on the inside. US Navy photo by Earl Lester

The NIXIE winch on *Missouri*. Its location and arrangement was almost identical on all four BBs.

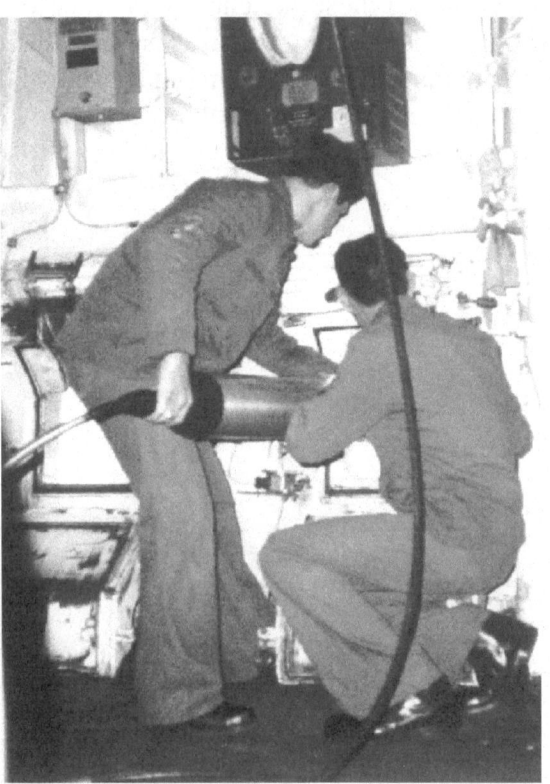

The NIXIE decoy being deployed on *Missouri*.

The NIXIE cable passing through the transom door on the *Missouri*. The *Missouri* doors are similar to *New Jersey* with only minor changes.

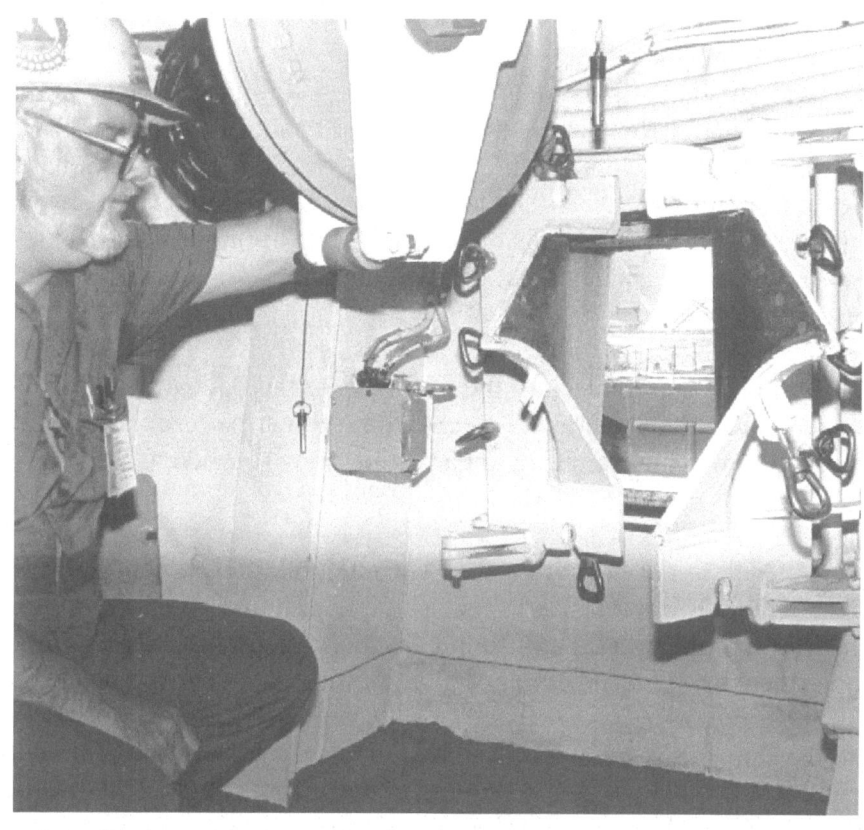

The author inspecting the design of the NIXIE transom doors on the *Wisconsin* during a shipcheck in Philadelphia in 1989.

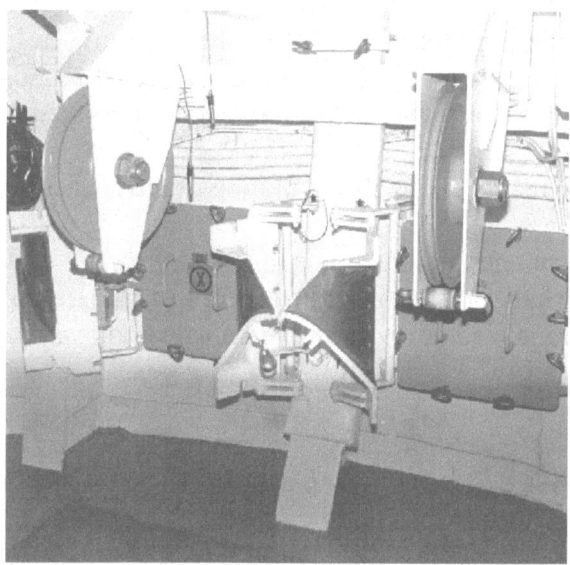

The NIXIE transom closure plates on *Wisconsin*.

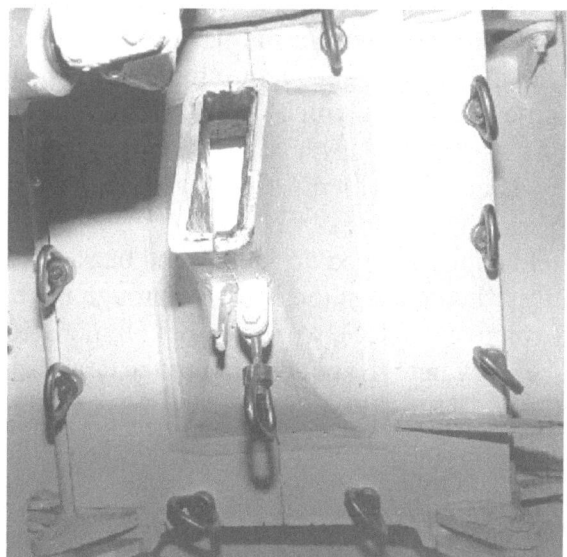

The NIXIE cable scuttle on *Wisconsin*. Simple but not totally watertight. However at speeds less than 26 knots it was quite sufficient.

US Navy photos as directed by author during his inspections of NIXIE transoms on all four ships.

Missing: (1) Towing Pelican Hook and (4) Boat Tending Booms:
This is not a class problem, but since this chapter mentioned cannibalization of winches, it's an appropriate place to tell about the missing Pelican Hook and boat booms on *New Jersey*.

When I was clandestinely assigned the *New Jersey* in 1968 for her Viet Nam deployment and the shipyard was officially designated the planning yard; we had to address certain Insurv items that were left unresolved when she left Philadelphia. One of the items was that she did not have the quick-release Pelican Hook for her emergency tow wire. The tow wire was stowed in its correct place by being wrapped around barbette III. The boatswain's mates had the appropriate size shackles and other fittings to attach the tow wire to the towing padeye, but they could not find the quick-release Pelican Hook to let go of the wire in case of emergency.

As an historical note, it was the lack of the invention of the Pelican Hook that led to the loss of the Cruiser *Milwaukee* in 1921 when it was trying to pull a submarine off a beach in Monterey, California. The boatswains mates were trying to hack saw the wire when a Tsunami washed the Cruiser up onto the beach.

I was assigned the job to find a plan for the Pelican Hook, draw a new plan if necessary or find a replacement. I pulled the microfilm reels and spent a couple of hours straining my eyes to find the right drawing listed in the drawing index. Finally I found the stowage drawing for the Pelican Hook to be on 3rd deck in the compartment below the machinery room of the boat and airplane crane on the fantail.

I went out to the ship, crawled down through the 15-inch by 21-inch manhole on the 2nd deck and found the ship's original Pelican Hook neatly secured in its stowage brackets on the deck. This is a monstrous rigging item and weighs about four hundred pounds. So everybody was glad my research was thorough and I found the Pelican Hook where it should be.

Jump forward to 1982. We are aboard the *New Jersey* during her mock Insurv sea trial with Eddie Felipe as the coordinator. Eddie has a bit of a puzzled look on his face as he hands me an Insurv item. "I have this item about the ship missing its towing Pelican Hook, whatever that is. It sounds like a rigging item and since you used to work in Fittings, you're probably the best one to investigate it."

I laughed out loud. "Hell, I got that very same item back in 1968. I know **exactly** where it is."

I happily jumped up and headed back to the boat and airplane crane machinery room. As I'm gleefully dancing down the 2nd deck through the mess hall, other thoughts start coming into my mind. "Oh (expletive deleted), we ripped out all the B&A crane machinery. But the Pelican hook was stowed down below where the bottom end of the crane's kingpost was mounted."

I entered the B&A crane machinery room, which is now the NIXIE winch room. I open the manhole and climb down to the 3rd deck. "Oh (expletive deleted)." The place was as bare as Mother Hubbard's Cupboard. When LBNSY does a rip-out, it does a rip-out including the Pelican Hook.

Almost in a panic I scoured the rest of the ship, especially the Boatswains Locker up in the bow. No Pelican Hook there either. Upon our return from sea trial I learned from the shops that everything that was anywhere near the Boat and Airplane crane was removed and scrapped, including the Pelican Hook.

The ship was also missing its boat tending booms. Philadelphia built four brand new tending booms out of aluminum in 1968. They are square booms, thirty-six feet long each that are swung out perpendicular to the sides of the ship so small boats can tie up to them while in port. A photo below shows two still on board *New Jersey* when she arrived from Bremerton in 1981 but now, they are also gone.

Well, the next week we were to go up to Bremerton for the first shipcheck of *Missouri*. So I took along the appropriate plans in case we had to strip the boat tending booms and Pelican Hook off of that ship so *New Jersey* could finish up her fitting out availability and deploy for duty.

On *Missouri*, we found she still had her original steel booms. Two of them were thirty-six feet long and two of them were fifty feet long. The longer ones were for the forward boat moorings but the specifications for the modernized Battleships were to have only thirty-six foot booms for moorings. We cannibalized the two short booms for *New Jersey* and had to draw a whole set of new rigging plans for the long booms that remained on *Missouri*.

I found *Missouri's* Pelican Hook, however, up in the Boatswains Locker instead of the space below the B&A crane machinery room. I took a couple of pictures of it because I had an idea.

Upon our return to Long Beach, Ron Stewart found a plan for a similar size Pelican Hook for Aircraft Carriers. The time and cost to make one would be quite high. I got copies of the plan and made extra copies of the photograph I took of *Missouri's* Pelican Hook. Then I called Captain Frank Conlon, USN (retired) who was in charge of the memorial Battleship *North Carolina*. He said to send him the plan and pictures and his crew would see if his ship still had her hook. He also gave me the names and phone numbers of the people in charge of the *Massachusetts* and *Alabama*.

I Then called Bill Diffly of the *Alabama* but, unfortunately, they were of no help. I then called Paul Vaitses of the *Massachusetts* and he said they would be very willing to do a search. I immediately mailed him copies of the plan and photograph as a guide.

About two weeks later, I received a call from Herbert Collins of the *Massachusetts* and he said they found their Pelican Hook to be exactly the same as the one in my photograph rather than the similar one shown on the plan. I then contacted our Integrated Logistics Supply officer and, via Cdr. Vandever of ISOD, San Diego, we cannibalized the Pelican Hook off of *Massachusetts* and installed it on *New Jersey*. Little did I know that I was probably starting a trend to strip parts off of other Battleships **and** Cruisers to make the *Iowas* keep on ticking.

The Towing Pelican Quick Release Hook aboard *Missouri*. The *Massachusetts* gave us their hook (identical to the *Iowa* class) to replace the inadvertently scrapped one on *New Jersey*. Photo by author

The tapered beam lying diagonally on the deck was one of the four 1968 aluminum boat tending booms built by Philadelphia for *New Jersey*. A second one can be seen stowed along the port gunwale. When the ship came into Long Beach, these were the only two left of the original four. But even they disappeared. Disappearing parts for all kinds of equipment from all kinds of ships was a common problem and was typical of "Midnight Requisition" in all armed services. US Navy photo by Sophie Chase

Boat Davits: The amidships boat davits, port and starboard, had to be new designs to handle the ship's new issue of liberty boats and Captain's gig. Lake Shore got the contract to design and build the new davits and they were delivered in time to *New Jersey* and *Iowa*. *Missouri's* davits were detoured for installation aboard the USS *Belknap* (CG-26) that was undergoing major modifications as a flagship. But Lake Shore, bless their hearts, made sure we got ours in plenty of time to meet our schedule.

But a weight test of *New Jersey's* port davits caused a problem to arise. Test weights were hung from the spreader bar to simulate the 1 1/2 times the weight of a boat. But as the forward and aft davit arms were being raised, one was moving faster than the other. The twist caused the spreader bar to pull out of the sockets at the ends of the davit arms. Since the lifting wires held the spreader bar, it did not drop to the deck. But the davit arms dropped down to their full overside positions. Damage was minimal basically consisting of bending over a line-handling cleat welded to the top of the green water bulwark.

Lake Shore came to the rescue by installing a speed monitoring unit between the two winches rather than extensively redesigning the spreader connections to the davit arms. This was a more efficient way to solve the problem for all davits of this design installed on other ships of the fleet besides just the Battleships.

On a weight test on *New Jersey*, the boat davit arms did not lower at the same rate and caused the davit beam to pull out of the sockets of the davit arms. This is not really a Battleship class problem but an operator problem with this davit design on all ships.
US Navy photo

Green water bulwarks: The green water bulwarks are definitely a class item. At full load, the Battleships only have eighteen feet of freeboard at amidships and a lot of water pours over the gunwales and floods the main deck. Enough water building up between the five-inch gun mount upper handling rooms on the main deck would lift the stowed boats out of their cradles and cause extensive damage. A rough sketch was sent to us from NAVSEA where a couple of bold strokes from a wide-tipped felt point pen were drawn on a very small plan view of the main deck indicating the need for bulwarks to keep most of the green water out of the boat stowage area.

This was after *New Jersey* was commissioned and was now in her fitting out availability. I decided to assign Lee Upshaw the task of drawing the plan. He took one look at the rough sketch and said that it was going to be ugly as hell with just a straight steel wall jutting up from the top edge of the shell. I agreed but also noted that water could still rush down the deck from around the 5"/38 upper handling room and still fill up the deck. We wondered if we could angle a section of the bulwark inboard so both of us went out to the ship and spent over two hours measuring up the decks on both sides. We found we could install a forward diagonal section cutting in thirty degrees to deflect water away from the boat cradles. Also, I decided to put a concave curve into the plating to act as a venturi and deflect water back away from the ship.

Lee spent quite a bit of time on that drawing. I took his first check prints home and redlined them on my dinette table in the kitchen. It took about two hours to check all the dimensions, piece numbers, number of pieces, etc. so I did the check at home so the changes could be made first thing in the morning (and I didn't charge overtime either). The bulwarks were built out of half-inch thick steel plate to resist the three hundred pounds per square foot water force, support cleats and tie-down fittings for Ed Felipe's stowage needs and to provide a little more armor to that area of the ship. That drawing was the best Lee had ever done and after the installation was complete we got a number of compliments from the ship's crew for coming up with something that not only did the job but looked good as well.

Unfortunately, the conflict of design philosophies between the East Coast and Long Beach resulted in a strict adherence to the rough (almost unreadable) sketch sent by NAVSEA. The bulwarks installed on the *Iowa* and *Wisconsin* are straight, blank faced walls of steel with a deflecting section (**un**attached to the gunwale section) forward of the starboard bulwark. Lee's design was also used on *Missouri*, so the West Coast based ships had the better green water shields. We were told later by the crew that the bulwarks worked very well except that when the water is really high and comes over their tops, they don't let water back out fast enough. There were a couple of times when the lower boat did start to become waterborne until the ship heeled that direction again to dump the water back aft and through the deck drains.

As we were finishing up *New Jersey*, Loren Perry, a friend of Lee's in the model building world, was hired by Revell to modify a model to the 1980's configuration. Loren did most of his work at home but did some finish work in Lee's shop. One day I noticed he didn't have the bulwarks in place (the plan was issued only a few days before). Lee said he didn't think he should tell Loren about them but since they had nothing to do with weapons and would be visible for all to see, I said they should be on the model. We chuckled over the fact that the Revell model was going to be very up to date since we heard that Tamiya was coming out with a similar, but larger, model. Loren Perry's version was the first out in the hobby shops **with** the bulwarks. But when the Tamiya model came out, it not only had the bulwarks, but also had them exactly perfect including the diagonal sections and the concave venturi curve. I want to know who was feeding them our drawings before the ink was even dry.

Now that is a problem, class or not, that needs some very serious attention.

The starboard high seas bulwark to protect the small boats. Port side is similar but further forward.

The aft end of the starboard bulwark showing the hefty stiffening. The purpose of the inboard slant and the curve on top was not only to direct high water back out, but if any enemy gunboat sped alongside firing machine guns, that curve was my secret "**RETURN TO SENDER**" bullet deflection design.

Above Photos by author

The flat bulwark on *Iowa*.   Photo by Lee Upshaw in 2006 ICPA/PBC inspection.

CHAPTER 28: *MISSOURI'S* BARBETTE CRACK

This is an appropriate time to address a "legendary" problem and that is concerning the crack in barbette III of the *Missouri*. It is not a class problem, it is not a structural problem, and it is not a problem with compromising the armor of the Battleships. It is a problem in misconception, censorship and misinformation played to the hilt by anti-Battleship people.

Two attempts have been made by me to publish responses to news articles extolling the imagined severity of the crack. One time was at the request of a reserve Navy Captain who was assigned to LBNSY at the time. But censors stonewalled all responses every time. After retirement, I finally was able to publish an article on the crack in the quarterly newsletter of the *Iowa* Class Preservation Association. The following is the basic content of that article.

There have been many rumors and sea stories about the crack with most of them attributing its cause to the ships grounding in Hampton Roads. This could hardly be the cause as the ship was bogged down in a sandbar and impaled on a rock several hundred feet forward. All damage in that area was strictly localized and since then expertly repaired. There have also been rumors that the ship's speed was restricted because the grounding damage had not been completed. This also is not true as on *Missouri's* sea trials during reactivation she clipped along at 31 plus knots with no problem at all.

As the hull Configuration Manager I was tasked by NAVSEA to inspect the crack, unrepaired grounding damage and submit recommendations for repair. Captain VinRoot of NAVSEA issued marching orders that included consideration of all possible repairs up to and including the entire replacement of the cracked barbette panel. Such a replacement, however, would have required removal of the Turret. That Turret weighs 1,800 tons and would have had to be stripped down to the bare substructure that would still weigh 425 tons. That would be just within the maximum test limits of the German Crane.

Prior to the issue of the orders, NAVSEA had already done an inspection of the barbette crack and X-rayed the barbette panel to see how deep it went. Additionally they cut a rectangular coupon out of it for analysis. That coupon cut, with its square corners to concentrate stresses, was just asking for more cracks to emanate from the corners. I inspected the crack, as well as areas of the ship that may still show grounding damage, in both the 1982 and 1983 shipchecks in Bremerton, Washington. I photographed the crack, measured it, sketched it up and noted the depths as indicated by NAVSEA markings written on the armor from their X-ray study. As for grounding damage, the triple bottom construction of the ship prevented me from going further down than the third bottom plating which showed no signs of buckling. If any damaged structure were still there, it would have to be below the third bottom deck plating.

When we dry docked *Missouri* the damaged area was my first priority of hull inspection even before all of the water was out of the dock. It took a few minutes to finally find the outline of welds that showed where new shell plating had been installed. There was no discontinuity of the shell lines and it looked perfect. Since we were going to install new twelve-inch and ten-inch diameter seawater intakes and discharges for the air conditioning plants in that area I asked the shipfitter foreman, Glenn Davis, to look for unrepaired damage and report it to our office immediately. After a couple of weeks went by I became concerned that Glenn had not called me and I went down in the dock to personally talk to him. Glenn said he didn't need to call, as there was nothing wrong. They were able to trace repaired structure up to its most inboard welds and found no damaged plating or structure beyond that. The ship's hull was in "as new" condition. Well, that shot that speed restriction rumor down.

As for the barbette crack, it was there from the time the armor was made and installed on the ship. It is not a crack going into the plating, but it is a peeling of the face-hardened area from the non-heat treated mass of the steel. It is called **laminar separation**. The barbette panel is seventeen inches thick and the face of it, on the threat side, was heat-treated to about 540 Brinnel hardness by a carburization method. Heat-treating may go as deep as 40% of the thickness of the plate. But the edges are kept "soft" (not heat-treated) by keeping them cool in wet asbestos blankets so they may be machined later for keyways to interlock the panels together.

The X-ray readings showed the laminar separation to go no more than six inches deep near the center of the panel, which is only about 35% of the depth of the armor. The purpose of making the face of class A armor so hard is to break up the casings of bombs or projectiles upon impact to lessen the effectiveness of the explosive. Therefore it was determined that the panel should remain as is except that we had to cut out some pieces around the coupon cut to eliminate the square corners. Then we just filled the whole thing in with hull fairing Epoxy and painted over it. Our shop 64 people did such a good job in the Epoxy fill; they even duplicated the lumpiness of the steel armor so when painted you cannot tell a crack was ever there.

Actually there are many panels of class A armor on *Missouri* that have laminar cracks, particularly near the soft edges. Officers in the pre-commissioning crew called me out a number of times to inspect cracks in armored bulkheads. Bulkhead 50 looks like an ant farm of surface fractures but is strictly cosmetic in nature. They are ugly as hell, but in no way detracts from the effectiveness of the armor.

The reason the other three Battleships do not have as much of a showing of laminar separation is because their class A armor was made by different companies. Bethlehem Steel made the armor for the *Iowa* and *New Jersey*. Carnegie-Illinois Steel made the armor for the *Wisconsin* and unfinished *Kentucky*. The Midvale Company made the armor for *Missouri* and unfinished *Illinois* but used a different heat-treating and/or quenching method than the other companies. Nathun Okun researched his references again and confirmed the differences of face-hardening methods between Midvale and the other companies. Therefore the cracks were of a factory-induced nature, not the result of battle or accidental damage and did not compromise the safety of the ship.

So, let's put those rumors to rest. The above is strictly from "The Horse's Mouth" and if someone does not want to believe it and would rather rewrite history to suit his own concepts, then I can't even feel sorry for him. But I can feel sorry for those that read and believe those misconceptions and will never know the true history and value of these magnificent ships.

"B" It's sort of like the fantasy theory that the detonation of two ammunition ships is Port Chicago was actually a test of the Neutron Atomic Bomb. Duh, why would we drop ANY type of bomb on our own ammunition loading base? The "theory" is somewhat based upon what witnesses (off base) saw in the form of a huge dome of water appearing and a "mushroom" shaped cloud of explosive coming up through it. Well, you can look up photos or videos of an ammunition ship blowing up after being hit by a Kamikazi. It looks exactly the same as Test Baker done in 1946 at Bikini. Therefore all this "exposure to the truth" is actually just afterthought and written by hacks who have nothing else better to do than belch out a bunch of B.S.

The infamous crack in Barbette III   Photo by author

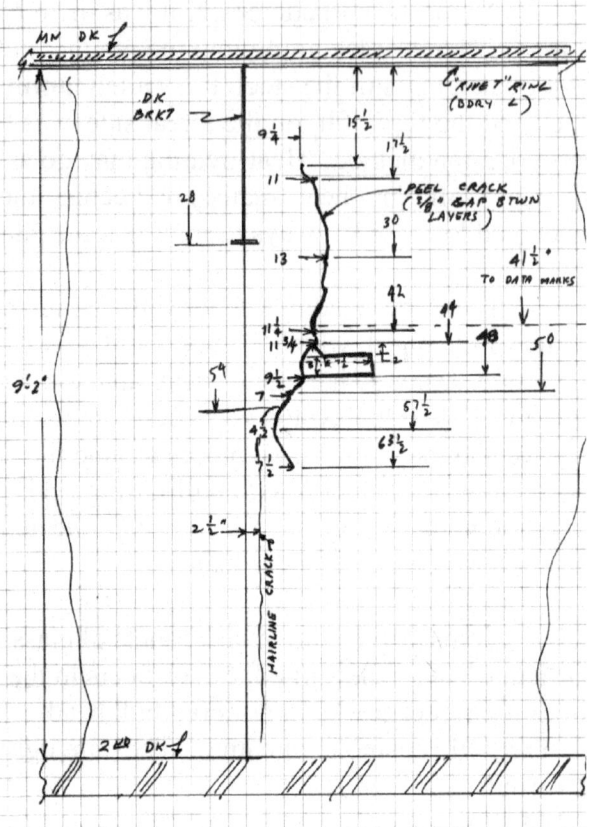
Detailed dimensions of the crack Author's field sketch

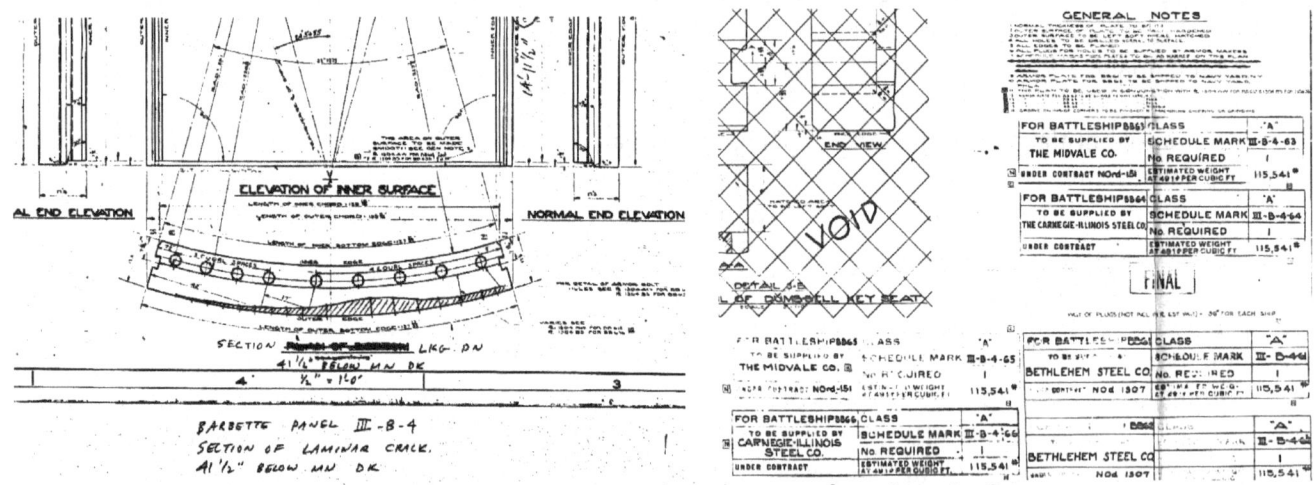
Plan view on the left shows the depth of the crack as taken by X-Rays.
Plan title on the right shows that Missouri's armor was built only by Midvale.

CHAPTER 29: TURRET II INCIDENT ON *IOWA*

I am constantly being asked what I think caused the "explosion" in Turret II of the USS *Iowa* that killed forty-seven crewmen. I have had a couple of theories but I am only going to describe one I had at the time of the incident and reported it to Norfolk. LBNSY didn't have that much to do with the investigation of the incident, but as planning yard we were called upon to provide technical assistance where needed. But there is a very eerie background to this incident.

As planning yard, we were called upon to provide a repair procedure when the list of damaged items was sent to us. Ken Bennett, who was then our chief engineer, was amazed that I had the procedure on his desk within minutes. "How the hell did you come up with that so fast?" he asked.

"Because we did this a year or so ago under operation *Proud Scout*." I answered.

"Huh? What was *Proud Scout*?" he asked.

"It was a secret drill NAVSEA put us through. *Wisconsin* was still undergoing reactivation and we were to assume *Iowa* had destroyed Turret II in an explosion. We were to come up with a procedure of taking one of *Wisconsin's* Turrets off and putting it on *Iowa*. We only had 24 hours to do it in but we passed the test. Ted Gallo even lined up a crane to lift the Turret sub-structure which is 425 tons."

Ken stared at me and asked, "How come I didn't know about this?"

I shrugged my shoulders but one of our planning coordinators with me answered, "I believe you were on travel that week and we were told to keep it secret after it was over. So, I guess nobody told you about it after you returned." Ken seemed to appreciate our dedication to security, though I'm sure he was miffed, as he should be, about not being briefed afterwards. I returned to my desk and had a heart stopping recollection of memory.

While I was still in the configuration manager's section a year or so before *Proud Scout*, I received a phone call from Jim Snyder in NAVSEA to contact the Damage Control officer of *Iowa* and investigate a problem they had with the Replenishment-at-Sea tripod on top of Turret II. I promptly called the officer and he said that the tripod problem was human error, not design. One of the boatswain's mates clipped off the end of his fingertip by having it where it should not have been while erecting the tripod.

He thought I was calling on another more serious problem they had where the center barrel of Turret II gets energized when the Discone/Discage antenna up on the bow is activated. He has had two men get zapped by high voltage from the muzzle of the gun when they were standing on top of Turret I and touched the barrel.

Al Perry, our electrical/electronics configuration manager, jumped up from his chair and dug the specs out on that antenna. He discovered that if the antenna goes out of synchronization, it could emit a longer wave than intended. The wave would be around 66-feet long, give or take two feet. I pulled out a profile drawing of the ship and scaled the distance from the antenna to the muzzle of a Turret II barrel. The distance was in increments of about 66 feet and the barrel itself is just 68-feet long. Therefore, the barrel could be turned into a secondary antenna storing high voltage. Al ran out to the *New Jersey* that was in port then and checked for any similar accidents. However, *New Jersey* reported that their antenna had never gone out of sync and they never had any near electrocutions on top of Turret I from the Turret II barrels.

While confusing reports and rumors ran rampant as to what caused the incident in *Iowa's* Turret, I thought I hit a real possibility when that recollection came back to me. I called Norfolk and contacted one of their investigators to give him the history of that antenna-to-gun barrel-energizing problem. I thought that possibly the center barrel was energized by the antenna and when the powder bags were loaded a spark caused the powder to ignite. That possibility was thoroughly investigated but came back negative for the following, very practical, reasons:

The barrel could only be energized while the antenna was on AND out of synchronization.

The barrel would have to be at zero degrees elevation at zero degrees azimuth aimed at the antenna.

The barrel would lose its charge once the antenna was turned off.

The barrel would lose its charge when trained away from the antenna even if the antenna was active.

If any electrical charge could be in the barrel, the loading of the inert practice projectile first would ground it out as it was rammed from the loading tray into the chamber.

The powder bags of linen do not conduct electricity and would not have created a spark during loading.

The antenna was NOT activated that day before the firing drill. Non-synchronization problems with that antenna had been resolved about two years previously due to the former accidents.

Well, I thought I had the answer there for a while. Many people have gotten into trouble over their personal opinions already and I don't want to argue it anymore. In truth, I don't think what really happened will ever be proved and it's time to lay the matter to rest. But just look at the spookiness, if you will that about a year or so after the electrical discharge accidents with the center barrel of Turret II, a secret Turret replacement drill is performed based upon the loss of Turret II. Then about a year after that Turret II actually blows. Even today, I have to warn our tour guides aboard the *Iowa* in San Pedro NOT to provide their own theories and just tell the visitors that we are keeping the Turret as a memorial for the lost 47 crewmen. Yes, we can manually rotate the Turret as well as elevate and depress the barrels for special viewings. **And** we do have a ceremony every year in honor of the lost crewmen.

"B"

After repairs were done in Norfolk, the crew covered 47 bolts of the Turret top plate with Memorial caps.

CHAPTER 30: ARMOR, STEALTH and SHIP STABILITY

ARMOR: Previous chapters mentioned adding armor to the *Tarawa*, *New Jersey* and *Spruance* class Destroyers. Actually, NAVSEA did not like to call it "armor" but "fragmentation protection" instead. However, many preferred the more generic term, "armor", as that describes anything to stop or deflect any chunk of metal, rock, bullets or shrapnel that is coming in fast enough to do you great bodily harm. NAVSEA was not concerned about direct hits from weaponry but the fragments and shrapnel that can punch through even 3/8-inch thick steel bulkheads and destroy critical electronics inside. But to me, being an ex-tank driver, I like lots of thick stuff between me and incoming regardless of what it is.

In 1980, Dan Clark was assigned to develop a SCOPE on adding appliqué type aluminum armor to protect the critical spaces of the *Spruance's*. However, he left the shipyard for a job in the petroleum industry and I took over writing the SCOPE. Mike Said worked closely with me on both the SCOPE and the detail installation drawings.

In November of that year, I went to Ingalls Shipbuilding in Pascagoula, Mississippi with Jim Bibeau the design branch supervisor, Ron Stuart of planning, Bud Cothern of the mold loft and Fred Messerschmitt the group superintendent of the shipfitter shop. Our task was to inspect how Ingalls was installing similar appliqué aluminum armor to the four *Kidd* class Destroyers. The *Kidd's* were also known as the "Ayatollah" class because they were originally intended for the Shah of Iran. But when the Shah was deposed, the Navy kept the ships AND the money initially paid for them.

Ingalls method was similar to what we envisioned except that the *Kidds* were heavier than the *Spruances* were and topside weight had to be kept to a minimum. Therefore, in many areas they made a "sandwich" of armor by placing a layer of resin reinforced aramid fiber (commercially known by DuPont's brand name of "Kevlar") plates between the structural bulkheads and external plates of thicker aluminum. The installation was complex and quite time consuming.

Upon our return to Long Beach, we studied the armor arrangements for the *Spruances* and decided to use a minimum of "Kevlar". It was used for interior lining of the wave-guide trunks running up the mast and as fragment velocity reducer inside the bulwarks port and starboard of the main deckhouse. Otherwise, we used HY-80 steel inserted into the port and starboard shell plating of the forward five-inch magazine and inserted into the deck over the top of the MK-46 torpedo compartment. The rest of the ship was all aluminum from the 01 level on up so aluminum appliqué armor was installed on the external bulkheads. The plating ranged from only one-half-inch thick to one and three quarters of an inch thick depending upon the thickness of the existing bulkheads behind the "armor" and how far **"B"** inboard the critical spaces were and how many other bulkheads would be in the way of shrapnel.

Attaching the thickest plates together and butt-welding them with the standard size bevels would have been very time consuming and use up tons of welding wire. Bud Cothern came up with an idea of beveling the top and bottom edges of the plates so that an upper plate would wedge into the bevel of the lower plate sort of like shiplap planks. Jim Bibeau didn't think it would work so when I went home that evening I dug out some 2 X 6 lumber scraps and made up some mock-ups with my radial arm saw. I took the pieces of wood in the next morning and showed Jim how they fitted and that Bud's idea would work. About the only critical space on the ships we could not effectively protect were the bridge windows. Well, we could, but NAVSEA had no idea how to do it yet and they didn't have any funding for a feasibility study. The best we could do was install aluminum appliqué armor to the bulkheads below the windows.

Mike Said had an idea of how to install 2-1/2" thick armored windows, identical to those on Aircraft Carriers, and even got their specs from the company that manufactures them. He wrote a Shipalt proposal, I did the sketches for him and we submitted it to NAVSEA. However, I don't think it was ever adopted or at least not until after I retired.

We were given general guidance of armor thickness and generally where to install it around the ammunition magazines of the *Tarawa* class LHA's. It was my job to design the details of how to install it. Since it was not designed to stop major caliber shells, its design had to be more precise to prevent any openings large enough for an AK-47 bullet to pass through. If it would stop small arms fire, it would certainly stop shrapnel from a near-by hit or from a warhead that explodes before hitting the ship.

The 5"/54 ammo magazines forward and aft on the *Tarawa's* had to be enclosed in three quarter-inch thick HY-80 steel. When the aft five-incher was replaced with a 20mm Vulcan Phalanx CIWS, that magazine also had to be armored. The detail design was not too complex until we came to designing an armored trunk for critical wiring up to the bridge.

The only area where we thought there was a goof up was in ordering about twice as much material as necessary. The reason for the over purchase was that NAVSEA had changed the guidance and removed one of the five-inch guns on the ships. Since three of the ships were home ported at Long Beach, we were not charged with stockpiling as initial funding was being raised to do the same job on the *Belleau Wood* and *Peleliu* as well as the *Tarawa*. Having that extra material came in very handy when we started building the armored Tomahawk deckhouses for *New Jersey* later.

We did not use any "Kevlar" on the LHA's or BB's as they are not as weight critical as the smaller ships. I'm not too keen about it anyway. Cutting with high-speed saws, all workers had to be in HAZMAT suits with dedicated air supply as the dust is toxic as well as abrasive. I also found that it doesn't stop bullets very well either. I collected a few pieces of scrap three-quarter inch thick Kevlar from the shop and took them up to some land we own in Oregon. I placed them against rocks and did some testing. No problem stopping a .22 caliber rim fire from my grandmother's rifle. A single piece just barely stopped a round from my .41 magnum Ruger. I then placed three pieces totaling 2-1/4" thick against a rock and fired one round from my M-1 Garand. But I cheated. I used an armor-piercing bullet. It went clean through all three pieces and didn't even strip the copper jacket off the penetrator core.

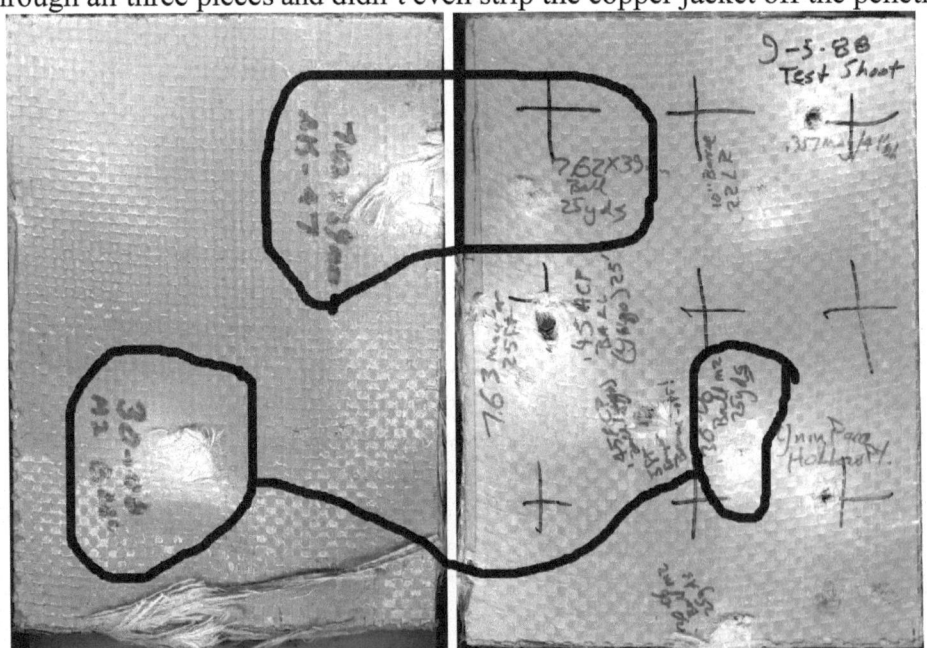

Front & back of a 3/4" thick "Kevlar" tested by Gordon Douglas. I'll stick to steel, thank you.

The armor covers for the wave guides and cableways going up the masts of the Spruance class were aluminum plate on the outside and "Kevlar" panels inside to save weight. US Navy photo by Sophie Chase

A DD-963 Class Destroyer getting Aluminum Clad armor installed.
Ship's hull number purposely blanked out by author. US Navy photo by Sophie Chase

Stand-Off armor plates were installed over vent openings.   US Navy photo by Sophie Chase

A big challenge to fit armor around the fittings of a Fueling-At-Sea station. US Navy photo by Sophie Chase

    Much of the armor we installed on *New Jersey* was also appliqué type. However, in most cases we did not have to butt plates together running up high bulkheads. The deck heights are only seven and one-half feet high and most areas requiring armor had an interruption with a platform or deck extension beyond the bulkhead. Making sure the armor stayed in place by only the edge welds, we cut diagonal "slashes" in the structural bulkhead behind and welded those cuts to the armor. This gave an additional attachment as well as take out the oil panning bulges in the bulkheads.

However, when we designed the outer bulkheads of CEC we did not do "slashing". Since there would be no deck on the outside to take the weight of some of the armor panels of 1-1/2 inch thick steel, that weighs 61.2 pounds per square foot (or 1,913 lbs each), we had panels of the bulkheads cut out between the stiffeners. This left the stiffeners with an "I" beam cross-section instead of a "T" and allowed a full peripheral weld to be placed around inside each armor panel hanging in sheer as well as the outer welds.

The forward fire control tower was already built of three-quarter inch thick STS and only required a sheathing of one-quarter inch thick HY-80 to be added on the outside. Also, we saved the main leg of the original mast and added one-quarter inch thick steel to it as well. But that gave us some problems later on though not our fault.

In every new space, or redesignated space, that received armor we also designed bolted access panels for equipment change-outs in future overhauls. Tim Douglass in the compartment and access design section designed the armored doors. All the doors were beveled on the edges to match the beveled cutouts in the armor panel. Cutting the radius corners in those panels gave Shop 11 some problems at first because the concentration of heat often melted out more metal than desired. They solved the problem by cutting out the door openings from the backside, thus spreading the torch heat out.

Armored trunks were a pain in the butt because we had to have a bolted access panel every few feet for installation of wiring or piping. However, we retained all of the armored ammo hoists and wiring trunks of the removed 5"/38 and 40mm gun mounts and we reused those trunks for new wiring and piping.

Now for the armor "problem" mentioned earlier. One day Bob Blount called me and he said that the Naval Investigative Service (NIS now NCIS) needed someone to assist in a fraud investigation for the FBI. I was the logical choice to help since it had to do with possible bad steel armor installed on the *New Jersey*.

Oh joy! About a year before, I received a letter from NAVSEA that was sent to them from a Senator who received it from a constituent. The letter complained about a loss of American jobs in the steel industry and was asking how much steel from Japan was installed aboard the *New Jersey*. Based upon my meeting with NSC a few months prior and actually seeing the procurement documents, I was able to respond that all of the steel used on the ship was from Lutjens Steel in Pennsylvania. Lutjens is a very highly regarded manufacturer and it is unbelievable that they would have sold inferior grade for such an important project.

As it turned out, however, it was not related to steel from Lutjens but from a sub-contractor. You see, the thicker the plate, the cheaper it is per pound because it doesn't have to go through the rolls as often. Lutjens found a supplier in Marietta, Georgia who claimed to have sufficient quantities of one-quarter inch thick HY-80 to supplement the overall order. Therefore Lutjens did not have to roll out any armor thinner than one-half inch and kept the total average cost down to only forty-five cents per pound.

To add a little more to the fraud fire, a few weeks before that phone call from Bob, the shipyard was building a new stainless steel uptake for a *Spruance* class ship. The design called for a very high grade of stainless steel to resist the tremendous heat put out by gas turbine exhaust. But the welder noticed one corner of the plate was stamped "Type 304" a lower grade of stainless steel. The welder called the metallurgical lab and they took some samples that tested as 304 rather than the higher grade.

Inspection of the shipping documents claimed it to be the higher grade and identified the supplier as that outfit in Marietta. At about the same time, a former foreman of the company called the fraud hotline in Washington, D.C. and claimed that the company was deliberately marking low-grade metals as high grade and charging the higher price. When Washington discovered that Lutjens contracted the company to supply some of the HY-80 armor for the *New Jersey*, flags went up all over the place.

I met with the NIS agent and we discussed our plan of investigation. The ship had already left on deployment, but tons of scrap remnants still remained in the shop. Dan Kline from the metallurgical lab came with his portable analysis machine and with the shop expeditor assisting in identifying the remnants; we tested pieces for a whole day. I was able to identify remnants just by the shape that was cut out from them and the expeditor could verify that as he was the one who had to have cranes put them in the storage racks. In the end, we found only some of the one-quarter inch thick plates, marked as HY-80, to be of ordinary medium steel.

We also involved the shop planners in digging up all shipping records and invoices. Along with photographs we had of the armor being installed, some showing the shipping stencils still on it, we were able to give NIS quite a package of documentation.

It was finally scheduled to test every plate of HY-80 on the ship upon her return, which didn't happen for another five years. When she did return, we had to stage all superstructure that received armor plating so Dan and his team could test the metal. We found everything over one-quarter inch thick to be within specs for HY-80. Most of the one-quarter inch also was within specs except for the sheathing we did on the mast leg and two plates on the front of the fire control tower. Rather than cutting all of those plates off, the mast being the most difficult, we merely added another quarter inch of armor over them. NIS turned over all results of our investigation to the FBI who in turn arrested the owners of the company for fraud.

"B" Excerpts from the outcome of the court trial printed in the New York Times, July 21, 1984:
2 GET 10 YEARS IN MILITARY STEEL FRAUD (NYTimes.com)
"A Federal district judge has sentenced two military contractors to 10 years in prison for selling inferior steel to the Navy for refitting the battleship **New Jersey** *and other warships, as well as for a space-shuttle engine-testing project"*

"Judge Marvin H. Shoob, sitting in Atlanta, called the deed 'sabotage' as he imposed the sentences Thursday on Jerald R. Hedden and Russell D. Roper of the Metal Service Center of Georgia."

"Information from the public record of the case showed that Mr. Hedden was the sales manager of Metal Service Center and the company's manager of quality control. Mr. Roper was a salesman. The two worked from a small office in Marietta, Ga."

"They had 400 contracts with the Government worth about $2.8 million."

"The court record showed that the method of operation for Mr. Hedden and Mr. Roper was to submit a low bid on a Government contract, such as with the Defense Industrial Supply Center in Philadelphia, then buy lower-grade material for a much lower price."

"The defendants removed the markings from the material, replaced them with markings to indicate that the material would meet Government specifications and forged certificates to that effect."

Please note: The judge used the word **SABOTAGE**. I agree and think 10 years each was too light of a sentence.

One unusual item I personally designed armor for, where even NAVSEA had to agree "armor" was the correct term, was the jettisonable dolly for the RPV gasoline bladder in the former 40mm gun tub on the stern of the ship. With terrorists getting bolder by the day, the Navy was concerned about a speedboat full of terrorists zipping alongside the ship while in harbor and raking it with machinegun fire. The 500-gallon gasoline bladder was used to store fuel for the Remote Piloted Vehicle (RPV) that is basically a large radio controlled "model" airplane equipped with cameras for precise target designation. The bladder was stowed in a steel dolly that was on a set of inclined tracks and held back with quick release hooks. The dolly could then be jettisoned overboard should there be a major fire on the helicopter deck.

Norfolk had designed and built armor plates around the gasoline bladder for the East Coast based ships. I reviewed their design and found a number of problems with it. First of all, it used only one-quarter inch thick HY-80 plates and was all bolted together with ¼-20 machine screws. I came up with an entirely new design that used one-half inch thick HY-80 where it would receive the most direct hits, one-quarter inch thick steel in more obliquely angled areas and all welded. It was also about fifty pounds lighter than the Norfolk design.

The greatest problem we had with armor, at the start, was not knowing what Class A and Class B armor were actually made of. There was no Mil-Spec on any of them as at the time of their manufacture in WW II as it was highly classified. I wrote to a couple of steel companies that were listed on the armor drawings and only US Steel came back with a one page letter thinking that the high grade armors were similar to STS.

Even the Mil-Spec on STS was vague and did not list a chemical content. It only listed a maximum allowable carbon content and a minimum allowable yield strength of 110,000 pounds per square inch (110 KPSI). I finally found an archival record of STS printed before WW II that gave the chemical tables. Because the original design of STS used fairly large quantities of chromium and nickel to attain its toughness, the war demanded that companies be allowed to alter their formulas so they could meet the millions of tons required for the construction of ships, light tanks, armored cars, etc. It didn't matter what other metals were used to make up for lower percentages of chromium or nickel as long as the steel met the basic requirements of carbon content and 110 KPSI yield. In any case, STS had to be welded with 25-20 stainless steel welding rod anyway, which would efficiently fuse any chemical mix of steel delivered.

Bill Garzke, of Gibbs and Cox, had written some valuable books on Navy ships that we used as our "bibles" in design. Gordon Douglas found Bill's phone number for me and I gave him a call asking if he knew where we could find the detailed information on Class A and B armor. Bill suggested I contact Nathan Okun up in Oxnard, California who had done an extensive personal study on armor manufacture.

I found Nathan worked at the Naval Research Center at Port Hueneme and I was able to call him at work. By the next week, I received a package two inches thick of all the research material he had including his own summaries high-lighting the information I needed. I then made several copies of all that material and distributed that to our welding engineers and metallurgical laboratory. I also pushed through a letter of commendation to be sent to the commander of Port Hueneme for Nathan's extra effort.

The "Gung Ho" attitude of bringing back the Battleships was not restricted to the Long Beach Naval Shipyard. Nathan Okun is just one example of many people outside the shipyard who went that extra mile.

On the C.E.C. outer bulkheads, the 3/8-inch thick panels of Medium Steel were cut out between the frames leaving just 3-inches on each side. Then the 1 ½-inch thick HY-80 armor panels were installed on the outside but were welded on both sides. US Navy photo by Sophie Chase

Welding in an armored deck of HY-80. Note the electrical heating straps to pre-heat and post-heat the steel for welding with Stainless Steel rod. US Navy photo by Sophie Chase

The armored vent duct of HY-80 steel for a 5"/38 upper handling room.   Photo by author

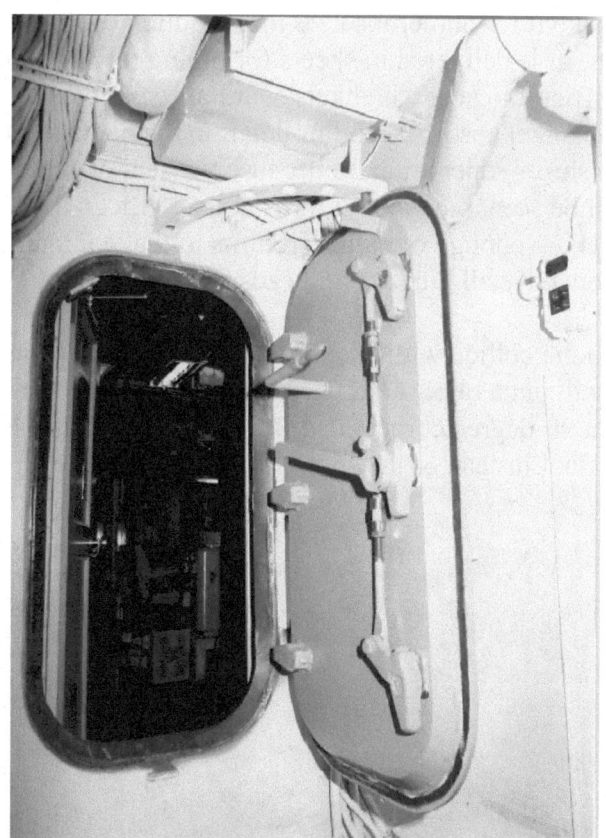

A 1 ½-inch thick HY-80 armored door going into C.E.C. All new armored doors were designed by Tim Douglass and all were built and installed by the shipfitter shop (Shop 11).   Note the ingenious method Tim designed above the door to easily hold it open at any position.
Photo by author

STEALTH: Another special project the shipyard was tasked to do was the Passive Countermeasures (PCM) installation on a class of ships. PCM is just a thinly veiled cover term for Stealth. One of the pipe dreams of airplane and ship designers from as early as WW I was how to make an airplane or a ship "invisible". One trick tried in the First World War was to cover the framework of an airplane with a clear "see through" material. But it reflected Sun light so well it could be seen further off than a lightly painted plane. Then RADAR came along in the Second World War. Various materials and methods were installed to absorb RADAR but from its own antennas to protect near-by electronic systems. To coat an entire ship with this material would be far too much topside weight and it couldn't be shaped around circular objects such as masts and kingposts as it was about an inch thick and as stiff as plywood.

However, fast drivers who wanted to get out of speeding ticket came up with another idea. Ever see one of those fancy sports cars zipping on down the road with a "car bra" over the front end? They are advertised as keeping the fronts of cars clean of splattered bugs. But that's not their true purpose. They are actually made of a series of rubber layers, with an aluminum foil backing, to absorb police RADAR. The rest of the car is streamlined enough to deflect RADAR beams off in another direction and the traffic cop cannot get a positive fix on your speed. Well, why can't we just glue that same type of stuff onto the metal bulkheads of a ship? So it was given a try on a ship berthed out at the Mole at LBNS. I went out there to check on another job to be done and saw shop people gluing rubber sheets down in various places. I wondered what the heck it was for but didn't ask. I assumed it was for some experiment with external insulation. One of the crewmen aboard the ship said it gave a soft surface for the crew members to beat their heads against.

No secrets here (as usual). The car bra that absorbs police RADAR was described in detail on the 1980's Australian TV show, "Beyond 2000". Even the exact material is not totally a military secret because several companies make it for numerous uses that require absorbing RADAR-type emissions such as in electronics test labs. It is delivered in sheets for gluing directly onto metal surfaces. For areas on a ship that would be too difficult to coat, "blankets" similar to car bras, are hung over the area. Norman Friedman described blanket absorbers in fair detail in his book on Desert Storm. It is obvious that we cannot coat the entire ship's superstructure because we cannot coat the entire hull. A ship's hull broadside to RADAR can still be seen, but when it turns at least fifteen degrees off of broadside, it will be difficult for RADAR to pick up enough of pattern returns to make it a target. You notice that our latest Zumwalt class Destroyers have all hull & bulkheads slanted inboard 15 degrees.

"B" So STEALTH ships don't collide with friendly ships, reflective panels are swung out to 90 degree angles so other ships will get a blip. Also we use a RADAR decoy that's an inflated "float". Internal reflective panels form 90-degree corners and is floated behind as a RADAR decoy so an incoming missile will hit the float instead of the ship. Love its nickname, the "Rubber Ducky."

Normally it takes up to three months to do the installation absolutely perfect in accordance with the Shipalt and Installation Instructions I was tasked to write. But time was VERY short.

However a Tiger Team could install the PCM material in less than two weeks if most of the preparatory work, such as scaling paint, repainting and cleaning with a solvent, were cut to a minimum. During Desert Storm, two ships were rapidly coated by the "Crash Program" method. One didn't work out too well because of peeling paint behind the material. But the other ship did very well and an errant Exocet actually lost acquisition of the ship and flew right over the top.

"Semi-funny side": an officer of that ship was in the "O" Club in Bahrain one evening and another officer remarked, "We are having a problem with our RADAR lately. There are times when your ship is turned at certain angles we don't pick it up at all." NAVSEA people there quickly told him to shut up. Ah, the shades of World War II; "Loose Lips Sink Ships". Just as true today as then.

SHIP STABILITY: Another consideration we had to take into account with the above addition of fragmentation armor and stealth material was the added weight above waterline. For every additional piece of steel or aluminum or every additional black box or every additional run of ventilation we had to calculate the weight of the addition to the closest pound and calculate the center of gravity of the addition for its height above the keel, distance port or starboard of centerline and distance fore or aft of amidships. Then the scientific section would combine all the estimated weight and moment calculations from each design section and then calculate the change in draft, trim and most importantly, the ship's overall stability.

The overhaul of the USS *Oklahoma City* (CL-5) in 1962 showed that we were not calculating the stability changes as accurately as we should when the ship experienced a dangerously extreme heel doing hard turns on her sea trial. But this was true of all shipyards and not just LBNSY. The addition of permanently installed heavy electronics above the main deck, to keep within fifty feet of their antennas per manufacturer's warranty restrictions, added tons of high weight to the ships. Hundreds of tons of lead ballast had to be added into the fuel tanks of *Oklahoma City* to compensate for the added topside weights.

I was mildly criticized for being so concerned about weight and moment of such a tremendously stable Battleship but I always referred back to the *Oklahoma City* we almost lost on sea trial. Ironically, one day as I was stating that excuse for being so weight and moment conscious, an engineer for the NAVSEA design agent agreed full-heartedly with me and quoted the exact tonnage of ballast that had to be added. It turned out he was the former XO of *Oklahoma City* at the time.

CHAPTER 31: REEVES FIELD VRF-3 NATS

Reeves Field was originally a private airfield called Allen Field. Most shipyard workers that came on board after 1947 never saw any air activity there and when we did have some work to do on it all we saw was acres of gray asphalt. During open houses, the visitor's shuttle would only take us as far as the building that served as the Naval Reserve Center and a mine warfare group. The mine warfare group would have a couple of inert mines and a torpedo on display and that was about it. An old four-engine flying boat, minus its wings, would be sitting out on the tarmac and was not open for tours. From the Reserve Center, you could see a row of cottages that actually served as married officers housing. But we were not allowed to tour that area. Only the old timers would tell the new hires that Reeves Field used to be a very busy air base attached to the Naval Base (Roosevelt Base). So very little of its history ever got recorded. At the southeast corner of the field was an indoor 25-yard pistol range that was used not only for training of military personnel but also by the Long Beach Naval Shipyard Gun Club for practice and matches. Photos of Reeves Field were collected from various sources. Maps were reconstructed from aerial photographs and the building layouts from other aerial photos.

The most definitive history of Reeves Field is taken directly from the website of The California State Military Museum and gives two historical accounts by **three** different historians. Their accounts are presented in their original form with full credit to the contributors.

The California State Military Museum
Preserving California's Military Heritage
Naval Air Station, Terminal Island
(Naval Air Station, San Pedro; Naval Air Base, San Pedro; Reeves Field.
HISTORICAL ACCOUNT
by WO1 Mark Denger

Allen Field was a small 410-acre civilian airport built in 1927 on a portion of the expanded section of Terminal Island. Terminal Island is a sand-filled island located adjacent to the port of Los Angeles and expanding between the harbors of San Pedro and Long Beach. Located approximately equally between three cities, San Pedro, Wilmington, and Long Beach, it was reached by each city by taking a foot ferry or one of the Red Cars that were operated by the Pacific R.R. Company. The field itself consisted of three paved runways (the largest being 4,200 feet long), a large seaplane ramp, and several hangars and other buildings.

The U.S. Navy began its use of Allen Field almost from the very beginning. In 1927 a Naval Air Reserve Training Facility was established there. With the U.S. Naval Reserve Training Camp located across the harbor at the Submarine Base in San Pedro, it was an ideal location. With its large seaplane ramp, the airfield at Terminal Island soon became the primary operating base for seaplanes assigned to ships of the Pacific Fleet.

In 1935 the Navy took complete control over Allen Field and in 1936 designated it as a Naval Air Base (NAB San Pedro) and renamed it Reeves Field, in honor of Rear Admiral Joseph M. Reeves, Naval Aviation Observer and farseeing pioneer in the tactical employment of Aircraft Carriers.

Terminal Island was one of the first islands seized from Japanese fishermen and cannery workers shortly after Pearl Harbor was attacked.

Early in 1942, the Naval Reserve Air Training Facility at Reeves Field was turned over, along with its facilities there, to other Naval units of the Pacific Fleet and relocated to NAS Los Alamitos, and NAB San Pedro was redesignated as a Naval Air Station (NAS Terminal Island). Even though Reeves Field was operational as a Naval Reserve Air Training Facility from 1927 to 1942, it continued to play an important training role to Naval Reserve Air personal through 1945.

In 1942, NAB San Pedro, now NAS Terminal Island, was now relegated to the task of equipping and performing flight-tests on a large number of military aircraft produced at the nearby plants of Lockheed, Douglas & Vultee. To facilitate delivery of these aircraft, the U.S. Navy established the Naval Air Ferry Command (NAFC) in 1943. This was a wing of the Naval Air Transport Service (NATS), and three Air Ferry Squadrons were commissioned, VRF-1 at NAS New York, VRF-2 at NAF Columbus, Ohio, and VRF-3 at NAS Terminal Island, California. Originally called Air Delivery Units (ADUs), the ADUs and ferry squadrons used small transports to ferry pilots to the manufacturer's plant to pick up the aircraft and then the transport would fly to the station where the aircraft were delivered to bring the pilots back to either the factory for another flight or to their home station.

The commander of NAS Terminal Island was Captain Kneflar "Socko" McGinnis, who had been awarded the Navy Cross for transporting the first mass flight of seaplanes from Northern California to Hawaii.

Also stationed at NAS Terminal Island were a small group of women, whose contribution to the war effort has often been overlooked. These women were part of an elite group of the Navy's WAVES (Women Accepted in Volunteer Emergency Services). Of the 25,000 WAVES and 1,900 SPARs who became part of naval aviation in jobs as mechanics, air traffic controllers, and radio and air navigators in World War II, about 200 of them worked at Terminal Island. These women played an important role in the Naval Air Transport Service. Day and night, hundreds of new planes roared in and out of Reeves Field, one of the busiest naval ferrying air stations on the West Coast. Planes just off assembly lines were flight-tested here and then "pickled" with a protective coating to protect them against salt air before they were shipped to the South Pacific.

Reeves Field also served as a training field for men having just completed Naval Air Navigation School. Interestingly enough, a few of the WAVES assigned to NAS Terminal Island were qualified as Navy aerial navigators and trained hundreds of men as naval aviators and navigators from the Naval Reserves at Reeves Field.

Even so, with the Naval Reserve Training Facility having been transferred in 1942, NAB San Pedro's status was downgraded to that of a Naval Air Station (NAS Terminal Island) in 1943. Both NAS Terminal Island and NAS Los Alamitos remained under the command of the Naval Operating Base at San Pedro, California, until August 10, 1944, when they both fell under the jurisdiction of the Eleventh Naval District. The Long Beach Naval Station (NAVSTA Long Beach), which was not established until 1941, became located adjacent to the airfield. Reeves Field as a Naval Air Station was disestablished in 1947, although the adjacent NAVSTA Long Beach would continue to utilize Reeves Field as an auxiliary airfield until the late 1970s, at which time the land was made available to Los Angeles for critically needed port expansion to the south. The name of Reeves Field was later transferred to the Naval Air Station in Lemoore, California, where a new airfield was established in 1961 for the U.S. Navy's fighter and attack bombers.

HISTORICAL ACCOUNT
by M.L. Shettle, Jr.

Long Beach and San Pedro serve as the harbor for the greater Los Angeles area. During World War I, the Navy established an operating base at San Pedro that remained in use through the 1920s and 30s. In 1935, a need arose for an aviation facility to support the floatplanes of battleships and cruisers. The harbor's sand-filled Terminal Island was leased for no charge from the City of Los Angeles. The WPA provided initial construction of the breakwater, a seaplane ramp, a concrete parking mat, and three runways that reached completion in June 1937. Work continued with the addition of hangars, barracks, and other facilities in the fall. The station was commissioned on March 1, 1938, as NAS San Pedro, and went through a series of name changes before finally settling on Terminal Island.

In early 1939, the Navy began construction of a training facility nearby, named Roosevelt Base, and a shipyard. On October 1, 1941, the Navy formed an Aircraft Delivery Unit (ADU) at the air station. Shortly after the attack on Pearl Harbor, the Army stationed P-40 and P-38 interceptors at the airfield with the permission of the Navy. In January 1942, VS-46 began operating the inshore patrol mission from the base with 12 OS2U Kingfishers. The same month, the Army built eight concrete revetments on the airfield to protect its aircraft. The primary mission of the air station became the major West Coast Aircraft Delivery Unit. In the last six months of 1942, the ADU commissioned 200 aircraft a month from the Douglas and Lockheed factories in the area including the SBD, SNV, PV, and the A-24 (SBDs for the Army). Meanwhile NATS's VR-2 began three flights a week.

During 1943, activity continued to rise. VR-2's service increased to daily with VR-3 beginning two daily transcontinental flights. Scouting squadrons continued operating from the station and from August to December of the year, VS-52 conducted operational training with SBDs. During the year, the ADU's deliveries averaged 434 aircraft a month including Culver TD2C drones, PB2Bs, PB2Y-3R transports, Canadian produced SB2Cs, and PBYs from Consolidated's new plant in New Orleans. Terminal Island reached the limit of its capacity; therefore, an Auxiliary Aircraft Acceptance Unit opened at Litchfield Park, Arizona, to accept the PB4Ys Liberators from San Diego. On December 1, the ferry squadron, VRF-3, was commissioned at Terminal Island. Army continued to operate interceptors and added antiaircraft guns plus barrage balloons. During 1944, the station started performing aircraft modifications. At the end of 1944, the ADU began receiving the new Lockheed PV-2 Harpoon. VJ-12 also arrived and remained to war's end.

Terminal Island had three asphalt runways with the longest at 4,900 ft. In March 1944, personnel totaled 341 officers, 1,274 enlisted men and 420 civilians. Billeting was available for 171 officers and 1,054 men. Peak utilization of the station occurred in the spring of 1945, with over 300 aircraft on board. VRF-3 operated 18 aircraft -- mostly light transports. The station proper had approximately 20 aircraft assigned. An Assembly and Repair Department maintained an aircraft pool that reached over 100.

Terminal Island closed in 1947, and its property assigned to the Bureau of Yards and Docks. Growth of the Long Beach Naval Shipyard and Naval Station eventually obliterated the former airfield's runways. The 1995 Base Realignment and Closure Commission recommended closing the shipyard.

"B" The WAVES by: Ceclia Rasmussen - Los Angeles Times staff writer.

Her April 14, 2002 account in the Los Angeles Times

Behind the U.S. Navy's World War II flyboys was a small band of women whose wing-and-a-prayer contribution to the war effort never made history books.

Almost 60 years ago (*as of 2002*), an elite group of WAVES--Women Accepted in Volunteer Emergency Services--charted a new course in air navigation and opened doors for other women into a male-dominated branch of the service.

These were the women--80 of them airborne, hundreds more on the ground--who served as stateside navigators, training male pilots in navigational skills and sometimes even riding shotgun on domestic military flights. They were the forebears of the Navy women who today fly as "top gun" pilots.

The Japanese bombing of Pearl Harbor on Dec. 7, 1941, ignited a war in the Pacific that changed the world. It also brought to Los Angeles' Terminal Island a new kind of Navy navigator.

To free up men to serve at sea, thousands of women joined the Navy in the newly organized women's unit called WAVES, and a few thousand more enlisted in the new Coast Guard's SPAR women units, short for Semper Paratus, "Always Ready".

Of those, 25,000 WAVES and 1,900 SPARs became part of naval aviation in jobs as mechanics, air traffic controllers, and radio and air navigators. **About 200 of them worked at Terminal Island**.

Only 80 female navigators, some of whom were already private pilots, were sent for further training, 50 flight hours in twin-engine military planes. That earned them prized gold wings as the nation's first female military personnel to share noncombat flight duties with men.

Before World War II. only wartime emergencies brought women into military work, and then only in a limited capacity. Female volunteers had participated in every war involving American men, and formalizing their participation started to take shape in 1901 and 1908 with the creation of the Army and Navy nurse corps.

In 1942, things changed. Joy Bright Hancock, a civilian pilot who had been a Navy yeoman in World War I, pressured the government to create the Navy WAVES, making her the highest-ranking Navy woman, a distinction she retained for years.

To boost enlistments from women, Eleanor Roosevelt arranged for the American-born couturier Mainbocher--birth name Maing Rousseau Bocher -- to design uniforms for the WAVES and SPARs. His prior experience included introducing the strapless evening dress in 1934.

In 1943, Marian Davis Skidmore and Marjorie Law Beringer were 21 year old UCLA graduates when they and six other women joined the Navy and then, in Navy uniform, became the first female radio navigators assigned to Reeves Field, a military airfield on Terminal Island.

Skidmore and Beringer had just finished naval boot camp at New York City's Hunter College, where they earned high marks in math and were among the first women selected to attend the Naval Air Navigation School in Atlanta. The 1 0-week course --- known as "coming on the beam" --- was tough. Those who did not maintain a 3.2 average were tossed out of school. Trainees studied meteorology, drew weather maps, learned temperature drops and forecasts. They navigated and charted hypothetical four-hour flights over the Pacific, learned Morse code and how to us basic instruments such as a compass, altimeter, tachometer and turn-and-back indicators.

They wangled sea duty in the Pacific, Skidmore recalled sardonically --- which meant "riding the San Pedro Ferry back and forth across the harbor" to a "glamour hot spot" on Terminal Island, "the best duty of and WAVES radio navigators."

Reeves Field was also known as the "Hollywood Country Club" because its wartime residents included such actors as Robert Taylor and Charles "Buddy" Rogers, who was married to Mary Pickford, as well as actress Norma Shearer's husband, ski instructor and Navy aviator Lt. Arrouge.

"B" *Charles Rogers is also listed in Appendix G as Rogers, C.E. Ltjg, Aircraft Delivery Unit.*

Since wartime gas rationing limited driving, Rogers rode a motorcycle to the field each day, while Skidmore ant the others hopped aboard the Pacific Electric trolley, *(the famous "RED CARS")* downtown for the ride to San Pedro.

WAVES seldom had to walk the last mile from the drop-off point to the gate. If Marines patrolling the area in Jeeps didn't happen by to give them a ride, they took a four-bit taxi ride, piling in eight to a car, WAVES sitting on sailor's laps.

For the WAVES that got off the RedCars, there were always Jeeps ready for them.. Tough work for the sailors already in them "requiring" the WAVES to sit on their laps. But somebody had to do it.

The famous "RED CARS" that was perhaps the best light rail transportation system in the country. They were not restricted to city lines but could cross over counties and provided fast and dependable transport to the Long Beach Naval Shipyard, Roosevelt Base and (especially) the WAVES of Reeves Field NAS that had to live off base.

Author's personal collection of brass & custom painted Red Car trolleys in HO scale.

Terminal Island was one of the first Islands seized from Japanese American fishermen and cannery workers shortly after Pearl Harbor was attacked. Its commander was Captain Kneflar "Socko" McGinnis, who had won the Navy Cross for transporting the first mass flight of seaplanes from Northern California to Hawaii.

"He ran a good station," recalled Skidmore, who along with Beringer still lives *(as of April 2002 when this historical report was written)* in Rancho Palos Verdes, not far from their old posting. "He was strict but fair and you always knew where you stood with him. If men showed up for inspection in tailor-made uniforms they'd purchased in the Far East [with silk jacket linings, zippers and tight fitting pants] instead of their GI-issue uniform, McGinnis had the tailor-made clothes collected and burned."

Day and night, hundreds of new planes roared in and out of Reeves Field, one of the busiest naval ferrying air stations on the West Coast. New planes just off assembly lines were flight-tested and then "pickled" with a protective coating against the salt air before they were shipped to the South Pacific.

But not all went smoothly. Seasoned pilots who had already served in the South Pacific and were now assigned states side, well as pilots too old for overseas assignments, resented having to learn radio navigation procedures from WAVES. They especially objected to WAVES evaluating their flying skills.

One of the 80 airborne WAVES, Betty Turbiville, was navigating on a training mission over the Pacific. The young male navigator she was teaching insisted that his charts were right. If the pilot had listened to him rather than to Turbiville, the plane would have run out of fuel and crashed in Mexico.

"I didn't have anyone insult me for being in the service," Skidmore said. "But once a pilot unfairly reported one of the WAVES who was bowlegged for not keeping her stocking seams straight.'

While the pilot n training sat in a mockup training cockpit wearing a headset, Skidmore sat at a desk just outside, also wearing a headset, sending Morse code signals to the pilot, changing wind speeds and charting his path on a map to see how well he could follow the course changes. She reckons she trained hundreds of naval navigators this way.

On March 30, 1945, as the war neared its end, the Navy authorized a distinctive gold wings insignia for the 80 airborne female navigators, all of whom until then had worn a 1920's "observer" wing with a compass in the center over crossed anchors.

In their purses these women carried copies of their orders authorizing them to wear wings because they were often stopped by senior officers who pointed out that they weren't allowed to wear their "boyfriend's" wings.

Reeves Field was decommissioned in 1947 and eventually swallowed up in the harbor development. As aircraft got bigger, its landing field became too small for safe touchdowns,

In 1948, all women on active military duty, including WAVES, were made an official part of the armed forces under the Women's Armed Services Integration Act. Even so, women had to wait until 1967 for the removal of restrictions on the rank that even career military women could achieve.

Celebrating the contributions these women made to the war effort and commemorating their 60th anniversary, the Los Angeles Maritime Museum in San Pedro recently opened its newest exhibit, "WAVES and SPARS: Navy and Coast Guard Women of World War II."

The show, which runs through July, chronicles an extraordinary group of women, some of whom earned the much-coveted U. S. Navy aerial navigator's wings despite sentiments expressed by some enlisted men that it would take "two women to do the work of one man." Turbiville's dress-blue uniform, with its gold wings, is on display there.

Women's contributions were noted contemporaneously as well. In 1944, the Navy estimated that the number of WAVES on duty that year equaled the number of men it would have taken in peacetime to man 10 Battleships, 10 Aircraft Carriers, 28 Cruisers and 50 Destroyers.

Maybe they are not in their fancy blue dress uniforms you may have expected me to print, but showing one of the jobs the WAVES really did is, in this author's opinion, deserves a standing salute.

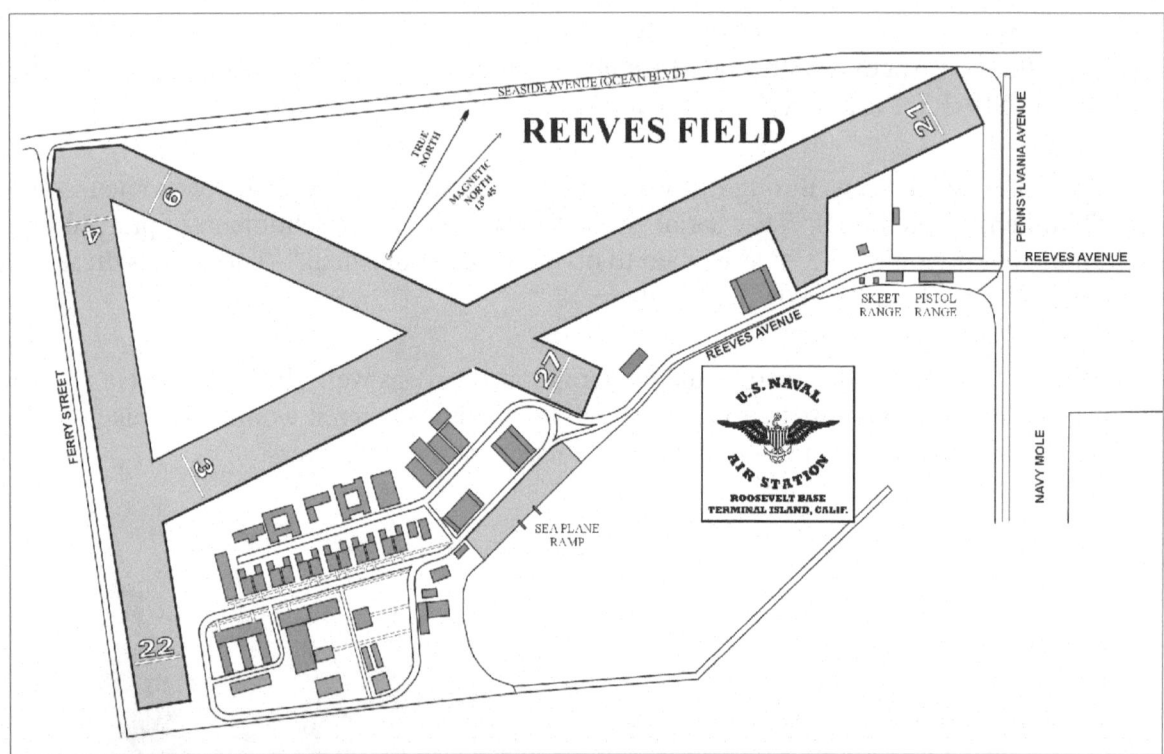

Map drawn by author after reconstructing from numerous photographs.

Opening Day cover (commemorative envelope) of April 30, 1938. Note the Blimp hangar that was planned for the Air Station but, as far as I know, was never built. Author's collection

Reeves Field in 1938 before Roosevelt Base began to be built the following year. Author's Collection

Reeves Field in 1968 showing Federal Immigration and Customs Center. The officer's quarters and hangars were still intact with a Martin Flying Boat and a Consolidated PBY near the seaplane ramp.

Reeves Field in WW II. Most of aircraft in this air view photo appear to be light Recon planes.

But then there were our "Don't Tread on Me" types. Photo looking North across the Main Channel.

Reeves Field was responsible for adding all the latest combat mods to Lockheed Harpoons.

Lockheed Harpoon bomber.   Above photo from Air Classics magazine-October 1997

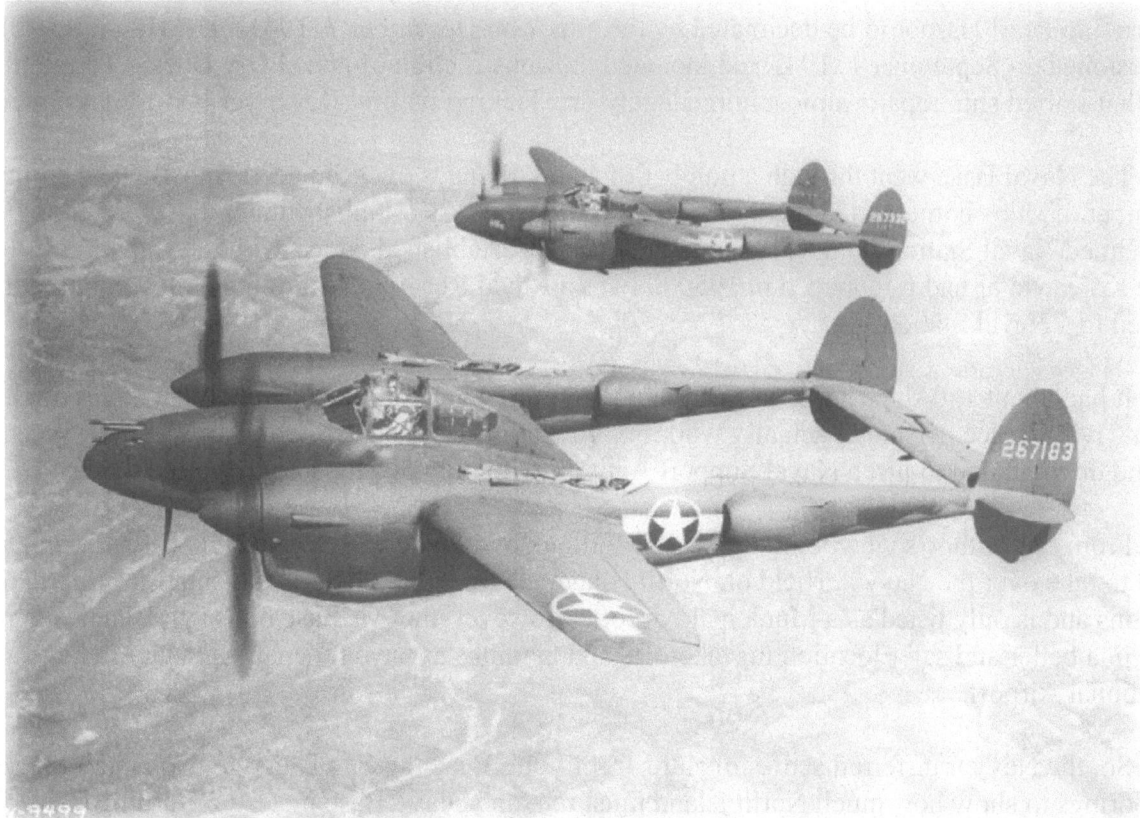

And now we have the "Fork Tailed Devils" (That's what the Luftwaffe called them) that were stowed at Reeves Field for transfer. Some did not have to go too far. The 5,000 foot runway (called the Lomita Air Strip - actually Torrance Airport now known as Zamperinni Field) but in WW II, that air strip was our Interceptor Fighter Base for possible carrier planes from Japan. Umm, the Japanese were not as figurative as the Germans and merely called them "Two Airplanes but only one pilot". You may argue that the P-51 Mustang was better. But neither the Germans or the Japanese wanted to encounter them. As Admiral Yamamoto found out the hard way.   Photo from the Internet.

CHAPTER 32: ROOSEVELT BASE

Though Reeves Field was the start of a complex of Naval Facilities, it was actually on the Los Angeles City side of the Boundary line between Los Angeles and Long Beach. With the air field becoming a Navy installation in 1938, plans for an adjoining Naval Base were drawn up in 1939 (or perhaps long before that) and with buying 104 acres from Long Beach for one-dollar, 1940 saw rapid construction of the Base.

It was named in honor of Franklin Delano Roosevelt, not that he was President but that he was a former Secretary of the Navy and was always very supportive of Naval advancement in technology and building up a Naval fleet of World importance as his uncle, Theodore Roosevelt, did in 1908. "Teddy" Roosevelt's Great White Fleet stopped off in Long Beach Harbor during its round the World trip and began a large Naval presence in the Long Beach and Los Angeles Harbors.

Starting in 1919, the fleet made San Pedro its home base with nine Battleships, twenty Submarines and nine support ships. With the construction of the breakwater to provide calm water anchorage and the construction of the Navy Landing in Long Beach, by 1932 the city was known as "The Navy Capitol of the United States" with fifty Pacific Fleet ships assigning about 2,200 officers and 26,500 enlisted men.

The construction of Roosevelt Base was a two year construction plan though most of its fleet transferred to Pearl Harbor to be decimated by the attack on December 7, 1941. The Base was officially commissioned on September 1, 1942 and included the construction of Naval Dry Docks, Terminal Island that started ship repairs almost immediately dry docking its first Destroyer just 12 days later.

The Naval Base went through a number of status changes over the years, mostly depending upon the number of ships home ported there or if Fleet Command was established there. In March of 1948 it was renamed Naval Station Long Beach and then was disestablished, along with the shipyard, in 1949. But the Korean War had it reopened in 1950 only as a Naval Receiving Station but almost immediately upgraded to a Naval Station.

It had about 140 ships home ported there with more than 40,000 personnel, not counting the civilian Civil Service personnel actually working the Station. It was disestablished again on June 30, 1974 and downgraded to just a Naval Support Activity with only 10 ships home ported there.

From this author's viewpoint, the reason for the downgrade was because the City of San Diego wanted to take over the Navy Airfield on North Island. The city's airfield is too small for International operations and is only listed as a Municipal Airport. However, the Air Base on North Island was much bigger, in a better and safer location for take-offs and landings and would enable the city to have an International Airport.

So, the Navy transferred scores of ships from Long Beach to San Diego to pack in all the piers and moorings to show how much North Island must remain a Navy Base instead of turning it over to the city. However, on October 1, 1979 the Support Facility was again upgraded to the status of a Naval Station. The Station supported post Viet Nam ships and Gulf War ships very effectively.

Unfortunately, container cargo ships were increasing their imports and land was needed to park them on. So the Base Realignment and Closure Committee (BRAC) voted it to be closed forever in 1991. The closure date was set for 1997, but the need for a container terminal for China Ocean Shipping Company had its closing date boosted up 3 years. Its closing ceremonies were held on September 30, 1994 after serving the Fleet in World War II, Korean War, Viet Nam War and the Gulf War (Desert Storm) only to become a parking lot.

Still there were the required re-use meetings to be held and the base would have been a perfect training facility for Police and Fire Departments. While closed, a number of Police training exercises were carried out there and the Fire Department had finally been given the order and funding to train for toxic chemical and biological warfare. This could have been done on the base that was equipped with all facilities needed and far away from the populated areas of Long Beach.

All ideas fell on deaf ears except the US Senate issued a proclamation that COSCO (which is owned by communist China) would not be allowed to lease any property that was formerly a US Government Defense Base.

So Hanjin of Korea now parks its containers there along with the shipyard (with all three dry docks filled in).

Looking East at the east end of Rattlesnake Island on February 2, 1928.
The short pier near the top was the original Fleet Landing for the Navy. Author's Collection

The "Mole" extending out from the Naval Base to form a double protected harbor, also called The West Basin. This was in its early stages without any permanent buildings or piers on it besides Pier 9 Fuel Pier as the photo was taken in 1944. Courtesy: Ken Britton

The other end of the Mole taken in 1944. Courtesy: Ken Britton

This was our Fire Department as of 1967. The Fire Truck on the far left has been seen in a dark (and unprintable) 1949 photo. So it was one of the first to be put in service as the Fire Station (Building 3) being the first one constructed on the new Navy Base near the start of WW II.   Photo by author

Building 1, the main Administration Building. It was also the Air Traffic Control Tower, "manned" by the WAVES.   Author's collection

Entrance to the Enlisted Men's Club, Stark Center.   Author's collection

Commissioned Officers Club, Allen Center, that was also a selection for Weddings, Promotion parties, Retirement parties and the first RAB meetings.   Author's collection

The Dispensary as it appeared in 1948.   Courtesy: "Salty"

A long shot of Roosevelt Base with Pier 9 Fuel Pier in the foreground. Author's collection

Oilers at Pier 9 that took on fuel to provide to ships either pierside or at anchorage.   Courtesy: "Salty"

The wide building in the foreground was the new Fleet Landing center, replacing the one in Long Beach. Later it became the Chief's Club and named the John Kennedy Center.   Author's collection

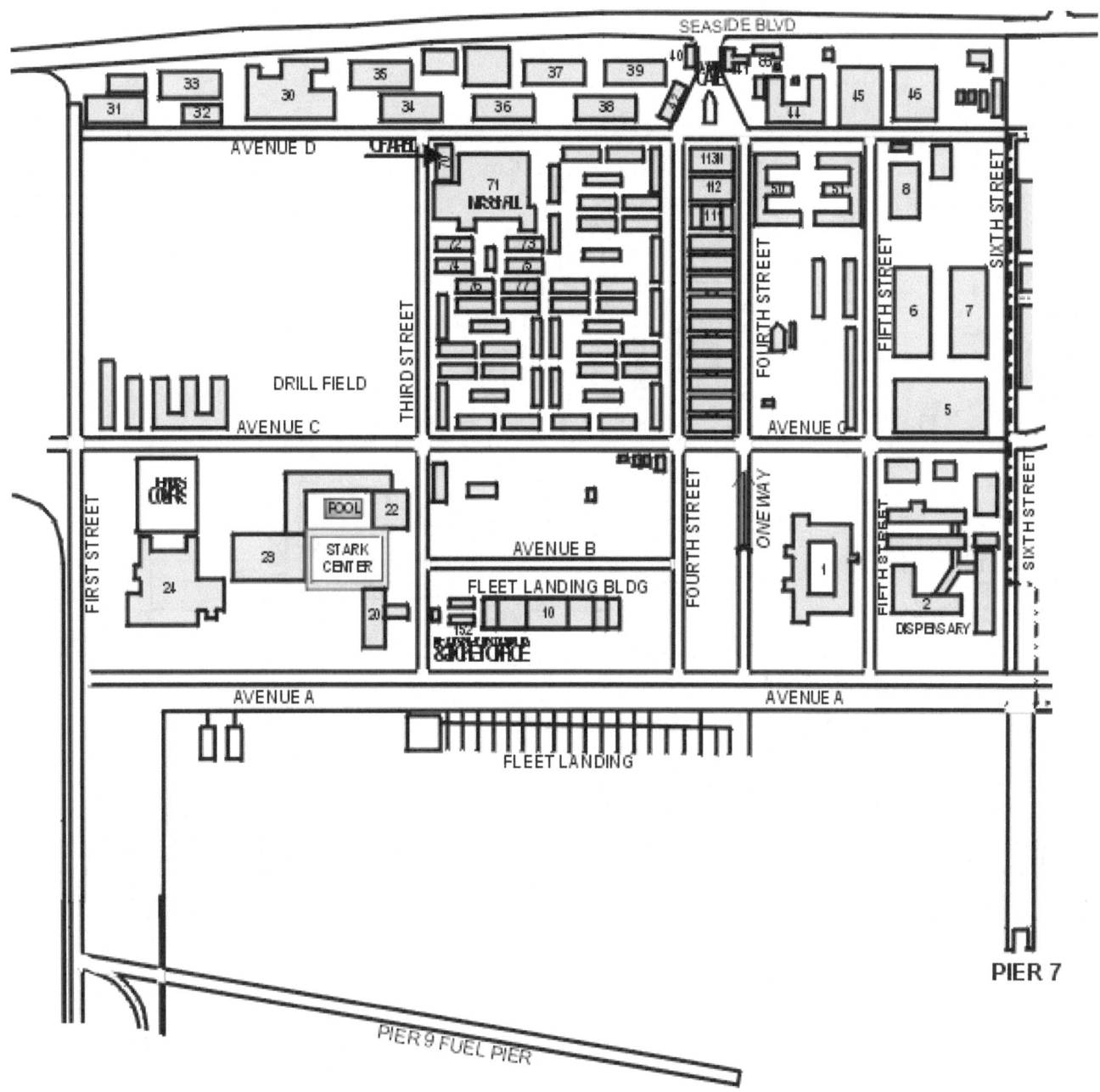

Roosevelt Base as it was arranged in 1945 between the Supply Center and Reeves Field. Author's drawing

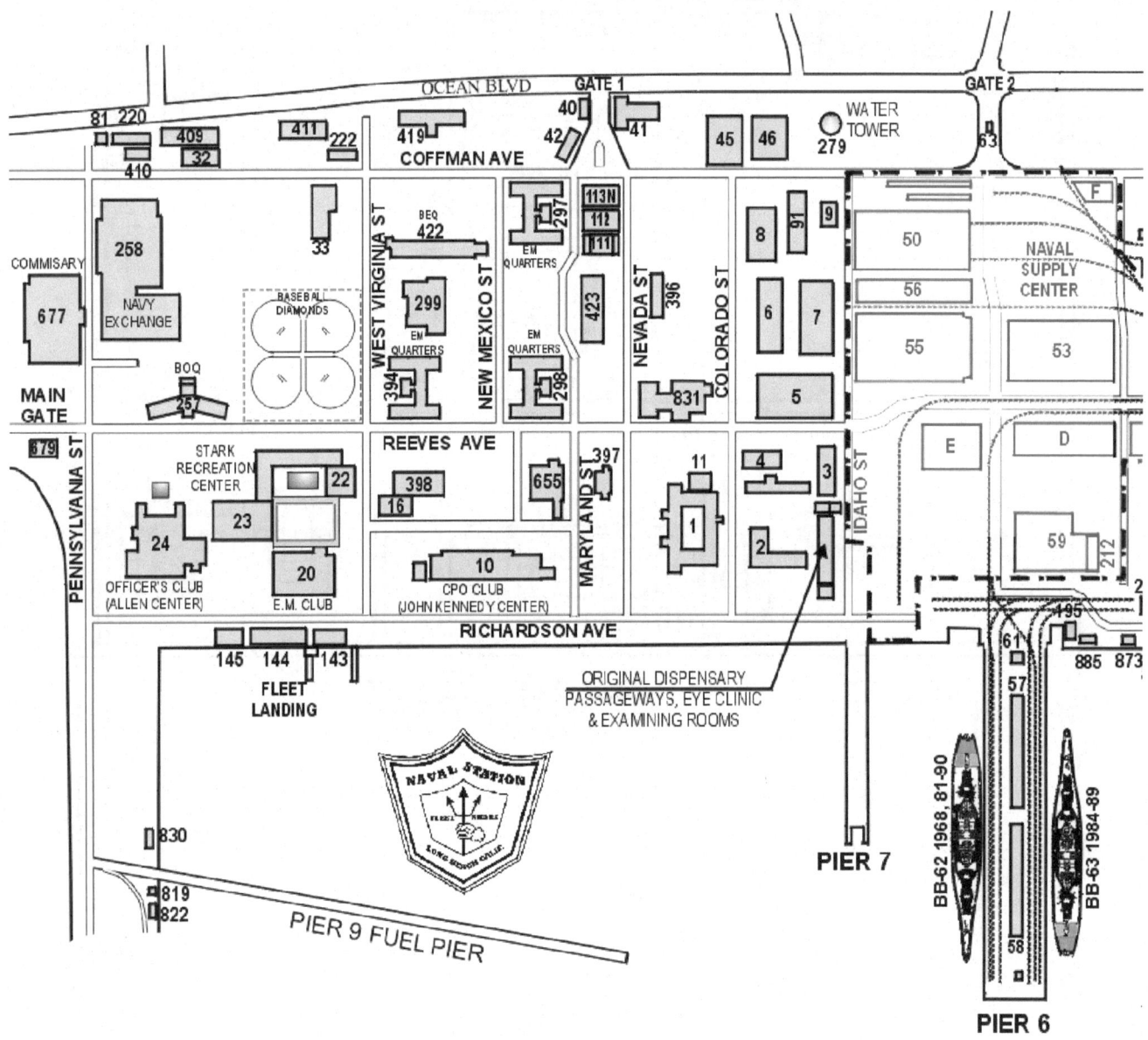

The Naval Station as laid out about 1990. Pier 6 was always part of the shipyard until 1982 when it was transferred to be part of the Station in order to legally load Tomahawk and Harpoon missiles aboard the Battleships, in BATTLESHIP COUNTRY of course.   Author's drawing

Two Roosevelt Base matchbooks. Sea Horse logo was developed by Walt Disney. Author's collection

The various matchbooks from the CPO club. Author's collection

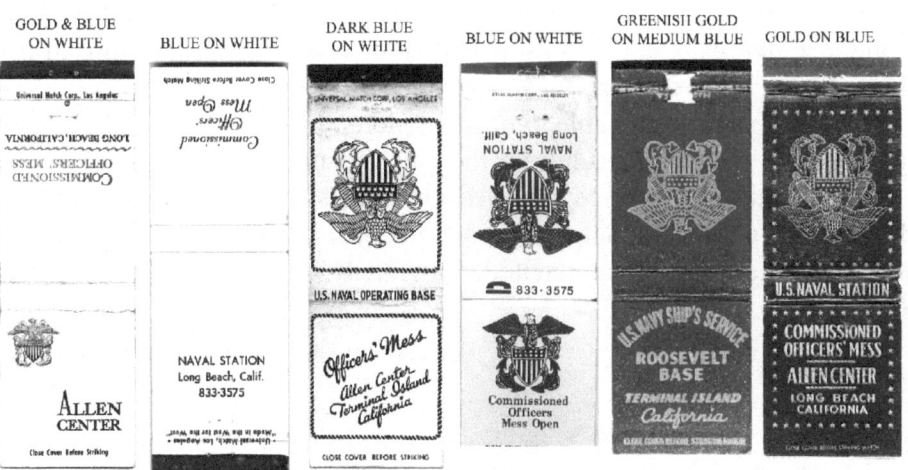

OFFICER'S CLUB (ALLEN CENTER) MATCHBOOKS

CHAPTER 33: THE FINAL COUNT

Previous chapters have expressed some negative opinions on the closing of both the Naval Station and the Naval Shipyard. A proofreader who read the first version of this book offered the advice to be a little more objective if this is to be an historical document. The loss of the Naval Complex in Long Beach was only one of many base closings throughout the Nation after the end of the Cold War. Army bases, Air Force bases as well as Naval bases were shut down and turned over to local governments to do with as they pleased. California was the hardest hit in base closings with the loss of Fort Ord and El Toro Marine Air Base as well as earlier losing Mare Island and Hunters Point Naval Shipyards. Today only the Naval Base in San Diego is still active. The mothball fleet in Benicia, California was packed with decommissioned ships but comes nowhere close to being considered a defense base. Most of the ships there are now melted down into park benches.

In 1969 America had a 900 ship Navy but by 1980 we were down to less than 450 ships. One of the criticisms of the Carter administration was that he allowed our active fleet to total less than the number of active ships we had when Pearl Harbor was attacked in 1941. President Reagan sought to bring our Navy back up to 600 ships and came pretty close to it. But the breakup of the Soviet Union, thus eliminating the big threat that required a large Navy, has forced later administrations to bow to demands to reduce defense spending since we presumably do not need a large military anymore. As of this writing, Communist China now has the largest Navy in the world.

Hundreds of inactive ships are in mothball fleets on both coasts and are not counted as being able to answer the call to duty. Some say that with the demise of the Soviet Union 300 ships is enough, disregarding the buildup of the Chinese Navy. One can't help but wonder if the Washington bean counters really know anything about the complex combination of machinery, electronics and weaponry that makes up a warship. An active ship is a ship that is in commission with a full crew assigned to it. However, that does not mean that ship is out to sea and on duty. In 1969 when we still had seven Naval Shipyards, at any one time you could count at least twenty ships in those shipyards receiving repair, overhaul or major modifications. That's one hundred and forty ships off line, in just public yards. Private yards had lobbied Congress to give them at least fifty percent of all Navy repair work by that time. Therefore another one hundred and forty ships would be undergoing at least moderate repair work scattered around privately owned shipyards. Then there's Yokosuka, Japan and Subic Bay, Philippines (now closed) where Navy work was done. Add another thirty ships from those two foreign yards and you have three hundred and ten ships off line reducing the numbers on duty, on both foreign and domestic patrol, to six hundred.

Based upon those figures, you can conservatively say that at least one-third of the ships in the active Navy will be off line while undergoing shipyard availability. With only a 300 ship Navy, it is hard to imagine only 200 of them being able to properly defend freedom while the rest are being overhauled. Both the Navy and Congress fell for the pipe dream that our older ships would be replaced with newer ships that had multi-mission capabilities and use less crewmen. Anti-submarine warfare would be with ship based hunter-killer helicopters and all with less men as they would also be more automated --- more automated --- more automated. Obviously confidence in automated systems is not universal between everyone.

The Navy has been spending millions of dollars on new long-range "gun" systems to out-perform the Battleships. One is the Extended Range Guided Munitions (ERGM) system. The way it was supposed to work was that a rocket-propelled projectile would be fired from a ship's gun. The rocket (one concept uses a ram jet instead of a rocket) would extend the range of the projectile out to sixty, eighty or a hundred miles. Its accuracy would be assured because Geophysical Positioning Satellites (GPS) would guide it. And that's not counting Rail Guns and High Intensity Lasers.

The purpose of GPS guidance for "pin point" accuracy is because to rocket a projectile that far, the actual warhead can be no larger than a 155mm howitzer shell. The Navy is hoping it can be reduced still to 127mm so it can be fired from the standard 5"/54 and 5"/62 gun mounts. If your target is a railroad bridge and the wind drifted the shell greater than GPS accuracy tolerances, the worst damage would be some dents from shrapnel of the near miss. There has also been the horror story (rumor?) that some GPS satellites have failed because of common cellular phone interference. That's scary. Dial a wrong number and a Cruise Missile or ERGM round will either miss its target or hit a wrong target of innocent bystanders.

Ummm, I think that has already happened when we hit a Hospital in Syria rather than ISIS headquarters.

With the success of the Pioneer Remote Piloted Vehicles used for air spotting during the Lebanon crises and the Gulf War, flyboy types have become more convinced that future aircraft will be pilotless and controlled via a monitor a safe distance away much like a video game. Such an aircraft is being used today not only for reconnaissance but is also capable of carrying weaponry in the form of small bombs and guided missiles. Perhaps that day has come where human "pilots" sit in padded chairs in front of large video screens, manipulating a joy stick in one hand and having a coffee and Danish with the other.

Disregarding the negative results and lack of proven hardware, Congress and the Military still bought the pipe dreams and started reducing ships, shipyards, air bases and army bases in dramatic numbers. Subic Bay was closed down when the Philippine government got too greedy and wanted to raise the rent exorbitantly. Subic was not on the list of closures and President H. W. Bush (Sr.) was more than happy to close the base as part of the post-Cold War cost cutting program. We were hoping that Long Beach, Charleston or Philadelphia shipyards would be removed from the closure list using Subic Bay as the replacement closure. However, that reprieve did not happen as too much had already been carved in stone.

One of the stone engravings was the container terminal expansion that the Port of Long Beach wanted to do with the Navy land. Though all bases had to go through hearings and studies for all other possible uses, as far as Long Beach was concerned it was just wasted effort because the Port had its plans laid out and was not going to change them come hell or high water. While the Navy owned the land, the Port could not collect any rent. No matter what other uses were suggested, none would generate as much revenue as the rents charged a shipping company.

All buildings have been demolished and dry docks two and three have been filled in. Even the great dry dock one was filled in as the Port supposedly could not find a dependable tenant to utilize it and eighteen acres of surrounding pier area. Of the three base closure sessions scheduled, the Naval Station lost out on the second vote and the Shipyard lost out on the third and final session. With no station or base to support the shipyard, container terminal construction on the Naval Base land and Mole would have actually interfered with shipyard work. So the shipyard had to go as well.

From a bean counter's point of view, if we were only going to have a 300 ship Navy, we do not need all those shipyards to support it. The remaining public facilities capable of doing major repair work are Norfolk NSY, Jacksonville Naval Base, San Diego Naval Base, Bremerton and Pearl Harbor. The private shipyards will gladly take up any excess work. That is what they wanted all along anyway. In the mid-1950's, Congress granted private shipyards twenty percent of all repair work. Twenty percent was all the lobbyists for the private shipyards called for. After they got twenty percent, they almost immediately said they really needed twenty-five to thirty percent of all Navy work to keep in business. Then it was fifty percent. That wasn't even counting new construction. Today, no Navy ships whether they are Destroyers, Aircraft Carriers or Submarines are built in public shipyards.

Mathematically, only three shipyards are needed to support only a 300 ship Navy. But one can't help wondering what could we do if the time came we had to build back up to a 500 or 600 ship Navy. Philadelphia has been converted over to a private shipyard and doing quite well. It could conceivably be drafted back into service. But Long Beach Naval Shipyard and Long Beach Naval Station physically do not exist anymore and can no longer serve this Nation in time of war. Literally, the Long Beach Naval Complex has become history.

As long as we are talking numbers, let's look at the final impact on jobs. Throughout the arguments to have the Naval Complex closed, the Port of Long Beach kept telling people of the new jobs the container terminal would create. Well, on January 14, 2005 the Government Accountability Office issued its report on job losses versus job gains on all base closures. At the time of closure, the Long Beach Naval Complex lost 4,487 civilian jobs. The installation of the container terminal has only taken on a mere 200 jobs. That's less than 4 ½% replacement. Also, for every DOD worker, five other people outside depended upon his employment. Those are people from the parts and hardware suppliers on down to the grocery clerk. So that's about 22,000 other people affected by the early retirements and transfers of the DOD personnel. In our heyday, employing about 12,000 DOD workers, that supported 60,000 people on the other side of Gate 5. But the amount of revenue those employees could provide to the money-strapped city of Long Beach was nowhere near the millions of dollars the Port of Long Beach could pull in from a shipping company renting container space. Obviously, the shipyard had to go.

The only way left to tell any more of the shipyard history is to provide the reader with as many photographs as possible. Some of them date back to the 1940's and were scanned from other shipyard publications such as the special booklets printed for the closing ceremonies of the shipyard. The booklets include *Memories*, *Our Finest Years* and the *Disestablishment Ceremony Program*. Others are from negatives John Saltalamachia found. Photographs I took at open houses in the 1960's are included. Some of them are from 2 ¼" X 2 ¼" slides and I had positive prints made of them.

Finally I started taking photographs in the year 2000 as the shipyard buildings were starting to fall to the bulldozers. The Naval Station was already gone but at least I had some negatives of some of its buildings when it was in its glory. I could not stop the destruction of the shipyard so the best I can do is record it for posterity. In order to have some continuity to the pictures, I have added sub-chapters to this chapter so there will be a lead page describing the set of pictures enclosed. As time went on I acquired more photos, many contributed by friends, but to put them all in one group overwhelmed the meanings of selected sets. So I have arranged them is sub-groups covering either an era or items of special interest. It is hard to say goodbye to the Naval Shipyard and the Naval Station, especially if you have spent most of your adult life there as I have. Any final words that come to my mind are too schmaltzy. We can't have that. After all, I'm Battleship tough. So from this point on, I will let the pictures speak for themselves.

CHAPTER 33-A: THE BEGININGS OF THE SHIPYARD

The following photos document some of the beginnings of the Naval Complex

In the beginning, there was a stretch of sand originally known as Rattlesnake Island later to have part of it called Brighton Beach and the home of many Japanese families living at the west end. Little did people realize it was to become a major National Defense installation of a Naval Shipyard, Naval Base, Naval Supply Center and Naval Air Station.

Courtesy: "Salty"

The beginning layouts of Dry Dock 1 and the piers.

Courtesy: Ken Britton

Dry Dock 1 under construction in 1941   Author's collection

Dry Docks 2 & 3 under construction in 1944.   Author's Collection

US Naval Dry docks Terminal Island and Roosevelt Base about 1943. Reeves Field can be seen above but the Mole has not been built yet though Pier 9 Fuel Pier is already installed. Courtesy: "Salty"

March 1, 1948: US Naval Dry docks renamed Long Beach Naval Shipyard. Author's collection

CHAPTER 33-B: LBNSY IN HER PRIME

The pictures in this group come from several sources. My first format was to arrange them as before and after photos showing also the demolition of the structures. But that was starting to ramble and hard to control for continuity. So I decided just to show the shipyard at her best and leave the heart breaking pictures for last.

A view of the shipyard on June 3, 1949 showing how well it was laid out with streets and buildings square to each other and using much less acreage than other shipyards. Author's collection

Gate 5 in World War II.   Courtesy: Gale Eastman

South end of the Machine Shop was the weapons shop, October 23, 1948.   Courtesy: "Salty"

The USS *Wilkinson* (DL-5) in Dry Dock 2, November 28, 1961 after installation of the very first all steel bow-mounted SONAR dome, built by LBNSY. The first ever on any Navy ship.   Author's collection

The Pacific Reserve Fleet of "mothballed" Destroyers in August of 1955. Courtesy: "Salty"

In July of 1967, LBNSY would have been "Ground Zero 1" in the event of a global war having six Carriers it was working on all at the same time. From left to right are USS *Kitty Hawk* (CV-63), USS *Bennington* (CVS-20), USS *Kearsarge* (CVS-33), USS *Princeton* (LPH-5), USS *Valley Forge* (LPH-8) and finally in Dry Dock 1 USS *Yorktown* (CVS 10).   Author's collection

Photo # NH 98310   First shipboard test firing of USS Hull's newly-installed 8" gun, 17 April 1975

"B" Thanks to a "SW4U" (a member of the WAB forum) who corrected me on the bore configuration. LBNSY put in many man-days in design, manufacture and installation of the 8-inch gun on the USS *Hull* (DD-945) for tests. The gun was for the *Spruance* DD's but the program was shut down because the barrel did not have "enough" rifling for accuracy as complained by a very influential Senator. In fact it was intended to be part smooth bore and partly rifled and it was a VERY good gun.   US Navy photo

Another weapons test system by LBNSY was to mount a Sheridan tank turret on the Hydrofoil USS Flagstaff (PGH-1). The top of the turret was cut out and a Plexiglas dome put over it for observation tests. If accepted, it would have been a fully armored turret.   US Navy photo

The Regulus Air Missile (Project RAM) was another special job assigned to LBNSY that we installed on the Cruisers USS *Helena* (CA-75) and USS *Los Angeles* (CA-135). This first type of missile, along with the Army's Matador, eventually evolved into the Tomahawk, ALCM and Harpoon missiles.   Author's collection

How is this for versatility? NASA sent one of their divers' training Apollo "boiler plate" capsules to LBNSY for modifications that involved Shops 11, 31, 64 & 71. So, when we say we worked on ships, that includes "Space Ships"   Jan 19, 1968 issue of THE DIGEST

This author is more familiar with the shipfitter shop, several photos will be of Bldg 128 that housed the shipfitters, welders, boilermakers, blacksmiths and foundrymen. Photo was taken in 1948 and shows the west assembly slab totally exposed and remained that way for many years afterwards.   Courtesy: "Salty"

This photo was taken before total demolition. The center roll-up doors had been replaced with smaller sliding doors but the west slab was completely weather enclosed. This was a great advantage to the night shift especially when the fog was so heavy the crane operator could not see his hook. This caused work delays until the morning sun burned away the fog.   The person in the cart is Vaughn Garvey who would take me anywhere in the shipyard for photos just for this book.   Photo by author in the year 2000

This is looking North inside the now fully enclosed west slab. The armored deckhouses for the *New Jersey* and *Missouri* reactivations were built here.   Photo by author in 2000

This photo of the west slab looking South was also taken by the author on the same day and standing exactly in the same place. Note how small my "escort" is compared to the doors.   Photo by author in 2000

This is an overall view looking Northwest of the shipfitter shop's heavy machinery section. Just beyond the hydraulic presses and up to the open door behind was the boilermaker shop. Photo by author in 2000

A closer look at the heavy hydraulic presses. The 1,000 ton press on the right was dismantled by the closure crew in hopes of finding a buyer for it. The 3,000 ton press to the left was salvaged from the New York NSY when it was closed . But there were no buyers were found for either one. Photo by author in 2000

The 30-foot planer in the shipfitter shop that cut bevels on the edges of metal plates. It was the machine that had a high pitched "squeal" in its compressed air one day that drove everyone out of the shop. But the operator, Ernie Lopez, was already deaf enough and continued beveling thick Metal Plates for an improved deck area on a certain class of ships to support some heavy "machinery". Photo by author in 2000

One of the hydraulic hammers in the Blacksmith's shop. It could pound out very large blocks of red hot steel into any shape. In the background is the door to the annealing oven. Photo by author in 2000

The Betts Turret Lathe in the Machine Shop (Bldg 132). Vaughn Garvey is standing by it to show its enormous size that, unfortunately, was too big for local sale.   Photo by author in 2000

The Niles draw mill that was the pride and joy of the Machine Shop. But there were no buyers, within the city of Long Beach or any city that abutted its borders, so it was destroyed.   Photo by author in 2000

One of the machines in Bldg 132 that did get sold. The problem of selling them is that sales were restricted to only Long Beach or adjoining community businesses rather than State-wide or out of State. Therefore most of them were cut to pieces with carbon-arc cutters.   Photo by author in 2000

The almost brand new paint shop, fully enclosed and meeting all environmental requirements. The bulldozers had quite a job tearing it down.   Photo by author in 2000

The sand blasting grit towers in front of the paint shop. We could recycle and clean all grit to remove "HAZMAT" type paints such as red lead and yellow chromate. Photo by author in 2000

The "Killer" ad in the local newspaper. Notice that it was restricted to businesses with only 250 employees or less. Any manufacturing company that small did not need or could not afford the dismantling and reassembling costs of the largest machines. From the Long Beach Press-Telegram.

The most popular air view photo of LBNSY taken in the late 1980's. AKA BATTLESHIP COUNTRY. The USS *New Jersey* is at Pier 6 and the USS *Missouri* is at Pier Echo. I think.   Author's collection

LBNSY in 1993 still in "Service to the Fleet"   Author's collection

THE SECRETARY OF THE NAVY
WASHINGTON

    The Secretary of the Navy takes pleasure in presenting the MERITORIOUS UNIT COMMENDATION to

    LONG BEACH NAVAL SHIPYARD

for service as set forth in the following

CITATION:

    For meritorious service in the performance of its mission from 1 May 1988 to 30 April 1990. Long Beach Naval Shipyard distinguished itself by excelling in the areas of schedule adherence, financial performance, production management, safety, and customer and community service. The men and women of the Shipyard accomplished these significant achievements while in a unique and difficult environment of direct competition with the private sector ship repair industry and in the midst of a downsizing and reorganization effort that was blazing the trail for the Naval Shipyard Community. The Shipyard's personnel responded in a bold, innovative fashion to the demands of competition. By their superb professionalism, total determination, and impressive dedication to duty, the officers, enlisted personnel, and civilian employees of Long Beach Naval Shipyard reflected credit upon themselves and upheld the highest traditions of the United States Naval Service.

Secretary of the Navy

Ribbon awarded to uniformed personnel

Pinback awarded to civilian personnel

The Meritorious Unit Commendation awarded LBNSY. The ONLY Naval Shipyard to be granted such status. Though it refers to cost savings in General, it was really for getting the Battleship USS New Jersey commissioned a month early and UNDER budget.

CHAPTER 33-C: THE FINAL BLOWS

Almost all of the pictures in this group I personally took. Vaughn Garvey, a former welder, was one of the supervisors for Earth Tech that had the contract to sell off the machinery, vehicles, equipment and to tear down the buildings. When I was ready to take some more photos, all I had to do (over beers at Curley's) was tell him what time I would be down there. He would take me in through the gate and drive me in his golf cart type scooter to where I wanted to start shooting as it was required he escort me. Usually he would just drop me off because I was going to be there up to an hour and he knew I wouldn't fall into a dry dock. I was supposed to be legally escorted through Building 128 but all the people there knew me and let me go about my business while they went about theirs.

The only pictures I had to sneak in were of the demolition of Building 300. The regular access at Gate 5 had been cut off and separate security guards wouldn't let me in. However, I found a back gate by the scrap yard open and would drive in through there within 200 feet of the building. I was driving a green Dodge Dakota pickup truck with a matching green low-profile camper shell. I was wearing a quilted white sleeveless (vest-type) jacket and a light gray hard hat. I would arrive just before noon when some of the men on the demolition machines were trying to break for an early lunch. But seeing me in that white vest and hard hat taking pictures, they all jumped back on their machines thinking I was some sort of inspector.

Bldg 300 that was our Administration, Planning and Design center in its prime.   Photo by author

This section may seem too emphatic of the demolition of the Naval Complex. But there is a reason for it. Many of us pleaded with our Congressmen and top Naval Admirals to save the shipyard particularly with its Dry Dock facilities. This author also wrote a letter to the CNO at the time but only received a formal outline of the BRAC process as a reply.

BUT. Here's the head banger. It was around the early part of the 21st Century (2005 to 2010 or there about) that the NAVY finally confessed they did NOT want the Long Beach facilities closed. But were ordered from higher up (????) to keep their mouths closed.

Bldg 300 being torn down to rubble and scrap metal. Photo by author

Gate 5 looking pretty much like it did during most of the shipyard's history. This photo by the author on February 7, 2000 and the truck going in is a Prospective buyer of some of the shop tools and machinery.

Bldg 210, Weapons & Electronics shop, gutted out of furniture & equipment thrown out of the windows. July, 2000.

Bldg 210 just a pile of rubble by October, 2000.

Looking South through razor wire at Bldg 128 - 80% crushed. April 30, 2001. The 1,000 ton press was dismantled in hopes of finding a buyer. The 3,000 ton press is awaiting the cutting torches.

Start of demolition of Bldg 132. Ironically, it was the first shop built at the Shipyard and served as the shipfitter shop, foundry and gun repair shop. Now it was the last to be torn down. Photo by author @ 2003.

Building the sea wall in Drydock 3

The demolishers added retaining walls to the dry dock caissons. Really, all they had to do was fill them with sand as they are hollow anyway.

Photo by Bill Perry

PC-14 demolition, June 2000

I guess it's much more dramatic to chop the supports off of a Portal Crane than it is to dismantle it in a safe way.

Photo by Bill Perry

"B"
CHAPTER 34: AROUND THE SCUTTLEBUTT

On a Navy ship, the water fountains are called scuttlebutts. Don't ask me why. I don't know. But they serve a secondary purpose as the coffee machine in an office does and that is to have a place to shoot the bull with some of the other folks. Well, I'm devoting this chapter to items that may or may not fit properly into any of the preceding chapters.

16" GUNS & THEIR POWDER BAGS:

So I think I'll start off with problems in loading 16" gun barrels. Now, this really has nothing to do with the turret incident on the *Iowa*. Actually a somewhat similar incident happened on the *New Jersey* in 1968. That involves using reduced service propellant bags. But I am also including some studies done on using lighter weight projectiles (smaller in diameter) fitted into a sabot. That started in the 1950's with Project Katy that was to fire nuclear warheads out the main guns. But even with standard Explosive D a lighter weight shell can go much further and the Navy was trying to extend the range from 25 miles to 65 miles.

Project Katy was cancelled, however, because all projectile loading into their magazines are done with slings, wire ropes, parbuckling lines and raw man power. The AEC would not accept that and insisted that all handling of nuclear warheads had to be "positive capture" in cradles and fail-safe elevator type hoists. We had a heck of a time installing such a system on the USS *Chicago*.

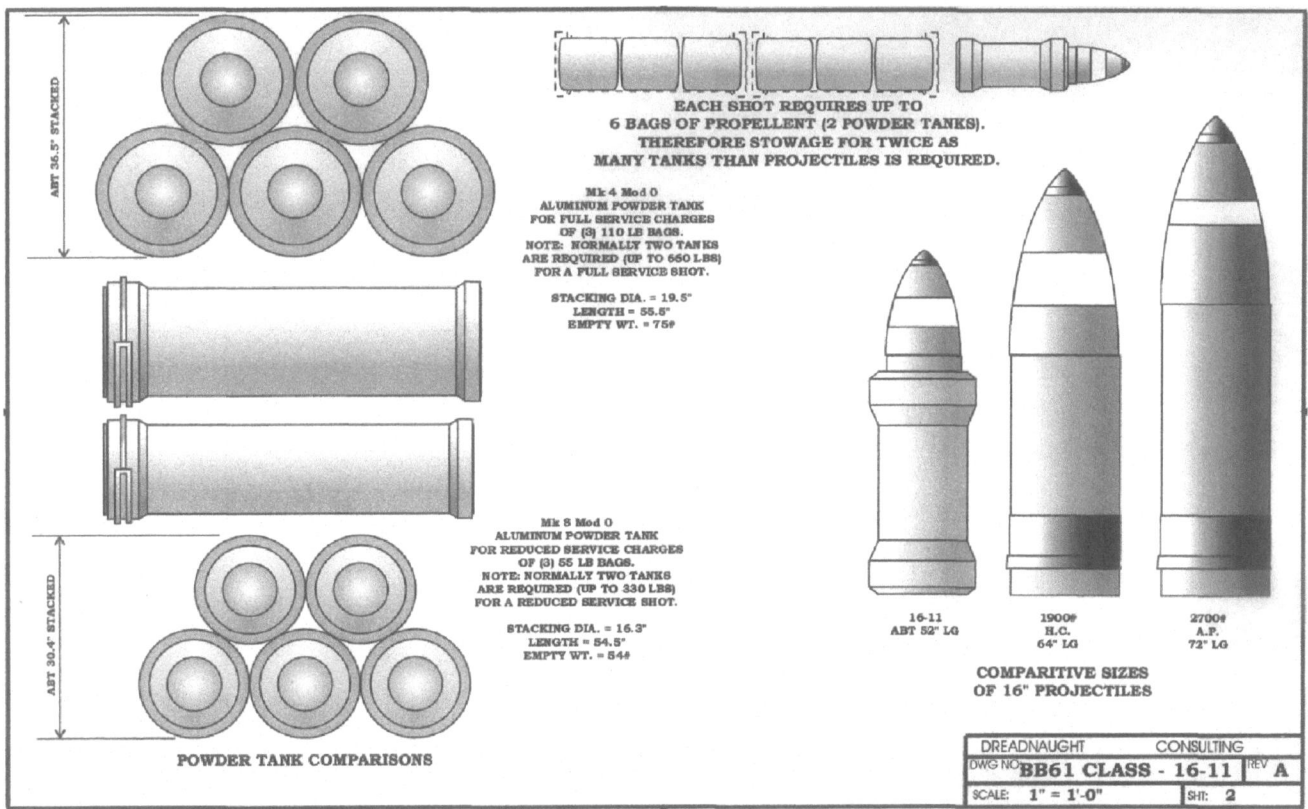

In this CAD drawing, the SABOT round is based upon the Army's 11" shell,
though larger sizes were considered and tested for stowage procedures.

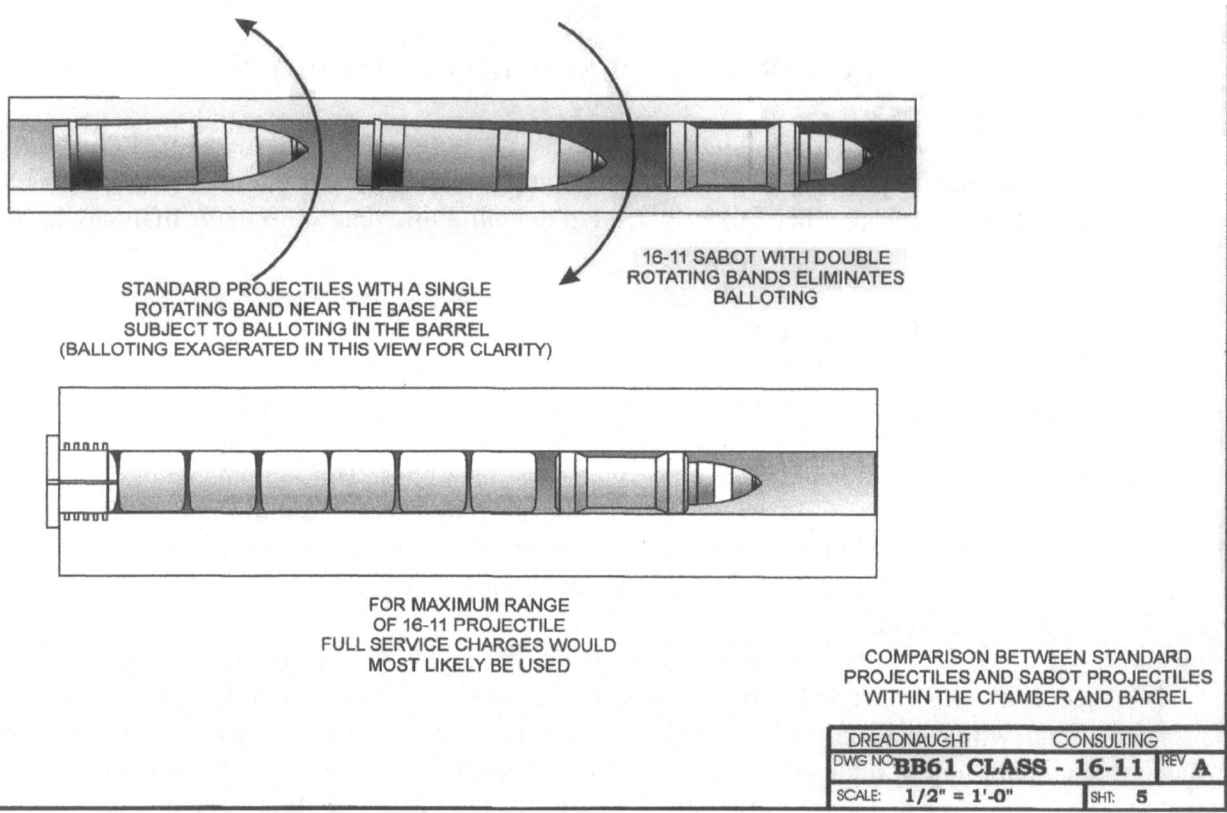

Just some things that can happen as a "bullet" goes down a barrel.

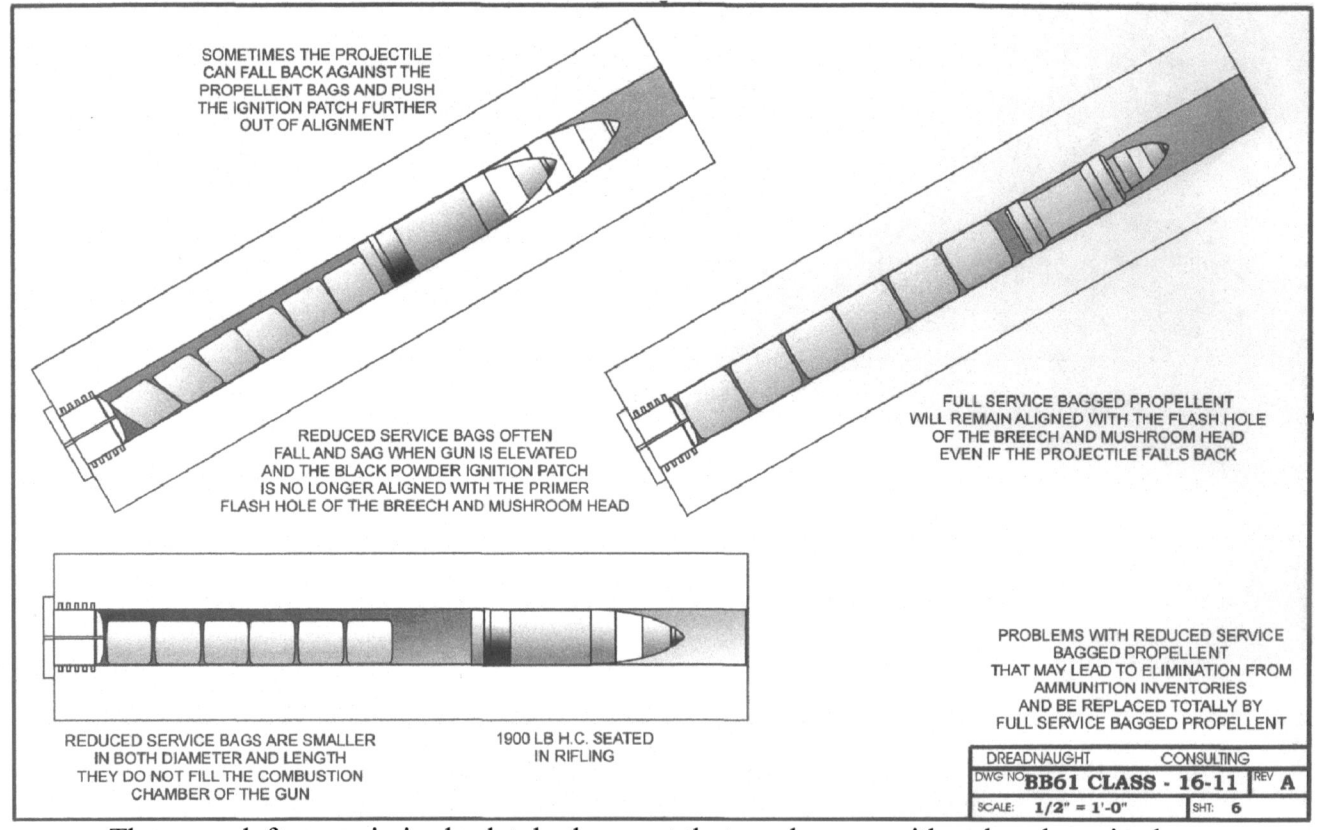

The upper left scenario is absolutely the worst that can happen with reduced service bags.

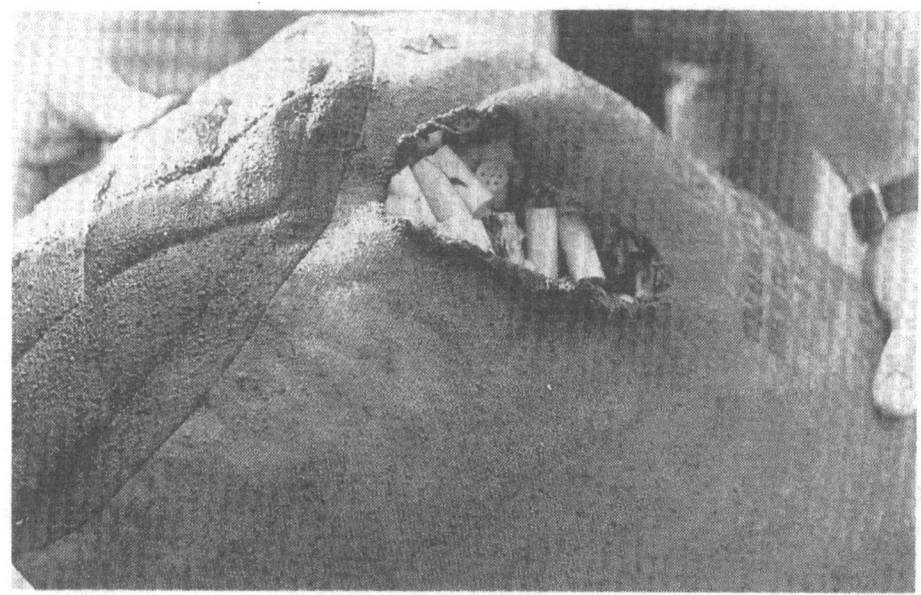

This is almost the worst that can happen if the primer hole in the mushroom head of the breach block is not lined up with the quilted patch of black powder that in turn ignites the main propellant. This happened with the center gun of turret II (why is it ALWAYS THAT turret?) on the USS *New Jersey* during her Viet Nam deployment in 1968. After this Admiral Snyder (then Captain of the ship) rejected the use of reduced service bags from then on. Unfortunately, the brainy people on the hill never learn from history and when the BB's were reactivated in the 1980's, 55 lb bags were stowed aboard.

The photo above was scanned from Paul Stillwell's excellent book on the history of the *New Jersey*. You will find it on page 227 with the full report of what happened.

As for sabot rounds, I do recall some loading tests were done with inert or dummy projectiles. But I don't think you will find any around anymore.

Unless you visit the USS *Iowa* in San Pedro, California.   Photo by author.

PREMATURE DETONATIONS:

As long as we are on the subject of problems with guns (AND when I thought I was finished with this book) a subject came up on the WAB about explosive shells detonating while in flight. Well, it took me a while to go through my library to find a photo I saw of a premie exploding just beyond the muzzle of the *Missouri* during the Korean War. Well, I didn't find the photo I was looking for but did find a couple of very interesting photos of that detonation in two other books.

Most Naval history buffs know of the premature when the 8" HE projectile exploded **INSIDE** the center barrel of Turret II on the US *Newport News* (CA-148) during her Viet Nam deployment on 1 October 1972. Rather than replacing the gun, the entire assembly was removed and the gun port of the turret was sealed off.

A beautiful ship, regardless of missing one of her main guns.

However, many people are more interested in Battleships and I have had much more experience with the BBs than with the CAs. So, let's start off with a cross-sectional drawing of a 16" Hi-Cap:

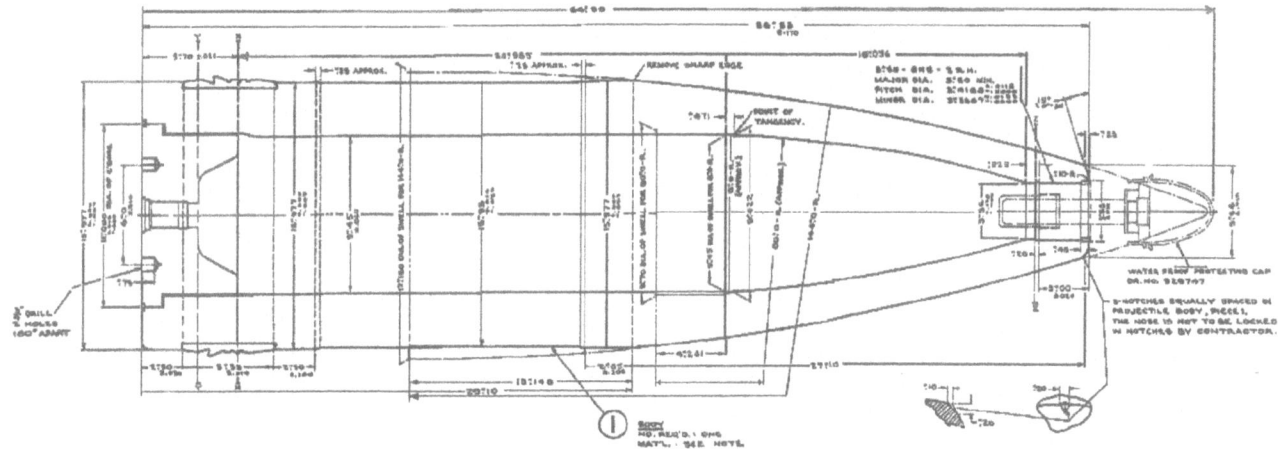

An overall cross section of a Mk 14 Mod 0 High Capacity 16" projectile

FUZES

BASE DETONATING FUZE MK 48 MODS 0, 1, AND 3
Projectiles Used in: 8-Inch HC; 12-Inch HC; 14-Inch HC; 16-Inch HC

Figure 2.34—Base Detonating Fuze Mk 48 Mod 3: External View (left) and Sectional View of Unarmed Position (right).

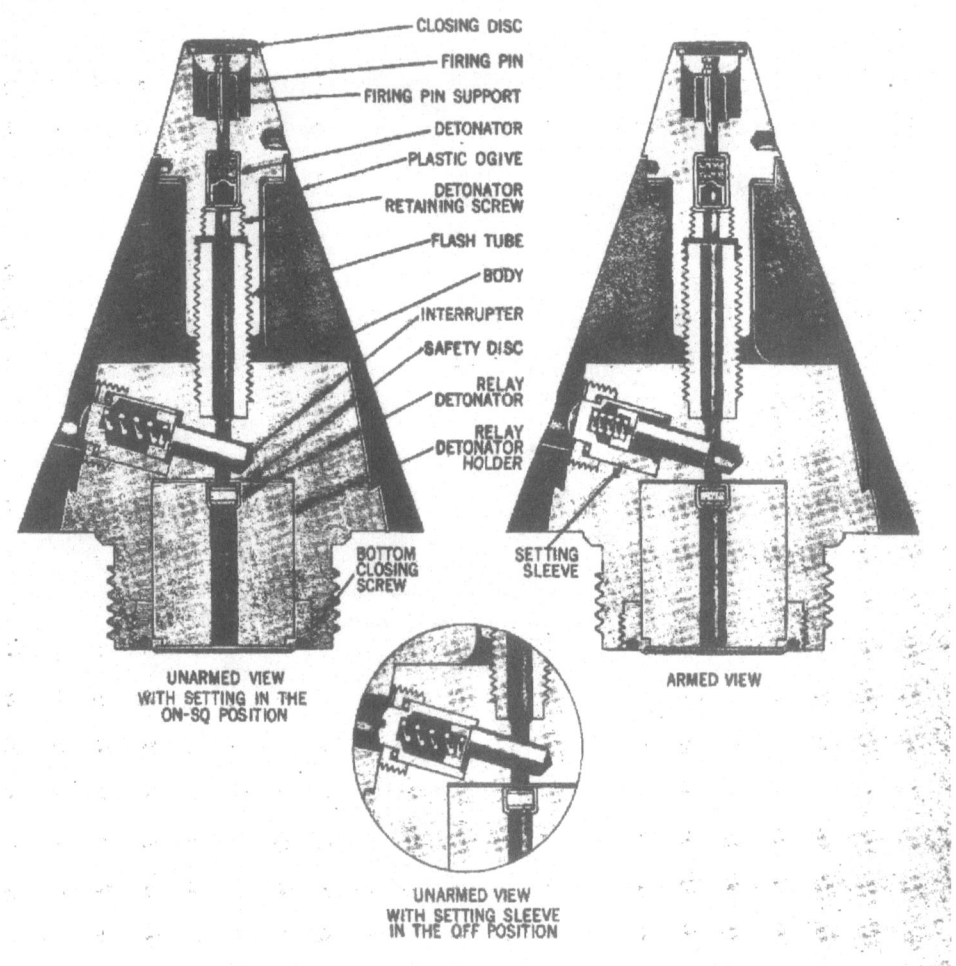

Figure 2.8—Point Detonating Fuze Mk 29 Mod 3, Unarmed Position, Sectional View.

Before we go any further, remember that all munitions are produced by the hundreds of thousands if not in the millions. Most loading of the explosive bombs and artillery rounds is done by women. This may have started in the "Rosie the Riveter" days of WW II but I think much earlier than that. A cousin of mine was a male safety inspector at a munitions factory here in Southern California. Almost all the employees who actually loaded and assembled high explosive weapons were women. Their work clothes were all white and they all had "bracelets" with a copper wire looped onto a copper pipe up above that in turn was attached to a vertical copper solid round bar driven 8 feet into the ground. Obviously this was to cancel out any possible sparks from even normal static electricity. And why women? They seem to have a natural instinct to observe repetitive detail. But regardless of how expert a person can be, Murphy's First Law takes precedence: "If there is anything that can **possibly** go wrong, IT WILL." The following photos of *Missouri's* premature in Korea prove that.

A premature ignition.   "MIGHTY MO" by Newell & Smith - page 123

Shrapnel fallout from the premature.   "BATTLESHIP MISSOURI" by Paul Stillwell - page 181

AS LONG AS WE ARE TALKING ABOUT GUNS:

The LBNSY Gun Club was organized for the purpose of competition style shooting. Trap, Skeet, Pistol, small bore rifle and centerfire rifles.. One of our fellow members was Chuck Dietl who retired as Assistant Chief Engineer of the Code 250 design sections, was also a past Triple A California State Champion in Skeet shooting.

Charles "Chuck" Dietl. California AAA skeet champion.
Assistant Chief Engineer displaying his own line of shooting jackets.

For pistol and .22 rifle shooting we practiced on a 25 yard indoor target range in the lower right hand corner of Reeves Field. Below is a posed photograph of some of the members explaining the workings of a very expensive .22 target pistol to one of our secretaries who "happened" to come by the pistol range on Reeves Field.

Photo by Edmund Stanley

SAVING THE BATTLESHIP *IOWA*

You have no idea how hard it was to save the USS *Iowa* (BB-61) from the scrappers. She was decommissioned on the East Coast and left at anchorage for two years off of Rhode Island. In the meantime, four of her Tomahawk ABLs were taken off amidships and her main analog fire control computer (one of two on board) was confiscated by a museum. Then when put back on Class B reserve the best thing California's two Senators did was to get her transferred to Siusun Bay above San Francisco, California. But to get her under a railroad bridge, the Navy cut off the top portion of the tripod mast in NINE pieces. And it was my job to figure out how to put it all back together again.

But that was only one of the last problems we had to overcome. Originally an organization, Historic Ship Museum of Pacific Square (HSMPS), in the Bay area put in a bid for the ship as a museum attraction. But every time they found a suitable pier, the city or county of San Francisco suddenly came up with another use for that spot. As a member of the *Iowa* Class Preservation Association (ICPA), we inspected the ship for them several times and I provided a number of drawings I developed for the *Missouri* and *New Jersey* museums.

Well, it was a useless effort when on You Tube I saw an interview of one of the San Francisco County Supervisors. He said, "I don't want that ship anywhere NEAR San Francisco." The Interviewer asked, "Why not?". The Supervisor said, "Because she's a weapon of WAR."

I think Tojo and Hirohito got the same impression when she came in alongside the *Missouri* for Japan to sign their unconditional surrender.

HSMPS didn't stand a chance with both city and county against them. So the ICPA changed its name to the Pacific Battleship Center (PBC) as a 501c3 charitable organization with the intent of berthing the ship in San Pedro instead. It took a lot of speech making to the Los Angeles Harbor Department (San Pedro is a division of the city of Los Angeles) but we got a berth for her.

One of the speeches I made was, "We have a preliminary Table of Organization. I'm listed as head of the design team and Naval Architecture. Every time I get together with some of the former Long Beach Naval Shipyard workers at a reunion many ask to have their names added to the list. Some are engineering staff, as myself, who have inspected all four Battleships. Many are shop workers who modernized the *New Jersey* and *Missouri* here in Long Beach. So, we are not just some people who have read a book on Battleships. WE are the PROFESSIONALS."

So we now OWN the Battleship USS *Iowa* (BB-61) but still with three Navy restrictions. In case the Navy wants to reactivate the ship again, we cannot reopen the Crew's Galley (But we can reopen the Wardroom Galley, Captain's Galley & Chief's Galley), we cannot unlock the propeller shafts for propulsion and we cannot reactivate the Navigation equipment - er - for navigation. Well, if we cannot go anywhere with locked propellers, we can't Navigate, but we can reactivate it's long range RADAR to add back up of weather conditions or look for ships in the fog. But we haven't got that far along yet as many of the consoles and repeaters are not on board -- yet. Oh, thirdly, we cannot reactivate the boilers or propulsion machinery "for propulsion". Well, with locked shafts, you can't go anywhere anyway.

We have restored the Captain's in-port cabin to President Roosevelt's quarters when he sailed aboard the *Iowa* to Casablanca for his meeting with Churchill and Stalin in Teheran to decide where the D-Day landings should be. We have also installed an elevator, close to where a temporary elevator for FDR was installed in WW II, for handicapped visitors to see his quarters and the only warship in the world that has a bathtub in it.

The upper part of the mast lying in pieces on the helicopter deck of the Iowa.

The entire mast top totally reassembled in Richmond, CA and lifted into place in one piece. The lift and installation (minus production welding) was done in less than two hours rather than two weeks as estimated to be maximum if installed in sections. Also a test of how long you can hold your breath.

The mast is fully in place and the joints are stronger than before. This pic was taken in 2013 celebrating with England the Victory in the Battle of the Atlantic over the Axis powers. You will notice a British Union Jack, donated by *Jamie Woodthorpe* of Cambridgeshire, England, flying from the forward/starboard yardarm. It is autographed by Jack M. Atkinson who was the helmsman aboard the HMS *Rodney* during its toe-to-toe battle with the DKM *Bismarck*.

We have procured the last remaining HUP helicopter in the World. Only one more exists in a museum. Ours was trucked from Pennsylvania to California and restored at the Torrance Airport (Zamperini Field) that was a P-38 interceptor base in WW II. Oh yes, we have the rotor blades but just have to move the HUP to a permanent display site on deck and then secure the rotors in place.

AIR CONDITIONING FOR MUSEUM STATUS BATTLESHIPS:

While reading some postings on the World Affairs Board a while ago, one contributor was wondering why the Battleship *Missouri* in Hawaii claims to be the cleanest ship around. Well, my answer was because she is using a special Air Conditioning design that Stan Lintner and I created using two Carrier plants that use fresh water from the pier rather than cutting open the intakes and discharges for the York plants down on 3rd deck and using Salt water.

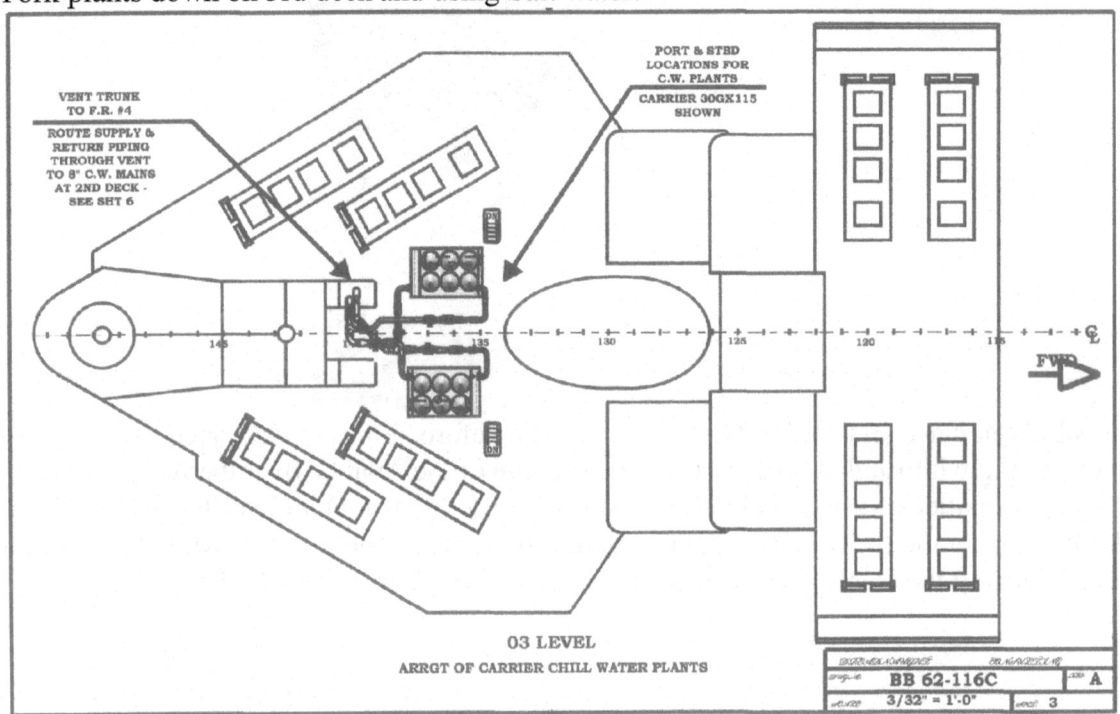

To stay out of everybody's way (and muffle some of the noise) the main chill water plants are mounted on the 03 level between the ABLs.

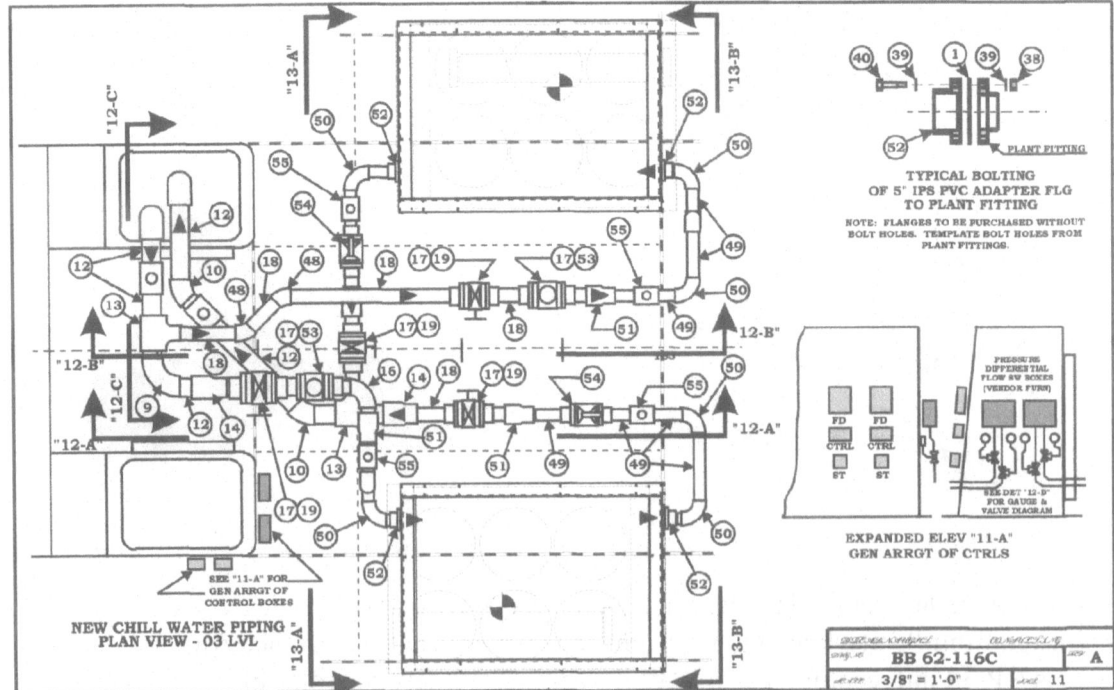

This may look like a plumber's nightmare, but to us Navy DOD people, just another day at the "office".

SLEP: What Could Have Been

SLEP is the acronym for "Ship Life Extension Program". As for the *Iowa* class Battleships, it was intended to extend their service life until the year 2010. But this also included a major reconstruction of the upper levels in order to install a Vertical Launch System (VLS) of 96 cells to launch any kind of missile you wanted. Only the 16 HARPOON tubes would have remained as they would be out of the way of rebuilding the aft and amidships sections of the super structure from 01 level up to a new 04 level.

I was given a copy of the general arrangement drawings done by a NAVSEA design agency that was in the process of throwing out all old and never to be used again drawings including all of the Battleship drawings. The Battleship drawings were "disposed" of by delivering them to a Battleship lover whom in turn shipped many of them out to me to use for Pacific Battleship Center's application for recovering the *Iowa* from the "Ghost Fleet" up in Suisun Bay.

The drawings for the VLS installation I kept for a while and copied them with Corel Draw and I had some beautiful 11 X 17 prints in a special folder on my computer. Unfortunately, when I was forced into installing the "latest and greatest" version of my computer's operating system, that file got devoured in the turnover. However, someone (I don't remember who) uploaded the following sketches to me. So, here they are to answer any technical questions.

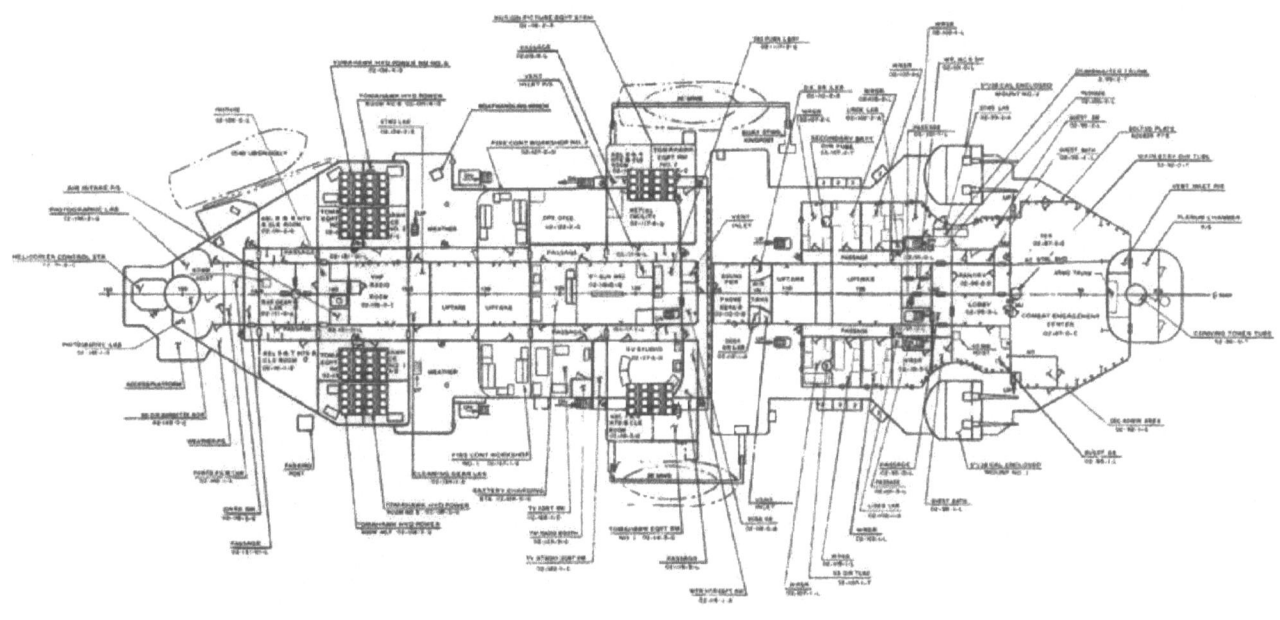

A plan view at the 02 level showing locations of 96 Vertical Launch Cells.

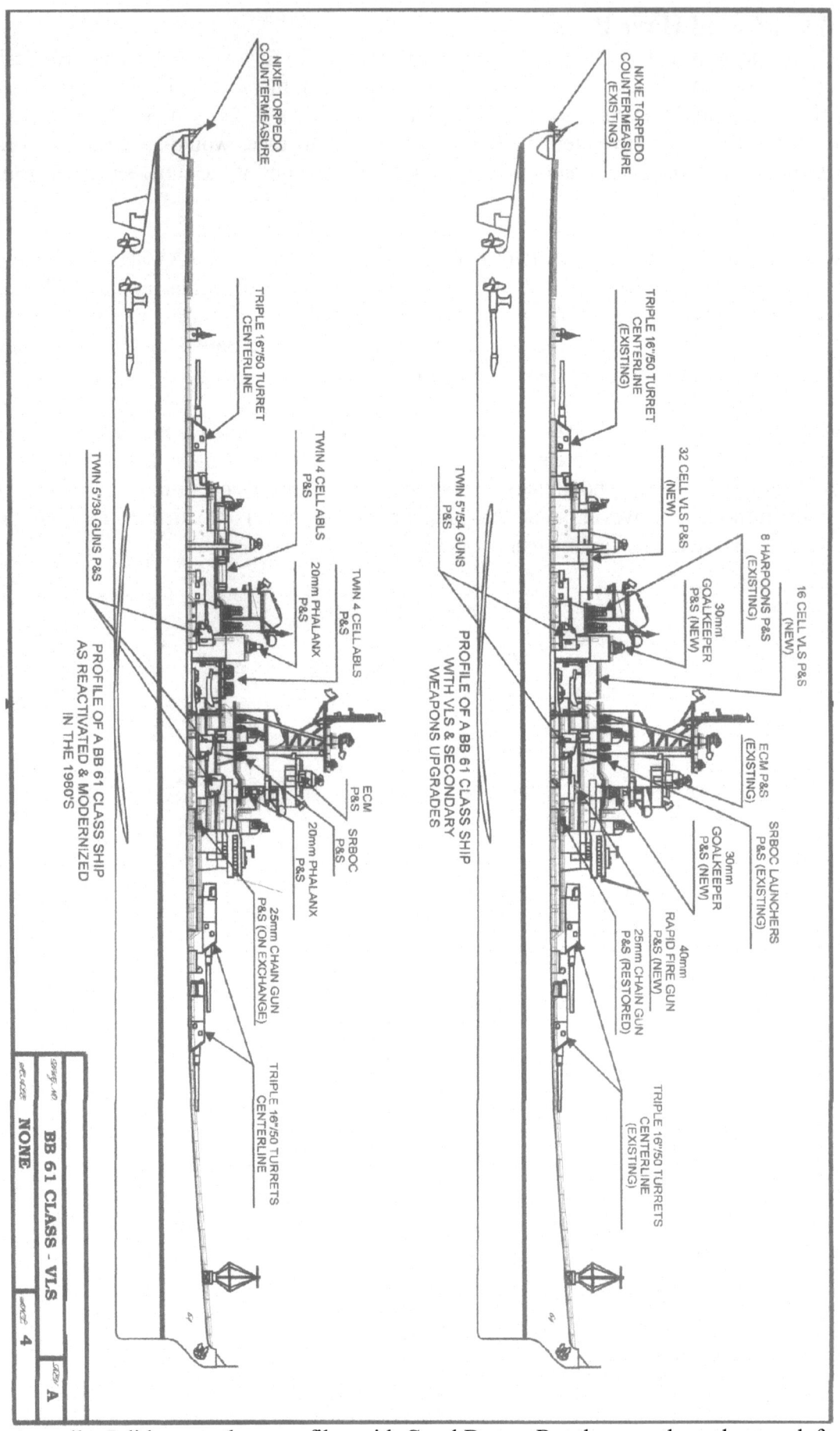

Actually, I did create these profiles with Corel Draw. But they are the only ones left.

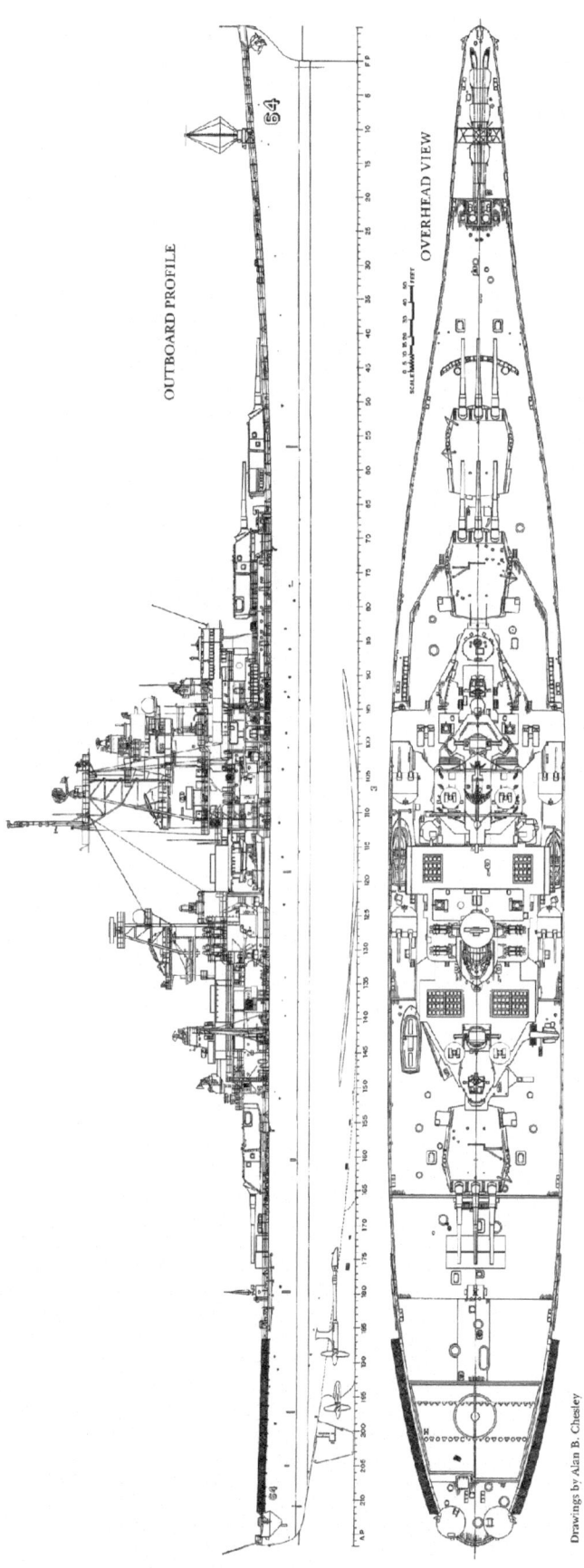

Then in trying to gain some more memory space on my idiot box,
I found this beautiful drawing done by the master of ship drawings; Alan B. Chelsy.

Missouri's enlisted head, latrine, water trough:

When LBNSY was inspecting the *Missouri* up in Bremerton for reactivation. We found this old relic that was in service up through the Korean War.

This is at the low end of the trough. Where the most worried person sat.

Why was the low end user worried? There was always some joker up at the high end that would wad up a bunch of toilet paper, light it and let the burning wad flow down making all the other guys jump up and down like people in a stadium doing the wave. (Was that the idea of where the wave came from)?.

LBNSY MEMORIAL PARK:

As a final note, through the efforts of Friends of the Navy and a couple of other organizations, a memorial park has been dedicated to honor all those who worked at the complex or even ships that docked there often.

When in Long Beach, California, you can drive down to The Aquarium of the Pacific. Just behind the Aquarium at the east side of the road going out to an historic light house is the park.

CAPTAIN JOHN PICKERING DEDICATING THE LONG BEACH NAVY MEMORIAL PARK
JULY 10, 2004

Captain Pickering passed on 2 years later. But we made sure he will always be remembered.

An overall view of the park. Notice the Queen Mary across the channel.
The flagpole is fashioned like a ship's mast but was actually the flag pole for the Naval Hospital on Carson Street near the Long Beach Police Academy.

A stocked anchor donated by the Al Larson Boat company. It is claimed that it was lost by one of the Battleships in Teddy Roosevelt's GREAT WHITE FLEET.

The park also has a special memorial honoring the loss of 74 crewmen who died when their ship, USS *Frank E. Evans* (DD-754), was cut in two by an Aircraft Carrier during Maneuvers. To add insult to injury; their names were NOT added to the Viet Nam wall just because the ship was not in the Tonkin Gulf (AT THAT TIME). But the ship WAS in the Gulf when called out to participate in the maneuvers and was then to RETURN TO GUNNERY DUTY IN VIET NAM.

We even salvaged the street sign of the main street that ran through the shipyard.
Originally it was named Reeves Avenue (an easterly extension from the Naval Air Station).
But it was renamed Sullivan Avenue in honor of the 5 Sullivan brothers who died together in battle.

My last order of bricks was to list the special projects of LBNSY.

You are now entering ---- The Twilight Zone (with apologies to Rod Serling)

Sci Fi:

My version of the infamous "Philadelphia Experiment": "Probably" a test of counter lighting to reduce the shadows cast by platforms, boats, etc. that identify what kind of a ship it was rather than just a hazy outline. Trying it out on a ship seemed logical and two extra generators were (supposedly) added to the USS *Eldridge* (DE-173) to supply the power needed for all those lights to lighten shadows under platforms and small boats. It should work, sort of, on a hazy day when even without counter lighting you only see a grayish silhouette of the ship. But it didn't work that well as the denseness of the haze/fog kept changing. So, what was seen (from a distance) was a Destroyer Escort of the USS *Cannon* (DE-99) class of which 78 were built exactly alike during WW II. Identification of the ship by the hull number (173) would indicate it was the *Eldridge*. But about the same time, the *Eldridge* was seen in Norfolk about 200 miles south, also identified by hull number.

How can that be? Simple. We were absolutely shocked when a night photograph of New York City was published through the periscope of a German Submarine (that was before we ordered "Black Out" drills at night). Also, when the B-25 bombers struck military and infrastructure targets in Japan in early 1942, President Roosevelt announced they were launched by the Aircraft Carrier *Shangrilla*. Though we know today it was the *Hornet*. We did not have a Carrier named after FDR's announcement. But it gave us an idea. So to merely confuse the enemy, particularly German U-Boats on the East coast, we painted duplicate hull numbers on different ships of the same class. Remember, it was WW II and all sides would try anything to be "stealthy".

UFOs:

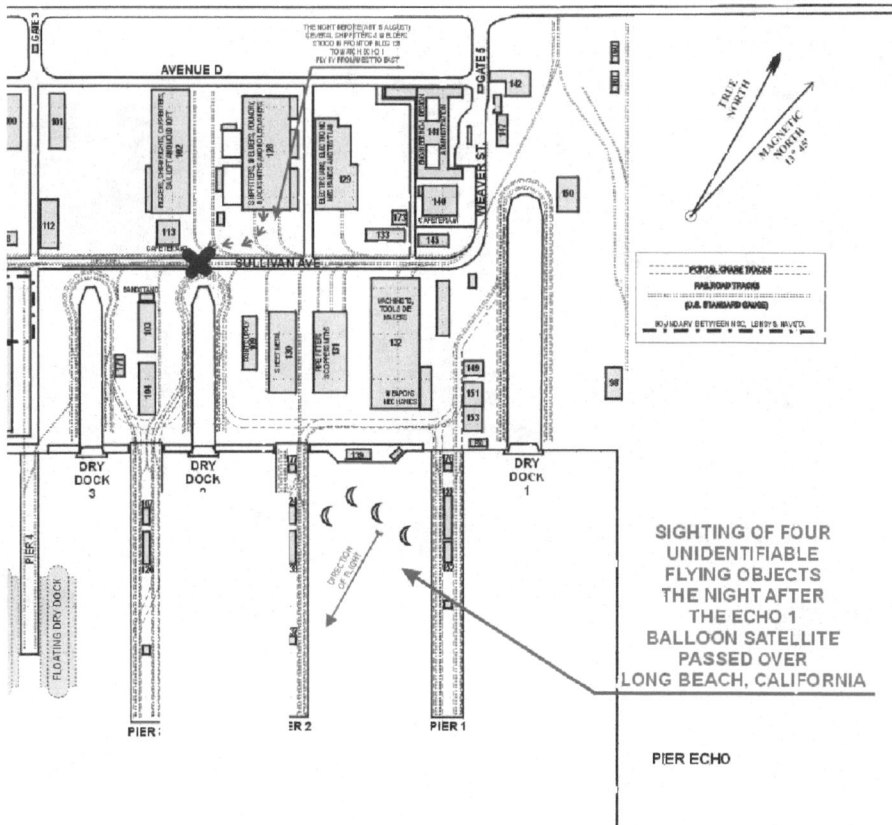

On August 15, 1960, right after the end of Swing Shift's lunch break, the sun was already set and the sky was perfectly clear with no clouds. One of our welders, called out all the workers of the shipfitter shop because our inflatable satellite, ECHO 1, was passing overhead and was perfectly clear to the naked eye.

The next night, August 16, was a bit different as we had some broken clouds and as I was walking out toward Dry Dock 2, I glanced up through a fairly large gap in the clouds and assumed we would not see ECHO 1 again. Instead, I saw 4 crescent shaped "lights" in a reverse echelon formation "fly" directly "true" south above a large break in the clouds. There was absolutely no sound at all but the crescent shape gave the impression that it was the refection of the setting sun (though now over the horizon) reflecting off the curved edges of those "things" which would mean that they were extremely high up. Of course, nobody believed me. The heavy "X" at the north end of DD-2 was where I was brought to a stop while crossing Sullivan Avenue. The crescents I added in are larger (in proportion to the shipyard map) than they actually were. But in the size they are shown on this page, that's just about the size I saw them in. I stepped back to see if it was a reflection of some ground based lights off of my glasses. Nope. And not a sound either except for minor "hissing" of air from LP air manifolds.

August 16, 1960: Four UFO crescents in reverse echelon heading true South above the clouds.

Here is what I think they really were. A squadron of Star Ships from the Federation of Planets got caught in a time warp. I think this is Captain Picard's ship with the setting sun reflecting off the edge of his upper section.

Well, that's just as good an explanation as anything else.

Hey! You gotta have some fun sometime. Yes, I did see those crescents, but as a Star Trek fan, I could not pass this up.

EPILOGUE & RETIREMENT

In the latter half of 1993, hundreds of LBNSY employees were sent questionnaires asking if they would take early out retirements. Most of us, as in my case, already had the minimum age and time in so to call it an "early out" was not quite accurate except for the fact that some of us would be retiring earlier than we planned to. Others were very close to retirement and had at least the time, if not the age, or had the age, if not the time, to qualify for some sort of annuity. My wife and I discussed this and I was planning to retire late in 1994 anyway with an even forty years service, we decided on February 1st as my last day at the shipyard (which was also our 25th wedding anniversary).

I finished up my volunteer time at Disaster Assistance Center 4 in Van Nuys on Sunday, January 30th, packed my bags from where I was staying at my brother's and drove back home to Long Beach. On Monday I started cleaning out my files and desk. Friends who valued my desire to preserve history took care of a lot of historical type items that were supposed to be thrown in the trash barrel. It was very strange how those items just bounced out of the trash barrel, down four flights of stairs, across the street into Parking Lot B and finally coming to rest in the back of my mini-van. I took one last tour of the shops and said goodbye to old friends and took one last look at the steel shaping machines I used to operate in the shipfitter shop.

On Tuesday, February 1, 1994 I packed up the last of my personal items from my desk and put them in the car. We went to the mustering out office and got our package of sign-off papers to clear our records at the tool crib, safety supply and various other offices. We had to take our cars out to the front of the main gate to have the window sticker removed and issued a temporary parking passes. We were handed a package containing our basic employment records and a shipyard plaque. Our badges were traded in for temporary passes. As many others did, I merely got in my car, looked around for what I thought would be the last time and drove out the gate handing my temporary parking permit to the guard and went home.

I never really expected to go back to the shipyard again except for the office Christmas parties. But that summer the BRAC decided to close the yard and there were no parties. In April I noticed an ad in the paper for volunteers to serve on the Restoration Advisory Board (RAB) overseeing identification and potential clean ups of toxic material in and under the Base and Shipyard (collectively called the Naval Complex).

When the Naval Station was abandoned for the bulldozers, we moved our RAB meetings into the executive dining room on the ground floor of building 300. Though the shipyard officially closed on September 30, 1997 one more year was needed for final shutdown and distribution of government material and records to storage centers. It was found that there were sixty-eight employees that would be able to attain minimum time of service within that year so they were kept on as the final closure crew.

Naturally I went to the closing ceremonies of the shipyard. I met a lot of other old friends there and we spent more time talking about old times than crying in our "beer". Hundreds of people took their retirements and then had to find some work outside to supplement it. It was not surprising to see an ex-yardbird in the plumbing department of Home Depot or another driving a truck.

Before the Naval Station was bulldozed, I attended a number of public meetings to hear proposals for re-use of the Naval Facilities there. I submitted a proposal to convert most of the Naval Station into a new Police Academy since the city bulldozed their own academy on Carson Street to make way for a used car lot.

Yes. I said **a used car lot**. AutoNation took over the entire academy area, except the pistol range, including the training field to sell used cars but went out of business in only 11 months. For a while, the cadets trained at Long Beach City College but that didn't work out at all. Finally they moved in trailers by the old pistol range, south of the original academy. Seeing the city's lack of respect for its own Police Academy confirmed suspicions that our attendance at reuse hearings, writing proposals and petitioning local officials was a waste of time. The city and the Port of Long Beach had their own agenda and they were not going to sway from it regardless of how many hearings were legally required.

At the reuse hearings, I proposed that the Naval Station could be used for all kinds of emergency response training. In particular the Poison Gas and Germ Warfare training the Fire Department was finally authorized to do. SWAT training could be done there at any time of day or night because of the miles of separation from any residences or businesses. Pier 6 could be converted into a Naval History museum pier with a Battleship on one side and any other ship we could get on the other. The shipyard itself could be converted into any type of heavy fabrication facility besides ships. The container terminal could still be built by filling in the outer harbor (as once proposed by the Port of Long Beach) **between the Mole and the outer Breakwater** (see map on page 382). It would give them even **more** acreage with railroad tracks run on the mole parallel to the wharves. Long Beach could have its container terminal and the entire historic Naval Facility would remain intact carrying on its **Service To The Fleet**. But all fell on deaf ears. The only uplifting note was that Congress passed a resolution not allowing any former Naval properties to be used by the China Ocean Shipping Company (COSCO). Since communist China owns COSCO, many people feared the terminal becoming a military landing zone.

"B" Some retirees started their own businesses as consultants or designers. I also formed a consulting business called DREADNAUGHT CONSULTING. I was basically the only "employee", though I did "contract out" a couple of retired LBNSY engineers to provide technical services for plans I drew for ship museum Associations and I also had quite a team of volunteers (former co-workers) ready to put hardhats back on to inspecting a Battleship. Our team shipchecked the *Missouri* in 1997 with the USS *Missouri* Memorial Association and the USS *Iowa* in 2006 up in Benicia's graveyard of ships.

"B" In late 1997 I sat myself down to start writing this book. Since then however, many of us became founding members of the Pacific Battleship Center (originally ICPA). Getting *Iowa* ready for tow out of Benicia I was very happy that Bob Rhia, Jr. drove up with me to photograph and film the ship's first tow. He is an excellent photographer and one of his photos is on the back cover of this edition. He also rode the ship with us and the photo below is him interviewing a veteran and former crewman of the ship. "Bobby" is like his father. If it has to be done, it must be done RIGHT.

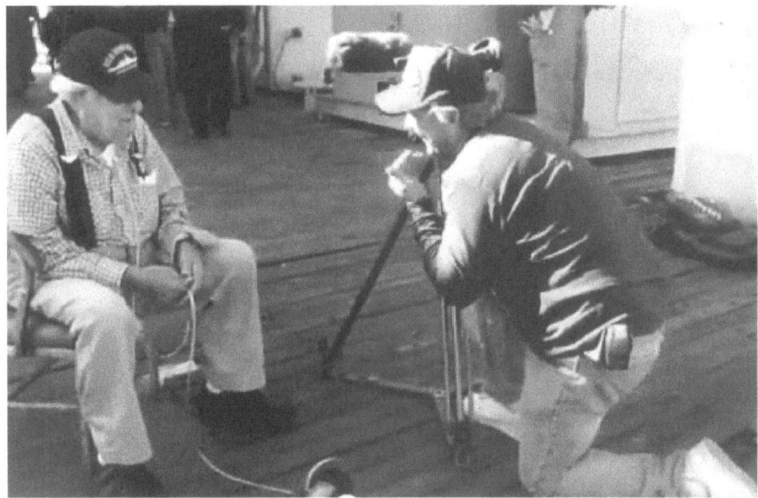

Bob Riha Jr. filming an *Iowa* veteran during our tow from Benicia to Richmond.

APPENDIX INDEX

APPENDIX A: Chronological list of all dockings at from 1942 to 1996.

APPENDIX B: Special or noteworthy dockings at LBNSY.

APPENDIX C: Crests, Logos and Memorabilia

APPENDIX D: Shipyard maps

APPENDIX E: List of Apprentice Graduates – 1947 to 1991.

APPENDIX F: List of Commanding Officers.

APPENDIX G: Roster of Officers – Reeves Field – December 10, 1942

APPENDIX H: A Deck Log of the USS *Missouri* (BB-63)

Revision "B" notes:

Appendices A and E took up a lot of time converting them from Excel to Word for later converting to PDF. Thankfully I have a neighbor who can help.

There were some corrections that had to be made for Appendix E. One was misspelling the name of a graduate. The worst was not recognizing another graduate who was a female. It's sort of hard to tell a person's gender just by the name.

Appendix C has been drastically shortened removing the pictures of plaques which are now all mounted on 2-foot by 4-foot pegboards and are now all aboard the Battleship *Iowa* awaiting a place to display them in honor of LBNSY that was the Planning Yard for the reactivation of the Battleships.

I also found a couple of nice photos for the beginning and the end of Appendix H. Naturally they include "MY" Battleship USS *Iowa* in them.

APPENDIX A
Chronology of Dry Dockings at LBNSY
1942-1996

This appendix is derived from a database in Micro Soft Excel provided to me by John Saltalamachia. I collected additional data from the Dictionary of American Naval Fighting Ships (DANFS) on the Internet (www.hazegray.org/danfs/). It is an excellent source of ship histories sponsored by the USS *Salem* historical group. However, even that exhaustive database has errors in it, most of them having to do with where specific ships were repaired or overhauled. Where LBNSY should be identified (at least by its original name of Naval Dry Docks Terminal Island) many of the DANFS' records indicate San Pedro instead. One record identified San Francisco as the repair yard for USS *Orestes* (AGP-10) that received extensive battle damage but in truth was repaired at LBNSY according to our docking logs.

The database was created from the 1987 issue of the Docking History of Long Beach Naval Shipyard covering dockings up to 1985. The information was compiled from original docking logs and record copies of the shipyard's newspaper *Digest*. It was assembled under the direction of C. C. (Bud) Miller who was the Service Shop Group Superintendent (Code 970) and shipyard historian. Dockings from 1985 to 1996 that were added in appear to be much more accurate than the previous year's thanks to computerized record keeping. Before forwarding the database to me, Salty found several typographical errors and made the necessary corrections. I found additional technical errors as well as date errors and added in those corrections. All told, it took Salty and I over three months to confirm and correct the docking list.

I found several MSOs merely listed as MINESWEEPERS with no names attached. Thanks to the Internet, I found that those particular ships were built for Norway, France, Portugal and Italy. From various Internet sources I was then able to add in their names as well as the hull numbers assigned by their countries. I found one line item merely listing *Cole* as being in dry dock 3 in late 1952 with absolutely no indication as to what kind of ship it was. Through the process of elimination and Internet browsing I found it was the USS *William C. Cole* (DE 641) that was decommissioned four years before but had some hull maintenance done with other decommissioned Destroyer Escorts of the same class just previous to or just after the *Cole's* dry dock period.

The most humorous error I found was that the USS *Cacapon* (AO 52) was dry docked four different times and her name was spelled four different ways with only one of them being correct.

One error/omission that struck home to me personally was that the Chinese ship RCS *Chung Chi* (LST-218) was not listed. We had to replace a 28-foot by 30-foot section of its bottom shell plating and tank top deck in November and December of 1955. But I could not find *Chung Chi* anywhere in the database. I worked on her, as well as another LST in the same dry dock at the same time, while I was an apprentice. Fortunately I saved my apprentice logbooks and confirmed the dry dock dates of the *Chung Chi* and the USS *Daviess County* (LST-692) in the same dry dock. The database, on the other hand, had the USS *Burton Island* (AGB-1) listed instead of the *Chung Chi*.

I have gone over these thousands of dockings several times and believe I have caught most, if not all, of the typographical and historical errors. The most common typographical error was inputting of dates. It is quite obvious when a ship's undocking was in February, eight months BEFORE its docking in October. Errors like this were easy to correct where the "10" for the "October" date was quickly changed to "01" for "January". The correctness of the change was of course double-checked against the previous and following dockings for that particular dry dock.

While talking about dry dock dates, some of them require some explanation so a reader or historical researcher can understand why consecutive dockings of the same ship are shown where it was undocked and docked again the same day. A typical example is the 1987 dockings of the *New Jersey* for her hull repairs.

This type of docking procedure is called a "bounce". Most ship's docking drawings show three positions for the docking blocks the hull rests upon. Most dry dockings that include a nearly total sandblasting and painting of the underwater hull are only in one of the three positions. This is why accurate docking records must be kept by both the shipyard and the ship to show if the ship's last docking was in position 1, 2 or 3. If the ship's last hull painting was done while the blocks were in position 1, her next docking will be in position 2 so the area of the hull covered by the docking blocks from the last event can be sandblasted and painted.

In a case where the entire hull must be painted 100% and/or hull repairs are required where docking blocks cover the repair area, then the ship is "bounced" to the next block position. It is not an off-the-cuff event either. Sight lines and winch lines must be rigged to position the ship over the next position just as soon as enough water has flooded the dock to float the ship. The instant the ship is in the next position over the blocks, the pumps are started to set her back down. This is all done in one day but because of the effort of time, equipment and personnel involved it is considered as a full docking cycle.

I felt the above explanation was necessary for clarification as I am sure some readers will make the effort to read all 3,532 line items one by one just to catch any errors I missed. If he does, he is welcome to forward the corrections to me for the next revision.

SHIP'S NAME	CLASS	NUMBER	DOCK	UNDOCK	DRYDOCK
A & P PILE DRIVER	BARGE/E	1200	8/15/1942	8/22/1942	1
KENDRICK	DD	612	9/13/1942	9/18/1942	1
WHARTON	AP	7	11/4/1942	11/18/1942	1
MACKENZIE	DD	614	11/22/1942	11/27/1942	1
McLANAHAN	DD	615	12/20/1942	12/26/1942	1
ZEILIN	AP	9	12/26/1942	2/19/1943	1
NEVADA	BB	36	2/24/1943	3/15/1943	1
ABNER READ	DD	526	3/30/1943	4/1/1943	1
STEROPE	AK	96	4/9/1943	5/10/1943	1
BOYD	DD	544	5/8/1943	5/19/1943	3
MOOSEHEAD	IX	98	5/14/1943	6/14/1943	1
DOYEN	AP	2	5/31/1943	6/5/1943	1
KANKAKEE	AO	39	5/31/1943	6/5/1943	1
BRADFORD	DD	545	6/14/1943	6/18/1943	3
PRUITT	DM	22	6/14/1943	6/29/1943	3
HERMITAGE	AP	54	6/28/1943	7/20/1943	1
NAVY HARBOR	BARGE/YNG	37	7/2/1943	7/16/1943	3
BROWN	DD	546	7/10/1943	7/16/1943	3
FELAND	APA	11	7/18/1943	7/24/1943	3
BALDHILL	PRIVATE/AO		7/20/1943	8/22/1943	1
OGLALA	ARG	1	7/22/1943	8/14/1943	2
SCULPTOR	AK	103	7/25/1943	7/31/1943	3
SABINE	AO	25	8/3/1943	8/16/1943	3
GULF QUEEN	PRIVATE/AO		8/16/1943	9/13/1943	2
COWELL	DD	547	8/23/1943	8/28/1943	3
CONCRETE CAISSON	CAISSON	1	8/24/1943	8/29/1943	1
BALDHILL	PRIVATE/AO		8/25/1943	8/29/1943	1
LACKAWANNA	AO	40	9/1/1943	9/7/1943	1
MILLICOMA	AO	73	9/1/1943	9/7/1943	1
TAPPAHANNOCK	AO	43	9/1/1943	9/7/1943	2
A & P PILE DRIVER	BARGE/E	1200	9/2/1943	9/6/1943	3
A & P WATER BARGE	BARGE	18	9/2/1943	9/6/1943	3
BROWN	DD	546	9/6/1943	9/12/1943	3
STEEL CAISSON	CAISSON		9/10/1943	9/21/1943	1
ENCHANTRESS	YACHT/YAG	6	9/17/1943	9/21/1943	3
RADIO	YACHT/YAG	7	9/17/1943	9/21/1943	3
REVENGE	AM	110	9/17/1943	9/21/1943	3
LANDING SHIP	LST	78	9/22/1943	9/29/1943	3
PENNSYLVANIA SUN	PRIVATE/AO		9/28/1943	10/1/1943	1
TEJON	PRIVATE/AO		9/28/1943	10/1/1943	1
HOPEWELL	DD	681	10/1/1943	10/6/1943	3
BAUGUST	DE	739	10/4/1943	10/6/1943	1
WATERMAN	DE	740	10/4/1943	10/6/1943	1
BELFAST	PF	35	10/7/1943	10/9/1943	1
CORONADO	PF	38	10/7/1943	10/9/1943	1

SHIP'S NAME	CLASS	NUMBER	DOCK	UNDOCK	DRYDOCK
EUGENE	PF	4	10/9/1943	10/11/1943	1
OGDEN	PF	3	10/9/1943	10/11/1943	1
CROSBY 1	BARGE/E	403	10/12/1943	10/21/1943	1
CROSBY 2	BARGE/E	404	10/12/1943	10/21/1943	1
MAURY	DD	401	10/12/1943	10/21/1943	1
ROTANIN	AK	108	10/12/1943	10/26/1943	1
SHENANDOAH	PRIVATE/AO		10/13/1943	10/16/1943	2
AJAX	AR	6	10/16/1943	10/29/1943	3
SARANAC	AO	7	10/18/1943	10/21/1943	2
BETHLEHEM. STEEL	FLT'G DRYDOCK		10/22/1943	11/3/1943	1
ROTANIN	AK	108	10/22/1943	11/3/1943	1
COWELL	DD	547	10/22/1943	10/24/1943	2
HERMITAGE	AP	5	10/26/1943	11/5/1943	2
PORTERFIELD	DD	682	10/30/1943	11/4/1943	3
CUMMINGS	DD	365	11/4/1943	11/16/1943	3
DUNLAP	DD	384	11/4/1943	11/16/1943	3
A & P WATER BARGE	BARGE	1	11/5/1943	11/8/1943	1
GEMINI	AP	7	11/5/1943	11/8/1943	1
BEDFORD	PRIVATE/AO		11/8/1943	11/10/1943	2
GEMINI	AP	7	11/9/1943	11/11/1943	1
LANDING CRAFT	LCT	350	11/15/1943	11/17/1943	2
PATROL CRAFT	PC	785	11/15/1943	11/17/1943	2
RACHEL JACKSON	PRIVATE/AK		11/18/1943	11/20/1943	3
YARD OILER	YOG	3	11/19/1943	11/20/1943	2
YARD OILER	YOG	3	11/19/1943	11/20/1943	2
WARREN	APA	5	11/20/1943	11/24/1943	1
HOPEWELL	DD	681	11/21/1943	11/26/1943	2
ALBERT HILL	PRIVATE/AO		11/22/1943	11/25/1943	3
MOBILITE	PRIVATE/AO		11/25/1943	11/28/1943	1
HOPE	AH	7	11/26/1943	12/12/1943	3
PAVO	AK	139	11/28/1943	12/15/1943	1
CALLAGHAN	DD	792	11/28/1943	12/1/1943	2
JOHN WHITICKER	AK	140	11/30/1943	12/15/1943	1
LININGRAD	PRIVATE	2	12/3/1943	12/6/1943	2
ASHTABULA	AO	5	12/14/1943	12/17/1943	3
NIEUW AMERSTERDAM	AP		12/17/1943	1/3/1944	1
HOPE	AH	7	12/19/1943	1/8/1944	2
BANGUST	DE	739	12/19/1943	12/24/1943	3
GLENDALE	PF	3	12/19/1943	12/24/1943	3
LONG BEACH	PF	3	12/19/1943	12/24/1943	3
NORTHWIND	CR	9	12/27/1943	12/30/1943	3
WEAVER	DE	741	12/27/1943	12/30/1943	3
A & P WATER BARGE	BARGE	1	12/31/1943	1/4/1944	3
BARGE DERRICK	RC	1	12/31/1943	1/4/1944	3
CASSIN YOUNG	DD	793	12/31/1943	1/4/1944	3
EPPING FOREST	LSD	4	1/4/1944	1/9/1944	1

SHIP'S NAME	CLASS	NUMBER	DOCK	UNDOCK	DRYDOC
GUNSTON HALL	LSD	5	1/4/1944	1/9/1944	1
EGG HARBOR	PRIVATE/AO		1/5/1944	1/7/1944	3
PEROTE	PRIVATE/AO		1/7/1944	1/10/1944	3
JAMES L. HOGG	AK	1	1/9/1944	1/14/1944	1
JOHN WHITICKER	AK	1	1/9/1944	1/14/1944	1
HOPE	AH	7	1/9/1944	3/1/1944	2
HOWARD	DMS	7	1/9/1944	3/1/1944	2
YARD OILER	YO	8	1/9/1944	3/1/1944	2
HILBERT	DE	7	1/11/1944	1/13/1944	3
WATER BARGE	YW	9	1/11/1944	1/13/1944	3
CORONADO	PF	3	1/14/1944	1/27/1944	3
SAN PEDRO	PF	3	1/14/1944	1/27/1944	3
LANDING SHIP	LST	4	1/27/1944	2/5/1944	1
MONONGAHELA	AO	4	1/27/1944	2/5/1944	1
CALLAGHAN	DD	7	1/27/1944	1/29/1944	3
EASTWIND	CR	9	1/29/1944	2/5/1944	3
WATERMAN	DE	7	1/29/1944	2/5/1944	3
LANDING SHIP	LSM	2	2/6/1944	2/11/1944	1
EL PASO	PF	4	2/7/1944	2/13/1944	3
OGDEN	PF	3	2/7/1944	2/13/1944	3
VAN BUREN	PF	4	2/7/1944	2/13/1944	3
YARD OILER	YOG		2/7/1944	2/13/1944	3
HERMITAGE	AP	5	2/11/1944	3/6/1944	1
HOPE	AH	7	2/13/1944	3/1/1944	2
HOWARD	DMS	7	2/13/1944	3/1/1944	2
YARD CRAFT	YC	8	2/13/1944	3/1/1944	2
IRWIN	DD	7	2/15/1944	2/10/1944	3
ORANGE	PF	4	2/15/1944	2/19/1944	3
BELFAST	PF	3	2/19/1944	2/27/1944	3
CORPUS CHRISTI	PF	4	2/19/1944	2/27/1944	3
WEAVER	DE	7	2/19/1944	2/27/1944	3
YARD OILER	YO	1	2/27/1944	3/1/1944	3
LAMONS	DE	7	3/1/1944	3/6/1944	3
YARD OILER	YO	1	3/1/1944	3/6/1944	3
FOOTE	DD	5	3/5/1944	6/4/1944	2
CASSIN YOUNG	DD	7	3/6/1944	3/7/1944	3
HECTOR	AR	7	3/7/1944	3/20/1944	1
SIR J. C. ROSS	T.S.M.V.	1	3/7/1944	3/25/1944	1
YARD OILER	YO	8	3/7/1944	3/27/1944	1
CACHE	AO	6	3/9/1944	5/27/1944	3
STEEL DRYDOCK CAISSON	CAISSON	2	3/9/1944	5/27/1944	3
STEEL DRYDOCK CAISSON	CAISSON	3	3/9/1944	5/27/1944	3
PRESTON	DD	7	3/21/1944	3/25/1944	1
ALEYONE	AK	2	3/27/1944	4/3/1944	1
FLOATING CRANE	YD	1	3/27/1944	4/3/1944	1
KYNE	DE	7	3/27/1944	4/3/1944	1

SHIP'S NAME	CLASS	NUMBER	DOCK	UNDOCK	DRYDOCK
SOUTHWIND	CR	98	3/27/1944	4/3/1944	1
YARD CRAFT	YC	965	3/27/1944	4/3/1944	1
JAMESTOWN	AGP	3	4/4/1944	4/15/1944	1
LANDING SHIP	LST	169	4/4/1944	4/15/1944	1
LANDING SHIP	LST	205	4/4/1944	4/15/1944	1
YARD OILER	YO	733	4/4/1944	4/15/1944	1
HARRIS	PA	2	4/18/1944	4/25/1944	1
LA SALLE	AP	102	4/18/1944	4/25/1944	1
SNYDER	DE	745	4/26/1944	5/3/1944	1
WESTWIND	CR	99	4/26/1944	5/3/1944	1
BISBEE	PF	46	5/5/1944	5/12/1944	1
HEMMINGER	DE	746	5/5/1944	5/12/1944	1
M. V. UNICOI	PRIVATE/AK		5/5/1944	5/12/1944	1
ADOPT	AM	137	5/12/1944	5/18/1944	1
FT. DEARBORN	PRIVATE/AO		5/12/1944	5/18/1944	1
GALLUP	PF	47	5/12/1944	5/18/1944	1
MILLICOMA	AO	73	5/18/1944	5/26/1944	1
JAMESTOWN	AGP	3	5/27/1944	6/9/1944	1
NECHES	AO	47	5/29/1944	6/20/1944	3
BARETA	AN	41	6/1/1944	6/9/1944	1
MUSKOGEE	PF	49	6/1/1944	6/9/1944	1
SATINLEAF	AN	43	6/1/1944	6/9/1944	1
SPICEWOOD	AN	53	6/1/1944	6/9/1944	1
FOOTE	DD	511	6/4/1944	6/18/1944	2
EASTWIND	CR	97	6/10/1944	6/18/1944	1
JASON	ARH	1	6/10/1944	6/18/1944	1
SHELIKOF	AVP	52	6/18/1944	6/26/1944	2
YARD OILER	YO	820	6/18/1944	6/23/1944	2
ATKINSON CO.	PRIVATE BARGE		6/23/1944	6/29/1944	2
BRIGHT	DE	747	6/23/1944	6/29/1944	2
PATROL CRAFT	PC	777	6/23/1944	6/29/1944	2
ARMY BARGE	FP	309	6/26/1944	7/17/1944	3
THORNTON	AVD	11	6/26/1944	7/17/1944	3
ATASCOSA	AD	66	6/28/1944	7/11/1944	1
STEEL CAISSON	CAISSON	1	6/28/1944	7/11/1944	1
PATROL CRAFT	PC	777	6/29/1944	7/3/1944	1
EMBA	WAR SHIP	BD	7/3/1944	7/11/1944	2
CONCRETE DOCK CAISSON	CAISSON	1	7/17/1944	7/19/1944	2
THORNTON	AVD	11	7/17/1944	7/20/1944	3
ASHTABULA	AO	51	7/20/1944	7/26/1944	1
BARGE	YPD	1	7/20/1944	7/26/1944	1
COLUMBIA DUCE	YMT	26	7/20/1944	7/26/1944	1
BRAINE	DD	630	7/20/1944	8/12/1944	2
CONCRETE DOCK CASSION	CAISSON	2 & 3	7/20/1944	8/12/1944	2
HEMMINGER	DE	746	7/20/1944	7/24/1944	3
LOWRY	DD	770	7/24/1944	7/29/1944	3

SHIP'S NAME	CLASS	NUMBER	DOCK	UNDOCK	DRYDOCK
CORNEL	AN	45	7/27/1944	8/5/1944	1
SARANAC	AO	74	7/27/1944	8/5/1944	1
SOUTHWIND	AGCR	98	8/1/1944	8/5/1944	3
TILLIS	DE	748	8/1/1944	8/5/1944	3
SUAMICO	AO	49	8/5/1944	8/20/1944	1
LANDING SHIP	LST	240	8/6/1944	8/20/1944	1
ARMY BARGE	BD	1337	8/7/1944	8/11/1944	3
WILLOUGHBY	AGP	9	8/7/1944	8/11/1944	3
ARMY BARGE	FB	173	8/11/1944	8/12/1944	3
ARMY BARGE	FP	174	8/11/1944	8/12/1944	3
ARMY BARGE	FP	174	8/14/1944	8/16/1944	2
ARMY BARGE	FS	173	8/14/1944	8/16/1944	2
ST. LOUIS	CL	49	8/16/1944	10/6/1944	3
LANDING SHIP	LST	119	8/20/1944	8/27/1944	1
LANDING SHIP	LST	274	8/20/1944	8/27/1944	1
MASTIC	AN	46	8/20/1944	8/27/1944	1
ROBERTS	DE	749	8/20/1944	8/25/1944	2
LINDSEY	DM	32	8/25/1944	8/30/1944	2
WEST VIRGINIA	BB	48	8/30/1944	9/6/1944	1
LINDSEY	DM	32	9/8/1944	9/9/1944	2
NEVILLE	APA	9	9/10/1944	9/22/1944	1
PRESIDENT MONROE	AP	104	9/10/1944	9/22/1944	1
PRESIDENT POLK	AP	103	9/10/1944	9/22/1944	1
McCLELLAND	DE	750	9/10/1944	9/15/1944	2
WESTWIND	CR	99	9/10/1944	9/15/1944	2
HASKELL	APA	117	9/15/1944	9/18/1944	2
BERING STRAIT	AVP	34	9/20/1944	9/27/1944	2
CANOTIA	AN	47	9/20/1944	9/27/1944	2
PRESIDENT ADAMS	AP	38	9/22/1944	10/1/1944	1
PRESIDENT JACKSON	AP	37	9/22/1944	10/1/1944	1
CHAUTAUQUA	CR	107	10/1/1944	10/6/1944	3
GWIN	DM	33	10/1/1944	10/6/1944	3
WINNEBAGO	CR	106	10/1/1944	10/6/1944	3
APPLING	APA	58	10/2/1944	10/8/1944	1
BARROW	APA	61	10/3/1944	10/8/1944	1
AUDRAIN	APA	59	10/8/1944	10/15/1944	1
BRACKEN	APA	64	10/8/1944	10/15/1944	1
La PORTE	AKA	151	10/8/1944	10/15/1944	1
SARASOTA	APA	204	10/8/1944	10/15/1944	1
LA PLACENTIA	PRIVATE/AO		10/9/1944	10/13/1944	3
VIKING	ARS	1	10/9/1944	10/13/1944	3
CHILDS	AVD	1	10/11/1944	11/3/1944	2
HOGAN	DMS	6	10/11/1944	10/27/1944	2
W. B. PRESTON	AVD	7	10/11/1944	11/3/1944	2
ZANE	DMS	14	10/11/1944	10/27/1944	2
DALE	DD	353	10/13/1944	10/17/1944	3

SHIP'S NAME	CLASS	NUMBER	DOCK	UNDOCK	DRYDOCK
OXFORD	APA	189	10/17/1944	10/19/1944	3
MILLICOMA	AO	73	10/19/1944	11/27/1944	1
OZARK	LSV	2	10/19/1944	10/24/1944	1
LOWNDES	APA	154	10/19/1944	10/20/1944	3
WARWICK	AKA	89	10/20/1944	10/23/1944	3
CLEVELAND	CL	55	10/25/1944	12/6/1944	3
SAN FRANCISCO	CA	38	10/28/1944	10/30/1944	1
AARON WARD	DM	34	10/29/1944	11/3/1944	2
CIMARRON	AO	22	11/2/1944	11/27/1944	1
CERRO AZUL	PRIVATE/AO		11/7/1944	11/22/1944	2
McCLELLAND	DE	750	11/22/1944	11/27/1944	ARDC-10
HUGH W. HADLEY	DD	774	11/26/1944	12/2/1944	2
LANDING SHIP	LSM	211	11/26/1944	12/2/1944	2
ATK CO.	WOOD BARGE	1	11/28/1944	12/1/1944	ARDC-10
ATK CO.	WOOD BARGE	2	11/28/1944	12/1/1944	ARDC-10
LANDING SHIP	LSM	252	12/2/1944	12/4/1944	ARDC-10
LANDING SHIP	LSM	447	12/4/1944	12/6/1944	ARDC-10
PLATTE	AO	24	12/5/1944	12/28/1944	1
SANTEE	CVE	29	12/5/1944	12/28/1944	1
KALININ BAY	CVE	68	12/5/1944	12/30/1944	2
LANDING SHIP	LSM	448	12/6/1944	12/7/1944	ARD-10
LANDING SHIP	LSM	220	12/7/1944	12/12/1944	ARD-10
KASKASKIA	AO	27	12/8/1944	12/11/1944	3
LANDING SHIP	LSM	70	12/12/1944	12/14/1944	ARD-10
LANDING SHIP	LSM	244	12/14/1944	12/16/1944	ARD-10
WICHITA	CA	45	12/16/1944	2/8/1945	3
LANDING SHIP	LSM	6	12/16/1944	12/21/1944	ARD-10
LANDING SHIP	LSM	69	12/21/1944	12/23/1944	ARD-10
WILLARD KEITH	DD	775	12/28/1944	1/3/1945	ARD-10
NORTON SOUND	AV	11	12/31/1944	1/6/1945	1
ST. LOUIS	CL	49	12/31/1944	2/6/1945	1
ASHTABULA	AO	51	1/1/1945	1/21/1945	2
METHA NELSON	IX (WOOD	74	1/4/1945	1/6/1945	1
OWASCO	CR	105	1/8/1945	1/1/1945	ARD-10
COOS BAY	AVP	25	1/20/1945	2/2/1945	ARD-10
SABINE	AO	25	1/21/1945	1/30/1945	2
MOBILE	CL	63	2/1/1945	2/24/1945	2
PATROL CRAFT	PCE	897	2/5/1945	2/9/1945	ARD-10
LACKAWANNA	AO	40	2/6/1945	2/15/1945	1
YARD REPAIR BARGE	YR	27	2/10/1945	2/14/1945	ARD-10
KANE	APD	18	2/10/1945	2/22/1945	ARD-8
COLUMBIA	CL	56	2/12/1945	3/18/1945	3
MASCOMA	AO	83	2/15/1945	2/19/1945	1
SEBAGO	CR	108	2/16/1945	2/19/1945	ARD-10
PATROL CRAFT	PC	787	2/19/1945	2/20/1945	1
WICHITA	CA	45	2/19/1945	2/28/1945	1

SHIP'S NAME	CLASS	NUMBER	DOCK	UNDOCK	DRYDOCK
ARMY SUPPLY CRAFT	FS	214	2/19/1945	2/21/1945	ARD-10
ARMY SUPPLY CRAFT	FS	219	2/19/1945	2/21/1945	ARD-10
MASCOMA	AO	83	2/20/1945	2/28/1945	1
PURDY	DD	734	2/22/1945	2/24/1945	ARD-10
OSTERHAUS	DE	164	2/23/1945	3/10/1945	ARD-8
JAMES C. OWENS	DD	776	2/24/1945	3/2/1945	ARD-10
LANDING SHIP	LST	222	2/25/1945	5/30/1945	ARD-10
BOTTINEAU	PA	235	2/26/1945	3/1/1945	2
CAPERTON	DD	650	2/27/1945	2/28/1945	ARD-4
KWAJALIEN	CVE	98	3/2/1945	3/7/1945	1
COGSWELL	DD	651	3/2/1945	3/21/1945	2
INGERSOLL	DD	652	3/2/1945	3/21/1945	2
WILEMAN	DE	22	3/3/1945	3/11/1945	ARD-10
CALIENTE	AO	53	3/7/1945	3/22/1945	1
KITKUN BAY	CVE	71	3/7/1945	3/22/1945	1
PARKS	DE	165	3/10/1945	3/24/1945	ARD-8
LANDING SHIP	LST	607	3/13/1945	4/5/1945	ARD-10
WINNEBAGO	CR	106	3/19/1945	3/22/1945	ARD-4
BRISTOL	DD	857	3/20/1945	3/24/1945	3
CAPERTON	DD	650	3/21/1945	3/29/1945	2
KNAPP	DD	653	3/21/1945	3/29/1945	2
IROQUOIS	CR	109	3/22/1945	3/26/1945	ARD-4
COLUMBIA	CL	56	3/25/1945	4/15/1945	3
ARMY SUPPLY CRAFT	FS	221	3/26/1945	3/29/1945	ARD-8
ARMY SUPPLY CRAFT	FS	355	3/26/1945	3/29/1945	ARD-8
ARMY SUPPLY CRAFT	FS	552	3/31/1945	4/4/1945	ARD-8
ARMY SUPPLY CRAFT	FS	553	3/31/1945	4/4/1945	ARD-8
BOSTON	CA	69	4/3/1945	4/29/1945	2
RAMSAY	DM	16	4/3/1945	4/17/1945	ARD-4
CAHABA	AO	82	4/4/1945	4/14/1945	1
NEOSHO	AO	48	4/4/1945	4/23/1945	1
BARGE DERRICK	BD	802	4/6/1945	4/10/1945	ARD-8
OWASCO	CR	105	4/7/1945	4/11/1945	ARD-10
YARD CRAFT	YMS	301	4/11/1945	4/14/1945	ARD-8
PATROL CRAFT	PC	802	4/12/1945	4/13/1945	ARD-10
YARD TUG (FIREBOAT)	YTB	394	4/12/1945	4/13/1945	ARD-10
LANDING SHIP	LST	240	4/15/1945	4/27/1945	ARD-8
PINE ISLAND	AV	12	4/17/1945	4/23/1945	1
CALABRE	PRIVATE/AK		4/17/1945	4/25/1945	3
DUNLIN	AM	361	4/23/1945	4/24/1945	ARD-10
LANDING SHIP	LSM	154	4/24/1945	5/1/1945	1
LANDING SHIP	LSM	165	4/24/1945	5/1/1945	1
LANDING SHIP	LSM	170	4/24/1945	5/1/1945	1
LANDING SHIP	LSM	273	4/24/1945	5/1/1945	1
LANDING SHIP	LSM	391	4/24/1945	5/1/1945	1
LANDING SHIP	LSM	392	4/24/1945	5/1/1945	1

SHIP'S NAME	CLASS	NUMBER	DOCK	UNDOCK	DRYDOCK
LANDING SHIP	LSM	341	4/25/1945	4/29/1945	ARD-10
SANTA FE	CL	60	4/27/1945	5/11/1945	3
LANDING SHIP	LSM	340	4/28/1945	5/2/1945	ARD-8
LANDING SHIP	LSM	388	4/28/1945	5/2/1945	ARD-8
WINNEBAGO	CR	106	5/1/1945	5/5/1945	ARD-10
CALIFORNIA	BB	44	5/3/1945	5/5/1945	1
BOGGS	DMS	3	5/3/1945	5/11/1945	ARD-8
ADMIRAL W. S. BENSON	AP	120	5/4/1945	5/11/1945	2
LANDING SHIP	LST	488	5/5/1945	5/11/1945	ARD-10
LANDING SHIP	LSM	371	5/12/1945	5/20/1945	2
LANDING SHIP	LST	38	5/12/1945	5/20/1945	2
LANDING SHIP	LSM	393	5/12/1945	5/15/1945	ARD-10
COOS BAY	AVP	25	5/13/1945	6/12/1945	3
HALSEY POWELL	DD	686	5/13/1945	6/12/1945	3
ORESTES	AGP	10	5/16/1945	5/25/1945	ARD-10
RAMSAY	DM	16	5/20/1945	5/22/1945	2
SANTA FE	CL	60	5/23/1945	6/8/1945	2
KENNEBAGO	AO	81	5/25/1945	6/2/1945	1
YARD CRAFT	YC	269	5/25/1945	6/2/1945	1
LANDING SHIP	LSM	264	5/30/1945	6/9/1945	ARD-10
CHELEB	AK	138	6/3/1945	6/8/1945	1
LANDING SHIP	LSM	241	6/3/1945	6/8/1945	1
MARIGOLD	USAHS		6/3/1945	6/8/1945	1
MIAMI	CL	89	6/9/1945	6/26/1945	2
COMFORT	AH	6	6/10/1945	6/29/1945	1
WYANDOT	AKA	92	6/10/1945	6/29/1945	1
ZELLARS	DD	777	6/10/1945	6/29/1945	1
LANDING SHIP	LSM	211	6/11/1945	6/19/1945	ARD-10
LANDING SHIP	LSM	261	6/11/1945	6/19/1945	ARD-10
OKLAWAHA	AO	84	6/13/1945	6/22/1945	3
LANDING SHIP	LSM	140	6/19/1945	6/29/1945	ARD-10
LANDING SHIP	LSM	266	6/19/1945	6/29/1945	ARD-10
PECOS	AO	65	6/22/1945	7/7/1945	3
ARCADIA	AD	23	6/27/1945	7/2/1945	2
LANDING SHIP	LSM	390	6/30/1945	7/5/1945	ARD-10
LANDING CRAFT	LCI	L17	7/1/1945	7/29/1945	1
LANDING CRAFT	LCI	L19	7/1/1945	7/29/1945	1
LANDING CRAFT	LCI	L190	7/1/1945	7/29/1945	1
LANDING CRAFT	LCI	L192	7/1/1945	7/29/1945	1
LANDING CRAFT	LCI	L195	7/1/1945	7/29/1945	1
LANDING CRAFT	LCI	L2	7/1/1945	7/29/1945	1
LANDING CRAFT	LCI	L41	7/1/1945	7/29/1945	1
LANDING CRAFT	LCI	L42	7/1/1945	7/29/1945	1
LANDING CRAFT	LCI	L43	7/1/1945	7/29/1945	1
LANDING CRAFT	LCI	L46	7/1/1945	7/29/1945	1
MUSTIN	DD	413	7/1/1945	7/30/1945	1

SHIP'S NAME	CLASS	NUMBER	DOCK	UNDOCK	DRYDOCK
PETROF BAY	CVE	80	7/1/1945	7/30/1945	1
CORMORANT	ATO	133	7/6/1945	7/9/1945	ARD-10
SANTA FE	CL	60	7/8/1945	7/8/1945	2
LEEDSTOWN	AP	56	7/9/1945	7/17/1945	3
YARD REPAIR BARGE	YR	23	7/9/1945	7/17/1945	3
CAPPS	DD	550	7/10/1945	8/22/1945	2
JENKINS	DD	447	7/10/1945	8/22/1945	2
SWAN	AVP	7	7/12/1945	7/16/1945	ARD-10
LANDING SHIP	LST	61	7/17/1945	7/26/1945	ARD-10
DOYEN	APA	1	7/18/1945	7/28/1945	3
SAN DIEGO	DREDGE		7/27/1945	7/31/1945	ARD-10
BOISE	CL	47	7/29/1945	8/10/1945	3
CHINCOTEAGUE	AVP	24	8/1/1945	8/7/1945	ARD-10
HALL	DD	583	8/8/1945	8/23/1945	1
TOLMAN	DM	28	8/8/1945	9/7/1945	1
PILOT	AM	104	8/8/1945	8/10/1945	ARD-10
HENDRY	PA	118	8/10/1945	8/18/1945	3
LANDING SHIP	LST	219	8/14/1945	9/7/1945	ARD-10
ADMIRALTY ISLANDS	CVE	99	8/20/1945	8/25/1945	3
SARGENT BAY	CVE	83	8/23/1945	9/7/1945	1
LANDING CRAFT	LCI	577	8/31/1945	9/16/1945	3
LANDING CRAFT	LCI	746	8/31/1945	9/16/1945	3
LANDING CRAFT	LCI	747	8/31/1945	9/16/1945	3
LANDING CRAFT	LCI	748	8/31/1945	9/16/1945	3
LANDING CRAFT	LCI	749	8/31/1945	9/16/1945	3
LANDING CRAFT	LCI	750	8/31/1945	9/16/1945	3
LANDING CRAFT	LCI	955	8/31/1945	9/16/1945	3
LANDING CRAFT	LCI	956	8/31/1945	9/16/1945	3
LANDING CRAFT	LCI	957	8/31/1945	9/16/1945	3
LANDING CRAFT	LCI	958	8/31/1945	9/16/1945	3
LANDING CRAFT	LCI	959	8/31/1945	9/16/1945	3
LANDING CRAFT	LCI	960	8/31/1945	9/16/1945	3
NORTHWIND	CR	184	9/5/1945	9/7/1945	2
LANDING CRAFT	LCI	1019	9/10/1945	9/14/1945	ARD-10
LANDING CRAFT	LCI	1060	9/10/1945	9/14/1945	ARD-10
EMILY H. M. WEBER	USAHS		9/11/1945	9/14/1945	2
FLOATING CRANE	YD	1	9/11/1945	9/14/1945	2
PAVO	AK	139	9/13/1945	9/27/1945	1
CASSIN YOUNG	DD	793	9/17/1945	10/10/1945	2
O'NEILL	DE	188	9/18/1945	9/27/1945	ARD-10
WHARTON	AP	7	9/20/1945	9/21/1945	3
ASTORIA	CL	90	9/25/1945	10/10/1945	3
LANDING CRAFT	LCI	956	9/27/1945	9/28/1945	ARD-10
LANDING CRAFT	LCI	577	9/28/1945	10/1/1945	ARD-10
GILLIS	AVD	12	10/2/1945	10/4/1945	ARD-10
GEO. E. BADGER	AVD	3	10/4/1945	10/5/1945	ARD-10

SHIP'S NAME	CLASS	NUMBER	DOCK	UNDOCK	DRYDOCK
TALBOT	DD	114	10/5/1945	10/8/1945	ARD-10
CHAUTAUQUA	WPG	41	10/8/1945	10/24/1945	1
GENERAL O. H. ERNST	AP	133	10/8/1945	10/26/1945	1
PALM	AN	28	10/8/1945	10/24/1945	1
GOLDSBOROUGH	DD	188	10/9/1945	10/10/1945	ARD-10
PRESTON	DD	795	10/10/1945	10/22/1945	2
CLEMSON	APD (EX-DD-186)	31	10/10/1945	10/11/1945	ARD-10
ELLIOT	DMS (EX DD-146)	4	10/11/1945	10/12/1945	ARD-10
WATERS	DD	115	10/12/1945	10/15/1945	ARD-10
MANATEE	AO	58	10/16/1945	11/5/1945	3
HAMILTON	DD	141	10/16/1945	10/17/1945	ARD-10
KILTY	DD	137	10/17/1945	10/18/1945	ARD-10
RAMSAY	DM	16	10/18/1945	10/19/1945	ARD-10
HUMPHREYS	DD	236	10/19/1945	10/22/1945	ARD-10
BEBAS	DE	10	10/23/1945	10/24/1945	ARD-10
DOGWOOD	USAHS		10/24/1945	10/31/1945	2
FLOATING CRANE	YD	139	10/24/1945	10/31/1945	2
LOVERING	DE	39	10/24/1945	10/25/1945	ARD-10
BURDEN H. HASTINGS	DE	19	10/25/1945	10/26/1945	ARD-10
LE HARDY	DE	20	10/26/1945	10/27/1945	ARD-10
ORANGE	PF	43	10/29/1945	11/2/1945	ARD-10
CACAPON	AO	52	11/1/1945	11/19/1945	1
HAROLD C. THOMAS	DE	21	11/6/1945	11/7/1945	ARD-10
LENAWEE	APA	195	11/7/1945	11/10/1945	3
CHARLES R. GREER	DE	23	11/7/1945	11/8/1945	ARD-10
URAGUAY	ARMY		11/8/1945	11/13/1945	2
WHITMAN	DE	24	11/8/1945	11/9/1945	ARD-10
WILEMAN	DE	22	11/9/1945	11/13/1945	ARD-10
GRIMES	APA	172	11/12/1945	11/16/1945	1
STEELE	DE	8	11/13/1945	11/14/1945	ARD-10
GRISWOLD	DE	7	11/14/1945	11/15/1945	ARD-10
TOPEKA	CL	67	11/15/1945	11/27/1945	2
BOWIE	APA	137	11/16/1945	11/23/1945	3
SEID	DE	256	11/16/1945	11/19/1945	ARD-10
CROUTER	DE	11	11/19/1945	11/20/1945	ARD-10
CARLSON	DE	9	11/20/1945	11/21/1945	ARD-10
DOHERTY	DE	14	11/21/1945	11/23/1945	ARD-10
LUNGA POINT	CVE	94	11/23/1945	11/28/1945	1
SERITA	AKA	39	11/23/1945	11/28/1945	1
EDWARD C. DALY	DE	17	11/28/1945	11/29/1945	ARD-10
ATLANTA	CL	104	11/29/1945	12/6/1945	2
GILMORE	DE	18	11/29/1945	11/30/1945	ARD-10
LOUIS A MILNE	USAHS		12/1/1945	12/7/1945	3
ELLIOT	DMS	4	12/2/1945	12/7/1945	1
GILLIS	AVD	12	12/2/1945	12/7/1945	1
NEVADA	BB	36	12/2/1945	12/7/1945	1

SHIP'S NAME	CLASS	NUMBER	DOCK	UNDOCK	DRYDOCK
DONEFF	DE	49	12/3/1945	12/4/1945	ARD-10
MEDEA	AKA	31	12/6/1945	12/10/1945	2
CRAFT	SC	1047	12/6/1945	12/10/1945	ARD-10
CRAFT	SC	1050	12/6/1945	12/10/1945	ARD-10
TEXAS	BB	35	12/8/1945	12/12/1945	1
McCRACKEN	PA	198	12/8/1945	12/10/1945	3
CRAFT	SC	1008	12/10/1945	12/12/1945	ARD-10
PILE DRIVER	YPD	1	12/10/1945	12/12/1945	ARD-10
NECHES	AO	47	12/11/1945	12/17/1945	2
PORT HUENEME	T	22	12/12/1945	12/18/1945	3
CRAFT	SC	1052	12/12/1945	12/18/1945	ARD-10
HUTCHINSON	PF	45	12/14/1945	12/20/1945	3
LOWRY	DD	770	12/14/1945	12/20/1945	3
YARD CRAFT	YC	1113	12/14/1945	12/20/1945	3
YARD CRAFT	YC	1114	12/14/1945	12/20/1945	3
IOWA	BB	61	12/16/1945	12/22/1945	1
CRAFT	SC	755	12/18/1945	12/19/1945	ARD-10
CRAFT	SC	992	12/18/1945	12/19/1945	ARD-10
FLOATING CRANE	YD	113	12/19/1945	12/26/1945	2
TURANDOT	AKA	47	12/19/1945	12/24/1945	2
LANDING SHIP	LSM	277	12/19/1945	12/26/1945	ARD-10
ELIZABETH STANTON	AP	69	12/21/1945	12/29/1945	2
60 TON CRANE BARGE	YD		12/21/1945	12/29/1945	3
ONEIDA	APA	221	12/26/1945	12/31/1945	2
YARD TUG	YTB	255	12/26/1945	12/29/1945	ARD-10
BARTON	DD	722	12/28/1945	1/10/1946	1
CHICAGO	CA	136	12/28/1945	1/18/1946	1
DAYTON	CL	105	12/28/1945	1/10/1946	1
MOALE	DD	693	12/28/1945	1/10/1946	1
CLINTON	APA	144	12/29/1945	1/4/1946	3
PERIDOT	PYC	18	12/29/1945	1/3/1946	ARD-10
ROCKINGHAM	APA	229	12/31/1945	1/7/1946	2
LANDING SHIP	LSM (R)	193	1/3/1946	1/7/1946	ARD-10
BRISCO	APA	65	1/5/1946	1/8/1946	3
TEREBINTH	AN	59	1/7/1946	1/14/1946	ARD-10
DEUEL	APA	160	1/8/1946	1/14/1946	2
COMMENCEMENT BAY	CVE	105	1/11/1946	1/18/1946	3
YARD TUG	YTB	397	1/14/1946	1/17/1946	ARD-10
RABY	DE	698	1/17/1946	1/29/1946	ARD-10
G. E. BADGER	DD	196	1/18/1946	2/4/1946	1
JOHN Q. ROBERTS	APD	94	1/18/1946	1/25/1946	1
LANDING CRAFT	LCT	647	1/18/1946	1/25/1946	1
SALT LAKE CITY	CA	25	1/18/1946	2/4/1946	1
RENDOVA	CVE	114	1/23/1946	1/29/1946	3
CORPUS CHRISTI	PF	44	1/25/1946	3/12/1946	2
LANDING SHIP	LST	205	1/25/1946	2/8/1946	2

SHIP'S NAME	CLASS	NUMBER	DOCK	UNDOCK	DRYDOCK
KULA GULF	CVE	108	1/29/1946	2/12/1946	3
MACKINAC	AVP	13	1/30/1946	2/7/1946	ARD-10
ARKANSAS	BB	33	2/4/1946	2/6/1946	1
ELVIDA	YP	109	2/7/1946	2/11/1946	AFDL-43
KEWAYDIN	ATO	24	2/7/1946	2/11/1946	AFDL-43
ALBEMARLE	AV	5	2/8/1946	2/17/1946	1
CUMBERLAND SOUND	AV	17	2/8/1946	2/17/1946	1
ORLECK	DD	886	2/11/1946	3/12/1946	2
ALERT	YP	264	2/12/1946	2/13/1946	AFDL-43
LANDING CRAFT	LCT	1359	2/14/1946	2/28/1946	AFDL-43
LANDING CRAFT	LCT	1361	2/14/1946	2/28/1946	AFDL-43
GILLIGAN	DE	508	2/20/1946	3/11/1946	1
LOUGH	DE	586	2/20/1946	3/11/1946	1
MERRIMACK	AO	37	2/20/1946	3/11/1946	1
SALAMONIE	AO	26	2/20/1946	3/11/1946	1
STEVENS	DD	479	2/20/1946	3/11/1946	1
WALKER	DD	517	2/25/1946	3/8/1946	3
WILLIAMS	DE	372	2/25/1946	3/8/1946	3
CRAFT	SC	628	3/1/1946	3/4/1946	AFDL-43
CRAFT	SC	1370	3/1/1946	3/4/1946	AFDL-43
LANDING CRAFT	LCI	609	3/4/1946	3/14/1946	AFDL-43
DAVID W. TAYLOR	DD	551	3/9/1946	3/22/1946	3
SHACKLE	ARS	9	3/9/1946	3/22/1946	3
STEVENS	DD	479	3/9/1946	3/22/1946	3
COWELL	DD	547	3/14/1946	3/26/1946	1
LANDING SHIP	LSM	300	3/14/1946	3/26/1946	1
TERRY	DD	513	3/14/1946	3/26/1946	1
VICKSBURG	CL	86	3/15/1946	4/2/1946	2
CRAFT	SC	728	3/15/1946	3/20/1946	AFDL-43
CRAFT	SC	994	3/15/1946	3/20/1946	AFDL-43
LANDING SHIP	LSM	360	3/21/1946	3/28/1946	AFDL-43
COMPTON	DD	705	3/23/1946	3/28/1946	3
LANDING CRAFT	LCI	947	3/23/1946	3/28/1946	3
YARD CRAFT	YNG	38	3/23/1946	3/28/1946	3
LANDING SHIP	LSM	60	3/29/1946	4/10/1946	1
DKM F EUGENE	IX (WAR PRIZE)	300	3/29/1946	4/10/1946	1
LANDING SHIP	LSM	494	3/29/1946	4/6/1946	AFDL-43
ERBEN	DD	631	3/30/1946	4/15/1946	3
LANDING CRAFT	LCI	735	3/30/1946	4/15/1946	3
NICHOLAS	DD	449	3/30/1946	4/15/1946	3
JASON	ARH	1	4/6/1946	4/26/1946	2
MARSH	DE	699	4/8/1946	4/16/1946	AFDL-43
AUCILLA	AO	56	4/15/1946	4/23/1946	1
LANDING SHIP	LST	666	4/15/1946	4/23/1946	1
LANDING SHIP	LST	842	4/15/1946	4/23/1946	1
TAYLOR	DD	468	4/15/1946	4/23/1946	1

SHIP'S NAME	CLASS	NUMBER	DOCK	UNDOCK	DRYDOCK
LANDING SHIP	LSM	60	4/16/1946	4/17/1946	AFDL-43
CINNAMON	AN	50	4/17/1946	4/29/1946	3
CLIFFROSE	AN	42	4/17/1946	4/29/1946	3
LANDING SHIP	LSM	231	4/17/1946	4/29/1946	3
SILVER BELL	AN	51	4/17/1946	4/29/1946	3
TORCHWOOD	AN	55	4/17/1946	4/29/1946	3
FLOATING CRANE	YD	87	4/18/1946	4/20/1946	AFDL-43
YARD CRAFT	YF	1136	4/18/1946	4/20/1946	AFDL-43
YARD CRAFT	YF	1137	4/18/1946	4/20/1946	AFDL-43
YARD TUG	YTB	509	4/22/1946	4/26/1946	AFDL-43
YARD TUG	YTB	510	4/22/1946	4/26/1946	AFDL-43
LANDING CRAFT	LCI	475	4/29/1946	5/7/1946	1
LANDING CRAFT	LCI	564	4/29/1946	5/7/1946	1
LANDING CRAFT	LCI	976	4/29/1946	5/7/1946	1
LANDING CRAFT	LCS	32	4/29/1946	5/7/1946	1
LANDING CRAFT	LCS	36	4/29/1946	5/7/1946	1
LANDING CRAFT	LCS	57	4/29/1946	5/7/1946	1
LANDING CRAFT	LCS	67	4/29/1946	5/7/1946	1
LANDING CRAFT	LCS	123	4/29/1946	5/7/1946	1
LANDING SHIP	LSM	355	4/29/1946	5/7/1946	1
LANDING SHIP	LSM	362	4/29/1946	5/7/1946	1
LANDING SHIP	LSM	371	4/29/1946	5/7/1946	1
LANDING SHIP	LSM	479	4/29/1946	5/7/1946	1
LANDING CRAFT	LCI	450	4/29/1946	5/7/1946	AFDL-43
LANDING CRAFT	LCI	947	4/29/1946	5/7/1946	AFDL-43
HECTOR	AR	7	4/30/1946	5/9/1946	2
FLUSSER	DD	368	5/2/1946	5/4/1946	3
OSMUS	DE	701	5/2/1946	5/4/1946	3
LANDING CRAFT	LCI	968	5/8/1946	5/15/1946	1
LANDING CRAFT	LCI	971	5/8/1946	5/15/1946	1
LANDING CRAFT	LCI	1052	5/8/1946	5/15/1946	1
LANDING CRAFT	LCI	1071	5/8/1946	5/15/1946	1
LANDING CRAFT	LCS	57	5/8/1946	5/15/1946	1
LANDING CRAFT	LCS	59	5/8/1946	5/15/1946	1
LANDING SHIP	LSM	30	5/8/1946	5/15/1946	1
LANDING SHIP	LSM	35	5/8/1946	5/15/1946	1
LANDING SHIP	LSM	219	5/8/1946	5/15/1946	1
LANDING SHIP	LSM	418	5/8/1946	5/15/1946	1
SEVERN	AO	61	5/8/1946	5/15/1946	1
SEER	AM	112	5/8/1946	5/18/1946	3
YARD CRAFT	YF	871	5/8/1946	5/18/1946	3
YARD CRAFT	YF	873	5/8/1946	5/18/1946	3
YARD CRAFT	YMS	430	5/8/1946	5/18/1946	3
SIOUX	ATF	75	5/8/1946	5/15/1946	AFDL-43
TALUGA	AO	62	5/10/1946	5/22/1946	2
LANDING CRAFT	LCI	31	5/16/1946	5/21/1946	AFDL-43

SHIP'S NAME	CLASS	NUMBER	DOCK	UNDOCK	DRYDOCK
LANDING SHIP	LSM	365	5/16/1946	5/21/1946	AFDL-43
AGAWAN	AOG	6	5/17/1946	5/26/1946	1
APPALACHIAN	AGC	1	5/17/1946	5/26/1946	1
OAHU	ARG	5	5/17/1946	5/26/1946	1
GENESEE	AOG	7	5/18/1946	5/26/1946	1
ELKHORN	AOG	7	5/21/1946	5/28/1946	3
SAN BERNARDINO CTY	LST	1110	5/21/1946	5/28/1946	AFDL-43
YARD CRAFT	YMS	430	5/22/1946	5/29/1946	AFDL-43
COLUMBUS	CA	74	5/27/1946	6/6/1946	2
LANDING SHIP	LST	1104	5/28/1946	6/11/1946	3
YARD CRAFT	YC	281	5/28/1946	6/11/1946	3
LANDING CRAFT	LCI	648	5/29/1946	6/13/1946	1
LANDING CRAFT	LCI	788	5/29/1946	6/13/1946	1
LANDING CRAFT	LCI	999	5/29/1946	6/13/1946	1
LANDING CRAFT	LCI	1053	5/29/1946	6/13/1946	1
LANDING CRAFT	LCI	1061	5/29/1946	6/13/1946	1
LANDING CRAFT	LCI (L)	1017	5/29/1946	6/13/1946	1
LANDING SHIP	LSM	261	5/29/1946	6/13/1946	1
YARD CRAFT	YF	872	5/29/1946	6/13/1946	1
YARD CRAFT	YF	874	5/29/1946	6/13/1946	1
YARD CRAFT	YF	875	5/29/1946	6/13/1946	1
YARD CRAFT	YF	882	5/29/1946	6/13/1946	1
YARD CRAFT	YF	883	5/29/1946	6/13/1946	1
IMPROVE	AM	247	5/29/1946	6/6/1946	AFDL-43
LANDING CRAFT	LCS	32	6/7/1946	6/13/1946	AFDL-43
REFRESH	AM	287	6/7/1946	6/13/1946	AFDL-43
TALUGA	AO	62	6/9/1946	6/11/1946	2
LANDING CRAFT	LCI	575	6/12/1946	6/21/1946	3
LANDING SHIP	LSM (R)	410	6/12/1946	6/21/1946	3
LAWRENCE COUNTY	LST	887	6/12/1946	6/21/1946	3
PAINTERS	BARGE		6/12/1946	6/21/1946	3
LANDING CRAFT	LCI	883	6/13/1946	6/24/1946	2
LANDING CRAFT	LCS	68	6/13/1946	6/24/1946	2
LANDING CRAFT	LCS	786	6/13/1946	6/24/1946	2
LANDING SHIP	LSM	128	6/13/1946	6/24/1946	2
PERRIS ISLAND	AG	72	6/14/1946	6/24/1946	AFDL-43
SUB CHASER	PC	1144	6/14/1946	6/24/1946	AFDL-43
LANDING CRAFT	LCI	440	6/19/1946	7/2/1946	1
LANDING CRAFT	LCI	732	6/19/1946	7/2/1946	1
LANDING SHIP	LSM	64	6/19/1946	7/2/1946	1
PONTOON	BARGE		6/19/1946	7/2/1946	1
WATER BARGE	YW	64	6/19/1946	7/2/1946	1
YARD CRAFT	YC	561	6/19/1946	7/2/1946	1
YARD CRAFT	YC	791	6/19/1946	7/2/1946	1
YARD CRAFT	YC	865	6/19/1946	7/2/1946	1
D CRAFT	YC	866	6/19/1946	7/2/1946	1

SHIP'S NAME	CLASS	NUMBER	DOCK	UNDOCK	DRYDOCK
YARD CRAFT	YC	867	6/19/1946	7/2/1946	1
YARD CRAFT	YC	870	6/19/1946	7/2/1946	1
YARD CRAFT	YC	871	6/19/1946	7/2/1946	1
YARD CRAFT	YC	872	6/19/1946	7/2/1946	1
YARD CRAFT	YF	654	6/19/1946	7/2/1946	1
CIMARRON	AO	22	6/24/1946	7/10/1946	3
SUB CHASER	PC	1078	6/24/1946	7/8/1946	AFDL-43
YARD TUG	YTB	400	6/26/1946	7/8/1946	AFDL-43
LANDING CRAFT	LCI	789	6/27/1946	7/26/1946	2
LANDING CRAFT	LCI	880	6/27/1946	7/26/1946	2
LANDING CRAFT	LCI	1063	6/27/1946	7/26/1946	2
LANDING SHIP	LSM	344	6/27/1946	7/26/1946	2
VALVE	ARS	28	6/27/1946	7/26/1946	2
VENT	ARS	29	6/27/1946	7/26/1946	2
COASTAL TRANSPORT	APC	9	7/9/1946	7/23/1946	1
FLOATING DRYDOCK	ARD	10	7/9/1946	7/22/1946	1
LANDING CRAFT	LCI	1031	7/9/1946	7/26/1946	1
LANDING CRAFT	LCI	1079	7/9/1946	7/26/1946	1
LANDING CRAFT	LCS	43	7/9/1946	7/26/1946	1
LANDING SHIP	LST	463	7/9/1946	7/22/1946	1
CHIPOLA	AO	63	7/12/1946	7/28/1946	3
ARISTAEUS	ARB	1	7/25/1946	8/9/1946	1
LANDING CRAFT	LCS	66	7/25/1946	8/9/1946	1
LANDING SHIP	LSM	368	7/25/1946	8/9/1946	1
OCEANUS	ARB	2	7/25/1946	8/9/1946	1
SARPEDON	ARB	7	7/25/1946	8/9/1946	1
STOCKHAM	DD	683	7/25/1946	8/9/1946	1
CACAPON	AO	52	7/29/1946	10/9/1946	3
SPARE CAISSON	CAISSON		7/30/1946	8/22/1946	2
INCREDIBLE	AM	249	7/30/1946	8/19/1946	ARD-10
LANDING CRAFT	LCI	975	7/30/1946	8/19/1946	ARD-10
DENNIS J. BUCKLEY	DD	808	8/3/1946	8/6/1946	ARD-8
HIDATSA	ATF	102	8/7/1946	8/19/1946	ARD-8
OCEAN TUG (RESCUE)	ATR	51	8/7/1946	8/19/1946	ARD-8
AUSTIN	DE	15	8/14/1946	8/28/1946	1
CHEWAUCAN	AOG	50	8/14/1946	8/28/1946	1
DONEFF	DE	49	8/14/1946	8/28/1946	1
LANDING CRAFT	LCI	546	8/14/1946	8/28/1946	1
PALAWAN	ARG	10	8/14/1946	8/28/1946	1
YARD CRAFT	YMS	445	8/20/1946	8/30/1946	AFDL-43
YARD TUG	YTB	255	8/20/1946	8/30/1946	AFDL-43
YARD CRAFT	YMS	438	8/21/1946	8/29/1946	ARD-8
FLOATING DRYDOCK	ARD	12	8/22/1946	9/7/1946	2
FLOATING DRYDOCK	ARD	9	8/30/1946	9/11/1946	1
TOLOVANA	AO	64	8/30/1946	9/11/1946	1
CINNAMON	AN	50	9/3/1946	10/15/1946	AFDL-43

SHIP'S NAME	CLASS	NUMBER	DOCK	UNDOCK	DRYDOCK
YARD CRAFT	YMS	296	9/3/1946	10/15/1946	AFDL-43
VAMMEN	DE	644	9/3/1946	9/7/1946	ARD-8
INCREDIBLE	AM	249	9/9/1946	9/11/1946	AFDL-43
ST. PAUL	CA	73	9/12/1946	9/27/1946	2
SUB CHASER	PC	1168	9/12/1946	9/20/1946	ARD-8
YARD TUG	YTB	511	9/12/1946	9/20/1946	ARD-8
KISHWAUKEE	AOG	9	9/14/1946	9/28/1946	1
OBERON	AKA	14	9/14/1946	9/28/1946	1
PASIG	AW	3	9/14/1946	9/28/1946	1
RONQUIL	SS	396	9/24/1946	9/27/1946	ARD-8
CHAWASHA	ATF	151	10/1/1946	10/8/1946	ARD-8
BENNER	DD	807	10/3/1946	10/17/1946	1
DIPHDA	AKA	59	10/3/1946	10/17/1946	1
HAWKINS	DD	873	10/3/1946	10/17/1946	1
MYLES C. FOX	DD	829	10/3/1946	10/17/1946	1
STEEL CAISSON	CAISSON	1	10/3/1946	10/17/1946	1
CHIMARIKO	ATF	154	10/10/1946	10/22/1946	2
GEAR	ARS	34	10/10/1946	10/22/1946	2
GRASP	ARS	24	10/10/1946	10/22/1946	2
SNATCH	ARS	27	10/10/1946	10/22/1946	2
ASHTABULA	AO	51	10/10/1946	10/23/1946	3
DIODON	SS	349	10/14/1946	10/17/1946	ARD-8
OCEAN TUG (RESCUE)	ATR	24	10/16/1946	10/20/1946	AFDL-43
BURTON ISLAND	AG	88	10/21/1946	10/27/1946	1
DIONYSUS	AR	21	10/21/1946	10/27/1946	1
CHIVO	SS	341	10/21/1946	10/25/1946	AFDL-43
SCABBARDFISH	SS	397	10/21/1946	10/24/1946	ARD-8
BLUE RIDGE	AGC	2	10/24/1946	11/5/1946	2
KASKASKIA	AO	27	10/26/1946	11/19/1946	3
CHOPPER	SS	342	10/28/1946	11/1/1946	ARD-8
GUNASON	DE	795	10/29/1946	11/14/1946	AFDL-43
CARTER HALL	LSD	3	10/30/1946	11/19/1946	1
OAK HILL	LSD	7	10/30/1946	11/19/1946	1
ARAPAHO	ATF	68	11/12/1946	11/25/1946	2
CARIB	ATF	82	11/12/1946	11/25/1946	2
SEGUNDO	SS	398	11/12/1946	11/25/1946	2
TOMBIGBEE	AOG	11	11/15/1946	12/2/1946	AFDL-43
PATROL CRAFT	PCE	857	11/18/1946	1/9/1947	YFD-8
PANAMINT	AGC	13	11/21/1946	12/4/1946	3
CREON	ARL	11	11/22/1946	12/7/1946	1
EPPING FOREST	LSD	14	11/22/1946	12/7/1946	1
LINDENWALD	LSD	6	11/22/1946	12/7/1946	1
STENTOR	ARL	26	11/22/1946	12/7/1946	1
HOLLAND	ARG	18	11/27/1946	12/11/1946	2
GANTNER	APD	42	12/3/1946	12/16/1946	AFDL-43
BARIOKO	CVE	115	12/6/1946	12/18/1946	3

SHIP'S NAME	CLASS	NUMBER	DOCK	UNDOCK	DRYDOCK
FLOATING CRANE	ARD	8	12/10/1946	1/3/1947	1
TAPPAHANNOCK	AO	43	12/10/1946	1/3/1947	1
YARD CRAFT	YF	340	12/10/1946	1/3/1947	1
FALL RIVER	CA	131	12/14/1946	12/23/1946	2
DUTTON	AGSC	8	12/17/1946	12/26/1946	AFDL-43
YARD TUG	YTB	400	12/17/1946	12/26/1946	AFDL-43
LANDING SHIP	LSM	451	12/20/1946	1/10/1947	3
LANDING SHIP	LSM (R)	409	12/20/1946	1/10/1947	3
LAYSAN ISLAND	ARS (T)	1	12/20/1946	1/10/1947	3
CHIEF	AM	315	12/27/1946	1/14/1947	2
IMPECCABLE	AM	320	12/27/1946	1/14/1947	2
WEEDEN	DE	797	12/27/1946	1/14/1947	2
YARD TUG	YTL	155	12/31/1946	1/9/1947	AFDL-43
YARD TUG	YTL	560	12/31/1946	1/9/1947	AFDL-43
LANDING CRAFT	LCI	1060	1/7/1947	1/21/1947	1
LANDING SHIP	LSM	37	1/7/1947	1/21/1947	1
PATROL CRAFT	PCS (S)	1403	1/10/1947	1/16/1947	AFDL-43
TOPEKA	CL	67	1/17/1947	2/6/1947	2
SPEAR	AM	322	1/20/1947	2/3/1947	AFDL-43
CALIENTE	AO	53	1/21/1947	2/5/1947	1
YARD CRAFT	YF	997	1/27/1947	2/4/1947	3
YARD CRAFT	YF	657	1/29/1947	2/7/1947	YFD-8
YARD TUG	YTB	285	1/29/1947	2/7/1947	YFD-8
FLOATING CRANE	YD	87	2/5/1947	2/14/1947	1
NEREUS	AS	17	2/5/1947	2/14/1947	1
LANDING SHIP	LSM	275	2/5/1947	2/13/1947	AFDL-43
YARD TUG	YTL	583	2/5/1947	2/13/1947	AFDL-43
AVERY ISLAND	AG	76	2/7/1947	2/18/1947	3
SIOUX	ATF	75	2/10/1947	2/19/1947	YFD-8
YARD TUG	YTB	539	2/10/1947	2/19/1947	YFD-8
GYPSY	ARSD	1	2/11/1947	3/28/1947	2
MENDER	ARSD	2	2/11/1947	3/28/1947	2
SAN BERNARDINO CTY	LST	1110	2/17/1947	2/19/1947	AFDL-43
CUMBERLAND SOUND	AV	17	2/20/1947	3/7/1947	1
SPERRY	AS	12	2/20/1947	3/7/1947	1
EDISTO	AG	89	2/20/1947	2/26/1947	3
CLAMP	ARS	33	2/21/1947	3/5/1947	YFD-47
SUB CHASER	PC (C)	1244	2/21/1947	3/5/1947	YFD-8
ARAWAK	YTB	702	2/24/1947	3/12/1947	AFDL-43
PRESERVER	ARS	8	2/24/1947	3/12/1947	AFDL-43
TELAMON	ARB	8	2/26/1947	3/10/1947	3
YARD CRAFT	YC	865	2/26/1947	3/10/1947	3
YARD CRAFT	YC	871	2/26/1947	3/10/1947	3
BULL	APD	78	3/6/1947	2/21/1947	YFD-8
SUB CHASER-RESCUE	EPCE (R)	857	3/10/1947	3/11/1947	3
APPALACHIAN	AGC	1	3/11/1947	3/24/1947	1

SHIP'S NAME	CLASS	NUMBER	DOCK	UNDOCK	DRYDOCK
PICKAWAY	APA	222	3/11/1947	3/24/1947	1
YARD CRAFT	YC	1336	3/11/1947	3/24/1947	1
YARD CRAFT	YC	1337	3/11/1947	3/24/1947	1
YARD CRAFT	YF	1138	3/11/1947	3/24/1947	1
YARD CRAFT	YF	1142	3/11/1947	3/24/1947	1
MATTABASET	AOG	52	3/13/1947	3/26/1947	3
YARD CRAFT	YC	269	3/13/1947	3/26/1947	3
YARD CRAFT	YC	791	3/13/1947	3/26/1947	3
BEGOR	APD	127	3/13/1947	3/28/1947	AFDL-43
HAVEN	AH	12	3/26/1947	4/8/1947	1
KENNETH WHITING	AV	14	3/26/1947	4/8/1947	1
YARD CRAFT	YC	919	3/26/1947	4/8/1947	1
YARD CRAFT	YC	926	3/26/1947	4/8/1947	1
MACAH	YTB	509	3/27/1947	4/8/1947	YFD-8
WAXWING	AM	389	3/27/1947	4/8/1947	YFD-8
GEORGE CLYMER	APA	27	3/28/1947	4/17/1947	3
LANDING CRAFT	LCT	1273	3/28/1947	4/17/1947	3
LANDING CRAFT	LCT	1459	3/28/1947	4/17/1947	3
PHAON	ARB	3	4/1/1947	4/18/1947	AFDL-43
COASTERS HARBOR	AG	74	4/2/1947	4/15/1947	2
ROMULUS	ARL	22	4/11/1947	4/23/1947	1
SPERRY	AS	12	4/11/1947	4/18/1947	1
SPHINX	ARL	24	4/11/1947	4/23/1947	1
GUADALUPE	AO	32	4/17/1947	4/30/1947	2
YARD CRAFT	YFN	1140	4/17/1947	4/30/1947	2
GARBAGE BARGE	YG	46	4/19/1947	4/23/1947	AFDL-43
LANDING SHIP	LSM	332	4/19/1947	4/23/1947	AFDL-43
FORT MARION	LSD	22	4/21/1947	5/2/1947	3
LANDING CRAFT	LC(FF)	790	4/21/1947	5/2/1947	3
CAHUILLA	ATF	152	4/22/1947	5/6/1947	AFDL-43
YARD TUG	YTL	310	4/22/1947	5/6/1947	AFDL-43
GARBAGE BARGE	YG	34	4/24/1947	5/6/1947	YFD-8
LANDING SHIP	LSM	424	4/24/1947	5/6/1947	YFD-8
GUNSTON HALL	LSD	5	4/28/1947	5/9/1947	1
PLATTE	AO	24	4/28/1947	5/9/1947	1
YARD CRAFT	YC	870	4/28/1947	5/9/1947	1
BURTON ISLAND	AG	88	5/5/1947	5/16/1947	2
NAMAKAGON	AOG	53	5/5/1947	5/16/1947	2
YARD CRAFT	YC	281	5/7/1947	5/19/1947	3
YARD CRAFT	YFN	654	5/7/1947	5/19/1947	3
YARD CRAFT	YFN	955	5/7/1947	5/19/1947	3
YARD OILER	YO	219	5/7/1947	5/19/1947	3
GARBAGE BARGE	YG	47	5/7/1947	5/20/1947	YFD-8
YARD CRAFT	YF	385	5/7/1947	5/20/1947	YFD-8
RECLAIMER	ARS	42	5/8/1947	5/20/1947	YFD-8
YARD TUG	YTB	397	5/8/1947	5/20/1947	YFD-8

SHIP'S NAME	CLASS	NUMBER	DOCK	UNDOCK	DRYDOCK
ASKARI	ARL	30	5/14/1947	6/3/1947	1
TYPHON	ARL	28	5/14/1947	5/26/1947	1
CARMICK	DMS	33	5/21/1947	6/3/1947	2
LANDING CRAFT	LCI	744	5/21/1947	6/3/1947	2
LANDING CRAFT	LCI	958	5/21/1947	6/3/1947	2
LANDING CRAFT	LCI	960	5/21/1947	6/3/1947	2
LANDING CRAFT	LCF	788	5/22/1947	6/2/1947	3
FLOATING CRANE	YD	148	5/22/1947	6/2/1947	YFD-8
YARD TUG-FIREBOAT	YTB	394	5/22/1947	6/6/1947	YFD-8
LANDING SHIP	LSM	462	5/23/1947	6/6/1947	AFDL-43
YARD TUG	YTB	398	5/23/1947	6/6/1947	AFDL-43
NET TENDER	YN	83	5/23/1947	6/1/1947	YFD-8
NECHES	AO	47	5/29/1947	6/20/1947	1
YANCEY	AKA	93	5/29/1947	6/20/1947	1
WEDDERBURN	DD	684	6/4/1947	6/13/1947	1
STEEL DRYDOCK CAISSON	CAISSON	2	6/5/1947	6/27/1947	3
STEEL DRYDOCK CAISSON	CAISSON	3	6/5/1947	6/27/1947	3
ASTORIA	CL	90	6/18/1947	7/26/1947	2
O'BRIEN	DD	725	6/19/1947	7/11/1947	YFD-8
LANDING CRAFT	LCT	1330	6/23/1947	7/3/1947	AFDL-43
CAVALIER	APA	37	6/25/1947	8/12/1947	1
FLOATING CRANE	YD	156	6/25/1947	7/21/1947	1
UVALDE	AKA	88	6/25/1947	7/21/1947	1
STEEL DRYDOCK CAISSON	CAISSON	1	6/27/1947	7/17/1947	3
HILSBOROUGH COUNTY	LST	827	7/15/1947	7/30/1947	AFDL-43
PICKING	DD	685	7/15/1947	7/30/1947	YFD-8
LANDING CRAFT	LCI	715	7/21/1947	8/12/1947	1
WASHBURN	AK	108	7/21/1947	8/12/1947	1
HELENA	CA	75	7/22/1947	8/1/1947	3
WILLIAM W. WOOD	DD	715	7/27/1947	8/13/1947	AFDL-44
TORTUGA	LSD	26	7/29/1947	8/11/1947	2
YARD CRAFT	YF	873	7/29/1947	8/11/1947	2
WANTUCK	APD	125	8/1/1947	8/15/1947	AFDL-43
MARIAS	AO	57	8/5/1947	8/19/1947	3
BROWN	DD	546	8/14/1947	9/5/1947	2
LANDING CRAFT	LCI	818	8/14/1947	9/5/1947	2
TWINING	DD	540	8/14/1947	9/5/1947	2
UHLMANN	DD	687	8/15/1947	9/8/1947	AFDL-44
BOYD	DD	544	8/18/1947	9/3/1947	1
BRONX	APA	236	8/18/1947	9/3/1947	1
FRONTIER	AD	25	8/18/1947	9/3/1947	1
HART	DD	594	8/18/1947	9/3/1947	1
LANDING CRAFT	YDG	9	8/18/1947	9/3/1947	1
CHILKAT	YTB	510	8/19/1947	9/2/1947	AFDL-43
WANNALANCET	YTB	385	8/19/1947	9/2/1947	AFDL-43
NANTAHALA	AO	60	8/23/1947	9/1/1947	3

SHIP'S NAME	CLASS	NUMBER	DOCK	UNDOCK	DRYDOCK
OCONOSTOTA	YTB	375	8/23/1947	9/1/1947	AFDL-43
O'BRIEN	DD	725	9/4/1947	10/1/1947	3
YARD CRAFT	YF	292	9/4/1947	9/17/1947	3
YARD CRAFT	YF	876	9/4/1947	9/17/1947	3
YARNALL	DD	541	9/4/1947	9/17/1947	3
SUB CHASER -RESCUE	EPCF (R)	855	9/4/1947	10/3/1947	AFDL-43
BADGER	DD	657	9/6/1947	9/22/1947	1
CONNER	DD	582	9/6/1947	9/22/1947	1
CURTISS	AV	4	9/6/1947	9/22/1947	1
KANKAKEE	AO	39	9/6/1947	9/22/1947	1
SAWFISH	SS	276	9/10/1947	9/24/1947	2
STEUBEN COUNTY	LST	1138	9/10/1947	9/24/1947	2
YARD REPAIR BARGE	YR	49	9/10/1947	9/24/1947	2
YARD TUG	YTB	384	9/10/1947	9/22/1947	AFDL-44
YARD TUG	YTB	516	9/10/1947	9/22/1947	AFDL-44
LANDING CRAFT	LC(FF)	790	9/19/1947	10/1/1947	3
MERTZ	DD	691	9/19/1947	10/1/1947	3
PASSAIC	AN	87	9/19/1947	10/1/1947	3
BUCKEYE	AN	13	9/24/1947	10/7/1947	AFDL-44
PASSACONAWAY	AN	86	9/24/1947	10/7/1947	AFDL-44
ELKHORN	AOG	7	9/25/1947	10/9/1947	1
HENRICO	APA	45	9/25/1947	10/9/1947	1
HORACE A. BASS	APD	124	9/25/1947	10/9/1947	1
STEMBEL	DD	644	9/25/1947	10/9/1947	1
YARD OILER	YO	223	9/25/1947	10/9/1947	1
BURTON ISLAND	AG	88	9/29/1947	10/10/1947	2
MONSSEN	DD	798	9/29/1947	10/10/1947	2
YARD CRAFT	YOS	26	9/29/1947	10/10/1947	2
DUXBURY BAY	AVP	38	10/3/1947	10/16/1947	3
HUDSON	DD	475	10/3/1947	10/16/1947	3
SUB CHASER	PC (C)	1169	10/3/1947	10/16/1947	3
LANDING SHIP	LST	1111	10/9/1947	10/20/1947	AFDL-44
SWAY	AM	120	10/9/1947	10/20/1947	AFDL-44
AMPHITRITE	ARL	29	10/13/1947	10/26/1947	1
JOHN A. BOLE	DD	755	10/13/1947	10/25/1947	1
LOFBERG	DD	759	10/13/1947	10/25/1947	1
WARWICK	AKA	89	10/13/1947	10/30/1947	1
CURRENT	ARS	22	10/14/1947	10/26/1947	2
HERALD	AM	101	10/14/1947	10/26/1947	2
SUMMIT COUNTY	LST	1146	10/14/1947	10/26/1947	2
PREVAIL	AM	107	10/15/1947	10/27/1947	AFDL-43
LANDING CRAFT	LC(FF)	790	10/16/1947	10/17/1947	3
MOTIVE	AM	102	10/21/1947	10/31/1947	AFDL-43
AUK	AM	57	10/22/1947	11/7/1947	3
HALL	DD	583	10/22/1947	11/7/1947	3
WILEY	DD	597	10/22/1947	11/7/1947	3

SHIP'S NAME	CLASS	NUMBER	DOCK	UNDOCK	DRYDOCK
MELVIN	DD	680	10/29/1947	11/20/1947	2
SYMBOL	AM	123	10/29/1947	11/20/1947	2
TERRY	DD	513	10/29/1947	11/20/1947	2
MATACO	ATF	86	10/29/1947	11/26/1947	AFDL-43
IZARD	DD	589	11/4/1947	11/25/1947	AFDL-44
GERMAN CRANE TITAN	YD	171	11/5/1947	12/1/1947	1
NAVASOTA	AO	106	11/5/1947	12/1/1947	1
NECHES	AO	47	11/14/1947	11/20/1947	3
YARD CRAFT	YFN	406	11/14/1947	11/20/1947	3
CURTISS	AV	4	11/20/1947	11/21/1947	3
LAWS	DD	558	11/24/1947	12/12/1947	2
RADFORD	DD	446	11/24/1947	12/12/1947	2
SUMMIT COUNTY	LST	1146	11/24/1947	11/25/1947	3
BUCKEYE	AN	13	12/2/1947	1/12/1948	AFDL-44
METIVIER	DE	582	12/3/1947	12/19/1947	3
PRITCHETT	DD	561	12/3/1947	12/19/1947	3
YARD OILER	YOG	87	12/3/1947	12/19/1947	3
YARD TUG	YTB	255	12/4/1947	12/18/1947	AFDL-43
YARD TUG	YTB	703	12/4/1947	12/18/1947	AFDL-43
BRUSH	DD	745	12/5/1947	12/26/1947	1
L. L. B. KNOX	DE	580	12/5/1947	12/26/1947	1
MADDOX	DD	731	12/5/1947	12/26/1947	1
ORLECK	DD	886	12/5/1947	12/26/1947	1
TAUSSIG	DD	746	12/5/1947	12/26/1947	1
MISSION SOLANO	AO	135	12/13/1947	1/7/1948	2
SAMUEL L. MOORE	DD	747	12/22/1947	1/12/1948	3
SAN BERNARDINO COUNTY	LST	1110	12/22/1947	1/12/1948	3
PAKANA	ATF	108	12/22/1947	1/13/1948	AFDL-43
GENESEE	AOG	8	12/31/1947	1/19/1948	1
NAIFEH	DE	352	12/31/1947	1/19/1948	1
SILVERSTEIN	DE	534	12/31/1947	1/19/1948	1
ULVERT M. MOORE	DE	442	12/31/1947	1/19/1948	1
Wm. SEIVERLING	DE	441	12/31/1947	1/19/1948	1
CHIMAERA	ARL	33	1/7/1948	1/22/1948	2
LANDING SHIP	LSM	462	1/7/1948	1/22/1948	2
LeRAY WILSON	DE	414	1/7/1948	1/22/1948	2
McGINTY	DE	365	1/14/1948	1/29/1948	AFDL-44
GEN. ANDERSON	AP	111	1/15/1948	2/6/1948	3
DOUGLAS A. MUNRO	DE	422	1/16/1948	2/2/1948	AFDL-44
LELAND E. THOMAS	DE	420	1/23/1948	2/14/1948	1
MELVIN R. NAWMAN	DE	416	1/23/1948	2/14/1948	1
PASSUMPSIC	AO	107	1/23/1948	2/14/1948	1
WHITESIDE	AKA	90	1/23/1948	2/14/1948	1
GOSSELIN	APD	126	1/23/1948	2/14/1948	2
SUB CHASER -RESCUE	EPCE (R)	857	1/27/1948	2/2/1949	AFDL-43
ST. PAUL	CA	73	1/28/1948	2/4/1948	2

SHIP'S NAME	CLASS	NUMBER	DOCK	UNDOCK	DRYDOCK
McCOY REYNOLDS	DE	440	1/30/1948	2/16/1948	AFDL-44
SHOVELER	AM	382	2/4/1948	2/26/1948	AFDL-43
SPRINGFIELD	CL	66	2/9/1948	2/28/1948	2
AGERHOLM	DD	826	2/11/1948	2/27/1948	3
LANDING CRAFT	LCI (L)	1017	2/11/1948	2/27/1948	3
MAJOR	DE	796	2/11/1948	2/27/1948	3
RAVEN	AM	55	2/11/1948	2/27/1948	3
FIEBERLING	DE	640	2/16/1948	2/28/1948	1
HENRY W. TUCKER	DD	875	2/16/1948	2/28/1948	1
LANDING SHIP	LSM (R)	401	2/16/1948	3/17/1948	1
MISSION SAN FERNANDO	USNT		2/16/1948	2/28/1948	1
THREAT	AM	124	2/18/1948	3/4/1948	AFDL-44
YARD TUG	YTB	539	2/18/1948	3/4/1948	AFDL-44
AUCILLA	AO	56	3/1/1948	3/13/1948	2
GARBAGE BARGE	YG	46	3/1/1948	3/13/1948	2
LANDING CRAFT	LCT	1362	3/2/1948	3/17/1948	1
LANDING CRAFT	LCT	1431	3/2/1948	3/17/1948	1
LANDING CRAFT	LCT	1460	3/2/1948	3/17/1948	1
RICHARD S. BULL	DE	402	3/2/1948	3/17/1948	1
SAN JOAQUIN COUNTY	LST	1122	3/2/1948	3/17/1948	1
THUBAN	AKA	19	3/2/1948	3/17/1948	1
WILLIAM C. COLE	DE	641	3/2/1948	3/17/1948	1
BLESSMAN	APD	48	3/3/1948	3/18/1948	3
DUNCAN	DD	874	3/3/1948	3/18/1948	3
LANDING SHIP	LSM	359	3/3/1948	3/18/1948	3
ZEAL	AM	131	3/3/1948	3/18/1948	3
YARD CRAFT	YFRN	385	3/4/1948	4/2/1948	AFDL-43
AIRCRAFT RESCUE	AVRC	77620	3/8/1948	4/2/1948	AFDL-43
CATFISH	SS	339	3/8/1948	3/12/1948	AFDL-44
CHIPOLA	AO	63	3/13/1948	3/27/1948	2
LANDING CRAFT	LCI (L)	1017	3/15/1948	3/19/1948	3
RONQUIL	SS	396	3/15/1948	3/20/1948	AFDL-44
COOK	APD	130	3/20/1948	4/3/1948	1
LANDING SHIP	LSM	406	3/20/1948	4/3/1948	1
LANDING SHIP	LSM (R)	508	3/20/1948	4/3/1948	1
SKAGIT	AKA	105	3/20/1948	4/3/1948	1
TOLOVANA	AO	64	3/20/1948	4/3/1948	1
YARD CRAFT	YF	882	3/20/1948	4/3/1948	1
CHIVO	SS	341	3/22/1948	3/27/1948	AFDL-44
DIACHENKO	APD	123	3/24/1948	4/8/1948	3
GUNASON	DE	795	3/24/1948	4/8/1948	3
LANDING CRAFT	LC(FF)	788	3/24/1948	4/8/1948	3
YARD TUG	YTL	560	3/24/1948	4/8/1948	3
CUSK	SS	348	3/29/1948	4/3/1948	AFDL-44
GOSSELIN	APD	126	3/31/1948	4/1/1948	2
GENDREAU	DE	639	4/2/1948	4/17/1948	2

SHIP'S NAME	CLASS	NUMBER	DOCK	UNDOCK	DRYDOCK
LAYSAN ISLAND	ARS (T)	1	4/2/1948	4/17/1948	2
SWIFT	AM	122	4/2/1948	4/17/1948	2
CHOPPER	SS	342	4/5/1948	4/9/1948	2
KEARSARGE	AB (EX-BB 05)	1	4/6/1948	4/7/1948	1
LOVELACE	DE	198	4/6/1948	4/19/1948	AFDL-43
LANDING CRAFT	LCT	1430	4/7/1948	4/21/1948	1
LANDING CRAFT	LCT	1458	4/7/1948	4/21/1948	1
LANDING CRAFT	LCT	1459	4/7/1948	4/21/1948	1
RAYMOND	DE	341	4/7/1948	4/21/1948	1
WASATCH	AGC	9	4/7/1948	4/21/1948	1
WEEDEN	DE	797	4/7/1948	4/21/1948	1
WHETSTONE	LSD	27	4/7/1948	4/21/1948	1
ALBERT T. HARRIS	DE	447	4/12/1948	4/29/1948	AFDL-44
BURTON ISLAND	AG	88	4/13/1948	5/15/1948	3
DUNCAN	DD	874	4/13/1948	5/15/1948	3
ORACLE	AM	103	4/13/1948	5/15/1948	3
BAYFIELD	APA	33	4/20/1948	5/6/1948	2
LANDING SHIP	LSM	419	4/21/1948	5/4/1948	AFDL-43
GERMAN CRANE	YD	171	4/27/1948	5/19/1948	1
HILSBOROUGH COUNTY	LST	827	4/27/1948	5/19/1948	1
LANDING SHIP	LSM (R)	403	4/27/1948	5/19/1948	1
LANDING SHIP	LSM (R)	404	4/27/1948	5/19/1948	1
MANNING	DE	199	4/27/1948	5/19/1948	1
BIVEN	DE	536	4/30/1948	5/13/1948	AFDL-44
DORAN	DMS	41	5/6/1948	5/21/1948	AFDL-43
NECHES	AO	47	5/7/1948	5/18/1948	2
BUNTING	AMS	3	5/14/1948	5/27/1948	AFDL-44
CARDINAL	AMS	4	5/14/1948	5/27/1948	AFDL-44
DOYLE	DMS	34	5/18/1948	5/25/1948	3
YARD CRAFT	YSD	57	5/18/1948	5/25/1948	3
GARBAGE BARGE	YG	24	5/20/1948	6/3/1948	2
OBERON	AKA	14	5/20/1948	6/3/1948	2
BENNER	DD	807	5/22/1948	6/15/1948	1
DENNIS J. BUCKLEY	DD	808	5/22/1948	6/15/1948	1
HAWKINS	DD	873	5/22/1948	6/15/1948	1
SAN BERNARDINO COUNTY	LST	1110	5/22/1948	6/15/1948	1
SUMMIT COUNTY	LST	1146	5/22/1948	6/15/1948	1
HORNBILL	AMS	19	5/25/1948	6/11/1948	AFDL-43
SUB CHASER	PCS	1401	5/25/1948	6/11/1948	AFDL-43
BAYFIELD	APA	33	5/28/1948	6/1/1948	3
BURTON ISLAND	AG	88	6/1/1948	6/2/1948	3
REMORA	SS	487	6/1/1948	6/5/1948	AFDL-44
IRWIN	DD	794	6/2/1948	6/20/1948	3
MYLES C. FOX	DD	829	6/2/1948	6/20/1948	3
SHELTON	DD	790	6/5/1948	6/10/1948	2
WATER BARGE	YWN	70	6/5/1948	6/10/1948	2

SHIP'S NAME	CLASS	NUMBER	DOCK	UNDOCK	DRYDOCK
YARD CRAFT	YC	1113	6/8/1948	6/16/1948	AFDL-44
YARD CRAFT	YC	1114	6/8/1948	6/16/1948	AFDL-44
ASHTABULA	AO	51	6/11/1948	6/25/1948	2
HIDATSA	ATF	102	6/17/1948	7/1/1948	AFDL-44
YARD CRAFT	YFN	561	6/17/1948	7/1/1948	AFDL-44
FLOATING DRYDOCK	AFDL	12	6/18/1948	7/6/1948	1
FLOATING DRYDOCK	AFDL	43	6/18/1948	7/6/1948	1
KEARSARGE	AB (EX-BB 05)	1	6/18/1948	7/6/1948	1
GANTNER	APD	42	6/22/1948	7/8/1948	3
SNOHOMISH COUNTY	LST	1126	6/22/1948	7/8/1948	3
YARD CRAFT	YFN	408	6/22/1948	7/8/1948	3
LANDING SHIP	LSM	419	6/24/1948	6/28/1948	2
DIPHDA	AKA	59	6/28/1948	7/12/1948	2
YARD CRAFT	YSR	25	6/28/1948	7/12/1948	2
JOHN R. PIERCE	DD	753	7/7/1948	7/20/1948	AFDL-44
DENNIS J. BUCKLEY	DD	808	7/8/1948	7/9/1948	1
FLOATING DRYDOCK	AFDL	9	7/9/1948	7/23/1948	1
FLOATING DRYDOCK	ARD	20	7/9/1948	7/23/1948	1
LANDING SHIP	LSM	250	7/9/1948	7/23/1948	1
LANDING SHIP	LSM (R)	412	7/9/1948	7/23/1948	1
LLOYD THOMAS	DD	764	7/13/1948	7/21/1948	3
HENRY W. TUCKER	DD	875	7/14/1948	7/27/1948	2
ROGERS	DD	876	7/14/1948	7/27/1948	2
TAWAKONI	ATF	114	7/19/1948	7/22/1948	AFDL-43
CHIMARIKO	ATF	154	7/22/1948	8/9/1948	AFDL-43
PATROL CRAFT	PCS	1423	7/22/1948	8/4/1948	AFDL-43
GANTNER	APD	42	7/23/1948	7/23/1948	3
HARADEN	DD	585	7/26/1948	8/6/1948	3
PERKINS	DD	877	7/26/1948	8/6/1948	3
SEGUNDO	SS	398	7/26/1948	7/30/1948	AFDL-44
A. A. CUNNINGHAM	DD	752	7/28/1948	7/30/1948	1
BERTHING BARGE	APL	27	7/28/1948	8/12/1948	1
THOMAS JEFFERSON	APA	30	7/28/1948	7/30/1948	1
DIPHDA	AKA	59	7/30/1948	7/30/1948	2
YANCEY	AKA	93	8/2/1948	8/18/1948	2
YARD CRAFT	YC	867	8/2/1948	8/18/1948	2
BLENNY	SS	324	8/2/1948	8/6/1948	AFDL-44
FLOATING CRANE	YD	148	8/10/1948	8/28/1948	3
GUEST	DD	472	8/10/1948	8/28/1948	3
LAFFEY	DD	724	8/10/1948	8/24/1948	AFDL-44
NUTHATCH	AM	60	8/11/1948	8/24/1948	AFDL-43
FLOATING DRYDOCK	ARD	24	8/17/1948	9/7/1948	1
KASKASKIA	AO	27	8/17/1948	9/7/1948	1
LANDING SHIP	LSM (R)	412	8/17/1948	9/7/1948	1
SUB CHASER (RESCUE)	EPCE (R)	857	8/17/1948	9/7/1948	1
SEDGWICK COUNTY	LST	1123	8/19/1948	9/3/1948	2

SHIP'S NAME	CLASS	NUMBER	DOCK	UNDOCK	DRYDOCK
THOMASON	DE	203	8/19/1948	9/2/1948	2
JAMES E. CRAIG	DE	201	8/26/1948	9/1/1948	AFDL-43
PHEASANT	AM	61	8/26/1948	9/2/1948	AFDL-43
SAN BERNARDINO COUNTY	LST	1110	8/31/1948	9/10/1948	3
SUMMIT COUNTY	LST	1146	8/31/1948	9/10/1948	3
TOUCAN	AM	387	9/3/1948	9/15/1948	AFDL-43
YARD CRAFT	YC	866	9/3/1948	9/12/1948	AFDL-44
DULUTH	CL	87	9/8/1948	9/25/1948	2
BAIROKO	CVE	115	9/10/1948	9/27/1948	1
FLOATING CRANE	ARD	8	9/10/1948	9/27/1948	1
PATROL CRAFT	PCS	1444	9/14/1948	9/28/1948	AFDL-44
PRESERVER	ARS	8	9/14/1948	9/28/1948	AFDL-44
BURTON ISLAND	AG	88	9/16/1948	9/29/1948	3
TOMBIGBEE	AOG	11	9/16/1948	9/29/1948	3
COMPETENT	AM	316	9/17/1948	9/30/1948	AFDL-43
YARD CRAFT	YC	865	9/17/1948	9/30/1948	AFDL-43
TAPPAHANNOCK	AO	43	9/29/1948	10/12/1948	2
CARTER	LSD	3	9/30/1948	10/15/1948	1
MANATEE	AO	58	9/30/1948	10/15/1948	1
WALKE	DD	723	9/30/1948	10/15/1948	1
EUGENE E. ELMORE	DE	686	10/1/1948	10/14/1948	AFDL-44
ABBOT	DD	629	10/4/1948	10/18/1948	3
WISEMAN	DE	667	10/4/1948	10/18/1948	3
CHAWASHA	ATF	151	10/4/1948	10/22/1948	AFDL-43
YARD CRAFT	YFN	268	10/11/1948	10/21/1948	AFDL-43
YANCEY	AKA	93	10/14/1948	10/26/1948	2
SUB CHASER	PC (C)	1244	10/18/1948	10/29/1948	AFDL-44
YARD CRAFT	YFN	406	10/18/1948	10/29/1948	AFDL-44
THOMPSON	DMS	38	10/19/1948	12/16/1948	3
CALIENTE	AO	53	10/20/1948	11/3/1948	1
FLOATING DRYDOCK	ARD	31	10/20/1948	11/3/1948	1
CHAS. J. KIMMEL	DE	584	10/25/1948	11/5/1948	3
CREON	ARL	11	10/25/1948	11/5/1948	3
MURRELET	AM	372	10/25/1948	11/5/1948	3
MAURICE J. MANUEL	DE	351	10/26/1948	11/8/1948	AFDL-44
BAIROKO	CVE	115	10/27/1948	10/28/1948	2
MADDOX	DD	731	10/28/1948	10/29/1948	2
YANCEY	AKA	93	11/2/1948	11/16/1948	2
STEPHEN POTTER	DD	538	11/2/1948	11/16/1948	AFDL-44
CRASH	ARS	24	11/8/1948	11/24/1948	1
GEORGE CLYMER	APA	27	11/8/1948	11/24/1948	1
JEFFERSON COUNTY	LST	845	11/8/1948	11/24/1948	1
O'BRIEN	DD	725	11/8/1948	11/24/1948	1
PALAWAN	ARG	10	11/8/1948	11/24/1948	1
TAPPAHANNOCK	AO	43	11/9/1948	11/18/1948	3
HAAS	DE	424	11/10/1948	11/23/1948	AFDL-44

SHIP'S NAME	CLASS	NUMBER	DOCK	UNDOCK	DRYDOCK
CALIENTE	AO	53	11/17/1948	12/31/1948	2
PATROL CRAFT	PCS	1448	11/18/1948	12/2/1948	AFDL-44
STARLING	AM	64	11/18/1948	12/2/1948	AFDL-44
DEXTROUS	AM	341	11/22/1948	12/5/1948	3
HANNA	DE	449	11/22/1948	12/6/1948	3
ROMULUS	ARL	22	11/22/1948	12/6/1948	3
DIODON	SS	349	11/29/1948	12/3/1948	AFDL-43
BROADBILL	AM	58	12/1/1948	12/16/1948	1
SHASTA	AE	6	12/1/1948	12/17/1948	1
STOCKHAM	DD	683	12/1/1948	12/16/1948	1
THOMPSON	DMS	38	12/1/1948	12/16/1948	1
WHETSTONE	LSD	27	12/1/1948	12/17/1948	1
BEGOR	APD	127	12/3/1948	12/16/1948	AFDL-44
BELL	DD	587	12/7/1948	12/20/1948	AFDL-43
BARTON	DD	722	12/8/1948	12/22/1948	3
SAN BERNARDINO COUNTY	LST	1110	12/8/1948	12/22/1948	3
YARD OILER	YO	223	12/8/1948	12/22/1948	3
YARD TUG	YTL	583	12/9/1948	1/4/1949	BARGE
BRADFORD	DD	545	12/17/1948	12/30/1948	AFDL-44
LANDING SHIP	LSM	462	12/21/1948	1/4/1949	AFDL-43
MARIAS	AO	57	12/22/1948	1/7/1949	1
PLATTE	AO	24	12/22/1948	1/7/1949	1
PRESIDENT HAYES	APA	20	12/27/1948	1/11/1949	3
BAYA	SS	318	1/1/1949	1/18/1949	AFDL-44
CHARR	SS	329	1/3/1949	1/7/1949	AFDL-44
HELENA	CA	75	1/5/1949	1/18/1949	2
WOODSON	DE	359	1/6/1949	1/18/1949	AFDL-43
BUNCH	APD	79	1/12/1949	1/26/1949	1
FLOATING CRANE	YD	113	1/12/1949	1/26/1949	1
JOHN R. PIERCE	DD	753	1/12/1949	1/26/1949	1
LANDING SHIP	LSM	275	1/12/1949	1/26/1949	1
STICKELL	DD	888	1/12/1949	1/26/1949	1
TABBERER	DE	418	1/12/1949	1/26/1949	1
PLATTE	AO	24	1/13/1949	2/11/1949	3
GURKE	DD	783	1/19/1949	2/1/1949	2
BENNION	DD	662	1/19/1949	2/1/1949	AFDL-44
YARD TUG (FIREBOAT)	YTB	394	1/20/1949	1/27/1949	AFDL-43
ST. PAUL	CA	73	1/27/1949	2/9/1949	2
CAVALIER	APA	37	2/1/1949	2/15/1949	1
HAMLIN	AV	15	2/1/1949	2/15/1949	1
HENRY R. KENYON	DE	683	2/1/1949	2/15/1949	1
WEDDERBURN	DD	684	2/1/1949	2/15/1949	1
YARD OIL BARGE	YON	99	2/1/1949	2/15/1949	1
HALE	DD	642	2/2/1949	2/15/1949	AFDL-44
SUB CHASER	PC (C)	1169	2/3/1949	2/4/1949	AFDL-43
YARD CRAFT	YFN	733	2/4/1949	2/14/1949	AFDL-43

SHIP'S NAME	CLASS	NUMBER	DOCK	UNDOCK	DRYDOCK
NICHOLAS	DD	449	2/14/1949	2/23/1949	2
O'BANNON	DD	450	2/14/1949	2/23/1949	2
THEO. E. CHANDLER	DD	717	2/16/1949	3/22/1949	3
JOHN R. PIERCE	DD	753	2/16/1949	2/17/1949	AFDL-44
KNUDSON	APD	101	2/17/1949	3/3/1949	AFDL-43
JOHN C. BUTLER	DE	339	2/18/1949	3/8/1949	1
KANKAKEE	AO	39	2/18/1949	3/8/1949	1
TETON	AGC	14	2/18/1949	3/8/1949	1
WATER BARGE	YWN	64	2/18/1949	3/8/1949	1
YARD OILER	YO	219	2/18/1949	3/8/1949	1
BALDUCK	APD	132	2/23/1949	3/8/1949	AFDL-44
GUADALUPE	AO	32	2/26/1949	3/29/1946	2
KITE	AMS	22	3/7/1949	3/22/1949	AFDL-43
JOHN R. PIERCE	DD	753	3/8/1949	3/8/1949	1
SHACKAMAWON	AN	88	3/9/1949	3/18/1949	AFDL-44
YARD CRAFT	YC	870	3/9/1949	3/18/1949	AFDL-44
CHICKADEE	AM	59	3/11/1949	3/25/1949	1
PICKAWAY	APA	222	3/11/1949	3/25/1949	1
RICHARD P. LEARY	DD	664	3/11/1949	3/25/1949	1
WASHBURN	AKA	108	3/11/1949	3/25/1949	1
YARD CRAFT	YFN	617	3/11/1949	3/25/1949	1
WANTUCK	APD	125	3/22/1949	4/4/1949	AFDL-44
CAPITAINE	SS	336	3/28/1949	4/1/1949	AFDL-43
FLOATING CRANE	YD	157	3/30/1949	4/14/1949	2
NECHES	AO	47	3/30/1949	4/14/1949	2
COASTERS HARBOR	AG	74	3/31/1949	4/14/1949	1
HOPEWELL	DD	681	3/31/1949	4/14/1949	1
UVALDE	AKA	88	3/31/1949	4/14/1949	1
WICKES	DD	578	3/31/1949	4/14/1949	1
BLOWER	SS	325	4/4/1949	4/8/1949	AFDL-43
IMPECCABLE	AM	320	4/5/1949	4/24/1949	3
OZBOURN	DD	846	4/5/1949	4/21/1949	3
CURLEW	AMS	8	4/5/1949	4/14/1949	AFDL-44
FIRECREST	AMS	10	4/5/1949	4/15/1949	AFDL-44
NEUENDORF	DE	200	4/12/1949	4/22/1949	AFDL-43
SAN BERNARDINO COUNTY	LST	1110	4/18/1949	5/20/1949	2
SUMMIT COUNTY	LST	1146	4/18/1949	5/20/1949	2
AUCILLA	AO	56	4/19/1949	5/5/1949	1
GILLETTE	DE	681	4/19/1949	5/5/1949	1
JEFFERSON COUNTY	LST	845	4/19/1949	5/5/1949	1
ROBERT H. SMITH	DM	23	4/19/1949	5/5/1949	1
TWINING	DD	540	4/19/1949	5/5/1949	1
PTARMIGAN	AM	376	4/20/1949	4/28/1949	AFDL-44
McNULTY	DE	581	4/25/1949	5/15/1949	AFDL-43
BENNETT	DD	473	4/26/1949	5/9/1949	3
BURTON ISLAND	AG	88	4/26/1949	5/5/1949	3

SHIP'S NAME	CLASS	NUMBER	DOCK	UNDOCK	DRYDOCK
REDSTART	AM	378	5/3/1949	5/12/1949	AFDL-44
GOSS	DE	444	5/9/1949	5/19/1949	AFDL-43
NAVASOTA	AO	106	5/10/1949	5/24/1949	1
PEIFFER	DE	588	5/10/1949	5/24/1949	1
SAUGUS	LSV	4	5/10/1949	5/24/1949	1
UHLMANN	DD	687	5/10/1949	5/24/1949	1
BERTHING BARGE	APL	8	5/12/1949	5/27/1949	3
KENNETH M. WILLETT	DE	354	5/12/1949	5/27/1949	3
COURSER	AMS	6	5/16/1949	5/24/1949	AFDL-44
PATROL CRAFT	PCS	1423	5/16/1949	5/24/1949	AFDL-44
ACCOMAC	APB	49	5/17/1949	5/31/1951	2
CARBONERO	SS	337	5/23/1949	5/23/1949	AFDL-43
HELENA	CA	75	5/25/1949	6/2/1949	2
EPCE(R)	EPCE	855	5/25/1949	6/8/1949	AFDL-43
YARD TUG	YTB	371	5/25/1949	6/8/1949	AFDL-43
REDBUD	AG	398	5/26/1949	6/7/1949	AFDL-44
YARD TUG	YTB	400	5/26/1949	6/7/1949	AFDL-44
CHIPOLA	AO	63	5/31/1949	6/20/1949	1
HIGBEE	DD	806	5/31/1949	6/13/1949	1
LOWRY	DD	770	5/31/1949	6/20/1949	1
OCEANUS	ARB	2	5/31/1949	6/20/1949	1
HORACE A. BASS	APD	124	6/1/1949	6/15/1949	3
PEORIA COUNTY	LST	1183	6/1/1949	6/15/1949	3
HENRICO	APA	45	6/6/1949	6/17/1949	2
HERON	AMS	18	6/9/1949	6/20/1949	AFDL-44
YARD TUG	YTB	416	6/9/1949	6/20/1949	AFDL-44
ADG-11	ADG	11	6/10/1949	6/22/1949	AFDL-43
YARD TUG	YTB	374	6/10/1949	6/22/1949	AFDL-43
BURTON ISLAND	AG	88	6/17/1949	6/23/1949	3
LANDING SHIP	LSM	419	6/17/1949	6/23/1949	3
FIRECREST	AMS	10	6/20/1949	6/21/1949	AFDL-44
WARWICK	AKA	89	6/21/1949	7/6/1949	2
PATROL CRAFT	PCC	1169	6/21/1949	7/8/1949	AFDL-44
FLOATING DOCK	YFD	68	6/24/1949	7/14/1949	1
LANDING SHIP	LSM (R)	405	6/27/1949	7/11/1949	3
LANDING SHIP	LSM (R)	409	6/27/1949	7/11/1949	3
CARP	SS	338	6/27/1949	7/8/1949	AFDL-44
BLUE RIDGE	AGC	2	7/7/1949	7/21/1949	2
PATROL CRAFT	PCS	1444	7/8/1949	7/14/1949	AFDL-44
ASKARI	ARL	30	7/13/1949	7/27/1949	3
EDMONDS	DE	406	7/13/1949	7/27/1949	3
HENRICO	APA	45	7/14/1949	7/14/1949	1
BARBERO	SS	317	7/18/1949	7/27/1949	AFDL-43
GARBAGE BARGE	YG	46	7/18/1949	7/28/1949	AFDL-44
PIONEER	AM	105	7/18/1949	7/28/1949	AFDL-44
FLOATING DRYDOCK	AFDL	42	7/20/1949	8/4/1949	1

SHIP'S NAME	CLASS	NUMBER	DOCK	UNDOCK	DRYDOCK
LANDING SHIP	LSM	441	7/20/1949	8/4/1949	1
TOLOVANA	AO	64	7/20/1949	8/4/1949	1
REDBUD	AG	398	7/21/1949	7/21/1949	2
LOWRY	DD	770	7/26/1949	8/5/1949	2
WILLIAM W. WOOD	DD	715	7/26/1949	8/5/1949	2
NICHOLAS	DD	449	7/29/1949	8/29/1949	3
O'BANNON	DD	450	7/29/1949	8/29/1949	3
CARBONERO	SS	337	7/29/1949	8/1/1949	AFDL-43
DIACHENKO	APD	123	8/1/1949	8/5/1949	AFDL-44
REDFISH	SS	395	8/2/1949	8/11/1949	2
LOWRY	DD	770	8/5/1949	8/9/1949	2
WALTON	DE	361	8/8/1949	8/19/1949	AFDL-44
HALFORD	DD	480	8/9/1949	8/26/1949	2
LOWRY	DD	770	8/9/1949	8/26/1949	2
BURNS	DD	588	8/11/1949	8/25/1949	1
INDRA	ARL	37	8/11/1949	8/25/1949	1
LA VALLETTE	DD	448	8/11/1949	8/25/1949	1
LANDING SHIP	LSI(L)	1092	8/11/1949	8/25/1949	1
ST. GEORGE	AV	16	8/11/1949	8/25/1949	1
LANDING SHIP	LSM	510	8/15/1949	8/25/1949	AFDL-43
YARD TUG	YTB	509	8/15/1949	8/25/1949	AFDL-43
ARDENT	AM	340	8/23/1949	9/2/1949	AFDL-44
HIGBEE	DD	806	8/29/1949	9/2/1949	2
ARIKARA	ATF	98	8/29/1949	9/9/1949	AFDL-43
YARD CRAFT	YF	873	8/29/1949	9/9/1949	AFDL-43
CABILDO	LSD	16	8/30/1949	9/14/1949	1
THUBAN	AKA	19	8/30/1949	9/14/1949	1
CAVALLERO	APD	128	9/1/1949	9/16/1949	3
TINSMAN	DE	589	9/1/1949	9/16/1949	3
METCALFE	DD	595	9/2/1949	9/16/1949	2
DEFENSE	AM	317	9/6/1949	9/19/1949	AFDL-44
GARBAGE BARGE	YG	47	9/6/1949	9/19/1949	AFDL-44
FLOATING DOCK	AFDM	9	9/14/1949	9/15/1949	1
PATROL CRAFT	PCS	1448	9/19/1949	9/23/1949	AFDL-43
WENONASK	YTB	148	9/19/1949	9/27/1949	AFDL-43
FLOATING DRYDOCK	AFDL	44	9/20/1949	10/4/1949	1
MARIAS	AO	57	9/20/1949	10/4/1949	1
YARD CRAFT	YRD(M)	5	9/20/1949	10/4/1949	1
DENNIS	DE	405	9/21/1949	10/4/1949	3
OSMUS	DE	701	9/21/1949	10/4/1949	3
BURTON ISLAND	AGB	1	9/22/1949	10/14/1949	2
LANDING SHIP	LSM	411	9/22/1949	10/14/1949	2
PRESLEY	DE	371	9/27/1949	10/7/1949	AFDL-43
DAMON M. CUMMINGS	DE	643	10/6/1949	10/18/1949	3
ROLF	DE	362	10/6/1949	10/18/1949	3
CHARETTE	DD	581	10/10/1949	10/21/1949	1

SHIP'S NAME	CLASS	NUMBER	DOCK	UNDOCK	DRYDOCK
FLOATING DRYDOCK	AFDL	19	10/10/1949	10/21/1949	1
MAZAMA	AE	9	10/10/1949	10/21/1949	1
MILLER	DD	535	10/10/1949	10/21/1949	1
OWENS	DD	536	10/10/1949	10/21/1949	1
PAUL HAMILTON	DD	590	10/11/1949	10/24/1949	AFDL-43
FRENCH	DE	367	10/17/1949	10/27/1949	AFDL-44
ROSS	DD	563	10/18/1949	10/28/1949	2
TAYLOR	DD	468	10/18/1949	10/28/1949	2
YARD CRAFT	YFN	821	10/18/1949	10/28/1949	2
LLOYD E. ACREE	DE	356	10/20/1949	11/1/1949	3
RILEY	DE	579	10/20/1949	11/1/1949	3
BENHAM	DD	796	10/26/1949	11/9/1949	1
LANDING SHIP	LSM (R)	401	10/26/1949	11/17/1949	1
MANATEE	AO	58	10/26/1949	11/9/1949	1
OAHU	ARG	5	10/26/1949	11/9/1949	1
THE SULLIVANS	DD	537	10/26/1949	11/9/1949	1
LAWRENCE TAYLOR	DE	415	10/27/1949	11/8/1949	AFDL-43
RICHARD SUESENS	DE	342	10/27/1949	11/10/1949	AFDL-44
HEERMAN	DD	532	11/1/1949	11/16/1949	2
ROOKS	DD	804	11/1/1949	11/16/1949	2
YARD CRAFT	YOS	9	11/1/1949	11/16/1949	2
AGAWAN	AOG	6	11/3/1949	11/16/1949	3
PRATT	DE	363	11/3/1949	11/16/1949	3
KENSHAW	YTB	255	11/10/1949	11/21/1949	AFDL-43
WILLIAMS	DE	372	11/14/1949	11/23/1949	AFDL-44
ASHLAND	LSD	1	11/17/1949	12/2/1949	1
CULEBRA ISLAND	ARG	7	11/17/1949	12/2/1949	1
HAILEY	DD	556	11/17/1949	12/2/1949	1
REMEY	DD	688	11/17/1949	12/2/1949	1
BULLARD	DD	660	11/18/1949	12/1/1949	2
CHESTER T. O'BRIEN	DE	421	11/18/1949	12/6/1949	3
GENTRY	DE	349	11/18/1949	12/6/1949	3
HUNT	DD	674	11/18/1949	12/1/1949	3
ALBERT W. GRANT	DD	649	11/22/1949	12/7/1949	AFDL-43
GEORGE W. INGRAM	APD	43	11/28/1949	12/8/1949	AFDL-44
NICHOLAS	DD	449	12/24/1949	12/27/1949	2
O'BANNON	DD	450	12/24/1949	12/27/1949	3
PAINTERS BARGE	BARGE SERIAL	011730	12/30/1949	1/15/1951	3
SERVICE BARGE	BARGE SERIAL	011731	12/30/1949	1/15/1951	3
SERVICE BARGE	BARGE SERIAL	017736	12/30/1949	1/15/1951	3
SLUDGE BARGE	YSR SERIAL	031422	12/30/1949	1/15/1951	3
STEEL DRYDOCK CAISSON	CAISSON	DD-1	12/30/1949	1/15/1951	3
WHEELER SYSTEM BARGE	BARGE	?	12/30/1949	1/15/1949	3
SEA MULE SERVICE BARGE	BARGE SERIAL	011340	1/19/1950	1/15/1951	2
STEEL CAISSON	CAISSON	DD-2	1/19/1950	1/15/1951	2
FULLAM	DD	474	2/1/1951	3/8/1951	2

SHIP'S NAME	CLASS	NUMBER	DOCK	UNDOCK	DRYDOCK
McNAIR	DD	679	2/1/1951	3/8/1951	2
YARD CRAFT	YC	866	2/1/1951	3/8/1951	2
HMCS HURON	DDG	216	2/9/1951	2/14/1951	1
WEEDEN	DE	797	2/10/1951	2/23/1951	3
YARD CRAFT	YFP	3	2/10/1951	2/23/1951	3
ADAMS	DM	27	2/19/1951	3/10/1951	1
FLOATING CRANE	YD	87	2/19/1951	3/10/1951	1
FLOATING DRYDOCK	ARD	31	2/19/1951	3/10/1951	1
YARD CRAFT	YSR	25	2/19/1951	3/10/1951	1
YARD TUG	YTB	397	2/19/1951	3/10/1951	1
YARD TUG	YTB	398	2/19/1951	3/10/1951	1
YARD TUG	YTL	450	2/19/1951	2/24/1951	3
YARD TUG	YTL	583	2/19/1951	2/24/1954	3
BUCKTHORN	AN	14	2/28/1951	3/19/1951	3
COHOES	AN	78	2/28/1951	3/19/1951	3
HENRY A. WILEY	DM	29	2/28/1951	3/19/1951	3
TOLMAN	DM	28	2/28/1951	3/19/1951	3
SICILY	CVE	118	3/12/1951	3/21/1951	2
YARD CRAFT	YFN	952	3/12/1951	3/21/1951	2
LANDING SHIP	LSM	236	3/22/1951	4/5/1951	3
LEWIS HANCOCK	DD	675	3/22/1951	4/5/1951	3
MILLER	DD	535	3/22/1951	4/5/1951	3
YARD TUG	YTB	400	3/22/1951	4/5/1951	3
ADG-8	ADG	8	3/24/1951	4/10/1951	2
BURTON ISLAND	AGB	1	3/24/1951	4/10/1951	2
COWIE	DMS	39	3/24/1951	4/10/1951	2
TINGEY	DD	539	4/6/1951	4/14/1951	3
WATER BARGE	YWN	64	4/6/1951	4/14/1951	3
YARD CRAFT	YFN	951	4/6/1951	4/14/1951	3
McNAIR	DD	679	4/9/1951	4/18/1951	AFDL-42
ADG-8	ADG	8	4/12/1951	4/23/1951	2
COWIE	DMS	39	4/12/1951	4/23/1951	2
GARBAGE BARGE	YG	29	4/12/1951	4/23/1951	2
LASSEN	AE	3	4/12/1951	4/23/1951	2
YARD CRAFT	YO	219	4/12/1951	4/23/1951	2
YARD TUG (FIREBOAT)	YTB	394	4/17/1951	5/8/1951	3
LANDING SHIP	LSU	1225	4/20/1951	5/4/1951	1
J. WILLIAM DITTER	DMS	31	4/20/1951	5/3/1951	AFDL-42
GURKE	DD	783	4/25/1951	4/27/1951	2
GURKE	DD	783	4/27/1951	5/15/1951	2
McGOWAN	DD	678	4/27/1951	5/15/1951	2
YARNALL	DD	541	5/3/1951	5/9/1951	AFDL-42
LANDING SHIP	LSU	1224	5/4/1951	5/14/1951	1
DAY	DE	225	5/10/1951	5/25/1951	AFDL-42
EARLE	DMS	42	5/11/1951	5/22/1951	3
UHLMANN	DD	687	5/11/1951	5/22/1951	3

SHIP'S NAME	CLASS	NUMBER	DOCK	UNDOCK	DRYDOCK
LANDING SHIP	LSU	1348	5/14/1951	5/23/1951	1
YARD CRAFT	YFN	953	5/17/1951	5/31/1951	2
LANDING SHIP	LSU	666	5/23/1951	6/28/1951	1
CECIL J. DOYLE	DE	368	9/25/1951	10/18/1951	1
HAMPSHIRE COUNTY	LST	819	9/25/1951	10/18/1951	1
LANDING SHIP	LSM	175	9/25/1951	10/18/1951	1
LANDING SHIP	LSM	268	9/25/1951	10/18/1951	1
ISLE ROYALE	AD	29	9/27/1951	10/4/1951	3
COURSER	AMS	6	10/1/1951	10/15/1951	AFDL-42
SWAN	AMS	37	10/1/1951	10/15/1951	AFDL-42
PINE ISLAND	AV	12	10/5/1951	10/24/1951	3
GUEST	DD	472	10/16/1951	10/19/1951	AFDL-42
DAVISON	DMS	37	10/24/1951	11/17/1951	1
FLOATING DRYDOCK	AFDB	6	10/24/1951	11/17/1951	1
JOHN L. WILLIAMSON	DE	370	10/24/1951	11/17/1951	1
PITKIN COUNTY	LST	1082	10/24/1951	11/17/1951	1
PRESLEY	DE	371	10/24/1951	11/17/1951	1
STEMBEL	DD	644	10/25/1951	10/29/1951	AFDL-42
BURTON ISLAND	AGB	1	10/29/1951	11/9/1951	3
SNOHOMISH COUNTY	LST	1126	10/29/1951	11/9/1951	3
GARBAGE BARGE	YG	47	10/30/1951	11/8/1951	AFDL-42
PATROL CRAFT	PCS	1423	10/30/1951	11/8/1951	AFDL-42
LANDING SHIP	LSU	715	11/6/1951	12/3/1951	1
LANDING SHIP	LSU	764	11/6/1951	12/3/1951	1
CROW	AMS	7	11/9/1951	11/20/1951	AFDL-42
LARK	AMS	24	11/9/1951	11/20/1951	AFDL-42
BROWN	DD	546	11/14/1951	12/10/1951	3
HARRY E. HUBBARD	DD	748	11/14/1951	12/10/1951	3
DIPHDA	AKA	59	11/21/1951	12/7/1951	1
JOHN L. WILLIAMSON	DE	370	11/21/1951	12/7/1951	1
LOUGH	DE	586	11/21/1951	12/7/1951	1
MACK	DE	358	11/21/1951	12/7/1951	1
PRESLEY	DE	371	11/21/1951	12/7/1951	1
BRYANT	DD	665	11/23/1951	12/19/1951	AFDL-42
LANDING SHIP	LSU	588	12/3/1951	1/8/1951	1
LANDING SHIP	LSU	667	12/3/1951	1/8/1951	1
AVENTINUS	ARVE	3	12/11/1951	12/27/1951	1
FABIUS	ARVA	5	12/11/1951	12/27/1951	1
FLICKER	AMS	9	12/11/1951	12/27/1951	1
HARRIS COUNTY	LST	822	12/11/1951	12/27/1951	1
LANDING SHIP	LSM	419	12/11/1951	12/27/1951	1
LANDING SHIP	LSM	462	12/11/1951	12/27/1951	1
STAFFORD	DE	411	12/11/1951	12/27/1951	1
NAVASOTA	AO	106	12/13/1951	1/2/1952	3
YARD CRAFT	YOS	9	12/13/1951	1/2/1952	3
DEFENSE	AM	317	12/20/1951	1/4/1951	AFDL-42

SHIP'S NAME	CLASS	NUMBER	DOCK	UNDOCK	DRYDOCK
CIMARRON	AO	22	1/3/1952	2/7/1952	1
ERNST G. SMALL	DD	838	1/3/1952	2/7/1951	1
SEYMOUR D. OWENS	DD	767	1/3/1952	2/7/1952	1
STEELHEAD	SS	280	1/3/1952	2/7/1952	1
WEEDEN	DE	797	1/3/1952	2/7/1952	1
DEVESTATOR	AM	318	1/4/1952	1/10/1952	AFDL-42
HEYWOOD L. EDWARDS	DD	663	1/5/1952	1/19/1952	3
STAFFORD	DE	411	1/5/1952	1/19/1952	3
LANDING SHIP	LSU	709	1/8/1952	2/11/1952	1
LANDING SHIP	LSU	1386	1/8/1952	2/11/1952	1
PATROL CRAFT	EPCE(R)	857	1/10/1952	1/24/1952	AFDL-42
RENDOVA	CVE	114	1/22/1952	1/29/1952	3
GLADIATOR	AM	319	1/22/1952	2/7/1952	AFDL-42
COMSTOCK	LSD	19	2/1/1952	2/16/1952	2
LEONARD F. MASON	DD	852	2/2/1952	2/13/1952	3
RUPERTUS	DD	851	2/2/1952	2/13/1952	3
HUMMER	AMS	20	2/8/1952	2/21/1952	AFDL-42
SATYR	ARL	23	2/20/1952	3/11/1952	2
YARD CRAFT	YFN	561	2/20/1952	3/11/1952	2
RILEY	DE	579	2/24/1952	10/10/1952	AFDL-42
BENNETT	DD	473	2/25/1952	2/29/1952	AFDL-42
NORMAN SCOTT	DD	690	2/29/1952	3/5/1952	AFDL-42
MERTZ	DD	691	3/5/1952	3/21/1952	1
TINGEY	DD	539	3/5/1952	3/21/1952	1
WILEY	DD	597	3/5/1952	3/21/1952	1
YARNALL	DD	541	3/5/1952	3/21/1952	1
SICILY	CVE	118	3/10/1952	3/12/1952	3
REPOSE	AH	16	3/13/1952	3/27/1952	2
YARD CRAFT	YC	791	3/13/1952	3/27/1952	2
NORMAN SCOTT	DD	690	3/13/1952	3/14/1952	AFDL-42
HUMMER	AMS	20	3/14/1952	3/17/1952	AFDL-42
HALL	DD	583	3/17/1952	3/31/1952	3
HART	DD	594	3/17/1952	3/31/1952	3
STEVENS	DD	479	3/18/1952	4/3/1952	AFDL-42
BOYD	DD	544	3/25/1952	4/10/1952	1
McDERMUT	DD	677	3/25/1952	4/10/1952	1
TALUGA	AO	62	3/25/1952	4/11/1952	1
DUVAL COUNTY	LST	758	3/28/1952	4/14/1952	2
YARD CRAFT	YC	870	3/28/1952	4/14/1952	2
MERTZ	DD	691	4/3/1952	4/4/1952	AFDL-42
CAPPS	DD	550	4/4/1952	4/17/1952	AFDL-42
LAWRENCE COUNTY	LST	887	4/14/1952	4/29/1952	2
JOHN C. BUTLER	DE	339	4/16/1952	5/2/1952	1
LANDING SHIP	LSM	355	4/16/1952	5/2/1952	1
LANDING SHIP	LSM	362	4/16/1952	5/2/1952	1
SAWFISH	SS	276	4/16/1952	5/2/1952	1

SHIP'S NAME	CLASS	NUMBER	DOCK	UNDOCK	DRYDOCK
TERRY	DD	513	4/16/1952	5/2/1952	1
COMPETENT	AM	316	4/18/1952	4/28/1952	AFDL-42
INCREDIBLE	AM	249	4/28/1952	5/1/1952	AFDL-42
DEXTROUS	AM	341	5/1/1952	5/14/1952	2
LSS (L-67)	LSS	67	5/1/1952	5/14/1952	2
LSS (L-68)	LSS	68	5/1/1952	5/14/1952	2
REDSTART	AM	378	5/1/1952	5/14/1952	2
BELL	DD	587	5/5/1952	5/9/1952	AFDL-42
CUMBERLAND SOUND	AV	17	5/8/1952	5/23/1952	1
DENNIS	DE	405	5/8/1952	5/23/1952	1
RUDDEROW	DE	224	5/8/1952	5/23/1952	1
ALBERT W. GRANT	DD	649	5/9/1952	5/28/1952	AFDL-42
BURTON ISLAND	AGB	1	5/20/1952	6/17/1952	2
PONTCHARTRAIN	WPG	70	5/20/1952	6/4/1952	2
CROW	AMS	7	5/29/1952	6/6/1952	AFDL-42
LARK	AMS	23	5/29/1952	6/6/1952	AFDL-42
BELLE ISLE	AKS	21	6/3/1952	6/19/1952	1
CATSKILL	LSV	1	6/3/1952	6/19/1952	1
KILLEN	DD	593	6/3/1952	6/19/1952	1
METCALFE	DD	595	6/3/1952	6/19/1952	1
TARGET RAFT	RAFT	125	6/4/1952	6/17/1952	2
JACKDAW	AMS	21	6/9/1952	6/26/1952	AFDL-42
PATROL CRAFT	PCEC	898	6/9/1952	6/26/1952	AFDL-42
LANDING SHIP	LSM	422	6/18/1952	6/30/1952	2
LANDING SHIP	LSM	546	6/18/1952	6/30/1952	2
TARGET RAFT	RAFT	96	6/18/1952	6/30/1952	2
TARGET RAFT	RAFT	122	6/18/1952	6/30/1952	2
FOSS	DE	59	6/24/1952	7/9/1952	1
POLK COUNTY	LST	1084	6/24/1952	7/9/1952	1
RUSSEL COUNTY	LST	1090	6/24/1952	7/9/1952	1
SURFBIRD	AM	383	6/27/1952	7/10/1952	AFDL-42
SALINE COUNTY	LST	1101	7/2/1952	7/22/1952	2
SAN JOAQUIN COUNTY	LST	1122	7/10/1952	7/28/1952	3
ST. PAUL	CA	73	7/12/1952	7/13/1952	1
THEO. E. CHANDLER	DD	717	7/14/1952	7/30/1952	1
WILTSIE	DD	716	7/14/1952	7/30/1952	1
JACKDAW	AMS	21	7/16/1952	7/31/1952	AFDL-42
MOLALA	ATF	106	7/16/1952	7/31/1952	AFDL-42
BELLEROPHON	ARL	31	7/22/1952	8/6/1952	2
CHARETTE	DD	581	7/29/1952	8/14/1952	3
WHEELER SYSTEM BARGE	BARGE	1	7/29/1952	8/14/1952	3
WHEELER SYSTEM BARGE	BARGE	2	7/29/1952	8/14/1952	3
BAIROKO	CVE	115	8/4/1952	8/20/1952	1
CHEVALIER	DD	805	8/4/1952	8/20/1952	1
HAMNER	DD	718	8/4/1952	8/20/1952	1
OAHU	ARG	5	8/12/1952	9/26/1952	2

SHIP'S NAME	CLASS	NUMBER	DOCK	UNDOCK	DRYDOCK
GANTNER	APD	42	8/15/1952	9/5/1952	AFDL-42
GREGORY	DD	802	8/16/1952	9/19/1952	3
MARSHALL	DD	676	8/16/1952	9/19/1952	3
CONNER	DD	582	8/25/1952	9/11/1952	1
EVERSOLE	DD	789	8/25/1952	9/11/1952	1
JAMES E. KYES	DD	787	8/25/1952	9/11/1952	1
SHELTON	DD	790	8/25/1952	9/11/1952	1
CORBESIER	DE	438	9/8/1952	9/23/1952	AFDL-42
KASKASKIA	AO	27	9/16/1952	9/26/1952	1
GENTRY	DE	349	9/23/1952	10/8/1952	3
KEY	DE	348	9/23/1952	10/8/1952	3
ERNST G. SMALL	DD	838	10/1/1952	10/16/1952	1
SEYMOUR D. OWENS	DD	767	10/1/1952	10/16/1952	1
WASHBURN	AKA	108	10/1/1952	10/16/1952	1
STEUBEN COUNTY	LST	1138	10/2/1952	10/21/1952	2
UNADILLA	ATA	182	10/2/1952	10/21/1952	2
RILEY	DE	579	10/10/1952	11/18/1952	3
TRAW	DE	350	10/10/1952	11/18/1952	3
DAMON M. CUMMINGS	DE	643	10/13/1952	10/28/1952	AFDL-42
BATAAN	CVL	29	10/19/1952	10/21/1952	1
DOYLE	DMS	34	10/24/1952	11/7/1952	1
ENDICOTT	DMS	35	10/24/1952	11/7/1952	1
PLATTE	AO	24	10/24/1952	11/7/1952	1
YARD CRAFT	YFN	821	10/24/1952	11/7/1952	1
BURTON ISLAND	AGB	1	10/24/1952	11/20/1952	2
GOSS	DE	444	10/27/1952	11/20/1952	2
IZARD	DD	589	10/29/1952	11/13/1952	AFDL-42
A. A. CUNNINGHAM	DD	752	11/9/1952	11/26/1952	1
LEONARD F. MASON	DD	852	11/9/1952	11/26/1952	1
RUPERTUS	DD	851	11/9/1952	11/26/1952	1
KEOSANQUA	ATA	198	11/17/1952	12/2/1952	AFDL-42
OSMUS	DE	701	11/19/1952	12/5/1952	3
ROLF	DE	362	11/19/1952	12/5/1952	3
CHIMAERA	ARL	33	11/21/1952	12/5/1952	2
CLEARWATER COUNTY	LST	602	12/2/1952	12/19/1952	1
GREER COUNTY	LST	799	12/2/1952	12/19/1952	1
OUTAGAMIE COUNTY	LST	1073	12/2/1952	12/19/1952	1
WILLIAMS	DE	372	12/3/1952	12/17/1952	AFDL-42
SAN BERNARDINO COUNTY	LST	1110	12/5/1952	1/8/1952	2
WILLIAM C. COLE	DE	641	12/9/1952	12/24/1952	3
PAUL G. BAKER	DE	642	12/18/1952	1/9/1953	AFDL-42
MAJOR	DE	796	12/24/1952	1/13/1953	3
CALIENTE	AO	53	12/27/1952	1/14/1953	1
McKEAN	DD	784	12/27/1952	1/14/1953	1
YARD CRAFT	YC	1088	12/27/1952	1/14/1953	1
FLOYD COUNTY	LST	762	1/9/1953	1/26/1953	2

SHIP'S NAME	CLASS	NUMBER	DOCK	UNDOCK	DRYDOCK
RICHARD SUESENS	DE	342	1/9/1953	1/26/1953	2
FIEBERLING	DE	640	1/14/1953	2/9/1953	3
FRANKS	DD	554	1/14/1953	2/9/1953	3
COURSER	AMS	6	1/15/1953	1/28/1953	AFDL-42
CROW	AMS	7	1/15/1953	1/28/1953	AFDL-42
ST. PAUL	CA	73	1/17/1953	1/27/1953	1
GENDREAU	DE	639	1/28/1953	2/13/1953	2
GUNASON	DE	795	1/28/1953	2/13/1953	2
FLAMINGO	AMS	11	1/28/1953	2/10/1953	AFDL-42
SWAN	AMS	37	1/28/1953	2/10/1953	AFDL-42
LANDING SHIP	LSM (R)	455	1/29/1953	2/12/1953	1
TOLOVANA	AO	64	1/29/1953	2/12/1953	1
LANDING SHIP	LSM	58	2/10/1953	2/20/1953	3
LANDING SHIP	LSM	226	2/10/1953	2/20/1953	3
HARADEN	DD	585	2/10/1953	2/13/1953	AFDL-42
RENDOVA	CVE	114	2/12/1953	2/28/1953	1
GENDREAU	DE	639	2/25/1953	3/20/1953	3
PATROL CRAFT	PCS	1401	2/25/1953	3/20/1953	3
FLOATING DRYDOCK	AFDB	6	3/4/1953	4/23/1953	1
FLOATING DRYDOCK	AFDL	42	3/4/1953	4/23/1953	1
GERMAN CRANE	YD	171	3/4/1953	4/23/1953	1
MAHONING COUNTY	LST	914	3/6/1953	3/25/1953	2
SICILY	CVE	118	3/24/1953	3/30/1953	3
SHOVELER	AM	382	3/25/1953	3/31/1953	2
LANDING SHIP	LSM (R)	404	3/31/1953	5/6/1953	2
MARION COUNTY	LST	975	3/31/1953	5/6/1953	2
BURTON ISLAND	AGB	1	4/7/1953	5/7/1953	3
MORGAN COUNTY	LST	1048	4/7/1953	5/7/1953	3
KIDD	DD	661	4/25/1953	5/11/1953	AFDL-42
COLLETT	DD	730	5/9/1953	6/3/1953	2
DEFENSE	AM	317	5/9/1953	5/21/1953	2
MARION COUNTY	LST	975	5/12/1953	6/1/1953	3
MORGAN COUNTY	LST	1048	5/12/1953	6/1/1953	3
TINGEY	DD	539	5/12/1953	5/15/1953	AFDL-42
KEARSARGE	CVA	33	5/14/1953	5/21/1953	1
COMPETENT	AM	316	5/22/1953	6/2/1953	AFDL-42
HARRY E. HUBBARD	DD	748	5/27/1953	6/16/1953	1
MANSFIELD	DD	728	5/27/1953	6/16/1953	1
O'BRIEN	DD	725	5/27/1953	6/16/1953	1
WALKE	DD	723	5/27/1953	6/16/1953	1
DEVASTATOR	AM	318	6/2/1953	6/17/1953	AFDL-42
CTBR-15	CTBR	15	6/5/1953	6/23/1953	3
SEYMOUR D. OWENS	DD	767	6/5/1953	6/23/1953	3
STICKELL	DD	888	6/5/1953	6/23/1953	3
De HAVEN	DD	727	6/9/1953	6/27/1953	2
LYMAN K. SWENSON	DD	729	6/9/1953	6/29/1953	2

SHIP'S NAME	CLASS	NUMBER	DOCK	UNDOCK	DRYDOCK
PATROL CRAFT	PCS	1423	6/19/1953	7/3/1953	AFDL-42
O'BRIEN	DD	725	6/22/1953	6/29/1953	1
O'BRIEN	DD	725	6/29/1953	8/14/1953	2
LANDING SHIP	LSM	419	7/1/1953	7/20/1953	3
LANDING SHIP	LSM	462	7/1/1953	7/20/1953	3
CONSOLATION	AH	15	7/8/1953	8/6/1953	1
DUKES COUNTY	LST	735	7/8/1953	8/6/1953	1
EVERSOLE	DD	789	8/7/1953	8/22/1953	3
STEEL CAISSON	CAISSON	DD-1	8/7/1953	8/22/1953	3
LYMAN K. SWENSON	DD	729	8/14/1953	8/17/1953	2
SHELTON	DD	790	8/17/1953	8/29/1953	2
HIGBEE	DDR	806	8/22/1953	9/12/1953	1
JAMES E. KYES	DD	787	8/22/1953	9/12/1953	1
MISPILLION	AO	105	8/22/1953	9/12/1953	1
YARD CRAFT	YC	1367	8/22/1953	9/12/1953	1
FECHTELER	DD	870	8/29/1953	9/19/1953	2
YARD CRAFT	YC	1088	8/29/1953	9/19/1953	2
YARD CRAFT	YFN	272	8/29/1953	9/19/1953	2
COURSER	AMS	6	9/2/1953	9/11/1953	3
CROW	AMS	7	9/2/1953	9/11/1953	3
FLAMINGO	AMS	11	9/2/1953	9/11/1953	3
SWAN	AMS	37	9/2/1953	9/11/1953	3
SPROSTON	DD	577	9/12/1953	9/14/1953	3
CHITTENDEN COUNTY	LST	561	9/13/1953	9/25/1953	1
HILSBOROUGH COUNTY	LST	827	9/13/1953	9/25/1953	1
SUMMIT COUNTY	LST	1146	9/13/1953	9/25/1953	1
SUB CHASER (RESCUE)	EPCE(R)	857	9/19/1953	10/2/1953	2
BAIROKO	CVE	115	9/22/1953	10/3/1953	3
FOX (SEC.)	AFBD	4	9/25/1953	10/13/1953	1
CHITTENDEN COUNTY	LST	561	10/3/1953	10/7/1953	2
COMSTOCK	LSD	19	10/7/1953	10/30/1953	3
HIGBEE	DDR	806	10/10/1953	10/20/1953	2
IMPECCABLE	AM	320	10/10/1953	10/20/1953	2
LANDING SHIP	LSM (R)	412	10/15/1953	11/19/1953	1
MANATEE	AO	58	10/15/1953	11/19/1953	1
GEORGE A. JOHNSON	DE	583	11/4/1953	11/18/1953	3
BURTON ISLAND	AGB	1	11/9/1953	11/25/1953	2
PINE ISLAND	AV	12	11/19/1953	12/4/1953	3
RENVILLE	APA	227	11/23/1953	12/11/1953	1
ST. CLAIR COUNTY	LST	1096	11/23/1953	12/11/1953	1
WHEELER SYSTEM	BARGE SERIAL	?	11/23/1953	12/11/1953	1
LANDING SHIP	LSM (R)	409	12/1/1953	12/18/1953	2
LANDING SHIP	LSM (R)	525	12/1/1953	12/18/1953	2
CALAVERAS COUNTY	LST	516	12/8/1953	1/4/1954	3
DUVAL COUNTY	LST	758	12/8/1953	1/4/1954	3
RUDDY	AM	380	12/8/1953	12/17/1953	AFDL-42

SHIP'S NAME	CLASS	NUMBER	DOCK	UNDOCK	DRYDOCK
NAVASOTA	AO	106	12/15/1953	1/29/1954	1
SECTION (E)	AFDB	4	12/15/1953	1/29/1954	1
BOBOLINK	AMS	2	12/21/1953	1/4/1954	AFDL-42
SHOVELER	AM	382	12/21/1953	1/4/1954	AFDL-42
FORD COUNTY	LST	772	12/23/1953	1/27/1954	2
HAMPDEN COUNTY	LST	803	12/23/1953	1/27/1954	2
JOHN C. BUTLER	DE	339	1/5/1954	1/27/1954	AFDL-42
LEONARD F. MASON	DD	852	1/6/1954	1/8/1954	3
CHOWANOC	ATF	100	1/11/1954	2/4/1954	3
HENRY W. TUCKER	DDR	875	1/11/1954	2/4/1954	3
WEEDEN	DE	797	1/11/1954	2/4/1954	3
BEGOR	APD	127	1/27/1954	2/19/1954	AFDL-42
FLOATING DOCK SEC. A	AFDB	11	1/29/1954	3/15/1954	1
HOLMES COUNTY	LST	836	2/1/1954	2/26/1954	2
ULVERT M. MOORE	DE	442	2/1/1954	2/26/1954	2
SPANGLER	DE	696	2/8/1954	2/9/1954	3
LEWIS	DE	535	2/11/1954	3/2/1954	3
WISEMAN	DE	667	2/11/1954	3/2/1954	3
Wm. SEIVERLING	DE	441	2/11/1954	3/2/1954	3
DASH	AMS	428	2/23/1954	3/23/1954	AFDL-42
BLUEBIRD	MSC	121	3/1/1954	3/19/1954	2
DUNCAN	DDR	874	3/1/1954	3/19/1954	2
YARD CRAFT	YC	1088	3/1/1954	3/19/1954	2
RUSSEL COUNTY	LST	1090	3/4/1954	4/13/1954	3
CURRIER	DE	700	3/9/1954	4/1/1954	3
MANCHESTER	CL	83	3/15/1954	3/16/1954	1
PASSUMPSIC	AO	107	3/30/1954	4/22/1954	1
SECTION (B)	AFDB	1	3/30/1954	4/22/1954	1
DYNAMIC	AM	432	3/30/1954	4/16/1954	AFDL-42
SAN JOAQUIN COUNTY	LST	1122	3/31/1954	4/21/1954	2
STONE COUNTY	LST	1141	3/31/1954	4/24/1954	2
SALINE COUNTY	LST	1101	4/13/1954	4/27/1954	3
TALUGA	AO	62	4/22/1954	5/18/1954	1
COMORANT	AMS	122	4/23/1954	5/7/1954	AFDL-42
PAQUERETTE	AMS	140	4/23/1954	5/7/1954	AFDL-42
PONTCHARTRAIN	WPG	70	4/27/1954	5/21/1954	2
FRASSIANO	AMS	89	5/7/1954	5/12/1954	AFDL-42
FLOYD B. PARKS	DD	884	5/8/1954	5/14/1954	3
ASHTABULA	AO	51	5/20/1954	6/14/1954	1
HAWK	AMS	17	5/24/1954	6/2/1954	3
ILLUSIVE	AM	448	5/24/1954	6/18/1954	AFDL-42
SYMBOL	AM	123	5/24/1954	6/7/1954	AFDL-42
BERNEVEL	AM	450	5/27/1954	6/2/1954	2
GOSS	DE	444	6/3/1954	6/16/1954	3
LEONARD F. MASON	DD	852	6/3/1954	6/16/1954	3
MOTOR MINESWEEPER	AMS	95	6/7/1954	6/18/1954	AFDL-42

SHIP'S NAME	CLASS	NUMBER	DOCK	UNDOCK	DRYDOCK
KEOSANQUA	ATA	198	6/8/1954	6/18/1954	2
PICTOR	AF	54	6/17/1954	7/9/1954	1
SECTION (C)	AFDB	4	6/17/1954	7/9/1954	1
BIR HACHEIM	AM	451	6/28/1954	7/2/1954	AFDL-42
KIDD	DD	661	6/29/1954	7/27/1954	3
UHLMANN	DD	687	6/29/1954	7/27/1954	3
SQUAW	FAUX MINI-SUB	N/A	7/12/1954	7/23/1954	2
HOPEWELL	DD	681	7/14/1954	8/13/1954	1
WEDDERBURN	DD	684	7/14/1954	8/13/1954	1
HAMILTON COUNTY	LST	802	7/30/1954	8/23/1954	2
INCREDIBLE	AM	249	8/3/1954	8/31/1954	3
MAINSTAY	AM	261	8/3/1954	8/31/1954	3
AM-480	AM	480	8/6/1954	8/19/1954	AFDL-42
COLAHAN	DD	658	8/17/1954	9/15/1954	1
FLOYD COUNTY	LST	762	8/17/1954	9/15/1954	1
SHIELDS	DD	596	8/17/1954	9/30/1954	1
IMPLICIT	AM	455	8/19/1954	9/10/1954	2
GARIGLIANO	AM	452	8/19/1954	9/2/1954	AFDL-42
INFLICT	AM	456	8/19/1954	9/2/1954	AFDL-42
ERBEN	DD	631	8/31/1954	9/24/1954	3
TWINING	DD	540	8/31/1954	9/24/1954	3
DETECTOR	PRIVATE		9/2/1954	9/22/1954	AFDL-42
DYNAMIC	AM	432	9/2/1954	9/22/1954	AFDL-42
SQUAW	FAUX MINI-SUB	N/A	9/10/1954	9/17/1954	2
SECTION (G)	AFBD	4	9/15/1954	9/30/1954	1
ENERGY	AM	436	9/17/1954	10/7/1954	2
ENGAGE	AM	433	9/17/1954	10/7/1954	2
FORTIFY	AM	446	9/17/1954	10/7/1954	2
LOYALTY	MSO	457	9/17/1954	10/7/1954	2
MURRETTE	AM	372	9/24/1954	10/8/1954	3
SYMBOL	AM	123	9/24/1954	10/8/1954	3
CHICKASAW	ATF	83	9/24/1954	10/6/1954	AFDL-42
SQUAW	FAUX MINI-SUB	N/A	10/4/1954	10/19/1954	2
HAMNER	DD	718	10/8/1954	10/29/1954	3
MINNETONKA	CR	114	10/8/1954	10/29/1954	3
ENDURANCE	AM	435	10/8/1954	10/22/1954	AFDL-42
ILLUSIVE	AM	448	10/8/1954	10/22/1954	AFDL-42
ALENCON	AM	453	10/25/1954	11/5/1954	AFDL-42
ENGAGE	AM	433	10/25/1954	11/5/1954	AFDL-42
BURTON ISLAND	AGB	1	10/26/1954	12/3/1954	2
ENDURANCE	AM	435	10/26/1954	12/3/1954	2
WILTSIE	DD	716	11/2/1954	11/30/1954	3
DYNAMIC	AM	432	11/5/1954	11/18/1954	AFDL-42
INFLICT	AM	456	11/5/1954	11/18/1954	AFDL-42
COMORANT	AMS	122	11/23/1954	12/7/1954	AFDL-42
DOMPAIRE	AM	454	11/23/1954	12/7/1954	AFDL-42

SHIP'S NAME	CLASS	NUMBER	DOCK	UNDOCK	DRYDOCK
THEO. E. CHANDLER	DD	717	11/25/1954	11/30/1954	3
KENNETH WHITING	AV	14	12/2/1954	12/17/1954	3
SHELTON	DD	790	12/3/1954	12/8/1954	2
ONBEVREESD (DUTCH)	AM (M 885)	481	12/7/1954	12/21/1954	AFDL-42
PLUCK	AM	464	12/7/1954	12/21/1954	AFDL-42
LANDING SHIP	LSM (R)	403	12/8/1954	12/28/1954	2
SATYR	ARL	23	12/8/1954	12/28/1954	2
FORTIFY	AM	446	12/21/1954	1/6/1955	AFDL-42
PRESTIGE	AM	465	12/23/1954	1/6/1955	AFDL-42
LOWE	DER	325	12/29/1954	2/1/1955	3
SEYMOUR D. OWENS	DD	767	12/29/1954	2/1/1955	3
HAVEN	AH	12	1/3/1955	1/19/1955	1
SECTION (C)	AFDB	4	1/3/1955	1/19/1955	1
CONSTANT	AM	427	1/6/1955	1/19/1955	AFDL-42
FIRM	AM	444	1/6/1955	1/19/1955	AFDL-42
CHEVALIER	DDR	805	1/11/1955	2/3/1955	2
MUNSEE	ATF	107	1/11/1955	2/3/1955	2
YARD CRAFT	YFN	272	1/11/1955	2/3/1955	2
IMPERVIOUS	AM	449	1/19/1955	2/2/1955	AFDL-42
MYTHO	AM	475	1/19/1955	2/2/1955	AFDL-42
POINT CRUZ	CVE	119	1/21/1955	1/24/1955	1
MORMAL GULF	PRIVATE		1/24/1955	1/26/1955	1
POINT CRUZ	CVE	119	1/26/1955	2/21/1955	1
ENDURANCE	AM	435	2/2/1955	2/4/1955	AFDL-42
SQUAW	FAUX MINI-SUB	N/A	2/3/1955	2/6/1955	2
GREER COUNTY	LST	799	2/3/1955	2/17/1955	3
YARD CRAFT	YC	705	2/3/1955	2/17/1955	3
LLABREGAT	AMS	143	2/4/1955	2/17/1955	AFDL-42
YASHIMA	AMS	144	2/4/1955	2/17/1955	AFDL-42
CURRIER	DE	700	2/8/1955	2/25/1955	2
GEORGE	DE	697	2/8/1955	3/3/1955	2
SQUAW	FAUX MINI-SUB	N/A	2/8/1955	2/25/1955	2
ENERGY	AM	436	2/17/1955	3/4/1955	AFDL-42
PRIME	AM	466	2/17/1955	3/4/1955	AFDL-42
GEO. K MACKENZIE	DD	836	2/24/1955	3/16/1955	3
RUPERTUS	DD	851	2/24/1955	3/16/1955	3
REAPER	AM	96	3/4/1955	3/17/1955	AFDL-42
CONSTANT	AM	427	3/7/1955	3/24/1955	2
PIVOT	AM	463	3/7/1955	3/24/1955	2
PLUCK	AM	464	3/7/1955	3/24/1955	2
PRESTIGE	AM	465	3/7/1955	3/24/1955	2
HENRY W. TUCKER	DDR	875	3/18/1955	4/6/1955	3
LEONARD F. MASON	DD	852	3/18/1955	4/6/1955	3
WALKE	DD	723	3/24/1955	3/31/1955	2
TRATHEN	DD	530	3/30/1955	4/11/1955	1
FORCE	AM	445	3/31/1955	4/21/1955	AFDL-42

SHIP'S NAME	CLASS	NUMBER	DOCK	UNDOCK	DRYDOCK
ALVIN C. COCKRELL	DE	366	4/4/1955	4/25/1955	2
DEXTROUS	AM	341	4/4/1955	4/25/1955	2
REDSTART	AM	378	4/4/1955	4/25/1955	2
BRADLEY COUNTY	LST	400	4/8/1955	4/22/1955	3
LANDING SHIP	LSM	279	4/8/1955	4/22/1955	3
ONVERVAARD (DUTCH)	AM (M 888)	482	4/8/1955	4/21/1955	AFDL-42
DUKES COUNTY	LST	735	4/11/1955	4/28/1955	1
HAMPSHIRE COUNTY	LST	819	4/11/1955	4/28/1955	1
ENERGY	AM	436	4/21/1955	4/26/1955	AFDL-42
ENDURANCE	MSO	435	4/26/1955	5/6/1955	AFDL-42
IMPLICIT	MSO	455	4/26/1955	5/6/1955	AFDL-42
CORMORANT	MSC	122	4/29/1955	5/17/1955	2
PTARMIGAN	MSF	376	4/29/1955	5/17/1955	2
TOUCAN	MSF	387	4/29/1955	5/17/1955	2
FORTIFY	MSO	446	5/2/1955	5/16/1955	3
INFLICT	MSO	456	5/2/1955	5/16/1955	3
LOYALTY	MSO	457	5/2/1955	5/16/1955	3
PRIME	MSO	466	5/2/1955	5/16/1955	3
ENGAGE	MSO	433	5/9/1955	5/19/1955	AFDL-42
ILLUSIVE	MSO	448	5/9/1955	5/19/1955	AFDL-42
HELENA	CA	75	5/10/1955	6/10/1955	1
MOTOR MINESWEEPER	AMSC	138	5/23/1955	6/9/1955	2
ORLECK	DD	886	5/23/1955	6/9/1955	2
DYNAMIC	MSO	432	5/24/1955	6/7/1955	AFDL-42
GUIDE	MSO	447	5/24/1955	6/7/1955	AFDL-42
FLOYD B. PARKS	DD	884	5/31/1955	6/28/1955	3
JOHN R. CRAIG	DD	885	5/31/1955	6/28/1955	3
INFLICT	MSO	456	6/2/1955	6/21/1955	AFDL-42
CANTHO (FRANCE)	MSO (M 615)	476	6/7/1955	6/20/1955	AFDL-42
LOYALTY	MSO	457	6/7/1955	6/20/1955	AFDL-42
BAYFIELD	APA	33	6/13/1955	7/11/1955	1
BURTON ISLAND	AGB	1	6/14/1955	6/21/1955	2
FIRM	MSO	444	6/21/1955	7/5/1955	AFDL-42
LOWE	DER	325	6/27/1955	7/6/1955	2
EMBATTLE	MSO	434	7/5/1955	7/19/1955	AFDL-42
REAPER	MSO	467	7/5/1955	7/19/1955	AFDL-42
TAWASA	ATF	92	7/6/1955	7/21/1955	2
ILLUSIVE	MSO	448	7/19/1955	8/2/1955	AFDL-42
VINH LONG (FRANCE)	MSO (M 619)	477	7/19/1955	8/2/1955	AFDL-42
OKANOGAN	APA	220	7/25/1955	8/10/1955	1
ST. CLAIR COUNTY	LST	1096	7/26/1955	8/11/1955	3
FORCE	MSO	445	8/2/1955	8/17/1955	AFDL-42
SAO JORGE (PORTUGAL)	MSO (M 415)	478	8/2/1955	8/17/1955	AFDL-42
CATAMOUNT	LSD	17	8/8/1955	9/9/1955	2
GERMAN CRANE	YD	171	8/10/1955	9/19/1955	1
LANDING SHIP	LSM (R)	536	8/10/1955	9/19/1955	1

SHIP'S NAME	CLASS	NUMBER	DOCK	UNDOCK	DRYDOCK
De HAVEN	DD	727	8/15/1955	9/14/1955	3
MANSFIELD	DD	728	8/15/1955	9/14/1955	3
PICO	PRIVATE		8/22/1955	9/7/1955	AFDL-42
COLLETT	DD	730	9/16/1955	10/4/1955	3
LYMAN K. SWENSON	DD	729	9/16/1955	10/4/1955	3
HALSEY POWELL	DD	686	9/21/1955	11/7/1955	2
HIGBEE	DDR	806	10/3/1955	10/24/1955	1
JAMES E. KYES	DD	787	10/3/1955	10/24/1955	1
LITCHFIELD COUNTY	LST	901	10/3/1955	10/24/1955	1
EVERSOLE	DD	789	10/7/1955	10/27/1955	3
SHELTON	DD	790	10/7/1955	10/27/1955	3
PEACOCK	MSC	198	10/10/1955	10/20/1955	AFDL-42
EXCEL	MSO	439	10/21/1955	11/4/1955	AFDL-42
GUIDE	MSO	447	10/21/1955	11/4/1955	AFDL-42
CARTER HALL	LSD	3	10/27/1955	12/15/1955	1
PINE ISLAND	AV	12	11/1/1955	11/16/1955	3
ENHANCE	MSO	437	11/7/1955	11/17/1955	AFDL-42
PHOEBE	MSC	199	11/7/1955	11/17/1955	AFDL-42
LANDING SHIP	LSM	279	11/9/1955	11/28/1955	2
ENERGY	MSO	436	11/18/1955	11/29/1955	AFDL-42
PIVOT	MSO	463	11/18/1955	11/29/1955	AFDL-42
CHUNG CHI (TAIWAN)	LST (ex LST-279)	218	11/21/1955	12/16/1955	3
DAVIESS COUNTY	LST	692	11/21/1955	12/16/1955	3
FORCE	MSO	445	11/30/1955	12/16/1955	2
LUCID	MSO	458	11/30/1955	12/16/1955	2
SAWFISH	SS	276	11/30/1955	12/16/1955	2
CONSTANT	MSO	427	12/5/1955	12/16/1955	AFDL-42
PRESTIGE	MSO	465	12/5/1955	12/16/1955	AFDL-42
HELENA	CA	75	12/17/1955	12/22/1955	1
ISLE ROYALE	AD	29	12/19/1955	12/30/1955	3
LUCID	MSO	458	12/19/1955	1/5/1956	AFDL-42
VIREO	MSC	205	12/19/1955	1/5/1956	AFDL-42
SHEA	DM	30	12/21/1955	1/10/1956	2
WEISS	APD	135	12/21/1955	1/10/1956	2
TOLEDO	CA	133	12/23/1955	12/29/1955	1
LOS ANGELES	CA	135	1/5/1956	2/3/1956	3
ENDURANCE	MSO	435	1/5/1956	1/6/1956	AFDL-42
BLACK	DD	666	1/6/1956	2/1/1956	1
COMSTOCK	LSD	19	1/6/1956	2/1/1956	1
FORSTER	DER	334	1/6/1956	2/1/1956	1
JARVIS	DD	799	1/6/1956	2/1/1956	1
ENDURANCE	MSO	435	1/6/1956	2/2/1956	AFDL-42
LEADER	MSO	490	1/6/1956	1/27/1956	AFDL-42
TRATHEN	DD	530	1/12/1956	2/2/1956	2
WATTS	DD	567	1/12/1956	2/2/1956	2
ENHANCE	MSO	437	1/28/1956	2/2/1956	AFDL-42

SHIP'S NAME	CLASS	NUMBER	DOCK	UNDOCK	DRYDOCK
LAGEN (NORWAY)	MSO (M 950)	498	2/2/1956	2/20/1956	AFDL-42
NAMSEN (NORWAY)	MSO (M 951)	499	2/2/1956	2/20/1956	AFDL-42
REAPER	MSO	467	2/3/1956	2/16/1956	2
WARBLER	MSC	206	2/3/1956	2/16/1956	2
De KALB COUNTY	LST	715	2/6/1956	2/21/1956	1
RUDDY	MSF	380	2/15/1956	3/8/1956	3
YARD CRAFT	YFP	2	2/15/1956	3/8/1956	3
TRATHEN	DD	530	2/16/1956	2/20/1956	2
MADDOX	DD	731	2/16/1956	3/8/1956	3
CONQUEST	MSO	488	2/20/1956	3/7/1956	AFDL-42
LAGEN (NORWAY)	MSO (M 950)	498	2/20/1956	3/7/1956	AFDL-42
CALVERT	APA	32	2/21/1956	3/16/1956	1
BRUSH	DD	745	2/29/1956	3/23/1956	2
FORTIFY	MSO	446	3/13/1956	4/27/1956	3
LOYALTY	MSO	457	3/13/1956	4/27/1956	3
ARTEVELDE (BELGIUM)	MSO (M 907)	503	3/16/1956	4/5/1956	AFDL-42
HERBERT J. THOMAS	DDR	833	3/23/1956	4/23/1956	1
SAMUEL L. MOORE	DD	747	3/23/1956	4/23/1956	1
CONQUEST	MSO	488	4/5/1956	4/16/1956	AFDL-42
ESTEEM	MSO	438	4/16/1956	5/2/1956	AFDL-42
GALLANT	MSO	489	4/16/1956	5/2/1956	AFDL-42
LANSING	DER	388	4/18/1956	5/7/1956	2
PRESTON	DD	795	4/18/1956	5/7/1956	2
YARD CRAFT	YFN	272	4/18/1956	5/7/1956	2
GEORGE CLYMER	APA	27	4/25/1956	5/21/1956	1
YARD CRAFT	YFP	3	4/25/1956	5/21/1956	1
HENRY A. WILEY	DM	29	5/5/1956	5/22/1956	3
MILLER	DE	410	5/5/1956	5/22/1956	3
LANSDALE	DD	766	5/8/1956	6/5/1956	2
ORIGNY (FRANCE)	MSO (M 621)	501	5/8/1956	6/5/1956	2
BREYDEL (BELGIUM)	MSO (M 906)	504	5/21/1956	6/8/1956	1
HAMILTON COUNTY	LST	802	5/21/1956	6/8/1956	1
STORIONE (ITALY)	MSO (M 5431)	506	5/21/1956	6/8/1956	1
CONFLICT	MSO	426	5/24/1956	7/18/1956	3
DYNAMIC	MSO	432	5/24/1956	7/18/1956	3
FLOYD B. PARKS	DD	884	5/24/1956	7/18/1956	3
BERLIAMONT (FRANCE)	MSO (M 620)	500	6/4/1956	6/20/1956	AFDL-42
SAMUEL L. MOORE	DD	747	6/7/1956	6/9/1956	2
ERNST G. SMALL	DDR	838	6/11/1956	7/6/1956	1
MULBERRY	AN	27	6/11/1956	7/6/1956	1
WALKE	DD	723	6/11/1956	7/6/1956	1
HARRY E. HUBBARD	DD	748	6/19/1956	7/11/1956	2
O'BRIEN	DD	725	6/19/1956	7/11/1956	2
ENHANCE	MSO	437	6/25/1956	7/10/1956	AFDL-42
LEADER	MSO	490	6/25/1956	7/10/1956	AFDL-42
AUTUN (FRANCE)	MSO (M 622)	502	7/10/1956	7/27/1956	AFDL-42

SHIP'S NAME	CLASS	NUMBER	DOCK	UNDOCK	DRYDOCK
BACCARAT (FRANCE)	MSO (M 623)	505	7/10/1956	7/27/1956	AFDL-42
HELENA	CA	75	7/13/1956	8/13/1956	2
BENNER	DDR	807	7/20/1956	7/25/1956	1
EVERETT F. LARSON	DDR	830	7/20/1956	7/25/1956	1
FORSTER	DER	334	7/23/1956	8/8/1956	3
MINESWEEPER	MSC	218	7/23/1956	8/8/1956	3
MINESWEEPER	MSC	219	7/23/1956	8/8/1956	3
CONFLICT	MSO	426	7/27/1956	7/31/1956	AFDL-42
PONCHATOULA	AO	148	7/30/1956	8/9/1956	1
ENHANCE	MSO	437	7/31/1956	8/3/1956	AFDL-42
DYNAMIC	MSO	432	8/4/1956	8/9/1956	AFDL-42
ENERGY	MSO	436	8/13/1956	10/5/1956	3
PIVOT	MSO	463	8/13/1956	10/5/1956	3
LeRAY WILSON	DE	414	8/16/1956	9/5/1956	3
FLOYDS BAY	AVP	40	8/20/1956	9/7/1956	1
YARNALL	DD	541	8/20/1956	9/7/1956	1
SALMONE (ITALY)	MSO (M 5430)	507	8/27/1956	9/12/1956	AFDL-42
NOBLE	APA	218	9/7/1956	9/28/1956	1
TINGEY	DD	539	9/7/1956	9/28/1956	1
CHICKASAW	ATF	83	9/10/1956	10/11/1956	2
McDERMUT	DD	677	9/10/1956	10/9/1956	2
OMOSUND	MSC	221	9/12/1956	9/26/1956	AFDL-42
TSUSHIMA	MSC	255	10/2/1956	10/16/1956	AFDL-42
SHANGRI LA	CVA	38	10/4/1956	10/6/1956	1
PERSISTENT	MSO	491	10/10/1956	12/6/1956	3
YARD CRAFT	YC	1115	10/10/1956	12/6/1956	3
HENRICO	APA	45	10/11/1956	11/5/1956	1
LANSING	DER	388	10/11/1956	11/5/1956	1
YARD CRAFT	YFN	272	10/11/1956	11/5/1956	1
JUCAR	MSC	220	10/16/1956	10/31/1956	AFDL-42
TINGEY	DD	539	10/30/1956	11/1/1956	2
FORSTER	DER	334	11/1/1956	11/6/1956	2
BENNER	DDR	807	11/6/1956	11/8/1956	2
CACAPON	AO	52	11/8/1956	11/26/1956	1
LENAWEE	APA	195	11/8/1956	11/26/1956	1
EVERETT F. LARSON	DDR	830	11/9/1956	11/10/1956	2
De HAVEN	DD	727	11/11/1956	11/13/1956	2
PLEDGE	MSO	492	11/14/1956	11/21/1956	AFDL-42
STEPHEN POTTER	DD	538	11/19/1956	11/27/1956	2
LANDING SHIP	LSM (R)	455	11/21/1956	11/28/1956	AFDL-42
ENOREE	AO	69	11/28/1956	12/10/1956	1
SABINE	AO	25	11/28/1956	12/10/1956	1
PLEDGE	MSO	492	11/28/1956	12/7/1956	AFDL-42
WORCESTER	CL	144	12/3/1956	1/3/1957	2
GRONSUND	MSC	256	12/10/1956	12/21/1956	AFDL-42
ULVSUND	MSC	263	12/10/1956	12/21/1956	AFDL-42

SHIP'S NAME	CLASS	NUMBER	DOCK	UNDOCK	DRYDOCK
EVERSOLE	DD	789	12/11/1956	12/12/1956	3
De HAVEN	DD	727	12/13/1956	12/18/1956	3
COLLETT	DD	730	12/19/1956	12/21/1956	3
OWENS	DD	536	12/26/1956	1/3/1957	3
HALSEY POWELL	DD	686	12/27/1956	1/28/1957	1
KNAPP	DD	653	12/27/1956	1/28/1957	1
MARSHALL	DD	676	12/27/1956	1/28/1957	1
ACME	MSO	508	12/27/1956	1/14/1957	AFDL-42
FIRM	MSO	444	1/7/1957	2/26/1957	3
FORCE	MSO	445	1/7/1957	2/26/1957	3
GREGORY	DD	802	1/9/1957	2/1/1957	2
PORTERFIELD	DD	682	1/9/1957	2/1/1957	2
PLEDGE	MSO	492	1/22/1957	1/24/1957	AFDL-42
KAWISHIWI	AO	146	1/28/1957	1/30/1957	1
ACME	MSO	508	2/2/1957	2/4/1957	AFDL-42
CALIENTE	AO	53	2/4/1957	3/29/1957	1
NEWELL	DER	322	2/4/1957	3/29/1957	1
YARD CRAFT	YFN	272	2/4/1957	3/29/1957	1
CONKLIN	DE	439	2/6/1957	3/1/1957	2
HOWARD F. CLARK	DE	533	2/6/1957	3/1/1957	2
GOLDBORGSUND	MSC	257	2/18/1957	3/4/1957	AFDL-42
VILSUND	MSC	264	2/18/1957	3/4/1957	AFDL-42
ACME	MSO	508	2/26/1957	2/27/1957	3
FORSTER	DER	334	2/27/1957	3/5/1957	3
MATACO	ATF	86	3/1/1957	3/14/1957	2
SIOUX	ATF	75	3/1/1957	3/14/1957	2
CARRONADE	IFS	1	3/5/1957	3/26/1957	3
ORCA	AVP	49	3/5/1957	3/26/1957	3
TAURUS	PRIVATE		3/17/1957	3/18/1957	2
DUKES COUNTY	LST	735	3/20/1957	4/16/1957	2
GUAYAS	PF	56	3/20/1957	4/16/1957	2
THEO. E. CHANDLER	DD	717	4/2/1957	5/3/1957	3
CHEVALIER	DDR	805	4/4/1957	5/10/1957	1
RAMSDEN	DER	382	4/4/1957	5/10/1957	1
WILTSIE	DD	716	4/4/1957	5/10/1957	1
YARD CRAFT	YFN	272	4/4/1957	5/10/1957	1
CAVALLERO	APD	128	4/18/1957	5/17/1957	2
HAMNER	DD	718	4/18/1957	5/17/1957	2
TASHIMA	SC	258	4/23/1957	5/9/1957	AFDL-42
ILLUSIVE	MSO	448	5/9/1957	5/24/1957	AFDL-42
PRESTON	DD	795	5/13/1957	5/23/1957	3
HAVEN	AH	12	5/16/1957	6/14/1957	1
MATHEWS	AKA	96	5/16/1957	6/14/1957	1
CHARETTE	DD	581	5/22/1957	6/11/1957	2
JOHN D. HENLEY	DD	553	5/22/1957	6/11/1957	2
STANLY	DD	478	5/27/1957	6/10/1957	3

SHIP'S NAME	CLASS	NUMBER	DOCK	UNDOCK	DRYDOCK
GUAYAS	PF	56	5/31/1957	6/6/1957	AFDL-42
CREE	ATF	84	6/10/1957	6/25/1957	AFDL-42
THEO. E. CHANDLER	DD	717	6/12/1957	6/13/1957	3
WILTSIE	DD	716	6/12/1957	6/13/1957	3
NEWELL	DER	322	6/13/1957	7/10/1957	2
SUMMIT COUNTY	LST	1146	6/13/1957	7/10/1957	2
ENHANCE	MSO	437	6/17/1957	8/9/1957	3
GUIDE	MSO	447	6/17/1957	8/9/1957	3
STEEL CAISSON	CAISSON	DD-3	6/17/1957	8/9/1957	3
GEO. K MACKENZIE	DD	836	6/20/1957	7/19/1957	1
HENRY W. TUCKER	DD	875	6/20/1957	7/19/1957	1
LEONARD F. MASON	DD	852	6/20/1957	7/19/1957	1
RUPERTUS	DD	851	6/20/1957	7/19/1957	1
ST. CLAIR COUNTY	LST	1096	7/10/1957	7/20/1957	2
KAWISHIWI	AO	146	7/25/1957	8/13/1957	1
CURTISS	AV	4	8/1/1957	8/27/1957	2
ENHANCE	MSO	437	8/13/1957	8/16/1957	AFDL-42
EVERSOLE	DD	789	8/15/1957	9/18/1957	3
HIGBEE	DDR	806	8/15/1957	9/18/1957	3
FORTIFY	MSO	446	8/16/1957	9/4/1957	AFDL-42
LOYALTY	MSO	457	8/16/1957	9/4/1957	AFDL-42
TOLEDO	CA	133	8/19/1957	9/13/1957	1
JAMES E. KYES	DD	787	9/3/1957	9/25/1957	2
SHELTON	DD	790	9/3/1957	9/25/1957	2
ENGAGE	MSO	433	9/4/1957	9/24/1957	AFDL-42
INFLICT	MSO	456	9/4/1957	9/24/1957	AFDL-42
RAMSDEN	DER	382	9/20/1957	10/1/1957	3
IMPERVIOUS	MSO	449	9/24/1957	10/11/1957	AFDL-42
FULLAM	DD	474	9/26/1957	10/16/1957	1
HOWORTH	DD	592	9/26/1957	10/16/1957	1
KILLEN	DD	593	9/26/1957	10/16/1957	1
HANNA	DE	449	10/2/1957	10/25/1957	3
CHOWANOC	ATF	100	10/15/1957	10/31/1957	AFDL-42
BLACK	DD	666	10/24/1957	11/15/1957	2
ESTEEM	MSO	438	10/29/1957	12/18/1957	3
PLEDGE	MSO	492	10/29/1957	12/18/1957	3
YARD CRAFT	YC	1115	10/29/1957	12/18/1957	3
ALGOL	AKA	54	10/30/1957	11/27/1957	1
EVERETT F. LARSON	DDR	830	10/30/1957	11/27/1957	1
IRWIN	DD	794	10/30/1957	11/27/1957	1
RAMSDEN	DER	382	11/1/1957	11/5/1957	AFDL-42
HOWORTH	DD	592	11/6/1957	11/12/1957	AFDL-42
FULLAM	DD	474	11/12/1957	11/22/1957	AFDL-42
ACME	MSO	508	11/18/1957	12/11/1957	2
LYMAN K. SWENSON	DD	729	11/18/1957	12/11/1957	2
YARD CRAFT	YC	791	11/18/1957	12/11/1957	2

SHIP'S NAME	CLASS	NUMBER	DOCK	UNDOCK	DRYDOCK
HARRY E. HUBBARD	DD	748	11/25/1957	12/2/1957	AFDL-42
HIGBEE	DDR	806	11/27/1957	12/3/1957	1
MICHAEL MORAN	MCE	3050	12/4/1957	1/3/1958	1
KILLEN	DD	593	12/4/1957	12/17/1957	AFDL-42
BLACK	DD	666	12/12/1957	12/16/1957	2
COLLETT	DD	730	12/17/1957	1/17/1958	2
MANSFIELD	DD	728	12/17/1957	1/17/1958	2
WEISS	APD	135	12/19/1957	1/24/1958	AFDL-42
BENNER	DDR	807	12/23/1957	1/24/1958	3
De HAVEN	DD	727	12/23/1957	1/24/1958	3
GERMAN CRANE	YD	171	1/3/1958	1/8/1958	1
YARD CRAFT	YC	875	1/3/1958	1/8/1958	1
CONCRETE DOCK CASSION	CAISSON	DD-1	1/13/1958	2/5/1958	1
MISPILLION	AO	105	1/13/1958	2/5/1958	1
SHEA	DM	30	1/13/1958	2/5/1958	1
YARD CRAFT	YC	872	1/13/1958	2/5/1958	1
PINE ISLAND	AV	12	1/22/1958	2/13/1958	2
RICE COUNTY	LST	1089	1/27/1958	2/17/1958	3
CONSTANT	MSO	427	1/29/1958	2/17/1958	AFDL-42
ENERGY	MSO	436	1/29/1958	2/17/1958	AFDL-42
TULARE	AKA	112	2/7/1958	2/22/1958	1
VERNON COUNTY	LST	1161	2/7/1958	2/22/1958	1
TRATHEN	DD	530	2/18/1958	3/11/1958	2
WATTS	DD	567	2/18/1958	3/11/1958	2
DENNIS J. BUCKLEY	DD	808	2/19/1958	3/31/1958	3
JARVIS	DD	799	2/19/1958	3/28/1958	3
MANATEE	AO	58	2/24/1958	3/19/1958	1
WHETSTONE	LSD	27	2/24/1958	3/19/1958	1
COWELL	DD	547	3/13/1958	4/10/1958	2
STEMBEL	DD	644	3/13/1958	4/10/1958	2
NAVASOTA	AO	106	3/20/1958	4/11/1958	1
DYNAMIC	MSO	432	4/1/1958	4/23/1958	AFDL-42
ENDURANCE	MSO	435	4/1/1958	4/23/1958	AFDL-42
CUSHING	DD	797	4/2/1958	4/24/1958	3
PRITCHETT	DD	561	4/2/1958	4/24/1958	3
GERMAN CRANE	YD	171	4/11/1958	4/14/1958	1
ENHANCE	MSO	437	4/14/1958	4/25/1958	2
EXCEL	MSO	439	4/14/1958	4/25/1958	2
GUIDE	MSO	447	4/14/1958	4/25/1958	2
WILKINSON	DL	5	4/17/1958	5/8/1958	1
EMBATTLE	MSO	434	4/23/1958	5/15/1958	AFDL-42
FIRM	MSO	444	4/23/1958	5/15/1958	AFDL-42
COWELL	DD	547	4/25/1958	4/29/1958	3
FECHTELER	DDR	870	4/30/1958	5/23/1958	3
FORCE	MSO	445	4/30/1958	5/23/1958	3
PRESTON	DD	795	4/30/1958	5/23/1958	3

SHIP'S NAME	CLASS	NUMBER	DOCK	UNDOCK	DRYDOCK
POP-UP (FBM POLARIS)	STAGING VESSEL		5/9/1958	6/3/1958	1
BEGOR	APD	127	5/13/1958	6/4/1958	2
PICKING	DD	685	5/13/1958	6/4/1958	2
CONFLICT	MSO	426	5/21/1958	6/12/1958	AFDL-42
ILLUSIVE	MSO	448	5/21/1958	6/12/1958	AFDL-42
MADDOX	DD	731	5/27/1958	7/3/1958	3
SAMUEL L. MOORE	DD	747	5/27/1958	7/3/1958	3
BRUSH	DD	745	6/6/1958	7/9/1958	2
HERBERT J. THOMAS	DD	833	6/6/1958	7/9/1958	2
COLONIAL	LSD	18	6/16/1958	7/17/1958	1
PASSUMPSIC	AO	107	6/16/1958	7/17/1958	1
CHICKASAW	ATF	83	6/17/1958	7/11/1958	AFDL-42
RENVILLE	APA	227	7/8/1958	7/29/1958	3
TALUGA	AO	62	7/18/1958	8/11/1958	1
BRINKLEY BASS	DD	887	7/21/1958	8/20/1958	2
DUNCAN	DDR	874	7/21/1958	8/20/1958	2
BRUSH	DD	745	7/31/1958	8/4/1958	3
CONFLICT	MSO	426	8/1/1958	8/4/1958	AFDL-42
CONFLICT	MSO	426	8/4/1958	8/5/1958	AFDL-42
ERNST G. SMALL	DDR	838	8/7/1958	8/28/1958	3
WALKE	DD	723	8/7/1958	8/28/1958	3
PENDER COUNTY	LST	1080	8/11/1958	9/4/1958	1
THETIS BAY	CVHA	1	8/11/1958	9/4/1958	1
HARRY E. HUBBARD	DD	748	8/25/1958	8/19/1958	2
O'BRIEN	DD	725	8/25/1958	9/19/1958	2
ASHTABULA	AO	51	9/3/1958	9/26/1958	3
EVERSOLE	DD	789	9/8/1958	9/10/1958	AFDL-42
PHILIPPINE SEA	CV	47	9/10/1958	10/15/1958	1
POP-UP (FBM POLARIS)	MONITOR BARGE		9/10/1958	10/15/1958	AFDL-42
ENHANCE	MSO	437	9/23/1958	10/14/1958	AFDL-42
BLUE	DD	744	9/24/1958	10/22/1958	2
FRANK E. EVANS	DD	754	9/24/1958	10/22/1958	2
BRINKLEY BASS	DD	887	9/30/1958	10/2/1958	3
HARRY LUCKENBACK	PRIVATE		10/3/1958	10/5/1958	3
A. A. CUNNINGHAM	DD	752	10/7/1958	11/6/1958	3
McKEAN	DDR	784	10/7/1958	11/6/1958	3
HECTOR	AR	7	10/20/1958	11/14/1958	1
PRAIRIE	AD	15	10/20/1958	11/14/1958	1
EXCEL	MSO	439	10/20/1958	11/7/1958	AFDL-42
GUIDE	MSO	447	10/20/1958	11/7/1958	AFDL-42
O'BRIEN	DD	725	10/22/1958	10/23/1958	2
WALKE	DD	723	10/22/1958	10/23/1958	2
ST. PAUL	CA	73	11/10/1958	12/9/1958	2
BLUE	DD	744	11/14/1958	11/17/1958	3
LEADER	MSO	490	11/17/1958	12/8/1958	AFDL-42
LUCID	MSO	458	11/17/1958	12/8/1958	AFDL-42

SHIP'S NAME	CLASS	NUMBER	DOCK	UNDOCK	DRYDOCK
BELL	DD	587	11/18/1958	12/17/1958	1
BURNS	DD	588	11/18/1958	12/17/1958	1
MONTICELLO	LSD	35	11/18/1958	12/17/1958	1
FRONTIER	AD	25	11/19/1958	12/16/1958	3
McDERMUT	DD	677	12/12/1958	1/12/1959	2
TINGEY	DD	539	12/12/1958	1/12/1959	2
POP-UP (FBM POLARIS)	FISH HOOK	N/A	12/19/1958	1/23/1959	1
WICKES	DD	578	12/19/1958	1/23/1959	1
BOYD	DD	544	12/19/1958	1/13/1959	3
WEDDERBURN	DD	684	12/19/1958	1/13/1959	3
O'BRIEN	DD	725	1/13/1959	1/19/1959	2
WEISS	APD	135	1/14/1959	1/26/1959	AFDL-42
HENRY A. WILEY	DM	29	1/15/1959	2/5/1959	3
UHLMANN	DD	687	1/15/1959	2/5/1959	3
HOPEWELL	DD	681	1/21/1959	2/13/1959	2
KIDD	DD	661	1/21/1959	2/13/1959	2
MAKASSAR STRAIT	CVE	91	1/23/1959	2/4/1959	1
JOHN C. BUTLER	DE	339	1/29/1959	2/9/1959	AFDL-42
KEARSARGE	CV	33	2/10/1959	3/23/1959	1
ELDORADO	AGC	11	2/11/1959	2/27/1959	3
BALDUCK	APD	132	2/12/1959	2/24/1959	AFDL-42
STEEL DRYDOCK CAISSON	CAISSON	1	2/17/1959	3/30/1959	2
DAY	DE	225	2/26/1959	3/13/1959	AFDL-42
HEYWOOD L. EDWARDS	DD	663	3/3/1959	3/9/1959	3
RICHARD P. LEARY	DD	664	3/3/1959	3/9/1959	3
CHARETTE	DD	581	3/16/1959	4/20/1959	3
MARSHALL	DD	676	3/16/1959	4/20/1959	3
ACME	MSO	508	3/18/1959	4/8/1959	AFDL-42
CONQUEST	MSO	488	3/18/1959	4/8/1959	AFDL-42
LEXINGTON	CVA	16	3/31/1959	4/1/1959	1
HOPEWELL	DD	681	4/3/1959	4/6/1959	2
CHEMUNG	AO	30	4/6/1959	5/8/1959	1
CONCRETE DOCK AISSON	CAISSON	1	4/10/1959	5/8/1959	1
HALSEY POWELL	DD	686	4/10/1959	5/1/1959	2
PLUCK	MSO	464	4/15/1959	5/6/1959	AFDL-42
GREGORY	DD	802	4/18/1959	5/1/1959	2
ADVANCE	MSO	510	4/23/1959	5/20/1959	3
TWINING	DD	540	4/23/1959	5/20/1959	3
PORTERFIELD	DD	682	5/6/1959	5/29/1959	2
SHIELDS	DD	596	5/6/1959	5/29/1959	2
GERMAN CRANE (TITAN II)	YD	171	5/8/1959	6/16/1959	1
TOLOVANA	AO	64	5/8/1959	6/16/1959	1
COVE	MSI	1	5/25/1959	6/12/1959	AFDL-42
PIVOT	MSO	463	5/25/1959	6/12/1959	AFDL-42
HAMUL	AD	20	5/28/1959	6/26/1959	3
CONNER	DD	582	6/3/1959	7/16/1959	2

SHIP'S NAME	CLASS	NUMBER	DOCK	UNDOCK	DRYDOCK
JOHN W. THOMASON	DD	760	6/3/1959	7/16/1959	2
LANDING SHIP	LSU	1446	6/15/1959	8/18/1959	AFDL-42
HALSEY POWELL	DD	686	6/19/1959	6/22/1959	1
TWINING	DD	540	6/19/1959	6/22/1959	1
FLICKER	AMS	9	6/27/1959	7/10/1952	AFDL-42
BENNER	DDR	807	6/30/1959	7/14/1959	3
PRINCETON	LPH	5	7/1/1959	7/24/1959	1
CAVALLARO	APD	128	7/17/1959	8/6/1959	3
HALL	DD	583	7/17/1959	8/6/1959	3
CHEVALIER	DDR	805	7/22/1959	8/21/1959	2
WILTZIE	DD	716	7/22/1959	8/21/1959	2
LOFBERG	DD	759	7/27/1959	7/29/1959	1
HAMNER	DD	718	8/3/1959	8/24/1959	1
KLONDIKE	AD	22	8/3/1959	8/24/1959	1
THEO. E. CHANDLER	DD	717	8/3/1959	8/24/1959	1
CHEMUNG	AO	30	8/10/1959	8/13/1959	3
HENRY COUNTY	LST	824	8/17/1959	9/25/1959	3
STEEL DRYDOCK CAISSON	CAISSON	2	8/17/1959	9/25/1959	3
CAPE	MSI	2	8/18/1959	9/1/1959	AFDL-42
ESTES	AGC	12	8/27/1959	10/1/1959	1
RICHARD S. EDWARDS	DD	950	8/27/1959	10/1/1959	1
FECHTELER	DD	870	9/3/1959	9/12/1959	2
YARD CRAFT	YC	705	9/3/1959	9/12/1959	2
HAMNER	DD	718	9/15/1959	9/18/1959	2
PRITCHETT	DD	561	9/15/1959	9/18/1959	2
GEO. K MACKENZIE	DD	836	9/23/1959	10/16/1959	2
RUPERTUS	DD	851	9/23/1959	10/16/1959	2
MADDOX	DD	731	9/30/1959	10/5/1959	3
EVANS	DE	1023	10/6/1959	10/28/1959	1
HENRY W. TUCKER	DDR	875	10/6/1959	10/28/1959	1
LEONARD F. MASON	DD	852	10/6/1959	10/28/1959	1
DENNIS J. BUCKLEY	DDR	808	10/7/1959	10/12/1959	3
SQUAW	FAUX MINI-SUB	29	10/12/1959	10/27/1959	3
MUNSIF	MSC	273	10/14/1959	10/23/1959	AFDL-42
HIGBEE	DD	806	10/21/1959	11/16/1959	2
JAMES E. KYES	DD	787	10/21/1959	11/16/1959	2
YUNG CHUAN	MSC	58	10/23/1959	10/30/1959	AFDL-42
JEROME COUNTY	LST	848	10/27/1959	11/25/1959	3
HENRY W. TUCKER	DDR	875	10/28/1959	11/12/1959	1
MUKHTAR	MSC	274	10/30/1959	11/6/1959	AFDL-42
LANDING CRAFT	LCU	1446	11/10/1959	12/7/1959	AFDL-42
EVERSOLE	DD	789	11/12/1959	12/4/1959	1
JASON	AR	8	11/12/1959	12/4/1959	1
HALL	DD	583	12/4/1959	12/11/1959	2
HULL	DD	945	12/9/1959	1/15/1960	3
FLOYD B. PARKS	DD	884	12/14/1959	12/21/1959	2

SHIP'S NAME	CLASS	NUMBER	DOCK	UNDOCK	DRYDOCK
PERKINS	DDR	877	12/14/1959	1/11/1960	2
JOHN W. THOMASON	DD	760	12/16/1959	12/21/1959	1
FORT MARION	LSD	22	12/21/1959	3/11/1960	1
NEREUS	AS	17	12/21/1959	3/11/1960	1
YARD CRAFT	YC	15	12/28/1959	1/14/1960	AFDL-42
JOHN R. CRAIG	DD	885	1/11/1960	1/28/1960	2
POP-UP	MONITOR BARGE	N/A	1/19/1960	2/5/1960	AFDL-42
LOS ANGELES	CA	135	1/21/1960	3/8/1960	3
EVERSOLE	DD	789	1/28/1960	2/12/1960	2
YARD CRAFT	YC	1115	2/5/1960	2/29/1960	AFDL-42
EVERETT F. LARSON	DDR	830	2/15/1960	3/14/1960	2
ROGERS	DDR	876	2/15/1960	3/14/1960	2
PRIME	MSO	466	3/9/1960	4/1/1960	AFDL-42
TOLEDO	CA	133	3/11/1960	4/8/1960	3
BENNER	DDR	807	3/16/1960	4/7/1960	2
A. A. CUNNINGHAM	DD	752	3/17/1960	3/31/1960	1
McKEAN	DDR	784	3/17/1960	3/31/1960	1
HENRY W. TUCKER	DDR	875	3/31/1960	4/4/1960	1
FIRM	MSO	444	4/1/1960	4/29/1960	AFDL-42
REAPER	MSO	467	4/1/1960	4/29/1960	AFDL-42
BAUER	DE	1025	4/4/1960	5/9/1960	1
SKAGIT	AKA	105	4/4/1960	5/9/1960	1
COLLETT	DD	730	4/11/1960	5/27/1960	2
MANSFIELD	DD	728	4/11/1960	5/27/1960	2
YARD CRAFT	YFN	1130	4/11/1960	5/23/1961	2
JAMES E. KYES	DD	787	4/11/1960	5/13/1960	3
STURTEVANT	DER	239	4/21/1960	5/13/1960	3
FLOATING CRANE	YD	87	5/10/1960	5/20/1960	1
JOYCE	DER	317	5/10/1960	5/20/1960	3
SERRANO	ATF	112	5/16/1960	6/2/1960	AFDL-42
BLACK	DD	666	5/18/1960	6/13/1960	3
TRATHEN	DD	530	5/18/1960	6/13/1960	3
BREMERTON	CA	130	5/20/1960	6/23/1960	1
WILKINSON	DL	5	5/20/1960	6/23/1960	1
CHARLES BERRY	DE	1035	5/31/1960	6/4/1960	2
CONSTANT	MSO	427	6/3/1960	6/17/1960	AFDL-42
DENNIS J. BUCKLEY	DDR	808	6/6/1960	6/29/1960	2
COWELL	DD	547	6/15/1960	7/13/1960	3
PRITCHETT	DD	561	6/15/1960	7/13/1960	3
FORT MARION	LSD	22	6/24/1960	6/27/1960	1
ESTEEM	MSO	438	6/27/1960	7/13/1960	AFDL-42
WHITE MARSH	LSD	8	7/5/1960	8/5/1960	2
AMMEN	DD	527	7/20/1960	8/3/1960	3
HERBERT J. THOMAS	DDR	833	7/26/1960	8/19/1980	1
THETIS BAY	CVHA	1	7/26/1960	8/19/1960	1
COLLETT	DD	730	8/3/1960	8/24/1960	3

SHIP'S NAME	CLASS	NUMBER	DOCK	UNDOCK	DRYDOCK
SEAMAN	DD	791	8/3/1960	8/24/1960	3
PROVIDENCE	CLG	6	8/11/1960	8/23/1960	2
EDSON	DD	946	8/25/1960	9/22/1960	1
PASSUMPSIC	AO	107	8/25/1960	9/22/1960	1
FECHTELER	DDR	870	8/29/1960	9/23/1960	2
PICKING	DD	685	8/29/1960	9/23/1960	2
TORTUGA	LSD	26	9/6/1960	10/7/1960	3
BLACK	DD	666	9/22/1960	10/3/1960	1
GREGORY	DD	802	9/26/1960	9/29/1960	2
CIMARRON	AO	22	10/3/1960	10/28/1960	1
COLLETT	DD	730	10/3/1960	10/7/1960	2
MADDOX	DD	731	10/14/1960	11/10/1960	3
SAMUEL L. MOORE	DD	747	10/14/1960	11/10/1960	3
ENDURANCE	MSO	435	10/18/1960	11/15/1960	AFDL-42
ILLUSIVE	MSO	448	10/18/1960	11/15/1960	AFDL-42
DYNAMIC	MSO	432	10/19/1960	11/10/1960	2
PRESTON	DD	795	10/19/1960	11/10/1960	2
FECHTELER	DDR	870	10/28/1960	10/31/1960	1
BRUSH	DD	745	10/31/1960	11/28/1960	1
TALUGA	AO	62	10/31/1960	11/28/1960	1
TOPEKA	CLG	8	11/15/1960	12/7/1960	3
SHELTON	DD	790	11/17/1960	12/23/1960	2
YARD CRAFT	YC	1116	11/17/1960	12/23/1960	2
YARD CRAFT	YFN	272	11/17/1960	12/23/1960	2
TINGEY	DD	539	11/28/1960	12/20/1960	1
De HAVEN	DD	727	12/12/1960	12/15/1960	3
PICKING	DD	685	12/12/1960	12/15/1960	3
DUNCAN	DDR	874	12/22/1960	2/21/1961	3
YARD CRAFT	YC	789	12/22/1960	2/21/1961	3
YARD CRAFT	YFN	1130	12/22/1960	2/21/1961	3
PRINCETON	LPH	5	12/28/1960	3/16/1961	1
PREBLE	DLG	15	12/29/1960	1/12/1961	2
CHEVALIER	DDR	805	1/17/1961	1/20/1961	2
ACME	MSO	508	1/27/1961	4/4/1961	AFDL-42
COWELL	DD	547	2/2/1961	2/9/1961	2
HARRY E. HUBBARD	DD	748	2/13/1961	3/15/1961	2
McKEAN	DD	784	2/13/1961	3/15/1961	2
COLLETT	DD	730	2/24/1961	3/3/1961	3
SAMUEL L. MOORE	DD	747	3/8/1961	3/23/1961	3
BOYD	DD	544	3/20/1961	4/6/1961	2
FLOATING DRYDOCK	AFDL	48	3/22/1961	4/12/1961	1
WEDDERBURN	DD	684	3/28/1961	4/26/1961	3
A. A. CUNNINGHAM	DD	752	4/11/1961	5/23/1961	2
FRANK E. EVANS	DD	754	4/11/1961	5/23/1961	2
YARD CRAFT	YFN	272	4/11/1961	5/23/1961	2
SHELTON	DD	790	4/25/1961	5/2/1961	1

SHIP'S NAME	CLASS	NUMBER	DOCK	UNDOCK	DRYDOCK
YARD CRAFT	YC	791	4/25/1961	5/2/1961	1
SPERRY	AS	12	5/3/1961	6/27/1961	1
ISHERWOOD	DD	520	5/5/1961	5/31/1961	3
MULLANY	DD	528	5/5/1961	5/31/1961	3
ACME	MSO	508	5/8/1961	5/16/1961	AFDL-42
YARD CRAFT	YC	791	5/8/1961	5/16/1961	AFDL-42
PRITCHETT	DD	561	5/23/1961	5/31/1962	1
THRASHER	MSC	203	5/23/1961	6/1/1961	AFDL-42
GREGORY	DD	802	5/26/1961	7/6/1961	2
UHLMANN	DD	687	5/26/1961	7/6/1961	2
COLLETT	DD	730	6/2/1961	6/9/1961	3
PRESTON	DD	795	6/2/1961	6/9/1961	3
FECHTELER	DDR	870	6/19/1961	6/23/1961	3
A & P WATER BARGE	BARGE	15	6/19/1961	6/30/1961	AFDL-42
POP-UP	MONITOR BARGE	N/A	6/19/1961	6/30/1961	AFDL-42
YARD CRAFT	YC	1396	6/19/1961	6/30/1961	AFDL-42
POP-UP (POLARIS)	STAGING VESSEL	N/A	6/27/1961	7/12/1961	1
HALSEY POWELL	DD	686	6/27/1961	8/8/1961	3
MARSHALL	DD	676	6/27/1961	8/8/1961	3
McDERMUT	DD	677	6/28/1961	4/26/1961	3
YARD CRAFT	YC	1383	6/30/1961	7/14/1961	AFDL-42
BRAINE	DD	630	7/12/1961	8/18/1961	1
COGSWELL	DD	651	7/12/1961	8/18/1961	1
INGERSOLL	DD	652	7/12/1961	8/18/1961	1
STODDARD	DD	566	7/12/1961	8/18/1961	1
WILKINSON	DL	5	7/17/1961	11/29/1961	2
HENRY B. WILSON	DDG	7	8/10/1961	8/16/1961	3
CHARLES BERRY	DE	1035	8/10/1961	8/16/1961	AFDL-42
De HAVEN	DD	727	8/18/1961	8/25/1961	3
MANSFIELD	DD	728	8/18/1961	8/25/1961	3
ELDORADO	AGC	11	8/24/1961	9/19/1961	1
POINT DEFIANCE	LSD	31	8/24/1961	9/19/1961	1
TURNER JOY	DD	951	8/31/1961	9/29/1961	3
WORK BARGE	BARGE	16	8/31/1961	9/29/1961	3
CALIENTE	AO	53	9/22/1961	10/27/1961	1
DELTA	AR	9	9/22/1961	10/27/1961	1
FRANK KNOX	DDR	742	9/29/1961	10/4/1961	3
TURNER JOY	DD	951	10/5/1961	10/9/1961	3
YARD CRAFT	YFU	39	10/5/1961	10/9/1961	3
PROVIDENCE	CLG	6	10/13/1961	10/18/1961	3
HARRY E. HUBBARD	DD	748	10/13/1961	10/18/1961	AFDL-42
EVANS	DE	1023	10/24/1961	11/28/1961	AFDL-42
ESTES	AGC	12	10/30/1961	11/24/1961	1
PARSONS	DD	949	10/30/1961	11/24/1961	1
CATAMOUNT	LSD	17	11/15/1961	1/31/1962	3
O'BRIEN	DD	725	12/1/1961	12/4/1961	2

SHIP'S NAME	CLASS	NUMBER	DOCK	UNDOCK	DRYDOCK
COGSWELL	DD	651	12/4/1961	12/11/1961	1
LYMAN K. SWENSON	DD	729	12/4/1961	12/11/1961	1
McMORRIS	DE	1036	12/4/1961	1/8/1962	AFDL-42
TOPEKA	CLG	8	12/8/1961	12/30/1961	2
EVANS	DE	1023	12/11/1961	1/9/1962	1
FRONTIER	AD	25	12/11/1961	1/9/1962	1
CHARLES BERRY	DE	1035	1/2/1962	1/8/1962	2
BRIDGET	DE	1024	1/8/1962	1/24/1962	2
GANNET	MSC	290	1/11/1962	1/17/1962	AFDL-42
LINCOLN COUNTY	LST	898	1/12/1962	1/18/1962	1
GURKE	DD	783	1/18/1962	2/8/1962	1
ROWAN	DD	782	1/18/1962	2/8/1962	1
CHARLES BERRY	DE	1035	1/19/1962	1/23/1962	AFDL-42
BUCK	DD	761	2/2/1962	3/2/1962	2
YARD CRAFT	YC	1115	2/2/1962	3/2/1962	2
YARD CRAFT	YFN	1130	2/2/1962	3/2/1962	2
CHARLES BERRY	DE	1035	2/5/1962	2/7/1962	3
CHARLES BERRY	DE	1035	2/7/1962	2/10/1962	3
ALBATROSS	MSC	289	2/9/1962	2/28/1962	AFDL-42
GERMAN CRANE (TITAN II)	YD	171	2/12/1962	3/8/1962	1
MORTON	DD	948	2/12/1962	3/8/1962	1
McMORRIS	DE	1036	2/27/1962	3/1/1962	3
CB-2	CB	2	2/28/1962	3/29/1962	AFDL-42
McMORRIS	DE	1036	3/5/1962	3/9/1962	3
CHEVALIER	DDR	805	3/6/1962	4/3/1962	2
YARD CRAFT	YC	1367	3/6/1962	4/3/1962	2
YARD CRAFT	YFN	272	3/6/1962	4/3/1962	2
RICHARD S. EDWARDS	DD	950	3/14/1962	4/18/1962	3
HERBERT J. THOMAS	DDR	833	3/28/1962	3/30/1962	1
TAUSSIG	DD	746	4/3/1962	5/10/1962	2
YARD CRAFT	YC	705	4/3/1962	5/10/1962	2
YARD CRAFT	YC	1120	4/3/1962	5/10/1962	2
EVANS	DE	1023	4/9/1962	4/13/1962	1
EVANS	DE	1023	4/16/1962	4/30/1962	1
WALKE	DD	723	4/18/1962	4/20/1962	3
STEEL CAISSON	CAISSON	3	4/20/1962	5/3/1962	3
TOPEKA	CLG	8	4/30/1962	5/11/1962	1
JOHN W. THOMASON	DD	760	5/3/1962	5/29/1962	3
WORLD CENTURION	PRIVATE		5/13/1962	5/20/1962	1
ACME	MSO	508	5/14/1962	5/27/1962	AFDL-42
BLACK	DD	666	5/17/1962	6/8/1962	1
LOS ANGELES	CA	135	5/17/1962	6/8/1962	2
McMORRIS	DE	1036	5/28/1962	6/7/1962	AFDL-42
HULL	DD	945	5/29/1962	7/5/1962	3
PERKINS	DDR	877	6/14/1962	7/24/1962	2
YARD CRAFT	YC	789	6/14/1962	7/24/1962	2

SHIP'S NAME	CLASS	NUMBER	DOCK	UNDOCK	DRYDOCK
YARD CRAFT	YC	1116	6/14/1962	7/24/1962	2
OKLAHOMA CITY	CLG	5	6/18/1962	6/29/1962	1
COONTZ	DLG	9	7/5/1962	7/9/1962	1
JOHN W. THOMASON	DD	760	7/7/1962	7/11/1962	3
POP-UP (POLARIS)	FISH HOOK	N/A	7/9/1962	7/26/1962	1
POP-UP (POSEIDON)	STAGING VESSEL	N/A	7/9/1962	7/26/1962	1
ISLE ROYALE	AD	29	7/17/1962	7/17/1962	3
PREBLE	DLG	15	7/27/1962	8/24/1962	2
CHEVALIER	DDR	805	8/1/1962	8/7/1962	1
RICHARD S. EDWARDS	DD	950	8/10/1962	8/17/1962	1
EVERETT F. LARSON	DDR	830	8/23/1962	10/5/1962	3
YARD CRAFT	YC	1088	8/23/1962	10/5/1962	3
YARD CRAFT	YFN	1130	8/23/1962	10/5/1962	3
TAUSSIG	DD	746	8/24/1962	8/29/1962	1
BENNER	DDR	807	9/5/1962	10/4/1962	2
YARD CRAFT	YC	1115	9/5/1962	10/4/1962	2
YARD CRAFT	YFN	272	9/5/1962	10/4/1962	2
FLOATING DRYDOCK	AFDL	42	9/6/1962	10/17/1962	1
JASON	AR	8	9/6/1962	10/17/1962	1
BRINKLEY BASS	DD	887	10/5/1962	10/8/1962	2
TAUSSIG	DD	746	10/6/1962	10/9/1962	3
PIEDMONT	AD	17	10/11/1962	11/19/1962	2
COLAHAN	DD	658	10/16/1962	11/9/1962	3
ST. PAUL	CA	73	10/25/1962	11/11/1962	1
BOYD	DD	544	11/15/1962	11/29/1962	3
RIGGER WORK BARGE	BARGE	72-1	11/27/1962	12/20/1962	2
YARD CRAFT	YC	789	11/27/1962	12/20/1962	2
YARD CRAFT	YC	1367	11/27/1962	12/20/1962	2
EDSON	DD	946	12/6/1962	1/4/1963	3
HERBERT J. THOMAS	DDR	833	12/18/1962	1/16/1963	1
PICKING	DD	685	12/18/1962	1/16/1963	1
WILKINSON	DL	5	12/27/1962	1/18/1963	2
HALSEY POWELL	DD	686	1/10/1963	1/25/1963	3
MARSHALL	DD	676	1/10/1963	1/25/1963	3
PERKINS	DDR	877	1/21/1963	1/24/1963	2
GREGORY	DD	802	1/22/1963	2/8/1963	1
KING	DLG	10	1/22/1963	2/13/1963	1
McDERMUT	DD	677	1/22/1963	2/8/1963	1
PRESTON	DD	795	1/30/1963	2/20/1963	3
MAHAN	DLG	11	2/5/1963	3/1/1963	2
STODDARD	DD	566	2/13/1963	3/1/1963	1
UHLMANN	DD	687	2/13/1963	3/1/1963	1
DIVING BOAT	N/A	72	2/19/1963	3/7/1963	AFDL-42
YARD REPAIR BARGE	YR	63	2/19/1963	3/12/1963	AFDL-42
COWELL	DD	547	2/26/1963	3/29/1963	3
TRATHEN	DD	530	2/26/1963	3/29/1963	3

SHIP'S NAME	CLASS	NUMBER	DOCK	UNDOCK	DRYDOCK
GERMAN CRANE (TITAN II)	YD	171	3/1/1963	3/2/1963	1
BLACK	DD	666	3/5/1963	3/27/1963	1
FLOATING CRANE	YD	197	3/5/1963	3/27/1963	1
FLOATING CRANE	YD	197	3/5/1963	3/30/1963	1
PRITCHETT	DD	561	3/5/1963	3/27/1963	1
ORLECK	DD	886	3/8/1963	4/23/1963	2
YARD CRAFT	YC	1088	3/8/1963	4/23/1963	2
YARD CRAFT	YC	1116	3/8/1963	4/23/1963	2
YARD CRAFT	YFN	1130	3/8/1963	4/23/1963	2
WILKINSON	DL	5	3/30/1963	4/25/1963	1
OKLAHOMA CITY	CLG	5	4/11/1963	5/14/1963	3
FECHTELER	DD	870	5/1/1963	3/13/1963	2
YARD CRAFT	YC	705	5/1/1963	6/13/1963	2
YARD CRAFT	YC	791	5/1/1963	6/13/1963	2
YARD CRAFT	YFN	272	5/1/1963	6/13/1963	2
BRYCE CANYON	AD	36	5/2/1963	6/4/1963	1
HENRY B. WILSON	DDG	7	5/2/1963	6/4/1963	1
YARD CRAFT	YC	789	5/2/1963	6/4/1963	1
YARD CRAFT	YC	1367	5/2/1963	6/4/1963	1
ACME	MSO	508	5/16/1963	6/18/1963	AFDL-42
COGSWELL	DD	651	5/20/1963	6/10/1963	3
INGERSOLL	DD	652	5/20/1963	6/10/1963	3
BERTHING BARGE	APL	18	6/18/1963	7/2/1963	3
BRUSH	DD	745	6/20/1963	7/24/1963	2
MADDOX	DD	731	6/20/1963	7/24/1963	2
ALOHA STATE	PRIVATE		7/8/1963	7/9/1963	1
VALLEY FORGE	LPH	8	7/17/1963	10/3/1963	1
ELDORADO	AGC	11	7/18/1963	8/14/1963	3
LOS ANGELES	CA	135	8/8/1963	9/17/1963	2
ORLECK	DD	886	8/28/1963	9/6/1963	3
MADDOX	DD	731	9/1/1963	9/5/1963	AFDL-42
MADDOX	DD	731	9/9/1963	9/21/1963	AFDL-42
GREGORY	DD	802	9/13/1963	10/18/1963	3
McDERMUT	DD	677	9/13/1963	10/18/1963	3
RONCADOR	SS	301	10/3/1963	10/23/1963	AFDL-42
R. B. ANDERSON	DD	786	10/4/1963	11/2/1963	2
WEDDERBURN	DD	684	10/4/1963	11/2/1963	2
COONTZ	DLG	9	10/24/1963	11/26/1963	3
FECHTELER	DD	870	11/4/1963	11/13/1963	2
BRINKLEY BASS	DD	887	11/12/1963	11/27/1963	1
JOSEPH STRAUSS	DDG	16	11/19/1963	12/10/1963	2
ERNST G. SMALL	DDR	838	12/2/1963	12/24/1963	3
YORKTOWN	CV	10	12/4/1963	1/10/1964	1
FORTIFY	MSO	446	12/5/1963	12/23/1963	AFDL-42
ESTES	AGC	12	12/17/1963	1/16/1964	2
ENGLAND	DLG	22	12/30/1963	1/17/1964	3

SHIP'S NAME	CLASS	NUMBER	DOCK	UNDOCK	DRYDOCK
BERKELEY	DDG	15	1/15/1964	2/5/1964	1
BLACK	DD	666	1/15/1964	2/5/1964	1
PORTERFIELD	DD	682	1/30/1964	3/5/1964	2
ROKS NAM YANG	MSC	526	2/10/1964	2/10/1964	AFDL-42
PRINCETON	LPH	5	2/11/1964	4/14/1964	1
ROBISON	DDG	12	2/13/1964	3/10/1964	3
OZBOURN	DD	846	3/5/1964	3/31/1964	2
CANBERRA	CAG	2	3/17/1964	4/15/1964	3
ST. CLAIR COUNTY	LST	1096	4/2/1964	5/13/1964	2
YARD CRAFT	YFN	1130	4/2/1964	5/13/1964	2
MARS	AFS	1	4/21/1964	5/7/1964	1
VANCOUVER	LPD	2	4/21/1964	5/7/1964	1
McKEAN	DDR	784	4/22/1964	6/8/1964	3
YARD CRAFT	YC	705	4/22/1964	6/8/1964	3
YARD CRAFT	YC	789	4/22/1964	6/8/1964	3
YARD CRAFT	YFN	272	4/22/1964	6/8/1964	3
FLOATING DOCK SEC. D	AFDB	4	5/12/1964	6/9/1964	1
FLOATING DOCK SEC. F	AFDB	4	5/12/1964	6/9/1964	1
KING	DLG	10	5/12/1964	6/9/1964	1
FLOATING CRANE	YD	192	5/19/1964	6/15/1964	2
MAHAN	DLG	11	5/19/1964	6/15/1964	2
ST. CLAIR COUNTY	LST	1096	6/7/1964	6/11/1964	AFDL-42
HIGBEE	DD	806	6/10/1964	6/16/1964	3
WATER BARGE	YWN	70	6/17/1964	6/23/1964	AFDL-42
YARD CRAFT	YFP	3	6/17/1964	6/23/1964	AFDL-42
DALE	DLG	19	6/18/1964	7/10/1964	2
ENGLAND	DLG	22	6/25/1964	7/22/1964	3
JARICHA	PRIVATE		7/13/1964	7/15/1964	1
SNOHOMISH COUNTY	LST	1126	7/14/1964	8/13/1964	2
YARD CRAFT	YFN	1130	7/14/1964	8/13/1964	2
WORDEN	DLG	18	7/23/1964	8/6/1964	3
BOYD	DD	544	7/29/1964	9/3/1964	1
FRANK E. EVANS	DD	754	7/29/1964	9/3/1964	1
IWO JIMA	LPH	2	7/29/1964	9/3/1964	1
WILTSIE	DD	716	8/26/1964	9/24/1964	3
FRONTIER	AD	25	8/31/1964	9/24/1964	2
ARNOLD J. ISBELL	DD	869	9/15/1964	10/13/1964	1
TINIAN	AKV	23	9/15/1964	10/13/1964	1
WALKE	DD	723	9/15/1964	10/13/1964	1
FRANK E. EVANS	DD	754	9/24/1964	9/26/1964	3
McKEAN	DD	784	9/26/1964	9/29/1964	3
BLUE	DD	744	9/30/1964	10/31/1964	2
COLLETT	DD	730	9/30/1964	10/3/1964	2
McKEAN	DD	784	10/2/1964	10/4/1964	3
COGSWELL	DD	651	10/12/1964	11/5/1964	3
FRANK KNOX	DDR	742	10/12/1964	11/5/1964	3

SHIP'S NAME	CLASS	NUMBER	DOCK	UNDOCK	DRYDOCK
GALVESTON	CLG	3	10/20/1964	11/16/1964	1
HOEL	DDG	13	10/20/1964	11/16/1964	1
INGERSOLL	DD	652	11/3/1964	12/10/1964	2
UHLMANN	DD	687	11/3/1964	12/10/1964	2
BUCK	DD	761	11/6/1964	11/18/1964	3
YARD CRAFT	YSR	25	11/6/1964	12/7/1964	3
CHEVALIER	DDR	805	11/20/1964	12/4/1964	1
HARRY E. HUBBARD	DD	748	11/20/1964	12/4/1964	1
WALKE	DD	723	11/30/1964	12/4/1964	3
A. A. CUNNINGHAM	DD	752	12/7/1964	1/7/1965	3
O'BRIEN	DD	725	12/7/1964	1/7/1965	3
BENNER	DDR	807	12/11/1964	12/28/1964	1
BRUSH	DD	745	12/11/1964	12/28/1964	1
REEVES	DLG	24	12/15/1964	12/28/1964	2
KHANAMUIE	MSI	310	12/17/1964	12/30/1964	AFDL-42
FRANK KNOX	DDR	742	1/8/1965	1/11/1965	3
ACME	MSO	508	1/11/1965	2/19/1965	AFDL-42
BRONSTEIN	DE	1037	1/14/1965	1/28/1965	2
FLOATING CRANE	YD	87	1/19/1965	2/24/1965	1
PRAIRIE	AD	15	1/19/1965	2/24/1965	1
SHIELDS	DD	596	1/19/1965	2/24/1965	1
TURNER JOY	DD	951	1/19/1965	2/24/1965	1
HALSEY POWELL	DD	686	1/27/1965	2/26/1965	3
MOLALA	ATF	106	1/27/1965	2/26/1965	3
YARD CRAFT	YFN	272	1/27/1965	2/26/1965	3
BRUSH	DD	745	1/30/1965	2/1/1965	2
BRINKLEY BASS	DD	887	2/12/1965	3/5/1965	2
KEARSARGE	CVS	33	3/4/1965	4/2/1965	1
WORDEN	DLG	18	3/5/1965	3/12/1965	3
BRIDGET	DE	1024	3/8/1965	4/7/1965	2
HENDERSON	DD	785	3/8/1965	4/7/1965	2
WALKE	DD	723	3/8/1965	3/15/1965	AFDL-42
TURNER JOY	DD	951	3/14/1965	3/19/1965	3
TRIAINA (GREECE)	S (ex SS-397)	86	3/18/1965	3/23/1965	AFDL-42
GRIDLEY	DLG	21	3/23/1965	4/19/1965	3
AGERHOLM	DD	826	4/7/1965	5/4/1965	1
EVANS	DE	1023	4/7/1965	5/4/1965	1
HOLLISTER	DD	788	4/7/1965	5/4/1965	1
THEO. E. CHANDLER	DD	717	4/7/1965	5/4/1965	1
ELDORADO	AGC	11	4/15/1965	6/3/1965	2
BERKELEY	DDG	15	4/26/1965	5/17/1965	3
YARD CRAFT	YOS	9	4/26/1965	5/17/1965	3
NAVASOTA	AO	106	5/7/1965	5/12/1965	1
EVANS	DE	1023	5/17/1965	5/18/1965	1
WEDDERBURN	DD	684	5/19/1965	6/14/1965	3
GERMAN CRANE (TITAN II)	YD	171	5/24/1965	6/17/1965	1

SHIP'S NAME	CLASS	NUMBER	DOCK	UNDOCK	DRYDOCK
POP-UP	MONITOR BARGE	N/A	5/24/1965	6/17/1965	1
POP-UP (POSEIDON)	FISH HOOK	N/A	5/24/1965	6/17/1965	1
POP-UP (SEALAB II MODS)	STAGING VESSEL	N/A	5/24/1965	6/17/1965	1
INGERSOLL	DD	652	6/6/1965	6/8/1965	3
RPS RIZAL	PS	69	6/8/1965	9/17/1965	AFDL-42
PICKING	DD	685	6/18/1965	6/28/1965	3
CARRONADE	IFS	1	6/22/1965	7/21/1965	1
CAVALIER	APA	37	6/22/1965	7/21/1965	1
WHITE RIVER	LSM (R)	563	6/22/1965	7/21/1965	1
CORSARO II (ITALY)	YAWL	N/A	6/24/1965	7/1/1965	AFDL-42
DUNCAN	DDR	874	7/6/1965	7/14/1965	3
YARD CRAFT	YC	1115	7/6/1965	7/14/1965	3
DIMIRHISAR	PC	1639	7/13/1965	7/20/1965	AFDL-42
FLORIKAN	ASR	9	7/15/1965	8/6/1965	2
MORTON	DD	948	7/15/1965	8/6/1965	2
YARD CRAFT	YC	1088	7/16/1965	7/23/1965	3
FLOATING DRYDOCK	AFDL	48	7/26/1965	8/3/1965	1
BAUER	DE	1025	7/27/1965	8/26/1965	3
HOOPER	DE	1026	7/27/1965	8/26/1965	3
RICHARD S. EDWARDS	DD	950	8/5/1965	9/9/1965	1
SQUAW	FAUX MINI-SUB	29	8/5/1965	9/9/1965	1
TAUSSIG	DD	746	8/5/1965	9/9/1965	1
ESTEEM	MSO	438	8/6/1965	8/12/1965	AFDL-42
BRONSTEIN	DE	1037	8/16/1965	8/24/1965	2
HOPEWELL	DD	681	8/25/1965	9/7/1965	2
ROBISON	DDG	12	9/6/1965	9/15/1965	3
YARD CRAFT	YC	1367	9/6/1965	9/15/1965	3
SQUAW	FAUX MINI-SUB	29	9/13/1965	10/6/1965	2
WILTSIE	DD	716	9/13/1965	10/6/1965	2
BAUSELL	DD	845	9/20/1965	10/4/1965	3
RPS RIZAL	PS	69	9/21/1965	9/24/1965	AFDL-42
USNS RANGE TRACKER	T-AGM	1	9/22/1965	9/26/1965	1
HECTOR	AR	7	9/28/1965	10/28/1965	1
BLACK	DD	666	10/25/1965	12/13/1965	AFDL-48
TAUSSIG	DD	746	10/26/1965	11/4/1965	2
KLONDIKE	AD	22	10/28/1965	11/24/1965	1
LOS ANGELES	CA	135	11/5/1965	11/22/1965	2
EVERETT F. LARSON	DD	830	11/22/1965	12/30/1965	3
STEEL CAISSON	CAISSON	3	11/22/1965	12/30/1965	3
ST. PAUL	CA	73	11/24/1965	12/23/1965	2
PORTERFIELD	DD	682	11/30/1965	12/9/1965	1
BENNINGTON	CVS	20	12/12/1965	2/2/1966	1
IMPERVIOUS	MSO	449	12/17/1965	12/21/1965	AFDL-42
BANKEO	MSC	6	12/22/1965	1/3/1966	AFDL-42
JAMES E. KYES	DD	787	1/3/1966	1/27/1966	3
STEEL CAISSON	CAISSON	3	1/3/1966	2/14/1965	3

SHIP'S NAME	CLASS	NUMBER	DOCK	UNDOCK	DRYDOCK
BAUER	DE	1025	1/12/1966	1/19/1966	2
HECTOR	AR	7	1/21/1966	1/24/1966	2
FLOATING CRANE	YD	197	2/1/1966	2/8/1966	3
HULL	DD	945	2/7/1966	3/3/1966	2
FLOATING CRANE	YD	197	2/8/1966	4/6/1966	1
WHITE SANDS	ARD	20	2/8/1966	4/6/1966	1
TAUSSIG	DD	746	2/14/1966	2/21/1966	3
FRANK E. EVANS	DD	754	2/15/1966	2/28/1966	AFDL-48
HALSEY	DLG	23	2/25/1966	3/9/1966	3
FRANK E. EVANS	DD	754	3/1/1966	3/7/1966	AFDL-48
OZBOURN	DD	846	3/8/1966	4/5/1966	2
PRITCHETT	DD	561	3/8/1966	4/5/1966	2
E. H. BIRD	COMMERCIAL	N/A	3/17/1966	3/23/1966	3
CAIMAN	SS	323	4/1/1966	4/24/1966	AFDL-42
COGSWELL	DD	651	4/11/1966	4/27/1966	2
DUNCAN	DDR	874	4/11/1966	4/27/1966	2
BON HOMME RICHARD	CVA	31	4/12/1966	7/7/1966	1
WALKE	DD	723	4/23/1966	5/2/1966	3
EVERSOLE	DD	789	5/3/1966	5/31/1966	2
BRINKLEY BASS	DD	887	5/9/1966	6/21/1966	AFDL-48
PARSONS	DD	949	5/17/1966	8/4/1966	3
STEEL CAISSON	CAISSON	2	5/17/1966	8/4/1966	3
YARD CRAFT	YC	1088	5/17/1966	8/4/1966	3
YARD CRAFT	YFN	1130	5/17/1966	8/4/1966	3
FOX	DLG	33	6/3/1966	6/28/1966	2
WALKE	DD	723	7/8/1966	7/16/1966	AFDL-48
PASSUMPSIC	AO	107	7/12/1966	7/27/1966	1
WADDELL	DDG	24	7/12/1966	8/30/1966	2
SHELTON	DD	790	7/22/1966	8/1/1966	AFDL-48
FECHTELER	DD	870	7/29/1966	8/25/1966	1
NORTON SOUND	AVM	1	7/29/1966	8/25/1966	1
HARRY E. HUBBARD	DD	748	8/3/1966	8/15/1966	AFDL-48
INGERSOLL	DD	652	8/3/1966	8/15/1966	AFDL-48
BRUSH	DD	745	8/11/1966	9/30/1966	3
SAMUEL L. MOORE	DD	747	8/11/1966	9/20/1966	3
YARD CRAFT	YFP	3	8/23/1966	1/10/1967	AFDL-42
OGDEN	LPD	5	8/30/1966	11/1/1966	1
GALVESTON	CLG	3	9/6/1966	9/29/1966	2
WEDDERBURN	DD	684	9/14/1966	10/21/1966	AFDL-48
RUPERTUS	DD	851	10/6/1966	11/9/1966	2
GEO. K MACKENZIE	DD	836	10/13/1966	11/19/1966	3
HENRY W. TUCKER	DDR	875	10/13/1966	11/19/1966	3
AGERHOLM	DD	826	10/24/1966	11/19/1966	AFDL-48
DULUTH	LPD	6	11/3/1966	12/29/1966	1
POP-UP (TRIDENT C-4)	FISH HOOK	N/A	11/3/1966	12/29/1966	1
POP-UP (TRIDENT C-4)	STAGING VESSEL	N/A	11/3/1966	12/29/1966	1

SHIP'S NAME	CLASS	NUMBER	DOCK	UNDOCK	DRYDOCK
COONTZ	DLG	9	11/16/1966	12/29/1966	2
HOOPER	DE	1026	11/22/1966	12/17/1966	AFDL-48
BRONSTEIN	DE	1037	11/28/1966	12/17/1966	3
FLOATING CRANE	YD	192	11/28/1966	12/17/1966	3
LYNDE McCORMICK	DDG	8	12/21/1966	1/23/1966	3
YARD CRAFT	YC	1395	12/21/1966	1/23/1967	3
CATFISH	SS	339	1/4/1967	1/9/1967	AFDL-48
MOUNT McKINLEY	AGC	7	1/5/1967	2/1/1967	1
ENGLAND	DLG	22	1/12/1967	1/23/1967	2
HOOPER	DE	1026	1/12/1967	1/16/1967	AFDL-48
TAUSSIG	DD	746	1/13/1967	1/27/1967	AFDL-42
ROGERS	DD	876	1/27/1967	2/23/1967	3
STEEL CAISSON	CAISSON	1	1/27/1967	3/31/1967	3
FOX	DLG	33	1/30/1967	2/13/1967	2
ASHEVILLE	PGM	84	2/1/1967	2/20/1967	AFDL-42
LYMAN K. SWENSON	DD	729	2/2/1967	2/24/1967	AFDL-48
VALLEY FORGE	LPH	8	2/9/1967	3/30/1967	1
BROOKE	DEG	1	2/20/1967	5/2/1967	2
YARD CRAFT	YC	1082	2/20/1967	5/2/1967	2
ROWAN	DD	782	2/28/1967	3/31/1967	3
HOOPER	DE	1026	3/4/1967	3/15/1967	AFDL-48
GALLUP	PGM	85	3/6/1967	3/20/1967	AFDL-42
WILTSIE	DD	716	3/29/1967	4/6/1967	AFDL-48
TAUSSIG	DD	746	4/1/1967	5/1/1967	AFDL-42
DALE	DLG	19	4/5/1967	4/29/1967	3
YORKTOWN	CVS	10	4/17/1967	8/5/1967	1
GURKE	DD	783	4/20/1967	5/16/1967	AFDL-48
BUCHANAN	DDG	14	5/3/1967	5/25/1967	3
YARD CRAFT	YC	705	5/3/1967	5/25/1967	3
PARSONS	DD	949	5/11/1967	6/20/1967	2
YARD CRAFT	YC	1088	5/11/1967	6/20/1967	2
YARD CRAFT	YFN	1130	5/11/1967	6/20/1967	2
BUCK	DD	761	5/20/1967	5/31/1967	AFDL-42
PRITCHETT	DD	561	5/23/1967	6/16/1967	AFDL-48
GURKE	DD	783	6/3/1967	6/9/1967	3
TOPEKA	CLG	8	6/14/1967	7/4/1967	3
MULLANY	DD	528	6/23/1967	7/25/1967	AFDL-48
EVERETT F. LARSON	DDR	830	7/1/1967	7/8/1967	2
GRIDLEY	DLG	21	7/12/1967	8/7/1967	2
ALAMO	LSD	33	7/19/1967	7/26/1967	1
CANBERRA	CAG	2	7/28/1967	9/7/1967	3
PRINCETON	LPH	5	8/9/1967	11/16/1967	1
A. A. CUNNINGHAM	DD	752	8/11/1967	9/12/1967	2
HANSON	DD	832	8/11/1967	9/12/1967	2
MULLANY	DD	528	8/18/1967	9/1/1967	AFDL-48
PRITCHETT	DD	561	8/25/1967	9/1/1967	AFDL-42

SHIP'S NAME	CLASS	NUMBER	DOCK	UNDOCK	DRYDOCK
TAUSSIG	DD	746	9/6/1967	9/15/1967	AFDL-42
PRITCHETT	DD	561	9/8/1967	9/20/1967	AFDL-48
WADDELL	DDG	24	9/11/1967	10/10/1967	3
O'BRIEN	DD	725	9/14/1967	10/14/1967	2
INGERSOLL	DD	652	10/17/1967	11/20/1967	2
STODDARD	DD	566	10/17/1967	11/20/1967	2
MADDOX	DD	731	10/30/1967	11/29/1967	3
SHELTON	DD	790	11/7/1967	12/4/1967	AFDL-48
ARNOLD J. ISBELL	DD	869	11/22/1967	12/19/1967	2
BRINKLEY BASS	DD	887	11/22/1967	12/19/1967	2
HORNET	CVS	12	11/27/1967	2/16/1968	1
MAHAN	DLG	11	12/4/1967	12/28/1967	3
YARD CRAFT	YOS	9	12/4/1967	12/28/1967	3
FLOYD B. PARKS	DD	884	12/6/1967	12/29/1967	AFDL-48
ENHANCE	MSO	437	12/12/1967	1/15/1968	AFDL-42
LUCID	MSO	458	12/12/1967	1/15/1968	AFDL-42
RAMSEY	DEG	2	12/22/1967	1/8/1968	2
EVANS	DE	1023	1/3/1968	3/13/1968	3
MORTON	DD	948	1/3/1968	1/22/1968	3
YARD CRAFT	YOS	9	1/3/1968	1/22/1968	3
GEO. K MACKENZIE	DD	836	1/3/1968	2/1/1968	AFDL-48
HENDERSON	DD	785	1/15/1968	2/2/1968	2
SAMUEL L. MOORE	DD	747	1/15/1968	2/2/1968	2
HALSEY POWELL	DD	686	1/25/1968	2/27/1968	AFDL-42
BRIDGET	DE	1024	1/31/1968	3/13/1968	3
DECATUR	DDG	31	2/5/1968	2/23/1968	AFDL-48
GALVESTON	CLG	3	2/8/1968	3/12/1968	2
DIXIE	AD	14	2/24/1968	3/18/1968	1
RAMSEY	DEG	2	2/24/1968	3/2/1968	1
RUPERTUS	DD	851	2/26/1968	3/5/1968	AFDL-48
COGSWELL	DD	651	3/5/1968	3/15/1968	AFDL-42
MERCER	APB	39	3/14/1968	4/8/1968	2
YARD CRAFT	YC	1088	3/14/1968	4/8/1968	2
YARD CRAFT	YC	1120	3/14/1968	4/8/1968	2
YARD CRAFT	YFN	1130	3/14/1968	4/8/1968	2
LUCID	MSO	458	3/19/1968	3/21/1968	AFDL-48
BRONSTEIN	DE	1037	3/20/1968	4/22/1968	3
LYMAN K. SWENSON	DD	729	3/20/1968	4/22/1968	3
LUCID	MSO	458	3/22/1968	3/26/1968	AFDL-42
PRESTON	DD	795	3/25/1968	4/12/1968	AFDL-48
SS QUEEN MARY	PRIVATE SHIP		4/6/1968	5/17/1968	1
READY	PGM	87	4/9/1968	4/17/1968	AFDL-42
DUNCAN	DDR	874	4/10/1968	5/9/1968	2
RICH	DD	820	4/13/1968	4/17/1968	AFDL-48
BRUSH	DD	745	4/23/1968	5/15/1968	AFDL-42
WEDDERBURN	DD	684	4/24/1968	5/17/1968	AFDL-48

SHIP'S NAME	CLASS	NUMBER	DOCK	UNDOCK	DRYDOCK
BELLE GROVE	LSD	2	5/1/1968	5/24/1968	3
HENRY W. TUCKER	DD	875	5/10/1968	6/8/1968	2
ORLECK	DD	886	5/10/1968	6/8/1968	2
SAMUEL L. MOORE	DD	747	5/16/1968	6/13/1968	AFDL-42
EVERETT F. LARSON	DD	830	5/18/1968	6/10/1968	AFDL-48
KEARSARGE	CVS	33	5/23/1968	8/5/1968	1
PRAIRIE	AD	15	5/27/1968	7/19/1968	3
FRANK E. EVANS	DD	754	6/10/1968	7/10/1968	2
WALKE	DD	723	6/10/1968	7/10/1968	2
HARRY E. HUBBARD	DD	748	6/11/1968	6/22/1968	AFDL-48
ANTELOPE	PGM	86	6/14/1968	6/24/1968	AFDL-42
READY	PGM	87	6/24/1968	6/26/1968	AFDL-42
SAMUEL L. MOORE	DD	747	6/24/1968	7/5/1968	AFDL-48
ANTELOPE	PGM	86	6/28/1968	7/3/1968	AFDL-42
READY	PGM	87	6/28/1968	7/3/1968	AFDL-42
JENKINS	DDE	447	7/4/1968	7/10/1968	AFDL-42
HMAS BRISBANE	D	41	7/13/1968	7/30/1968	2
PERKINS	DD	877	7/15/1968	8/16/1968	AFDL-48
READY	PGM	87	7/22/1968	8/19/1968	AFDL-42
LYMAN K. SWENSON	DD	729	7/23/1968	8/1/1968	3
NORTON SOUND	AVM	1	8/8/1968	9/26/1968	3
JAMES E. KYES	DD	787	8/20/1968	9/12/1968	AFDL-48
CHICAGO	CG	11	8/22/1968	9/18/1968	2
YARD CRAFT	YC	1395	8/22/1968	10/1/1968	AFDL-42
YARD CRAFT	YOS	13	8/22/1968	10/1/1968	AFDL-42
TICONDEROGA	CVA	14	8/26/1968	10/7/1968	1
GURKE	DD	783	9/26/1968	10/23/1968	AFDL-48
HOPEWELL	DD	681	10/1/1968	10/22/1968	2
HIGBEE	DD	806	10/2/1968	10/14/1968	3
YARD REPAIR BARGE	YR	63	10/4/1968	10/22/1968	AFDL-42
FLOATING DOCK SEC. A	AFDB	4	10/10/1968	12/6/1968	1
IWO JIMA	LPH	2	10/10/1968	12/6/1968	1
HERBERT J. THOMAS	DD	833	10/16/1968	11/15/1968	3
JOHN W. THOMASON	DD	760	10/16/1968	11/15/1968	3
MANSFIELD	DD	728	10/24/1968	11/21/1968	2
READY	PGM	87	10/24/1968	11/1/1968	AFDL-42
YARD REPAIR BARGE	YR	63	11/4/1968	11/13/1968	AFDL-42
ROGERS	DD	876	11/4/1968	11/21/1968	AFDL-48
BRADLEY	DE	1041	11/19/1968	12/23/1968	3
YARD CRAFT	YFN	272	11/19/1968	12/23/1968	3
HOLLISTER	DD	788	11/25/1968	12/27/1968	2
THEO. E. CHANDLER	DD	717	11/25/1968	12/27/1968	2
MULLANY	DD	528	12/5/1968	1/7/1969	AFDL-48
BON HOMME RICHARD	CVA	31	12/9/1968	1/2/1969	1
TURNER JOY	DD	951	12/9/1968	1/20/1969	3
UHLMANN	DD	687	12/30/1968	1/28/1969	2

SHIP'S NAME	CLASS	NUMBER	DOCK	UNDOCK	DRYDOCK
BENNINGTON	CVS	20	1/7/1969	3/19/1969	1
JOHN R. CRAIG	DD	885	1/9/1969	2/3/1969	AFDL-48
PICKING	DD	685	1/21/1969	2/12/1969	3
YARD CRAFT	YC	1116	1/21/1969	2/12/1969	3
YARD CRAFT	YC	1366	1/21/1969	2/12/1969	3
READY	PG	87	2/4/1969	2/17/1969	AFDL-42
De HAVEN	DD	727	2/6/1969	3/13/1969	AFDL-48
PERSISTENT	MSO	491	2/12/1969	2/14/1969	3
BLUE	DD	744	2/13/1969	3/19/1969	2
COLLETT	DD	730	2/13/1969	3/19/1969	2
EVERSOLE	DD	789	2/27/1969	3/28/1969	3
McKEAN	DD	784	2/27/1969	3/28/1969	3
BENNER	DD	807	3/14/1969	4/16/1969	AFDL-48
MANATEE	AO	58	3/21/1969	4/18/1969	2
SCHOFIELD	DEG	3	3/23/1969	3/30/1969	1
O'BRIEN	DD	725	3/26/1969	4/19/1969	AFDL-42
CANON	PG	90	3/30/1969	4/4/1969	3
LONG BEACH	CGN	9	4/2/1969	4/25/1969	1
O'CALLAHAN	DE	1051	4/2/1969	4/25/1969	1
CANBERRA	CA	70	4/7/1969	5/16/1969	3
MADDOX	DD	731	4/22/1969	5/20/1969	AFDL-42
MARYSVILLE	PCER	857	4/28/1969	5/28/1969	2
REXBURG	PCER	855	4/28/1969	5/28/1969	2
STONE COUNTY	LST	1141	4/28/1969	5/28/1969	2
McKEAN	DD	784	4/28/1969	5/5/1969	AFDL-48
FLOATING DOCK SEC. B	AFDB	4	4/30/1969	5/30/1969	1
FLOATING DOCK SEC. C	AFDB	4	4/30/1969	5/30/1969	1
VANCOUVER	LPD	2	4/30/1969	5/26/1969	2
ANTELOPE	PG	86	5/6/1969	5/26/1969	AFDL-48
NORTON SOUND	AVM	1	5/16/1969	5/24/1969	3
BERKELEY	DDG	15	5/27/1969	6/19/1969	3
FLOYD B. PARKS	DD	884	5/28/1969	6/17/1969	AFDL-48
DENVER	LPD	9	6/3/1969	7/26/1969	1
OGDEN	LPD	5	6/3/1969	7/26/1969	1
ADVANCE	MSO	510	6/10/1969	7/12/1969	2
BAUER	DE	1025	6/10/1969	7/12/1969	2
CONSTANT	MSO	427	6/10/1969	7/12/1969	2
READY	PG	87	6/10/1969	7/12/1969	2
MARSH	DE	699	6/19/1969	7/11/1969	AFDL-42
KLONDIKE	AD	22	6/30/1969	8/4/1969	3
EDSON	DD	946	7/1/1969	7/30/1969	AFDL-48
MARSH	DE	699	7/11/1969	7/31/1969	AFDL-42
READY	PG	87	7/12/1969	7/14/1969	2
BROOKE	DEG	1	7/16/1969	8/12/1969	2
DENVER	LPD	9	7/26/1969	8/13/1969	1
SHELTON	DD	790	8/1/1969	9/4/1969	AFDL-48

SHIP'S NAME	CLASS	NUMBER	DOCK	UNDOCK	DRYDOCK
ANTELOPE	PG	86	8/4/1969	8/7/1969	3
CANON	PG	90	8/4/1969	8/15/1969	AFDL-42
BAUSELL	DD	845	8/11/1969	9/9/1969	3
LOFBERG	DD	759	8/11/1969	9/9/1969	3
DENVER	LPD	9	8/13/1969	9/22/1969	1
DULUTH	LPD	6	8/13/1969	9/22/1969	1
ROGERS	DD	876	9/11/1969	10/8/1969	3
SOUTHERLAND	DD	743	9/11/1969	10/8/1969	3
PARSONS	DDG	33	9/16/1969	10/10/1969	AFDL-48
TALUGA	AO	62	9/18/1969	10/16/1969	2
LYMAN K. SWENSON	DD	729	9/24/1969	10/4/1969	AFDL-42
FLOATING DOCK SEC. E	AFDB	4	9/25/1969	10/9/1969	1
WICHITA	AOR	1	9/25/1969	10/9/1969	1
FLOATING DOCK SEC. E	AFDB	4	10/9/1969	11/17/1969	1
LYNDE McCORMICK	DDG	8	10/10/1969	11/7/1969	3
YARD CRAFT	YC	789	10/10/1969	11/7/1969	3
OKINAWA	LPH	3	10/13/1969	11/17/1969	1
McKEAN	DD	784	10/13/1969	10/16/1969	AFDL-48
MARATHON	PG	89	10/16/1969	11/5/1969	AFDL-42
KNOX	DE	1052	10/20/1969	11/18/1969	2
McKEAN	DD	784	11/3/1969	11/22/1969	AFDL-48
GURKE	DD	783	11/10/1969	12/4/1969	3
O'CALLAHAN	DE	1051	11/10/1969	12/4/1969	3
KEARSARGE	CVS	33	11/20/1969	12/12/1969	1
ST. PAUL	CA	73	11/24/1969	12/29/1969	2
MORTON	DD	948	12/9/1969	1/22/1970	3
YARD CRAFT	YC	1116	12/9/1969	1/22/1970	3
YARD CRAFT	YFN	1130	12/9/1969	1/22/1970	3
TICONDEROGA	CVA	14	12/15/1969	3/31/1970	1
FLOATING CRANE	YD	197	1/2/1970	1/15/1970	2
YARD CRAFT	YSR	25	1/2/1970	1/15/1970	2
BUCK	DD	761	1/8/1970	1/23/1970	AFDL-42
FLOATING CRANE	YD	197	1/19/1970	2/13/1970	2
SCHOFIELD	DEG	3	1/19/1970	2/13/1970	2
YARD CRAFT	YC	1367	1/19/1970	2/13/1970	2
DECATUR	DDG	31	1/22/1970	2/4/1970	AFDL-48
PEORIA	LST	1183	2/5/1970	2/16/1970	3
NEUCES	APB	40	2/17/1970	3/4/1970	AFDL-48
LUCID	MSO	458	2/20/1970	2/22/1970	2
POINT DEFIANCE	LSD	31	2/22/1970	2/26/1970	3
TRIPOLI	LPH	10	2/23/1970	2/27/1970	2
HOOPER	DE	1026	3/2/1970	3/26/1970	3
TOWERS	DDG	9	3/2/1970	3/26/1970	3
HEPBURN	DE	1055	3/3/1970	3/13/1970	2
JOHN R. CRAIG	DD	885	3/6/1970	4/1/1970	AFDL-48
JOHN S. McCAIN	DDG	36	3/16/1970	3/27/1970	2

SHIP'S NAME	CLASS	NUMBER	DOCK	UNDOCK	DRYDOCK
JAMES E. KYES	DD	787	3/27/1970	4/23/1970	3
CONCRETE CAISSON	CAISSON	1	3/30/1970	4/27/1970	2
FIRM	MSO	444	3/30/1970	4/27/1970	2
FLOATING DOCK SEC. G	AFDB	4	4/3/1970	5/6/1970	1
EVERETT F. LARSON	DD	830	4/10/1970	5/6/1970	1
FLOATING CRANE	YD	192	4/10/1970	5/6/1970	1
TAUSSIG	DD	746	4/16/1970	4/27/1970	AFDL-48
TACOMA	PG	92	4/18/1970	4/24/1970	AFDL-42
WELCH	PG	93	4/22/1970	4/29/1970	AFDL-42
EVERSOLE	DD	789	4/24/1970	5/4/1970	3
GLACIER	AGB	4	5/5/1970	6/19/1970	2
RICHARD S. EDWARDS	DD	950	5/8/1970	6/22/1970	3
YARD CRAFT	YC	1082	5/8/1970	6/22/1970	3
YARD CRAFT	YC	1115	5/8/1970	6/22/1970	3
HULL	DD	945	5/12/1970	7/28/1970	AFDL-48
WALKE	DD	723	5/13/1970	6/8/1970	AFDL-42
HOLLISTER	DD	788	5/14/1970	6/2/1970	1
SQUAW	FAUX MINI-SUB	29	5/14/1970	6/2/1970	1
CACAPON	AO	52	6/12/1970	7/27/1970	1
FRESNO	LST	1182	6/16/1970	6/24/1970	AFDL-42
FLOYD B. PARKS	DD	884	6/25/1970	7/24/1970	3
MEYERKORD	DE	1058	7/10/1970	8/3/1970	2
SCHOFIELD	DEG	3	7/10/1970	8/3/1970	2
PLEDGE	MSO	492	7/14/1970	8/25/1970	AFDL-42
PLUCK	MSO	464	7/14/1970	8/25/1970	AFDL-42
GRIDLEY	DLG	21	7/27/1970	8/26/1970	3
BARGE	NSY	27454	8/1/1970	9/1/1970	1
BARGE	NSY	27820	8/1/1970	9/1/1970	1
JOUETT	DLG	29	8/1/1970	8/24/1970	1
REPOSE	AH	16	8/1/1970	8/24/1970	1
EMBATTLE	MSO	434	8/6/1970	9/1/1970	2
RAMSEY	DEG	2	8/6/1970	9/1/1970	2
YARD CRAFT	YC	1088	8/6/1970	9/1/1970	2
REPOSE	AH	16	8/24/1970	9/1/1970	1
HENRY B. WILSON	DDG	7	8/29/1970	10/1/1970	3
YARD CRAFT	YFP	3	8/29/1970	10/1/1970	3
JOUETT	DLG	29	9/2/1970	9/8/1970	1
DEFIANCE	PG	95	9/2/1970	9/25/1970	AFDL-42
SURPRISE	PG	97	9/2/1970	9/25/1970	AFDL-42
BROOKE	DEG	1	9/3/1970	10/29/1970	2
PEORIA	LST	1186	9/11/1970	9/20/1970	1
WHITE SANDS	ARD	20	9/11/1970	9/20/1970	1
BRINKLEY BASS	DD	887	9/15/1970	10/13/1970	AFDL-48
MORTON	DD	948	9/20/1970	9/23/1970	1
POINT DEFIANCE	LSD	31	9/23/1970	11/9/1970	1
EVERSOLE	DD	789	10/5/1970	10/20/1970	3

SHIP'S NAME	CLASS	NUMBER	DOCK	UNDOCK	DRYDOCK
HOOPER	DE	1026	10/5/1970	10/20/1970	3
EMBATTLE	MSO	434	10/16/1970	10/27/1970	AFDL-42
COLLETT	DD	730	10/19/1970	11/16/1970	AFDL-48
STERETT	DLG	31	10/26/1970	11/23/1970	3
BENICIA	PG	95	10/27/1970	11/13/1970	AFDL-42
GRAY	DE	1054	10/31/1970	11/4/1970	2
RUPERTUS	DD	851	11/5/1970	12/9/1970	2
YARD CRAFT	YSR	26	11/5/1970	1/14/1970	2
MANITOWOC	LST	1180	11/9/1970	12/2/1970	1
BLUE	DD	744	11/17/1970	12/16/1970	AFDL-42
HENRY W. TUCKER	DD	875	11/18/1970	12/17/1970	AFDL-48
ALBERT DAVID	DE	1050	11/25/1970	1/6/1971	3
YARD CRAFT	YFN	272	11/25/1970	1/6/1971	3
FLOATING CRANE	YD	87	12/4/1970	1/18/1971	1
ISLE ROYALE	AD	29	12/4/1970	1/18/1971	1
MANSFIELD	DD	728	12/4/1970	1/18/1971	1
PARSONS	DDG	33	12/4/1970	1/18/1971	1
McKEAN	DD	784	12/12/1970	1/14/1971	2
JOHN W. THOMASON	DD	760	12/29/1970	1/26/1971	AFDL-48
FRANCIS HAMMOND	DE	1067	1/11/1971	2/3/1971	3
TAUSSIG	DD	746	1/13/1971	2/4/1971	AFDL-42
A. A. CUNNINGHAM	DD	752	1/19/1971	2/8/1971	2
MAHAN	DLG	11	1/20/1971	2/17/1971	1
DECATUR	DDG	31	1/28/1971	2/25/1971	AFDL-48
BRONSTEIN	DE	1037	2/9/1971	2/19/1971	3
BEACON	PG	99	2/12/1971	3/25/1971	2
CHEHALIS	PG	94	2/12/1971	3/25/1971	2
GREEN BAY	PG	101	2/12/1971	3/25/1971	2
LEONARD F. MASON	DD	852	2/12/1971	3/25/1971	2
YARD CRAFT	YOS	13	2/12/1971	3/25/1971	2
SUMTER	LST	1181	2/18/1971	3/2/1971	1
TAUSSIG	DD	746	2/18/1971	2/19/1971	AFDL-42
ARNOLD J. ISBELL	DD	869	2/22/1971	4/13/1971	3
HERBERT J. THOMAS	DD	833	2/22/1971	4/13/1971	3
DUNCAN	DDR	874	3/2/1971	3/31/1971	1
FLOATING DRYDOCK	AFDL	42	3/2/1971	3/31/1971	1
WATER BARGE	YWN	70	3/2/1971	3/31/1971	1
BENICIA	PG	96	3/17/1971	3/25/1971	AFDL-48
TALUGA	AO	62	3/29/1971	4/2/1971	2
GEO. K MACKENZIE	DD	836	3/30/1971	5/11/1971	AFDL-48
GERMAN CRANE (TITAN II)	YD	171	4/2/1971	5/10/1971	1
JOHN PAUL JONES	DDG	32	4/2/1971	5/10/1971	1
HIGBEE	DD	806	4/15/1971	5/27/1971	3
STEEL CAISSON	CAISSON	3	4/15/1971	5/27/1971	3
ASHTABULA	AO	51	4/16/1971	6/3/1971	2
ENGAGE	MSO	433	4/16/1971	5/7/1971	AFDL-42

SHIP'S NAME	CLASS	NUMBER	DOCK	UNDOCK	DRYDOCK
FORTIFY	MSO	446	4/16/1971	5/7/1971	AFDL-42
GREEN BAY	PG	101	5/10/1971	5/14/1971	AFDL-42
ALAMO	LSD	33	5/13/1971	6/18/1971	1
ARNOLD J. ISBELL	DD	869	5/18/1971	6/1/1971	AFDL-48
De HAVEN	DD	727	6/2/1971	6/10/1971	AFDL-48
GRAND RAPIDS	PG	98	6/3/1971	6/15/1971	AFDL-42
FRANCIS HAMMOND	DE	1067	6/15/1971	7/2/1971	2
HAMNER	DD	718	6/17/1971	7/30/1971	AFDL-48
CAMDEN	AOE	2	6/22/1971	8/17/1971	1
SUMTER	LST	1181	6/28/1971	7/8/1971	3
JOUETT	DLG	29	7/21/1971	8/19/1971	2
ANTELOPE	PG	86	7/22/1971	8/23/1971	3
READY	PG	87	7/22/1971	8/23/1971	3
WHITE SANDS	ARD	20	8/20/1971	9/3/1971	1
HOEL	DDG	13	8/23/1971	9/22/1971	3
CALIENTE	AO	53	8/24/1971	9/11/1971	2
DOUGLAS	PG	100	8/26/1971	9/3/1971	AFDL-42
WILTSIE	DD	716	8/27/1971	10/5/1971	AFDL-48
SOMERS	DDG	34	9/3/1971	10/4/1971	1
YARD CRAFT	YC	1395	9/3/1971	10/4/1971	1
SCHOFIELD	DEG	3	9/28/1971	11/10/1971	2
YARD CRAFT	YOS	9	9/28/1971	11/10/1971	2
SAN BERNARDINO	LST	1189	9/30/1971	11/9/1971	2
BLUE RIDGE	LCC	19	10/7/1971	11/11/1971	1
EVERSOLE	DD	789	10/7/1971	11/11/1971	1
OZBOURN	DD	846	10/7/1971	11/11/1971	1
CONCRETE CAISSON	CAISSON	2 & 3	10/26/1971	1/6/1979	1
FLOATING DOCK	YFD (CENTER	71	10/26/1971	11/6/1971	1
GERMAN CRANE (TITAN II)	YD	171	10/26/1971	1/6/1971	1
HOLLISTER	DD	788	10/28/1971	12/13/1971	AFDL-48
MAHAN	DLG	11	11/15/1971	11/30/1971	1
BRONSTEIN	DE	1037	11/16/1971	12/30/1971	3
YARD CRAFT	YC	799	11/16/1971	12/30/1971	3
HOLT	DE	706	11/30/1971	12/8/1971	3
BRADLEY	DE	1041	12/1/1971	3/20/1972	2
HOEL	DDG	13	12/8/1971	12/17/1971	1
IWO JIMA	LPH	2	12/17/1971	2/7/1972	1
YARD OIL BARGE	YON	2	12/17/1971	2/7/1972	1
SOMERS	DDG	34	12/22/1971	1/2/1972	AFDL-48
O'CALLAHAN	DE	1051	1/19/1972	5/2/1972	3
ANTELOPE	PG	86	2/14/1972	2/16/1972	AFDL-42
CONCRETE CAISSON	CAISSON	1	2/17/1972	4/4/1972	1
NEW ORLEANS	LPH	11	2/17/1972	4/4/1972	1
HENDERSON	DD	785	3/14/1972	5/12/1972	AFDL-48
MARVIN SHIELDS	DE	1066	3/28/1972	4/5/1972	2
TURNER JOY	DD	951	3/29/1972	5/11/1972	YFD-71

SHIP'S NAME	CLASS	NUMBER	DOCK	UNDOCK	DRYDOCK
BAINBRIDGE	DLGN	25	4/10/1972	5/3/1972	1
REASONER	DE	1063	4/11/1972	5/2/1972	2
ANTELOPE	PG	86	4/25/1972	5/10/1972	AFDL-42
READY	PG	87	4/25/1972	5/10/1972	AFDL-42
OGDEN	LPD	5	5/5/1972	6/19/1972	1
TOLOVANA	AO	64	5/9/1972	6/28/1972	3
TRUXTON	DLGN	35	5/10/1972	6/6/1972	2
HARLAN COUNTY	LST	1196	5/20/1972	5/25/1972	YFD-71
THEO. E. CHANDLER	DD	717	6/2/1972	7/25/1972	AFDL-48
SOUTHERLAND	DD	743	6/26/1972	8/17/1972	2
YARD CRAFT	YC	1120	6/26/1972	8/17/1972	2
YARD CRAFT	YSR	25	6/26/1972	8/17/1972	2
EDSON	DD	946	6/26/1972	8/17/1972	3
WABASH	AOR	5	7/17/1972	8/7/1972	1
LYNDE McCORMICK	DDG	8	8/9/1972	10/2/1972	1
AGERHOLM	DD	826	8/10/1972	10/4/1972	3
STEEL CAISSON	CAISSON	1	8/10/1972	10/4/1972	3
REASONER	DE	1063	9/9/1972	9/25/1972	2
HORNE	DLG	30	9/16/1972	10/2/1972	1
CHICAGO	CG	11	10/4/1972	1/17/1973	2
STEIN	DE	1065	10/12/1972	11/2/1972	3
FLOATING DRYDOCK	AFDL	48	10/17/1972	12/5/1972	1
PRAIRIE	AD	15	10/17/1972	12/5/1972	1
SPREADER CAMEL	NSY	377	10/17/1972	12/4/1972	1
SPREADER CAMEL	NSY	378	10/17/1972	12/4/1972	1
SPREADER CAMEL	NSY	379	10/17/1972	12/4/1972	1
DOUGLAS	PG	100	10/25/1972	12/4/1972	AFDL-42
GRAND RAPIDS	PG	98	10/25/1972	12/3/1972	AFDL-42
WHITE SANDS	ARD	20	11/8/1972	11/28/1972	3
BARBOUR COUNTY	LST	1195	12/6/1972	1/4/1973	YFD-71
NORTON SOUND	AVM	1	12/27/1972	3/14/1973	3
TUSCALOOSA	LST	1187	1/8/1973	2/21/1973	YFD-71
DENVER	LPD	9	1/30/1973	3/28/1972	1
FLOATING DOCK	YFD	71	1/30/1973	2/19/1973	1
YARD CRAFT	YC	1120	1/30/1973	3/28/1973	1
YARD CRAFT	YFN	1130	1/30/1973	3/28/1973	1
OKINAWA	LPH	3	2/6/1973	5/1/1973	2
FLOATING CRANE	YD	192	4/3/1973	7/3/1973	1
HEPBURN	DE	1055	4/3/1973	7/3/1973	1
ROBISON	DDG	12	4/3/1973	7/3/1973	1
YARD CRAFT	YFN	1130	4/3/1973	7/3/1973	1
YARD CRAFT	YFP	3	4/3/1973	7/3/1973	1
YARD CRAFT	YSR	26	4/3/1973	7/3/1973	1
BARBEY	DE	1088	6/5/1973	10/9/1973	2
STEEL CAISSON	CAISSON	2	6/5/1973	10/9/1973	2
YARD CRAFT	YC	1116	6/28/1973	8/6/1973	AFDL-48

SHIP'S NAME	CLASS	NUMBER	DOCK	UNDOCK	DRYDOCK
HEPBURN	DE	1055	7/3/1973	7/9/1973	1
PLEDGE	MSO	492	7/5/1973	7/19/1973	3
TOWERS	DDG	9	7/9/1973	8/27/1973	1
YARD CRAFT	YC	1082	7/9/1973	8/27/1973	1
YARD CRAFT	YC	1115	7/9/1973	8/27/1973	1
MECOSTA	YTB	818	7/9/1973	7/17/1973	AFDL-42
LANG	DE	1060	7/23/1973	10/25/1973	3
PLEDGE	MSO	492	7/27/1973	8/2/1973	AFDL-42
UTE	ATF	76	8/8/1973	8/31/1973	AFDL-48
MEYERKORD	DE	1058	10/23/1973	10/30/1973	2
HENRY B. WILSON	DDG	7	10/30/1973	2/19/1974	1
MEYERKORD	DE	1058	10/30/1973	2/19/1974	1
HEPBURN	DE	1055	11/2/1973	12/27/1973	3
RAMSEY	DEG	2	11/8/1973	3/12/1974	2
YARD CRAFT	YC	789	11/8/1973	3/12/1974	2
YARD CRAFT	YFN	272	11/8/1973	3/12/1974	2
FOX	DLG	33	1/11/1974	5/13/1974	3
BARBEY	DE	1088	1/15/1974	1/22/1974	AFDL-48
MARVIN SHIELDS	DE	1066	1/29/1974	2/3/1975	3
McKEAN	DD	784	2/11/1974	4/1/1974	AFDL-48
DUBUQUE	LPD	8	2/25/1974	5/29/1974	1
THOMASTON	LSD	28	2/25/1974	5/29/1974	1
LANG	DE	1060	3/14/1974	3/25/1974	2
LANG	DE	1060	3/26/1974	4/1/1974	2
STERETT	DLG	31	4/5/1974	6/2/1974	2
TURNER JOY	DD	951	4/18/1974	4/22/1974	AFDL-48
BARBEY	DE	1088	5/3/1974	5/15/1974	AFDL-48
MEYERKORD	DE	1058	5/4/1974	6/24/1974	1
FLOATING CRANE	YD	87	5/17/1974	8/13/1974	3
ROARK	DE	1053	5/17/1974	8/13/1974	3
HULL	DD	945	5/17/1974	9/4/1974	AFDL-48
GERMAN CRANE (TITAN II)	YD	171	6/4/1974	7/19/1974	1
POP-UP (INACTIVATION)	STAGING VESSEL	N/A	6/4/1974	7/19/1974	1
LANG	DE	1060	6/27/1974	7/30/1974	2
WICHITA	AOR	1	7/19/1974	9/12/1974	1
FRANCIS HAMMOND	DE	1067	8/5/1974	11/18/1974	2
MARVIN SHIELDS	DE	1066	8/15/1974	10/3/1974	3
YARD CRAFT	YC	1085	8/15/1974	1/14/1974	3
YARD CRAFT	YOS	9	8/15/1974	10/10/1974	3
BARBEY	DE	1088	9/6/1974	10/3/1974	AFDL-48
ORISKANY	CVA	34	9/24/1974	1/22/1975	1
QUELLET	DE	1077	10/10/1974	1/14/1975	3
HMAS PERTH	D	38	11/22/1974	12/19/1974	2
YARD CRAFT	YC	789	11/22/1974	12/19/1974	2
YARD CRAFT	YC	1499	11/22/1974	12/19/1974	2
HOEL	DDG	13	2/4/1975	5/29/1975	1

SHIP'S NAME	CLASS	NUMBER	DOCK	UNDOCK	DRYDOCK
PIGEON	ASR	21	2/4/1975	5/29/1975	1
YARD CRAFT	YC	1120	2/4/1975	5/29/1975	1
BARBEY	DE	1088	2/4/1975	4/2/1975	3
CAYUGA	LST	1186	2/10/1975	4/16/1975	YFD-71
WADDELL	DDG	24	3/4/1975	5/22/1975	2
YARD CRAFT	YC	1383	3/4/1975	5/22/1975	2
BUCHANAN	DDG	14	4/14/1975	6/23/1975	3
YARD CRAFT	YC	789	4/14/1975	6/23/1975	3
A. A. CUNNINGHAM	DD	752	4/18/1975	5/19/1975	YFD-71
DECATUR	DDG	31	5/29/1975	8/4/1975	2
YARD CRAFT	YC	1116	5/29/1975	8/4/1975	2
JOUETT	DLG	29	6/5/1975	7/29/1975	1
YARD CRAFT	YC	1088	6/5/1975	7/29/1975	1
JOHN S. McCAIN	DDG	36	7/14/1975	9/18/1975	3
BRADLEY	DE	1041	8/11/1975	10/15/1975	2
YARD CRAFT	YC	1383	8/11/1975	10/15/1975	2
CORAL SEA	CVA	43	8/27/1975	12/30/1975	1
LYNDE McCORMICK	DDG	8	10/7/1975	12/23/1975	3
YARD CRAFT	YC	1499	10/7/1975	12/23/1975	3
GUDGEON	SS	567	12/11/1975	3/10/1976	AFDL-48
BARBEY	FF	1088	1/13/1976	3/22/1976	2
BLUE RIDGE	LCC	19	1/19/1976	3/19/1976	1
EDSON	DD	946	1/27/1976	4/1/1976	3
WORK BARGE 80'	N/A	N/A	1/27/1976	4/1/1976	3
YARD CRAFT	YC	1120	1/27/1976	4/1/1976	3
DECATUR	DDG	31	2/13/1976	2/15/1976	YFD-71
JOHN PAUL JONES	DDG	32	2/18/1976	4/16/1976	YFD-71
CANON	PG	90	3/16/1976	4/15/1976	AFDL-48
LANG	FF	1060	3/22/1976	4/8/1976	2
O'CALLAHAN	DE	1051	4/2/1976	6/22/1976	1
SCHOFIELD	DEG	3	4/2/1976	6/22/1976	1
YARD CRAFT	YC	983	4/2/1976	6/22/1976	1
YARD CRAFT	YC	1116	4/2/1976	6/22/1976	1
ALBERT DAVID	FF	1050	5/4/1976	8/3/1976	3
YARD CRAFT	YC	1088	5/4/1976	8/3/1976	3
REASONER	FF	1063	5/11/1976	8/18/1976	2
YARD CRAFT	YC	1367	5/11/1976	8/18/1976	2
HENDERSON	DD	785	6/15/1976	7/30/1976	YFD-71
DENVER	LPD	9	7/1/1976	9/16/1976	1
WATER BARGE	YWN	70	7/1/1976	9/16/1976	1
HULL	DD	945	7/9/1976	7/20/1976	AFDL-48
CONCRETE CAISSON	CAISSON	2 & 3	9/8/1976	11/8/1976	3
YARD CRAFT	YC	1394	9/8/1976	11/2/1976	3
YARD CRAFT	YC	1487	9/8/1976	11/2/1976	3
YARD CRAFT	YOS	20	9/8/1976	11/2/1976	3
SQUAW	FAUX MINI-SUB	29	9/16/1976	10/26/1976	1

SHIP'S NAME	CLASS	NUMBER	DOCK	UNDOCK	DRYDOCK
WATER BARGE	YWN	70	9/16/1976	10/26/1976	1
HORNE	CG	30	10/1/1976	1/24/1977	2
CONSTELLATION	CVA	64	10/28/1976	11/17/1976	1
DOLPHIN	AGSS	555	10/29/1976	11/22/1976	AFDL-48
LEAHY	CG	16	11/10/1976	2/24/1977	3
CONCRETE CASSION	CAISSON	2 & 3	12/7/1976	2/28/1977	1
ROBISON	DDG	12	12/7/1976	2/28/1977	1
YARD CRAFT	YC	1366	12/7/1976	2/28/1976	1
REASONER	FF	1063	2/16/1977	2/18/1977	AFDL-48
O'CALLAHAN	DE	1051	2/27/1977	4/19/1977	3
DOWNES	FF	1070	3/1/1977	5/13/1977	2
CLEVELAND	LPD	7	3/2/1977	5/19/1977	1
ALBERT DAVID	FF	1050	3/7/1977	3/11/1977	AFDL-48
BAGLEY	DE	1069	3/16/1977	3/30/1977	AFDL-48
FLOATING DOCK	YFD (N. END SEC.)	71	4/28/1977	9/27/1977	1
JOUETT	CG	29	5/18/1977	5/26/1977	2
RAMSEY	FFG	2	5/20/1977	9/16/1977	3
YARD OIL BARGE	YON	2	5/20/1977	9/16/1977	3
CONCRETE CAISSON	CAISSON	1	6/6/1977	6/7/1977	1
OKINAWA	LPH	3	6/7/1977	7/29/1977	1
DURHAM	LKA	114	7/12/1977	9/29/1977	2
HEWITT	DD	966	8/11/1977	8/22/1977	1
TARAWA	LHA	1	9/13/1977	11/22/1977	1
CONSTANT	MSO	427	9/22/1977	10/4/1977	AFDL-48
HENRY B. WILSON	DDG	7	9/23/1977	12/1/1977	3
STEEL CAISSON	CAISSON	3	9/23/1977	12/1/1977	3
HALSEY	CG	23	10/7/1977	12/22/1977	2
TURNER JOY	DD	951	12/14/1977	3/7/1978	3
GLOMAR EXPLORER	N/A	N/A	1/11/1978	1/17/1979	1
PAUL F. FOSTER	DD	964	1/24/1978	2/22/1978	1
YARD CRAFT	SWOB	20	1/24/1978	2/22/1978	1
GRIDLEY	DLG	21	2/1/1978	4/19/1978	2
KINKAID	DD	965	2/25/1978	3/15/1978	1
YARD CRAFT	SWOB	20	2/25/1978	3/15/1978	1
BARBEY	FF	1088	3/14/1978	5/25/1978	3
ELLIOTT	DD	967	3/18/1978	4/6/1978	1
YARD CRAFT	SWOB	20	3/18/1978	4/6/1978	1
BROOKE	DEG	1	4/12/1978	5/18/1978	AFDL-48
BAGLEY	FF	1069	4/25/1978	7/19/1978	2
ANCHORAGE	LSD	36	5/4/1978	6/25/1978	1
CONCRETE CAISSON	CAISSON	1	5/4/1978	10/18/1978	1
RAMSEY	FFG	2	7/6/1978	7/24/1978	AFDL-48
HEWITT	DD	966	7/20/1978	8/10/1978	3
NORTON SOUND	AVM	1	8/1/1978	10/18/1978	1
DAVID R. RAY	DD	971	8/2/1978	10/24/1978	2
O'BRIEN	DD	975	8/17/1978	9/19/1978	3

SHIP'S NAME	CLASS	NUMBER	DOCK	UNDOCK	DRYDOCK
BRADLEY	FF	1041	9/23/1978	9/28/1978	3
CONCRETE CAISSON	CAISSON	1	10/26/1978	2/20/1979	1
TOWERS	DDG	9	11/30/1978	3/21/1979	3
YARD CRAFT	YSD	60	11/30/1978	3/21/1979	3
JOHN YOUNG	DD	973	12/21/1978	1/9/1979	2
GLOMAR EXPLORER	WELL GATES	N/A	1/12/1979	1/17/1979	1
ROBISON	DDG	12	1/18/1979	1/29/1979	2
CONCRETE CAISSON	CAISSON	2 & 3	1/26/1979	2/20/1979	1
GERMAN CRANE (TITAN II)	YD	171	1/26/1979	2/20/1979	1
JOHN YOUNG	DD	973	2/13/1979	2/26/1979	2
OGDEN	LPD	5	2/28/1979	5/24/1979	1
PROTEUS	AS	19	2/28/1979	5/24/1979	1
HULL	DD	945	3/6/1979	6/1/1979	2
O'BRIEN	DD	975	5/15/1979	7/9/1979	3
COOK	FF	1083	6/6/1979	7/29/1979	2
YARD CRAFT	YC	1120	7/1/1979	8/14/1979	AFDL-48
FLOATING CRANE	YD	192	7/9/1979	7/16/1979	3
HOEL	DDG	13	7/10/1979	10/3/1979	2
STEEL CAISSON	CAISSON	1	7/10/1979	10/3/1979	2
O'BRIEN	DD	975	7/16/1979	7/20/1979	3
FLOATING CRANE	YD	192	7/26/1979	8/30/1979	3
PAINTERS BARGE	N/A	234	7/26/1979	8/30/1979	3
BRONSTEIN	FF	1037	8/20/1979	9/5/1979	AFDL-48
STERETT	CG	31	8/30/1979	12/17/1979	3
BELLEAU WOOD	LHA	3	9/20/1979	11/30/1979	1
FLOATING CHT TANK	N/A	N/A	11/8/1979	12/18/1979	AFDL-48
BROOKE	FFG	1	12/6/1979	4/3/1980	1
BUCHANAN	DDG	14	12/6/1979	4/3/1980	1
CONCRETE CAISSON	CAISSON	2 & 3	12/6/1979	4/9/1980	1
MEYERKORD	DE	1058	12/12/1979	1/9/1980	2
ENGLAND	CG	22	2/26/1980	5/8/1980	2
HEWITT	DD	966	3/25/1980	4/4/1980	3
KINKAID	DD	965	4/8/1980	4/16/1980	3
CONCRETE CAISSON	CAISSON	2 & 3	4/9/1980	7/8/1980	1
FRESNO	LST	1182	4/9/1980	4/11/1980	1
DAVID R. RAY	DD	971	5/1/1980	5/8/1980	3
WATER BARGE	YWN	70	5/1/1980	5/8/1980	AFDL-48
HOEL	DDG	13	5/20/1980	5/23/1980	1
JOUETT	CG	29	5/21/1980	8/29/1980	2
BERTHING BARGE	APL	2	7/8/1980	8/28/1980	1
CONCRETE CAISSON	CAISSON	1	7/8/1980	8/28/1980	1
FLOATING CRANE	YD	87	7/8/1980	8/28/1980	1
YARD CRAFT	YFP	3	7/8/1980	10/2/1980	1
YARD CRAFT	YSR	25	7/8/1980	8/28/1980	1
YARD CRAFT	YSR	26	7/8/1980	10/2/1980	1
CONCRETE CAISSON	CAISSON	2 & 3	7/17/1980	10/15/1980	3

SHIP'S NAME	CLASS	NUMBER	DOCK	UNDOCK	DRYDOCK
SCHOFIELD	FFG	3	7/17/1980	10/15/1980	3
JOHN YOUNG	DD	973	8/28/1980	9/5/1980	1
JOHN PAUL JONES	DDG	32	9/8/1980	12/10/1980	2
PAUL F. FOSTER	DD	964	10/5/1980	12/22/1980	1
TUSCALOOSA	LST	1187	10/22/1980	10/27/1980	3
JOUETT	CG	29	11/3/1980	11/20/1980	3
BRONSTEIN	FF	1037	12/2/1980	3/3/1981	3
PELELIU	LHA	5	1/5/1981	3/20/1981	1
DUNCAN	FFG	10	1/6/1981	3/5/1981	2
LEAHY	CG	16	3/11/1981	5/22/1981	2
DAVID R. RAY	DD	971	3/11/1981	4/7/1981	3
FLOATING DOCK	YFD (CENTER	71	3/30/1981	5/14/1981	1
FLOATING DOCK	YFD (N. END SEC.)	71	3/30/1981	5/14/1981	1
FLOATING DOCK	YFD (S. END SEC.)	71	3/30/1981	5/14/1981	1
KINKAID	DD	965	4/14/1981	7/22/1981	3
OLDENDORF	DD	972	5/20/1981	6/26/1981	1
HMAS ADELAIDE	FFG	17 (01)	6/1/1981	8/4/1981	2
STEEL CAISSON	CAISSON	2	6/1/1981	8/4/1981	2
HEWITT	DD	966	7/24/1981	10/25/1981	3
O'BRIEN	DD	975	7/25/1981	8/3/1981	1
BARBEY	FF	1088	8/8/1981	8/22/1981	2
TARAWA	LHA	1	8/12/1981	10/10/1981	1
HORNE	CG	30	8/31/1981	11/24/1981	2
BRONSTEIN	DE	1037	11/6/1981	11/16/1981	3
NEW JERSEY	BB	62	11/18/1981	3/13/1982	1
RAMSEY	FFG	2	1/7/1982	2/5/1982	3
JOHN YOUNG	DD	973	1/12/1982	2/25/1982	2
PAUL F. FOSTER	DD	964	2/26/1982	3/16/1982	2
HEWITT	DD	966	4/15/1982	5/9/1982	2
BERKELEY	DDG	15	4/27/1982	7/16/1982	3
HALSEY	CG	23	5/27/1982	10/1/1982	2
BROOKE	FFG	1	7/29/1982	8/9/1982	3
ELLIOTT	DD	967	8/20/1982	10/20/1982	1
FIFE	DD	991	9/1/1982	10/6/1982	3
CONCRETE CAISSON	CAISSON	1	10/22/1982	12/7/1982	1
YARD CRAFT	YC	1119	10/22/1982	12/7/1982	1
GRIDLEY	CG	21	11/2/1982	2/10/1983	3
BERTHING BARGE	YRBM	32	1/11/1983	3/13/1983	1
PAUL F. FOSTER	DD	964	1/11/1983	3/13/1983	1
HEWITT	DD	966	1/28/1983	3/14/1983	2
JOHN YOUNG	DD	973	2/23/1983	6/9/1983	3
CHRIS ZEPPA	BARGE		3/14/1983	3/16/1983	2
SSTV	N/A	N/A	3/15/1983	6/11/1983	2
OBSERVATION ISLAND	TAGM	23	3/21/1983	3/26/1983	2
FOX	CG	33	3/22/1983	7/5/1983	1
LANG	FF	1060	4/4/1983	8/6/1983	2

SHIP'S NAME	CLASS	NUMBER	DOCK	UNDOCK	DRYDOCK
CHRIS ZEPPA/SSTV	N/A	N/A	6/10/1983	6/11/1983	3
SHOP 72 DIVE BOAT	DIVE BOAT	N/A	6/16/1983	7/1/1983	3
CUSHING	DD	985	7/6/1983	8/16/1983	3
OGDEN	LPD	5	7/7/1983	10/6/1983	1
PIGEON	ASR	21	8/8/1983	12/9/1983	2
BRADLEY	FF	1041	8/22/1983	1/24/1984	3
HOEL	DDG	13	10/12/1983	1/31/1984	1
RAMSEY	FFG	2	10/12/1983	1/31/1984	1
O'CALLAHAN	FF	1051	12/9/1983	1/16/1984	2
POINT LOMA	AGDS	2	1/23/1984	3/10/1984	2
LANG	FF	1060	1/24/1984	3/21/1984	3
BARBEY	FF	1088	2/7/1984	5/15/1984	1
CONCRETE CAISSON	CAISSON	1	2/7/1984	7/24/1984	1
FLOATING CRANE	YD	159	2/7/1984	5/15/1984	1
FLOATING CRANE	YD	236	2/7/1984	5/15/1984	1
GERMAN CRANE (TITAN II)	YD	171	2/7/1984	5/15/1984	1
OLDENDORF	DD	972	3/19/1984	5/16/1984	2
MEYERKORD	FF	1058	3/27/1984	7/10/1984	3
STEEL CAISSON	CAISSON	3	3/27/1984	7/10/1984	3
WATER BARGE	YWN	70	5/23/1984	7/24/1984	1
YARD CRAFT	YC	1487	5/23/1984	7/24/1984	1
JOHN YOUNG	DD	973	6/29/1984	7/31/1984	2
MISSOURI	BB	63	8/11/1984	3/23/1985	1
GRAY	FF	1054	9/17/1984	12/14/1984	2
MARVIN SHIELDS	FF	1066	9/25/1984	1/28/1985	3
WADSWORTH	FFG	9	1/7/1985	3/14/1985	2
LANG	FF	1060	2/11/1985	2/25/1985	3
WADDELL	DDG	24	3/11/1985	7/31/1985	3
BERKELEY	DDG	15	5/4/1985	5/22/1985	2
FLOATING CRANE	YD	192	7/9/1985	9/17/1985	2
YARD CRAFT	YFN	1178	7/9/1985	9/17/1985	2
BUCHANAN	DDG	14	8/12/1985	1/9/1985	3
FLETCHER	DD	992	9/26/1985	10/31/1985	2
BERTHING BARGE	APL	4	11/12/1985	12/6/1985	2
BERTHING BARGE	APL	5	11/12/1985	12/6/1985	2
PELELIU	LHA	5	1/6/1986	4/7/1986	1
CHRIS ZEPPA/SSTV	N/A	N/A	1/14/1986	4/2/1986	2
BERTHING BARGE	YRBM	37	4/2/1986	6/16/1986	2
CLEVELAND	LPD	7	4/21/1986	8/12/1986	1
BUCHANAN	DDG	14	6/16/1986	6/17/1986	2
BERTHING BARGE	IX	503	6/17/1986	8/22/1986	2
CONCRETE CAISSON	CAISSON	2 & 3	8/12/1986	1/5/1987	1
BERTHING BARGE	IX	503	8/22/1986	8/28/1986	2
YARD CRAFT	SWOB	14	8/28/1986	10/9/1986	2
FLETCHER	DD	992	10/2/1986	4/4/1987	3
YARD CRAFT	SWOB	14	10/9/1986	10/21/1986	2

SHIP'S NAME	CLASS	NUMBER	DOCK	UNDOCK	DRYDOCK
ENGLAND	CG	22	10/21/1986	3/24/1987	2
VALLEY FORGE	CG	50	1/5/1987	1/20/1987	1
NEW JERSEY	BB	62	3/9/1987	7/25/1987	1
JOHN A. MOORE	FFG	19	3/31/1987	6/12/1987	2
JOHN A. MOORE	FFG	19	5/12/1987	6/10/1987	2
FORD	FFG	54	6/14/1987	6/17/1987	2
ALAMO	LSD	33	7/1/1987	8/6/1987	2
NEW JERSEY	BB	62	7/25/1987	8/13/1987	1
LEAHY	CG	16	8/11/1987	1/26/1988	3
NEW JERSEY	BB	62	8/13/1987	8/29/1987	1
TARAWA	LHA	1	9/10/1987	2/4/1988	1
FLOATING CRANE	YD	244	10/20/1987	6/16/1988	2
PIGEON	ASR	21	10/20/1987	6/16/1988	2
LEAHY	CG	16	1/26/1988	2/2/1988	3
JOUETT	CG	29	4/15/1988	10/3/1988	3
DAVID R. RAY	DD	971	6/9/1988	1/17/1989	1
CHANDLER	DDG	996	8/17/1988	8/29/1988	2
LOCKWOOD	FF	1064	9/1/1988	12/13/1988	2
HORNE	CG	30	10/28/1988	5/2/1989	3
MISSOURI	BB	63	2/3/1989	4/25/1989	1
MOBILE	LKA	115	4/11/1989	7/6/1989	2
VINCENNES	CG	49	6/5/1989	8/1/1989	3
STEADFAST	AFDM	14	6/8/1989	9/14/1989	1
STEEL CAISSON	CAISSON	1	6/8/1989	14/9/89	1
MARVIN SHIELDS	FF	1066	8/15/1989	10/26/1989	2
CALLAGHAN	DDG	994	9/19/1989	3/23/1990	3
RANGER	CV	61	9/29/1989	11/20/1989	1
HAMMOND	FF	1067	12/12/1989	3/6/1990	1
JOHN YOUNG	DD	973	1/3/1990	8/16/1990	2
SAN ONOFRE	ARD	30	3/20/1990	7/24/1990	1
INGRAHAM	FFG	61	3/28/1990	5/11/1990	3
FLETCHER	DD	992	6/26/1990	7/10/1990	3
NEW JERSEY	BB	62	8/23/1990	11/6/1990	1
STEEL CAISSON	CAISSON	2	9/6/1990	11/9/1990	2
YARD CRAFT	SWOB	51	9/6/1990	11/9/1990	2
YARD CRAFT	YSR	26	9/6/1990	11/9/1990	2
YARD CRAFT	YC	789	10/5/1990	1/10/1991	3
YARD CRAFT	YC	1487	10/5/1990	1/10/1991	3
YARD CRAFT	YFN	1130	10/5/1990	1/10/1991	3
NEW JERSEY	BB	62	11/6/1990	11/13/1990	1
KNOX	FF	1052	11/15/1990	12/18/1990	2
BELLEAU WOOD	LHA	3	12/6/1990	4/30/1991	1
CONCRETE CAISSON	CAISSON	2 & 3	12/6/1990	8/20/1991	1
YARD CRAFT	SWOB	14	1/31/1991	3/21/1991	3
YARD CRAFT	SWOB	20	1/31/1991	3/21/1991	3
YARD CRAFT	YOS	20	1/31/1991	3/21/1991	3

SHIP'S NAME	CLASS	NUMBER	DOCK	UNDOCK	DRYDOCK
ANTIETAM	CG	54	3/25/1991	6/14/1991	3
JOHN A. MOORE	FFG	19	4/9/1991	7/2/1991	2
YARD CRAFT	YFN	820	4/30/1991	6/26/1991	1
REUBEN JAMES	FFG	57	6/26/1991	7/23/1991	1
YARD CRAFT	YO	47	7/23/1991	8/20/1991	1
OLDENDORF	DD	972	7/29/1991	3/10/1992	2
PAUL F. FOSTER	DD	964	8/27/1991	11/26/1991	3
ANCHORAGE	LSD	36	10/1/1991	1/9/1992	1
YARD CRAFT	YC	1383	10/1/1991	1/9/1992	1
YARD CRAFT	YC	1499	10/1/1991	1/9/1992	1
PELELIU	LHA	5	1/28/1992	7/9/1992	1
VINCENNES	CG	49	4/16/1992	4/24/1992	2
ROANOKE	AOR	7	7/21/1992	11/14/1992	1
BREWTON (EX)	FF	1086	8/15/1992	11/15/1992	3
MERRILL	DD	976	10/3/1992	4/8/1993	2
PEARY (EX)	FF	1073	11/15/1992	1/20/1993	3
MOBILE	LKA	115	1/9/1993	2/17/1993	1
DAVID R. RAY	DD	971	1/30/1993	4/8/1993	3
OGDEN	LPD	5	2/24/1993	5/27/1993	1
KIRK (EX)	FF	1087	4/17/1993	6/3/1993	3
INGRAHAM	FFG	61	4/18/1993	5/4/1993	2
MOUNT VERNON	LSD	39	5/15/1993	7/18/1993	2
ANTIETAM	CG	54	6/5/1993	6/12/1993	1
RANGER	CV	61	7/24/1993	10/16/1993	1
YARD CRAFT	YC	789	8/14/1993	10/26/1993	3
YARD CRAFT	YC	1119	8/14/1993	10/26/1993	3
TARAWA	LHA	1	10/30/1993	5/14/1994	1
CONCRETE CAISSON	CAISSON	2 & 3	1/8/1994	7/15/1994	3
PRINCETON	CG	59	2/25/1994	5/26/1994	2
WATER BARGE	YWN	70	6/10/1994	9/30/1994	2
YARD CRAFT	SWOB	20	6/10/1994	9/30/1994	2
YARD CRAFT	SWOB	51	6/10/1994	9/30/1994	2
HEWES (EX)	FF	1087	7/29/1994	10/25/1994	3
BARBEY (EX)	FF	1088	9/16/1994	1/6/1994	1
COOK (EX)	FF	1083	9/16/1994	1/6/1994	1
ANTIETAM	CG	54	10/7/1994	3/23/1995	2
PAUL F. FOSTER	DD	964	1/20/1995	6/23/1995	3
GERMAN CRANE (TITAN II)	YD	171	4/21/1995	1/8/1996	1
KINKAID	DD	965	7/21/1995	2/9/1996	2
DECATUR (EX)	DDG	31	9/8/1995	10/31/1995	3
DAVID R. RAY	DD	971	11/7/1995	3/15/1996	3
STEADFAST	AFDM	14	1/8/1996	5/22/1996	1

APPENDIX B
Special or noteworthy dockings at LBNSY

One Thursday evening at Curley's Café in Signal Hill, where a few ex-shipyarders and Naval Station people meet, I was bragging to Vaughn Garvey about the dry docking database Joseph Saltalamachia uploaded to me. Vaughn said he had a hard copy of that list though it only went up to 1985. However, in addition he also had a breakdown of dry dockings of special meaning relating to war damaged ships.

Well, I certainly had to have that for this book.. A couple of days later I met him in his office at EarthTech on the former shipyard property and he loaned me his copy. The cover also gave me another inspiration as it had four of the old shipyard logos on it and they appear in a later appendix (I also found a fifth logo that has been added in as well).

Reading the special dockings was a trip back into time. It listed ships that had received serious damage from collisions, bombs, torpedoes and Kamikazes that required our healing touch. It also included the dates of first dry dockings of the ships of major classes and, thanks to Salty's updated database, I was able to add in the last ships prior to shipyard closure. Where the list identified battle damage inflicted on a ship, I verified it through the DANFS web site and was even able to add more information (such as what kind of plane was sacrificed in the Kamikaze attack). I also verified ship identifications and war records from the Naval Vessel Register and other Internet resources.

The list did have some errors in it, however, particularly in bow replacements of a couple of the Destroyers. The list claimed that Shop 11 made new bows for the ships when, in fact, bows from unfinished Destroyers were used instead. Through DANFS and other web sites I was able not only able to verify that bows from unfinished ships were used, but precisely what the hull numbers were of the unfinished ships. Actually only the USS *Ozbourn* and USS *Cook* had to have their bows built anew.

I was also able to add in a couple more special interest dockings such as the hull repair on the Chinese LST *Chung Chi* and the unusual SONAR dome replacement of the USS *Stein* because a mysterious sea creature nibbled on it.

Thanks to the complete database I had going up to 1996 I was able to add more to this list including the last page tabulating the grand total of all dry dockings from Day One to closure. I think I have been able to highlight all of the most interesting dry dockings and have triple checked their accuracy for historians to rely on.

Long Beach Naval Shipyard, originally known as U.S. Naval Dry Docks Terminal Island from August of 1942 to 30 November 1945 and then known as Terminal Island Naval Shipyard from 30 November 1945 to 29 February 1948. It was known as the Long Beach Naval Shipyard since then even during its closure from 1 July 1950 to 1 February 1951. It was reopened in 1951 due to the Korean War and served the fleet during the Viet Nam War, Lebanon action and Gulf War.

Dry Docks utilized with first and last usage:

Dock	1st docking	Craft or Ship	Last undocking	Craft or Ship
DD #1	08/15/42	A&P Pile Driver	05/22/96	AFDM *Steadfast*
DD #2	07/22/43	USS *Oglala* (ARG-1	07/21/96	USS *Kinkaid* (DD-965)
DD #3	04/09/43	USS *Sterope* (AK-96)	03/15/96	USS *David R. Ray* (DD-971)
ARD-10	11/22/44	USS *McClelland* (DE-750)	08/19/46	LCI 975
ARD-8	02/10/45	USS *Kane* (APD-18)	11/01/46	USS *Chopper* (SS-342)
ARD-4	02/27/45	USS *Carpenter* (DD-650)	04/17/45	USS *Ramsay* (DM-16)
YFD-8	1/18/46	PCE (R) 857	07/30/47	USS *Picking* (DD-685)
*AFDL-43	07/02/46	USS *Kewaydin* (ATO-34)	12/07/49	USS *Kenshaw* (YTB-255)
*AFDL-44	07/24/47	USS *Wood* (DD-715)	12/08/49	USS *George W. Ingram* (APD-43)
AFDL-42	04/09/51	USS *McNair* (DD-679)	08/02/73	USS *Pledge* (MSO-492)
AFDL-48	10/25/66	USS *Black* (DD-666)	05/08/80	YWN-70 (Water Barge)
YFD-71	05/20/72	USS *Marlan County* (LST-1196)	09/27/77	YFD End Section (Floating Dock)

*First usage with the AFDL classification. Originally classified as ARD (C) 10 and ARD (C) 11 respectively. The ARD (C) 10 was referred to as ARD-10 in the docking logs.

First ship docked at U.S. Naval Dry Docks:
    USS *Kendrick* (DD-612)   09/13/42   Dry Dock 1

First Battleship docked at U.S. Naval Dry Docks:
    USS *Nevada* (BB-36)   02/24/43   Dry Dock 1

First Aircraft Carriers docked at U.S. Naval Dry Docks:
    USS *Kalinin Bay* (CVE-68)   12/05/44   Dry Dock 2 (First Escort Carriers)
    USS *Santee* (CVE-29)   12/05/44   Dry Dock 1 (First Escort Carriers)
    USS Kearsarge (CVA-33)   05/14/53   Dry Dock 1 (First Attack Carrier)

First gun Cruiser docked at U.S. Naval Dry Docks:
    USS *St. Louis* (CL-49)   08/16/44   Dry Dock 3

First Submarine docked at U.S. Naval Dry Docks:
    USS *Ronquil* (SS-396)   09/24/46   ARD-8

DOCKINGS OF MAJOR SHIPS BY CLASS

<u>BATTLESHIPS: (All in Dry Dock 1)</u>

USS *Nevada* (BB-36)	02/23/43 to 03/15/43	*(1)*
" " "	12/02/45 to 12/07/45	
USS *West Virginia* (BB-48)	08/30/44 to 09/06/44	
USS *California* (BB-44)	05/03/45 to 05/05/45	
USS *Texas* (BB-35)	12/08/45 to 12/12/45	
USS *Iowa* (BB-61)	12/16/45 to 12/22/45	
USS *Arkansas* (BB-33)	02/04/46 to 02/06/46 (Prepared for Bikini Atomic tests)	
USS *New Jersey* (BB-62)	11/18/81 to 03/13/82 (Reactivation and Modernization)	
" " " "	03/09/87 to 08/29/87 (Hull repairs with two "bumps")	
" " " "	08/23/90 to 11/13/90 (Inactivation)	*(2)*
USS *Missouri* (BB-63)	08/11/84 to 03/23/85 (Reactivation and Modernization)	
" " "	02/03/89 to 04/25/89 (Hull modifications)	

(1) First docking of a Battleship at LBNSY
(2) Last docking of a Battleship at LBNSY

<u>OTHER BATTLESHIP AVAILABILITY'S (PIERSIDE ONLY – NO DRY DOCKING):</u>

USS *Mississippi* (BB-41)	1945	
USS *Maryland* (BB-46)	1945	
USS *Pennsylvania* (BB-38)	1945	
USS *Nevada* (BB-36)	1946	(Prepared for Bikini Atomic tests)
USS *Missouri* (BB-63)	04/12/51	
USS New Jersey (BB-62)	04/01/53	
USS *Wisconsin* (BB-64)	04/19/52	
" " "	09/23/53	
" " "	04/14/54	

<u>SPECIAL DOCKINGS (Dry Dock 1)</u>

German Crane (YD-171)	11/05/47 to 12/01/47 (Reassembly)
" " "	01/26/79 to 02/29/79 (Repaint inner ballast tanks)
" " "	04/21/95 to 01/08/96 (Inactivation)
Prinz Eugen (IX-300) ex-German Cruiser	03/29/46 to 04/10/46 (Prepared for Bikini Atomic tests)
Pop-Up Staging Vessel	05/09/58 to 06/03/58 (Assembly of Catamaran barges)
Pop-Up Fish Hook	12/19/58 to 01/23/59 (Assembly of Catamaran barges)
Queen Mary	04/06/68 to 05/17/68 (Hull sealing for museum status)
USS *Long Beach* (CGN-9)	04/03/69 to 04/25/69 (Only nuclear ship docked)
Glomar Explorer	01/11/79 to 01/17/79

WORLD WAR II TYPE (GUN) CRUISER DOCKINGS: (Reclassified DLGs not included)

Ship	Drydock	Dock – Undock	Notes
USS *St. Louis* (CL-49)	DD #3	08/16/43 – 10/06/44	Bomb damage
" " "	DD #1	12/31/44 – 02/06/45	
USS *Cleveland* (CL-55	DD #3	10/25/44 – 12/06/44	
USS *San Francisco* (CA-38)	DD #1	10/28/44 – 10/30/44	
USS *Wichita* (CA-45)	DD #3	12/16/44 – 02/08/45	Torpedo/bomb damage
" " "	DD #2	02/19/45 – 02/28/45	
USS *Mobile* (CL-63)	DD #2	02/01/45 – 02/24/45	
USS *Columbia* (CL-56)	DD #3	02/12/45 – 03/18/45	Kamikaze damage
" " "	DD #3	03/25/45 – 04/15/45	
USS *Boston* (CA-69)	DD #2	04/03/45 – 04/29/45	
USS *Santa Fe* (CL-60)	DD #3	04/27/45 – 05/11/45	
" " " "	DD #2	05/23/45 – 06/08/45	
" " " "	DD #2	07/08/45 – 07/08/45	
USS *Boise* (CL-47)	DD #3	07/29/45 – 08/10/45	
USS *Astoria* (CL-90)	DD #3	09/25/45 – 10/10/45	
" " "	DD #2	06/18/47 – 07/26/47	
USS *Miami* (CL-89)	DD #2	06/09/45 – 06/26/45	
USS *Topeka* (CL-67)	DD #2	11/15/45 – 11/27/45	
" " "	DD #2	01/17/47 – 02/06/47	
USS *Atlanta* (CL-104)	DD #2	11/29/45 – 12/06/45	
USS *Dayton* (CL-105)	DD #1	12/28/45 – 01/10/46	
USS *Chicago* (CA-136)	DD #1	12/28/45 – 01/18/46	(CG-11 mod not shown)
USS *Salt Lake City* (CA-25)	DD #1	01/18/46 – 02/04/46	
USS *Vicksburg* (CL-46)	DD #2	03/15/46 – 04/02/46	
USS *St. Paul* (CA-73)	DD #2	09/12/46 – 09/27/46	
" " "	DD #2	01/28/48 – 02/04/48	
" " "	DD #2	01/27/49 – 02/09/49	
" " "	DD #1	07/12/52 – 07/13/52	
" " "	DD #1	01/17/53 – 01/27/53	
" " "	DD #2	11/10/58 – 12/09/58	
" " "	DD #1	10/25/62 – 11/11/62	
" " "	DD #2	11/24/65 – 12/23/65	
" " "	DD #2	11/24/69 – 12/29/69	
USS *Fall River* (CA-131)	DD #2	12/14/46 – 12/23/46	
USS *Helena* (CA-75)	DD #3	07/22/47 – 08/01/47	
" " "	DD #2	01/05/49 – 01/18/49	
" " "	DD #2	05/25/49 – 06/02/49	
" " "	DD #1	05/10/55 – 06/10/55	
" " "	DD #1	12/17/55 – 12/22/55	
" " "	DD #2	07/13/56 – 08/13/56	
USS *Springfield* (CL-66)	DD #2	02/09/48 – 02/28/48	
USS *Dutluth* (CL-87)	DD #2	09/08/48 – 09/25/48	
USS *Manchester* (CL-83)	DD #3	03/15/54 – 03/16/54	
USS *Toledo* (CA-133)	DD #1	12/23/55 – 12/29/55	
" " "	DD #1	08/19/57 – 09/13/57	
" " "	DD #3	03/11/60 – 04/08/60	

WORLD WAR II TYPE (GUN) CRUISER DOCKINGS (continued):

Ship	Dry Dock	Dock Undock	Notes
USS *Los Angeles* (CA-135)	DD #3	01/05/56 – 02/03/56	
" " " "	DD #3	01/21/60 – 03/08/60	
" " " "	DD #2	05/17/62 – 06/08/62	
" " " "	DD #2	08/08/63 – 09/17/63	
" " " "	DD #2	11/05/65 – 11/22/65	
USS *Worchester* (CL-144)	DD #2	12/03/56 – 01/03/57	
USS *Bremerton* (CA-130)	DD #1	05/20/60 – 06/23/60	
USS *Providence* (CLG-6)	DD #2	08/11/60 – 08/23/60	
" " "	DD #3	10/13/61 – 10/18/62	
USS *Oklahoma City* (CLG-5)	DD #1	06/18/62 – 06/29/62	
" " " "	DD #3	04/11/63 – 05/14/63	
USS *Canberra* (CAG-2)	DD #3	03/17/64 – 04/15/64	
" " "	DD #3	07/28/67 – 09/07/67	
USS *Galveston* (CLG-3)	DD #1	10/20/64 – 11/16/64	
" " "	DD #2	09/06/66 – 09/29/66	
" " "	DD #2	02/08/68 – 03/12/68	

AIRCRAFT CARRIER DOCKINGS (Escort and Light Carriers):

Ship	Dry Dock	Dock Undock	Notes
USS *Kalinin Bay* (CVE-68)	DD #2	12/05/44 – 12/30/44	
USS *Santee* (CVE-29) (ex *Esso Seakay*)	DD #1	12/05/44 – 12/28/44	Converted (AO-29)
USS *Kwajalein* (CVE-98)	DD #1	03/02/45 – 03/07/45	
USS *Kitkun Bay* (CVE-71)	DD #1	03/07/45 – 03/22/45	
USS *Petrof Bay* (CVE-80)	DD #1	07/01/45 – 07/30/45	
USS *Admiralty Islands* (CVE-99)	DD #3	08/20/45 – 08/25/45	
USS *Sargent Bay* (CVE-83)	DD #1	08/23/45 – 09/07/45	
USS *Lunga Point* (CVE-94)	DD #1	11/23/45 – 11/28/45	
USS *Commencement Bay* (CVE-105)	DD #3	01/11/46 – 01/18/46	
USS *Rendova* (CVE-114)	DD #3	01/23/46 – 01/29/46	
" " "	DD #3	01/22/52 – 01/29/52	
" " "	DD #1	01/12/53 – 02/28/53	
USS *Kula Gulf* (CVE-108)	DD #3	01/29/46 – 02/12/46	
USS *Bairoko* (CVE-115)	DD #3	12/06/46 – 12/18/46	
" " "	DD #1	09/10/48 – 09/27/48	
" " "	DD #2	10/27/48 – 10/28/48	
" " "	DD #1	08/04/52 – 08/20/52	
" " "	DD #3	09/22/53 – 10/03/53	
USS *Sicily* (CVE-118)	DD #2	03/12/51 – 03/21/51	
" " "	DD #3	03/10/52 – 03/12/52	
" " "	DD #3	03/24/53 – 03/30/53	
USS *Bataan* (CVL-29) (ex USS *Buffalo*)	DD #1	10/19/52 – 10/21/52	ex (CL-29)
USS *Point Cruz* (CVE-119)	DD #1	01/21/55 – 01/24/55	
" " " "	DD #1	01/26/55 – 02/21/55	
USS *Thetis Bay* (CVE-90) – Later (CVHA-1)	DD #1	08/11/58 – 09/04/58	
" " " (CVHA-1) – Later (LPH-1)	DD #1	07/26/60 – 08/19/60	
USS *Makassar Straight* (CVE-91)	DD #1	01/23/59 – 02/04/59	

AIRCRAFT CARRIER DOCKINGS (Attack & ASW Carriers):

Ship	Dry Dock	Dock – Undock	Notes
USS *Kearsarge* (CVA-33)	DD #1	05/14/53 – 05/21/53	Later CV-33
" " (CV-33)	DD #1	02/10/59 – 03/23/59	Later CVS-33
" " (CVS-33)	DD #1	03/04/65 – 04/02/65	
" " (CVS-33)	DD #1	05/23/68 – 08/05/68	
" " (CVS-33)	DD #1	11/20/69 – 12/12/69	Inactivation
USS *Shangri-La* (CVA-38)	DD #1	10/04/56 – 10/06/56	
USS *Philippine Sea* (CV-47)	DD #1	09/10/58 – 10/15/58	
USS *Lexington* (CVA-16)	DD #1	03/31/59 – 04/01/59	
USS *Yorktown* (CV-10)	DD #1	12/04/63 – 01/10/64	Later CVS-10
" " (CVS-10)	DD #1	04/17/67 – 08/05/67	
USS *Bennington* (CVS-20)	DD #1	12/12/65 – 02/02/66	
" " "	DD #1	01/07/69 – 03/19/69	
USS *Bon Homme Richard* (CVA-31)	DD #1	04/12/66 – 07/07/66	
" " " " "	DD #1	12/09/68 – 01/02/69	
USS *Hornet* (CVS-12)	DD #1	11/27/67 – 02/16/68	
USS *Ticonderoga* (CVA-14)	DD #1	08/26/68 – 10/07/68	
" " "	DD #1	12/15/69 – 03/31/70	
USS *Oriskany* (CVA-34)	DD #1	09/24/74 – 01/22/75	
USS *Coral Sea* (CVA-43)	DD #1	08/27/75 – 12/30/75	
USS *Constellation* (CVA-64)	DD #1	10/28/76 – 11/17/76	
USS *Ranger* (CV-61)	DD #1	09/29/89 – 11/20/89	
" " "	DD #1	07/24/93 – 10/16/93	Inactivation *

HELICOPTER CARRIER AND HELICOPTER ASSAULT SHIP DOCKINGS:

Ship	Dry Dock	Dock – Undock	Notes
USS *Princeton* (LPH-5)	DD #1	07/01/59 – 07/24/59	ex CV-37
" " "	DD #1	12/28/60 – 03/16/61	
" " "	DD #1	02/11/64 – 04/14/64	
" " "	DD #1	08/09/67 – 11/16/67	
USS *Valley Forge* (LPH-8)	DD #1	07/17/63 – 10/03/64	ex CV-45
" " " "	DD #1	02/09/67 – 03/30/67	
USS *Iwo Jima* (LPH-2)	DD #1	07/29/64 – 09/03/64	
" " " "	DD #1	10/10/68 – 12/06/68	
" " " "	DD #1	12/17/71 – 02/07/72	
USS *Okinawa* (LPH-3)	DD #1	10/13/69 – 11/17/69	
" " "	DD #2	02/06/73 – 05/01/73	
" " "	DD #1	06/07/77 – 07/29/77	
USS *Tripoli* (LPH-10)	DD #2	02/23/70 – 02/27/70	
USS *New Orleans* (LPH-11)	DD #1	02/17/72 – 04/04/72	
USS *Tarawa* (LHA-1)	DD #1	09/13/77 – 11/22/77	
" " "	DD #1	08/12/81 – 10/10/81	
" " "	DD #1	09/10/87 – 02/04/88	
" " "	DD #1	10/30/93 – 05/14/94	**
USS *Belleau Wood* (LHA-3)	DD #1	09/20/79 – 11/30/79	
" " " "	DD #1	12/06/90 – 04/30/91	
USS *Peleliu* (LHA-5)	DD #1	01/05/81 – 03/20/81	
" " "	DD #1	01/06/86 – 04/07/86	
" " "	DD #1	01/28/92 – 07/09/92	

Though LBNSY was not considered to be a Submarine yard, as compared to Mare Island, 34 dockings of 25 Submarines over its history says something about the versatility of the shipyard.

The dockings of the unmanned *Squaw* research submarines are not included as identification of which vessel was in which dry dock cannot be made.

SUBMARINE DOCKINGS:

Ship	Dry Dock	Dock	Undock	Notes
USS *Ronquil* (SS-396)	ARD-8	09/24/46	09/27/46	First docking of a Sub
" " "	AFDL-44	03/15/48	03/20/48	
USS *Diodon* (SS-349)	ARD-8	10/14/46	10/17/46	
" " "	AFDL-43	11/29/48	12/03/48	
USS *Chivo* (SS-341)	AFDL-43	10/21/46	10/25/46	
" " "	AFDL-44	03/22/48	03/27/48	
USS *Scabbardfish* (SS-397)	ARD-8	10/21/46	10/24/46	
USS *Chopper* (SS-342)	ARD-8	10/28/46	11/01/46	
" " "	DD #2	04/05/48	04/09/48	
USS *Segundo* (SS-398)	DD #2	11/12/46	11/25/46	
" " "	AFDL-44	07/26/48	07/30/48	
USS *Sawfish* (SS-276)	DD #2	09/10/47	09/24/47	Home ported at Naval Station until replaced by Roncador.
" " "	DD #1	04/16/52	05/02/52	
" " "	DD #2	11/30/55	12/16/55	
USS *Catfish* (SS-339)	AFDL-44	03/08/48	03/12/48	
" " "	AFDL-48	01/04/67	01/09/67	
USS *Cusk* (SS-348)	AFDL-44	03/29/48	04/03/48	
USS *Remora* (SS-487)	AFDL-44	06/01/48	06/05/48	
USS *Blenny* (SS-324)	AFDL-44	08/02/48	08/06/48	
USS *Baya* (SS-318)	AFDL-44	01/01/49	01/18/49	
USS *Barbero* (SS-317)	AFDL-43	07/18/49	07/27/49	
USS *Charr* (SS-329)	AFDL-44	01/03/49	01/07/49	
USS *Capitaine* (SS-336)	AFDL-43	03/28/49	04/01/49	

SUBMARINE DOCKINGS (Continued):

Ship	Dry Dock	Dock – Undock	Notes
USS *Blower* (SS-325)	AFDL-43	04/04/49 – 04/08/49	
USS *Carbonero* (SS-337)	AFDL-43	05/23/49 – 05/23/49	
" " "	AFDL-43	07/29/49 – 08/01/49	
USS *Carp* (SS-338)	AFDL-44	06/27/49 – 07/08/49	
USS *Redfish* (SS-395)	DD #2	08/02/49 – 08/11/49	
USS *Steelhead* (SS-280)	DD #1	01/03/52 – 02/07/52	
USS *Roncador* (SS-301)	AFDL-42	10/03/63 – 10/23/63	"Acted" as Pink Submarine for TV series. The Conning Tower is on display in San Diego.
RGN *Triaina* (S-86) (ex SS-397)	AFDL-42	03/18/65 – 03/23/65	
USS *Caiman* (SS-323)	AFDL-42	04/01/66 – 04/24/66	
USS *Gudgeon* (SS-567)	AFDL-48	12/11/75 – 03/10/76	
USS *Dolphin* (AGSS-555)	AFDL-48	10/29/76 – 11/22/76	Last docking of a Sub

SHIPS REPAIRED AT LBNSY THAT WERE LATER LOST AT SEA:

Ship	Date lost	Where & How lost
USS *Abner Read* (DD-526)	11/01/44	Philippines – "Val" Kamikazi & bomb.
USS *Callaghan* (DD-792)	07/28/45	Okinawa - sunk by Kamikaze hit.
USS *Thornton* (AVD-11)	04/05/45	Ryukus – Collision with *Ashtabula* (AO-51) and *Escalante* (AO-70) – Abandoned on beach.
USS *Frank E. Evans* (DD-754)	06/03/69	Collision with Carrier HMAS *Melbourn* in South China Sea.

MAJOR COLLISION REPAIRS (BOW REPLACEMENTS):

Ship	Dry Dock	Dock – Undock	Notes
USS *Ozbourn* (DD-846)	DD #3	04/05/49 – 04/21/49	Collision in China Sea with USS *Theodore E. Chandler* (DD-717) - New bow built and installed by Shop 11.
USS *Ernst G. Small* (DD-838)	DD #1	10/01/52 – 10/16/52	Hit enemy mine in Korea – Bow from unfinished DD-767 installed.
USS *Floyd B. Parks* (DD-730)	DD #3	05/24/56 – 07/18/56	Collision at Tachen Islands with USS *Columbus* (CA-70) – Bow from unfinished DD-766 installed.

SHIPS REPAIRED AT LBNSY THAT WERE LATER LOST AT SEA (continued):

Ship	Date lost	Where & How lost
USS *Collett* (DD-730)	DD #3	08/03/60 – 08/24/60 Collision off San Diego with USS *Ammen* (DD-527) Bow from unfinished DD-791 installed.
USS *Brinkley Bass* (DD-887)	AFDL-48	05/09/66 – 06/21/66 Collision off Viet Nam with USS *Waddell* (DDG-24) Bow from decommissioned USS Tingey (DD-539) installed.
USS *Cook* (FF-1083)	DD #2	06/06/79 – 07/29/79 Collision off San Diego with tender New bow built and installed by Shop 11.

MAJOR SIDE OR BOTTOM DAMAGE REPAIRS:

Ship	Dry Dock	Dock Undock	Notes
RCS *Chung Chi* (LST-218)	DD #3	11/21/55 – 12/16/55	Grounded on sand bar – replaced 28' X 30' section of bottom shell and tank top deck.
USS *Ammen* (DD-527)	DD #3	07/20/60 – 08/03/60	Rammed by USS *Collett* (DD-730). Installed cofferdam as ship was sold for scrap shortly afterwards.
USS *Brooke* (DEG-1)	AFDL-48	04/12/78 – 05/18/78	Over 100 feet of starboard shell plating damaged against Seal Beach NWS pier during a "Santanna" wind storm.

MAJOR SIDE OR BOTTOM DAMAGE REPAIRS (continued):

Ship	Dry Dock	Dock Undock	Notes
USS *Belleau Wood* (LHA-3)	DD #1	12/06/90 – 04/30/91	Port shell plating of bow caved in from a freak wave in the Pacific. This was in the era of "The Perfect Storm" that ravaged ships in both the Atlantic and the Pacific. USS *Saipan* (LHA-2) in the Atlantic suffered identical damage in her starboard bow also from a freak wave.

TOTAL BOILER REPLACEMENTS:

Ship	Dry Dock	Dock Undock	Notes
USS *Jenkins* (DD-447)	DD #2	07/10/45 – 08/22/45	Mine damage.
USS *O'Brien* (DD-725)	DD #2	06/29/53 – 08/14/53	Boiler melt down (no feed water while on hot iron).

MAJOR BATTLE DAMAGE REPAIRS (As reported in USN Dry Docks Digest of 10/27/45):

Ship	Dry Dock	Dock — Undock	Notes
USS *Foote* (DD-511)	DD #2	03/05/44 – 06/04/44	First battle damage customer. Propellers and 70 feet of stern replaced from a torpedo hit on 11/02/43. 71,650 mandays expended.
USS *St. Louis* (CL-49)	DD #3	08/16/44 – 10/01/44	Bomb damage received on 02/15/44 and torpedo hit on 07/13/44 resulting in propeller loss next day.
" " "	DD #1	12/31/44 – 02/06/45	Hit by two Kamikazis on 11/27/44 causing major damage.
USS *Millicoma* (AO-73)	DD #1	05/18/44 – 05/26/44	Hull damage
" " "	DD #1	10/19/44 – 11/27/44	Major Typhoon damage to hull and topside rigging systems.
USS *Cleveland* (CL-55)	DD #3	10/25/44 – 12/06/44	General battle damage.
USS *Santee* (CVE-29)	DD #1	12/05/44 – 12/28/44	Major hull damage from a torpedo and major damage on hangar deck from a Kamikazi on 10/25/44.
USS *Wichita* (CA-45)	DD #3	12/16/44 – 02/08/45	Broken propeller shaft shaft, broken propeller strut on another shaft from various torpedo and air attacks.
USS *Ashtabula* (AO-51)	DD #1	01/01/45 – 01/21/45	Major hull damage from a direct hit of a torpedo on 10/24/44.
USS *Coos Bay* (AVP-25)	ARD-10	01/20/45 – 02/02/45	Various hull damage.
" " " "	DD #3	05/13/45 – 06/12/45	Various hull damage.
USS *Columbia* (CL-56)	DD #3	02/12/45 – 03/18/45	Major hull damage and topside fire damage from two Kamikazi hits and three bombs on 01/06/45 hits in Lingayen Gulf, Philippines.
USS *Kitkun Bay* (CVE-71)	DD #1	03/07/45 – 03/22/45	Major hull damage from a "Zeke" Kamikazi on 10/25/44 and an "Oscar" Kamikazi on 01/01/45 creating large hole in port hull.

MAJOR BATTLE DAMAGE REPAIRS (continued):

Ship	Dry Dock	Dock — Undock	Notes
USS *Santa Fe* (CL-60)	DD #3	04/27/45 – 05/11/45	General battle damage.
" " " "	DD #2	05/23/45 – 06/08/45	General battle damage. 89,950 mandays for complete overhaul.
USS *Halsey Powell* (DD-686)	DD #3	05/13/45 – 06/12/45	Major hull damage in stern when a Kamikazi overshot Carrier *Hancock* and hit *Halsey Powell* on 03/20/45.
SS *Orestes* (AGP-10)	ARD-10	05/16/45 – 05/25/45	A "Val" Kamikazi with a 500 lb. bomb and a mine blowing out one end of the boiler on 12/10/44 caused extensive hull and topside damage. 202,500 manhours (25,313 mandays) were expended to repair the ship.
USS *Comfort* (AH-6)	DD #1	06/10/45 – 06/29/45	Major topside damage at 01 level amidships by a Kamikazi hit on 04/29/45.
USS *Wyandot* (AKA-92)	DD #1	06/10/45 – 06/29/45	Hit in hull from a 250 lb. bomb.
USS *Zellars* (DD-777)	DD #1	06/10/45 – 06/29/45	"Jill" Kamikazi hit on 04/02/45 created 25-foot wide hole in side from main deck to waterline.
USS *Jenkins* (DD-447)	DD #2	07/10/45 – 08/22/45	Hit by a mine on 04/30/45 blew out a fire room. 30 feet of keel bent. Entire boiler replaced.
USS *Caisson Young* (DD-793)	DD #2	09/17/45 – 10/10/45	Extensive damage from two Kamikazi hits on 04/12/45 & 07/28/45.

DOCKINGS FOR MYSTERIOUS DAMAGE:

Ship	Dry Dock	Dock — Undock	Notes
USS *Stein* (DE-1065)	DD#3	10/12/72 – 11/02/72	Replacement of SONAR dome after a (then unknown) Megamouth shark gnawed on it.
Berthing Barge (APL-2)	DD#1	07/08/80 – 08/28/80	When the barge was towed out of Pearl Harbor, it bounced off of an underwater object and nearly sunk. Four "L" shaped holes punched in the bottom speculated that the barge bounced off of the ice breaking studs of a submarine making a covert exit from Hawaii.

TOTAL DRY DOCKINGS (INCLUDING BUMPS) OF ALL DRYDOCKS:

Dry Dock 1: 1,120

Dry Dock 2: 780

Dry Dock 3: 857

ARD-4: 4

ARD-8: 25

ARD-10: 92

ARDC-10 5

BARGE 1

YFD-8: 20

YFD-47: 1

YFD-71: 10

AFDL-42: 325

AFDL-43: 127

AFDL-44: 79

AFDL-48: 91

Total: **3,532** dockings from 1942 to 1996.

APPENDIX C
Crests, Logos
& Memorabilia

Various crests, logos and official seals relating to the shipyard, station or special projects have been designed and incorporated since the Navy first took over Rattlesnake Island. Each shop had its own logo as well. Most of the plaques I collected can be seen in Revision "A" of this book. But they take up an awful lot of room and I have decided to delete them from this edition. Besides, all of them are now mounted on 2-foot by 4-foot framed peg boards and stored aboard the Battleship Iowa in San Pedro awaiting a place to be set aside for a small museum of the Long Beach Naval Shipyard that was the Planning Yard for the reactivation of all four ships of that class.

The black and white logos appeared on the letterhead of the shipyard weekly newspaper, The Digest. They went through six major designs with the last one showing the USS *Long Beach* (CGN-9) with the greatest longevity even after the cruiser was stricken from the Navy rolls and the superstructure cut up for scrap. My source for four of the logos came from the cover of a study listing shipyard dry dockings up to 1985 but was missing the German Crane logo. After rummaging through my memorabilia, I found a 1956 issue of The Digest with that logo and was able to include it in this appendix. Then in a scrapbook from the Safety Office just before the bull dozers came in I found yet a sixth logo used from 1957 through 1958 showing a Regulus I missile mounted on one of the Cruisers we modified for that installation. In an ancient copy of the Shipyard weekly newspaper the back page showed the early badges worn by supervisors and lead workers.

All of these are now aboard the (ex) USS *Iowa* (BB-61) in San Pedro - Berth 87

1944

1959 to 1996

THE 6 KNOWN
LOGOS ON THE
DIGEST LETTERHEAD
OF LBNSY

1945 to 1948

1957-1958

1948 to 1950

1951 to 1957

U. S. Naval Drydocks   September 3, 1943   Page 10

MASTER'S BADGE

FOREMAN'S BADGE

LUNCH BADGE
ISSUED TO EMPLOYEES FOR PURPOSE OF EARLY OR LATE LUNCH HOUR

DOCKING CREW BADGE
ISSUED TO EMPLOYEES ENGAGED IN DOCKING AND UNDOCKING VESSELS

SNAPPER'S BADGE

SHOP BUTTON

SUPERVISOR'S BADGE

The only crest known of the Naval Air Station
also known as Reeves Field.
Variations of this design were printed on
several different matchbooks so it is
logical to assume that this is the best
one to represent the Air Arm of the
Long Beach Naval Complex

1944

If this author were to judge what shipyard logo would be the best,
THIS IS THE ONE.

APPENDIX D
Shipyard maps

It was difficult finding any map of the shipyard that was clear enough to even read let alone reproduce for publication. I commandeered a map out of one of the RAB manuals that was reasonably accurate but sharpness was lost when scanning it. It was difficult telling the difference between a building outline and the boundary of a parking lot because the cartographer used the same line style for both. But I was able to use it for a basic tracing and using aerial photos and other maps (though somewhat inaccurate or out of date) was able to put buildings in where they belonged and totally disregarded the parking lots and material lay-down areas. Of all the shipyard maps I used for reference, no two were alike. In some the building shapes were different than shown on the others, building numbers did not coincide and some were cluttered with identification of non-people "structures" such as electrical vaults, sub stations and pump sumps.

I e-mailed Bob Zimmerman who finished up his career at the shipyard as an Assistant Program Manager. Bob had to bounce back and forth between all the buildings coordinating work schedules and material delivery. He uploaded a listing of all number identified structures in both the shipyard and station. The listing is accurate for about the year 1990 and even lists all of the unglamorous sumps, sheds, shacks and shanties. **"B" I have deleted this long, boring list from the first edition to save space. Former "yard birds" know which building was their home shop and what the piers and dry docks are for. But if you are a cartographer and have a magnifying glass handy, buy the first edition as these two editions really should go together as a set. Apologies to Bob Zimmerman who provided me this rare and accurate list. But I have to save room somewhere for additional and more accurate information to include in this edition.**

I also modified the map and the list to include buildings of historical importance that were torn down when replaced by newer buildings prior to 1990. Unfortunately I cannot totally detail the Roosevelt Base/Reeves Field layout that was all on land west of Navy Way and was turned back to the City of Los Angeles when the lease terminated on 31 December 1979. The original Navy Reserve Center, Mine Warfare Group and Married Officers Housing were on that portion of the base. I did scan and trace a 1953 aerial photo and with some computer magic was able to get outlines of the airstrips and most of the buildings.

Some of my research materials included photos taken of a model of the shipyard and some watercolor paintings showing the proposed expansion of the shipyard (they were found at an estate sale). The expansion would have occurred had funding become available and there was no danger of closure. Therefore I have included a small map of what the shipyard and expanded Naval base would have looked like by the 21st century. The first major step would have been to add a dry dock 4 extending out into the West Basin. Its quay walls would have served as a new pier 4 (replacing the old wooden pier 4 removed around 1980) and a new pier 5 (replacing a stub pier that was used only as a garbage pier). At one time it was considered to extend dry dock 4 inland as well and adding an internal caisson. A ship with a long-term dry dock period would be at the North end while ships with shorter schedules could use the South end. However that idea was abandoned as being not only too radical but the sealing of the internal caisson would present problems without having water on one side to press it into the sill. Therefore I do not show that option.

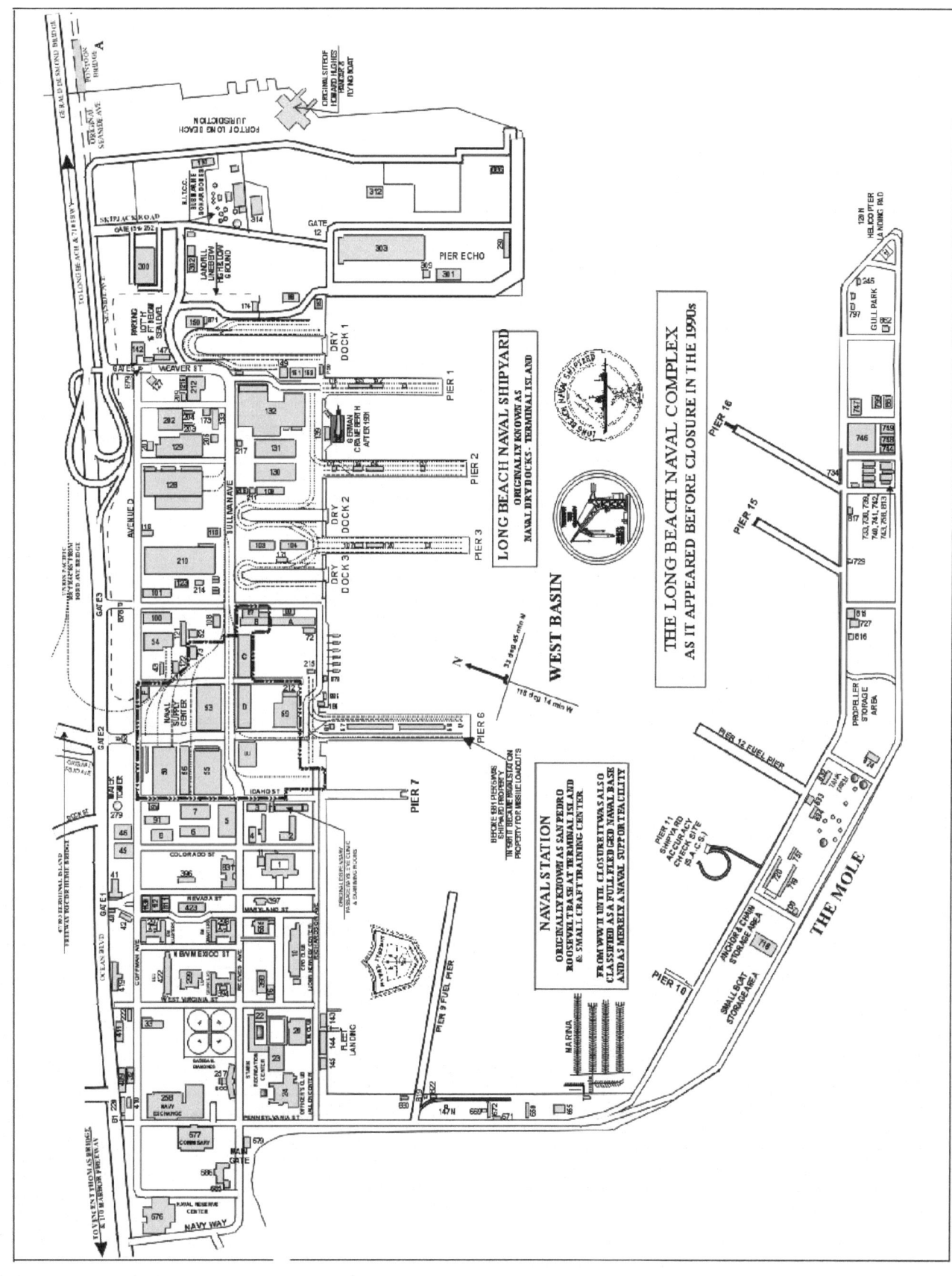

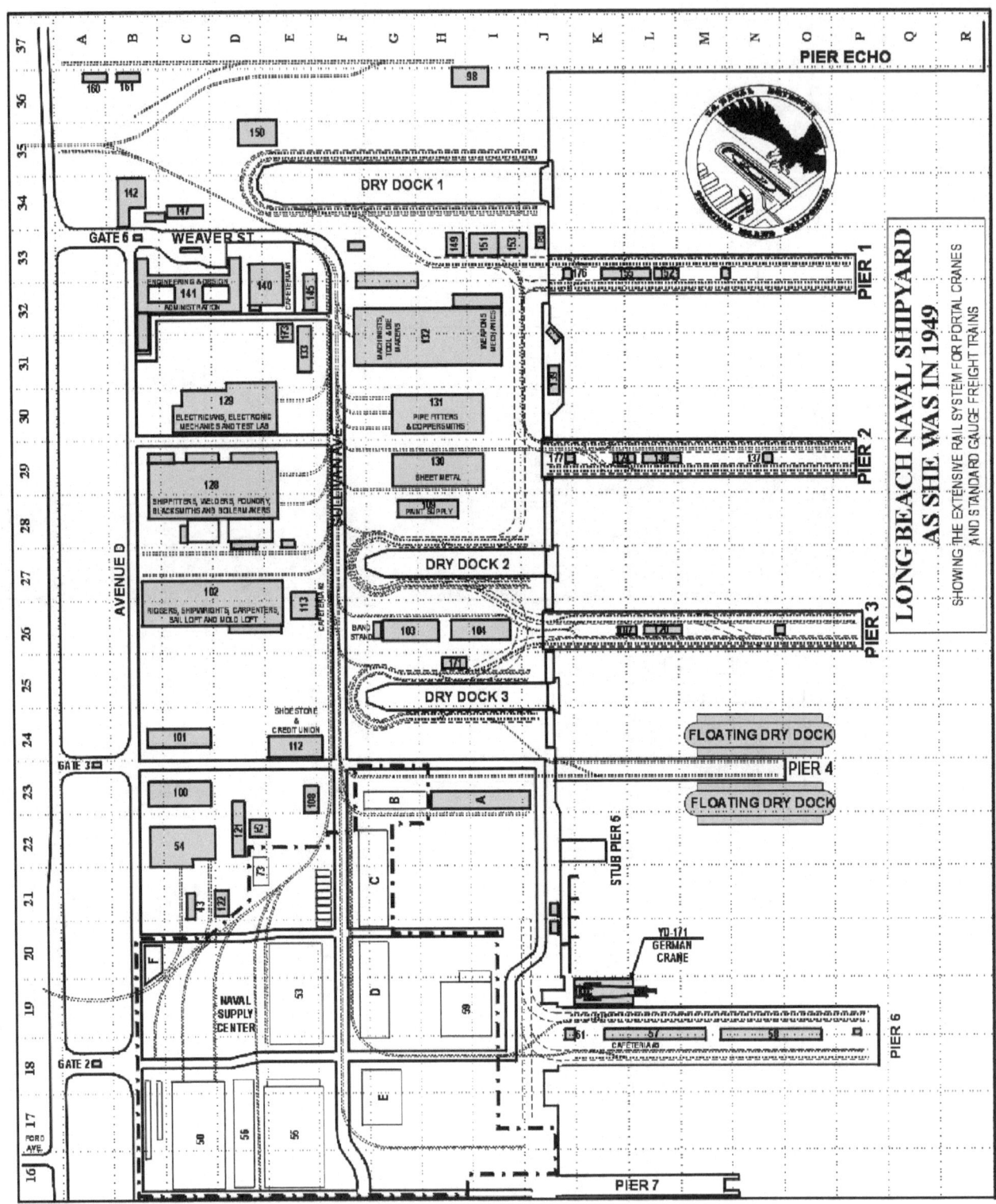

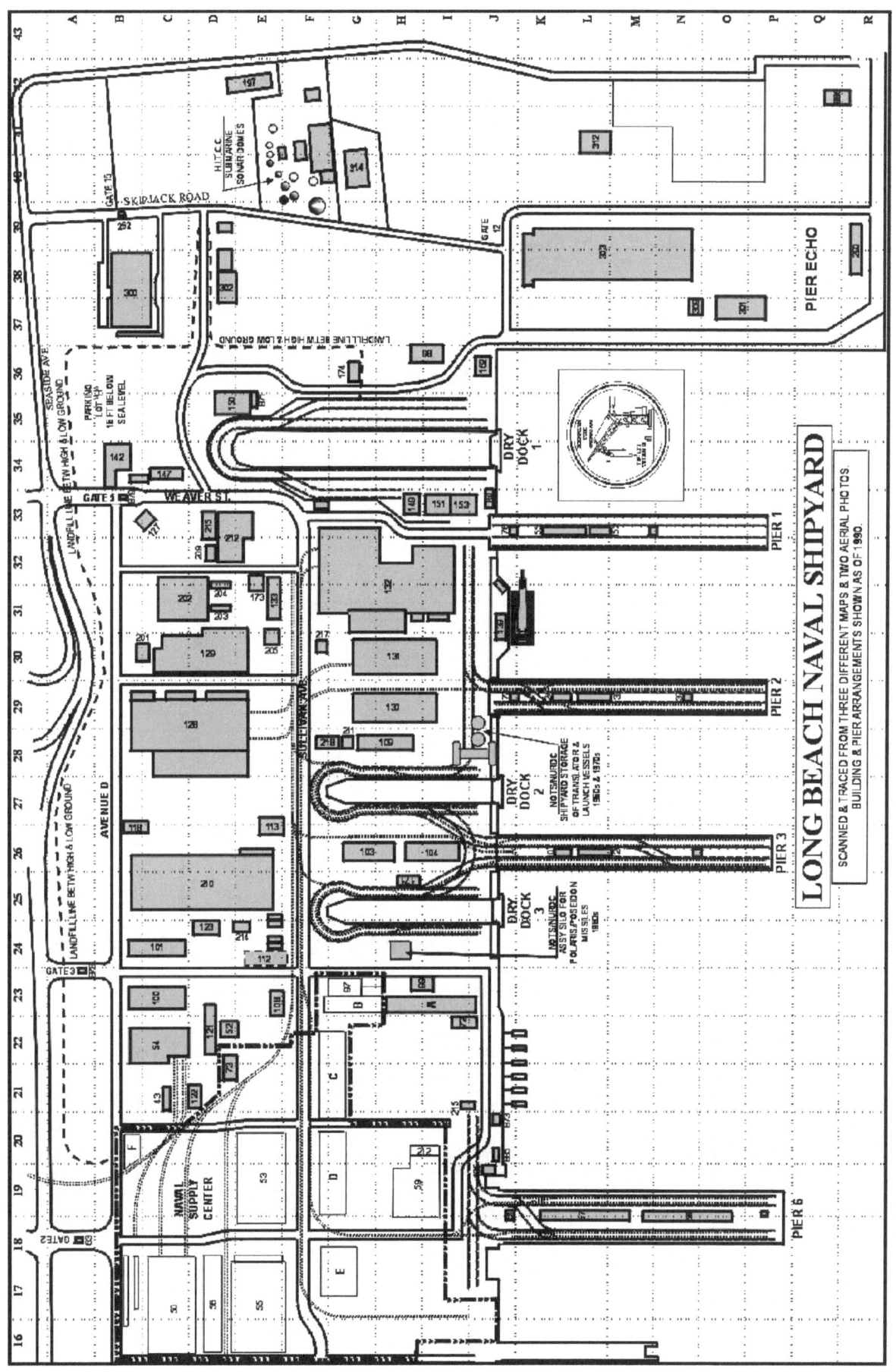

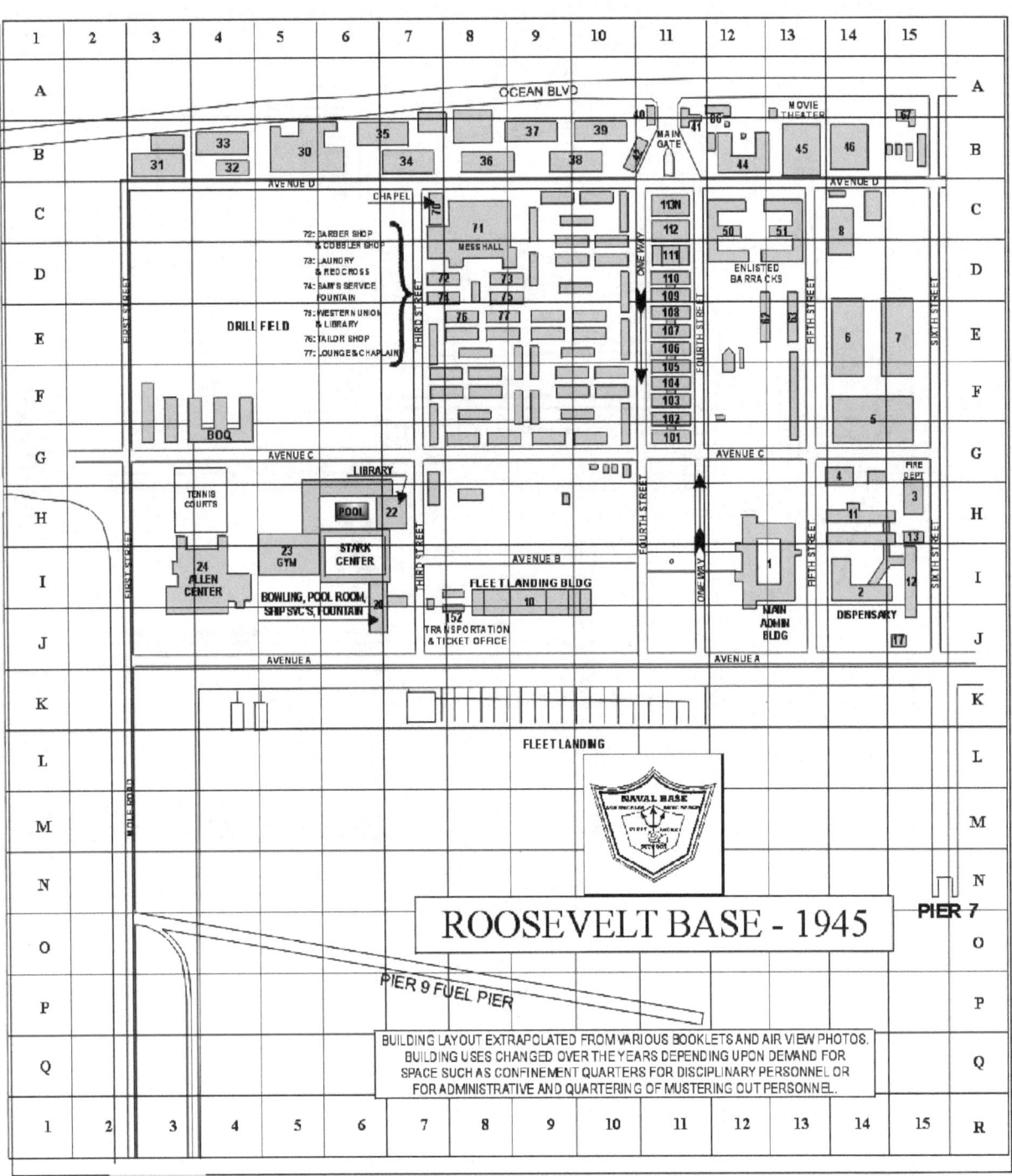

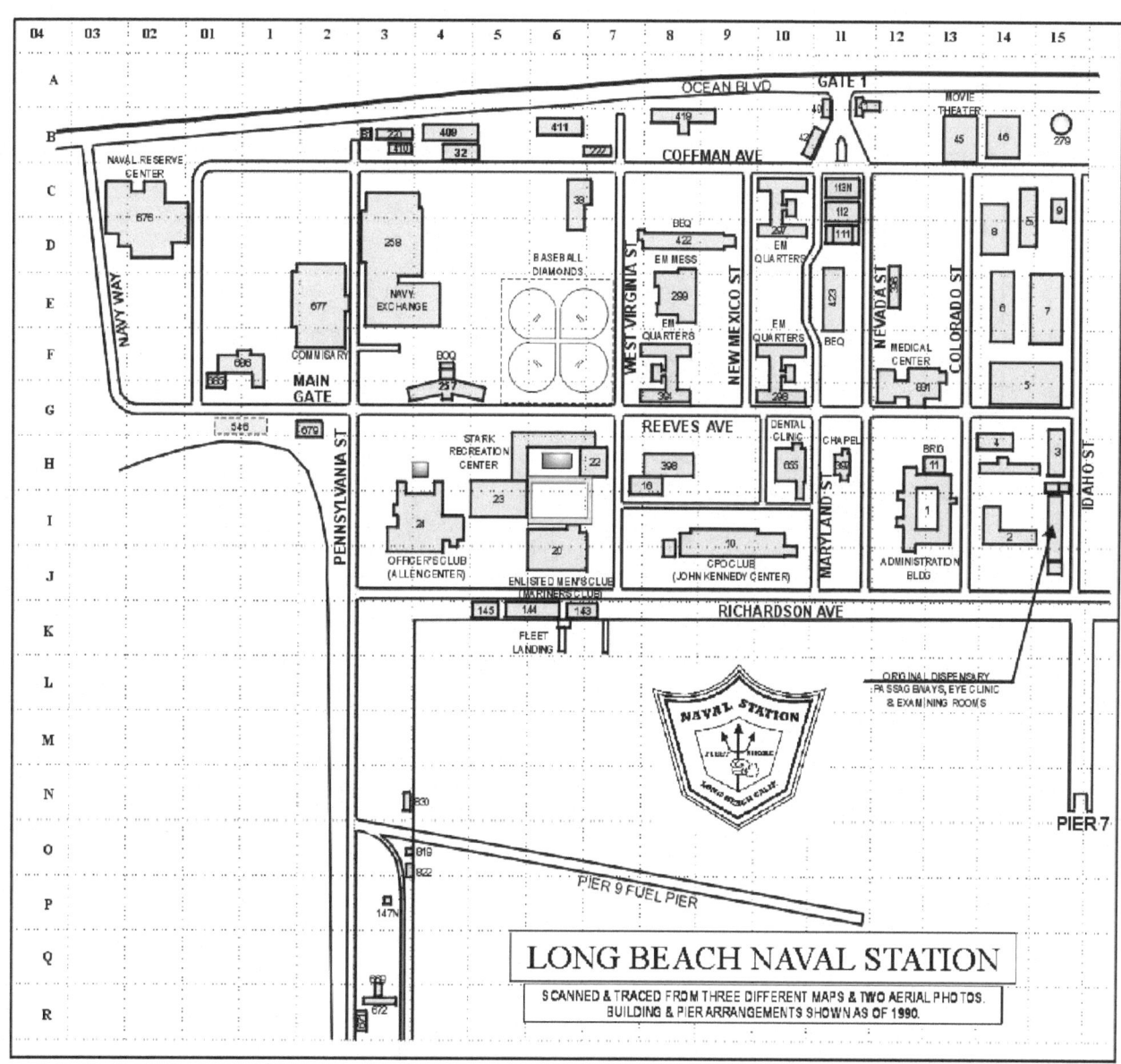

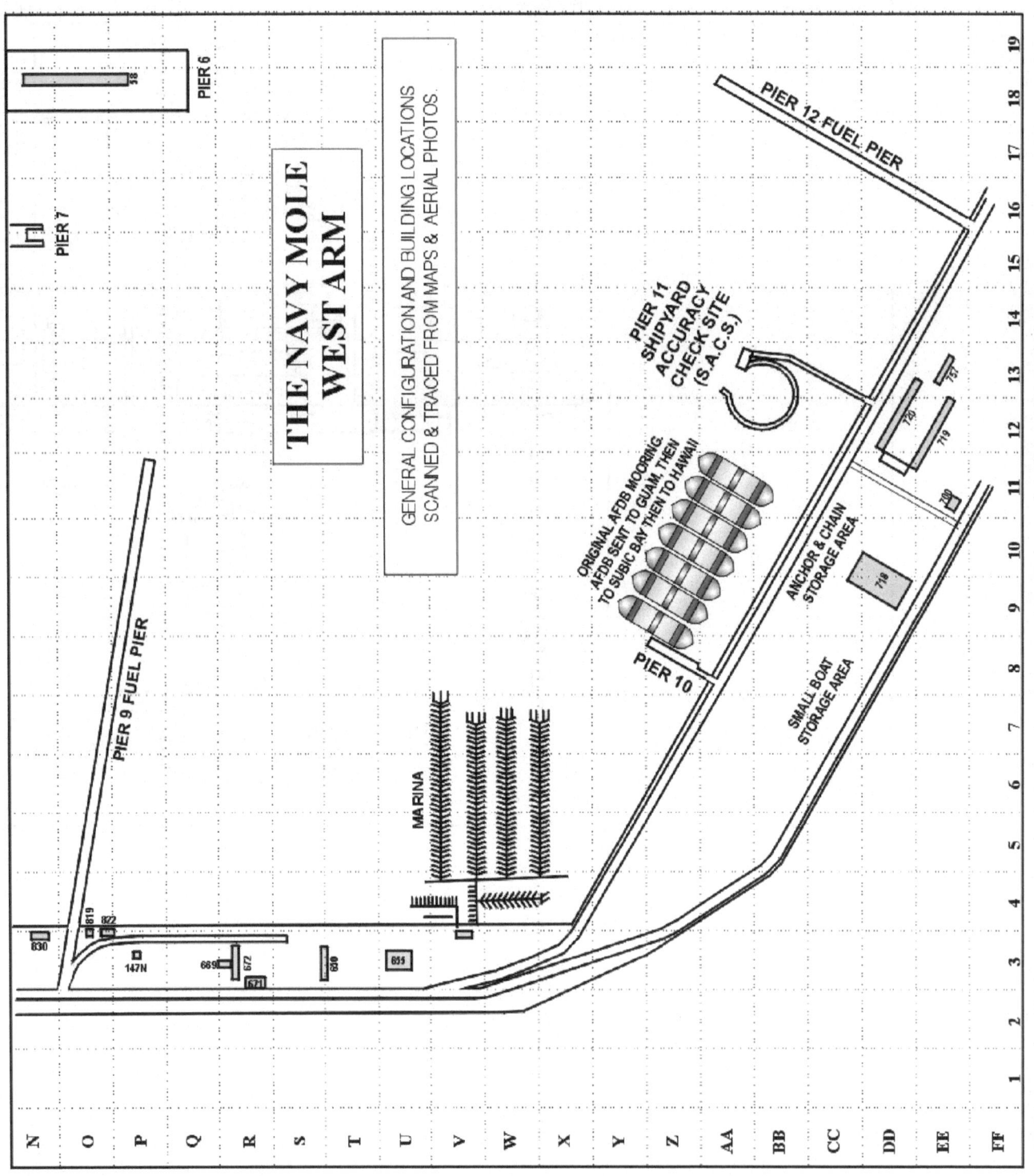

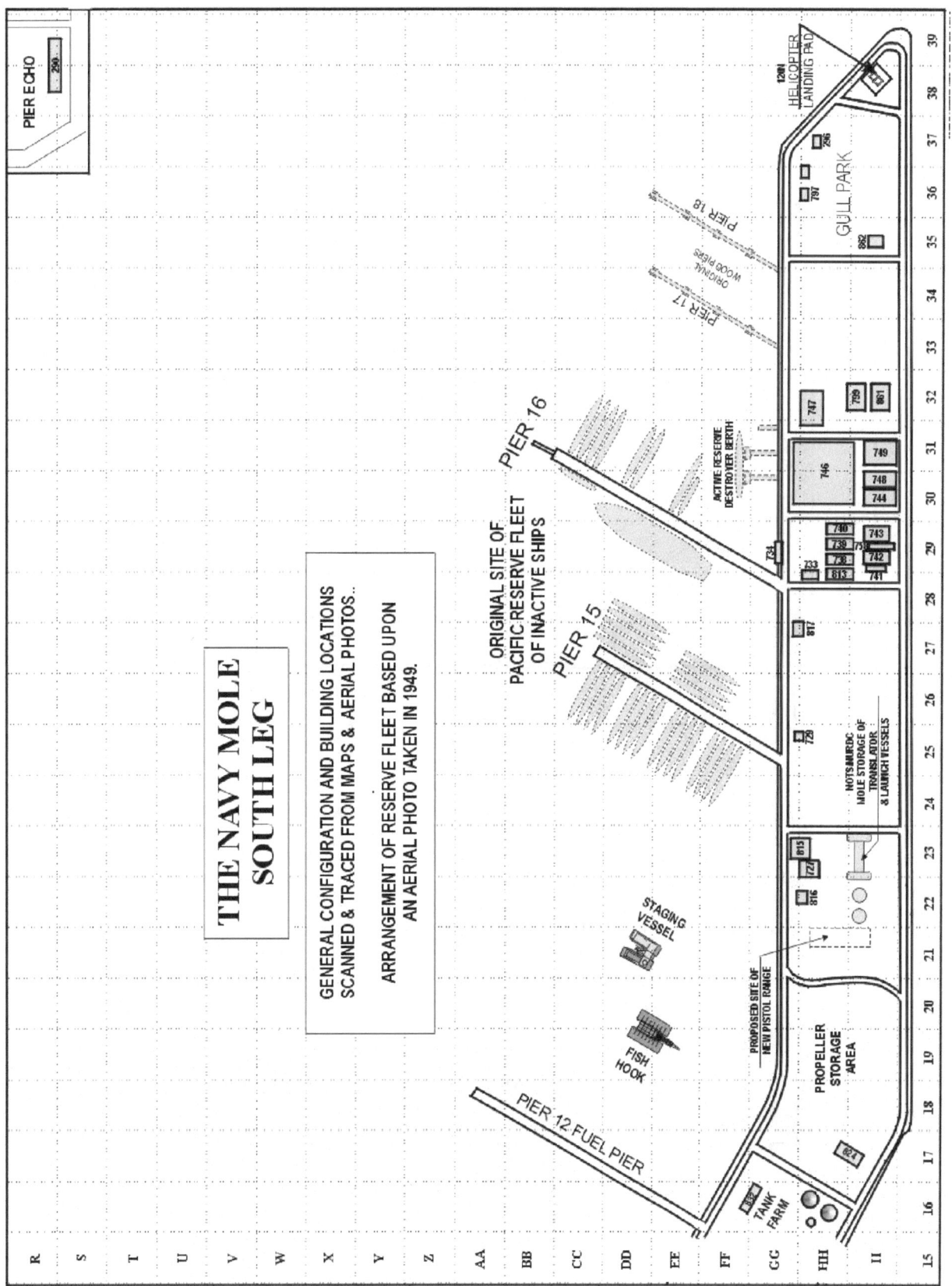

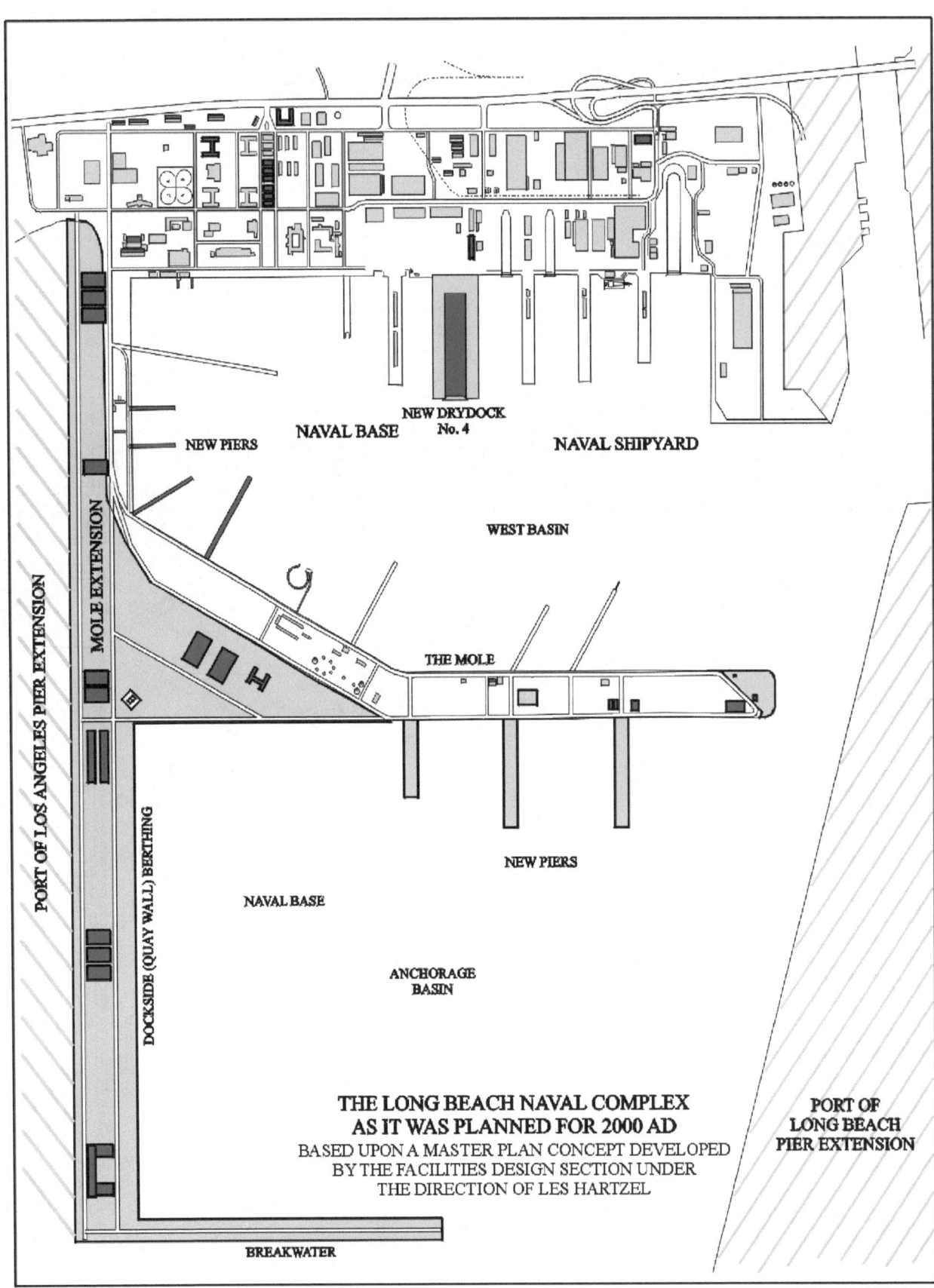

A model of the shipyard with the proposed Dry Dock 4 replacing piers 4 & 5.
The model is gone and the color lithograph of it was nearly destroyed by flood water.
So this is all we are going to see of it. *Author's collection*

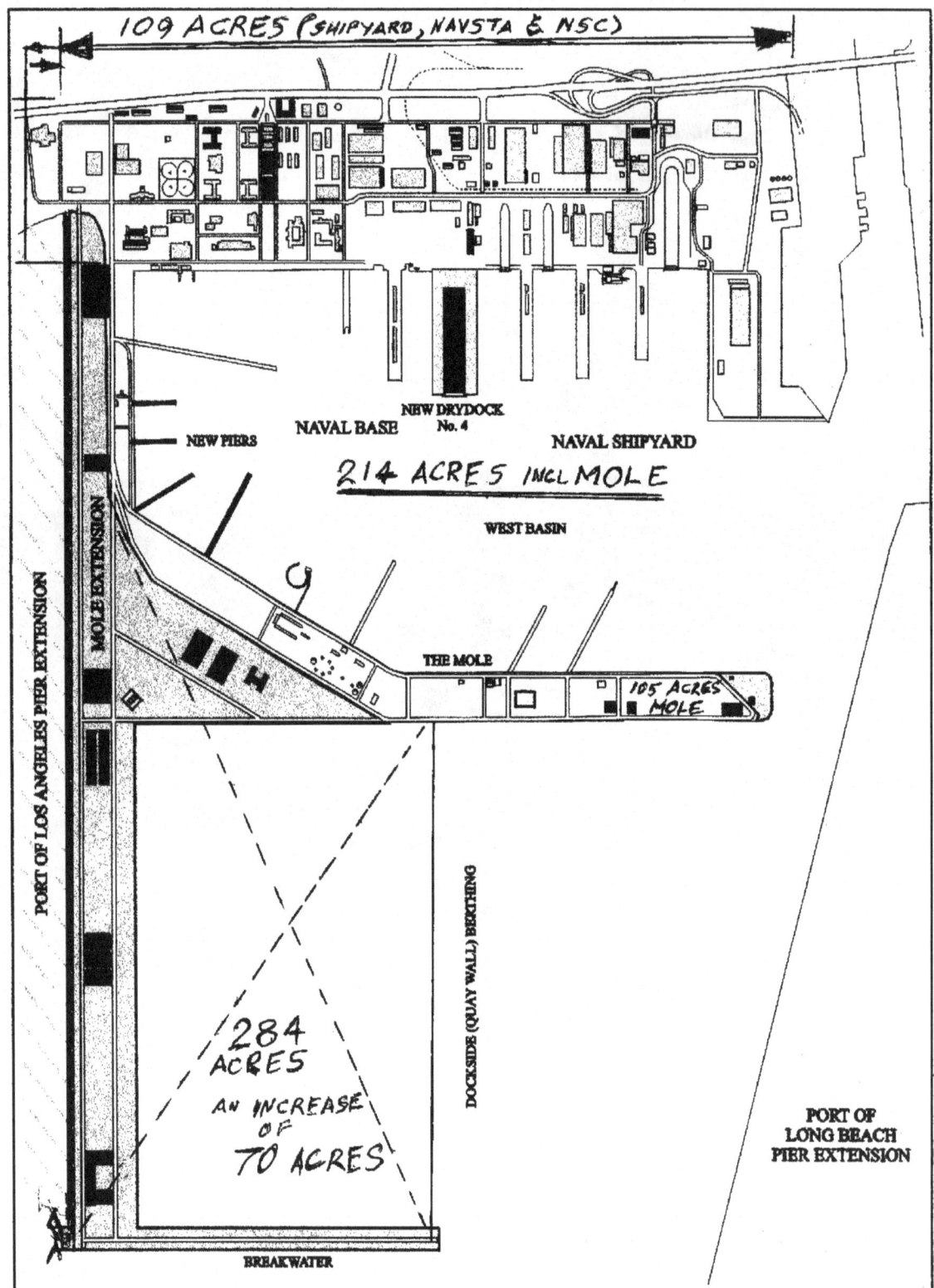

"B" Hindsight is usually better than Foresight, this is not really that type. Since there were already plans drawn up to extend the shipyard to the breakwater, they could have been altered to have the Container Island extended and the Naval complex, not only kept intact but improved upon with the super Dry Dock 4 that could take the largest Aircraft Carriers we now have. But the politicians, Port of Long Beach and Container shipping lines didn't want to wait an extra year or so for the fill in, Hanjin Lines took over a "filled in" shipyard instead. As you can see, the wait would have given them an extra 70 acres for their personal parking lot. Oh, by the way, Hanjin has gone bankrupt.

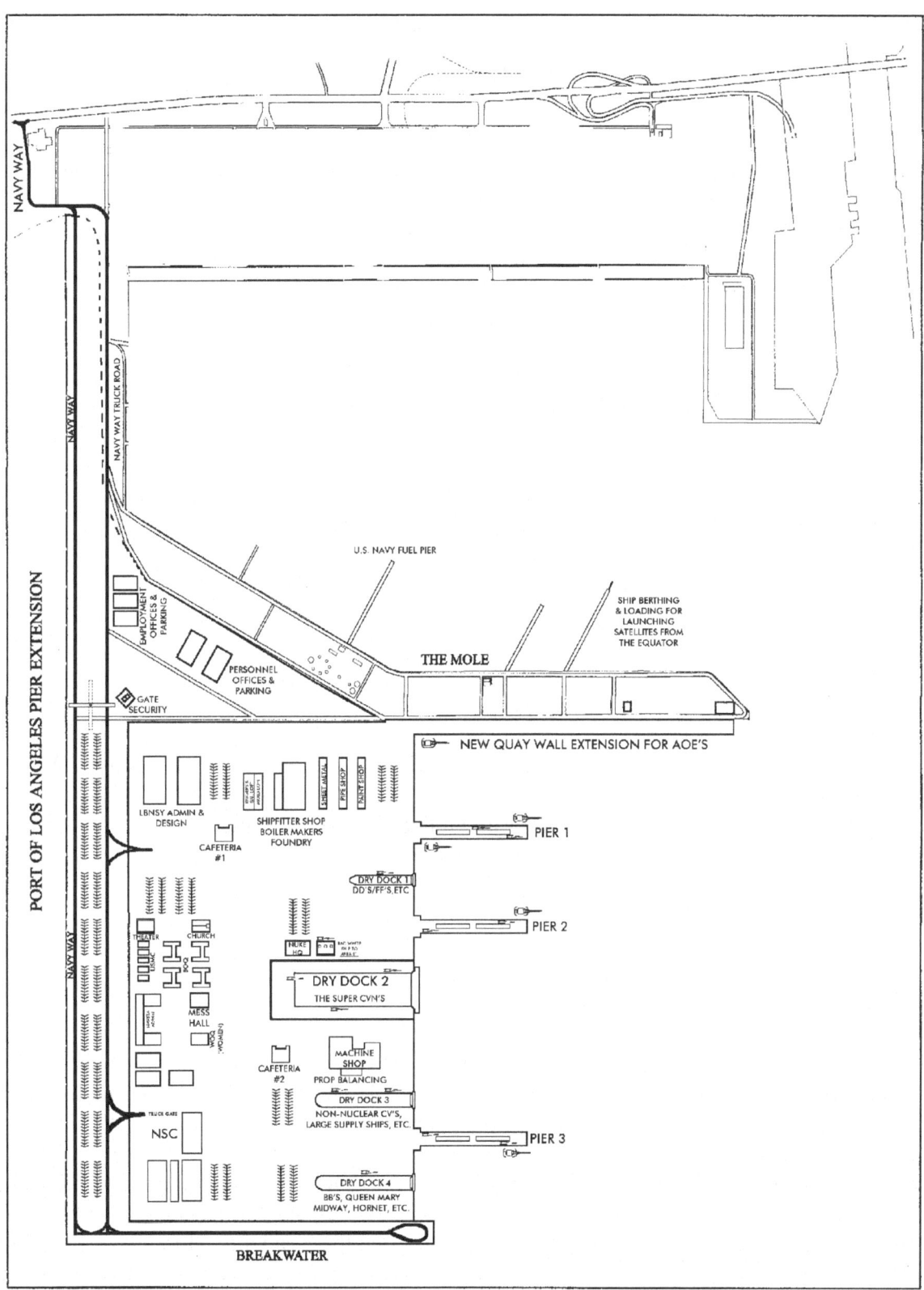

So, where can we build a new LBNSY? Where we wanted to extend it before but widen it as the container terminal could have. We could have the super dry dock for Nuclear Carriers, at least 3 piers, all the shop buildings, 3 dry docks to include upkeep and repair of memorial ships (including the QM that's rotting away), jobs for 6,000 Civil Service workers (plus 24 to 30,000 jobs for civilians outside the SY that depend upon those 6K employees). Naw. I guess that's just too simple for a Congressman to understand. Plus the cost would dig too deep into his personal pickle barrel like the Gulf War. If we kept going to Baghdad then, we would not have had to go back later. But that's only my opinion.

APPENDIX E
List of Graduate Apprentices

    2,870 people completed the shipyard's apprentice program from 1947 to 1991. The following list is based upon two sources. From 1947 to February of 1978 the list was copied from a handwritten ledger that was found in an abandoned desk by Vaughn Garvey after the shipyard was closed. Charlie Sprenger made a copy of that ledger for me and I have transcribed it line by line but reorganized it by year, by shop and then the graduate's names alphabetically so readers can find a name more readily. The list from 1978 to 1991 was copied from various issues of the Digest. Steve Gwinn had all of them, except the issue showing the class of 1988, and gave them to me for this appendix.

    Honor graduates are identified in the lists based upon a name plaque of the award John Pfeiffer received. There were no awards given in a couple of years either due to the 1949 shipyard closure or no graduating class in 1989. In 1972 the Dr. Plusch awards were initiated and I was able to add those in.

    The Honor award, also known as the Faculty Academic award, was based upon six factors of the candidate's four years taking the classes sponsored by Long Beach City College:
1. Trade Theory
2. Trade Mathematics
3. Trade Science
4. Trade drawing and blueprint reading
5. Applied English
6. Organization and management

    The Dr. James O. Plusch Work Experience Achievement Award, established in 1972, was based upon seven factors:
1. Observance of work hours and reliability in attendance
2. Observance of rules and regulations
3. Observance of safety
4. Quantity of work
5. Quality of work
6. Compliance with work instruction
7. Performance in new or changing situations

    The Dr. Plusch award was established in honor of Dr. James O. Plusch who was the Director of Occupation Preparation for Long Beach City College. He was instrumental in establishing Vocation Education College Credits for the Apprentice program.

    The lists up to 1977 may be a bit confusing. Some graduates received their certificates in the first one to three months of the year following their class. For example Alan Lees received his certificate in 1971 but he was of the class of 1970 and was even awarded the Academic Honors for 1970. Therefore it was difficult to separate some of the January through March certificate recipients from those that received them later in the year.

    The reasons for a graduate receiving his certificate later than others are varied. In most cases it was because he was hired in later off of a waiting list to fill a spot left open by a non-reporting applicant or an applicant that left the program early for another job – or was drafted into the Army. However, those that were drafted were able to return to their exact same job after release from active service. In most cases that was only two years and the shops adjusted the number of apprentice openings in anticipation of returning draftees.

Because of this confusion, in 1978 it was decided to wait until March or April of the following year to award all graduates their certificates at the same time. Though a graduate may have completed his minimum number of academic and work hours well before the end of his class year, he did not receive his certificate until the first quarter of the following year. It did simplify record keeping unless the editor of the Digest that week wasn't feeling too well. The Digest issue for the class of 1982 was confusing because the dateline on the issue was also 1982 instead of 1983. Also that Digest issue said there were 88 graduates but 89 names were listed. There are two Lewis' as insulators and two Lawson's as machinists but which one may be the extra name is unknown so I left all of them in the list.

I almost did not have the graduating class of 1988 because of all the Digests Steve Gwinn gave me, he was missing the 1989 issue that listed the graduates. I only had the names of the honor graduate and the recipient of the Dr. Plusch Award. However, Joanne McCaughey in Hawaii contacted me and she stated she was a sheetmetal worker apprentice in that graduating class. Fortunately she still had a copy of that Digest and she transcribed the entire list of names for me into MS Word. Therefore, we now have a complete list of all 2,870 apprentices who graduated from Long Beach Naval Shipyard.

Due to a hiring freeze in 1985 and 1986, there was no graduating class in 1989. Some 1986 applicants were hired in later in 1987 and constituted the class of 1990. Since the apprenticeship was winding down to extinction, few others were hired that year to make up the class of 1991. The "Lean and Mean" requirements, to make us better competitors with private shipyards, were being pushed down the throats of the shipyard command staff. To cut down on overhead costs and keep the manday rate as low as possible, deleting the apprentice program was one of sacrificial lambs.

"B" Now the lists in this edition seem to have lots of spaces in them. Well, that's because I copied them directly from the first edition which was only in a 7"X9" format. This larger format spreads them out, but it's just too much trouble for me to readjust. After all, in less than two weeks from the time I'm writing this paragraph, I will be 80 years old and I seriously doubt I will ever write another book.

	NAME OF GRADUATE	SKILLED TRADE	NOTES
17 February 1947	Womeldurf, John D.	Machinist	
18 August 1947	Swensen, J. G.	Electrician	
			2 for 1947
23 October 1948	Downing, Clarence	Shipfitter	
28 June 1948	Atkins, Wayne H.	Rigger	
1 November 1948	Benson, Ralph W.	Rigger	
October 1948	Guttry, James C.	Boilermaker	
18 October 1948	Paxton, Daniel S.	Patternmaker	
17 May 1948	Miller, Kenneth W.	Pipefitter	
27 September 1948	Nielsen, Jess L.	Boilermaker	
16 August 1948	Barsby, James B.	Machinist	
29 November 1948	Burris, Ernest	Machinist	
3 May 1948	Harper, Kent	Machinist	
28 June 1948	Haytack, Robert S.	Machinist	
22 March 1948	Johnson, Ralph L.	Machinist	
2 August 1948	Kimmons, Don C	Machinist	
18 October 1948	Ransom, Thomas L.	Machinist	
5 January 1948	Rinnert, Gerhard	Machinist	
June 1948	Rozar, Robert L.	Machinist	
17 May 1948	Sprague, Ted G.	Machinist	
13 September 1948	Sprenger, Charles E.	Machinist	
22 March 1948	Bateman, William R.	Electrician	Honor Graduate
17 May 1948	Cauley, J. E.	Electrician	
27 December 1948	Lawler, Joe	Electrician	
27 September 1948	Ross, Kenneth J.	Electrician	
2 February 1948	Sampson, Alfred R.	Electrician	
			23 for 1948
			25 Total

DA	NAME OF GRADUATE	SKILLED TRADE	NOTES
17 October 1949	Bost, William	Shipfitter	
28 March 1949	Cothern, Leon	Shipfitter	
26 December 1949	Dodd, Oliver	Shipfitter	
25 April 1949	Dowd, Perry D.	Shipfitter	
12 December 1949	Frank, Wyburn L.	Shipfitter	
126 December	Freyermuth, Donald L.	Shipfitter	
5 December 1949	Humberstan, Kenneth	Shipfitter	
14 November 1949	Lynch, Justin J.	Shipfitter	
26 December 1949	Rosvurm, Ray E.	Shipfitter	
12 September 1949	Winans, Dean	Shipfitter	
29 November 1948	Horton, Willard L.	Boilermaker	Honor Graduate
19 September 1949	Chase, Theodore	Sheetmetal Worker	
9 May 1949	Custer, Lon L	Sheetmetal Worker	
30 May 1949	Montgomery, Harold R.	Sheetmetal Worker	
14 February 1949	Sexton, J.C.	Sheetmetal Worker	
19 September 1949	Whisner, Charles A.	Sheetmetal Worker	
19 September 1949	Baker, James H.	Pipefitter	
19 September 1949	Esposito, Umberto	Pipefitter	
19 September 1949	Estes, Cotton E.	Pipefitter	
8 August 1949	Heflin, Bernard L.	Pipefitter	
19 September 1949	Morehead, James F.	Pipefitter	
7 November 1949	Nielsen, David J.	Pipefitter	
3 January 1949	Ramirez, Frank J.	Pipefitter	
19 September 1949	Salcido, Manuel	Pipefitter	
7 November 1949	Alford, John A.	Coppersmith	
1 August 1949	Ayers, Charles	Coppersmith	
19 September 1949	Jeneks, Horace M.	Coppersmith	
7 November 1949	Jensen, Roger	Coppersmith	
18 April 1949	Holmes, James	Joiner	
31 January 1949	Johnson, James D.	Joiner	
3 January 1949	Smith, Billie L.	Joiner	
24 January 1949	Pugh, Charles R.	Boatbuilder	
24 July 1949	Farrar, Merlin K.	Patternmaker	
1 August 1949	Ballou, Glen S.	Rigger	
12 December 1949	Lenox, P. A.	Rigger	
17 January 1949	Workman, Charles A.	Rigger	
17 January 1949	Smith, Richard R.	Sailmaker	
12 September 1949	Davey, James F.	Painter	
31 October 1949	Pierce, Floyd A.	Painter	
8 August 1949	Bathe, Edward C.	Machinist	
15 August 1949	Bjerke, D.A.	Machinist	
13 June 1949	Boyles, New W.	Machinist	
21 November 1949	Brown, Robert L.	Machinist	
15 August 1949	Christeansen, A.	Machinist	
18 April 1949	Collins, Marshall P.	Machinist	
14 March 1949	Downing, Gordon A.	Machinist	
10 October 1949	Finch, Edward P.	Machinist	
17 October 1949	Gilmer, R. E.	Machinist	
11 April 1949	Heitsche, Zane E.	Machinist	
17 October 1949	Klaren, Donald A.	Machinist	
10 October 1949	Kot, Eugene	Machinist	

1949 Continued next page

DA	NAME OF GRADUATE	SKILLED TRADE	NOTES
26 December 1949	LaCost, J. N.	Machinist	
10 October 1949	McClintock, Orvel H.	Machinist	
29 August 1949	Nelson, Harold F.	Machinist	
24 Ocotober 1949	Peterson, Kenneth B.	Machinist	
30 May 1949	Riffel, Richard	Machinist	
29 August 1949	Ross, Harold	Machinist	
19 September,	Ross, John A.	Machinist	
7 November 1949	Scott, Floyd E.	Machinist	
30 May 1949	Sunley, William	Machinist	
19 September,	Vinzant, Linford	Machinist	
10 October 1949	Wilhelm, Milford D.	Machinist	
16 May 1949	Clark, Charles	Electrician	
29 August 1949	Connell, Arthur	Electrician	
3 October 1949	Hoover, E. R.	Electrician	
21 April 1949	Keith, S. W.	Electrician	
3 October 1949	Koerner, John	Electrician	
12 September 1949	Larson, Robert L.	Electrician	
18 April 1949	Miller, Donald	Electrician	
23 May 1949	Mohar, William	Electrician	
14 November 1949	Myers, Harry	Electrician	
17 October 1949	Pawneshing, Alex	Electrician	
14 March 1949	Payne, Aaron	Electrician	
21 April 1949	Quinzel, A. E.	Electrician	
7 April 1949	Sanchez, James	Electrician	
19 September,	Smeallie, Donnan R.	Electrician	
6 June 1949	Stevens, Carl	Electrician	
14 April 1949	Young, Gene C.	Electrician	
			78 for 1949

103 Total

DA	NAME OF GRADUATE	SKILLED TRADE	NOTES
30 January 1950	Cordova, Augustine	Shipfitter	
30 January 1950	Davis, Philip	Shipfitter	
2 January 1950	Holdstack, Wifred H.	Shipfitter	
9 January 1950	Letcher, Robert D.	Shipfitter	
8 May 1950	Miller, Rondald	Shipfitter	
23 January 1950	Parks, Myron B.	Shipfitter	
2 January 1950	Benhom, Jack	Sheetmetal Worker	
16 January 1950	Benjestorf, Stanley C.	Sheetmetal Worker	
13 April 1950	Cobb, Lynn	Sheetmetal Worker	
16 January 1950	Holman, Eugene	Sheetmetal Worker	
23 January 1950	Larson, Lyle	Sheetmetal Worker	
27 February 1950	Lupac, Harold G.	Sheetmetal Worker	
6 February 1950	Pattison, Louis R.	Sheetmetal Worker	
2 February 1950	Pond, Herbert	Sheetmetal Worker	
13 February 1950	Sargeant, Clifford	Sheetmetal Worker	
9 January 1950	Wedge, Warren S.	Sheetmetal Worker	
2 January 1950	Ferguson, James	Blacksmith	
27 February 1950	Phillips, Jack A.	Blacksmith	
16 January 1950	Coons, Ralph C.	Boilermaker	
8 May 1950	Honodel, Thomas	Boilermaker	
16 January 1950	Nolan, Arnold	Boilermaker	
2 January 1950	Smith, Robert M.	Boilermaker	
27 February 1950	Young, James E.	Boilermaker	
13 March 1950	Winblad, Earl V.	Boilermaker	
27 February 1950	O'Neal, Thomas E.	Coppersmith	
2 January 1950	Adams, Paul	Painter	
2 January 1950	Hill, Milton	Painter	
2 January 1950	Knowles, Jesse	Painter	
13 February 1950	Richards, Jerry	Painter	
23 January 1950	Short, Thomas E.	Painter	
6 March 1950	Smith, Robert H.	Painter	
2 January 1950	Touw, Marion A.	Painter	
12 February 1950	Barney, Albert	Rigger	
13 February 1950	Hahn, C. H.	Rigger	
27 February 1950	Keane, Joseph	Rigger	
2 January 1950	Krebill, Robert C.	Rigger	
30 January 1950	Mitchell, John A.	Rigger	
13 March 1950	Raley, Barney	Rigger	
13 February 1950	Reed, Thomas S.	Rigger	
27 February 1950	Ross, Alfred S.	Rigger	
30 January 1950	Villa, V. C.	Rigger	
6 February 1950	Wright, Richard W.	Joiner	
3 April 1950	LeGrande, W. M.	Sailmaker	
23 January 1950	Dreigbaum, Robert A.	Boatbuilder	
23 January 1950	Foyle, Alan D.	Boatbuilder	
23 January 1950	Krugbaum, Robert A.	Boatbuilder	
26 May 1950	Mosher, Horace E.	Boatbuilder	
17 January 1950	Murdock, Carl	Boatbuilder	
2 January 1950	Bair, Charles N.	Pipefitter	
9 January 1950	Griess, Cornelius C.	Pipefitter	
2 January 1950	Hyatt, Elwin	Pipefitter	

1950 Continued next page

DA	NAME OF GRADUATE	SKILLED TRADE	NOTES
12 September 1950	Hickey, Rexford T.	Pipefitter	
12 September 1950	McClanahan, Homer	Pipefitter	Honor Graduate
30 January 1950	Morris, Earl W.	Pipefitter	
9 January 1950	Riggins, Glen R.	Pipefitter	
17 January 1950	Romanoski, Walter C.	Pipefitter	
13 March 1950	Russell, William C.	Pipefitter	
9 January 1950	Sanders, LeRoy	Pipefitter	
2 February 1950	Bailey, William C.	Machinist	
16 January 1950	Boss, Edward C.	Machinist	
9 January 1950	Carroll, Thomas W.	Machinist	
27 February 1950	Cheek, Robert	Machinist	
2 January 1950	Dilly, Archie E.	Machinist	
10 April 1950	Eubanks, Robert L.	Machinist	
16 January 1950	Hanna, Averil M.	Machinist	
27 February 1950	Harris, Earl G.	Machinist	
23 January 1950	Judd, Gene	Machinist	
9 January 1950	Liever, Urban J.	Machinist	
3 April 1950	Linn, Earl V.	Machinist	
13 February 1950	O'Rourke, Frank P.	Machinist	
24 April 1950	Sanchez, Arthur	Machinist	
9 January 1950	Sapin, Abraham	Machinist	
6 March 1950	Scherer, Clifford	Machinist	
30 January 1950	Shreffner, Clair	Machinist	
3 April 1950	Sperling, John A.	Machinist	
9 January 1950	Takahashi, Suco	Machinist	
27 February 1950	Teubert, Richard	Machinist	
6 February 1950	Wilson, Joseph	Machinist	
June 1950	Mulhern, Austin	Marine Machinist	
20 February 1950	Bishop, Byron	Electrician	
10 October 1950	Borden, Otis A.	Electrician	
3 October 1950	Brenner, William B.	Electrician	
13 March 1950	Brueggemann, Ralph	Electrician	
30 January 1950	Clammer, C. C.	Electrician	
3 April 1950	Elliott, J. D.	Electrician	
13 February 1950	Goetz, John G.	Electrician	
23 January 1950	Hewins, Irwin M.	Electrician	
13 February 1950	MacDiarmid, N. A.	Electrician	
3 April 1950	May, Samuel A.	Electrician	
27 March 1950	Olson, Leonard	Electrician	
23 January 1950	Robinson, C. P.	Electrician	
20 February 1950	Sanchez, Frank Jr.	Electrician	
20 March 1950	Schlange, Merline D.	Electrician	
17 January 1950	Smith, Edward E.	Electrician	
16 January 1950	Storm, C. L.	Electrician	
6 March 1950	Sutherland, Don	Electrician	
27 March 1950	Swisher, William H.	Electrician	

97 for 1950

200 Total

DA	NAME OF GRADUATE	SKILLED TRADE	NOTES
14 April 1951	Walsh, Charles D.	Shipfitter	
10 September 1951	Dawson, Donald	Sheetmetal Worker	
15 October 1951	Pharney, Walter	Sheetmetal Worker	
15 October 1951	Sexton, William	Sheetmetal Worker	
23 July 1951	Mize, Donald L.	Plumber	
6 August 1951	Warner, Clyde	Plumber	
9 July 1951	Miller Herman L.	Painter	
			7 for 1951

207 Total

29 September 1952	Watson, John R.	Shipfitter	
26 May 1952	Liggett, Thomas W.	Sheetmetal Worker	
15 June 1952	Ross, Valorus	Sheetmetal Worker	
1 December 1952	LaFond, Raymond C.	Boatbuilder	
1 December 1952	Smith, Vern E.	Boatbuilder	
12 January 1952	DiGiacomo, John	Rigger	
28 July 1952	Howard, Raleigh S.	Pipefitter	
17 November 1952	Richards, John D.	Pipefitter	
19 March 1052	Siegfried, Roy	Pipefitter	
25 February 1952	Andress, Harold W.	Pipe Coverer & Insulator	
25 February 1952	Lindell, Roy C.	Pipe Coverer & Insulator	
27 October 1952	Beristain, Joe L.	Machinist	
27 October 1952	Clark, Alvin M.	Machinist	
28 January 1952	Dabulis, Leonard A.	Machinist	
4 February 1952	Garstka, Raymond P.	Machinist	
28 January 1952	Smith, Dale M.	Machinist	
2 June 1952	Harris, Paul T.	Machinist	
6 October 1952	Hotze, Earl W.	Machinist	
20 October 1952	Modlin, Charles A.	Machinist	
27 October 1952	Nuncio, Daniel L.	Machinist	
13 October 1952	Stasko, Carl L. D.	Machinist	
13 October 1952	Yennel, Clifford H.	Machinist	
27 October 1952	Daffron, Howard B.	Electrician	
13 October 1952	Kalench, John Jr.	Electrician	
28 January 1952	Moore, Robert A.	Electrician	
21 July 1952	Morgan, John W.	Electrician	
28 July 1952	Germaneri, Domenic	Instrument Maker	Honor Graduate
			27 for 1952

234 Total

DA	NAME OF GRADUATE	SKILLED TRADE	NOTES
27 April 1953	Whitmire, Edward A.	Sheetmetal Worker	
15 June 1953	Hunker, Vard F.	Shipwright	
27 July 1953	Hawke, Howard H.	Joiner	
7 December 1953	Carlson, Calvin A.	Rigger	
30 June 1953	Frazier, Bennie	Rigger	
6 July 1953	Lane, Richard	Sailmaker	
14 April 1953	Mahen, William E.	Painter	
7 December 1953	Bailey, Walter	Machinist	
27 July 1953	Berlin, Albert F.	Machinist	
16 March 1953	Culpepper, Earl S.	Machinist	
20 April 1953	Gonzales, Gilbert	Machinist	
26 October 1953	Greer, Robert K.	Machinist	
9 March 1953	Hartzell, William H.	Machinist	
19 October 1953	Hornbeck, Charles J.	Machinist	
2 February 1953	Munoz, Ernest A.	Machinist	Honor Graduate
12 October 1953	Smallwood, Robert J.	Machinist	
26 January 1953	Snow, James M.	Electrician	

17 for 1953

251 Total

DA	NAME OF GRADUATE	SKILLED TRADE	NOTES
11 October 1954	Cresey, Harvey L. Jr.	Boilermaker	
17 May 1954	Roy, George F. Jr.	Pipe Coverer & Insulator	
8 February 1954	Brown, Daniel E.	Machinist	
24 May 1954	Brunner, Henry A.	Machinist	
18 January 1954	Ferguson, Paul E. Jr.	Machinist	
12 July 1954	Lambe, William T. Jr.	Machinist	
1 February 1954	Robson, John E.	Machinist	
16 November 1954	Dougherty, Charles	Electrician	Honor Graduate
15 February 1954	Hall, Durell E.	Electrician	
5 April 1954	Perea, Paul O.	Electrician	

10 for 1954

261 Total

DA	NAME OF GRADUATE	SKILLED TRADE	NOTES
4 July 1955	Ellis, Walter	Shipfitter	
25 July 1955	Henry, Robert W.	Boatbuilder	
11 July 1955	Legaspi, Norman S.	Shipwright	
4 July 1955	Chabot, Frederick	Pipefitter	
4 July 1955	Frandsen, Donald	Pipefitter	
4 July 1955	Lopez, Isabel	Pipefitter	
4 July 1955	Redkahl, Monty J.	Pipefitter	
11 July 1955	Smith, Merle	Pipefitter	
25 July 1955	Reed, Paul G.	Pipe Coverer & Insulator	
1 August 1955	Scherer, Chalres	Pipe Coverer & Insulator	
21 February 1955	Green, Rondall	Rigger	
18 July 1955	Stuart, Robert	Rigger	
18 July 1955	Violante, Ralph	Rigger	
22 August 1955	Hargrove, Romie D.	Painter	
4 July 1955	Van Valkenberg,	Optical Instrument Maker	
22 August 1955	Bookout, Donald E.	Machinist	
18 July 1955	Charles, Larry B.	Machinist	
1 August 1955	Christoffers, H. H.	Machinist	
25 July 1955	Davis, Melvin J.	Machinist	
8 August 1955	Dominquez, Manuel	Machinist	
22 August 1955	Drummond, J. O.	Machinist	
1 August 1955	Ewing, Robert	Machinist	
18 July 1955	Hanna, Robert E.	Machinist	
4 July 1955	Harvey, Paul L.	Machinist	
25 July 1955	Heim, John T.	Machinist	
29 August 1955	Judge, Porter Jr.	Machinist	
11 July 1955	Kluge, Ervin E.	Machinist	
11 July 1955	Landress, James C.	Machinist	
25 July 1955	Nielsen, Lester	Machinist	
25 July 1955	Pace, Lawrence E.	Machinist	
4 July 1955	Provorse, Kemble	Machinist	
11 July 1955	Sherritt, Stanley	Machinist	
4 July 1955	Tentle, George H.	Machinist	
13 June 1955	Ward, Ralph M.	Machinist	
22 August 1955	Williams, Howard	Machinist	
15 August 1955	Whiting, Leon	Machinist	
25 July 1955	Alvarado, Edward	Electrician	
1 August 1955	Ballentine, William	Electrician	
23 July 1955	Brown, Walter	Electrician	
4 July 1955	Fredericksen, Adrian	Electrician	
8 August 1955	Hughey, William	Electrician	
4 July 1955	Meyer, Vernon	Electrician	Honor Graduate
25 July 1955	Patz, Lowell	Electrician	
4 July 1955	Price, Eric	Electrician	
4 July 1955	Vetrovec, William	Electrician	
25 July 1955	Bryant, William C.	Electronics Mechanic	
18 July 1955	Daw, Albert Thomas	Electronics Mechanic	
4 July 1955	Dein, George C.	Electronics Mechanic	
18 July 1955	Jansen, Edwin	Electronics Mechanic	
1 August 1955	Laird, Jack	Electronics Mechanic	
15 August 1955	Lamb, Richard R.	Electronics Mechanic	
11 July 1955	Worden, Robert D.	Electronics Mechanic	

52 for 1955

313 Total

DATE	NAME OF GRADUATE	SKILLED TRADE	NOTES
25 June 1956	Hammond, Milt	Shipfitter	
10 September 1956	Peyton, Geoffrey	Shipfitter	
10 September 1956	Ward, James	Shipfitter	
19 March 1956	McKinney, Ralph J.	Boilermaker	
27 August 1956	Shurtle, Jerry M.	Boilermaker	
10 September 1956	Cassity, Wayne E.	Combination Welder	
26 June 1956	Labs, David	Combination Welder	
25 June 1956	Bell, Charles	Boatbuilder	
26 June 1956	Bommelje, Ralph	Boatbuilder	
10 September 1956	VanDyke, Kenneth R.	Boatbuilder	
10 September 1956	Stallings, Charles E.	Joiner	
26 June 1956	Edgecomb, Harry Jr.	Sheetmetal Worker	
25 June 1956	Ichikawa, Robert S.	Optical Instrument Maker	
17 September 1956	Adams, Donald	Pipefitter	Honor Graduate
17 September 1956	Mulkey, Lonnie J.	Pipefitter	
17 September 1956	Beu, James G.	Pipe Coverer & Insulator	
1 October 1956	Eck, Dan L.	Pipe Coverer & Insulator	
10 September 1956	Francis, Cecil D.	Painter	
2 July 1956	Ackelson, Robert L.	Machinist	
8 October 1956	Beland, Russell R.	Machinist	
31 October 1956	Bernabe, Benjamin	Machinist	
8 October 1956	Blanchard, Richard W.	Machinist	
22 October 1956	Chmielewski, Arthur	Machinist	
2 July 1956	Crom, Thomas L. Jr.	Machinist	
23 January 1956	Eisenbauer, Kenneth	Machinist	
10 September 1956	Graham, Ronnie L.	Machinist	
2 July 1956	Gross, Jack D.	Machinist	
26 June 1956	Jackson, Roland J.	Machinist	
6 July 1956	Karan, Jack	Machinist	
10 September 1956	McCain, Wallace C.	Machinist	
2 July 1956	Mims, Rodney E.	Machinist	
1 October 1956	Pearson, Charles E.	Machinist	
13 August 1956	Poor, Fred E.	Machinist	
9 July 1956	Shipp, Elmer R.	Machinist	
9 July 1956	Williams, John C.	Machinist	
26 June 1956	Humble, Paul E.	Electrician	
4 June 1956	Nies, Clarence F.	Electrician	
11 June 1956	Maglica, Anthony E.	Electronics Mechanic	
			38 for 1956

351 Total

DAT	NAME OF GRADUATE	SKILLED TRADE	NOTES
16 September 1957	Sorenson, Thomas N.	Shipfitter	
16 September 1957	Storms, John C.	Shipfitter	
16 September 1957	Clark, Kenneth	Combination Welder	
16 September 1957	Witt, Albert D.	Combination Welder	
25 February 1957	Beasley, Mervyn	Sheetmetal Worker	
14 October 1957	Matthis, Robert	Sheetmetal Worker	
9 September 1957	Wright, Donald V.	Sheetmetal Worker	
10 June 1957	Dickson, William	Boatbuilder	
11 March 1957	Moore, lugher L. Jr.	Joiner	
16 September 1957	Logan, Thomas	Rigger	
25 February 1957	Longo, Joseph A.	Pipefitter	
23 September 1957	Mauser, Lawrence A.	Pipefitter	
25 March 1957	Morris, Lugher H.	Pipefitter	
11 March 1957	King, Rodney G.	Pipe Coverer & Insulator	
3 June 1957	Ropczycki, Gerald M.	Pipe Coverer & Insulator	
30 September 1957	Williams, Floyd G.	Pipe Coverer & Insulator	
18 February 1957	Barton, Donald W.	Machinist	
27 May 1957	Bartholomew, Charles	Machinist	
23 September 1957	Daley, Donald K.	Machinist	
6 May 1957	Griffin, Robert	Machinist	
18 February 1957	Lindsey, James Y. Jr.	Machinist	
4 March 1957	Marino, Domenic	Machinist	
18 February 1957	Riggle, Robert D.	Machinist	
15 July 1957	Shupe, Joseph P.	Machinist	
18 February 1957	Thompson, Darryl W.	Machinist	
16 September 1957	Turner, Cleo	Machinist	
18 February 1957	Wisneskie, Raymond	Machinist	
16 September 1957	Lorenzana, Simon Jr.	Marine Machinist	
16 September 1957	Petkow, Raymond	Marine Machinist	
30 September 1957	Shade, Harry	Marine Machinist	
14 October 1957	Vasquez, Guillermo O.	Marine Machinist	Honor Graduate
16 September 1957	Winars, James P.	Marine Machinist	
9 September 1957	King, Norman	Electrician	
23 September 1957	McBeath, Harry	Electrician	
11 March 1957	Nunez, Francisco A. Jr.	Electrician	
4 March 1957	Price, Eunice	Electrician	
1 April 1957	Robinson, Maurice	Electrician	
16 September 1957	Spears, Andrew	Electrician	
9 September 1957	Graham, James A.	Electronics Mechanic	
2 December 1957	Morris, Aubrey D.	Electronics Mechanic	
			40 for 1957

391 Total

DA	NAME OF	SKILLED TRADE	NOTES
15 September	Cunningham,	Shipfitter	
15 September	Dickson, David R.	Shipfitter	
15 September	Fedak, William D.	Shipfitter	
15 September	Hastings, Charles L.	Shipfitter	
15 September	Landgraff, Richard A.	Shipfitter	
15 September	Hillis, Albert D.	Welder	
22 September	Ambe, Gerald G.	Blacksmith	
22 September	Butler, Edward	Boilermaker	
22 September	Kurtz, Sherman L.	Boilermaker	
22 September	Wildgoose, Leslie E.	Boilermaker	
15 September	Hartzell, Lester F. Jr.	Shipwright	
15 September	Wallace, John M.	Boatbuilder	
15 September	Tomasello, Joseph	Joiner	
15 September	Wolbers, John E.	Joiner	
8 September 1958	Rossman, Edwiin C.	Rigger	
6 October 1958	Worth, Arthur J.	Rigger	
15 September	Bennett, Charles S.	Painter	
15 September	Gonzales, Pablo	Painter	
15 September	Bowser, Allen Jr.	Sheetmetal Worker	
8 September 1958	Crane, Lyle W.	Sheetmetal Worker	
24 November 1958	Downing, Darrel D.	Sheetmetal Worker	
15 September	Scott, Freddy J.	Sheetmetal Worker	
15 September	Sergent, Roy O.	Sheetmetal Worker	
15 September	Thompson, Robert V.	Sheetmetal Worker	
15 September	Dial Jack	Pipefitter	
20 October 1958	Rios, Dannie V.	Pipefitter	
23 June 1958	Bateman, Bennett L.	Machinist	
8 September 1958	Hatch, Glenn M.	Machinist	
8 September 1958	Mumford, William F.	Machinist	
8 September 1958	Vernon-Cole, Michael	Machinist	
15 September	Vickry, William J.	Machinist	
27 October 1958	Clontz, Dean E.	Marine Machinist	
8 September 1958	Dodge, Carl E.	Marine Machinist	
8 September 1958	Doughty, John S.	Marine Machinist	
27 January 1958	Holder, Russell G.	Marine Machinist	
8 September 1958	Larson, Donald A.	Marine Machinist	
8 September 1958	Peck, Thomas A.	Marine Machinist	
8 September 1958	Quintana, Pablo E.	Marine Machinist	
24 November 1958	Cartwright, John E.	Electrician	
15 September	Gaminde, Augustine	Electrician	Honor
8 September 1958	Mascarenas, Alex	Electrician	
20 October 1958	Stover, Thomas C.	Electrician	
16 June 1958	Rudolph, Ronald V.	Electronics Mechanic	
			43 for 1958

434 Total

DAT	NAME OF GRADUATE	SKILLED TRADE	NOTES
14 September 1959	Carpenter, Kenneth W.	Shipfitter	
14 September 1959	Strolsee, Daniel L.	Shipfitter	
14 September 1959	Vessells, Robert W.	Shipfitter	
21 September 1959	Bodnar, Stephen	Welder	
21 September 1959	Francis, Gale A.	Welder	
14 September 1959	Riddle, Robert C.	Welder	
14 September 1959	Shirran, Clifton A.	Welder	
14 September 1959	Hardy, Arthur W.	Blacksmith	
14 September 1959	Swenson, Benjamin A.	Shipwright	
14 September 1959	DiNapoli, Rocco Jr.	Joiner	
14 September 1959	Stockton, James R.	Joiner	
12 October 1959	Goodrich, Edward E.	Rigger	
14 September 1959	Cowherd, Ray T.	Sheetmetal Worker	
14 September 1959	Gritton, Robert L.	Sheetmetal Worker	
25 May 1959	Landry, John C.	Sheetmetal Worker	
14 September 1959	Ussery, Charles B.	Sheetmetal Worker	
13 July 1959	Fish, Lawrence E.	Pipefitter	
28 December 1959	Hiller, Charles H.	Pipefitter	
28 September 1959	Lacy, Bill E.	Pipefitter	
7 September 1959	Dennis, Wayne D.	Pipe Coverer & Insulator	
28 September 1959	Shadduck, Jack P.	Pipe Coverer & Insulator	
27 April 1959	Autry, Delbert D.	Machinist	
12 October 1959	Bishop, Robert N.	Machinist	
7 September 1959	Coopeland, James R.	Machinist	
7 September 1959	Denton, Monroe C.	Machinist	
7 September 1959	Ford, Charles L.	Machinist	
7 September 1959	Houillion, David E.	Machinist	
7 September 1959	Ichikawa, Mahanu	Machinist	
19 January 1959	McGlinchey, Eugene R.	Machinist	
7 September 1959	Parker, James A.	Machinist	
4 September 1959	Purcaro, Richard W.	Machinist	
7 September 1959	Shoemaker, Charles J.	Machinist	
7 September 1959	Smith, Norman P.	Machinist	
5 October 1959	Thirion, Robert F.	Machinist	
23 March 1959	Torres, Edward V.	Machinist	
26 October 1959	Wilson, James W. Jr.	Machinist	
30 November 1959	Alson, Grover L.	Marine Machinist	
7 September 1959	Donoho, Paul O.	Marine Machinist	
26 October 1959	Geary, Thomas L.	Marine Machinist	
7 September 1959	Irvine, Douglas G. Jr.	Marine Machinist	
7 September 1959	Roberts, Edward J.	Marine Machinist	
14 September 1959	Brown, Dale M.	Electrician	
7 September 1959	Hubbard, Louis D.	Electrician	
7 September 1959	Smith, James C. Jr.	Electrician	
7 September 1959	Cox, Robert T.	Electronics Mechanic	Honor Graduate
7 September 1959	Gall, John W.	Electronics Mechanic	
7 September 1959	Hoppes, William J.	Electronics Mechanic	
7 September 1959	Lehan, Richard A.	Electronics Mechanic	
7 September 1959	McCorduck, John E.	Electronics Mechanic	
			49 for 1959

483 Total

	NAME OF GRADUATE	SKILLED TRADE	NOTES
11 September 1960	Cook, George W.	Shipfitter	
11 September 1960	Davis, Glenn G.	Shipfitter	
11 September 1960	Hunsaker, Paul W.	Shipfitter	
11 September 1960	Perry, James E.	Shipfitter	
2 October 1960	Cantara, Henry O.	Welder	
11 September 1960	Holt, Glen Dale	Welder	
30 October 1960	Murphy, Dennis M.	Blacksmith	
4 September 1960	Rodriquez, Louis A.	Boilermaker	
18 September 1960	Morales, Carlos G.	Shipwright	
28 March 1960	Staxrud, Sidney C. Jr.	Boatbuilder	
18 September 1960	Moses, Robert E.	Joiner	
18 September 1960	Portugal, Edward L.	Joiner	
27 November 1960	Gossett, James	Rigger	
22 August 1960	Miller, Clarence C.	Rigger	
25 September 1960	Fritshchmann, Gary	Painter	
25 September 1960	Wilson, James E.	Painter	
18 September 1960	Eck, Eddie J.	Sheetmetal Worker	
28 August 1960	Jacobson, David V.	Sheetmetal Worker	
25 September 1960	Wilson, Edgar C.	Sheetmetal Worker	
11 September 1960	Zeller, Glenn E.	Sheetmetal Worker	
25 September 1960	Harper, Logan E.	Pipefitter	
11 September 1960	Holshouser, Troy L.	Pipe Coverer & Insulator	
18 September 1960	McWherter, Joy L.	Pipe Coverer & Insulator	
11 September 1960	Nidever, Wade C.	Pipe Coverer & Insulator	
11 September 1960	Owens, Robert A.	Pipe Coverer & Insulator	
4 September 1960	Burdeno, Paul L.	Machinist	
4 September 1960	Dixon, James R.	Machinist	
15 February 1960	Palmer, Malcolm E.	Machinist	
25 September 1960	Peterson, Erhardt H.	Machinist	
1 January 1960	Treadway, Theland E.	Machinist	
11 September 1960	Burnett, Raymond D.	Marine Machinist	
18 April 1960	Davis, Leondard J.	Marine Machinist	
18 September 1960	Dunne, Charles U.	Marine Machinist	
11 September 1960	Larsen, Richard W.	Electrician	
11 September 1960	Pelton, Richard E.	Electrician	
25 September 1960	Pfadt, Frederick R.	Electrician	
11 September 1960	Reed, Carl M.	Electrician	
6 November 1960	Belcher, Charles W.	Electronics Mechanic	
11 September 1960	Benigno, Flore T.	Electronics Mechanic	Honor Graduate
11 September 1960	Claborne, James H.	Electronics Mechanic	
18 January 1960	Dollens, Lindsay R.	Electronics Mechanic	
11 September 1960	Eckman, Robert B.	Electronics Mechanic	
25 September 1960	Mays, Walter E.	Electronics Mechanic	
			43 for 1960

526 Total

DAT	NAME OF GRADUATE	SKILLED TRADE	NOTES
10 September 1961	Bishop, Robert J.	Shipfitter	
4 June 1961	Edmondson, Darryl R.	Shipfitter	
19 November 1961	Reynolds, Robert A.	Shipfitter	
10 September 1961	Richardson, Robert E.	Shipfitter	
10 September 1961	Husband, Ray B.	Welder	
17 September 1961	Alger, Ronald L.	Blacksmith	
17 September 1961	Smith, Kenley M.	Blacksmith	
24 September 1961	Rimmer, O'Dell	Boilermaker	
17 September 1961	Davison, Kenneth V.	Boatbuilder	
17 September 1961	Hojaboom, Richard L.	Boatbuilder	
17 September 1961	Billetts, Frederick D.	Joiner	
17 September 1961	Douglas, Julius E.	Joiner	
21 May 1961	Duran, Oscar	Sheetmetal Worker	
10 September 1961	Morris, Raymon Lee	Sheetmetal Worker	
24 September 1961	Strohman, William	Sheetmetal Worker	
10 September 1961	Wilson, Bobby A.	Sheetmetal Worker	
23 July 1961	Cassingham, Donald	Pipefitter	
24 September 1961	Cornwall, John L.	Pipefitter	
10 September 1961	Ciolek, Richard J.	Machinist	
10 September 1961	Mahr, John G.	Machinist	
15 October 1961	Moore, Dennis A.	Machinist	
16 July 1961	Renouard, James L.	Machinist	
15 October 1961	Silva, Daniel A.	Machinist	
10 September 1961	Smith, Donald F.	Machinist	
29 October 1961	Treadway, Charles B.	Machinist	
10 September 1961	Weinstein, Robert L.	Machinist	
24 September 1961	Baccus, Charles R. Jr.	Marine Machinist	
24 September 1961	Baker, Norman C.	Marine Machinist	
24 September 1961	Bryant, George T.	Marine Machinist	
8 October 1961	Gadberry, Charles W.	Marine Machinist	
10 September 1961	Hird, Robert L.	Marine Machinist	
24 September 1961	Murphy, John A.	Marine Machinist	
24 September 1961	Ashbridge, Vernon L.	Electrician	
24 September 1961	Boehm, Lester A.	Electrician	
15 January 1961	Jackson, Steven A.	Electrician	
24 September 1961	Stewart, Hollis A.	Electrician	
24 September 1961	Warner, Thomas M.	Electrician	
17 September 1961	Brown, Donald C.	Electronics Mechanic	
17 September 1961	Craig, Curtis D.	Electronics Mechanic	
17 September 1961	Davis, Douglas K.	Electronics Mechanic	
17 September 1961	Gaden, Glenn V.	Electronics Mechanic	
17 September 1961	King, Darrell R.	Electronics Mechanic	Honor Graduate
			42 for 1961

568 Total

DAT	NAME OF GRADUATE	SKILLED TRADE	NOTES
16 September 1962	Davis, Donald R.	Shipfitter	
16 September 1962	Hanson, Donald L.	Shipfitter	
16 September 1962	Millington, Joseph D.	Shipfitter	
11 November 1962	Nightingale, Gordon M.	Shipfitter	
16 September 1962	Plambeck, Christian A.	Shipfitter	
28 October 1962	Harbour, Ernest W.	Welder	
16 September 1962	Stoner, Donald F.	Welder	
16 September 1962	Zidek, Albert M.	Welder	
24 June 1962	Wastell, Martin G. Jr.	Boilermaker	
16 September 1962	Setran, Arnold R.	Rigger	
8 July 1962	Stone, Oscar P.	Rigger	
16 September 1962	Fernandez, Renald	Sheetmetal Worker	
16 September 1962	Grigg, Arthur R.	Sheetmetal Worker	
16 September 1962	Manis, James C.	Pipefitter	
16 September 1962	Nelson, Henry E. Jr.	Pipefitter	
16 September 1962	Massoth, Frank T.	Pipe Coverer & Insulator	
16 September 1962	Baiguga, Clifford L.	Machinist	
16 September 1962	Clawson, Royce B.	Machinist	
16 September 1962	Crist, Charles E.	Machinist	
18 March 1962	Graham, Gary G.	Machinist	
30 September 1962	Hawkins, Richard L.	Machinist	
16 September 1962	Justice, Paul G.	Machinist	
16 September 1962	Leon, Salvador J.	Machinist	
28 October 1962	Lewis, Myrll E.	Machinist	
16 September 1962	Siebert, Richard K.	Machinist	
30 September 1962	Anderson, Edward L.	Marine Machinist	
16 September 1962	Beckman, Charles H.	Marine Machinist	
16 September 1962	Bitney, Richard P.	Marine Machinist	
16 September 1962	Garrison, Franklin T.	Marine Machinist	Honor Graduate
16 September 1962	Manning, Clyde E.	Marine Machinist	
16 September 1962	Ramsay, William A.	Marine Machinist	
16 September 1962	Boomer, Daniel M.	Electrician	
14 October 1962	DePreker, John F.	Electrician	
16 September 1962	Gregg, Orville H.	Electrician	
16 September 1962	Jordan, Marshall C.	Electrician	
16 September 1962	Kurai, Yasuo	Electrician	
16 September 1962	Kuroda, Kobai	Electrician	
16 September 1962	Mitchell, Joseph L.	Electrician	
16 September 1962	Nichols, Martin L.	Electrician	
16 September 1962	Sparbel, Donald H.	Electrician	
16 September 1962	Wheeler, Douglas I. Jr.	Electrician	
16 September 1962	Butler, Donny E.	Electronics Mechanic	
16 September 1962	Harper, Garland L.	Electronics Mechanic	
16 September 1962	Scammahorn, Donald	Electronics Mechanic	
16 September 1962	Uchimiya, Ray	Electronics Mechanic	
			45 for 1962
			613 Total

DAT	NAME OF GRADUATE	SKILLED TRADE	NOTES
22 December 1963	Clark, David L.	Shipfitter	
15 September 1963	Duncan, Ronald C.	Shipfitter	
15 September 1963	Lepper, Raymond H.	Shipfitter	
15 September 1963	Martin, Bryan G.	Shipfitter	
13 October 1963	Perry George G.	Shipfitter	
1 September 1963	Elliott, David L.	Welder	
1 September 1963	Herman, Robert H.	Welder	
15 September 1963	Malin, Ronald E.	Welder	
1 September 1963	Rogers, Hal R.	Welder	
15 September 1963	Curran, Joseph G.	Boilermaker	
1 September 1963	Rugg, Francis J.	Boilermaker	
1 September 1963	Ashby, Charles R.	Shipwright	
15 September 1963	Jones, Gayle A.	Joiner	
1 September 1963	Newell, Tommy W.	Rigger	
1 September 1963	Cook, Lawrence K.	Sheetmetal Worker	
6 January 1963	Henton, James P.	Sheetmetal Worker	
1 September 1963	Meusch, John J.	Sheetmetal Worker	
29 September 1963	Fulton, Shirley A.	Pipefitter	
1 September 1963	Dennis, William R.	Pipe Coverer & Insulator	
1 September 1963	Humphrey, Bobby R.	Refrigeration Mechanic	
1 September 1963	Bjerke, Stanley G.	Machinist	
15 September 1963	Ely, Frederick D.	Machinist	
1 September 1963	Elzea, George E.	Machinist	
29 September 1963	Galloway, James F.	Machinist	
29 September 1963	Isham, Ted J.	Machinist	
1 September 1963	Martin, Eugene H.	Machinist	
1 September 1963	Norcross, Frank L.	Machinist	Honor Graduate
29 September 1963	Reid, Wayne E.	Machinist	
1 September 1963	Simpson, Norman B.	Machinist	
1 September 1963	Brucker, Jacob A.	Marine Machinist	
1 September 1963	Coll, Orlie E.	Marine Machinist	
1 September 1963	Franco, Dario S.	Marine Machinist	
1 September 1963	Howse, Walter F.	Marine Machinist	
15 September 1963	Simpson, Norman E.	Marine Machinist	
17 November 1963	Winget, George W.	Marine Machinist	
1 September 1963	Alt, LeRoy D.	Electrician	
15 September 1963	Carr, Robert W.	Electrician	
1 September 1963	Deinstadt, Larry W.	Electrician	
1 September 1963	Stauffer, Harold R.	Electrician	
1 September 1963	Thomas, Ralph E.	Electrician	
27 October 1963	Crumby, Hardy L. Jr.	Electronics Mechanic	
1 September 1963	Jordon, Robert T.	Electronics Mechanic	
1 September 1963	Priebe, Lloyd W.	Electronics Mechanic	
			43 for 1963

656 Total

DAT	NAME OF GRADUATE	SKILLED TRADE	NOTES
13 September 1964	Fuller, Rufus	Shipfitter	
13 September 1964	Klug, Peter Jr.	Shipfitter	
13 September 1964	Messersmith, Alfred W	Shipfitter	
13 September 1964	Munoz, William R.	Shipfitter	
13 September 1964	Tighe, Walter B.	Shipfitter	
5 January 1964	Wright, Royce C.	Shipfitter	
22 November 1964	Spika, Michael S.	Welder	
30 August 1964	Macknicki, Stanley W.	Boilermaker	
11 October 1964	Ennis, Jon P.	Boilermaker	
11 October 1964	Owens, Norman P.	Boilermaker	
30 August 1964	Barbes, Richard G.	Shipwright	
30 August 1964	Wariner, Max E.	Joiner	
13 September 1964	Armstrong, Paul D.	Sheetmetal Worker	
13 September 1964	Mumford, Malcom	Sheetmetal Worker	
13 September 1964	Werner, James E. Jr.	Sheetmetal Worker	
27 September 1964	Parsons, William H. Jr.	Refrigeration Mechanic	
30 August 1964	Garden, James J.	Refrigeration Mechanic	
10 May 1964	Prickett, Johnny F. Jr.	Refrigeration Mechanic	
13 September 1964	Day, Albert W.	Pipefitter	
13 September 1964	DeMooy, Richard	Pipefitter	
13 September 1964	Johnson, Julius Jr.	Pipefitter	
6 December 1964	Edwards, Cecil E.	Machinist	
13 September 1964	Erb, Terrill D.	Machinist	
30 August 1964	Hanbury, Thomas D.	Machinist	
30 August 1964	Marabito, Raymond J.	Machinist	
13 September 1964	Moore, Marvin K.	Machinist	Honor Graduate
13 September 1964	Nance, Fredrick M.	Machinist	
30 August 1964	Nelson, Arthur G.	Machinist	
13 September 1964	Phineas, Mike	Machinist	
13 September 1964	Sanchez, Jose R.	Machinist	
13 September 1964	Vasquez, Louis M.	Machinist	
30 August 1964	Anderson, William F.	Marine Machinist	
30 August 1964	Due, William H.	Marine Machinist	
27 September 1964	Elliot, Bruce G.	Marine Machinist	
30 August 1964	Anderson, Jon E.	Electrician	
30 August 1964	Bennett, James D.	Electrician	
16 August 1964	Charles, Walter C.	Electrician	
30 August 1964	Cudney, Charles R.	Electrician	
30 August 1964	Eastman, David L.	Electrician	
13 September 1964	Rose, Duane E.	Electrician	
30 August 1964	Womack, James E.	Electrician	
			41 for 1964

697 Total

	NAME OF GRADUATE	SKILLED TRADE	NOTES
12 September 1965	Sanchez, John	Shipfitter	
12 September 1965	Satterfield, Albert E.	Shipfitter	
12 September 1965	DeMatto, Gabriel	Boilermaker	
15 August 1965	Peterson, Dwight	Boilermaker	
26 September 1965	Powers, William A.	Boilermaker	
12 September 1965	Galati, Anthony L.	Blacksmith	
12 September 1965	Adler, Mitchell J.	Sheetmetal Worker	
12 September 1965	King, Chester A.	Sheetmetal Worker	
12 September 1965	Quatrone, Larry J.	Sheetmetal Worker	
12 September 1965	Batryn, Eugene B.	Pipefitter	
12 September 1965	Denham, Charles V.	Pipefitter	
12 September 1965	Guianen, John J.	Pipefitter	
26 September 1965	Railston, Jim C.	Pipefitter	
10 October 1965	Warrick, James W.	Pipefitter	
12 September 1965	Barker, Charles P	Machinist	
12 September 1965	Boaz, James C.	Machinist	
12 September 1965	Christmas, Ernest M.	Machinist	
12 September 1965	Eickelberger, John E.	Machinist	
26 September 1965	Franson, Donald L.	Machinist	
20 June 1965	Waters, James W.	Machinist	
12 September 1965	Young, Norman C. Jr.	Machinist	
12 September 1965	Casserly, Clyde M.	Marine Machinist	
12 September 1965	Bruggeman, Charles	Marine Machinist	
12 September 1965	Rattner, David J.	Marine Machinist	
12 September 1965	Sugita, Toru	Marine Machinist	
12 September 1965	Alther, Edward A.	Electrician	
12 September 1965	Fish, Donald D.	Electrician	
12 September 1965	Hill, Delwin W.	Electrician	
12 September 1965	Jones, Richard D.	Electrician	
12 September 1965	McMillen, Jacob Jr.	Electrician	
12 September 1965	Montana, John	Electrician	
21 November 1965	Peterson, Richard J.	Electrician	
12 September 1965	Petkow, Louois H.	Electrician	
12 September 1965	Billiet, Edgar P.	Electronics Mechanic	
12 September 1965	Faulkner, Charles A.	Electronics Mechanic	
12 September 1965	Russell, Denny R.	Electronics Mechanic	Honor Graduate
7 November 1965	Iskowitz, Stuart A.	Fire Control Mechanic	
			37 for 1965

734 Total

DAT	NAME OF GRADUATE	SKILLED TRADE	NOTES
25 September 1966	Crum, Bill W.	Shipfitter	
25 September 1966	Kelly, John A.	Shipfitter	
11 September 1966	Jones, Dale A.	Shipfitter	
16 January 1966	Bauer, John E.	Welder	
16 January 1966	Churchill, David L.	Welder	
16 January 1966	Friedman, Joseph S.	Welder	
16 January 1966	Fortenberry, Jerry L.	Welder	
27 February 1966	Kenney, Wilbur L.	Welder	
16 January 1966	Miller, Dewey C.	Welder	
16 January 1966	Valadez, Angel R.	Welder	
9 October 1966	Blake, John L.	Boilermaker	
11 September 1966	Hatfield, Russell	Boilermaker	
11 September 1966	Mitchell, Matthew J.	Boilermaker	
11 September 1966	Alden, Charles W.	Sheetmetal Worker	
11 September 1966	Dills, Ralph E.	Sheetmetal Worker	
11 September 1966	Eastman, Gale M.	Sheetmetal Worker	
11 September 1966	Mattina, Vincent C.	Sheetmetal Worker	
6 November 1966	Mullen, George E.	Sheetmetal Worker	
11 September 1966	Rowland, Edward L.	Sheetmetal Worker	
9 October 1966	Tilzer, Gary	Sheetmetal Worker	
11 September 1966	Miller, Edward A.	Pipefitter	
9 October 1966	Price, Charles V. III	Pipefitter	
11 September 1966	Purris, Lee A.	Pipefitter	
11 September 1966	Chipperfield, William	Pipe Coverer & Insulator	
9 October 1966	Price, Joe R.	Pipe Coverer & Insulator	
11 September 1966	Risko, Joseph M.	Pipe Coverer & Insulator	
6 November 1966	Webb, Perry R.	Pipe Coverer & Insulator	
9 October 1966	Wixom, Joseph N.	Pipe Coverer & Insulator	
11 September 1966	Allen, earl B.	Machinist	
11 September 1966	Avery, Douglas M.	Machinist	
11 September 1966	Behunin, Maughn R.	Machinist	
11 September 1966	Bishop, Raymond J.	Machinist	
28 August 1966	Cash, Michael S.	Machinist	
11 September 1966	Cluney, William M.	Machinist	
11 September 1966	Haas, David R.	Machinist	
11 September 1966	Ortega, Angel F.	Machinist	
10 April 1966	Ridgley, David H.	Machinist	
11 September 1966	Wiley, Tacoma W.	Machinist	
23 October 1966	Clark, Noman J. Jr.	Marine Machinist	
11 September 1966	Crupa, Carlos, M.	Marine Machinist	
11 September 1966	Hollingsworth, Ronald	Marine Machinist	
30 January 1966	Humphries, Harold L.	Marine Machinist	
11 September 1966	Smeltzer, John H.	Marine Machinist	
11 September 1966	Smith, Bernard D.	Marine Machinist	
11 September 1966	Thomas, Ronald W.	Marine Machinist	
11 September 1966	Watson, William A.	Marine Machinist	
11 September 1966	Weinstein, Harry	Marine Machinist	
11 September 1966	Brunner, Robert P.	Electrician	
25 September 1966	Cirasale, Peter	Electrician	
25 September 1966	Jimenez, Anthony	Electrician	
14 August 1966	O'Conner, Bernard M.	Electrician	

1966 Continued next page

DAT	NAME OF GRADUATE	SKILLED TRADE	NOTES
11 September 1966	Proffitt, Wilbert B.	Electrician	
11 September 1966	Taylor, John A.	Electrician	
14 August 1966	Cooper, Arthur M.	Electronics Mechanic	
11 September 1966	Flores, Raul M.	Electronics Mechanic	
11 September 1966	Pfeiffer, John R.	Electronics Mechanic	Honor Graduate
25 September 1966	Martinez, Jose T.	Electronics Mechanic	
9 October 1966	Gresham, Marvin E.	Fire Control Mechanic	
27 March 1966	Harrod, James E.	Fire Control Mechanic	
11 September 1966	Maddux, Robert S.	Fire Control Mechanic	
11 September 1966	Seigford, Kenneth C.	Fire Control Mechanic	
			61 for 1966

795 Total

5 November 1967	Erkes, Vernon Loyd	Shipfitter	
10 September 1967	McKnight, Glen E.	Shipfitter	
10 September 1967	Seely, Mitt A.	Shipfitter	
10 September 1967	Stewart, Ronald G.	Shipfitter	
10 September 1967	Washington, Frank E.	Shipfitter	
10 September 1967	Adams, Paul T.	Welder	
10 September 1967	Doak, Floyd A.	Welder	
10 September 1967	Wilkinson, David G.	Welder	
10 September 1967	Young, Michael D.	Welder	
10 September 1967	Erspamer, Walter L.	Boilermaker	
10 September 1967	Gerdes, John H.	Boilermaker	
10 September 1967	Chandler, Donald S.	Blacksmith	
10 September 1967	Berger, Nicolas	Sheetmetal Worker	
10 September 1967	Mendenhall, Carey R.	Sheetmetal Worker	
10 September 1967	Davis, Christopher	Pipefitter	
24 September 1967	McKay, David L.	Pipefitter	
10 September 1967	Yates, Gerald G.	Pipefitter	
10 September 1967	Allen, Craig R.	Machinist	
10 September 1967	Banar, Joseph C.	Machinist	
10 September 1967	Bullock, Elmer G.	Machinist	
10 September 1967	Cassady, Kenneth E.	Machinist	
10 September 1967	Fujioka, Tadao	Machinist	
10 September 1967	James, Barry P.	Machinist	
10 September 1967	LeBlanc, Walter C.	Machinist	
10 September 1967	Mintz, Melvyn B.	Machinist	
10 September 1967	Mustasa, A. J. Jr.	Machinist	
10 September 1967	Wright, Larry G.	Machinist	
24 September 1967	Carlwell, James R.	Marine Machinist	
2 February 1967	Holmes, Thomas P.	Marine Machinist	Honor Graduate
24 September 1967	Humphreys, James R.	Marine Machinist	
27 August 1967	Muldrew, Dorsie L.	Marine Machinist	
10 September 1967	Tandoi, Joseph A.	Marine Machinist	
10 September 1967	Wall, Larry G.	Marine Machinist	
10 September 1967	Alvarez, J. R.	Electrician	
30 July 1967	Davis, Robert G.	Electrician	
10 September 1967	Fishbeck, Jack D.	Electrician	
13 August 1967	Howatin, Fred M.	Electrician	
10 September 1967	Leming, Howard A. Jr.	Electrician	

1967 Continued next page

DAT	NAME OF GRADUATE	SKILLED TRADE	NOTES
10 September 1967	Simpkins, Robert L.	Electrician	
4 June 1967	Taylor, Jerry D.	Electrician	
10 September 1967	Turgeon, Arthur F.	Electrician	
10 September 1967	Gallo, Armondo J.	Electronics Mechanic	
24 September 1967	Jackson, Ray J. III	Electronics Mechanic	
27 August 1967	Joseph, John C.	Electronics Mechanic	
27 August 1967	Prince, Leonard H.	Electronics Mechanic	
10 September 1967	Sawyer, Victor L.	Electronics Mechanic	
13 August 1967	Williams, Stephen T.	Electronics Mechanic	
10 September 1967	Butler, Kenneth	Fire Control Mechanic	
10 September 1967	Erickson, Thomas H.	Fire Control Mechanic	
27 August 1967	Gibbons, John J.	Fire Control Mechanic	
27 August 1967	Karlson, Henry	Fire Control Mechanic	
			51 for 1967

846 Total

DAT	NAME OF GRADUATE	SKILLED TRADE	NOTES
8 May 1968	Denton, Paul D.	Boilermaker	
25 February 1968	Rigsby, Bill K.	Pipe Coverer & Insulator	
20 October 1968	Monar, Chester	Machinist	
7 April 1968	Tyler, Charles H.	Machinist	
22 September 1968	Abrams, Howard	Electrician	
8 November 1968	Brownlee, Walter H. Jr.	Electrician	
1 December 1968	Smith, Gary D.	Electrician	
			7 for 1968

853 Total

DAT	NAME OF GRADUATE	SKILLED TRADE	NOTES
5 October 1969	Anast, William A. Jr.	Shipfitter	
5 October 1969	Burr, Isaac D.	Shipfitter	
5 October 1969	Fish, Randolf L.	Shipfitter	
5 October 1969	Jankowski, Bernard E.	Shipfitter	
27 July 1969	Smith, William E.	Shipfitter	
10 August 1969	Raike, Jess L.	Welder	
10 August 1969	Smith, Thomas E.	Welder	
19 October 1969	Cedarholm, Henry A.	Shipwright	
19 October 1969	Joseph, Faheem G.	Boatbuilder	
19 October 1969	Bradshaw, Marion	Sheetmetal Worker	
19 October 1969	Marshall, Oliver V. E.	Sheetmetal Worker	
29 June 1969	Mullen, Keith E.	Sheetmetal Worker	
19 October 1969	Wallace Donald E.	Pipefitter	
27 July 1969	Robinson, John C.	Pipe Coverer & Insulator	
10 August 1969	Burk, Jimmie L.	Refrigeration Mechanic	
2 November 1969	Barrett, Donald R.	Machinist	
9 February 1969	Davies, Thomas H.	Machinist	
19 October 1969	Farmer, Michael E.	Machinist	
2 November 1969	Obritz, Robert J.	Machinist	
30 November 1969	Reid, Robert H.	Machinist	
5 October 1969	Stucker, Craig A.	Machinist	
6 April 1969	Huckaby, John R. Jr.	Marine Machinist	
6 April 1969	Gamble, Donald A.	Marine Machinist	
19 October 1969	Simpson, Gregory J.	Marine Machinist	
5 October 1969	Denny, William B.	Electrician	
5 October 1969	Ekizian, Martin D.	Electrician	
21 September 1969	Pace, Larry R.	Electrician	
2 November 1969	Amaro, Raymond D.	Electronics Mechanic	
5 October 1969	Hanson, Larry E.	Electronics Mechanic	
7 September 1969	Woolsey, James W.	Electronics Mechanic	
5 October 1969	Guimond, Michael J.	Fire Control Mechanic	Honor Graduate
5 October 1969	Nickell, Virgil L.	Fire Control Mechanic	
			32 for 1969

885 Total

DATE	NAME OF GRADUATE	SKILLED TRADE	NOTES
*10 January 1971	Lees, Alan A.	Shipfitter	Honor Graduate
18 October 1970	McFadden, Bruce L.	Shipfitter	
*10 January 1971	Montrose, Howard J.	Shipfitter	
1 November 1970	Renfrow, Robert F.	Shipfitter	
*10 January 1971	Thomas, William A.	Shipfitter	
18 October 1970	Thompson, Kenneth R.	Shipfitter	
*10 January 1971	Tollison, David R.	Shipfitter	
*10 January 1971	Anderson, Lawrence	Welder	
*10 January 1971	May, Buddy P.	Welder	
31 May 1970	Sperling, Ashley M.	Welder	
*10 January 1971	Thirion, Hary G.	Welder	
13 December 1970	Barker, Theo G. II	Boilermaker	
*24 January 1971	Lomelino, Gary D.	Boilermaker	
*24 January 1971	Massie, Charles T.	Boilermaker	
13 December 1970	Accursi, Geoffrey S.	Joiner	
29 November 1970	Fliegner, Harold A. Jr.	Joiner	
*24 January 1971	Jones, Freddie L.	Rigger	
*7 February 1971	Parent, Bruce O.	Rigger	
27 December 1970	Hoppe, Frederick W.	Sheetmetal Worker	
15 November 1970	Lambert, Michael E.	Sheetmetal Worker	
*7 March 1971	Muse, Kirk E.	Sheetmetal Worker	
*7 February 1971	Snyder, Glen O.	Sheetmetal Worker	
18 October 1970	Spence, Arthur L.	Sheetmetal Worker	
6 September 1970	Elliott, Terry W.	Pipefitter	
1 November 1970	Harrison, Michael A.	Pipefitter	
*21 March 1971	Sanders, David A.	Pipe Coverer & Insulator	
6 September 1970	Beckner, Albert M. Jr.	Machinist	
6 September 1970	Cooper George A. Jr.	Machinist	
4 October 1970	Dunio, Edward W.	Machinist	
6 September 1970	Fabisiak, John E.	Machinist	
20 September 1970	Fox, George E. Jr.	Machinist	
6 September 1970	Jackson, Charles R.	Machinist	
4 October 1970	Jensen, Carl R.	Machinist	
20 September 1970	Kahrs, William J.	Machinist	
5 April 1970	Leonard, Kurt E.	Machinist	
*18 April 1971	Lewis, Gerald L.	Machinist	
*4 April 1971	McCleary, Stephen J.	Machinist	
6 September 1970	Peterson, Craig A.	Machinist	
6 September 1970	Smith, Gerald D.	Machinist	
22 February 1970	Torres, Vincent L.	Machinist	

* Denotes members of 1970 Class eceiving their degrees in 1971

1970 Continued next page

DAT	NAME OF GRADUATE	SKILLED TRADE	NOTES
6 September 1970	Wildman, Harry B.	Machinist	
1 November 1970	Whiteker, Steven C.	Machinist	
18 October 1970	Black, Daniel M.	Marine Machinist	
8 February 1970	Cromer, Howad E.	Marine Machinist	
*March 1971	Fritz, Arthur A.	Marine Machinist	
18 October 1970	Hansen Kenneth S.	Marine Machinist	
20 September 1970	Hansen, Louis F.	Marine Machinist	
6 September 1970	Haslock, Steven W.	Marine Machinist	
1 November 1970	Holt, Chester D. Jr.	Marine Machinist	
1 November 1970	Mauser, Raymond L.	Marine Machinist	
18 October 1970	Olson, Donald C.	Marine Machinist	
13 December 1970	Spratt, Michael T.	Marine Machinist	
13 December 1970	Upcroft, Latta T.	Marine Machinist	
8 March 1970	Cromer, Paul B.	Electrician	
6 September 1970	Shuman, Robert C. Jr.	Electrician	
6 September 1970	Wells, James H.	Electrician	
6 September 1970	Wolf, Kenneth R. Jr.	Electrician	
6 September 1970	Amador, Samuel Jr.	Electronics Mechanic	
18 October 1970	Delahanty, Richard M.	Electronics Mechanic	
6 September 1970	Estrada, Phillip J.	Electronics Mechanic	
20 September 1970	Foster, Robert L.	Electronics Mechanic	
22 February 1970	Gallegas, Jow M.	Electronics Mechanic	
20 September 1970	Geer, Frank V.	Electronics Mechanic	
18 October 1970	Howell, Alvin B.	Electronics Mechanic	
20 September 1970	Johnson, James T.	Electronics Mechanic	
6 September 1970	Kauble, Edward L.	Electronics Mechanic	
18 October 1970	Myrwold, Richard K.	Electronics Mechanic	
18 October 1970	Chun, Michael King Wo	Fire Control Mechanic	
6 September 1970	Collins, Eugene S.	Fire Control Mechanic	
18 October 1970	Cudisk, Bennett C.	Fire Control Mechanic	
6 September 1970	Evans, Lewis W.	Fire Control Mechanic	
18 October 1970	Walker, Delton H.	Fire Control Mechanic	
			72 for 1970

* Denotes members of Class of 1970 receiving their certificates in 1971   957 Total

DAT	NAME OF GRADUATE	SKILLED TRADE	NOTES
19 September 1971	Asuega, Tasi T.	Shipfitter	
5 September 1971	Cady, Roger D.	Shipfitter	
5 September 1971	Eckmayer, Jacob P.	Shipfitter	
5 September 1971	Jackson, Melvin D.	Shipfitter	
31 October 1971	Lewis, Thomas	Shipfitter	
22 August 1971	Merritt, Donald A.	Shipfitter	
5 September 1971	Sanchez, Salvador	Shipfitter	
5 September 1971	Baker, Samuel N. III	Welder	
3 October 1971	Doughty, George W.	Welder	
22 August 1971	Earwood, Ralph B.	Welder	
22 August 1971	Lapera, David M. Jr.	Welder	
22 August 1971	Massey, Raymond M.	Welder	
22 August 1971	May, Stanley F.	Welder	
5 September 1971	Ochoa, David P.	Welder	
3 October 1971	Riddle, David L.	Welder	
5 September 1971	Rodriguez, George A.	Welder	
27 June 1971	Rollefson, Duane L.	Welder	
25 July 1971	Siebert, Walter E.	Welder	
22 August 1971	Venturato, Gary A.	Welder	
22 August 1971	Wilbur, Neal P.	Welder	
11 July 1971	Sabol, Robert T.	Shipwright	
5 September 1971	Vetrovec, William J.	Shipwright	
17 October 1971	Walker, Duane	Shipwright	
12 December 1971	Pharis, Donald R.	Boilermaker	
5 September 1971	Ichicawa, Freddie P.	Boatbuilder	
5 September 1971	Monath, Jerry L.	Boatbuilder	
5 September 1971	Swenson, James E.	Boatbuilder	
5 September 1971	Leuschner, Carl J.	Patternmaker	
5 September 1971	Grisamer, Gary L.	Rigger	
5 September 1971	Janowicz, John R.	Rigger	
3 October 1971	Turner, Eddie A.	Rigger	
19 September 1971	Valler, Orel N.	Rigger	
5 September 1971	Edmond, Edward L.	Painter	
19 September 1971	Force, King M.	Painter	
22 August 1971	Gartin, Michael M.	Painter	
31 October 1971	Glazener, Walter H.	Painter	
5 September 1971	Rice, Ray E.	Painter	
14 November 1971	Stokes, Raymond	Painter	
3 October 1971	Anderson, Robert W.	Sheetmetal Worker	
19 September 1971	Larkin, Thomas E.	Sheetmetal Worker	
3 October 1971	Martin, Joseph F.	Sheetmetal Worker	
5 September 1971	Renz, Kenneth J.	Sheetmetal Worker	
5 September 1971	Smith, Robert D.	Coppersmith	
22 August 1971	Castro, Rodolfo T.	Pipefitter	
22 August 1971	Dillon, Ronald L.	Pipefitter	
3 October 1971	Dougherty, Michael D.	Pipefitter	
3 October 1971	Fuller, Larry F.	Pipefitter	Honor Graduate
14 November 1971	Gordon, Amos	Pipefitter	
3 October 1971	Gray, Duke, Jr.	Pipefitter	
5 September 1971	Malin, David E.	Pipefitter	
14 November 1971	Savala, Edward P.	Pipefitter	

1971 Continued next page

DAT	NAME OF GRADUATE	SKILLED TRADE	NOTES
5 September 1971	Smith, Gilbert J.	Pipefitter	
12 December 1971	Spease, Terry R.	Pipefitter	
19 September 1971	Williams, Wilbert L.	Pipe Coverer & Insulator	
22 August 1971	Crabtree, Robert E.	Refrigeration Mechanic	
12 December 1971	Vardeman, Ralph L.	Refrigeration Mechanic	
14 November 1971	Anderson, Ronald E.	Machinist	
28 November 1971	Araon, Keith A.	Machinist	
22 August 1971	Blanco, Rosendo D.	Machinist	
22 August 1971	Bledsoe, George M.	Machinist	
5 September 1971	Bonachita, Gary W.	Machinist	
22 August 1971	Callahan, Nolan	Machinist	
11 July 1971	Crane, James R.	Machinist	
22 August 1971	Ferguson, Clinton T.	Machinist	
31 October 1971	Flores, Frank J.	Machinist	
31 October 1971	Gernule, Edward A.	Machinist	
5 September 1971	Hanson, Clifton W.	Machinist	
5 September 1971	Johnson, James W.	Machinist	
22 August 1971	Alday, Al R.	Marine Machinist	
22 August 1971	Bennett, German W.	Marine Machinist	
22 August 1971	Bergamini, Jay	Marine Machinist	
22 August 1971	Gomez, Samuel R.	Marine Machinist	
17 October 1971	Hammond, Cornelius	Marine Machinist	
22 August 1971	H;umphries, James B.	Marine Machinist	
22 August 1971	Lofstrom, Jack D.	Marine Machinist	
31 October 1971	Manriquez, Steve J.	Marine Machinist	
22 August 1971	Scott, John P.	Marine Machinist	
22 August 1971	Williams, Theodore A.	Marine Machinist	
26 December 1971	Casillan, Daniel	Machinist (Ship's Weapons)	
5 September 1971	Howell, Stephen W.	Machinist (Ship's Weapons)	
22 August 1971	McKercher, Thomas D.	Machinist (Ship's Weapons)	
22 August 1971	Nost, Hubert E.	Machinist (Ship's Weapons)	
5 September 1971	Smetana, Mark A.	Machinist (Ship's Weapons)	
5 September 1971	Solis, Armando	Machinist (Ship's Weapons)	
5 September 1971	Bird, Richard T.	Electrician	
22 August 1971	Campbell, Douglas R.	Electrician	
22 August 1971	Jensen, Lester H. Jr.	Electrician	
5 September 1971	Vaught, Charles V. Jr.	Electrician	
22 August 1971	Zuheke, Robert E.	Electrician	
22 August 1971	Anast, James	Electonics Mechanic	
19 September 1971	Dunham, James H.	Electonics Mechanic	
22 August 1971	Earnest, Richard K.	Electonics Mechanic	
22 August 1971	Gramenz, Dennis D.	Electonics Mechanic	
5 September 1971	Jackson, Nathaniel G.	Electonics Mechanic	
3 October 1971	Noel, Thomas L.	Electonics Mechanic	
22 August 1971	Puskarick, Mark S.	Electonics Mechanic	
22 August 1971	Rivera, Patrick K.	Electonics Mechanic	
5 September 1971	Ash, Charles B.	Fire Control Mechanic	
5 September 1971	Reeves, Thomas J.	Fire Control Mechanic	
22 August 1971	Savellano, Stanley S.	Fire Control Mechanic	
22 August 1971	Toulouse, Dennis J.	Fire Control Mechanic	
22 August 1971	Widrig, Myron D.	Fire Control Mechanic	
3 October 1971	Williams, Curtis, W.	Fire Control Mechanic	

103 for 1971

1,060 Total

DATE	NAME OF GRADUATE	SKILLED TRADE	NOTES
19 October 1972	Barnes, George D.	Shipfitter	
3 September 1972	Davis, Philip S.	Shipfitter	
26 November 1972	Francis, Allen G.	Shipfitter	
10 December 1972	Lewis, Gerald R.	Shipfitter	
15 October 1972	Morris, Billy L.	Shipfitter	
11 June 1972	Moen, Michael E.	Shipfitter	
11 June 1972	Viloria, Francisco M.	Shipfitter	
3 September 1972	JcBrayer, Jack L. Jr.	Welder	
9 July 1972	Moser, Wayne O.	Welder	
3 September 1972	Venable, Palmer V.	Welder	
12 November 1972	Baker, Richard E.	Boilermaker	
29 October 1972	Gamble, Frank	Boilermaker	
5 March 1972	Hicks, Phillip II	Boilermaker	
12 November 1972	Liversedge, Frank E.	Boilermaker	
29 October 1972	Mendez, Armando E.	Boilermaker	
19 March 1972	Beauvois, Rolly L.	Shipwright	
15 October 1972	Stice, Allen L.	Shipwright	
15 October 1972	Hughes, Thomas J.	Joiner	
20 February 1972	Levy, Phillip J.	Patternmaker	
1 October 1972	Barrett, Colorado M.	Rigger	
9 January 1972	Melanson, Michael E.	Rigger	
17 September 1972	Perry, William A.	Rigger	
1 October 1972	Sorensen, Thomas A.	Rigger	Honor Graduate
3 September 1972	Carichoff, Robert D.	Painter	
29 October 1972	Makaena, Paul H.	Pipefitter	
15 October 1972	Operchuck, Terry L.	Pipefitter	
20 August 1972	Smith, John E.	Pipefitter	
2 April 1972	Vail, Paul F.	Pipefitter	
17 September 1972	Lough, Thomas A.	Coppersmith	
20 August 1972	Viazanko, Larry J.	Coppersmith	
12 November 1972	Barba, Elias	Machinist	
15 October 1972	Cardin, Paul E.	Machinist	
17 September 1972	Eaton, Lloyd L.	Machinist	
26 November 1972	Hamilton, Richard E.	Machinist	
15 October 1972	Hendrix, Charles E.	Machinist	
29 October 1972	Lawson, Burline	Machinist	
1 October 1972	Lewis, Charlie W. Jr.	Machinist	
29 October 1972	MacInnes, Kenneth M.	Machinist	
24 December 1972	Markham, James A. Jr.	Machinist	
29 October 1972	Meredith, Donald P.	Machinist	
17 September 1972	Nieto, Roque	Machinist	
29 October 1972	Pangelinan, Ignacio G.	Machinist	
25 June 1972	Rigsby, George A.	Machinist	
1 October 1972	Sinclair, Dennis E.	Machinist	
26 November 1972	Staber, David W.	Machinist	
19 March 1972	Coates, Thomas W.	Marine Machinist	Dr. Plusch Award
15 October 1972	Ellison, James B.	Marine Machinist	

1972 Continued next page

DAT	NAME OF GRADUATE	SKILLED TRADE	NOTES
12 November 1972	Guglielmo, Albert P.	Marine Machinist	
17 September 1972	Munoz, Alfred R.	Marine Machinist	
24 December 1972	Newton, Jerry W.	Marine Machinist	
1 October 1972	Vance, William F.	Marine Machinist	
17 September 1972	Amaro, Richard R.	Machinist (Ship's Weapons)	
17 September 1972	Brezner, Richard B.	Machinist (Ship's Weapons)	
1 October 1972	Briggs, Norman N.	Machinist (Ship's Weapons)	
17 September 1972	Figuerero, Robert E.	Machinist (Ship's Weapons)	
15 October 1972	Henry, Nathaniel	Machinist (Ship's Weapons)	
3 September 1972	Mullen, Charles H.	Machinist (Ship's Weapons)	
15 October 1972	Rizer, David H. III	Machinist (Ship's Weapons)	
17 September 1972	Allen, Melvin L.	Electrician	
3 September 1972	Beauchamp, Don A.	Electrician	
1 October 1972	Hernandez, Gregory D.	Electrician	
3 September 1972	LeVine, Richard M.	Electrician	
1 October 1972	Otramba, Mark S.	Electrician	
17 September 1972	Robinson, Charles L.	Electrician	
23 January 1972	Shridan, Richard P.	Electrician	
17 September 1972	Swenson, Robert E.	Electrician	
9 July 1972	Borja, Joseph G.	Electronics Mechanic	
3 September 1972	Congleton, Ira F.	Electronics Mechanic	
17 September 1972	Dooley, Gilbert R. Jr.	Electronics Mechanic	
3 September 1972	Heiden, John M.	Electronics Mechanic	
3 September 1972	Mann, Delbert L.	Electronics Mechanic	
17 September 1972	McClendon, John L.	Electronics Mechanic	
25 June 1972	Oliveras, Louie M.	Electronics Mechanic	
29 October 1972	Robitaille, Charles E.	Electronics Mechanic	
29 October 1972	Bergevin, Daryl G.	Fire Control Mechanic	
17 September 1972	Kuwahara, Toshio	Fire Control Mechanic	
17 September 1972	March, Earl M.	Fire Control Mechanic	
17 September 1972	Marshall, Gary D.	Fire Control Mechanic	
3 September 1972	Paikai, Gaylen L.	Fire Control Mechanic	
			79 for 1972

1,139 Total

DAT	NAME OF GRADUATE	SKILLED TRADE	NOTES
2 September 1973	Baumann, Dwight A.	Shipfitter	
16 September 1973	Forsha, John P.	Shipfitter	
4 March 1973	Bean, Windsor Lee III	Welder	
2 September 1973	Earwood, Larry D.	Welder	
2 September 1973	Garvey, Vaughn D.	Welder	
1 April 1973	Higginbotham, Harold	Welder	
1 April 1973	Johnson, Bruce A.	Welder	
22 July 1973	Randolph, Samuel	Welder	
30 September 1973	Washington, Callie Jr.	Welder	
22 July 1973	Crane, Michael P.	Boilermaker	
22 July 1973	Stanfield, Ben E.	Boilermaker	
2 September 1973	Kaskaneas, Andrew	Shipwright	
16 September 1973	Kerley, Noble K.	Joiner	
23 December 1973	McGary, Alvin	Molder (Plastic)	
2 September 1973	Conn, Douglas W.	Rigger	
14 October 1973	Downey, Tedford W.	Rigger	
14 October 1973	Peres, Pedro A. Jr.	Rigger	
16 September 1973	Springgate, Alvin L.	Rigger	
16 September 1973	Wolf, Lawrence S.	Rigger	
2 September 1973	Graham, Leonard D.	Painter	
16 September 1973	Stubbs, Thomas E.	Painter	
2 September 1973	Yoder, Raymond C.	Painter	
14 October 1973	Hicks, Gregory L.	Sheetmetal Worker	
2 September 1973	O'Dell, James F.	Sheetmetal Worker	
2 September 1973	Wyzykowski, Dennis	Sheetmetal Worker	
11 November 1973	Burns, Thomas R.	Pipefitter	
30 September 1973	Dougherty, Timothy D.	Pipefitter	
4 March 1973	Sowinski, Rober E.	Pipefitter	
24 June 1973	Thomas, Tommy	Pipefitter	
2 September 1973	Ahumada, Mike Jr.	Pipe Coverer & Insulator	
10 June 1973	Cheke, Donald A.	Pipe Coverer & Insulator	
16 September 1973	Masher, Roland C.	Pipe Coverer & Insulator	
2 September 1973	Thompson, James W.	Pipe Coverer & Insulator	
16 September 1973	Wallick, Douglas A.	Pipe Coverer & Insulator	
2 September 1973	Beckett, Leon W.	Machinist	
11 November 1973	Buck, Charles W.	Machinist	
28 October 1973	Coronado, Julian A.	Machinist	
21 January 1973	Delucia, Joseph E.	Machinist	
2 September 1973	Fisher, John T.	Machinist	
10 December 1973	Flores, George M.	Machinist	
22 July 1973	Gamez, Albert R.	Machinist	
2 September 1973	Kasparson, Andrew G.	Machinist	
16 September 1973	Ledbetter, Walter J.	Machinist	
30 September 1973	Lingener, Paul W. III	Machinist	
21 January 1973	Locklear, Kennet	Machinist	
1 April 1973	Martinez, Ernest	Machinist	
28 October 1973	McClanahan, Roger	Machinist	
2 September 1973	Phillips, Jesse	Machinist	
16 September 1973	Wheeler, Henry A.	Machinist	
16 September 1973	Behrendt, Albert R.	Marine Machinist	
2 September 1973	Black, Michael E.	Marine Machinist	

1973 Continued next page

DAT	NAME OF GRADUATE	SKILLED TRADE	NOTES
30 September 1973	Brown, Timothy P.	Marine Machinist	
2 September 1973	Cabrera, Daniel F.	Marine Machinist	
14 October 1973	Cousins, Wallace D.	Marine Machinist	
11 November 1973	David, Ricky W.	Marine Machinist	
2 September 1973	Girton, Benjamin F.	Marine Machinist	
11 November 1973	Holland, Joseph S.	Marine Machinist	
16 September 1973	Johnson, Henry L.	Marine Machinist	
14 October 1973	Rodriquez, Louis F.	Marine Machinist	
16 September 1973	Shows, James N.	Marine Machinist	
16 September 1973	Urria, John B.	Marine Machinist	
16 September 1973	Wasick, Thomas	Marine Machinist	
23 December 1973	Allen, Ronald L.	Machinist (Ship's Weapons)	
2 September 1973	Banzet, James D.	Machinist (Ship's Weapons)	
16 September 1973	Bromley, Gary W.	Machinist (Ship's Weapons)	
2 September 1973	Catkin, Gary C.	Machinist (Ship's Weapons)	
30 September 1973	Halley, Richard M. Jr.	Machinist (Ship's Weapons)	
23 December 1973	Havener, James M.	Machinist (Ship's Weapons)	
16 September 1973	Meehan, John F.	Machinist (Ship's Weapons)	
2 September 1973	Nieto, John A.	Machinist (Ship's Weapons)	
14 October 1973	Robinson, William B.	Machinist (Ship's Weapons)	
23 December 1973	Smith, Clinton A.	Machinist (Ship's Weapons)	
2 September 1973	Townsend, Charles G.	Machinist (Ship's Weapons)	
16 September 1973	George, Donald A.	Electrician	
2 September 1973	Hennig, Fred	Electrician	Dr. Plusch Award
2 September 1973	Jennings, Rodrix L. Jr.	Electrician	
16 September 1973	LaBonte, David R.	Electrician	
30 September 1973	Milek, Stee D.	Electrician	
11 November 1973	Powell, Emmett B.	Electrician	
2 September 1973	Taylor, Robert P.	Electrician	
2 September 1973	Zurin, Manfred D.	Electrician	
1 April 1973	Belvel, Michael L.	Electronics Mechanic	
1 April 1973	Curran, John E.	Electronics Mechanic	
27 May 1973	Garrison, Gary L.	Electronics Mechanic	
2 September 1973	Herara, Manuel	Electronics Mechanic	
8 July 1973	Lemier, Richard A.	Electronics Mechanic	
27 May 1973	Lumsdaine, Phillip	Electronics Mechanic	
8 July 1973	MacDiamid, Robert E.	Electronics Mechanic	
27 May 1973	Onken, Bruce A.	Electronics Mechanic	
27 May 1973	Riebau, Robert A.	Electronics Mechanic	Honor Graduate
27 May 1973	Taylor, Gary A.	Electronics Mechanic	
15 April 1973	Fenton, Ernest C.	Fire Control Mechanic	
27 May 1973	Ingram, Joseph J.	Fire Control Mechanic	
2 September 1973	Pogue, James S.	Fire Control Mechanic	
2 September 1973	Phol, Kenneth T.	Fire Control Mechanic	
2 September 1973	Sifuentis, Augustine C.	Fire Control Mechanic	
			96 for 1973
			1,235 Total

DAT	NAME OF GRADUATE	SKILLED TRADE	NOTES
1 September 1974	Fiorella, Louis P.	Shipfitter	
1 September 1974	Fobb, Herbert Jr.	Shipfitter	
28 April 1974	Kuaea, Victory M.	Shipfitter	
15 September 1974	Utley, William L.	Shipfitter	
1 September 1974	Bromley, James A.	Welder	
1 September 1974	Denison, John C.	Welder	
3 March 1974	O'Connell, Liam	Welder	
1 September 1974	Robedeauz, Richard	Welder	
23 June 1974	Trammeh, Jo A.	Welder	
1 September 1974	Ward, Ronald M.	Welder	
1 September 1974	Warth, Frank R. R.	Welder	
23 June 1974	Burns, Robert J.	Boilermaker	
22 December 1974	Owens, Mariun R.	Blacksmith	
23 June 1974	Blair, Kenneth C.	Shipwright	
18 August 1974	Ferguson, Sylvester	Shipwright	
15 September 1974	Nelson, Richard J.	Joiner	
23 June 1974	Rodriguez, Robert	Joiner	
23 June 1974	Szymanski, Richard L.	Joiner	
15 September 1974	Nieto, Tony B.	Rigger	
23 June 1974	Stapp, Everett L.	Rigger	
23 June 1974	Johnson, Dwayne P.	Painter	
18 August 1974	Marshall, Haywood	Painter	
13 October 1974	McNeal, Bruce L.	Painter	
1 September 1974	DeSoto, Paul	Sheetmetal Worker	
1 September 1974	Seymour, Walter S.	Sheetmetal Worker	
14 April 1974	Barry, Richard M.	Pipefitter	
18 August 1974	Cole, Thomas L.	Pipefitter	
17 March 1974	Crees, Martel	Pipefitter	
1 September 1974	Hauer, Rudolph J.	Pipefitter	
17 February 1974	Jordan, John J.	Pipefitter	
7 July 1974	London, Emanuel	Pipefitter	"B"
18 August 1974	Smith, John L.	Pipefitter	
29 September 1974	Tkos, Alan W.	Pipefitter	
15 September 1974	Newton, James L.	Pipe Coverer & Insulator	
7 July 1974	Rivera, Louis R.	Pipe Coverer & Insulator	
23 June 1974	DiGiovanni, Dennis	Pipe Coverer & Insulator	
21 July 1974	Starnes, James M.	Pipe Coverer & Insulator	
29 September 1974	Cheek, Royce E.	Machinist	
13 October 1974	Jarrett, Arthur C.	Machinist	
29 September 1974	Nieto, Frederic B.	Machinist	
13 October 1974	Rahm, Harold E.	Machinist	
23 June 1974	Renfroe, Eddie Jr.	Machinist	
9 June 1974	Yatsui, Tom Y.	Machinist	
9 June 1974	Beason, Victor L. Jr.	Marine Machinist	
13 October 1974	Bonniwell, Benjamin R.	Marine Machinist	
27 October 1974	Carsten, Thomas A. Jr.	Marine Machinist	
15 September 1974	Douglas, William L.	Marine Machinist	
15 September 1974	George, James L.	Marine Machinist	
7 July 1974	Murphy, Louis B.	Marine Machinist	
29 September 1974	Olson, Donald B.	Marine Machinist	
15 September 1974	Pavelee, Randolph E.	Marine Machinist	

1974 Continued next page

DAT	NAME OF GRADUATE	SKILLED TRADE	NOTES
10 November 1974	Shepard, James E.	Marine Machinist	
29 September 1974	Thomas, Philip S.	Marine Machinist	
20 January 1974	Turks, Roy R.	Machinist (Ship's Weapons)	
23 June 1974	Austin, Bradford R.	Electrician	
23 June 1974	Barbour, James A.	Electrician	
23 June 1974	Baysinger, Bruce A.	Electrician	
23 June 1974	Craycraft, James L.	Electrician	
23 June 1974	Hubbard, Frank R.	Electrician	Dr. Plusch
15 September 1974	Morrison, John C.	Electrician	
23 June 1974	Nieto, John E.	Electrician	
23 June 1974	Thibodo, Eduard D.	Electrician	
13 October 1974	Guerrero, Anthony	Electronics Mechanic	
13 October 1974	Horton, Robert E.	Electronics Mechanic	
17 March 1974	Kryda, Frank	Electronics Mechanic	Honor Graduate
17 February 1974	Sanchez, Jose S.	Electronics Mechanic	
29 September 1974	Schultz, Donald W.	Electronics Mechanic	
31 March 1974	Smith, Charles L. Jr.	Electronics Mechanic	
17 March 1974	Stavros, Leon	Electronics Mechanic	
1 September 1974	Wickliff, Oscar B.	Electronics Mechanic	
31 March 1974	Herold, Rodney L.	Fire Control Mechanic	
29 September 1974	Isenhower, Jerry L.	Fire Control Mechanic	
22 December 1974	Markel, Emmer E. Jr.	Fire Control Mechanic	
23 June 1974	Marquez, Jesse N.	Fire Control Mechanic	
14 April 1974	Montez, Joe L.	Fire Control Mechanic	
			77 for 1974

1,312 Total

22 June 1975	Alojado, William F.	Shipfitter	
19 January 1975	Buck, Neil R.	Shipfitter	
14 September 1975	Gordon, Charlie	Shipfitter	
14 September 1975	Hackett, Stephen H.	Shipfitter	
14 September 1975	Matthews, Neal	Shipfitter	
14 September 1975	O'Brien, John J.	Shipfitter	
14 September 1975	Quinn, Cheser J. Jr.	Shipfitter	
12 October 1975	Rose, Eugene	Shipfitter	
14 September 1975	Swanson, Charles E.	Welder	
11 May 1975	Clyne, Jackie K.	Welder	
22 June 1975	Duncan, Lowell J.	Welder	
22 June 1975	Gerosin, Dennis C.	Welder	
22 June 1975	Haley, Robert C.	Welder	
22 June 1975	Hyatt, James R.	Welder	
22 June 1975	King, Dale E.	Welder	
22 June 1975	Parra, Joseph Jr.	Welder	
22 June 1975	Doddroe, Bernard C.	Blacksmith	
6 July 1975	Lewis, Jack M.	Shipwright	
14 September 1975	Quirez, Manuel Jr.	Shipwright	
31 August 1975	Cleveland, Oakley T.	Joiner	
31 August 1975	Fuertes, Domingo F.	Joiner	
28 September 1975	Pennington, John Jr.	Joiner	
31 August 1975	Eccles, Alfred E.	Rigger	
6 July 1975	Gillott, Randolph	Rigger	

1975 Continued next page

DAT	NAME OF GRADUATE	SKILLED TRADE	NOTES
5 January 1975	Fuentes, Johny L..	Painter	
31 August 1975	Hamilton, Tommy E.	Painter	
31 August 1975	Johnson, Gregory O.	Painter	
22 June 1975	Allen, Teddy D.	Sheetmetal Worker	
22 June 1975	Carroll, Philip F.	Sheetmetal Worker	
28 September 1975	Cruz, Roman	Sheetmetal Worker	
22 June 1975	Marino, Philip C.	Sheetmetal Worker	
22 June 1975	Wilson, Larry A.	Sheetmetal Worker	
14 September 1975	Barrett, Richard J.	Pipefitter	
22 June 1975	Carveters, Robert M.	Pipefitter	
22 June 1975	Galing, James E.	Pipefitter	
22 June 1975	Gehrts, James G.	Pipefitter	
20 July 1975	Gonzales, Oscar V.	Pipefitter	
22 June 1975	Haislip, Samuel J.	Pipefitter	
22 June 1975	Shepherd, Harold J.	Pipefitter	
16 February 1975	Swallow, Leo P.	Pipefitter	
22 June 1975	Uqulini, Stephen A.	Pipefitter	
17 August 1975	Watt, Percy L.	Pipefitter	
22 June 1975	Wherry, Max D.	Pipefitter	
23 November 1975	Jones, James W.	Pipe Coverer & Insulator	
6 July 1975	Reich, Jack	Pipe Coverer & Insulator	
28 September 1975	Concepcion, David C.	Machinist	
14 September 1975	Doyel, Tommie E.	Machinist	
3 August 1975	Gagnon, Edmund J.	Machinist	
19 January 1975	Gibbs, Bennie L.	Machinist	
19 January 1975	Marins, Mike W.	Machinist	
22 June 1975	Ridgeway, Charles J.	Machinist	
31 August 1975	Smith, James W.	Machinist	
14 September 1975	Thompson, Murl J.	Machinist	
14 September 1975	Till, Robert R.	Machinist	
28 September 1975	Webb, Samuel E.	Machinist	
30 March 1975	Zimmerman, Bruce	Machinist	
31 August 1975	Diehl, Robert Jr.	Marine Machinist	
12 October 1975	Dysart, John T.	Marine Machinist	
22 June 1975	Gill, David A.	Marine Machinist	
19 January 1975	Hooper, Robert D.	Marine Machinist	
22 June 1975	Hopkins, Harold E.	Marine Machinist	
31 August 1975	Laurant, Glendell J.	Marine Machinist	
5 January 1975	Leighton, Michael E.	Marine Machinist	
31 August 1975	Llopis, Robert E.	Marine Machinist	
31 August 1975	McIntosh, Bruce R.	Marine Machinist	
31 August 1975	Merrill, Thomas O.	Marine Machinist	
31 August 1975	Oati, Victor J. Jr.	Marine Machinist	
31 August 1975	Watson, Jeffery B.	Marine Machinist	
16 February 1975	Backer, Chester F.	Machinist (Ship's Weapons)	
22 June 1975	Cartwright, Peter J.	Machinist (Ship's Weapons)	
22 June 1975	Huey, Michael H.	Machinist (Ship's Weapons)	
22 June 1975	Otellio, Phillip H.	Machinist (Ship's Weapons)	
3 August 1975	Rudnisky, George N.	Machinist (Ship's Weapons)	
14 September 1975	Ayala, Arthur	Electrician	
26 October 1975	Corpuz, Samuel B.	Electrician	

1975 Continued next page

DAT	NAME OF GRADUATE	SKILLED TRADE	NOTES
14 September 1975	Fehemann, John E. Jr.	Electrician	
20 July 1975	Gasbarra, Jerry A.	Electrician	
28 September 1975	Hash, Omar D. Jr.	Electrician	
14 September 1975	Johnson, Benjamin V.	Electrician	
14 September 1975	Jurvic, Thomas F.	Electrician	
22 June 1975	Maddock, Duane T.	Electrician	Dr. Plusch
14 September 1975	Siegfried, Terry L.	Electrician	
14 September 1975	Byllesby, Michael L.	Electronics Mechanic	
14 September 1975	Coronado, Juan Q.	Electronics Mechanic	
30 March 1975	Hale, Presley E.	Electronics Mechanic	Honor Graduate
28 September 1975	Hartman, Kelly B.	Electronics Mechanic	
30 March 1975	Jacob, Joseph A.	Electronics Mechanic	
14 September 1975	Laraille, Louis	Electronics Mechanic	
28 September 1975	Reinisch, Frederick R.	Electronics Mechanic	
22 June 1975	Otto, Kurt J.	Electronics Mechanic	
14 September 1975	Westerfield, Kelly S.	Electronics Mechanic	
14 September 1975	Halkens, David J.	Fire Control Mechanic	
			93 for 1975

1,405 Total

20 June 1976	Baily, Kenneth R.	Shipfitter	
12 September 1976	Bellenbaum, Frederick	Shipfitter	
5 December 1976	Escanuelas, Antonio R.	Shipfitter	
20 June 1976	King, Curtis	Shipfitter	
12 September 1976	Lopez, Mechael	Shipfitter	
20 June 1976	Winders, Melville T.	Shipfitter	
20 June 1976	Dickson, Harry O.	Welder	
20 June 1976	Flaherty, Frank W.	Welder	
12 September 1976	Hill, Paul D.	Welder	
6 June 1976	Shilling, Edward J.	Welder	
20 June 1976	Wachter, Gregory R.	Welder	
24 October 1976	Daley, Gary F.	Boilermaker	
12 September 1976	Klebusits, Larry	Boilermaker	
24 October 1976	Jones, Ernest E.	Boilermaker	
7 November 1976	Milton, Eugene	Boilermaker	
12 September 1976	Tuttle, Marshall K.	Boilermaker	
29 August 1976	Ellis, Richard P.	Blacksmith	
4 July 1976	Bauer, Kenneth J.	Rigger	
4 July 1976	Cooksie, Robert L.	Rigger	
4 July 1976	Ernst, Gary O.	Rigger	
4 July 1976	Nelson, Robert T.	Rigger	
12 September 1976	Bachman, Robert E.	Painter	
20 June 1976	Gutierrez, Leonard	Painter	
20 June 1976	Jones, Clarence G.	Painter	
21 November 1976	Porter, William F.	Painter	
26 September 1976	McDonald, Ronald S.	Painter	
20 June 1976	White, Thomas C.	Painter	
12 September 1976	Parr, Mark A.	Sheetmetal Worker	
12 September 1976	Williams, Charles T.	Sheetmetal Worker	
4 July 1976	Williams, Henry L.	Sheetmetal Worker	
26 September 1976	Armijo, Henry R.	Pipefitter	

1976 Continued next page

DATE	NAME OF GRADUATE	SKILLED TRADE	NOTES
10 October 1976	Calderon, Antonio	Pipefitter	
26 September 1976	Campbell, Daniel L.	Pipefitter	
26 September 1976	Cunes, Jose	Pipefitter	
26 September 1976	Mitchell, John M.	Pipefitter	
26 September 1976	Peterson, David G.	Pipefitter	
26 September 1976	Skrit, Thomas Jr.	Pipefitter	
21 November 1976	Edwards, Kenneth	Pipe Coverer & Insulator	
18 July 1976	Markham, Robert	Pipe Coverer & Insulator	
29 August 1976	Clark, David	A/C & Refrigeration Mechanic	
12 September 1976	Beria, Philip L.	A/C & Refrigeration Mechanic	
29 August 1976	Portillo, Carlos Jr.	A/C & Refrigeration Mechanic	
12 September 1976	Achman, Gary W.	Machinist	
7 November 1976	Anello, Thomas J.	Machinist	
7 November 1976	Chaufauros, William L.	Machinist	
4 July 1976	Delgadillo, Ignacio	Machinist	
9 May 1976	Gabriel, Roger R. Jr.	Machinist	
26 September 1976	Garcia, Gabriel	Machinist	
20 June 1976	Kumai, Tom H.	Machinist	
26 September 1976	Leininger, George W.	Machinist	
12 September 1976	Malauulu, Laisene	Machinist	
12 September 1976	Mamaradio, Faustino	Machinist	
15 February 1976	Marin, Mike W.	Machinist	
12 September 1976	Marinas, Gregory D.	Machinist	
18 July 1976	McCullough, Nickie B.	Machinist	
21 November 1976	Millman, Gordon	Machinist	
15 August 1976	Mojica, Marion	Machinist	
4 July 1976	Molica, Michail D.	Machinist	
12 September 1976	Peretic, Mark A.	Machinist	
20 June 1976	Sabo, Paul S.	Machinist	
26 September 1976	Wallin, Robert L.	Machinist	
20 June 1976	Watson, Robert	Machinist	
10 October 1976	Gonzales, Juan J.	Ordnance Equipment	
24 October 1976	Holley, Daniel	Ordnance Equipment	
20 June 1976	Renard, Alan	Ordnance Equipment	
20 June 1976	Robertson, Steve A.	Ordnance Equipment	
20 June 1976	Barclay, Alan J.	Electrician	
12 September 1976	Castro, Richard G.	Electrician	
12 September 1976	Grabowski, Thomas J.	Electrician	
12 September 1976	Perez, Larry	Electrician	
12 September 1976	Pickle, Aubrey C.	Electrician	
20 June 1976	Riehle, William K.	Electrician	Dr. Plusch
20 June 1976	Vara, Hector A.	Electrician	
12 September 1976	Brown, Delbert L.	Electronics Mechanic	
5 December 1976	Carroll, Ronald A.	Electronics Mechanic	
12 September 1976	Cook Christopher N.	Electronics Mechanic	
19 December 1976	Gollnick, Christopher	Electronics Mechanic	
19 December 1976	Henson, John S.	Electronics Mechanic	Honor Graduate
10 October 1976	Kocher, Bruce A.	Electronics Mechanic	
12 September 1976	Jilinski, Donald E.	Electronics Mechanic	
4 July 1976	Anderson, Michail W.	Fire Control Mechanic	
12 September 1976	Blanchard, Stephen R.	Fire Control Mechanic	
12 September 1976	Letchworth, Lathan T.	Fire Control Mechanic	
4 July 1976	Miles, Dennis J.	Fire Control Mechanic	
12 September 1976	Ramos, Robert R.	Fire Control Mechanic	

85 for 1976

1,490 Total

Date	Name	Trade	Notes
13 March 1977	Nicholson, Leon T.	Shipfitter	
11 September 1977	Ouren, Steven C.	Shipfitter	
11 September 1977	Stegmann, Gary A.	Shipfitter	
28 August 1977	Cody, David S.	Welder	
30 January 1977	Compagnon, James F.	Welder	
28 August 1977	Green Lucky	Welder	
28 August 1977	Mahoney, Matthew J.	Welder	
28 August 1977	Deighan, James F.	Boilermaker	
27 February 1977	Lindsey, Harry M.	Boilermaker	
23 October 1977	Richard, Oscar L.	Boilermaker	
25 September 1977	Sillett, Gary L.	Boilermaker	
11 September 1977	Jauri, Robert R.	Shipwright	
13 March 1977	Martin, Terry A.	Shipwright	
6 November 1977	Queen, Donald R.	Shipwright	
31 July 1977	Dela, Garza Octavio	Joiner	
28 August 1977	Hoover, Steven R.	Joiner	
28 August 1977	Ramirez, Eugene	Molder (Plastics)	
*19 February 1978	Colt, Terry L.	Patternmaker	
19 June 1977	Beato, Nemesio A.	Rigger	
19 June 1977	Boitel, Richard E.	Rigger	
23 October 1977	Dotson, Harold E.	Rigger	
19 June 1977	Marcy, Wayne S.	Rigger	
31 July 1977	Moega, Fitiaumua N.	Rigger	
19 June 1977	Newquest, Robert N.	Rigger	
19 June 1977	Riley, Michael C.	Rigger	
19 June 1977	Warnock, Wesley W.	Rigger	
24 April 1977	James, William W.	Painter	
3 July 1977	Maldonado, Joe L.	Painter	
16 January 1977	Brown, Clarence H.	Sheetmetal Worker	
10 April 1977	Cornelius, Harold B.	Sheetmetal Worker	
27 March 1977	Decker, Francis W.	Sheetmetal Worker	Dr. Plusch
23 October 1977	Garcia, Albert C.	Sheetmetal Worker	
11 September 1977	Kimbrough, Lester A.	Sheetmetal Worker	
11 September 1977	Miller, Dennis M.	Sheetmetal Worker	
11 September 1977	Cox, Floyd R.	Pipefitter	
17 July 1977	Berger, William O.	Pipefitter	
28 August 1977	Dambrowski, Thomas	Pipefitter	
11 September 1977	Fife, Albert B.	Pipefitter	
11 September 1977	Gottowski, Bruce H.	Pipefitter	
11 September 1977	Hunt, Hayward A.	Pipefitter	
25 September 1977	Lomas, Arturo	Pipefitter	
13 February 1977	Washington, Albert E.	Pipefitter	
19 June 1977	Broughton, Darrell R.	Pipe Coverer & Insulator	
6 November 1977	Brown, Everett E.	Pipe Coverer & Insulator	
11 September 1977	Douglas, James R.	Machinist	

1977 Continued next page

DATE	NAME OF GRADUATE	SKILLED TRADE	NOTES
25 September 1977	Garcia, James	Machinist	
27 March 1977	Kesler, Richard	Machinist	
11 September 1977	Reddman, Alan W.	Machinist	
6 November 1977	Richardson, Willie L.	Machinist	
11 September 1977	Talentino, Conrado A.	Machinist	
11 September 1977	Winn, George R.	Machinist	
11 September 1977	Crosby, Reginald	Marine Machinist	
2 January 1977	Curtis, Raymond A.	Marine Machinist	
28 August 1977	Farrell, Jack E.	Marine Machinist	
2 January 1977	Hammerton, George H.	Marine Machinist	
11 September 1977	Matanane, Edmund C.	Marine Machinist	
11 September 1977	Morgan, Johnny L.	Marine Machinist	
6 November 1977	Pittman, Robert M.	Marine Machinist	
2 January 1977	Scott, Duane D.	Marine Machinist	
28 August 1977	Trahan, Kenneth R.	Marine Machinist	
18 December 1977	Whitsell, Thomas L.	Marine Machinist	
19 June 1977	Thomas, Herman L.	Maintenance Machinist	
*15 January 1978	Heath, Cecil L.	Ordnance Equipment	
*15 January 1978	Lupo, William	Ordnance Equipment	
11 September 1977	Raker, John A.	Ordnance Equipment	
11 September 1977	Schutt, Dennis A.	Ordnance Equipment	
4 December 1977	Barnes, Rick W.	Electrician	
11 September 1977	Bower, Joseph E.	Electrician	
19 June 1977	Duggins, Michael K.	Electrician	
11 September 1977	Kerekes, Ernest R.	Electrician	
19 June 1977	Marincovich, Mark	Electrician	
19 June 1977	McArdle, Kenneth L.	Electrician	
19 June 1977	Speiser, Douglas L.	Electrician	Honor Graduate
11 September 1977	Callaway, Earl	Electronics Mechanic	
9 October 1977	Chaney, Ronald L.	Electronics Mechanic	
11 September 1977	Christoff, William J.	Electronics Mechanic	
11 September 1977	Cottom, Robert N.	Electronics Mechanic	
25 September 1977	Delos Reys, David M.	Electronics Mechanic	
27 March 1977	Franck, Richard E.	Electronics Mechanic	
13 March 1977	Patenza, Donald A.	Electronics Mechanic	
25 September 1977	Edwards, Kenneth F.	Fire Control Mechanic	
11 September 1977	Padilla, Armando H.	Fire Control Mechanic	
17 July 1977	Scott, William L.	Fire Control Mechanic	
			83 for 1977

*

1573 Total

Handwritten list ends here

GRADUATION DATE	NAME OF	SKILLED TRADE	NOTES
1978	Mayer, James L.	Shipfitter	
(01/29/79) DIGEST	Mingo, William C.	Shipfitter	
	O'Neill, Edward M.	Shipfitter	
	Steele, Donald F.	Shipfitter	
	Tolman, Sidney J.	Shipfitter	
	Bower, Frank R.	Welder	
	Carolan, Michael T.	Welder	
	Hamilton, Johnny R.	Welder	

1978 Continued next page

GRADUATION DATE	NAME OF	SKILLED TRADE	NOTES
1978	High, Brady E.	Welder	
(01/29/79) DIGEST	Hiltbold, Gary D.	Welder	
	Honey, Karen L.	Welder	"1st" Female
	Lowry, Bruce H.	Welder	
	Rhoades, Larry S.	Welder	
	Hemingway, Robert S.	Boilermaker	
	Minami, Lawrence T.	Boilermaker	Dr. Plusch
	Potter, John A.	Boilermaker	
	Ware, Herman J. W.	Boilermaker	
	Wolfe, Wesley R.	Boilermaker	
	Fox, Peter J.	Shipwright	
	Kaanoi, Wendall W. M.	Shipwright	
	Patterson, Michael A.	Shipwright	
	Rivers, Kenneth M.	Shipwright	
	Putnam, William N.	Molder (Plastics)	
	Shank, Ronald S.	Molder (Plastics)	
	Blackmon, Tommie	Rigger	
	McCarty, Michael R.	Rigger	
	Moreno, Frank J. Jr.	Rigger	
	Mulholland, Harry A.	Rigger	
	O'Connor, Patrick J.	Rigger	
	Tucay, Thomas A.	Rigger	
	Beckwith, Gerald S.	Painter	
	Miller, Randolph	Painter	
	Gressman, Richard F.	Painter	
	Valek, Stanley W.	Painter	
	Watson, Catherine	Painter	"1st" Female
	Ferrell, Robert L.	Sheetmetal Mechanic	
	Heggie, Robert S.	Sheetmetal Mechanic	
	Hernandez, Juan J.	Sheetmetal Mechanic	
	Stokes, Sidney	Sheetmetal Mechanic	
	Payne, David B.	Sheetmetal Mechanic	
	Armenta, Michael L.	Pipefitter	
	Irland, Lynn H.	Pipefitter	
	Jackson, Allen L.	Pipefitter	
	Johnson, Willoughby	Pipefitter	
	Miehl, John N	Pipefitter	
	Oja, William L.	Pipefitter	
	Owens, John H.	Pipefitter	
	Roberts, Jerome	Pipefitter	
	Smith Terry W.	Pipefitter	
	Spears, James F.	Pipefitter	
	Spohn, Rickey L.	Pipefitter	
	Blanchard, Robert W.	Pipe Coverer & Insulator	
	Catello, Michael F.	Pipe Coverer & Insulator	
	Conley, Paul T.	Pipe Coverer & Insulator	
	Meeks, Monroe J.	Pipe Coverer & Insulator	
	Meijer, Buddy J.	Pipe Coverer & Insulator	
	Ambe, Victor J.	Machinist	
	Asada, David D.	Machinist	
	Dolengewicz, William	Machinist	

1978 Continued next page

GRADUATION DATE	NAME OF GRADUATE	SKILLED TRADE	NOTES
1978	Ennis, David M.	Machinist	
(01/29/79) DIGEST	Flores, Enrique J. Jr.	Machinist	
	Grimmett, Jun P.	Machinist	
	Kennedy, Roy E. Jr.	Machinist	
	Kiyuna, Bruce J.	Machinist	
	Long, James R.	Machinist	
	Mendelson, David L.	Machinist	
	Randolph, Kenneth L.	Machinist	
	Risley, Gary D.	Machinist	
	Starwalt, Darrell L.	Machinist	
	Trujullo, Richard A.	Machinist	
	Vogel, Louis F.	Machinist	
	Williams, William L.	Machinist	
	Adam, Craig R.	Marine Machinist	
	Bins, Steven R.	Marine Machinist	
	Bradley, John D.	Marine Machinist	
	Clodfelder, Gary N.	Marine Machinist	
	Janus, Donald J.	Marine Machinist	
	Kursawe, Michael G.	Marine Machinist	
	Landri, Neil P.	Marine Machinist	
	McCue, Steven F.	Marine Machinist	
	McKenna, William D.	Marine Machinist	
	Millman, Gordon	Marine Machinist	
	Rieger, Ralph B.	Marine Machinist	
	Robinson, Edward S.	Marine Machinist	
	Sanchez, William M.	Marine Machinist	
	Chang, Clifford K. H.	A/C & Refrigeration Mechanic	
	Jarrett, Keith P.	A/C & Refrigeration Mechanic	
	Cooper, Gary	Ordance Equipment	
	Garcia, Alfredo	Ordance Equipment	
	Kumro, Roger N.	Ordance Equipment	
	Osborne, Dennis M.	Ordance Equipment	
	Smith, Emmitt III	Ordance Equipment	
	Warren, Ronald W.	Ordance Equipment	
	Bald, Harry C.	Electrician	
	Blabagno, Oscar C.	Electrician	
	Duran, David	Electrician	
	Forrest, Paul D.	Electrician	
	Hinchcliff, Leo M.	Electrician	
	Johnson, Gary L.	Electrician	
	Linson, David A.	Electrician	
	McNeil, Bruce K.	Electrician	
	Mills, Carl E.	Electrician	
	Mooney, John K.	Electrician	
	Nakamura, Tom T.	Electrician	
	Nieto, Richard D.	Electrician	
	Parsi, Richard F.	Electrician	
	Pluard, Fred D.	Electrician	
	Shaffell, Paul A.	Electrician	
	Brock, Donald L.	Electronics Mechanic	
	Edginton, Alfred G.	Electronics Mechanic	

1978 Continued next page

GRADUATION DATE	NAME OF	SKILLED TRADE	NOTES
1978	English, Joe L. Jr.	Electronics Mechanic	
(01/29/79) DIGEST	Ferguson, Robert D.	Electronics Mechanic	
	Huizar, Epifanio	Electronics Mechanic	
	Hunter, Francis K.	Electronics Mechanic	
	Jackson, Jolland S.	Electronics Mechanic	
	Joly, Michael E.	Electronics Mechanic	
	Jones, Clark M.	Electronics Mechanic	
	Mosher, Jeffrey M.	Electronics Mechanic	
	Rios, Manuel L.	Electronics Mechanic	
	Smith, Albert	Electronics Mechanic	
	Thomas, John W.	Electronics Mechanic	Honor Graduate
	Wade, Joseph M.	Electronics Mechanic	
	Black, Alan M.	Elex Fire Control Mechanic	
	Lopez, Gilbert	Elex Fire Control Mechanic	
	Wayne, Steven L.	Elex Fire Control Mechanic	
			125 for 1978

1,698 Total

GRA	NAME OF GRADUATE	SKILLED TRADE	NOTES
1979	Koczwara, Edward J.	Shipfitter	
(01/25/80) DIGEST	McLendon, Terry L.	Shipfitter	
	Maestas, Joe O.	Shipfitter	
	Pechar, Jerome C.	Shipfitter	
	Pelletier, Henry A.	Shipfitter	
	Rendrow, Rodney L.	Shipfitter	
	Smith, Deryn L.	Shipfitter	
	Woods, Eugene P.	Shipfitter	
	Zimmers, James M. Jr.	Shipfitter	
	Byrd, David D.	Welder	
	Hadlett, Christopher S.	Welder	
	Hamilton, John R.	Welder	
	Hayes, Robert L.	Welder	
	Korak, John I.	Welder	
	Pacheco, Rupert D.	Welder	
	Rankins, Archie A. Jr.	Welder	
	Thraen, David K.	Welder	
	Wilhelm, Bernhardt Jr.	Welder	
	Caron, Rdolph J.	Boilermaker	
	Chavez, Javier J.	Boilermaker	
	Compton, Ronald L.	Boilermaker	
	Johnson, Michael J.	Boilermaker	
	Lawrence, James E.	Boilermaker	
	Lowman, Donald J.	Boilermaker	
	Meininger, Gorden D.	Boilermaker	
	Renteria, Vicor	Boilermaker	
	Wade, Stephen M.	Boilermaker	
	Rich, Santiago III	Patternmaker	
	Beery, Don M.	Painter	
	Aldrich, Adrian O. III	Molder (Plastics)	
	Ayon, Abel A.	Molder (Plastics)	
	Mayer, James R.	Molder (Plastics)	
	Sanchez, Albert A.	Molder (Plastics)	

1979 Continued next page

GRADUATION DATE	NAME OF	SKILLED TRADE	NOTES
1979	Leonard, David L.	Rigger	
(01/25/80) DIGEST	Willey, Clyde E.	Rigger	
	Schaub, Melvin H.	Rigger	
	Dawes, Ernest H.	Sheetmetal Mechanic	
	Gramling, Jerry C.	Sheetmetal Mechanic	
	Macabuhay, Cipriano	Sheetmetal Mechanic	
	Martinez, Paul	Sheetmetal Mechanic	
	Wolfslau, Henry J. III	Sheetmetal Mechanic	
	Colby, Maurice H. Jr.	Pipefitter	
	Gonyer, Michael D.	Pipefitter	
	Lazzerini, Edwin	Pipefitter	
	Marquiss, Glenn W.	Pipefitter	
	May, Terral D.	Pipefitter	
	Mason, Robert L.	Pipefitter	
	Talbot, Edward L.	Pipefitter	
	Varga, Robert J.	Pipefitter	
	Yonan, Robert	Pipefitter	
	Dee, Philip A.	Pipe Coverer & Insulator	
	Maldonaldo, Victor M.	Pipe Coverer & Insulator	
	Poelvoorde, Robert S.	Pipe Coverer & Insulator	
	Wilson, Elwood	Pipe Coverer & Insulator	
	Tomlin, Kenneth L.	A/C & Refrigeration Mechanic	
	Adamson, Christopher	Heavy Equipment Mechanic	
	Hufford, Scott T.	Heavy Equipment Mechanic	
	Planas, Juan A.	Heavy Equipment Mechanic	
	Alvarez, Ruben P.	Machinist	
	Benskin, Richard A.	Machinist	
	Burrows, Earl D.	Machinist	
	Ceja, Michael J.	Machinist	
	Fernandez, Don F.	Machinist	
	Fleischer, Isidore	Machinist	
	Gallo, Sam S.	Machinist	
	Gelbmann, Gregory L.	Machinist	
	Rittmer, Gary F.	Machinist	
	Burnstein, Rex L.	Marine Machinist	
	Dasca, Cesar B.	Marine Machinist	
	Harrod, Ricky A.	Marine Machinist	
	Kerbyson, Edward A.	Marine Machinist	
	Larson, Lawrence R.	Marine Machinist	
	Pratt, Robert L.	Marine Machinist	
	Rose, Harold E.	Marine Machinist	
	Sarsfield, Craig R.	Marine Machinist	
	Serles, Craig R.	Marine Machinist	
	Vega, Steven S.	Marine Machinist	
	Freund, Daniel F.	Ordnance Mechanic	
	Martinez, Steven D.	Ordnance Mechanic	
	Babineau, Steven R.	Electrician	
	Beatty, Larry L.	Electrician	
	Douglass, Dennis P.	Electrician	
	Green, Cicero Jr.	Electrician	
	Lau, Tong W.	Electrician	Dr. Plusch

1979 Continued next page

GRADUATION DATE	NAME OF	SKILLED TRADE	NOTES
1979	Sala, Brian A.	Electrician	
(01/25/80) DIGEST	Floyd, Timothy W.	Electronics Mechanic	
	Footdale, Larry D.	Electronics Mechanic	
	Kubala, James J.	Electronics Mechanic	
	Natale, Ralph C.	Electronics Mechanic	
	Nimtz, Michael C.	Electronics Mechanic	
	Ornelas, Daniel T.	Electronics Mechanic	
	Torres, Jesse J.	Electronics Mechanic	
	Tucay, Bernardo S. Jr.	Electronics Mechanic	Honor Graduate
	Wathen, James A. III	Electronics Mechanic	
	Roberts, Alfred L.	Fire Control Mechanic (Elex)	
	Walker, James V.	Fire Control Mechanic (Elex)	
			96 for 1979

1794 Total

GRADUATION DATE	NAME OF	SKILLED TRADE	NOTES
1980	Ardoin, Joseph C. Jr.	Shipfitter	
(01/30/81) DIGEST	Leary, Thomas, A. Jr.	Shipfitter	
	Leland, Daniel	Shipfitter	
	Martin, Alexander	Shipfitter	
	Phipps, Barbara J.	Shipfitter	
	Sunia, Toaono A.	Shipfitter	
	Byrd, William D.	Welder	
	Hrmon, Charles E.	Welder	
	King, David R.	Welder	
	Martin, Edward G.	Welder	
	Sampson, Robert L.	Welder	
	Saylor, Lee	Welder	
	Svendor, Thomas A.	Welder	
	Tilzer, Edward A.	Welder	
	Dondero, Alan W.	Boilermaker	
	Hellickson, Gregory L.	Boilermaker	
	King, Henry D. Sr.	Boilermaker	
	Kosinski, John G.	Boilermaker	
	Limon, James D.	Boilermaker	
	Louie, Wai M.	Boilermaker	
	McCann, Robert J.	Boilermaker	
	Nalley, Charles M.	Boilermaker	
	Sheddy, Kristopher K.	Boilermaker	
	Thomson, James K.	Boilermaker	
	Gonzales, Frank M.	Shipwright	
	Murakami, Terumasa	Shipwright	
	Thompson, Gary S.	Shipwright	
	Jensen, Steven D.	Rigger	
	Nelson, James S.	Rigger	
	Staudt, Louis B.	Rigger	
	Wallace, Theodore	Rigger	
	Bolinger, Gary D.	Sheetmetal Mechanic	
	McCoy, mes	Sheetmetal Mechanic	
	Pickens, William C.	Sheetmetal Mechanic	
	Shetrone, Joseph B.	Sheetmetal Mechanic	
	Spilky, Richard I.	Sheetmetal Mechanic	
	Desilva, Mario D.	Pipefitter	

1980 Continued next page

GRADUATION DATE	NAME OF	SKILLED TRADE	NOTES
1980	Jeffrey, Aaron Jr.	Pipefitter	
(01/30/81) DIGEST	Moore, Virgil R.	Pipefitter	
	Perry, Henry Jr.	Pipefitter	
	Rodriquez, Fred	Pipefitter	
	King, Bertram T.	Pipe Coverer & Insulator	
	Sanchez, Ronald J.	Pipe Coverer & Insulator	
	Uehara, Stanley M.	Pipe Coverer & Insulator	
	Eccles, Gordon J.	A/C & Refrigeration Mechanic	
	Ferriera, Barry A.	A/C & Refrigeration Mechanic	
	Astorga, David	Machinist	
	Burton, Frank F.	Machinist	
	Barley, Danny L.	Machinist	
	Carlock, Philip B.	Machinist	
	Caviness, John E.	Machinist	
	Emory, Patricia A.	Machinist	
	Endo, Jun	Machinist	
	Gallo, Theodore D.	Machinist	
	Lenox, Michael J.	Machinist	
	Roman, Alan R.	Machinist	
	Earl, James M.	Marine Machinist	
	Espinoza, Arthur R.	Marine Machinist	
	Highnight, Talbert L.	Marine Machinist	
	Horvat, Joseph M.	Marine Machinist	
	Lakowski, Charles	Marine Machinist	
	McAfee, Henry L.	Marine Machinist	
	Perez, Robert A.	Marine Machinist	
	Ribas, Jose P.	Marine Machinist	
	Shephard, Eddie L. Jr.	Marine Machinist	
	Slocum, Charles A.	Marine Machinist	
	Vasques, Arthur R.	Marine Machinist	
	Williams, Lamont	Marine Machinist	
	Writz, James C.	Marine Machinist	
	Cruz, Alexander	Ordnance Equipt Mechanic	
	King, William C.	Ordnance Equipt Mechanic	
	Rose, William F.	Ordnance Equipt Mechanic	
	Cichoski, Stephen V.	Heavy Duty Equipt Mechanic	
	Hamilton, Delvon A. Jr.	Heavy Duty Equipt Mechanic	
	Lamontagne, Phillip L.	Heavy Duty Equipt Mechanic	
	Spillman, Charles E.	Heavy Duty Equipt Mechanic	
	Bell, Vinson C.	Fire Control Mechanic (Elex)	
	Breeding, Dennis L.	Fire Control Mechanic (Elex)	
	Dorset, Jeffrey L.	Fire Control Mechanic (Elex)	Honor Graduate
	Fournier, Noman C.	Fire Control Mechanic (Elex)	
	Jenkins, Robert A.	Fire Control Mechanic (Elex)	
	Noble, Cynthia A.	Fire Control Mechanic (Elex)	
	Ridley, Larry J.	Fire Control Mechanic (Elex)	
	Stunek, Stanley R.	Fire Control Mechanic (Elex)	
	Wallin, Glenna S.	Fire Control Mechanic (Elex)	
	Mestmoreland, Michae	Fire Control Mechanic (Elex)	
	Cardenas, Tony F.	Electrician	
	Harmon, Edward A.	Electrician	

1980 Continued next page

GRADUATION DATE	NAME OF GRADUATE	SKILLED TRADE	NOTES
1980	Hattan, Dennis W.	Electrician	
(01/30/81) DIGEST	Heath, George A.	Electrician	
	Koperski, Kenneth J.	Electrician	
	Larson, Vincent H.	Electrician	
	Lee, James M.	Electrician	
	Pagaling, Fermin M.	Electrician	
	Szczatko, Michael A.	Electrician	
	Fisher, Craig E.	Electronics Mechanic	
	Gonzales, Rodolfo A.	Electronics Mechanic	
	Hermosura, Fernando	Electronics Mechanic	
	Koener, Charles R.	Electronics Mechanic	Dr. Plusch
	McDonald, Sherman E.	Electronics Mechanic	
	Menes, Bernard M.	Electronics Mechanic	
	Milbery, James M.	Electronics Mechanic	
	Sacdalan, Eileen G.	Electronics Mechanic	
			103 for 1980

1,897 Total

GRADUATION DATE	NAME OF GRADUATE	SKILLED TRADE	NOTES
1981	Bankston, Richard	Shipfitter	
(01/29/82) DIGEST	Barrows, Avelino R. Jr.	Shipfitter	
	Bellenbaum, Richard	Shipfitter	
	Landry, Scott W.	Shipfitter	
	Ross, Donald R.	Shipfitter	
	Rowse, William S.	Shipfitter	
	Smith, Don R.	Shipfitter	
	Wallace, Michael R.	Shipfitter	
	Wilcher, Michael	Shipfitter	
	Cunningham, Wardlow	Welder	
	Hubbartt, Ronald D.	Welder	
	Huegel, Thomas R.	Welder	
	Koracka, John J.	Welder	
	Little, James R.	Welder	
	Ray, Patricia D.	Welder	
	Speck, Marvin J.	Welder	
	Udarbe, Herbi R.	Welder	
	Benham, William B.	Boilermaker	
	Campos, Gustavo A.	Boilermaker	
	Campos, Luis C.	Boilermaker	
	Caro, Michael D.	Boilermaker	
	Christofferson, Jerry	Boilermaker	
	Collie Michael A.	Boilermaker	
	Garcia, David P. Jr.	Boilermaker	
	Gurney, Robert N.	Boilermaker	
	Harber, Michael G.	Boilermaker	
	Hernandez, Fernando	Boilermaker	
	Johnson, William	Boilermaker	
	Muro, David J.	Boilermaker	
	Mercier, George L. Jr.	Boilermaker	
	McCord, George	Boilermaker	
	Rexach, Joseph O.	Boilermaker	
	Romick, Anthony	Boilermaker	

1981 Continued next page

GRADUATION DATE	NAME OF	SKILLED TRADE	NOTES
1981	Starnes, James E.	Boilermaker	
(01/29/82) DIGEST	Sutton, Lindley D.	Boilermaker	
	Williams, John M.	Boilermaker	
	Zerra, Anthony F.	Boilermaker	
	Joyner, patricia A.	Shipwright	
	LeFever, Steven C.	Shipwright	
	Vivao, Violet	Shipwright	
	Aldridge, Katherine F.	Shipwright	
	McKenzie, John R.	Plastic Fabricator	
	Rousseau, Arthur	Plastic Fabricator	
	Novak, Daniel E.	Rigger	
	Nomura, Edward T.	Rigger	
	Neubauer, David R.	Rigger	
	Solis, Daniel	Rigger	
	Bradley, John W. Jr.	Painter	
	Clarke, Chancy O.	Painter	
	Hester, Sherry M.	Painter	
	Cl;audette, James E.	Sheetmetal Mechanic	
	Cocca, Greg A.	Sheetmetal Mechanic	
	Lagana, Paul F.	Sheetmetal Mechanic	
	Walsh, Patrick J.	Sheetmetal Mechanic	
	Williams, Edwin P.	Sheetmetal Mechanic	
	Youseff, Gilbert S.	Sheetmetal Mechanic	
	Apodaca, arturo S.	Pipefitter	
	Devoy, Daniel J.	Pipefitter	
	Durham, Lee S.	Pipefitter	
	Gallagher, Tim R.	Pipefitter	
	Hohlman, Gregory W.	Pipefitter	
	Holm, Terry S.	Pipefitter	
	Jennings, Rex J.	Pipefitter	
	Huhn, Robert J.	Pipefitter	
	Laughlin, Milton M.	Pipefitter	
	Mayhew, Frederick J.	Pipefitter	
	Osborn, Thomas O.	Pipefitter	
	Patnaude, Herbert, M.	Pipefitter	
	Salazar, Aaron L.	Pipefitter	
	Suarez, George	Pipefitter	
	MacDonald, John D.	Pipe Coverer & Insulator	
	Risko, James E.	Pipe Coverer & Insulator	
	Scott, Ronald M.	Pipe Coverer & Insulator	
	Williams, Kenneth J.	Pipe Coverer & Insulator	
	Donlow, George E.	Machinist	
	Garcia, Patrick	Machinist	
	Henry, Ronnie	Machinist	
	McMahan, Michael R.	Machinist	
	Morante, Victor F.	Machinist	
	Simpson, Gary J.	Machinist	
	Collie, James L.	Fire Control Mechanic (Elex)	
	Irvine, Ellen K.	Fire Control Mechanic (Elex)	Dr. Plusch
	Cutler, Marvin P.	Fire Control Mechanic (Elex)	
	Howdershell, Thomas	Fire Control Mechanic (Elex)	

1981 Continued next page

GRADUATION DATE	NAME OF	SKILLED TRADE	NOTES
1981	Lenox, Michael M.	Fire Control Mechanic (Elex)	
(01/29/82) DIGEST	Pozniakoff, Robin	Fire Control Mechanic (Elex)	
	Rainey, Louis R. Jr.	Fire Control Mechanic (Elex)	
	Alaniz, Charlie	Marine Machinist	
	Caldwell, Pat D.	Marine Machinist	
	Carroll, Buddie U.	Marine Machinist	
	Engle, Paul M.	Marine Machinist	
	Gutierrez, Raymond M.	Marine Machinist	
	Naus, Joseph S.	Marine Machinist	
	Nelson, Kenneth C.	Marine Machinist	
	Price, David A.	Marine Machinist	
	Teti, Ronald H.	Marine Machinist	
	Kincheloe, Donald F.	Ordnance Equipment	
	Matz, James G. IV	Ordnance Equipment	
	Sanford, Thomas A.	Ordnance Equipment	
	Allen, Raymond	Electrician	
	Bensberg, William C.	Electrician	
	Charo, Albert	Electrician	
	Duffin, James M.	Electrician	
	Gillion, Ronald L.	Electrician	
	Herold, Mark G.	Electrician	
	McFarland, Charles E.	Electrician	
	O'Neil, Jimmie A.	Electrician	
	Pikelis, George S.	Electrician	
	Schuett, Robert B.	Electrician	
	Stewart, William A.	Electrician	
	Thompson, Norman	Electrician	
	Tyler, Anthony W.	Electrician	
	White, James F. Sr.	Electrician	
	Wu, Stanley Jr.	Electrician	Honor Graduate
	Connell, James C.	Electronics Mechanic	
	Correa, Clifford J.	Electronics Mechanic	
	Gonzales, Manuel A.	Electronics Mechanic	
	Manriques, Mario	Electronics Mechanic	
	P:otter, Corwin L.	Electronics Mechanic	
	Perl, Randall H.	Electronics Mechanic	
	Riveria, Daniel V.	Electronics Mechanic	
	Sakauskas, Peter	Electronics Mechanic	
	Smith, Clifford	Electronics Mechanic	
	Sumlin, Robert E.	Electronics Mechanic	
	Strobel, Michael A.	Electronics Mechanic	
	Wilkes, Larry J.	Electronics Mechanic	
			126 for 1981

2,023 Total

DUA	NAME OF GRADUATE	SKILLED TRADE	NOTES
1982	Caldwell, Robert L.	Shipfitter	
(04/29/83) DIGEST	Glazier, Jeffrey	Shipfitter	
	Jaroch, Eugene P.	Shipfitter	
	Meza, Richard J.	Shipfitter	
	Oliveria, David	Shipfitter	

1982 Continued Next Page

GRADUATION DATE	NAME OF	SKILLED TRADE	NOTES
1982	Sanchez, Jon	Shipfitter	
(04/29/83) DIGEST	Viatle, James A.	Shipfitter	
	Cloud, William J.	Welder	
	Hill, James M.	Welder	
	Hoodenpyle, John L.	Welder	
	Javier, John P.	Welder	
	Kirby, Joseph L.	Welder	
	Lovett, Tony F.	Welder	
	Lee, Calvin K.	Welder	
	Pizzuto, Joseph A.	Welder	
	Smith, Cynthia J.	Welder	
	Groendyke, Harold W.	Blacksmith	
	Vales, Michael	Blacksmith	
	Gran, James G.	Boilermaker	
	Gumataotao, Albert D.	Boilermaker	
	Lambert, Milledge	Boilermaker	
	Ploar, Larry G.	Boilermaker	
	Skoblar, Mate	Boilermaker	
	Tipton, Michael C.	Shipwright	
	Polk, Beverly J.	Shipwright	
	Quinata, James J.	Shipwright	
	Quintana, Emeteria A.	Shipwright	Honor
	Ramirez, Jacinto R.	Shipwright	
	Smith, Steven M.	Shipwright	
	Wells, Robert J.	Shipwright	
	Meston, Donald A.	Shipwright	
	Aguon, Joseph P.	Rigger	Dr. Plusch
	Alvarez, Anthony P.	Rigger	
	Esrada, Carles W.	Rigger	
	Lee, James M.	Rigger	
	Lavery, Robert F.	Rigger	
	Schorman, Richard P.	Rigger	
	Brooks, Gregory V.	Painter	
	Olaiz, Raymond	Painter	
	Soto, William Jr.	Painter	
	Stoefen, David T.	Painter	
	Crisostomo, Ponciano	Painter	
	Romana, Reynado R.	Painter	
	Davis, Willie A.	Sheetmetal Worker	
	Gearring, Isac L.	Sheetmetal Worker	
	Grandberry, Loretta I.	Sheetmetal Worker	
	Lee, Willie Jr.	Sheetmetal Worker	
	Mastro, Steve	Sheetmetal Worker	
	Hadnott, James H.	Pipefitter	
	Harmon, John G.	Pipefitter	
	Johnson, Walter C.	Pipefitter	
	Strack, Dennis C.	Pipefitter	
	Ubina, Mark	Pipefitter	
	Wells, Kenneth M.	Pipefitter	
	Cruz, Gilbert B.	Pipe Coverer & Insulator	
	Herte, Virginia L.	Pipe Coverer & Insulator	

1982 Continued next page

GRADUATION DATE	NAME OF	SKILLED TRADE	NOTES
1982	Kleidon, Clifford K.	Pipe Coverer & Insulator	
(04/29/83) DIGEST	Lewis, Frank L.	Pipe Coverer & Insulator	
	Mitchell, Phillip T.	Pipe Coverer & Insulator	
	Saltalamachia, Joseph	Pipe Coverer & Insulator	
	Cannon, Robert H. Jr.	Machinist	
	Harris, Alfred R.	Machinist	
	Lawson, Otis Jr.	Machinist	
	Lawson, Walter	Machinist	
	Rivera, John G.	Machinist	
	Sales, Robert C.	Machinist	
	Yoshizawa, Arnold R.	Machinist	
	Adam, Brian A.	Marine Machinist	
	Finley, Charles D.	Marine Machinist	
	Marquez, Joe R.	Marine Machinist	
	Mejia, Edward J.	Marine Machinist	
	Polk, Willie E. Jr.	Marine Machinist	
	Anderson, Trollope F.	A/C & Refrigeration Mechanic	
	Bradford, Charles E.	A/C & Refrigeration Mechanic	
	Figueroa, Ildefonso T.	A/C & Refrigeration Mechanic	
	Moran, Joseph F.	A/C & Refrigeration Mechanic	
	Arrington, Harry Jr.	Electronics Mechanic	
	Boker, Gerald J.	Electronics Mechanic	
	Campbell, Raymond L.	Electronics Mechanic	
	Dodson, James T.	Electronics Mechanic	
	Farris, Michael P.	Electronics Mechanic	
	Hausken, Jeffrey L.	Electronics Mechanic	
	Irvin, Robert F. Jr.	Electronics Mechanic	
	Morgan, Robert G.	Electronics Mechanic	
	Popper, Joseph C.	Electronics Mechanic	
	Thompson, Bruce E.	Electronics Mechanic	
	Torres, Johnny M.	Electronics Mechanic	
	Salisbury, Edana L.	Fire Control Mechanic (Elex)	Honor Graduate
			88 for 1982

2,11 Total

GRA	NAME OF GRADUATE	SKILLED TRADE	NOTES
1983	Anast, Ronald W.	Shipfitter	
(01/20/84) DIGEST	Buybee, Gary B.	Shipfitter	
	Groves, Robert P.	Shipfitter	
	Nunez, Richard A.	Shipfitter	
	Soard, Charles E.	Shipfitter	
	Spears, Mack T.	Shipfitter	
	Benson, Larry D.	Welder	
	Gabasa, Raymond M.	Welder	
	Elkins, Robert C.	Welder	
	Markowitz, Michael F.	Welder	
	Puccio, Stephen F.	Welder	
	Vega, Daniel A.	Welder	
	Chaney, Lawton	Welder	
	Hamilton, Dennis C.	Welder	
	Eakins, John F.	Blacksmith	
	Henry, Darrell A.	Blacksmith	

1983 Continued next page

GRADUATION DATE	NAME OF	SKILLED TRADE	NOTES
1983	Perkins, Clifton A.	Molder Foundry Workers	
(01/20/84) DIGEST	Johnson, Lynn L.	Molder Foundry Workers	
	Blackburn, Dick W.	Boilermaker	
	Crayton, Ray A.	Boilermaker	
	Escalante, Frank J.	Boilermaker	
	Flannigan, Roosevelt	Boilermaker	
	Hopkins, Arthur N.	Boilermaker	
	Jewell, Mart T.	Boilermaker	
	Shoemaker, Charles T	Boilermaker	
	Raposa, John A.	Boilermaker	
	Scriven, Ronald L.	Boilermaker	
	Wallace, Ronald C.	Boilermaker	
	Palacio, Lorenzo S.	Shipwright	
	Searcy, Kenneth L.	Shipwright	
	Sweard, Kenneth G.	Shipwright	
	Milburn, Clyde	Rigger	
	Nomura, Tomio A.	Rigger	
	Tejero, Franklin E.	Rigger	
	Duby, Arthur P.	Rigger	
	Heurter, Jeffrey E.	Rigger	
	Link, Mark M.	Rigger	
	Postma, John Jr.	Rigger	
	Viramontes, Ismael	Rigger	
	Thompson, John W.	Rigger	
	Argueta, Henry	Plastic Fabricator	
	Barela, Ben E.	Plastic Fabricator	
	Brazile, Chester L.	Plastic Fabricator	
	Lane, William W.	Plastic Fabricator	
	Oka, Reginald K.	A/C & Refrigeration Mechanic	
	Carro, John J.	Sheetmetal Mechanic	
	Garske, Gordon J.	Sheetmetal Mechanic	
	Metcalf, Harry W. Jr.	Sheetmetal Mechanic	
	Powers, Thomas J.	Sheetmetal Mechanic	
	Siu, Michael L.	Sheetmetal Mechanic	
	Unpingco, Jesus G.	Sheetmetal Mechanic	
	Rios, Danny V.	Sheetmetal Mechanic	
	Caron, John R.	Pipefitter	
	Heinig, Edward D. Jr.	Pipefitter	
	Jennings, Charles H.	Pipefitter	
	Kelley, Reuben Jr.	Pipefitter	
	Acosta, Oswald]	Pipefitter	
	Westland, Dean J.	Pipefitter	
	Savoie, Roger J.	Pipefitter	
	Kennedy, Michael, J.	Pipefitter	
	Harshman, Earl D.	Pipefitter	
	Cavalier, Kirk A.	Pipe Coverer & Insulator	
	Murphy, Arnett M.	Pipe Coverer & Insulator	
	Ramirez, Antoinetta	Pipe Coverer & Insulator	
	Tracy, Michael	Pipe Coverer & Insulator	
	Camagong, Junn E.	Machinist	
	Cipriano, Wilson F.	Machinist	

1983 Continued next page

GRADUATION DATE	NAME OF	SKILLED TRADE	NOTES
1983	Gallo, Samuel D.	Machinist	
(01/20/84) DIGEST	Houts, Jimmie D.	Machinist	Honor Graduate
	Kennedy, James P.	Machinist	
	McCabe, Owen J.	Machinist	
	Navarro, Benjamin A.	Machinist	
	Earnes, Robert J.	Machinist	
	Johnson, Lloyd D.	Machinist	
	Pariseau, Dennis J.	Machinist	
	Sato, Dennis	Machinist	
	Sifuentes, George C.	Machinist	
	Yoshizawa, Susan G.	Machinist	
	Clark, Walter J.	Marine Machinist	
	Curry, John H. Jr.	Marine Machinist	
	Ford, James W.	Marine Machinist	
	Heard, William J.	Marine Machinist	
	Hernandez, Rodelio F.	Marine Machinist	
	Lewandowski, John A.	Marine Machinist	
	Lewis, Laswan	Marine Machinist	
	Merriman, Delmer H.	Marine Machinist	
	Melson, Mark P.	Marine Machinist	
	Sagrillo, Jon A.	Marine Machinist	
	Sanchez, Tommy P.	Marine Machinist	
	Smith, Larry S.	Marine Machinist	
	Taite, Jake	Marine Machinist	
	Weida, David M.	Marine Machinist	
	Black, Douglas L.	Metal Inspector	
	Pacho, Robert W.	Metal Inspector	
	Palmer, Jimmy D.	Metal Inspector	
	Espejo, Emilio F.	Ordnance Mechanic	
	Frazier, Lyle E.	Ordnance Mechanic	
	Pittman, Lawrence	Ordnance Mechanic	
	Sardella, Joseph S.	Ordnance Mechanic	
	Dopazo, John J.	Fire Control Mechanic (Elex)	
	Levasseur, Michael J.	Fire Control Mechanic (Elex)	
	Sinsheimer, Harry E.	Fire Control Mechanic (Elex)	
	Terry, Joseph E. Jr.	Fire Control Mechanic (Elex)	
	Armador, Edward W.	Electrician	
	Atkins, David C.	Electrician	
	Autry, Donald E.	Electrician	
	Banister, Donald L.	Electrician	
	Breunig, David A.	Electrician	
	Campbell, Nathaniel W	Electrician	
	Hayes, Michale G.	Electrician	
	Herte, Michael J.	Electrician	
	Larkin, John N.	Electrician	
	Lenox, Mary Kate	Electrician	
	Patterson, Patrick A.	Electrician	
	Reyna, Philip	Electrician	
	Richmond, Thomas W.	Electrician	
	Sherman, Brad T.	Electrician	
	Stark, Douglas W.	Electrician	

1983 Continued next page

GRADUATION DATE	NAME OF	SKILLED TRADE	NOTES
1983	Stratton, Barry R.	Electrician	
(01/20/84) DIGEST	Andrews, Michael J.	Electonics Mechanic	
	Andrewin, Fitzpatrick	Electonics Mechanic	
	Balacano, Dante G.	Electonics Mechanic	
	Bustamante, David	Electonics Mechanic	
	Funkhouser, Dale C.	Electonics Mechanic	
	Harper-Rodriguez,	Electonics Mechanic	
	Kuhnke, Barry H.	Electonics Mechanic	
	Langston, Reynard D.	Electonics Mechanic	
	Nogawa, Ken C.	Electonics Mechanic	Dr. Plusch
	Pacheco, Gerry A.	Electonics Mechanic	
	Shaw, John A.	Electonics Mechanic	
	Stromberg, Thomas F.	Electonics Mechanic	
	Ulmer, William J.	Electonics Mechanic	
	Salcido, Ned L.	Electronics Industrial Control	
			133 for 1983

2,243 Total

GRADUATION DATE	NAME OF	SKILLED TRADE	NOTES
1984	Atuatasi, Johnny T.	Shipfitter	
(12/21/84) DIGEST	Barkwell, Charles E.	Shipfitter	
	Buckman, Raymond J.	Shipfitter	
	Conrad, Dennis J.	Shipfitter	
	Escue, Bobby R.	Shipfitter	
	Glaser, Edward E.	Shipfitter	
	Graff, Thomas L.	Shipfitter	
	Grepo, Luisito G.	Shipfitter	
	Jackson, Coy D.	Shipfitter	
	Martinez, Christopher	Shipfitter	
	Mutu, Panama Jr.	Shipfitter	
	Reyes, Richard D.	Shipfitter	
	Mothershed, Don J.	Shipfitter	
	Thomas, Robert E.	Shipfitter	
	Appel, Steve A.	Welder	
	Briggs, Marshall Q.	Welder	
	Day, Ronald L.	Welder	
	Ellison, John H.	Welder	
	Morris, Edward Jr.	Welder	
	Phelps, William T.	Welder	
	Reese, Frenchie R.	Welder	
	Rivers, Michael B.	Welder	
	Rivers, William E.	Welder	
	Webster, David D.	Welder	
	Weir, William F.	Welder	
	Aldredge, John J.	Boilermaker	
	Brown, Robert A.	Boilermaker	
	Steven, Marlin O. III	Boilermaker	
	Powers, Carl L.	Boilermaker	
	Huntress, Jerry D.	Shipwright	
	McKay, Louis A.	Shipwright	
	Spring, John J.	Shipwright	
	McCullough, Charles	Rigger	

1984 Continued next page

GRADUATION DATE	NAME OF	SKILLED TRADE	NOTES
1984	Brandon, James	Painter	
(12/21/84) DIGEST	Gomes, Donna R.	Sheetmetal Mechanic	Honor Graduate
	Jones Terry E.	Sheetmetal Mechanic	
	Morris, Robert A.	Sheetmetal Mechanic	
	Rogers, Jamal	Sheetmetal Mechanic	
	Yannette, Donald J.	Sheetmetal Mechanic	
	Auglar, Charles E.	A/C & Refrigeration Mechanic	
	Dahl, Terrance L.	A/C & Refrigeration Mechanic	
	Miller, John G.	A/C & Refrigeration Mechanic	
	Rogers, Charles W.	A/C & Refrigeration Mechanic	
	Davis, Duwayne V.	Pipefitter	
	Davies, Daniel R.	Pipefitter	
	Haines, Robert E.	Pipefitter	
	Krauser, Peter III	Pipefitter	
	Murdock, Stephen M.	Pipefitter	
	Negrete, Reynaldo	Pipefitter	
	Nibley, Victor S.	Pipefitter	
	Smith, William T.	Pipefitter	
	Steinel, Donald A. Jr.	Pipefitter	
	Taylor, James	Pipefitter	
	Welch, Deramus B.	Pipefitter	
	Young, De Andre	Pipefitter	
	Hamilton, Douglas R.	Pipe Coverer & Insulator	
	Migi, Matasaua A.	Pipe Coverer & Insulator	
	Norfolk, James D.	Pipe Coverer & Insulator	
	Olagues, Edward G.	Pipe Coverer & Insulator	
	Rollins, Donald L.	Pipe Coverer & Insulator	
	Anderson, William L.	Machinist	El Toro
	Blair, David S.	Machinist	
	Castellanos, Byron D.	Machinist	El Toro
	Concklin, James W.	Machinist	
	Dole, Burden	Machinist	El Toro
	Johnson Roy L.	Machinist	
	Kline, Everett K.	Machinist	
	MacPherson, Gary S.	Machinist	
	Matthews, Frank R.	Machinist	
	Napolitano, Steven	Machinist	
	Young, David A.	Machinist	
	Allen, Jeffrey L.	Marine Machinist	
	Barr, Robert J.	Marine Machinist	
	Batson, Forrest W.	Marine Machinist	
	Biscocho, Eddie P.	Marine Machinist	
	Cochran, William M.	Marine Machinist	
	Deshay, Charles W.	Marine Machinist	
	Dodderer, Thomas A.	Marine Machinist	
	Felix Mark A.	Marine Machinist	
	Garcia, Victor M.	Marine Machinist	
	Hohlman, Jeffrey A.	Marine Machinist	
	Horvath, Jeffrey G.	Marine Machinist	
	Langlois, Marc R.	Marine Machinist	
	Saputo, Anthony	Marine Machinist	

1984 Continued next page

GRADUATION DATE	NAME OF	SKILLED TRADE	NOTES
1984	Sween, Scott B.	Marine Machinist	
(12/21/84) DIGEST	Torena, Kenneth M.	Marine Machinist	
	Baysinger, Blane C.	Ordnance Mechanic	
	Garrett, Daniel	Ordnance Mechanic	
	Lingenfelter, Albert M.	Ordnance Mechanic	
	Mason, David B.	Ordnance Mechanic	
	Poissant, Joseph L.	Ordnance Mechanic	
	Rebollido, Frederick J.	Ordnance Mechanic	
	Viramontes, Louis	Ordnance Mechanic	
	Adamson, Scott B.	Electrician	
	Banuelos, Benjamin R.	Electrician	
	Crawford, Kenneth L.	Electrician	
	Dolan, Gary B.	Electrician	
	Maldonado, Jose F.	Electrician	
	Menes, Constantino M.	Electrician	
	Rainey, David P.	Electrician	
	Routh, Paul D.	Electrician	
	Smith, John E.	Electrician	
	Zike, Kenneth P.	Electrician	
	Brown, Willie L.	Electronics Mechanic	
	Elhardt, Dale G.	Electronics Mechanic	
	Jordan, William P. III	Electronics Mechanic	
	Kimbrough, Lester A.	Electronics Mechanic	
	Lewis, Charlotte M.	Electronics Mechanic	
	Mills, Dennis C.	Electronics Mechanic	
	Tabios, Arturo L.	Electronics Mechanic	Dr. Plusch
	Bonachita, Dennis A.	Fire Control Mechanic (Elex)	
	Bunn, Charles G.	Fire Control Mechanic (Elex)	
	Givens, Howard D.	Fire Control Mechanic (Elex)	
	Gonzales, Antonio A.	Fire Control Mechanic (Elex)	
	Knight, Jeffrey M.	Fire Control Mechanic (Elex)	
	Weller, Gary A.	Fire Control Mechanic (Elex)	
			117 for 1984

2.360 Total

GRADUATION DATE	NAME OF	SKILLED TRADE	NOTES
1985	Acebedo, Tommy A.	Shipfitter	
(03/29/86) DIGEST	Davis, Shermaine Y.	Shipfitter	
	Dawson, Edward	Shipfitter	
	Delgado, Fernando	Shipfitter	
	Ellinor, Anthony B.	Shipfitter	
	Gobert, Allen J.	Shipfitter	
	Mayo, Thomas E.	Shipfitter	
	Yonan, Andrew A.	Shipfitter	
	Cory, Robbie L.	Welder	
	D'Arcy-Garcia, Jaime	Welder	
	Delgado, Carol J.	Welder	
	Ford, Horace Jr.	Welder	
	Gutierrez, Brenda L.	Welder	
	Guillory, Rodney M.	Welder	
	Haas, Joseph R.	Welder	
	Hoffman, Richard S.	Welder	

1985 Continued next page

GRADUATION DATE	NAME OF	SKILLED TRADE	NOTES
1985	Kolstad, Bruce N.	Welder	
(03/29/86) DIGEST	Longstreth, Kerry A.	Welder	
	Mahoney, William R.	Welder	
	McDonald, Heather D.	Welder	
	McInnis, Larry R.	Welder	
	Seumanutafa, Talosaga	Welder	
	Stewart, John J.	Welder	
	Torres, Eduardo J.	Welder	
	Batiste, Tyrone J.	Boilermaker	
	Carter, Keith	Boilermaker	
	Hedgcorth, Daniel L.	Boilermaker	
	Llena, Danilo Q.	Boilermaker	
	Machado, Rudy M.	Boilermaker	
	Monahan, Cory S.	Boilermaker	
	Moss, Curtis L. Sr.	Boilermaker	
	Porter, Kevin S.	Boilermaker	
	Rettey, Mark E.	Boilermaker	
	Seraile, Mervin L.	Boilermaker	
	Branch, Sylvester J.	Shipwright	
	Crowley, Daniel W.	Shipwright	
	Cunningham, Stephen	Shipwright	
	Gibb, Michael D.	Shipwright	
	Otis, John V. Jr.	Shipwright	
	Varela, Daniel R.	Shipwright	
	Alexander, Kevin B.	Rigger	
	Jackson, Donald	Rigger	
	Malley, Reed K.	Rigger	
	Barcelou, Robert L.	Plastics Fabricator	
	Leon-Guerrero,	Plastics Fabricator	
	Little, Jerry W.	Plastics Fabricator	
	McVey, Johnnie R.	Plastics Fabricator	
	Beacham, Wendall T.	Sheetmetal Mechanic	
	Estrada, Dave L.	Sheetmetal Mechanic	
	Galvan, Henry L.	Sheetmetal Mechanic	
	Hughes, Richard A.	Sheetmetal Mechanic	
	Hunter, David W.	Sheetmetal Mechanic	
	Jamerson, Ronald L.	Sheetmetal Mechanic	
	Jordan, Walter L.	Sheetmetal Mechanic	
	Kenieutubbe, Howard	Sheetmetal Mechanic	
	McKinstry, John W.	Sheetmetal Mechanic	
	Neal, Darwin L. Jr.	Sheetmetal Mechanic	
	Stewart, Anthony B.	Sheetmetal Mechanic	
	Taylor, Kirk R.	Sheetmetal Mechanic	
	Watson, Alex	Sheetmetal Mechanic	
	Wright, Anthony C.	Sheetmetal Mechanic	
	Zito, Joseph	Sheetmetal Mechanic	
	Cunningham, Wallace	Pipefitter	
	Cutcher, Jerry J.	Pipefitter	
	Glasco, Rhodell	Pipefitter	
	Hernandez, Joe	Pipefitter	
	Ornelas, Xavier A.	Pipefitter	

1985 Continued next page

GRADUATION DATE	NAME OF GRADUATE	SKILLED TRADE	NOTES
1985	Paul, Leo M.	Pipefitter	
(03/29/86) DIGEST	Pillen, John C.	Pipefitter	
	Raposa, Mark F.	Pipefitter	
	Richmond, Timothy	Pipefitter	
	Roberts, Gregory K>	Pipefitter	
	Schatz, Todd W.	Pipefitter	
	Smith, Herman L.	Pipefitter	
	Vasquez, Miguel	Pipefitter	
	Weekworth, Carl H. Jr.	Pipefitter	
	Zepeda, Albert F.	Pipefitter	
	Ball, Jasper T.	Pipe Coverer & Insulator	
	Brown, Arthur R.	Pipe Coverer & Insulator	
	Middlebrooks,	Pipe Coverer & Insulator	
	Sandoval, Jose M.	Pipe Coverer & Insulator	
	Ivelia, Johnnie	A/C & Refrigeration Mechanic	
	Smith, Richard	A/C & Refrigeration Mechanic	
	Williams, Curtis B.	A/C & Refrigeration Mechanic	
	Nunez, Leonor	Metals Inspector	Female "B"
	Villegas, Julio E.	Metals Inspector	
	Alegre, Bonnie L.	Machinist	
	Angulo, Ernesto E.	Machinist	
	Arnold, Jerome M.	Machinist	
	Baldwin, Robert H. Jr.	Machinist	
	Cochran, Steven V.	Machinist	
	Colson, Phillip C.	Machinist	
	Cunningham, Anthony	Machinist	
	Flannery, Jack R.	Machinist	
	Lee, Vicent D.	Machinist	
	Oliver, Michael C.	Machinist	
	Sacayan, Henry E.	Machinist	
	Shimizu, Richard J.	Machinist	
	Stephens, Ronnie L.	Machinist	
	Barnes, John W.	Marine Machinist	
	Brown, William D.	Marine Machinist	
	Clare, Norman C.	Marine Machinist	
	Cody, Edward P.	Marine Machinist	
	Davis, Larry	Marine Machinist	
	Faamuli, Pete A.	Marine Machinist	
	Gutierrez, Danny M.	Marine Machinist	
	Hanley, Robert A.	Marine Machinist	
	Hiltz, William L.	Marine Machinist	
	Johnson, George N.	Marine Machinist	
	Long, Richard W.	Marine Machinist	
	Mercado, Guadalupe	Marine Machinist	
	Ponce, Richard	Marine Machinist	
	Rose, Robert E.	Marine Machinist	
	Williams, Paul V.	Marine Machinist	
	Aguon, Manuel N.	Industrial Electronics	
	Becker, Kenneth R.	Industrial Electronics	
	Cott, Terry E.	Industrial Electronics	
	Evans, Roy E.	Industrial Electronics	

1985 Continued next page

GRADUATION DATE	NAME OF	SKILLED TRADE	NOTES
1985	Perry, Carvin W.	Industrial Electronics	
(03/29/86) DIGEST	Scott, Abe E.	Industrial Electronics	
	Daniels, John W.	Ordnance Mechanic	
	Fruhnwirth, Kevin A.	Ordnance Mechanic	
	Geyer, Jeffrey T.	Ordnance Mechanic	
	Howell, Clifford C.	Ordnance Mechanic	
	King, Jeffrey L.	Ordnance Mechanic	
	Leidholdt, Robert D.	Ordnance Mechanic	
	Rahe, Dona C.	Ordnance Mechanic	
	Ullom, Markham M.	Ordnance Mechanic	
	Nelson, Arthur J. Jr.	Maintenance Machinist	
	Thompson, James K.	Maintenance Machinist	
	Allen, Rory C.	Electrician	
	Almozara, Mario R.	Electrician	
	Amendt, Kenneth C.	Electrician	
	Bodle, Lawrence J.	Electrician	
	Bostic, Wendall M.	Electrician	
	Boyer, John A.	Electrician	
	Bunch, Jean P.	Electrician	
	Clougherty, Paul E.	Electrician	
	Dent, Frank Jr.	Electrician	
	Dolan, Gary B.	Electrician	
	Henry, Anthony J.	Electrician	
	Johnson, Donald L.	Electrician	
	Kittinger, Stephen F.	Electrician	
	Montemayor, Enruque	Electrician	
	O'Mailia, John W.	Electrician	
	Ortiz, Daniel L.	Electrician	
	Perez, Thomas C.	Electrician	
	Ramierez, Samuel	Electrician	
	Stark, Daniel J.	Electrician	
	Stratton, Cathy D.	Electrician	Dr. Plusch
	Sohl, John J.	Electrician	
	Solan, William C.	Electrician	
	Torres, Joe B.	Electrician	
	Winders, Eric J.	Electrician	
	Austin, Ivan H.	Electronics Mechanic	
	Cantano, Artemio G.	Electronics Mechanic	
	Conn, Wendall	Electronics Mechanic	
	Courtney, Gwendolyn	Electronics Mechanic	
	Dacut, Gerard D.	Electronics Mechanic	
	Fraser, Brenda E.	Electronics Mechanic	Dr. Plusch
	Griffin, Jerry S.	Electronics Mechanic	
	Harris, Reuben O.	Electronics Mechanic	
	Medici, Johnnie	Electronics Mechanic	
	Pattishall, James H.	Electronics Mechanic	
	Rinkes, William A.	Electronics Mechanic	
	Roberts, Bruce F.	Electronics Mechanic	Dr. Plusch & Honor
	Sandland, William T.	Electronics Mechanic	
	Traub, Joseph M.	Electronics Mechanic	

1985 Continued next page

GRADUATION DATE	NAME OF	SKILLED TRADE	NOTES
1985	Valiente, Alfonso Jr.	Electronics Mechanic	
(03/29/86) DIGEST	Voetee, Michael E.	Electronics Mechanic	
	Begley, Vicki L.	Fire Control Mechanic (Elex)	
	Bolo, Andrew O.	Fire Control Mechanic (Elex)	Dr. Plusch
	Buruns, Marvin M.	Fire Control Mechanic (Elex)	
	Crouch, James W.	Fire Control Mechanic (Elex)	
	Czausz, William S.	Fire Control Mechanic (Elex)	
	Gilman, Randy H.	Fire Control Mechanic (Elex)	
	Gleason, Patrick F.	Fire Control Mechanic (Elex)	
	York, Edward E.	Fire Control Mechanic (Elex)	
			178 for 1985
			2,538 Total

1986	Cureton, Marcus K.	Shipfitter	
(02/27/87) DIGEST	Gaxiola, Luiz A.	Shipfitter	
	Guiste, James F.	Shipfitter	
	Jacobs, Collion C.	Shipfitter	
	James, Bishop Jr.	Shipfitter	
	Lindsey, Marvin W.	Shipfitter	
	Mayo, Thomas E.	Shipfitter	
	Rivera, Carmelo	Shipfitter	
	Slay, Marvin R. Jr.	Shipfitter	
	Stoyanoff, Jordan D.	Shipfitter	
	Woodard, Mark D.	Shipfitter	
	Allen, Thomas L.	Welder	
	Anderson, Lawrence	Welder	
	Briggs, Irvin N.	Welder	
	Cabotaje, Greg C.	Welder	
	Cisneros, Henry D.	Welder	
	Clemons, Richard C.	Welder	
	Duran, Alex	Welder	
	Hall, Oliver R.	Welder	
	Harper, James O.	Welder	
	Hebert, Jack	Welder	
	Hill, Louis W.	Welder	
	Jackson, Carlos E.	Welder	
	Mason, David O.	Welder	
	Nowell, Raymond L.	Welder	
	Ramirez, Dagober Jr.	Welder	
	Rothman, Elliott	Welder	
	Starkey, Robert J.	Welder	
	Bell, Kirk A.	Boilermaker	
	Calvin, Harold III	Boilermaker	
	Fitzgerald, Michael L.	Boilermaker	
	Fitzhugh, Elijah	Boilermaker	
	Gray, Michael S.	Boilermaker	
	Hilton, Michael E.	Boilermaker	
	Monahan, Gary P.	Boilermaker	
	Perkins, Tyler E.	Boilermaker	
	Salas, Jose J.	Boilermaker	
	Wagner, Kevin L.	Boilermaker	

1986 Continued next page

GRADUATION DATE	NAME OF GRADUATE	SKILLED TRADE	NOTES
1986	Concepcion, Jose B.	Shipwright	
(02/27/87) DIGEST	McHaney, Laverne I.	Shipwright	
	Armstrong, Norwood	Rigger	
	Buckley, Robert S.	Rigger	Dr. Plusch
	Daily, Timothy A.	Rigger	
	Jackson, Larry D.	Rigger	
	Jones, Kent R.	Rigger	
	Lindsey, Larry J. M.	Rigger	
	Mackner, Adolph W.	Rigger	
	Main, Kenneth L.	Rigger	Dr. Plusch
	Shafer, Jerry L.	Rigger	
	Lara, Stephen L.	A/C & Refrigeration	
	Walsh, Patrick	A/C & Refrigeration	
	Davis, Clarence L.	Painter	
	Hammond, Anthony A.	Painter	
	Hicks, Donald K.	Painter	
	Jones, Eddie	Painter	
	Milne, Alfred	Painter	
	Rivera, Chris P.	Painter	
	Shorter, Patricia A.	Painter	
	Swing, Michael B.	Painter	
	Anderson, Robert W.	Sheetmetal Mechanic	
	Cary, Christopher L.	Sheetmetal Mechanic	
	Gutierrez, David W.	Sheetmetal Mechanic	
	Hudson, James E.	Sheetmetal Mechanic	
	Matsukawa, Glen H.	Sheetmetal Mechanic	
	McKenna, John F.	Sheetmetal Mechanic	
	Medeiros, Michael K.	Sheetmetal Mechanic	
	Miller, Daniel M.	Sheetmetal Mechanic	
	Salazar, George G.	Sheetmetal Mechanic	
	Albright, Roger A.	Pipefitter	
	Barycki, Anthony V.	Pipefitter	
	Bradley, John W. Jr.	Pipefitter	
	Byler, Lawrence L.	Pipefitter	
	Chavis, George T.	Pipefitter	
	Cisneros, Fernando A.	Pipefitter	
	Clare, Richard E.	Pipefitter	
	Clemons, Herbert Jr.	Pipefitter	
	Finch, Lawrence L.	Pipefitter	
	Hultquist, Robert W.	Pipefitter	
	Jasenka, Richard A.	Pipefitter	
	Lewis, Kenneth W.	Pipefitter	
	Longo, Stephen A.	Pipefitter	
	Luiz, Dave P.	Pipefitter	
	Malan, Paul J.	Pipefitter	
	Martindale, Benjamin	Pipefitter	
	McDuell, Paul P.	Pipefitter	
	Pearson, Thomas V. III	Pipefitter	
	Tio, Christopher E.	Pipefitter	
	Tkacs, Richard F.	Pipefitter	
	Yetman, Michael E.	Pipefitter	

1986 Continued next page

GRADUATION DATE	NAME OF GRADUATE	SKILLED TRADE	NOTES
1986	Pulis, Joseph J.	Pipe Coverer & Insulator	
(02/27/87) DIGEST	Robinson, Wayne A.	Pipe Coverer & Insulator	
	Castaneda, Freddy	Production Machinery	
	Alangui, Eugene Q.	Industrial Control Mech	
	Bartolome, Napoleon P.	Industrial Control Mech	
	Bellemyh, Odell	Industrial Control Mech	
	Owens, Rebecca A.	Industrial Control Mech	
	Aurelius, Mathew J.	Machinist	
	Began, Joseph M.	Machinist	
	Bliss, Rand L.	Machinist	
	Coleman, Lyle III	Machinist	
	Collins, Timothy C.	Machinist	
	Corey, Paul J.	Machinist	
	Jiminez, Leonardo A.	Machinist	
	Klunk, Stephen G.	Machinist	
	Marquez, Larry T.	Machinist	
	Martinez, Henry Jr.	Machinist	
	McManigal, Philip R.	Machinist	
	Mestas, Lance A.	Machinist	
	Miller, Michael	Machinist	
	Palaganas, Jaime B.	Machinist	
	Santos, Alfredo D.	Machinist	
	Schumacher, Dennis R.	Machinist	
	Tavis, Peter J.	Machinist	
	Valdez, Michael R.	Machinist	
	Virgil, Arthur L.	Machinist	
	Duncan, Alex B.	Marine Machinist	
	Durbin, Stephen P.	Marine Machinist	
	Moore, Willie L.	Marine Machinist	
	Morsk, Daniel K.	Marine Machinist	
	Norvell, George L.	Marine Machinist	
	Sandstrom, Randy E.	Marine Machinist	
	Salvio, Ernesto S.	Marine Machinist	
	Savolski, Michael W.	Marine Machinist	
	Throne, Robin L.	Marine Machinist	
	Ughoc, James K.	Marine Machinist	
	Whaley, Russel E. Jr.	Marine Machinist	
	Campbell, Gregory D.	Fire Control Mechanic (Elex)	
	Fabio, Roy M.	Fire Control Mechanic (Elex)	
	Fleury, Vincent	Fire Control Mechanic (Elex)	
	Hale, Wayne E.	Fire Control Mechanic (Elex)	
	Magno, Herbert J.	Fire Control Mechanic (Elex)	
	Reyes, Kenneth B.	Fire Control Mechanic (Elex)	
	Richards, Vicki J.	Fire Control Mechanic (Elex)	
	Riley, Larry E.	Fire Control Mechanic (Elex)	
	Sanchez, John	Fire Control Mechanic (Elex)	
	Sebren, Thomas V.	Fire Control Mechanic (Elex)	Honor Graduate
	Sipes, Marlin J.	Fire Control Mechanic (Elex)	
	Sherman, Garry D.	Fire Control Mechanic (Elex)	
	Sherman, Sherry M.	Fire Control Mechanic (Elex)	
	Blahnik, Robert F.	Electrician	

1986 Continued next page

GRADUATION DATE	NAME OF GRADUATE	SKILLED TRADE	NOTES
1986	Bryan, George F.	Electrician	
(02/27/87) DIGEST	Gonzales, Enrique N.	Electrician	
	Hawes, Jess	Electrician	
	Jones, Larry L.	Electrician	
	Manfre, Clifford D.	Electrician	
	Newton, Donald R.	Electrician	
	Reines, William B.	Electrician	
	Tebeau, Rick L.	Electrician	
	Trulock, John M.	Electrician	
	Yeargin, Jeffrey L.	Electrician	
	Ansorge, Harry P.	Electronics Mechanic	Dr. Plusch
	Banania, Edmund F.	Electronics Mechanic	Dr. Plusch
	Cooper, Kevin T.	Electronics Mechanic	
	Crigler, Lizzie	Electronics Mechanic	
	Danner, Carl L.	Electronics Mechanic	
	Hellstrom, Karl F.	Electronics Mechanic	
	Johnson, Daniell B.	Electronics Mechanic	
	Kolone, Alava	Electronics Mechanic	
	McCall, Vicky R.	Electronics Mechanic	
	Miller, David M.	Electronics Mechanic	Dr. Plusch
	Owens, Steven W.	Electronics Mechanic	
	Poggio, Alberto V.	Electronics Mechanic	
	Rocha, Oscar L.	Electronics Mechanic	
	Romero, Eileen S.	Electronics Mechanic	
	Romero, Michael R.	Electronics Mechanic	Dr. Plusch
	Tio, Christian L.	Electronics Mechanic	Dr. Plusch
	Trembley, David A.	Electronics Mechanic	
	Wells, Gary B.	Electronics Mechanic	
	Young, Thomas P.	Electronics Mechanic	
	Black, Daniel C.	Ordnance Equipment	
	Eggleton, Andrew P.	Ordnance Equipment	
	Garcia, Louis	Ordnance Equipment	
	Misener, Kathy L.	Ordnance Equipment	
	Quiet, Victor A.	Ordnance Equipment	
	Williams, Mark D.	Ordnance Equipment	
			175 for 1986

2,713 Total

GRADUATION DATE	NAME OF GRADUATE	SKILLED TRADE	NOTES
1987	Bernardo, Nicanor N.	Shipfitter	
(03/25/88) DIGEST	Buckley, Donald W. Jr.	Shipfitter	
	Butler, Tony L.	Shipfitter	
	Brown, Vincent A. Jr.	Shipfitter	
	Davis, Clarence	Shipfitter	
	Logan, Reginald W. Jr.	Shipfitter	
	McCormick, Daniel T.	Shipfitter	
	Miles, Wilton R.	Shipfitter	
	Pecora, Salvatore W.	Shipfitter	
	Rodriguez, Miguel A.	Shipfitter	
	Smith, Timothy M.	Shipfitter	
	Watts, Robert W.	Shipfitter	
	Crist, Michael D.	Welder	

1987 Continued next page

GRADUATION DATE	NAME OF GRADUATE	SKILLED TRADE	NOTES
1987	McWhorter, Robert M.	Welder	
(03/25/88) DIGEST	Stewart, James E.	Welder	
	Barlow, Lance A.	Boilermaker	
	Hill, Robert C.	Boilermaker	
	Kincade, David L.	Boilermaker	
	Livingston, William F.	Boilermaker	
	Wilson, Douglas L.	Boilermaker	
	Gentry, Mona	Shipwright	
	Korgan, Robert M.	Shipwright	
	McHaney, Laverne I.	Shipwright	
	Clemons, Arlen G.	Painter	
	Hadley, Gregory A.	Painter	
	Hammond, Anthony A.	Painter	
	Huff, Robert W.	Metals Inspector	
	Phillips, Wayne F.	Metals Inspector	
	Harrel, Randall K.	Machinist	
	Hirsch, Paul M.	Machinist	
	Warren, Claraneda L.	Machinist	
	Funiestas, Teodorico A.	Marine Machinist	
	Noble, Robert G.	Marine Machinist	
	Cail, Arvid	Pipefitter	
	Menes, Anthony M.	Pipefitter	
	Mudd, Edward N.	Pipefitter	
	Cayton, Noah	Pipe Coverer & Insulator	
	Nicholson, Vickie M.	Production Machinery	
	Do, Janet M.	Industrial Control Mech	
	imenez, Jerry L.	Industrial Control Mech	
	Savoie, Roger J. Jr.	Industrial Control Mech (Elex	Honor Graduate
	Culton, Thomas H.	Ordnance Equipment	
	Cabrera, Arnel J.	Electrician	
	Conder, Gerald L.	Electronics Mechanic	
	Cushenberry, Karen B.	Electronics Mechanic	
	Dejusus, Samuel D.	Electronics Mechanic	Dr. Plusch
	Garcia, Peter N.	Electronics Mechanic	
	Gillett, Michael J.	Electronics Mechanic	
	Howes, Kenneth W.	Electronics Mechanic	
	Kawanari, Dean Y.	Electronics Mechanic	
	Keeler, David J.	Electronics Mechanic	
	Kolbush, Ralph E.	Electronics Mechanic	
	Mederios, Lawrence	Electronics Mechanic	
	Millan, Segismundo P.	Electronics Mechanic	
	Mooney, John M.	Electronics Mechanic	
	Nessler, Richard J.	Electronics Mechanic	
	Richard, Daniel L.	Electronics Mechanic	
	Soliven, Edgardo R.	Electronics Mechanic	
	Yancy, Willie J. Jr.	Electronics Mechanic	
			59 for 1987

2.772 Total

GRADUATION	NAME OF GRADUATE	SKILLED TRADE	NOTES
1	Amargo, Patricio D.	Shipfitter	
(McCaughey's	Cabug, Candido G.	Shipfitter	
	Cardenas, Raymond E.	Shipfitter	
	Croteau, Dean A.	Shipfitter	
	Herrick, Keith F.	Shipfitter	
	Kenyon, Leonard J.	Shipfitter	
	Loaiga, Bernard	Shipfitter	
	Manai, Isaako Jr.	Shipfitter	
	Sperling, Gilbert Jr.	Shipfitter	
	Vilano, Virgilio H.	Shipfitter	
	Behrens, Robert S.	Welder	
	Cagle, Michael E.	Welder	
	Carlton, Marvette	Welder	
	Franks, Charles A.	Welder	
	Jones, Paul J.	Welder	
	Laurason, Cynthia K.	Welder	Honor
	Mondain, Roderick Q.	Welder	
	Organ, Jeffery G.	Welder	
	Sullivan, Michael J.	Welder	
	Tafolla, Robert A.	Welder	
	Walker, Sidney L.	Welder	
	Warner, Larry D.	Welder	
	Washington, Donell	Welder	
	Acosta, Arnold A.	Boilermaker	
	Ebbat, Robert E.	Boilermaker	
	Stannard, Richard A.	Boilermaker	
	Acheson, Steven J.	Rigger	
	Campos, John V.	Rigger	
	Chambers, Cynthia R.	Rigger	
	Lozo, Frederick R. Jr.	Rigger	
	Martin, George F.	Rigger	
	Pasillas, Adrian J.	Rigger	Dr. Plusch
	Remick, Bruce D.	Rigger	
	Sutliff, James H.	Rigger	
	Vanderhider, Donahue	Rigger	
	Young, Caple	Rigger	
	Asher, Sidney E. Jr.	Painter	
	Brown, James R.	Painter	
	Chamness, John M.	Sheetmetal Mechanic	
	Hughes, Jerry L.	Sheetmetal Mechanic	
	Kia, Yong K.	Sheetmetal Mechanic	
	McCaughey, Joanne C.	Sheetmetal Mechanic	
	Schabel, Steve J.	Sheetmetal Mechanic	
	Veek, Karl A.	Sheetmetal Mechanic	
	Weimer, William S.	Sheetmetal Mechanic	
	Draper, Ralph T.	Plastic Fabricator	
	Wesolowski, Joseph	Plastic Fabricator	
	Begley, Judson P.	Electrician	
	Bell, Kelly	Electrician	
	Majdali, Walid T.	Electrician	
	Means, Phillip G.	Electrician	
19	Rendon, Esther R.	Electrician	
McCaughey's	Correnti, Mark A.	Production Machinist - Shop	
List from her	McMillan, Floyd L.	Production Machinist - Shop	
Persnoel record	Grimes, Michael A.	Industrial Elex Tech - Shop	
	Hayden, James C.	Industrial Elex Tech - Shop	
	Saylor, Ola	Industrial Elex Tech - Shop	
			58 for 1988

No graduating class in 1989 due to hiring freeze of 1985 & 1986   2.830 Total

| 1990/91 | Davids, Joseph | Pipefitter | |

(05/31/91) DIGEST	Yorker, Ferrell	Electrician	
	Claravall, Carmelo	Machinist	
	Garton, Ronald	Machinist	Dr. Plusch
	Goode, Frederick	Machinist	
	Harmonson, Mark	Machinist	
	Hill, William	Machinist	
	Kelly, John	Machinist	
	Legarreta, Debora	Machinist	
	Leyva, Steven	Machinist	
	Mangold, Steven	Machinist	
	Markowski, Moses	Machinist	
	Sanchez, Janet B.	Machinist	
	Williams, Michael	Machinist	
	Young, Derrick	Machinist	
	Gonzalez, Albert	Marine Machinist	
	Gorlinski, Joseph	Marine Machinist	
	Hoffert, John	Marine Machinist	
	Karl, James	Marine Machinist	
	Lawrence, Richard	Marine Machinist	
	Lloyd, Sherman	Marine Machinist	
	Niser, Harry	Marine Machinist	
	O'Donnell, Bert	Marine Machinist	
	Owens, Carl	Marine Machinist	
	Ribas, Jaime	Marine Machinist	
	Butler, Gary	Electronics Mechanic	
	Castro, Leonard	Electronics Mechanic	
	Cecil, Cathy J.	Electronics Mechanic	
	Cecil, David	Electronics Mechanic	Honor
	Eck, Vincent	Electronics Mechanic	
	Fabunan, Ruben	Electronics Mechanic	
	Fife, Arthur	Electronics Mechanic	
	Hanshew, Arthur	Electronics Mechanic	
	Mullen, John	Electronics Mechanic	
1990/91	Jarrett, Jary	Electronics Mechanic	
(05/31/91) DIGEST	Kuhn, Rosemary A.	Electronics Mechanic	
	Witherspoon, Curtis	Electronics Mechanic	
	Echevia, John	Elex Measurement Epqt Mech	
	Good, Winifred	Elex Measurement Epqt Mech	
	Taitague, Benny	Elex Measurement Epqt Mech	
			40 for 1990/91

FINAL GRADUATING CLASS   **2,870 TOTAL**

YEAR	HONOR GRADUATE	TRADE
1948	Bateman, William	Electrician
1949	Horton, Willard	Boilermaker
1950	McClanahan, Homer W.	Pipefitter
1951 (0)		
1952	Germaneri, Dominic P.	Instrument Maker
1953	Munoz, Ernest A.	Machinist
1954	Dougherty, Charles S.	Electrician
1955	Meyer, Vernon H.	Electrician
1956	Adams, Donald E.	Pipefitter
1957	Vasquez, Guillermo O.	Marine Machinist
1958	Gaminde, Augustine	Electrician
1959	Cox, Robert T.	Electronics Mechanic
1960	Benigno, Fiore T.	Electronics Mechanic
1961	King, Darrell R.	Electronics Mechanic
1962	Garrison, Franklin T.	Marine Machinist
1963	Norcross, Frank L.	Machinist
1964	Moore, Marvin K.	Machinist
1965	Russell, Denny R.	Electronics Mechanic
1966	Pheiffer, John R.	Electronics Mechanic
1967	Holmes Thomas P.	Marine Machinist
1968 (0)		
1969	Guimond, Michael J.	Fire Control Mechanic
1970	Lees, Alan A.	Shipfitter
1971	Fuller, Larry F.	Pipefitter
1972	Sorensen, Thomas A.	Rigger (Master Diver)
1973	Ribeau, Robert A.	Electronics Mechanic
1974	Kryda, Frank	Electronics Mechanic
1975	Hale, Presely E.	Electronics Mechanic
1976	Henson, John S.	Electronics Mechanic
1977	Speiser, Douglas L.	Electrician
1978	Thomas, John W.	Electronics Mechanic
1979	Tucay, Bernardo S.	Electronics Mechanic
1980	Dorset, Jeffrey L.	Fire Control Mechanic (Electronics)
1981	Wu, Stanley Jr.	Electrician
1982	Quintana, Emeteria A.	Shipwright
1983	Houts, Jimmie D.	Machinist
1983	Salisbury, Edana L.	Fire Control Mechanic (Electronics)
1984	Gomes, Donna R.	Sheetmetal Mechanic
1985	Roberts, Bruce F.	Electronics Mechanic
1986	Sebren, Thomas V.	Fire Control Mechanic (Electronics)
1987	Savoie, Roger J. Jr.	Industrial Control Mechanic (Elex)
1988	Jones, Paul J.	Welder
1989 (0)		
1990	Cecil, Cathy J.	Electronics Mechanic
1991	Harmansen, Mark	Machinist

YEAR	DR. PLUSCH AWARD	SKILLED TRADE
1972	Coates, Thomas W.	Marine Machinist
1973	Hennig, Fred	Electrician
1974	Hubbard, Frank R.	Electrician
1975	Maddock, Duane T.	Electrician
1976	Riehle, William K.	Electrician
1977	Decker, Frances W.	Sheetmetal Worker
1978	Minami, Lawrence T. Jr.	Boilermaker
1979	Lau, Tong W.	Electrician
1980	Koerner, Charles R.	Electronics Mechanic
1981	Irvine, Ellen K.	(Electronics)
1982	Aguon, Joseph P.	Rigger
1983	Nogawa, Ken C.	Electronics Mechanic
1984	Tabios, Arturo L.	Electronics Mechanic
1985	Stratton, Cathy D.	Electrician
1985	Fraser, Brenda E.	Electronics Mechanic
1985	Roberts, Bruce F.	Electronics Mechanic
1985	Bolo, Andrew O.	(Electronics)
1986	Ansorge, Harry P.	Electronics Mechanic
1986	Banania, Edmund F.	Electronics Mechanic
1986	Miller, David M.	Electronics Mechanic
1986	Romero, Michael R.	Electronics Mechanic
1986	Tio, Christian L.	Electronics Mechanic
1986	Buckley, Robert S.	Rigger
1986	Main, Kenneth L.	Rigger
1987	Dejesus, Samuel D.	Electronics Mechanic
1988	Pasillas, Adrian J.	Rigger
1990/91	Garton, Ronald	Machinist

YEAR	FEMALE GRADUATES	SKILLED TRADE
1978	Honey, Karen	Welder
1978	Watson, Catherine	Painter
1980	Phipps, Barbara J.	Shipfitter
1980	Emory, Patricia A.	Machinist
1980	Noble, Cynthia A.	Fire Control Mechanic (Electronics)
1980	Wallin, Glenna S.	Fire Control Mechanic (Electronics)
1980	Sacdalan, Eileen G.	Electronics Mechanic
1981	Ray, Patricia D.	Welder
1981	Joyner, Patricia A.	Shipwright
1981	Vivao, Violet	Shipwright
1981	Aldridge, Katherine F.	Shipwright
1981	Hester, Sherry M.	Painter
1981	Irvine, Ellen K.	Fire Control Mechanic (Electronics)
1982	Polk, Beverly J.	Shipwright
1982	Grandberry, Loretta I.	Sheetmetal Worker
1982	Smith, Cynthia J.	Welder
1982	Herte, Virginia L.	Pipe Coverer & Insulator
1982	Salisury, Edana L.	Fire Control Mechanic (Electronics)
1983	Johnson, Lynn L.	Molder Foundry Workers
1983	Ramirez, Antoinetta Maria	Pipe Coverer & Insulator
1983	Yoshizawa, Susan G.	Machinist
1983	Lenox, Mary Kate	Electrician
1984	Gomes, Donna R.	Sheetmetal Worker
1984	Lewis, Charlotte M.	Electronics Mechanic
1985	Delgado, Carol J.	Welder
1985	Gutierrez, Brenda L.	Welder
1985	McDonald, Heather D.	Welder
1985	Leon-Guerrero, Carmen C.	Plastics Fabricator
1985	Alegre, Bonnie L.	Machinist
1985	Rahe, Dona C.	Ordnance Equipment Mechanic
1985	Bunch, Jean P.	Electrician
1985	Stratton, Cathy D.	Electrician
1985	Courtney, Gwendolyn M.	Electronics Mechanic
1985	Fraser, Brenda E.	Electronics Mechanic
1985	Begley, Vicki L.	Fire Control Mechanic (Electronics)
1986	McHaney, Laverne I.	Shipwright
1986	Shorter, Patricia A.	Painter
1986	Owens, Rebecca A.	Industrial Control Mechanic (Elex)
1986	Palaganas, Jaime B.	Machinist

Year	Name	Trade
1986	Sherman, Sherry M.	Fire Control Mechanic (Electronics)
1986	Crigle, Lizzie	Electronics Mechanic
1986	McCall, Vicky R.	Electronics Mechanic
1986	Romero, Eileen S.	Electronics Mechanic
1986	Misener, Kathy L.	Ordnance Equipment Mechanic
1987	Gentry, Mona	Shipwright
1987	McHaney, Laverne I.	Shipwright
1987	Micholson, Vickie M.	Production Machinery Mechanic
1987	Do, Janet M.	Industrial Control Mechanic (Elex)
1987	Cushenberry, Karen B.	Electronics Mechanic
1988	McCaughey, Joanne C.	Sheetmetal Mechanic
1988	Laurason, Cynthia K.	Welder
1988	Chambers, Cynthia R.	Rigger
1988	Rendon, Esther R.	Electrician
1990/91	Legarreta, Debora	Machinist
1990/91	Sanchez, Janet B.	Machinist
1990/91	Ribas, Jaime	Marine Machinist
1990/91	Cecil, Cathy J.	Electronics Mechanic
1990/91	Kuhn, Rosemary A.	Electronics Mechanic

"B"
1985   Leonore, Nunez   "
        Metals Inspector

59 Female Graduates
"B"

For the reader: When copying this list, the computer worked in cahoots with MS Windows 7 and it wound up only partley editable. The only way I could add in a female graduate that I had overlooked (due to missinterpretation of the name) was as the add-on at the bottom.

APPENDIX F

List of Commanding Officers of the Long Beach Naval Base/Station and the Long Beach Naval Shipyard

LIST OF COMMANDING OFFICERS

Naval Base Los Angeles (Roosevelt Base) – 25 September 1941 to 15 April 1950

Captain Richard B. Coffman	25 September 1941 to 25 June 1942
Commodore S. F. Heim	25 June 1942 to June 1944
Captain Frank R. Walker	June 1944 to 15 January 1946
Rear Admiral L. J. Wiltse	15 January 1946 to 2 December 1946
Rear Admiral P. Hendren	2 December 1946 to 8 July 1949
Rear Admiral G. C. Crawford	8 July 1949 to 7 April 1950
Captain J. Y. Dannenberg	7 April 1950 to 15 April 1950

Disestablished 15 April 1950 – re-established as Naval Base Long Beach 1 February 1951

Captain J. Y. Dannenberg	1 February 1951 to 30 June 1952
Captain M. C. Heine	30 June 1952 to 30 June 1954
Captain J. L. Melgaard	30 June 1954 to 30 June 1955
Captain J. C. Woelfel	30 June 1955 to 30 September 1955
Captain G. G. Crissman	30 September 1955 to 19 November 1955
Rear Admiral R. L. Campbell	19 November 1955 to 17 April 1958
Captain R. N. S. Clark	17 April 1958 to 28 May 1958
Rear Admiral W. H. Price	28 May 1958 to 1 April 1960
Captain T. K. Bowers	1 April 1960 to 30 September 1960
Rear Admiral F. J. Becton	30 September 1960 to 7 October 1961
Rear Admiral K. L. Veth	7 October 1961 to 27 February 1964
Rear Admiral O. D. Waters Jr.	27 February 1964 to 12 August 1965
Rear Admiral C. B. Jones	12 August 1965 to 12 May 1967
Captain E. F. Leonard	12 May 1967 to 22 May 1967
Rear Admiral H. V. Bird	22 May 1967 to 31 July 1971
Captain C. E. Stastny	31 July 1971 to 30 June 1972
Captain M. J. Carpenter	30 June 1972 to 19 July 1972
Rear Admiral V. G. Lambert	19 July 1972 to 31 July 1973
Captain D. A. Smith	31 July 1973 to 18 September 1973
Rear Admiral W. S. Miller	18 September 1973

Disestablished as Naval Base on 18 September 1973

LIST OF COMMANDING OFFICERS
(continued)

Naval Station Long Beach

Renaming and reassignments of duties between Station status and Base status was mildly confusing at best with some commanding officers overlapping their titles while in other years there were two separate commanding officers.

Captain C. B. Hunt	January 1947 to January 1949
Captain J. Y. Dannenberg	April 1950 to February 1951
Captain M. C. Heine	February 1951 to June 1953
Captain J. C. Woelfel	July 1953 to September 1955
Captain G. G. Crissman	September 1955 to June 1956
Captain R. N. S. Clark	June 1956 to May 1959
Captain R. P. Fiala	May 1959 to October 1959
Captain J. C. G. Wilson	October 1959 to June 1961
Captain F. W. Silk	July 1961 to June 1963
Captain H. A. Cleveland	June 1963 to September 1963
Captain R. E. Dornin	September 1963 to June 1965
Captain M. H. Lytle	June 1965 to January 1967
Captain E. F. Leonard	February 1967 to July 1969
Captain C. E. Stastny	August 1969 to January 1972
Captain D. A. Smith	January 1972 to January 1974
Captain J. J. Meyer Jr.	January 1974 to June 1974

Disestablished as Naval Station on 30 June 1974
Reestablished as Naval Support Activity in July 1974

Naval Support Activity Long Beach

Captain J. J. Meyer Jr.	July 1974 to June 1975
Commander W. L. Lowe	June 1975 to August 1975
Captain R. E. Flynn	August 1975 to August 1978
Captain J. K. Thomas	August 1978 to October 1979

Disestablished as Naval Support Activity on 1 October 1979
Reestablished as Naval Station on 1 October 1979

Naval Station Long Beach

Captain J. K. Thomas	1 October 1979 to 26 November 1980
Captain J. P. Cornell	26 November 1980 to 12 January 1983
Captain D. H. Barnhart	12 January 1983 to 9 January 1985
Captain K. M. Healy	9 January 1985 to 29 May 1986
Captain W. R. Heinecke	29 May 1986 to 29 July 1988
Captain G. W. Dunne	29 July 1988 to 22 August 1990
Captain P. A. Tracey	22 August 1990 to 21 July 1992
Captain I. J. Jones	21 July 1992 to 30 September 1994

Disestablished permanently on 30 September 1994

LIST OF COMMANDING OFFICERS

LONG BEACH NAVAL SHIPYARD
U. S. Naval Dry Docks (established 25 February 1943)

Captain Fred M. Earle	25 February 1943 to 20 August 1945

Terminal Island Naval Shipyard (established 30 November 1945)

Commodore George T. Paine	20 August 1945 to 8 November 1946

Long Beach Naval Shipyard (established 1 March 1948)

Rear Admiral Thomas P. Wynkoop*	8 November 1946 to 26 January 1949
Captain Dale Quarton	26 January 1949 to 6 July 1949
Captain William E. Sullivan	6 July 1949 to 1 January 1950
Captain Dale Quarton	1 January 1950 to 1 June 1950

Disestablished on 1 June 1950

Long Beach Naval Shipyard (re-established 1 February 1951)

Captain Emmett E. Sprung	1 February 1951 to 1 October 1952
Rear Admiral George C. Weaver*	1 October 1952 to 23 September 1954
Rear Admiral Leroy V. Honsinger*	23 September 1954 to 19 August 1955
Rear Admiral Ralph K. James*	19 August 1955 to 27 June 1958
Rear Admiral Charles J. Palmer*	27 June 1958 to 25 January 1961
Rear Admiral John J. Fee*	25 January 1961 to 2 April 1963
Captain Jamie Adair	2 April 1963 to 22 December 1965
Rear Admiral John W. Dolan Jr.*	22 December 1965 to 20 September 1967
Rear Admiral C. Monroe Hart*	20 September 1967 to 8 October 1970
Captain Richard C. Fay	8 October 1970 to 14 August 1973
Captain Anthony W. Duacsek	14 August 1973 to 19 August 1975
Captain Edmund A. Miller	19 August 1975 to 30 August 1977
Captain James E. Kaune	30 August 1977 to 29 August 1979
Captain Joseph A. Gildea	29 August 1979 to 31 January 1983
Captain George E. Fink	31 January 1983 to 29 June 1987
Captain Larry D. Johnson	29 June 1987 to 27 June 1991
Captain Bernard Janov	27 June 1991 to 28 July 1994
Captain John A. Pickering	28 July 1994 to 30 September 1997

Disestablished permanently 30 September 1997

*Denotes promotion to Rear Admiral while serving as Shipyard Commander.

APPENDIX G

List of Officers of Naval Air Station
Terminal Island
(Reeves Field)
10 December 1942

While browsing on E bay one evening, I ran across an item listed as the Roster of Officers that were assigned to Naval Air Station, Terminal Island in 1942. I bid on it and won it. The 17-page roster was printed (one-sided) on a heavy paper and was in absolutely perfect shape. Only the two staples barely holding it together were rusted.

The list starts off alphabetically and even gives the addresses and phone numbers of the officers. Many of those residences no longer exist, especially those that were on the base that has been totally flattened. Many of the off base residences have also been leveled for urban expansion. Those that still may exist certainly no longer house the officer who lived there temporarily during World War II. Since the roster is actually a public record it is safe to list those addresses. However, I censored out the house numbers so some overly enthusiastic historian doesn't knock on the door and ask if the family of (*rank and name*) still lives here. Never mind trying to call the phone number. Those numbers with real names for prefixes were assigned decades before area codes. Some of them, such as in Lomita and Redondo Beach, were still only four-digit.

The only markings on the roster is on the cover where its original owner signed his name, Ensign P. D. Nugent who was one of the Naval Aviators assigned to Scouting Squadron 1-D11.

It is absolutely amazing that this roster has survived for over half a century in such remarkable shape. It is amazing that any rosters from that era still exist. Because of its rarity, I am including it as an appendix. Who knows? Perhaps a reader may find the name of his grandfather or great uncle in it and it will close a loop on his family history.

To top it all off, another E bay item I found was a July 4, 1944 menu for the Chief Petty Officers' Mess. I have collected other menus for display purposes at Navy memorial functions and placed a winning bid on it. When I received it, I couldn't believe what I found on the menu that was not described in E bay. That menu included the names of all the Chiefs assigned to the Naval Air Station. There are no addresses of course, but the list of names are included in this appendix.

ROSTER OF OFFICERS

NAVAL AIR STATION
TERMINAL ISLAND
CALIFORNIA

NAVAL AIR STATION, ROOSEVELT BASE,
TERMINAL ISLAND, CALIFORNIA.
December 10, 1942.

ROSTER of OFFICERS

	NAME	RANK	DUTY	RESIDENCE	PHONE
	ALLISON, R.T.	Lt.Comdr. SC-V(G)	Asst.S&A Off.	Lorain Rd., San Marino, Calif.	Atlantic 210-16
	ALLMAN, T.L.	Lt.Comdr. (MC)	Sr.Med.Off.	Williamsburg Lane, Rolling Hills, Calif.	Redondo 7514
	AMBROSINI, B.	Lt.(jg) A-V(S)	Asst.to A&R	Euclid Ave., Long Beach, Calif.	LB 355-28
	BRYANT, E.J.	Lieut. (SC)	Asst.to S&A	Brayton Ave., Long Beach, Calif.	LB 451-18
	BURCHFIEL, B.E.	Lt.Comdr. I-V(S)	Intelligence Officer	Mira Mar Ave., Long Beach, Calif.	LB 890-12
H	CADENBACH, J.B.	Lt.(jg)	Asst. Photo. Officer	Fries Ave., Wilmington, Calif.	Wilm. 1577
	CHRISTENSEN, E.W.	Lt.Comdr. D-V(S)	Security Off.	Rivo Alto Canal, Long Beach, Calif.	LB 310-68
	COKE, J.B.	Lt.(jg) A-V(S)	Photographic Officer.	Marber Ave., Long Beach, Calif.	LB 522-10
	CRAIG, J.B.	Lt.(jg) SC-V(S)	Asst.to S&A	Altura Ave., La Crescenta, Calif.	Churchill 915-06
	DANA, F.E.	Ensign A-V(S)	Physical Educ.	BOQ 1, Room 13	
	DEAN, J.R.	Lt.(jg) O-V(S)	Armory Off.	Via Wasiers, Newport Beach, Calif.	
*	DODSON, L.F.	Lt.Comdr.	A&R & Radar Officer.	Lime Ave., Long Beach, Calif.	LB 436-15
	DONAHUE, E.J.	Ch.Mach.	Asst.to A&R	- 26th Street, Manhattan Beach, Calif.	Redondo 6048
	DOWER, J.J.,Jr.	Mach.	Asst.to A&R	West 31st Street, Long Beach, Calif.	
	DUKE, L.M.	Lieut. D-V(S)	Ordnance & Gunnery Off.	MOQ "C"	Ext. 272
	ELSTON, C.S.	Aero.	Asst. Aero.Off.	Caspian Ave., Long Beach, Calif.	
Z	FERGUSON, D.S.	Ensign SC-V(P)	Asst.to S&A	Glen Ivy Dr., Glendale, Calif.	Citrus 335-44
	FIGROUID, A.J.	Gunner D-V(G)	Asst.Gunnery Officer.	Carson, Long Beach, Calif.	
	GERNAND, H.C.	Lt.Comdr. MC-V(G)	Asst.Med.Off.	Tremaine Ave., Los Angeles, Calif.	Walnut 4553
Z	GHOLZ, C.E.	Ensign SC-V(P)	Asst.to S&A	BOQ 1, Room 13	
*	GREEN, J.W.	Ensign	Asst.to Oper. ADU-Pilot	Haroross Dr., Los Angeles, Calif.	Ax. 102-49

	NAME	RANK	DUTY	RESIDENCE	PHONE
	HALL, R.E.	Lieut. C-V(S)	Asst.Comm.Off.	▆ - 246th St., Lomita, Calif.	Lomita 1160
	HANSON, G.	Elect.	Asst.to A&R	▆ Telford St., Los Angeles, Calif.	Angelus 1-2191
	HARRIS, L.P.	Lt.Comdr. (RA)	Court Martial Officer.	▆ Paseo de LosDelicios, Hollywood Riviera,Calif.	Redondo 7769
	HARTLEY, R.E.	Ch.Bos'n (RA)	Transportation	▆ E. 73rd Street, Los Angeles, Calif.	La. 5862
	HAYES, A.J.	Gun'r	Gunnery Duty-ADU	BOQ 1, Room 5	
	HERRMANN, O.D.F.	Lieut. ChC	Chaplain	▆ Newport Ave., Long Beach, Calif.	LB 817-42
	HOLLADAY, J.	Ensign D-V(S)	Coding Off.	BOQ 3, Room 16	
	HOOPER, W.W.	Lt.(jg) D-V(S)	Asst.Security Officer.	▆ Alcalde Drive, Glendale, Calif.	Ci. 160-90
	JONES, A.A.	Lieut. A-V(S)	Ship's Sec'y	▆ ,Portuguese Pt. Palos Verdes Est.,Cal.	Redondo 7544
*	JULIAN, N.N.	Ensign	Asst.to Oper. ADU-Pilot	▆ Glendora Ave., Long Beach, Calif.	LB. 349-41
	KENNEDY, T.L.	Lt.Comdr. CEC-V(S)	Public Works Officer.	▆ Elm Street, Long Beach, Calif.	LB 668-424
	LEICHTER, H.L.,Jr.	Lt.(jg) A-V(S)	Asst.to A&R	▆ E. 2nd Street, Long Beach, Calif.	LB 734-27
**	MacCALMAN, D.J.	Lt.Comdr. (RA)	Executive Off.	▆ E. Hadley Street, Whittier, Calif.	Whittier 427-184
Z	MALONE, W.E.	Ensign SC-V(P)	Asst.to S&A	▆ E. 1st Street, Long Beach, Calif.	
*	McGINNIS, K.	Comdr.	Commanding Off.	MOQ "A"	Ext. 259
	MUNSELL, D.W.	Lt.(jg) MC-V(G)	Asst.to Med.	▆ Pomona, Long Beach, Calif.	LB 317-26
	NEEDHAM, R.J.	Lieut. C-V(S)	Communications Officer.	▆ Balsam Ave., W.Los Angeles, Calif.	Ar. 325-55
	NEWTON, C.B.	Elect.	Public Works Dept.	▆ Cota Ave., Long Beach, Calif.	LB 733-96
X	OLSON, C.E.	Lt.(jg)	Temp.Duty at Bethlehem Stl.	▆ - 14th Street, San Pedro, Calif.	Harbor 297-J
**	OVERALL, F.N.C.	Lt.(jg)	1st Lieut.	▆ Chestnut Ave., Long Beach, Calif.	LB 438-43
	PATNAUDE, E.D.	Lieut. DC-V(S)	Asst.Dental Off.	BOQ 1, Room 9	
Z	PORTER, R.K.,Jr.	Ensign SC-V(P)	Asst.to Disb.	BOQ 1, Room 13	
	PRIDDAY, J.E.,Jr.	Ensign D-V(S)	Coding Off.	▆ E. Ocean Blvd., Long Beach, Calif.	LB 608-94
	RATTRAY, F.J.	Lieut. A-V(S)	Personnel Off.	BOQ 1, Room 15	
	REYNOLDS, F.M.	Lt.(jg) SC-V(G)	Asst.to S&A	BOQ 3, Room 8	

	NAME	RANK	DUTY	RESIDENCE	PHONE
	REYNOLDS, G.R.	Lieut. (DC)	Dental Officer.	▅ E. 1st Street, Long Beach, Calif.	LB 313-55
	RHIND, R.W.	Lieut. MC-V(G)	Asst.to Med.	▅ Manhattan Ave., Hermosa Beach, Calif.	Redondo 5414
	RICHARDS, E.E.	Lt.(jg) A-V(S)	Asst.to Oper.	BOQ 3, Room 6	
	RICHARDSON, J.F.	Lt.(jg) SC-V(S)	Asst.to S&A	▅ S. Edris Drive, Los Angeles, Calif.	Cr. 6-5894
	SCHINDLER, G.E.	Lieut. SC-V(G)	Disb.& Commissary Officer.	▅ E.2nd Street, Long Beach, Calif.	LB 329-02
	SCHRADER, E.D.	Lt.(jg) A-V(RS)	Asst.Radar Off.	▅ Lowena Drive, Long Beach, Calif.	LB 332-83
**	SCHUR, M.A.	Lt.Comdr. (RA)	Unassigned	▅ Kinsington Dr., San Diego, Calif.	R-8525
Z	SMITH, B.H.	Lt.(jg) A-V(S)	Asst. Air Transport Off.	▅ Esplanade, Redondo Beach, Calif.	
	SMITH, M.F.	Lieut. A-V(S)	Asst.Synthetic Training Off.	BOQ 3, Room 12	
Z	STAMPLEY, R.M.	Ensign SC-V(P)	Asst. to Commissary	BOQ 1, Room 6	
X	TATMAN, E.L.	Mach.	Temp.Duty at El Segundo		
	WAGNER, J.J.	Mach.	Asst.to Oper.	▅ Scott Street, Long Beach, Calif.	LB 249-26
	WALDRON, F.M.	Lt.Comdr. (SC),(RA)	S&A Officer	▅ E. 2nd Street, Long Beach, Calif.	LB 887-89
	WHEELOCK, J.L.	Ensign (RA)	Asst.to Exec. Officer.	▅ Gentry, Huntington Park, Calif.	Je. 6824
	WILLIAMS, C.R.	Act. Pay Clerk	Asst.to Disb.	▅ E. 2nd Street, Long Beach, Calif.	
	WILLIAMS, W.J.	Ensign	Temp.Duty at Bethlehem Stl.	▅ S. Gaffey Street, San Pedro, Calif.	Wilm. 1890

MARINE CORPS

	NAME	RANK	DUTY	RESIDENCE	PHONE
	COLOMY, J.D.	Major USMC(RA)	Commanding Off.	BOQ 2, Room 16	
	STAMPER, W.J.	1st Lt., USMC(RA)	Post-Adjutant	▅ W. 19th Street, San Pedro, Calif.	Harbor 2825-W
	TYSON, R.L.	2nd Lt., USMC.	Company Off.	BOQ 3, Room 2	

AIRCRAFT DELIVERY UNIT

NAME	RANK	DUTY	RESIDENCE	PHONE
ADAMS, R.L.	Ch.Gun'r	ADU	▓▓▓ Williams St., Long Beach, Calif.	
* ATCHLEY, J.R.	Lt.(jg) A-V(T)	ADU	BOQ 3, Room 3	
* ATHERTON, W.H.	Lt.(jg) A-V(T)	ADU	BOQ , Room	
* BALLARD, W.R.	Lieut. A-V(T),(RA)	ADU	▓▓▓ Colorado Pl., Long Beach, Calif.	LB 898-16
* BARTO, R.I.	Ensign A-V(T)	ADU	BOQ 3, Room 10	
* BATTAN, F.L.	Lieut. A-V(T)	ADU	▓▓▓ E. 1st Street, Long Beach, Calif.	
* BERGEY, G.L.	Ensign A-V(N)	ADU	▓▓▓ - 8th Street, Huntington Beach, Calif.	Phone 3632
* BLACK, J.	Ensign A-V(N)	ADU	BOQ 3, Room 8	
* BOEHCK, J.A.	Lt.(jg) A-V(N)	ADU	▓▓▓ Carson, Long Beach, Calif.	LB 488-15
* BOOCOCK, K.	Lieut. A-V(T)	ADU	▓▓▓ San Vicente Blvd., Santa Monica, Calif.	Sta.Mon. 5-8806
* BOWEN, J.C.	Lieut. A-V(T)	ADU	▓▓▓ E. 2nd Street, Long Beach, Calif.	LB 605-98
* BOWMAN, F.A.	Lieut. A-V(T)	ADU		
* BOYD, J.R.	Lt.(jg) A-V(N)	ADU	BOQ 3, Room 15	
* BREGEL, J.M.	Lt.(jg) A-V(N)	ADU	▓▓▓ E. 2nd Street, Long Beach, Calif.	LB 688-117
* BRITTON, E.O.	Lieut. A-V(T)	ADU	▓▓▓ E. Ocean Blvd., Long Beach, Calif.	LB 672-63
* BROWN, G.W.,Jr.	Lt.(jg) A-V(N)	ADU	BOQ 2, Room 29	
* BROWN, R.W.	Lt.Comdr. A-V(T)	ADU Flight Training Off.	▓▓▓ Apt.14 Long Beach, Calif.	LB 674-535
* BROWN, T.G.	Lt.(jg) A-V(T)	ADU	▓▓▓ Manhattan Ave., Hermosa Beach, Calif.	
* BUSH, B.T.,Jr.	Lt.(jg) A-V(N)	ADU	▓▓▓ Argonne Ave., Long Beach, Calif.	LB 872-43
* BUSHONG, J.H.	Lt.(jg) A-V(N)	ADU	BOQ 1, Room 14	
* CALLAHAN, J.D.	Ensign A-V(T)	ADU	▓▓▓ E. 5th Street, Long Beach, Calif.	
* CARTER, R.K.	Lt.(jg) A-V(T)	ADU	BOQ 3, Room 5	
* CHURCH, J.	Lieut. A-V(T)	ADU	▓▓▓ Pomona Long Beach, Calif.	
* COLE, A.M.	Lt.(jg) A-V(T)	ADU	▓▓▓ Roswell Ave., Long Beach, Calif.	LB 819-68
* COOLEY, C.P.	Lieut. A-V(T)	ADU		

	NAME	RANK	DUTY	RESIDENCE	PHONE
*	COTTRELL, L.H.	Ensign A-V(N)	ADU		
*	COWDREY, D.E.	Ensign A-V(N)	ADU	▊▊ E. Ocean Blvd., Long Beach, Calif.	LB 611-243
*	COX, J.H.	Ensign A-V(N)	ADU	BOQ , Room	
*	CRAWFORD, C.M.	Lt.(jg) A-V(T)	ADU	▊▊ Park Circle, Long Beach, Calif.	LB 683-465
	DAHL, R.E.	Mach.	ADU	▊▊ E. Ocean Blvd., Long Beach, Calif.	LB 612-52
	DAVIDSON, T.	Ensign	ADU	▊▊ Mira Mar Ave., Long Beach, Calif.	LB 870-88
*	DAVIS, S.G.E., Sr.	Lt.(jg) A-V(T)	ADU	▊▊ E. 2nd Street, Long Beach, Calif.	LB 605-98
*	DeBAUN, T.L.	Lieut. A-V(T)	ADU	BOQ 3, Room 41	
*	DEMING, W.E.	Lieut. A-V(T)	ADU Officer Training	▊▊ E. Ocean Blvd., Long Beach, Calif.	LB 672-63
*	DIXON, H.F.	Ensign	ADU	▊▊ Williams Street, Long Beach, Calif.	LB 691-298
*	FINNEGAN, W.J.	Lieut. A-V(T)	ADU	▊▊ W. 3rd Street, Long Beach, Calif.	LB 632-24
*	FITZGERALD, J.E., Jr.	Ensign A-V(N)	ADU	BOQ 3, Room 14	
*	FLICK, W.L.	Ensign A-V(N)	ADU	BOQ 1, Room 6	
*	FRENCH, H.S.	Ensign A-V(N)	ADU	▊▊ E. 3rd Street, Long Beach, Calif.	
*	GERMERAAD, D.P.	Ensign A-V(N)	ADU	BOQ 3, Room 4	
*	GOODMAN, W.A.	Ensign A-V(N)	ADU	▊▊ E. 3rd Street, Long Beach, Calif.	LB 670-575
*	GRAHAM, G.	Ensign A-V(N)	ADU	BOQ 1, Room 3	
	GRANT, M.H.	Ensign A-V(S)	ADU & Asst.Ship's Serv.Off.	▊▊ Livingston Ave., Long Beach, Calif.	LB 665-55
H*	GRAY, J.L.	Ensign A-V(N)	ADU	BOQ 3, Room 9	
*	HACKLEMAN, O.W.	Lt.(jg) A-V(N)	ADU	BOQ 3, Room 39	
*	HAHN, L.	Ensign A-V(N)	ADU	BOQ 1, Room 6	
*	HANCOCK, H.M.	Lieut. A-V(T)	ADU	BOQ 3, Room 41	
*	HARRIS, J.B.	Ensign A-V(N)	ADU	BOQ 3, Room 11	
	HARRIS, W.Jr.	Ensign A-V(P)	ADU	▊▊ E. 3rd Street, Long Beach, Calif.	LB 675-575
	HEIMBURGER, R.A.	Lieut. A-V(S)	ADU	BOQ 3, Room 12	

NAME	RANK	DUTY	RESIDENCE	PHONE
HELD, S.	Lieut. A-V(P)	ADU	▓▓▓ Miranda Street, N.Hollywood, Calif.	Sunset 140-94
* HENDERSON, C.M.	Lieut. A-V(T)	ADU	BOQ 1, Room 9	
* HERBST, F.W.	Ensign A-V(T)	ADU	▓▓ Hermosa Ave., Long Beach, Calif.	
* HILL, H.E.	Ensign A-V(N)	ADU	BOQ 1, Room 6	
* HINMAN, R.S.	Ensign A-V(N)	ADU	▓▓▓ E. 3rd Street, Long Beach, Calif.	LB 670-575
* HUNT, W.E.	Lieut. A-V(T)	ADU	▓▓▓▓▓▓▓,.,Shorham Dr. Cr. Los Angeles, Calif.	5-2894
* JAMES, R.C.	Ensign A-V(T)	ADU	▓▓▓ Earl Ave., Long Beach, Calif.	LB 466-40
* JONES, H.W., Jr.	Ensign A-V(N)	ADU	BOQ 3, Room 18	
* JONES, J.E.	Lt.(jg) A-V(T)	ADU	BOQ 3, Room 3	
* JONES, W.D.	Ensign A-V(N)	ADU	BOQ 3, Room 18	
* KIRK, W.T.	Lt.(jg) A-V(T)	ADU	BOQ 3, Room 11	
* KOEHLER, C.D.	Ensign A-V(N)	ADU	▓▓▓ Magnolia Ave., Long Beach, Calif.	LB 733-03
* LAING, W.M.	Lt.(jg) A-V(N)	ADU	BOQ 3, Room 15	
* LAWRENCE, R.E.	Lieut. A-V(T)	ADU	▓▓▓ E. 7th Street, Long Beach, Calif.	
* LEACH, E.S.W.	Ensign A-V(T)	ADU	▓▓▓ E. Ocean Blvd., Long Beach, Calif.	
* LENHART, G.J.	Lt.(jg) A-V(T)	ADU	▓▓▓ Lime Ave., Long Beach, Calif.	LB 657-576
* LEONARD, J.E.	Lieut. A-V(T)	ADU	▓▓▓▓▓ ▓▓▓ Motel Long Beach, Calif.	LB 410-54
* LESLIE, J.M.	Lieut. A-V(G)	ADU	▓▓▓ Chestnut Ave., Long Beach, Calif.	LB 685-312
* LINCOLN, Kirke P.	Lt.(jg) A-V(T)	ADU	BOQ 3, Room 10	
* LOHSEN, W.C.	Ensign A-V(N)	ADU	▓▓▓ E. 2nd Street, Long Beach, Calif.	
* LOWE, W.E., Jr.	Lt.(jg) A-V(N)	ADU	▓▓▓ E. Ocean Blvd., Long Beach, Calif.	LB 646-440
* MARTIN, H.	Lieut. A-V(T)	ADU	▓▓▓ Magnolia Ave., Long Beach, Calif.	LB 446-38
* MARTIN, M.T.	Lt.Comdr.	Operations & Sr.Officer ADU	▓▓▓ Linden Ave., Long Beach, Calif.	LB 444-61
MARTIN, W.H.	Rdo.Elec. C-V(G)	ADU	▓▓▓ Wilson Ave., San Diego, Calif.	Ra-7160
* McGAUGHEY, H.M.	Lieut. A-V(T)	ADU	▓▓▓ E.Ocean Blvd., Long Beach, Calif.	LB 662-53

	NAME	RANK	DUTY	RESIDENCE	PHONE
*	McNEAL, C.L.	Lt.(jg) A-V(N)	ADU	BOQ 3, Room 17	
*	McNEILL, G.E.	Lt.(jg) A-V(N)	ADU	▇ Pomona, Long Beach, Calif.	LB 835-10
*	MILLER, R.F.	Ensign A-V(N)	ADU	BOQ 2, Room 29	
*	MOORE, D.E.	Ensign A-V(N)	ADU	BOQ , Room	
*H	MOSS, C.W.	Lt.(jg) A-V(N)	ADU	▇ Coronada, Long Beach, Calif.	
*	MULVIHILL, T.P.	Lieut. A-V(T)	ADU	▇ Santa Ana, Long Beach, Calif.	LB 853-97
*	MUNDY, E.M.	Lt.(jg) A-V(N)	ADU	BOQ 3, Room 6	
*	MYERS, J.R.	Lt.(jg) A-V(T)	ADU	▇ E. Ocean Blvd., Long Beach, Calif.	LB 662-53
	NASH, J.J.	Mach.	ADU	▇ Via de Ansar, San Pedro, Calif.	
*	NEWTON, E.F.	Ensign A-V(N)	ADU	BOQ 1, Room 5	
*	NIEUKIRK, J.P.	Ensign A-V(N)	ADU	BOQ 3, Room 4	
*	OSBORNE, R.E.	Lieut. A-V(T)	ADU	▇ W. Ocean Blvd., Long Beach, Calif.	LB 622-31
*	PEARSON, G.W.	Lt.(jg) A-V(N)	ADU	BOQ 3, Room 7	
*	PEEK, R.L.	Lt.(jg) A-V(N)	ADU	BOQ 3, Room 39	
*	PELZER, L.P.	Lt.(jg) A-V(N)	ADU	BOQ 3, Room 9	
*	PIERCE, L.L.	Lieut. A-V(T)	ADU	▇ - 219th Place, Long Beach, Calif.	
*	PORTER, D.K.,Jr.	Lt.(jg) A-V(N)	ADU	BOQ 3, Room 7	
*	PRUYN, R.L.	Lieut. A-V(T)	ADU	▇ Via de Monte Palos Verdes, Calif.	
*	PULLIAM, W.W.	Lt.(jg) A-V(N)	ADU	▇ E. 3rd Street, Long Beach, Calif.	LB 611-345
*	RAINEY, J.B.,Jr.	Lt.(jg) A-V(N)	ADU	BOQ 3, Room 16	
*	RANDALL, W.B.	Lt.Comdr. A-V(T)	ADU Flight Off.	▇ E. Ocean Blvd., Long Beach, Calif.	LB 672-63
*	RENNEKER, R.C.	Lt.(jg) A-V(N)	ADU	▇ E. 1st Street, Long Beach, Calif.	LB 326-41
*	RICE, S.J.,Jr.	Ensign A-V(T)	ADU	▇ Lowena Drive, Long Beach, Calif.	LB 805-13
*	RIETZ, D.W.	Lt.(jg) A-V(T)	ADU	▇ Chestnut Ave., Long Beach, Calif.	LB 662-75
*	RILEY, V.F.	Ensign A-V(N)	ADU	BOQ 3, Room 38	

	NAME	RANK	DUTY	RESIDENCE	PHONE
*	ROBINSON, E.S.	Ensign A-V(T)	ADU	▬ Quincy Ave., Long Beach, Calif.	LB 831-05
*	ROGERS, C.E.	Lt.(jg) A-V(T)	ADU	▬ Summit Drive., Beverly Hills, Calif.	Cr. 171-36
*	ROW, C.L.	Ensign A-V(T)	ADU	▬ Peterson, Long Beach, Calif.	LB 600-59
*	RUSSELL, E.P.,Jr.	Ensign A-V(N)	ADU	BOQ , Room	
*	RYAN, E.B.	Ensign A-V(N)	ADU	▬ Orizaba Ave., Long Beach, Calif.	LB 877-47
*	SAWIN, F.L.	Ensign A-V(N)	ADU	BOQ 3, Room 13	
*	SCHATZ, V.E.	Lieut. A-V(G)	ADU	▬ Ximeno Ave., Long Beach, Calif.	
*	SCHUCK, R.D.	Lieut. A-V(T)	ADU	BOQ 3, Room 2	
*	SHEPHERD, G.R.	Ensign A-V(N)	ADU	▬ E. Ocean Blvd., Long Beach, Calif.	
	SMYTH, N.E.	Ensign A-V(S)	ADU	BOQ , Room	
*	SPRINGER, H.S.	Ensign	ADU	▬ Giralda Walk, Long Beach, Calif.	LB 848-55
*	STRAWN, H.B.	Lt.(jg) A-V(T)	ADU	BOQ 3, Room 17	
*	SULLIVAN, L.J.	Lt.(jg) A-V(N)	ADU	BOQ 3, Room 5	
	THOMPSON, D.	Lieut. A-V(S)	ADU	BOQ 3, Room 1	
*	THRUN, A.G.	Lieut. A-V(T)	ADU	▬ Mira Mar., Long Beach, Calif.	
*X	TINSLEY, J.S.	Lieut. A-V(T)	ADU	▬ Glendora, Long Beach, Calif.	LB 320-69
	VEILE, E.Y.	Lieut. A-V(S)	ADU	BOQ 3, Room 1	
*	WALDEN, C.	Lt.(jg) A-V(N)	ADU	▬ Covina Ave., Long Beach, Calif.	LB 349-92
*	WILLIAMS, J.A.	Ensign A-V(N)	ADU	▬ E. 1st Street, Long Beach, Calif.	LB 606-70
*	WINGERD, J.C.	Ensign A-V(N)	ADU	BOQ 1, Room 5	
*	WITTERS, M.K.	Ensign A-V(T)	ADU	BOQ 2, Room 29	
*	YAMBERT, R.F.	Lieut. A-V(T)	ADU & Asst.Oper.	▬ LaVerne, Long Beach, Calif.	LB 315-68

```
 *  Designates Naval Aviator (Flying Status)
 ** Designates Naval Aviator (Non-Flying Status)
 X  Detached on Temporary Status
 Z  Attached on Temporary Status
 H  Naval Hospital at Corona, as Patient.
```

ROSTER OF OFFICERS FOR PRECEDENCE PURPOSES

NAME	RANK	Date of Rank For Precedence
McGINNIS, K.	Comdr., USN	2- 1-37
SCHUR, M.A.	Lt.Comdr., USN, (RA)	5-15-41
MacCALMAN, D.J.	Lt.Comdr., USN, (RA)	2-25-42
DODSON, L.F.	Lt.Comdr., USN	6-15-42
MARTIN, M.T.	Lt.Comdr., USN	6-15-42
BROWN, R.W.	Lt.Comdr., A-V(T), USNR	6-15-42
HARRIS, L.P.	Lt.Comdr., USN, (RA)	6-16-42
RANDALL, W.B.	Lt.Comdr., A-V(T), USNR	7-15-42
BURCHFIEL, B.E.	Lt.Comdr., I-V(S), USNR	10- 1-42
CHRISTENSEN, E.W.	Lt.Comdr., D-V(S), USNR	10- 1-42
DEMING, W.E.	Lieut., A-V(T), USNR	12-10-41
LESLIE, J.M.	Lieut., A-V(G), USNR	1- 2-42
BOOCOCK, K.	Lieut., A-V(T), USNR	1-25-42
PRUYN, R.L.	Lieut., A-V(T), USNR	2-13-42
THOMPSON, D.	Lieut., A-V(S), USNR	3-23-42
RATTRAY, F.J.	Lieut., A-V(S), USNR	3-25-42
OSBORNE, R.E.	Lieut., A-V(T), USNR	3-27-42
VEILE, E.Y.	Lieut., A-V(S), USNR	3-29-42
HANCOCK, H.M.	Lieut., A-V(T), USNR	4- 7-42
PIERCE, L.L.	Lieut., A-V(T), USNR	4-21-42
YAMBERT, R.F.	Lieut., A-V(T), USNR	4-25-42
DeBAUN, T.L.	Lieut., A-V(T), USNR	5-14-42
BOWEN, J.C.	Lieut., A-V(T), USNR	5-23-42
COOLEY, C.P.	Lieut., A-V(T), USNR	5-25-42
FINNEGAN, W.J.	Lieut., A-V(T), USNR	5-25-42
HELD, S.	Lieut., A-V(P), USNR	6-11-42
HENDERSON, C.M.	Lieut., A-V(T), USNR	6-12-42
BRITTON, E.O.	Lieut., A-V(T), USNR	6-15-42
SCHATZ, V.E.	Lieut., A-V(G), USNR	6-15-42
DUKE, L.M.	Lieut., D-V(S), USNR	6-15-42
NEEDHAM, R.J.	Lieut., C-V(S), USNR	6-15-42
BOWMAN, F.A.	Lieut., A-V(T), USNR	6-15-42
THRUN, A.G.	Lieut., A-V(T), USNR	6-15-42
MULVIHILL, T.P.	Lieut., A-V(T), USNR	6-15-42
TINSLEY, J.S.	Lieut., A-V(T), USNR	6-15-42
McGAUGHEY, H.M.	Lieut., A-V(T), USNR	6-15-42
HALL, R.E.	Lieut., C-V(S), USNR	6-15-42
CHURCH, J.	Lieut., A-V(T), USNR	6-17-42
LAWRENCE, R.E.	Lieut., A-V(T), USNR	6-18-42
BATTAN, F.L.	Lieut., A-V(T), USNR	6-18-42
SCHUCK, R.D.	Lieut., A-V(T), USNR	7- 2-42
LEONARD, J.E.	Lieut., A-V(T), USNR	8-11-42
MARTIN, H.	Lieut., A-V(T), USNR	7- 3-42
SMITH, M.F.	Lieut., A-V(S), USNR	10- 1-42
JONES, A.A.	Lieut., A-V(S), USNR	10- 1-42
HUNT, W.E.	Lieut., A-V(T), USNR	10- 1-42
HEIMBURGER, R.A.	Lieut., A-V(S), USNR	10- 1-42
BALLARD, W.R.	Lieut., A-V(T), USNR, (RA)	10-23-42

NAME	RANK	Date of Rank For Precedence
ATCHLEY, J.R.	Lt.(jg), A-V(T), USNR	4- 8-42
DEAN, J.R.	Lt.(jg), O-V(S), USNR	4-11-42
RIETZ, D.W.	Lt.(jg), A-V(T), USNR	5-18-42
KIRK, W.T.	Lt.(jg), A-V(T), USNR	5-19-42
CRAWFORD, C.M.	Lt.(jg), A-V(T), USNR	5-20-42
CARTER, R.K.	Lt.(jg), A-V(T), USNR	6- 2-42
BROWN, T.G.	Lt.(jg), A-V(T), USNR	6- 4-42
DAVIS, S.G.E.,Sr.	Lt.(jg), A-V(T), USNR	6- 8-42
COKE, J.B.	Lt.(jg), A-V(S), USNR	6- 8-42
LINCOLN, K.P.,Jr.	Lt.(jg), A-V(T), USNR	6-11-42
ROGERS, C.E.	Lt.(jg), A-V(T), USNR	6-12-42
STRAWN, H.B.	Lt.(jg), A-V(T), USNR	6-13-42
BOYD, J.R.	Lt.(jg), A-V(N), USNR	6-15-42
MOSS, C.W.	Lt.(jg), A-V(N), USNR	6-15-42
RENNEKER, R.C.	Lt.(jg), A-V(N), USNR	6-15-42
PEARSON, G.W.	Lt.(jg), A-V(N), USNR	6-15-42
SULLIVAN, L.J.	Lt.(jg), A-V(N), USNR	6-15-42
RAINEY, J.B.,Jr.	Lt.(jg), A-V(N), USNR	6-15-42
BOEHCK, J.A.	Lt.(jg), A-V(N), USNR	6-15-42
PORTER, D.K.,Jr.	Lt.(jg), A-V(N), USNR	6-15-42
PULLIAM, W.W.	Lt.(jg), A-V(N), USNR	6-15-42
BUSHONG, J.H.	Lt.(jg), A-V(N), USNR	6-15-42
McNEILL, G.E.	Lt.(jg), A-V(N), USNR	6-15-42
BUSH, B.T.,Jr.	Lt.(jg), A-V(N), USNR	6-15-42
PEEK, R.L.	Lt.(jg), A-V(N), USNR	6-15-42
BREGEL, J.M.	Lt.(jg), A-V(N), USNR	6-15-42
MUNDY, E.M.	Lt.(jg), A-V(N), USNR	6-15-42
LOWE, W.E.,Jr.	Lt.(jg), A-V(N), USNR	6-15-42
WALDEN, C.	Lt.(jg), A-V(N), USNR	6-15-42
LEICHTER, H.L.,Jr.	Lt.(jg), A-V(S), USNR	6-15-42
HOOPER, W.W.	Lt.(jg), D-V(S), USNR	6-15-42
AMBROSINI, B.	Lt.(jg), A-V(S), USNR	6-15-42
LAING, W.M.	Lt.(jg), A-V(N), USNR	6-15-42
OVERALL, F.N.C.	Lt.(jg), USN	6-15-42
JONES, J.E.	Lt.(jg), A-V(T), USNR	6-18-42
CADENBACH, J.B.	Lt.(jg), USN	6-22-42
OLSON, C.E.	Lt.(jg), USN	6-22-42
RICHARDS, E.E.	Lt.(jg), A-V(S), USNR	6-28-42
ATHERTON, W.H.	Lt.(jg), A-V(T), USNR	7- 1-42
LENHART, G.J.	Lt.(jg), A-V(T), USNR	7- 2-42
SMITH, B.H.	Lt.(jg), A-V(S), USNR	7- 5-42
COLE, A.M.	Lt.(jg), A-V(T), USNR	7-15-42
PELZER, L.P.	Lt.(jg), A-V(N), USNR	10- 1-42
McNEAL, C.L.	Lt.(jg), A-V(N), USNR	10- 1-42
MYERS, J.R.	Lt.(jg), A-V(T), USNR	10- 1-42
HACKLEMAN, O.W.	Lt.(jg), A-V(N), USNR	10- 1-42
SCHRADER, E.D.	Lt.(jg), A-V(RS), USNR	10- 1-42
BROWN, G.W., Jr.	Lt.(jg), A-V(N), USNR	10- 1-42

NAME	RANK	Date of Rank For Precedence
WHEELOCK, J.L.	Ensign, USN, (RA)	6-21-30
GRAY, J.L.	Ensign, A-V(N), USNR	8- 6-41
COX, J.H.	Ensign, A-V(N), USNR	1- 9-42
HOLLADAY, J.	Ensign, D-V(S), USNR	1-13-42
BERGEY, G.L.	Ensign, A-V(N), USNR	2- 7-42
GRAHAM, G.	Ensign, A-V(N), USNR	2- 9-42
COWDREY, D.E.	Ensign, A-V(N), USNR	2-26-42
GERMERAAD, D.P.	Ensign, A-V(N), USNR	3- 7-42
ROBINSON, E.S.	Ensign, A-V(T), USNR	3- 7-42
COTTRELL, L.H.	Ensign, A-V(N), USNR	3-14-42
MOORE, D.E.	Ensign, A-V(N), USNR	3-14-42
HARRIS, J.B.	Ensign, A-V(N), USNR	3-17-42
BLACK, J.	Ensign, A-V(N), USNR	3-17-42
GREEN, J.W.	Ensign, USN	3-21-42
FLICK, W.L.	Ensign, A-V(N), USNR	3-25-42
GOODMAN, W.A.	Ensign, A-V(N), USNR	3-25-42
JONES, W.D.	Ensign, A-V(N), USNR	3-25-42
ROW, C.L.	Ensign, A-V(T), USNR	4- 3-42
JONES, H.W., Jr.	Ensign, A-V(N), USNR	4- 3-42
HINMAN, R.S.	Ensign, A-V(N), USNR	4- 3-42
SMYTH, N.E.	Ensign, A-V(S), USNR	4-12-42
PRIDDAY, J.E., Jr.	Ensign, D-V(S), USNR	4-14-42
CALLAHAN, J.D.	Ensign, A-V(T), USNR	4-16-42
GRANT, M.H.	Ensign, A-V(S), USNR	4-18-42
RILEY, V.F.	Ensign, A-V(N), USNR	4-23-42
LOHSEN, W.C.	Ensign, A-V(N), USNR	4-23-42
RYAN, E.B.	Ensign, A-V(N), USNR	4-23-42
FITZGERALD, J.E., Jr.	Ensign, A-V(N), USNR	5- 1-42
NIEUKIRK, J.P.	Ensign, A-V(N), USNR	5- 1-42
WINGERD, J.C.	Ensign, A-V(N), USNR	5- 1-42
MILLER, R.F.	Ensign, A-V(N), USNR	5- 1-42
FRENCH, H.S.	Ensign, A-V(N), USNR	5- 1-42
RUSSELL, E.P., Jr.	Ensign, A-V(N), USNR	5- 1-42
HILL, H.E.	Ensign, A-V(N), USNR	5- 1-42
NEWTON, E.F.	Ensign, A-V(N), USNR	5- 1-42
WILLIAMS, J.A.	Ensign, A-V(N), USNR	5- 4-42
SHEPHERD, G.R.	Ensign, A-V(N), USNR	5-15-42
KOEHLER, C.D.	Ensign, A-V(N), USNR	5-15-42
BARTO, R.I.	Ensign, A-V(T), USNR	5-21-42
HAHN, L.	Ensign, A-V(N), USNR	5-22-42
RICE, S.J., Jr.	Ensign, A-V(T), USNR	5-24-42
HARRIS, W., Jr.	Ensign, A-V(P), USNR	5-29-42
DAVIDSON, T.	Ensign, USN	6-15-42
SPRINGER, H.S.	Ensign, USN	6-15-42
JULIAN, N.N.	Ensign, USN	6-15-42
WITTERS, M.K.	Ensign, A-V(T), USNR	6-16-42
LEACH, E.S.W.	Ensign, A-V(T), USNR	6-20-42
WILLIAMS, W.J.	Ensign, USN	6-22-42

NAME	RANK	Date of Rank For Precedence
SAWIN, F.L.	Ensign, A-V(N), USNR	6-27-42
JAMES, R.C.	Ensign, A-V(T), USNR	6-27-42
HERBST, F.W.	Ensign, A-V(T), USNR	7-20-42
DANA, F.E.	Ensign, A-V(S), USNR	9- 9-42
DIXON, H.F.	Ensign, USN	10-15-42
ALLMAN, T.L.	Lt.Comdr., (MC), USN	1-18-42
GERNAND, H.C.	Lt.Comdr., MC-V(G), USNR	6-15-42
RHIND, R.W.	Lieut., MC-V(G), USNR	1- 2-42
MUNSELL, D.W.	Lt.(jg), MC-V(G), USNR	9- 3-42
WALDRON, F.M.	Lt.Comdr.,(SC), USN, (RA)	6-30-36
ALLISON, R.T.	Lt.Comdr., SC-V(G), USNR	10- 1-42
SCHINDLER, G.E.	Lieut., SC-V(G), USNR	6-15-42
BRYANT, E.J.	Lieut., (SC) USN	6-15-42
REYNOLDS, F.M.	Lt.(jg), SC-V(G), USNR	6-15-42
CRAIG, J.B.	Lt.(jg), SC-V(S), USNR	8-21-42
RICHARDSON, J.F.	Lt.(jg), SC-V(S), USNR	11- 6-42
MALONE, W.E.	Ensign, SC-V(P), USNR	8-24-42
GHOLZ, C.E.	Ensign, SC-V(P), USNR	9- 1-42
STAMPLEY, R.M.	Ensign, SC-V(P), USNR	9- 9-42
FERGUSON, D.S.	Ensign, SC-V(P), USNR	9-10-42
PORTER, R.K.,Jr.	Ensign, SC-V(P), USNR	9-20-42
HERRMANN, O.D.F.	Lieut., ChC, USN	2- 2-42
KENNEDY, T.L.	Lt.Comdr., CEC-V(S), USNR	10- 1-42
REYNOLDS, G.R.	Lieut., (DC), USN	1- 2-42
PATNAUDE, E.D.	Lieut., DC-V(S), USNR	5-17-42
HARTLEY, R.E.	Ch.Bos'n, USN, (RA)	10-15-37
ADAMS, R.L.	Ch.Gun'r, USN	8-15-42
FIGROUID, A.J.	Gun'r, D-V(G), USNR	4-11-42
HAYES, A.J.	Gun'r, USN	6-25-42
HANSON, G.	Elect., USN	6-22-42
NEWTON, C.B.	Elect., USN	6-25-42
MARTIN, W.H.	Rdo.Elect.,C-V(G), USNR	2-21-42
DONAHUE, E.J.	Ch.Mach., USN	10- 1-42
DAHL, R.E.	Mach., USN	6-25-42
DOWER, J.J.,Jr.	Mach., USN	6-25-42
NASH, J.J.	Mach., USN	6-25-42
WAGNER, J.J.	Mach., USN	6-25-42
TATMAN, E.L.	Mach., USN	6-25-42
WILLIAMS, C.R.	Act.PayClk., USN	8-15-42
ELSTON, C.S.	Aero., USN	6-25-42
COLOMY, J.D.	Major, USMC, (RA)	
STAMPER, W.J.	1st Lt., USMC, (RA)	
TYSON, R.L.	2nd Lt., USMC	10- 9-42

ORDERED to REPORT

	NAME	RANK	DUTY
*	BENSON, R.K.	Lieut. A-V(P)	ADU
*	CARANER, L.H.	Lieut. A-V(P)	ADU
*	DAILY, S.P.,Jr.	Lieut. A-V(P)	ADU
*	DAY, R.	Lt.(jg) A-V(P)	ADU
*	GALLO, O.A.	Ensign, A-V(T)	ADU
*	HIGGINS, R.G.	Ensign, A-V(T)	ADU
*	KELLER, B.S.	Lieut. A-V(P)	ADU
	KOEPKE, R.D.	Lt.Comdr. (DC)	Dental
	MAY, H.C.	Lt.(jg) A-V(S)	ADU
*	OLSON, R.	Lieut. A-V(P)	ADU
*	RICH, S.J.,Jr.	Ensign, A-V(P)	ADU

469

GENERAL COURT MARTIAL

Lt.Comdr.	GERNAND, H.C.	MC-V(G), USNR	Mbr.
1st Lieut.	STAMPER, W.J.	USMC, (RA)	Judge Adv.

SUMMARY COURT MARTIAL #1

Lt.Comdr.	DODSON, L.F.	USN	Sr.Mbr.
Lieut.	DUKE, L.M.	D-V(S), USNR.	Mbr.
Lieut.	HALL, R.E.	C-V(S), USNR.	Mbr.
Lieut.	JONES, A.A.	A-V(S), USNR.	Recorder.

SUMMARY COURT MARTIAL #2

Lt.Comdr.	HARRIS, L.P.	USN, (RA).	Sr.Mbr.
Lt.Comdr.	ALLISON, R.T.	SC-V(G), USNR.	Mbr.
Lieut.	RHIND, R.W.	MC-V(G), USNR.	Mbr.
Lt.(jg)	AMBROSINI, B.	A-V(S), USNR.	Recorder.

DECK COURT

Lt.Comdr.	HARRIS, L.P.	USN, (RA).

B O Q MESS

Auditing Board

Lt.Comdr.	WALDRON, F.M.	(SC), USN, (RA).	Sr.Mbr.
Lt.(jg)	MONAHAN, R.J.	A-V(N), USNR.	Mbr.
Lt.(jg)	WILLARD, C.S.	A-V(N), USNR.	Mbr.

President
  Lieut.   THOMPSON, D.   A-V(S), USNR.

Treasurer
  Lieut.   HEIMBURGER, R.A. A-V(S), USNR.

B O Q WINE MESS

Auditing Board

Lt.Comdr.	CHRISTENSEN, E.W.	D-V(S), USNR.	Sr.Mbr.
Lt.(jg)	LEICHTER, H.L.	A-V(S), USNR.	Mbr.
Ensign	GRANT, M.H.	A-V(S), USNR.	Mbr.

Treasurer
  Lieut.   DUKE, L.M.   D-V(S), USNR

Asst.Treas.
  Ensign   HOLLADAY, J.   D-V(S), USNR

CPO MESS & WINE MESS AUDITING BOARD

Lt.Comdr.	MARTIN, M.T.	USN	Sr.Mbr.
Lieut.	BRYANT, E.J.	(SC), USN	Mbr.
Lieut.	JONES, A.A.	A-V(S), USNR.	Mbr.

SHIP'S SERVICE AUDITING BOARD

Lt.Comdr.	WALDRON, F.M.	(SC), USN, (RA).	Sr.Mbr.
Lt.Comdr.	ALLISON, R.T.	SC-V(G), USNR.	Mbr.
Lieut.	HEIMBERGER, R.A.	A-V(S), USNR.	Mbr.
Ensign	DANA, F.E.	A-V(S), USNR.	Mbr.

WELFARE FUND

Auditing Board

Lt.Comdr.	ALLISON, R.T.	SC-V(G), USNR.	Sr.Mbr.
Lt.(jg)	RICHARDS, E.E.	A-V(S), USNR.	Mbr.
Ensign	GRANT, M.H.	A-V(S), USNR.	Mbr.

Treasurer
  Lieut.   DUKE, L.M.   D-V(S), USNR.

EXAMINING BOARDS

For Advancement in Rating of Enlisted Men
#1	Lt.Comdr.	MARTIN, M.T.	USN.	Sr.Mbr.
	Lieut.	HALL, R.E.	C-V(S), USNR.	Mbr.
	Lieut.	JONES, A.A.	A-V(S), USNR.	Recorder.
#2	Lt.Comdr.	DODSON, L.F.	USN.	Sr.Mbr.
	Lt.Comdr.	CHRISTENSEN, E.W.	D-V(S), USNR.	Mbr.
	Lieut.	RATTRAY, F.J.	A-V(S), USNR.	Recorder
#3	LT.Comdr.	DODSON, L.F.	USN.	Sr.Mbr.
	Lieut.	RHIND, R.W.	MC-V(G), USNR.	Mbr.
	Lieut.	RATTRAY, F.J.	A-V(S), USNR.	Recorder.

For Advancement in Rating of Photographers.
Lt.Comdr.	CHRISTENSEN, E.W.	D-V(S), USNR.	Sr.Mbr.
Lieut.	RATTRAY, F.J.	A-V(S), USNR.	Mbr.
Lieut.	JONES, A.A.	A-V(S), USNR.	Recorder.

For Advancement in Rating of Storekeepers, Ship's Cooks & Bakers.
Lieut.	SCHINDLER, G.E.	SC-V(G), USNR.	Sr.Mbr.
Lieut.	BRYANT, E.J.	(SC), USN.	Mbr.

Medical Examiners.
Lt.Comdr.	ALLMAN, T.L.	(MC), USN.	Sr.Mbr.
Lt.Comdr.	GERNAND, H.C.	MC-V(G), USNR.	Mbr.
Lieut.	RHIND, R.W.	MC-V(G), USNR.	Mbr.
Lieut.	PATNAUDE, E.D.	DC-V(S), USNR.	Mbr.

SCOUTING SQUADRON 1-D11

NAME	RANK	DUTY	RESIDENCE	PHONE
ALVERSON, A.R.	Mach.	Asst.to Eng.	▓ Constitution Lane, Long Beach, Calif.	
* BELIKOW, A.W.	Lt.(jg) A-V(N)	Asst.Eng.Off.	BOQ 3, Room 40	Ext.280
* BRENNER, A.S.	Lt.(jg) A-V(N)	Communications Officer.	▓ E. Ocean Blvd., Long Beach, Calif.	LB 608-94
BUNTING, J.B.	Lieut. A-V(S)	Material Off.	▓ E. Ocean Blvd., Long Beach, Calif.	LB 672-63
* BUTLER, J.D.	Ensign A-V(N)	Asst. Flight	BOQ 3, Room 36	Ext.280
* CANFIELD, W.B.	Ensign A-V(N)	Asst. Flight	BOQ 3, Room 35	Ext.280
* CARLON, R.P.	Ensign A-V(N)	Asst.to Eng.	BOQ 3, Room 37	Ext.280
* CHADWICK, J.P.	Ensign, A-V(N)	Asst.Navigation Officer.	BOQ 3, Room 38	Ext.280
* DOBBS, N.E.	Ensign A-V(N)	Athletic Off.	BOQ 3, Room 34	Ext.280
* HANNALA, R.E.	Ensign A-V(N)	Asst.Athletic Officer.	BOQ 3, Room 38	Ext.280
* HICKS, T.G.	Ensign A-V(N)	Asst.to Material	BOQ 3, Room 37	Ext.280
* HIRSCHY, H.H.	Lieut. A-V(N)	Commanding Off.	▓ Magnolia Ave., Long Beach, Calif.	LB 670-358
* MONAHAN, R.S.	Lt.(jg) A-V(N)	Gunnery Officer.	BOQ 3, Room 33	Ext.280
* MURPHY, D.J.	Lt.(jg) A-V(N)	Engineer Off.	▓ Magnolia Ave., Long Beach, Calif.	LB 648-434
* NUGENT, P.D.	Ensign A-V(N)	Asst.Comm.Off.	BOQ 3, Room 35	Ext.280
* OSTROSKI, E.J.	Ensign A-V(N)	Asst.Gunnery Officer.	BOQ 3, Room 34	Ext.280
* PEEVEY, L.H.	Lt.(jg) A-V(N)	Asst.Material Officer.	▓ Appleton Street, Long Beach, Calif.	
* ROBERTS, A.M.	Lieut. A-V(N)	Executive Off.	BOQ 3, Room 42	Ext.280
* SAUNDERS, H.F.	Lieut. A-V(N)	Flight Officer.	BOQ 3, Room 36	Ext.280
* SUMMERS, R.W.	Ensign A-V(N)		BOQ 3, Room 40	Ext.280
THURMON, C.W.	Lieut. A-V(S)	Personnel Off.	BOQ 3, Room 42	Ext.280
* WILLARD, C.S.	Lt.(jg) A-V(N)	Navigation Off.	BOQ 3, Room 33	Ext.280

* Designates Naval Aviator (Flying Status).

Roster of Chief Petty Officers
Naval Air Station Terminal Island
4 July 1944

Anderson, J. V., CSK
Andrew, A. W., ACRM
Backers, B. A., CphoM
Blumberg, E. R., CRM
Branum, G. M., CMoMM
Cody, L. G., CPhM
Carlson, G. J., CSK
Carter, D. F., ACMM
Conklin, F., CCM
Conner, L. R., CY
Childs, T. R., CSP
Dawson, R. G., CCM
Dobson, E. F., CSK
Elam, C. R., CPhM
Faeh, W. H., CMM
Finley, C. N., CMM
Floren, C. J., ACEM
Goesman, W. H., ACMM
Jalenic, E. P., CBM
Jennings, S. O., ACMM
Jones, J. H., CCM
Jones, S., ACMM
Laird, R. C., CRM
Langneau, A. F. C., ACOM
Lavoria, A. J., ACMM
Lawler, W. J., ACMM
Lemcke, H. M., CAP
Martin, S., ACM
KcPheeters. G/ E/. CSp(M)
Meade, C. T., ACM
Monroe, C. T., CSK
Morris, B. C., ACM
Morrison, M., CCM
Murphy, J. H., ACCM

Phelps, O. R., ACRM
Ramos, F. B., CWT
Roche, B. F., CSK
Schleiter, G. H., ACMM
Shepherd, J. E., CCM
Smith, F. T., CEM
Stalter, J. L., ACMM
Stepp, H. J., ACRM
Tripp, A. C., ACMM
Taylor, W. H., CMoMM
Van Ry, R. E., CMM
Wahl, J., CBM
Walker, M. G., ACOM
Wagner, A. F., ACMM
Ward, J. W., ACMM
Wass, C. W., CSP
Weyrauch, R. C., CSp(A)
Wilson, G. D., CMM
Windlinger, J. S., ACM
Reed, A. J.
Dorothy, B. E., ACMM
Jernigan, S. R. CY
Lord, C. W., ACMM
Gardner, R. L., ACMM
Koerner, A. J., ACMM
Lovett, L. G., ACMM
Starren, B. G., ACMM
Skinner, O. E., ACMM
Two Mey, G. P., CBM
Taylor, W. E., ACRT
Buck, B.
Curley, J. P.
Cow, C. M., CCST

APPENDIX H
A Deck Log of the
USS *Missouri* (BB-63)

When the *Missouri* was brought down to Long Beach, many items and records were still aboard going back to World War II. *Missouri* was the only ship of the four *Iowa* class Battleships not inactivated between the Second World War and the Korean War. After all ships were reactivated in the 1980's, some old records or old copies of older records of the *Missouri* were found to be still intact aboard ship. Somehow, Charles Sprenger (a supervisor machinist and apprentice graduate of the first class of apprentices) was given a copy of one of the deck logs detailing the events of one day of the ship's service in WW II. He gave me that copy, which was a blurry and misaligned copy, and I have done my best to recreate it word for word in this appendix. It may only be of some interest to a few historians but in another way I look at it as representing the contribution Long Beach Naval Shipyard did to have that particular deck log written.

Iowa & *Missouri* heading for Tokyo Bay

Navpers-134 (Rev 1-44)   DECK LOG – REMARKS SHEET

United States Ship MISSOURI   Sunday 2 September, 1945

===

0400
Anchored in berth F 71, Tokyo Bay, in 10 fathoms of water, mud bottom, with 50 fathoms of Chain to the starboard anchor on the following anchorage bearings: right tangent Port #! 168°T, Yokosuka Breakwater Light 325°T. Port #2 193°T. Boilers #1, #4, #5 and #6 are in use. Condition of readiness III is set. S.O.P.A. is in the U.S.S. SOUTH DAKOTA (BB57). Administrative S.O.P.A. is in the U.S.S. SAN DIEGO (CL53). Various units of the Pacific Fleet and British Fleet are present.

J. H. Hofman, Lt. (jg), U.S.N.

0800
Anchored as before. 0707, U.S.S. TAYLOR (DD468) came alongside to port with Lt. Col. R. Powell and about 170 press agents to attend surrender ceremonies of the Japanese Imperial Forces. 0733 U.S.S. TAYLOR (DD468) cast off. 0750, exercised crew at quarters for scheduled ceremony.

L. Olson, Lt.(jg), U.S.N,

1200
Anchored as before. 0803, U.S.S.BUCHANAN (DD484) came alongside to port with various general officers of the Army and foreign representatives to witness surrender ceremonies. 0805, Fleet Admiral C.W. Nimitz came aboard and his personal flag was broken at the mainmast. 0824, U.S.S. BUCHANAN (DD484) cast off. 0838, U.S.S. NICHOLAS (DD449) came alongside to port with General of the Army Douglas Mac Arthur. 0843, General of the Army Douglas Mac Arthur came aboard and his personal flag was broken at the mainmast alongside of the personal flag of Fleet Admiral C.W. Nimitz. 0848, U.S.S. NICHOLAS (DD449) cast off. 0856, Japanese representatives came aboard. At 0902, with the following present, the ceremony commenced and the Instrument of Surrender
was presented to all parties:

United States

Colonel Q.S. Lander (SCAP Liaison)

Republic of China

Gen. Hau Yung-Chang   Vice Adm. Yang Hauan Chang
Lt. Gen. Chu Shih Ming   Maj. Gen. Wang Chih
Co. Li Sho Chang   Col. Wang Pei Cheng

United Kingdom

Admiral Sir Bruce Fraser   Capt. A.D. Nicholl
Comdr. R.H. Courage   Comdr. (S) A.P. Cartwright
Surgeon Lieut. G.R. Gayman   Lt. V.C. Merry

Representing British Pacific Fleet

Vice Adm. Sir H.S. Hawling   Commodore J.P.L. Reid
Lt. G.E. Cook   Rear Adm. E.J.P. Brind
Lt. H.B. Ashmore

United Soviet Socialist Republic

Lt. Gen. Kuzma Nikolasvish Derevyanko	Maj. Gen. Nikolai Vasilevich Voronov
Rear Adm. Andry Mitrofanovich Stetzenko	Maj. Ivan Joseph Borovsky
Capt. Nikolai Michallovich Karamishev	Lt. Nidolai Nikolaevich Tulinov

Commonwealth of Australia

Gen. Sir Thomas Blamey	Lt. Gen. F.H. Berryman
Rear Adm. George D. Moore	Air Vice Marshall Jones
Air Vice Marshall Bostick	Commodore J.A. Collins
Capt. J. Balfour	

Dominion of Canada

Col. L. Moore Cosgrave

Republic of France

Gen. LeClere

Commonwealth of New Zealand

Air Vice Marshall Isitt Lt. J.D. Alfingham

United Kingdom of Netherlands

Adm. Helfrich	Lt. Gen. L.H. Van Oyen
Col. C. Giebel	Comdr. A.A. Fresco

Japanese Empire

Mr. Mamoru Shigemitsu, Foreign Minister	Gen. Yoshijiro Umezo
Ka suo Okazaki	Saburo Ohta
Sh nichi Kase	L. Gen. Shuichi Miyakazi
Major Gen. Yatsuki Nagai	Col. Kaziyi Sugita
Rear Admiral Tadatoshi Tomioka	Rear Admiral Ichiro Yokoyama
Captain Katsuo Shiba	

Navy

Fleet Admiral Chester W. Nimitz	Admiral William F. Halsey, jr.
Admiral Richmond K. Turner	Vice Admiral John H. Towers
Vice Admiral John S. McCain	Vice Admiral Charles A. Lockwood, jr.
Vice Admiral Theodore S. Wilkinson	Vice Admiral Frederick C. Sherman
Lt. General Roy S. Goiger, USMC	Rear Admiral John F. Shafroth, jr.
Rear Admiral Donald B. Beary	Rear Admiral Oscar C. Badger
Rear Admiral Howard F. Kingman	Rear Admiral James C. Jones, jr.
Rear Admiral Wilder D. Baker	Rear Admiral Lynde D. Mc Cormick
Rear Admiral Ingram C. Sowell	Rear Admiral Lloyd J. Wiltse
Rear Admiral Gerald F. Bogan	Rear Admiral Robert B. Carney
Rear Admiral Arthur W. Radford	Rear Admiral Donald B. Duncan
Rear Admiral Thomas R. Cooley	Rear Admiral Forrest P. Sherman
Rear Admiral Thomas L. Sprague	Rear Admiral John J. Ballentine
Rear Admiral C.A.F. Sprague	Rear Admiral Carl Holden
Brigadier Gen. Herman C. Feldman, USA	Commodore Oliver O. Kessing
Commodore Joel T. Boone (MC)	Commodore John P. Womble
Brigadier Gen. Wm. T. Clement, USMC	Brigadier Gen. J.H. Fellows, USMC
Commodore Roland N. Smoot	Commodore Roger W. Simpson
Commodore John M. Higgins	Commodore Joseph C. Cronin
Captain Tom B. Hill	Colonel Theodore J. Dayharsh, USA
Captain Harold B. Krick	Captain William D. Anderson

Captain Ralph K. Wilson
Captain John C. Cross
Captain Marion C. Cheek
Captain Arthur M. Taylor
Commander Howell A. Lamar
Lt. Commander Kaufman

General of the Army Mac Arthur
Maj. Gen. Kean
Maj. Gen. Ryan
Maj. Gen. Sverdrup
Maj. Gen. Willoughby
Maj. Gen. Byers
Lt. Gen. Gairdner
Maj. Gen. Marshall
Maj. Gen. Frink
Maj. Gen. Stivers
Maj. Gen. Casey
General Stilwell
General Hodges
General Kenney
Lt. Gen. Richardson
Lt. Gen. Styer
Lt. Gen. Wainwright

Captain Edwin J. Layton
Captain Fitzhugh Lee
Captain Herbert L. Hoerner
Commander M. Ward
Major Roy Owsley, USMCR
Lieutenant Stringer

Army

Maj. Gen. Valdes
Maj. Gen. Whitlock
Maj. Gen. Bertrandias
Maj. Gen. Wurtsmith
Brig. Gen. Chambers
Lt. Gen. Whitehead
Maj. Gen. Swing
Maj. Gen. Chamberlin
Maj. Gen. Akin
Maj. Gen. Marquet
General Krueger
General Spaatz
General Eichelberger
Lt. Gen. Sutherland
Lt. Gen. Giles
Lt. Gen. Percival

and various other general officers. 0904, Mamoru Shigemitsu, Japanese Foreign Minister signed for Japan. 0906. General Yoshijiro Umezo, Chief of Staff, Japanese Army Headquarter, signed for Japan. 0908, General of the Army Douglas Mac Arthur, the Supreme Commander for the Allied Powers, signed for all nations. 0912, Fleet Admiral C.W. Nimitz signed for the United States. 0913, Gneral Hsu Yung-Chang signed for China. 0914, Admiral Sir Bruce Fraser signed for the United Kingdom. 0916, Lt. General Kuzma Nikolasvish Derevyanko signed for the United Soviet Socialist Republic. 0917, General Sir Thomas Blamey signed for Australia. 0918, Colonel L. Moore Cosgrave signed for Canada. 0920, General LeClere signed for France. 0921, Admiral Helfrich signed for the Netherlands. 0922, Air Vice Marshall Isitt signed for New Zealand. 0925, ceremony completed. 0926, U.S.S. TAYLOR (DD468) came alongside to port to embark correspondents and photographers. 0929 Japanese representatives left the ship. 0940, U.S.S. TAYLOR (DD468) cast off. 0945 U.S.S. NICHOLAS (DD449) came alongside to port to embark General of the Army Douglas Mac Arthur. 0958, General of the Army Douglas Mac Arthur left the ship and his personal flag was hauled down. 1003, U.S.S. NICHOLAS (DD449) cast off. 1005, U.S.S. BUCHANAN (DD584) came alongside to port to embark allied representatives. 1027, U.S.S. BUCHANAN (DD584) cast off. 1044, Fleet Admiral C.W. Nimitz left the ship. 1052, secured the crew from quarters. 1059, CinCPac's flag was broken in the U.S.S. SOUTH DAKOTA (BB57). Hauled down CincPac's flag; broke flag of Commander of Third Fleet.

J.L. Starnes, Jr., Lt.Comdr.,
U.S.N.R.

APPROVED: EXAMINED:

S.S. MURRAY, Captain U.S.N. COMMANDING   H.B. Lyon, Commander,
U.S.N.

The rest of the deck log for that day recorded only normal ship's routine and is really of no historical interest. But again I must say that along with the efforts of the overall defense structure of America, the efforts of Naval Dry Docks Terminal Island (Long Beach Naval Shipyard), Naval Base Long Beach (Roosevelt Base) and Naval Air Station Terminal Island (Reeves Field) contributed much to that very special day recorded in the deck log of the USS *MISSOURI* (BB-63).

A foot tall solid brass paperweight this author retrieved from the Estate Sale of the late Walt Miller-Weapons Control-Combat Systems Office.

INDEX

This index is divided into two parts. The first part are what pages the names of ships mentioned in the main text appear. You will note that the identification of USS is not on the index as my word search only looked for those letters. Where the name of a ship appears somewhere else without the USS would be technically insignificant. The index has some ship names in quotes (" "). That identifies the ship as privately "owned", such as the *Queen Mary*. I missed a few, but I'm only human (I think).

The second part lists the names of people involved with the various projects and ships or were invaluable contributors to this book. Even if they "only" provided some photographs, they have enhanced this edition well over the first edition.

I am very greatful for the photo of the "Queen's Box" that John "Jack" Whitmire took while the ship was in dry dock. Jack was also a member of a model train club I belong to and was a terrific photographer of trains and ships throughout his world travels. He was also a docent at the Los Angeles Maritime Museum and I signed him up as a docent for the Battleship *Iowa* when we would bring her in. Jack also served in the United States Navy in WW II and was at the helm of the USS *Canberra* (CA-70) when a Japanese aerial torpedo struck the ship. Unfortunately, about 3 months after I took this photo of Jack with the model of his ship that he personally built,----- he passed away. Jack; May you always have fair winds, following seas and a steam locomotive to drive while on liberty call.

SHIP NAME	PAGE	SHIP NAME	PAGE
Albany	175	Maryland	157
Allen M. Sumner	30	Missouri	25, 65, 108, 246
Ammen	51, 52	Moctobi	30, 61
Avalon (DSRV)	75, 79, 80	Monticello	30
		Mt.McKinley	30
Bagley	100	Mustin	14
Barbey	119, 120	Mystic (DSRV)	75, 80, 82
Belleau Wood	11, 194	Nevada	11, 13, 28, 29, 30
Belknap	185	New Jersey	11, 16, 22, 41, 60>61, 66, 97, 104, 106, 109, 111, 125>126, 130, 141, 142>150, 151>191
Bennington	11, 194		
"Berkone" (Unofficial)	69, 70		
Bronstein	143, 144	North Carolina	105, 146, 158, 184
Brooke	119, 124	Norton Sound	78, 153
Cacapon	30, 277	O'Brien	31
Cannon	271	Oklahoma City	204
Chicago	175, 176	Ortolan	75, 77, 79, 80
Collett	30		
Columbus	141, 175	Peleliu	11, 195
Cree	30	Perkins	30
		Petroff Bay	12
Dehaven	30	Pigeon	75, 77, 79, 80
		Point Loma	56, 58
Eldridge	271	"Porcupine"	144
England	143, 148	Princeton	234
Essex	114, 135, 165	"Prinz Eugen" (German)	29
Flagstaff	235	Quapaw	60, 61
Floyd B. Parks	30	"Queen Mary" (Private)	9, 10, 13, 16, 24, 26, 27, 87, 96, 101, 113, 115, 268
George Clymer	30	Ramsey	118
George Eastman	31	Ranger	11
Granville S. Hall	31		
		San Francisco	79
Halibut	77, 78. 79	Sims	123
Hancock	158	South Dakota	144
Haven	30, 63, 96	Squalus	75
Helena	236	Stein	87, 115
Henrico	30		
Higbee	56	Tarawa	11, 109, 110, 152, 194, 197
Hull	235,	Texas	11, 109, 144
		Thresher	75
Iowa	8, 11, 13, 27, 97, 99, 141, 153 159, 160, 162, 172, 178, 191 219, 261	"Triest" Bathyscaphe	55>57, 71, 99, 135
		Turner	30
Ingraham	30	Valley Forge	234
		Walke	30
Kearsage	11, 15, 16, 116, 234	White Sands	55>57
Kitty Hawk	234	Wilkinson	233
		Wisconsin	33, 102, 145, 153, 160, 167
Lansing	30		
Laffey	30	Yorktown	11, 234
Leahy	129		
Lockwood	123		
Los Angeles	9, 236		
Lowe	114		
Lowry	30		

PEOPLE INDEX (NAMES)	PAGE
Abbot, Grayden	68
Alpazzar, George	50, 51
Ashford, William "Bill", "Pal"	55
Archambeau, Dean	154
Arthurs, Jeff	155, 156, 177
Ayon, Abel	131
Bartow, Mike	102
Bauer, John	10, 24, 104, 141
Berkich, Joe (NOTS/SEALAB)	69
Bevis, Floyd	51
Bibeau, James "Jim"	24>27, 77, 141, 152, 154
Blanchard, Richard "Dick"	158
Blount, Robert "Bob"	151, 197
Blake, Neal	52
Bond, George (Capt SEALAB)	68, 69, 70
Cavalier, Issac	42, 76, 130, 132, 154
Choate, Nat	154, 159
Cannon, Berry	71
Carpenter, Scott (Cdr, USN)	69
Chavez, Joe (FEMA)	131
Clark, Dan	193
Clarson, Keith	52
Concepcion, Vince	155
Cook, Gary	10
Cooper, Bob	5, 107, 108, 125
Cox, Glen	94, 156
Davis, George	34
Davis, Glenn	188
Davis, Les	50, 52
DeFriest, John	69
DeVries, Paul	132
Dickson, David "Dave"	17, 65
Dickson, William "Bill"	26, 175, 176
Dietl, Charles "Chuck"	76, 155, 258
Dillenbeck, Ralph	37
Dillenbeck, Randolf "Randy"	37
Dixon, Homer	104, 152, 158
Don, Henry	131
Duacsek, Diane	23
Douglas, Gordon	5, 175, 194, 199
Douglass, Tim	197, 201
Ellis, Richard "Dick"	52
Filipe, Ed	176, 177
Fernandez, Nate	152, 155
Finkelstein, Phillip	10, 11, 87
Fletcher, Daniel	131
Foster, Donald "Don"	29, 49, 52, 53, 113
Fraser, Don	56, 118
Garzke, Bill	199
Garvey, Vaughn	5, 237, 241, 246
Gildea, J. A. (Captain LBNSY)	25, 151, 156
Goodman, Bill	71
Gorshkov, Sergei (USSR Admiral)	162
Grant, John "Johnny"	52

PEOPLE INDEX (NAMES)	PAGE
Hamilton, Doug	129
Harris, William "Bill"	34, 68
Heath, Cicil	131
Hedden &Roper ("Saboteurs")	198
Herr, Donald "Don"	165
Hock, Fred	42, 55, 76
Kirk, Jan	151
Kline, Dan	198
Jensen, Rick	108
LeBlanc, Alred	140
Lichti, Don	76, 77, 130, 155
Lintner, Stan	262
Malia, Mchael "Mike"	97, 106, 137
Maldonado, Victor	131, 132
Malin, Ron	6
Mason, Dave	125, 131
Mazzone, Walter (Capt SEALAB)	68, 69
Marsh, Larry	96
Marshall, Linda	95, 155
McCarthy, Mike	140
McFaul, John	144
Meza, Rick	155
Neft, Darryl	130
Nikolai, Frank	52, 113
Okun, Nathan	189, 199
Pickering, John (Captain LBNSY)	155, 157, 267
Priftakis, John	10. 41, 42
Raines, Tom (Cdr, BB Mgr)	104, 158
Reid, Willam "Bill"	124, 156
Reagan, Ronald (President)	96, 163
Riha, Robert "Bob"	87, 121>123, 141
Riha, Robert Jr. "Bob"	24, 28, 275
Rios, Danny	161
Rodriguez, Lou	130
Said, Michael "Mike"	89, 104, 155, 193, 194
Saltalamachia "Salty"	7, 228, 272, 277, 356
Sanchez, John	131
Schull, Ray	153, 159
Shelton, Dr. (LBNSY)	65
Shuey, John	151
Spears, Gerald	131
Stashak, George	104, 158
Steiner, Charles "Charlie"	50, 51
Theobald, Rod	141, 146
Upshaw, William "Lee"	104, 155, 167, 186, 187
Walker, Ted	34
Whitmeyer, "Jack"	12, 479
White, Lawrence	131
Wong, Peggy	161
Zimmerman, Bob	5, 372

Made in United States
Troutdale, OR
03/10/2025